P- 34

The Church's

EDUCATIONAL

Ministry:

A CURRICULUM PLAN

This book has been developed through the cooperative efforts of many denominations working through the Cooperative Curriculum Project and is published by an interdenominational agency, the Cooperative Publication Association, in order to provide a resource of sound educational and theological value, and of practical usefulness to curriculum developers in the church.

The Church's
EDUCATIONAL
Ministry:

A CURRICULUM PLAN

The work of the
Cooperative Curriculum Project

THE BETHANY PRESS • ST. LOUIS, MISSOURI

ACKNOWLEDGMENTS

Appreciation is expressed for the assistance of the following persons in acting as consultants, in preparing study materials, and in reading documents.

Bernhard W. Anderson, Dean of Drew Theological Seminary, Madison, New Jersey

Alfred C. Bartholomew, Professor of Church and Community, Lancaster Theological Seminary, Lancaster, Pennsylvania

J. Donald Butler, Professor of the History and Philosophy of Education, Princeton Theological Seminary, Princeton, New Jersey

L. Harold DeWolf, Professor of Systematic Theology, Boston University School of Theology, Boston, Massachusetts

Paul Eiserer, Professor of Psychology and Education, Teachers College, Columbia University, New York, New York

Arthur W. Foshay, Associate Dean, Research and Field Services, Teachers College, Columbia University, New York New York

Robert J. Havighurst, Professor of Education, Committee on Human Development, University of Chicago, Chicago, Illinois

Byron L. Johnson, Administrator for International Aid, Washington, D. C.

James Gilmour Ranck, Psychologist, New York, New York

D. Campbell Wyckoff, Professor of Christian Education, Princeton Theological Seminary, Princeton, New Jersey

J. Carter Swaim, Executive Director of the Department of the English Bible, Division of Christian Education, National Council of the Churches of Christ in the United States of America

MANUFACTURED IN THE UNITED STATES OF AMERICA

To

Joseph V. Nash and Charles M. Eve

Contents

PART III

Source for Teaching-Learning Opportunities

ix

PART IV

The Relation of Administration to the Curriculum Plan

xiv

A Statement
About
the Project

This Curriculum Plan is the direct result of almost a decade of study and work. It represents the concern of the church in the midtwentieth century to be as thorough and careful as human insights will allow in the designing of the church's educational ministry, appropriate to the urgency of the church's mission.

The motivation for this Cooperative Curriculum Project was not new, for the churches have repeatedly revised their curricula out of concern to do the best possible job in Christian education. The means whereby the Project was undertaken were not revolutionary. For ever since the last century, denominations have worked together through interdenominational channels to bring to bear on curriculum developed the best insights from the various churches.

The approach in the Project and the resources brought to it have been significant and have resulted in a comprehensive curriculum plan for an educational ministry which will undergird the church's total mission.

The Cooperative Curriculum Project grew out of a series of curriculum studies, sponsored jointly by the Committee on Graded Curriculum and the Committee on the Uniform Series, constituent to the Commission on General Christian Education of the National Council of the Churches of Christ in the United States of America. This sequence of curriculum studies dealt with various issues inherent in the basic question, "What kind of curriculum is needed by our churches today in the task of Christian education?" The study was understaken by denominational leaders concerned with curriculum building and embraced such subjects as these: the relationship of theological foundation and psychological insights in Christian nurture; the philosophy of curriculum development; the use of the Bible in curriculum; theological view of scope and sequence in the curriculum; motivation in learning; evaluation in teaching-learning; learning theory; developments in contemporary education.

From this study and because of the urgent need felt by the denominations for a curriculum plan adequate for today's task in Christian education, there resulted the formation of a sixteen-member partnership in curriculum building.

In December, 1960, conditions of partnership were drawn up and the basic foundations of curriculum Design were agreed upon. The partnership agreements involved the assignment of personnel by partner denominations to the Cooperative Curriculum Project; the commitment of time and money to undergird the project; the responsibility of interpretation of the Project to nonparticipating staff of the partner denominations; and the schedule of work meetings that would anticipate finishing the project by March, 1964.

It was very soon evident that one characteristic of any curriculum adequate to the church's educational task would be that it be coextensive with the church's total mission and that it would undergird that mission. This led to the essential involvement in the project of denominational and National Council appointees from many phases of the church's life and work, such as, evangelism, stewardship, social action, mission, the laity, leadership, research, higher education (including colleges and seminaries), Christian education. This Project was carried out under the auspices of the National Council of Churches. It was possible for solid dependable work to move rapidly because of the work plan devised for the Project. Each partner denomination had named a representative to an Administrative Committee in whose hands rested the decisions for the Project. The approval of all stages of the Curriculum Plan rested with this group; the direction of the work of the Project and the provision for adequate review rested with them.

A group of persons known as the Cooperative Staff for the Project worked under the authority and direction of the Administrative Committee. Made up of staff members, part of whose time was assigned by their denominations to this responsibility, the Cooperative Staff did interim work of a preparatory or refining nature on behalf of the total Project membership.

The major portion of the work was accomplished through five work groups made up of the membership of the Project, a chairman and a secretary for each work group guided and preserved the work accomplished for the Project.

Under the direction of the Administrative Committee two task groups worked on major issues related to curriculum planning; the concept of leadership and the preparation of leaders; and the use of the product of the Cooperative Curriculum Project.

On the decision of the Administrative Committee, biblical scholars and consultants from various disciplines, such as economics, sociology, psychology, education, theology, served the project in a consultative manner as readers, formulators, reviewers, and critics.

Over the four-year period the Project's total membership of over 125 persons put in seven work sessions of one week each, to which were added months of work by subcommittees, special task groups, Administrative Committee, and the Project Staff.

This project has resulted in a Curriculum Plan usable by denominations nationally as a basis for designing curriculum and as a basis for developing materials to support curriculum. It is anticipated that denominations would use this resource both as single denominations and as denominations working cooperatively.

PARTICIPATING DENOMINATIONS

ADVENT CHRISTIAN CHURCH

AFRICAN METHODIST EPISCOPAL CHURCH

AMERICAN BAPTIST CONVENTION

CHRISTIAN CHURCHES (DISCIPLES OF CHRIST)

CHURCH OF THE BRETHREN

CHURCH OF GOD

CHURCH OF THE NAZARENE

CUMBERLAND PRESBYTERIAN CHURCH

THE EVANGELICAL UNITED BRETHREN CHURCH

MENNONITE CHURCH

THE METHODIST CHURCH

PRESBYTERIAN CHURCH IN CANADA

PRESBYTERIAN CHURCH IN THE U.S.

THE PROTESTANT EPISCOPAL CHURCH

SOUTHERN BAPTIST CONVENTION

UNITED CHURCH OF CANADA

xix

ADMINISTRATIVE COMMITTEE

OF THE

COOPERATIVE CURRICULUM PROJECT

*CHAIRMAN, REV. RAY L. HENTHORNE, Christian Churches (Disciples of Christ)

*VICE CHAIRMAN, ROWENA FERGUSON, The Methodist Church

REV. CLIFTON J. ALLEN, Southern Baptist Convention

REV. GLENN H. ASQUITH, American Baptist Convention

REV. ALVIN J. COOPER, United Church of Canada

*BETTIE CURRIE, Presbyterian Church in the U. S. and Cumberland Presbyterian

LOTTIE M. FRANKLIN, Church of God

REV. W. H. FULLER, Presbyterian Church in Canada

*RICHARD K. GLADDEN, American Baptist Convention, 1962-1965

*REV. CHARLES W. GRIFFIN, American Baptist Convention, 1960-1961

MARY ALICE JONES, The Methodist Church, 1960-1963

REV. ALBERT F. HARPER, Church of the Nazarene

*REV. WARREN J. HARTMAN, The Evangelical United Brethren Church

REV. HAROLD HAZENFIELD, The Evangelical United Brethren Church

ERCELL V. LYNN, Church of the Brethren

REV. PAUL M. LEDERACH, Mennonite Church

---

*Members of Cooperative Staff

REV. LESTER MCMANIS, The Protestant Episcopal Church

*REV. EDWARD C. PETERSON, The Methodist Church, 1960-1964

MRS. ESTHER S. REED, Advent Christian Church

REV. HOLMES ROLSTON, Presbyterian Church in the U. S.

REV. GEORGE OLIVER TAYLOR, Christian Churches (Disciples of Christ)

REV. HORACE W. WILLIAMS, The Methodist Church, 1963-1965

REV. ANDREW WHITE, African Methodist Episcopal Church

---

*Members of Cooperative Staff

COOPERATIVE STAFF

OF THE

COOPERATIVE CURRICULUM PROJECT

CHAIRMAN, REV. RAY L. HENTHORNE, Director, Youth Publications, Christian Churches (Disciples of Christ)

BETTIE CURRIE, Director of Educational Research, Presbyterian Church in the United States

ROWENA FERGUSON, Editor, Youth Publications, The Methodist Church

REV. RICHARD K. GLADDEN, Director of Curriculum Development, American Baptist Convention (1962-1965)

ALICE L. GODDARD, National Council of Churches, Department of Educational Development, Staff Associate—Curriculum

REV. CHARLES W. GRIFFIN, Director of Curriculum Development, American Baptist Convention (1960-1961)

REV. WARREN J. HARTMAN, Director of Curriculum Research and Development, Evangelical United Brethren Church

REV. EDWARD C. PETERSON, Editor, Children's Publications, The Methodist Church (1960-1964)

MURIEL F. WALKER, National Council of Churches, Department of Educational Development, Administrative Assistant—Curriculum

MEMBERSHIP

OF THE

COOPERATIVE CURRICULUM PROJECT

RAY L. HENTHORNE, Chairman

Advent Christian Church

FRED CLOTHEY,
(1960-1961)

ESTHER REED

African Methodist Episcopal Church

J. R. COAN

ANDREW WHITE

American Baptist Convention

GLENN H. ASQUITH

JOSEPH BAN

LOIS BLANKENSHIP

RODNEY BRITTEN

MARION BRAWN

BENJAMIN P. BROWNE,

(1960-1961)

KENNETH COBER

DAVID EVANS

HARVEY EVERETT

JAMES FIDLER
RICHARD GLADDEN
CHARLES GRIFFIN,
  (1960-1961)
JOSEPH J. HANSON,
  (1960-1961)
BLANCHE HOKE
BERTHOLD JACKSTEIT
WILLIAM KEECH
ELMER MILLION

WILLIAM C. NELSON,
  (1960-1963)
MIRIAM PETERSON
PEARL ROSSER
RONALD SCHLOSSER
DOROTHY SILL
NATHAN TURNER
FRANCIS WHITING,
  (1960-1961)

Christian Churches (Disciples of Christ)

JESSIE CARLSON,
  (1960-1963)
GEORGE CAROLAND
LEWIS DEER
KARL CROEL,
  (1960-1961)
IRIS FERREN
D. A. HOLT
*BARTON HUNTER
THOMAS INABINETT
*STUART JOHNSTON
WALTER J. LANTZ
RICHARD E. LENTZ

MARY ELIZABETH MASON,
  (1960-1962)
MABEL METZE
E. LEE NEAL
JACK REEVE
DONALD SALMON
MARVIN E. SMITH
MARETA SMOOT
ARTHUR SYVERSON
GEORGE OLIVER TAYLOR
FRANCES WOOLERY

Church of the Brethren

S. LOREN BOWMAN
RICHARD COFFMAN
*ROBERT GREINER
HAZEL KENNEDY
JOSEPH M. LONG
ERCELL LYNN

CARL E. MYERS
GLEN E. NORRIS
MARY SPESSARD WORK-
  MAN
DONALD L. STERN

*Appointed, but did not serve

Church of God (Anderson)

CECIL BROWN

LOTTIE FRANKLIN

MILDRED HATCH

ESTHER KIRKPATRICK

HAROLD PHILLIPS

CARL WILLIAMS

Church of the Nazarene

MILDRED EDWARDS

A. F. HARPER

ROY E. SWIM

Cumberland Presbyterian Church

M. F. ALLEN, JR., (1960-1963)

The Evangelical United Brethren Church

DONALD APP

MARION L. BAKER,
 (1960-1961)

E. CRAIG BRANDENBURG

CURTIS CHAMBERS

BERNARD COOK

WARREN J. HARTMAN

HAROLD H. HAZENFIELD

BRUCE HILTON

L. L. HUFFMAN

JOHN KNECHT

LEO KISROW

QUENTIN C. LANSMAN

EDITH LOOSE,
 (1960-1963)

HARRIET MILLER

W. R. MONTGOMERY,
 (1960-1961)

HELEN MOON

NORDAN MURPHY

PAUL PRICE

CAWLEY H. STINE

RAYMOND VEH

Mennonite Church

PAUL LEDERACH

The Methodist Church

LEON M. ADKINS

HENRY M. BULLOCK

WILLIAM F. CASE

ROBERT S. CLEMONS

NEWMAN S. CRYER

M. EARL CUNNINGHAM

RICHARD EDGAR

RUTH EMORY

ROWENA FERGUSON
B. F. JACKSON, JR.
*SEWELL B. JACKSON
RONALD K. JOHNSON
MARY ALICE JONES
MARGIE McCARTY
EDWARD C. PETERSON

LESLIE J. ROSS
EDWARD D. STAPLES
HORACE WEAVER
FRANK E. WIER
HORACE WILLIAMS
MARGERY ZERKOWITZ,
(1960-1963)

National Council of Churches

MALCOLM BLACKBURN
ALVA I. COX, JR.
J. BLAINE FISTER
WILLIAM H. GENNE'
ALICE L. GODDARD
WARD KAISER
BERNHARD E. OLSON
BARBARA P. POPPE

J. ALLAN RANCK
J. CARTER SWAIM
W. RANDOLPH THORN-
TON
MARY E. VENABLE
RUTH WAGNER
JOHN WOOD

Presbyterian Church in Canada

*J. S. CLARKE
W. H. FULLER

D. M. WARNE

Presbyterian Church in the U. S.

BETTIE CURRIE

HOLMES ROLSTON

The Protestant Episcopal Church

LESTER W. McMANIS

Southern Baptist Convention

CLIFTON J. ALLEN
HOWARD P. COLSON

RAYMOND RIGDON

United Church of Canada

ALVIN JOHN COOPER
ELTON DAVIDGE

CLARENCE FERGUSON
CHARLES STEWART

---

*Appointed, but did not serve

Foreword

The clue to the nature of this book is found in the words, "A Curriculum Plan." The Plan is essentially a document to be used as a resource in the educational ministry of Protestant churches. Specifically, it is a kind of high-operational tool to assist in the total process of constructing curriculum plans. The book does not purport to be "a curriculum," much less "the curriculum," of any church or churches. Rather, it displays a way of approaching the business of planning and offers some means for building specific curriculum plans for any educational situation in the life and work of the church.

Sixteen denominations have developed this Plan cooperatively through various groups of people working together in a way to produce a responsible approach to the task, coordination of effort, and coherence of content. This interdenominational effort was called "the Cooperative Curriculum Project." (See "A Statement about the Project.") The book is, therefore, a committee document and not the work of a single author. The book is not one to be read straight through from beginning to end. Some suggestions for becoming familiar with the book and for understanding how to use it as a resource are indicated following the Foreword.

This Curriculum Plan and the Project which produced it are based upon a number of assumptions:

> That "curriculum" properly understood cannot be separated from "program" because each is an essential aspect of the educational ministry; in a final analysis, but not necessarily at every stage of development, "curriculum" and "program" can be thought of as the same thing;

That "curriculum" is the concern of the whole church as it goes about its educational task; "curriculum" cannot be conceived as the province only of a single institutional arm of the church because the educational ministry is conceived as the educational aspect of each of the ministries of the church's life and work; thus, the curriculum enhances and undergirds all educational activity sponsored or initiated by any institutional unit of the church. Plans for curriculum at each level of the church's life and work may provide opportunity for the several agencies, commissions, boards, and the like, to consider the possibilities inherent in a common ministry of education. This kind of consideration will include:

plans which reduce the possibility of fragmentation and divisiveness among the various boards and agencies

the possibility of cooperative decisions and plans among various institutional and organizational units

the testing of the usefulness and value of all structures as a means of achieving the one Objective of the church

opportunity for each segment of the institutional life of the church to make its distinctive contribution while not fragmenting or duplicating its educational ministry;

That plans for such curriculum should be constructed within a single framework in which every educational effort of the church, wherever initiated, shall have an appropriate place;

That matters concerning the development of leadership are integral in curriculum and, hence, in the Curriculum Plan;

That there is sufficient common ground, theologically and educationally speaking, among a number of Protestant churches to make a cooperative effort in curriculum planning valid in terms of the Christian faith and serviceable in education; the divergencies among the churches as seen in their particular emphases complement and enlarge the perspective of every other one;

That curriculum planning will place major emphasis upon the quality of involvement which is achieved when the teacher and learner are in dialogue with respect to their understandings and perceptions of meanings and experiences. This emphasis will allow:

> all the resources of curriculum to be arranged so as to evoke and facilitate the imaginative potential of all of the persons involved as distinguished from resources that present only one course of action, one response, or one mode of communication
>
> persons involved in the educational ministry in particular churches to be free to make decisions in light of their own situations about how to arrange and order their curriculum within the overall Plan
>
> the cognitive aspects of the curriculum to have an essential place in the dialogue without being the only determining factor.

The book as a whole reflects these assumptions in many ways.

The Functions of this Plan

The Curriculum Plan functions only as it is employed by one or more agencies of the church engaged in the educational ministry. It should be a valuable resource, in whole or in part, to interdenominational and denominational planners of curriculum, to persons who interpret curriculum in the educational ministry, to professors and students in seminaries and divinity schools.

Parts of the book may be used by curriculum planners in countries other than the United States and Canada, the two countries represented in the development of this book.

In addition to Parts I through IV which set forth the substance of the Curriculum Plan, a detailed "Contents" gives an overview of the substance and displays the way it is organized; an "Afterword" describes a process of deriving teaching-learning units from the Plan; a "Glossary" lists and defines words that are used with a specialized meaning in the book; an "Appendix" describes certain principles for the development of leadership in the Christian community.

The Context of the curriculum, that is to say the milieu in which it becomes actualized, is the Christian community—the church. References to Context, its place and function in the Curriculum Plan, will be found in the "Preface to Part III" and in the "Afterword."

When appropriately used, this book will give perspective on the whole process of planning curriculum and will instruct and inform the process by offering check points for making and assessing curriculum plans for designated groups and settings. Also, the Plan describes a way in which the varied tasks in the designing of curricula may be conceived, carried out, and related to one another within the total curriculum enterprise. Aside from assisting in the process, this book offers the substance for making specific curriculum plans at each level of the church's life—local, regional, national—with any segment of the church's total constituency. The way in which each Part of this book may be employed is set forth in the Preface in each case.

The Curriculum Plan as a whole brings to bear a unifying factor among the varied elements of the ministry of education and helps mobilize within the framework of a common task the variety of persons from all units of the church responsible at their several levels for this ministry.

A Note on

Reading this Book

In order to become familiar with the book as a whole the following order of reading is suggested.

Read first the table of Contents which reveals the outline or skeleton of the book, and indicates the nature of each Part plus the way it is related to the whole. Read next "A Statement about the Project," page xv for a description of how the Curriculum Plan was developed. These two sections will provide a bird's-eye view not only of the book itself but also of its background.

Read next Part I, "The Design for the Curriculum of the Church's Educational Ministry," which describes the components of the curriculum from a Protestant point of view. Then read the Prefaces to Parts II and III. This reading will provide an accurate bearing on the course taken by Part II, "The Scope of the Curriculum" and Part III, "Source of Development of Teaching-Learning Opportunities."

This much reading will contribute to a readiness to understand the way in which the components of the Design have been explicated and put to work in the Plan as a whole. Mastering the content of Parts II and III will require study and careful assimilation, which probably may best be done through some such usage of the book as described above.

After becoming familiar with Parts I, II, and III read the "Afterword" which explains how to use these Parts to derive teaching-learning units.

For the purpose of this curriculum plan there are a number of words used in a specialized sense to express meanings in this plan. Refer to the Glossary frequently to be sure you understand the way in which words are being used.

When you are ready to implement your Curriculum Plan, Part IV may help you administer the Plan.

PART I

The Design for the Curriculum of the Church's Educational Ministry

Christian education is that ministry of the church which provides the educational undergirding for the church's entire ministry of worship, witness, and work. In this Design, Christian education is construed as related to all opportunities offered to persons primarily for the purpose of education in the Christian faith and for the Christian mission.

The curriculum for Christian education is the sum of all learning experiences resulting from the Curriculum Plan, under the guidance of the church and directed toward accomplishing the church's objective. The Curriculum Plan is not to be confused with the curriculum since the Curriculum Plan is resident in resources while the curriculum is what happens in the teaching-learning situation. The Curriculum Plan for the church's educational ministry must be so designed as to aid the church in its task of nurturing persons in the faith, thus preparing them for the mission of the church.

An adequate and satisfactory curriculum plan must be built according to sound principles of construction. Before any curriculum can be initiated, there must be some more-or-less clear picture of the theory on which it will be based. These foundation-principles are called "The Design for the Curriculum of the Church's Educational Ministry."

These principles, as incorporated into the Design, must answer certain questions about curriculum and about education in the church. Before beginning work on the curriculum itself, educators in the church must ask such questions as:

What is the purpose of the curriculum? To what end is the curriculum directed? These questions are answered for this Curriculum Design in the section on *The Objective of Christian Education* (page 7).

3

What is to be taught and learned that this purpose may be achieved? What are the various areas of learning—the range of subject matter and the experiences to which subject matter is related? How are the areas delineated, described, and organized? These questions are considered in the section on *The Scope of the Curriculum for Christian Education* (page 12).

Where does the curriculum function? What is the learning environment in which it will operate? Answers to these questions become the basis for the section on *The Context of the Curriculum* (page 23).

4

How does learning take place? When is it believed that learning has been achieved? These questions are dealt with in the section on *Learning Tasks in Christian Education* (page 24).

How are the components of the Design related to one another and to the learner? How is the learner taken into account in the curriculum? In dealing with these questions the clue to the *Organizing Principle of the Curriculum* is set forth in this Design (page 34).

Five components in the Curriculum Design—Objective, Scope, Context, Learning Tasks, Organizing Principle—have been identified. These five components are interdependent and interactive with one another. For example, each component must be seen in light of the objective in order that it may facilitate progress toward the Objective. Also, learning tasks must be in harmony with the Objective; they must be congenial to the Context; they must be appropriate to the learner in his situation; and they must give promise of dealing dynamically with Scope.

The components of the Design are separated here only for purposes of analysis and description. The Organizing Principle of the Design describes the way the components are related to one another.

The Design exhibits a potential for being used in a variety of ways. These ways can be categorized as those that are immediately functional and those that have possibilities of becoming functional.

The Design is immediately functional in that it can be used:

a. as the basis for planning, at the national level, the structure for denominational Christian education curriculum —uniting what has in the past often been seen as program-design-and-materials and curriculum-design-and-materials;

b. as the vehicle to foster conversations among denominational boards and agencies, looking toward the conscious coordination of all educative activities suggested to local churches by each of the several boards and agencies;

c. as the foundation for the planning of a unified denominational curriculum design, the synthesis of all national planning activities into one program of mission, geared to the vocation of the denomination's local congregations;

d. in colleges, universities, and seminaries for the study of curriculum planning in Christian education; the Design defines operationally and interrelatedly the components that must be taken into account in the art and science of curriculum development in the church.

The Design can become functional in that it may be used:

a. to interpret to local church leaders the skeletal structure of a denomination's curriculum plan, the dynamics of curriculum development, and the rootage and rationale of the curriculum materials;

b. as a statement of shared presuppositions that define the matrix for interdenominational, and even ecumenical, development of plans for the teaching-learning opportunities of the church;

c. by seminary faculties and college departments of Christian education to suggest a model for helping to organize their own curricular offerings.

5

Further, there is resident in the Design a potential for planning coordinated Christian education curricula that takes into account the person at all his ages and stages of development and the several institutions through which he is educated. Within a denomination, or among several working together, planners of curriculum from all levels of denominational education (local church including the home, national staff servicing local church education, church-related colleges, seminaries) may find this Design a base for conversations that look toward articulated curricula among these educational levels.

6

A common awareness of Objective, Scope, Context, Learning Tasks, and Organizing Principle can facilitate the construction of an overall design that defines a conscious linkage among the curricula at all the institutional levels, from the home through the seminary. The Design provides the functional categories for planning and integrating curricula for such articulated, multi-level Christian education.

The Design for
the Curriculum of
the Church's
Educational Ministry

The Objective of Christian Education

In making a design for the curriculum of Christian education, curriculum planners find themselves at the outset faced with this kind of question: What is to be accomplished? What is the end in view? What is the ultimate purpose? Questions of structure, process, and ways and means can be resolved only in light of the ends to be achieved. Therefore, the beginning of a curriculum foretells the end, and the end reflects the beginning. In this way an inner consistency and harmony among the various components of the curriculum are possible.

In this Design the end in view or the ultimate purpose will be called "the objective." The term "objective" was decided upon because it seems to suggest the intent of the entire process, the achievement toward which all the experiences of Christian education, comprehended in the curriculum, are directed. Accordingly, the nature of the objective is comprehensive, complete, ultimate. It must not be conceived as partial, fragmented, or intermediate.

It seems clear, also, at the beginning that the objective of the curriculum can be only the objective of the church's educational ministry. The curriculum in a sense is an implement or the carrier of the process of Christian education; therefore, the objective of the curriculum in this Design is designated as the objective of the church's educational ministry.

STATEMENT OF THE OBJECTIVE

The objective for Christian education is that all persons be aware of God through his self-disclosure, especially his redeeming love as revealed in Jesus Christ, and that they respond in faith and love—to the end that they may know who they are and what their human situation means, grow as sons of God rooted in the Christian community, live in the Spirit of God in every relationship, fulfill their common discipleship in the world, and abide in the Christian hope.

The Functions of the Objective

The functions of the objective have been suggested by the nature of the objective as indicated above. In general, the functions of the objective are three:

1. To chart the direction in which the educational experiences should be planned. These experiences when planned and organized under guidance constitute the curriculum. Every component of the curriculum—Scope, Context, Learning Tasks, Organizing Principle—is brought into focus by the objective.

2. To serve as a standard or measure by which the short-term goals, the ways and means employed in the curriculum, and the resources which implement the curriculum, may be planned. The Objective is functioning in this way when planners at each level of curriculum development (interdenominational and denominational) on both national and local levels, ask such questions as: Is this statement of scope comprehensive enough to make possible the working

out of the objective? Is this educational method in harmony with the objective?

3. To serve as a means of evaluation of the curriculum. The objective serves also indirectly when educational experiences in the church are being evaluated in the light of short-term goals consistent with the objective.

Characteristics of the Objective

When the functions of the objective of Christian education are viewed thus, a clear and precise formulation of the objective becomes a difficult matter. Obviously many kinds of formulations are possible and even desirable. Each one may contribute some degree of clarity, insight, utility, flexibility. No statement can claim to be *the* statement but the statement on page 8 is consistent with the views described above, and further, exhibits two important characteristics.

The first characteristic of this statement is that it displays the lifelong nature of the Objective of Christian education. That is, the Objective reflects the conviction that the Christian faith and life can never be thought of as finally accomplished in the sense that no further fulfillment is necessary. At the same time, it should be emphasized that the Objective is valid at any given moment of time and at every level of maturity. Persons may achieve the objective—that is, they may be aware of God through his self-disclosure and respond in faith and love—at each age and stage of development. There will be differences of awareness and response at various ages and stages but the differences will be in terms of maturity and of appropriateness of expression. The objective implies a kind of paradox. The person may achieve the objective and continue toward it at the same time. This is the experience of *becoming* in the Christian faith and life.

The second charcteristic is that this statement of the Objective is firmly in the Christian perspective and is formulated in terms of the Christian vocabulary. In other words, this statement is cast

9

in the framework of theology. This type of formulation seemed necessary if the Objective is to function in the ways described above. Christian education is closely related to other disciplines, especially the behavioral and social sciences, as will be evident in the curriculum plan at later stages. This statement, then, is not to be construed as overlooking or minimizing the contribution of these disciplines in Christian education.

Implications of the Objective

This statement of the Objective of the church's educational task is both general and basic.

It is general (as distinguished from specific) in that it does not attempt to specify responses in terms of convictions, attitudes, and behavior. It does not describe or even hint at the precise details of "who they are and what their human situation means." This means that it attempts to be genuinely an objective. Specific convictions (Christian doctrine and beliefs), designated attitudes of the Christian, and described behavior exemplified in the Christian life are sometimes listed as "purposes" or "outcomes" or "objectives" of Christian education. In this design, however, these matters are classified and become active elsewhere. Concepts or doctrine, convictions or beliefs are dealt with in Scope. Attitudes and behavior are taken into account in the various themes in the curriculum and are related to pupil goals or motivations present in every teaching-learning situation.

This statement of Objective is basic in that it indicates that the church's teaching ministry is addressed to man's fundamental and universal questions: Who am I? Why am I here? Where am I going? Who is God? Who is my neighbor? This is the import of the phrase "who they are and what their human situation means." The basic quality of the Objective is shown also by the fact that it indicates the distinguishing mark of education in the Christian church (as differentiated from general education), that is, that people and their particular human situations are seen first and always in relation to God—awareness of the redeeming love of God. This awareness is the initial step in becoming disciples, in becoming "new creatures in Christ," or in "being born again."

Certain important implications may be drawn from this Objective of Christian education that are pertinent to later stages in the Design.

First, the phrase "all persons," implies the outreach and evangelistic thrust of the church's teaching ministry. In other words, the church's teaching ministry is not limited to those already within the Christian fellowship.

Second, "rooted in the Christian community" provides the clue to the fact that Christian education may be viewed as the nurturing ministry of the church, and indicates the centrality of the life of the entire Christian fellowship in that ministry of education. The church in its total life and work is the matrix of Christian nurture.

Third, the ideas of awareness and response show the church's educational ministry as aiming at both an inward reality and an outward mission. The two are seen as interdependent and mutually supporting. Together they bring to full circle the Christian faith and life, that is, being the Christian in the inward spirit and doing the Christian way in all the outward affairs of life, especially as they are related to the social and ethical implications of the gospel.

Fourth, the church in its educational ministry as well as in all other ministries seeks the redemption of man in all his relationships, personal and social—"live in the Spirit of God in every relationship, fulfill their common discipleship in the world." No aspect of man's existence in all its ramifications is outside the purview of the Christian gospel. The objective, then, relates the process of Christian education redemptively to the specific life situation of every person.

Finally, the value of the Objective is that it provides direction and perspective for the entire educational ministry. It gives unity, direction, and selectivity to the curriculum.

11

The Scope of the Curriculum for Christian Education

The function of Scope in the Design of the curriculum is to provide a standard of comprehensiveness for the curriculum. It fulfills this function both at the stage of describing the total content for the curriculum and also at the stage of describing any subdivision of the content. Content is used in the Design to include both information and experience.

12

The term "scope of curriculum" is used to describe what is appropriate to be dealt with in the curriculum. It is distinctive from the term "content of curriculum" in that this latter term has to do with what is in fact dealt with in the curriculum. "Scope" is the broader term; it refers to what *may* be dealt with; it includes more than can possibly be used in the curriculum. "Content" is the narrower term; it refers to what *is* to be dealt with. Scope may be said to describe the field over which the church has legitimate purview for its educational ministry and from which the church may appropriately draw the content for its curriculum.

The Scope of the curriculum is coextensive with what God has revealed through his redemptive action and the implications of this redemptive action for man in the whole field of relationships—God, man, nature, and history. The Scope of the curriculum is thus identical with the scope of the church's educational concerns.

This concept of Scope is based on the conviction of the church that God comes to man in the Word, calling man into relationship with him. This invitation to relationship, which is witnessed to and disclosed in the Bible and in the life of the church, is continually being extended to man through the eternal Word, that is, God revealed in Jesus Christ, his person and work. God calls man to discipleship, whether or not man hears and heeds the call. In order to hear, man must involve himself with the Word, experience the Word. When man does indeed hear, a response is inevitable, though this response may be one of acceptance or of rejection. As man responds to God in faith, love, commitment, and obedience, he finds that light is thrown on all relationships, and that he is empowered and enriched within those relationships.

Light is thrown on man's relationship with God, the sovereign Creator, Father, Redeemer, Judge, so that man may relate to him as a faithful and obedient son. Light is thrown on man's relationship with man (himself and others in society—family, community, world) so that he may relate to man as he was created, in the image of God; as he is, sinner; and as he may become, redeemed. Light is thrown on man's relationship with nature, created and sustained by God, ruled over, cared for, and used by man as a steward, so that he may relate to nature as the setting in which God has created man to live. Light is thrown on man's relationship with history, ruled and overruled by the sovereign Lord, moving forward toward his designed consummation of it, so that man may relate to history as the continuum of God's activity and the temporal aspect of man's response to God's activity.

In view of this conviction, it is proper to identify the Scope of the curriculum for Christian education as the whole field of relationships viewed in light of, or from the perspective of, the gospel—God's whole continuous redemptive action toward man, known especially in Jesus Christ.

In this statement of Scope, the crucial phrase from the point of view of content is "in light of the gospel." This is what makes it a statement of Scope for Christian education. Therefore in the delineation of content of the curriculum, the gospel is the crucial factor. It is the given in Christianity and therefore becomes the given in the church's educational work. Accordingly, the gospel must be so communicated through the curriculum that it will shed light on man's whole field of relationships.

13

Everything that has been said above concerning the gospel is firmly anchored in the Scriptures. Insight into the gospel is gained through man's knowledge of the Bible informed and illuminated by the Holy Spirit. Therefore in Christian education the Bible is not one concern among many; it is the ground and guide of all concerns, and permeates in various ways the entire enterprise of Christian education.

The gospel as understood and interpreted by Christians is reflected in the church's past and current heritage as the church has dealt with its major concerns, such as faithful proclamation of the gospel; thoughtful formulation and interpretation of doctrines of man, of the church, of mission; responsible provision for worship and for the Christian nurture of persons; guidance in Christian ethics.

14

The whole field of relationships embraces the gamut of man's experiences and needs and their expression in specific situations. These are seen in such lifelong, persistent concerns of persons as interpersonal relations, self-image, sex, sense of destiny, survival, affection, usefulness, power, security, authority, trust, love, forgiveness, reconciliation.

The content of the curriculum is derived from the interaction between the gospel and the lifelong persistent concerns of the learner. The gospel comes alive and is recognized by the learner as relevant only when he sees the gospel in connection with his persistent lifelong concerns. Therefore the description of the content of the curriculum is the comprehensive delineation of the points of dynamic interaction between the gospel and the concerns of the person in his whole field of relationships.

Delineation of Elements of Scope

In order to arrive at a description of content of the curriculum, the Scope is further analyzed and delineated in terms of its basic elements. These elements are seen as three dimensions of reality with which every man is concerned—the divine, the human, the natural. These dimensions of reality are aspects of man's experience in the whole field of relationships. The church's curriculum by its inherent Christian character must deal with these dimensions from the point of view of the gospel.

Therefore the elements of the scope for the curriculum are identified as these three:

> The Christian experience of man under God—the divine dimension of reality in light of the gospel

> The Christian experience of man's relation to man—the human dimension of reality in light of the gospel

> The Christian experience of man within the world—the natural dimension of reality in light of the gospel

The Christian experience of man under God—the divine dimension of reality in light of the gospel. This element reflects the Christian view of God as the Creator and as one who continuously seeks a personal relationship with man as disclosed in the gospel.

The Christian experience of man's relation to man—the human dimension of reality in light of the gospel. This element includes one's own person as well as other persons individually and in society (family, community, world). It identifies men as fellow creatures under God with responsibility for one another and for society, consistent with the law of love disclosed through the gospel.

The Christian experience of man within the world—the natural dimension of reality in light of the gospel. Man's setting is the world of space-time; he is a part of it and dependent on it. This element takes account of the physical and natural order as created by God, to be used by man as a steward for purposes consistent with God's purposes as seen in the gospel.

Together these elements comprehend the entire scope—God's redemptive action and its implications for man in the whole field of relationships. The field of relationships always includes its three dimensions of reality. Therefore, wherever scope (the whole field of relationships in light of the gospel) is dealt with, it must reflect these three elements. These elements of scope find their

15

rootage in Scripture. The disclosure of God and his will through the Bible is integral to each element of scope and normative for its nature. Each of the elements has a historical aspect and hence history, including the Christian heritage, becomes a resource related to each.

General Description of Curriculum Areas

In order for the Scope to be dealt with in further stages of the Curriculum Plan it is organized into *areas of curriculum*. Their function is (1) to serve as a test for comprehensiveness of the curriculum and (2) to form the basis for the selection of themes appropriate in every span of life. A designation of areas of curriculum is the first step in deciding what is actually to be the content of the curriculum.

The following principles were used in arriving at the areas of curriculum: (1) all areas together comprehend the scope; (2) each area reflects all elements of the scope; (3) each area envisions something to learn about and something to participate in.

There are several ways of devising curriculum areas using these guiding principles. For the purpose of the Curriculum Plan, it seemed that the Objective of Christian Education offered some clues for the selection and formulation of the areas. When the objective is analyzed, five major facets emerge as distinctive and also integral to the whole: God's self-disclosure; man's human situation; the Christian's response to God as a son; his life of discipleship resulting from his acceptance of himself as a son of God, and his response to God in faith and love; his experience in the church in community with fellow Christians. Each of these facets reflects the three elements of the Scope.

God in his self-disclosure calls to man in his human situation and as he is related to other men and to his setting in the natural world.

Man's human situation embraces his relation to God, to other men, and to space-time.

When man accepts himself as God's son, the experience has meaning for his relationship to other men and to his space-time orientation.

Man's answer to God's call through Christian discipleship is in terms of his personal and social involvements including those of his setting in the natural world.

The community of Christians (gathered and dispersed), the church as a divine-human institution, in but not of the world, becomes the company of those who hear and heed God's call.

Applying the three principles, and using these five cross sections of scope, five areas of curriculum can be designated as follows:

Life and Its Setting: the Meaning and Experience of Existence

Revelation: the Meaning and Experience of God's Self-Disclosure

Sonship: the Meaning and Experience of Redemption

Vocation: the Meaning and Experience of Discipleship

The Church: the Meaning and Experience of Christian Community

There is no significance in the order of the listing of these curriculum areas. Each is as important as the others, and they are not thought of in sequence.

17

The five curriculum areas are not five separate slices of the total scope, but rather five vantage points, each of which deals with all elements of the scope of the curriculum. Thus each area is holistic in its nature which means that in the curriculum the learner is always seen as a whole person in his total field of relationships, and as experiencing the three dimensions of reality—divine, human, natural—in light of the gospel.

These areas of curriculum are, however, not only holistic in relation to Scope, they are also distinctive in relation to one another. The distinctiveness of each area is determined by its particular focus or perspective, which is indicated in the descriptions below. Since each area provides for the most elementary to the most culminating experiences of the learner, it is conceivable that he might experience the comprehensiveness of the Scope through only one curriculum area. It is expected, however, that since one area easily opens the door to other areas, most persons would experience the Scope from more than one vantage point.

The five curriculum areas are further organized into themes in order that the Scope may be more manageable as it is integrated with Context and Learning Tasks as the learner moves toward the Objective.

18

A theme is a major motif within an area which has significance throughout the life span. It describes in detail the intersection of the concerns of the Christian faith with basic persistent life issues. Within the curriculum areas there are several themes, each one bearing the perspective on Scope characteristic of its curriculum area. Together the themes constituent to an area comprehend the major lifelong motifs in the Scope as seen from the perspective of that area.

The purpose of organizing the Scope into themes is to identify more precisely the relevance of the gospel, in order that teaching-learning units may have built-in significance to the learner insofar as content is concerned.

LIFE AND ITS SETTING: THE MEANING AND EXPERIENCE
OF EXISTENCE

The focus, or vantage point, of this area is the significance and purpose of life; what it means to be a human being; the origin, meaning, and destiny of the natural order; the import of history.

Comprehended in this area of curriculum is such content from Christian thought and life as: the doctrine of creation; the doctrine of man including his relation to the natural world; interpretation of personal and social development; struggle and conflict; the concept of eternal life; interpretation of world view including human history and eschatology.

In order to have educational value as an area of curriculum this content must be viewed in terms of its pertinence to the persistent issues of man's life. Some of these issues are: What can I make of the universe? Does it have significance and purpose? Who am I? In what way, if any, does my life have meaning? What is my destiny and that of the world? Does the past tell me anything of value about the present and the future?

The themes within this area are:

Man Discovering and Accepting Himself
Man Living in Relationship with Others
Man's Relation to the Natural Order
Man's Involvement in Social Forces
Man's Coping with Change and the Absolute
Man's Creativity within Life's Daily Routines

REVELATION: THE MEANING AND EXPERIENCE OF GOD'S
SELF-DISCLOSURE

The focus, or vantage point, of this area of curriculum is the character of God and his work, the nature and significance of God's self-disclosure—the modes of God's action, and the way he has spoken and still speaks to man's search and man's need.

Comprehended in this area of curriculum is such content from Christian thought and life as: the doctrine of God; the doctrine of the Trinity; interpretation of the person, teaching, and work of Jesus Christ; interpretation of the work of the Holy Spirit; the relation of revelation to reason; interpretation of the nature and meaning of the gospel.

In order to have educational value as an area of curriculum this content must be viewed in terms of its pertinence to the persistent issues of man's life. Some of these issues are: Is there a God? Does God speak? If so, how? Does this tell me what I can live for? Does God disclose himself? If so, how? How is God known? What is the Bible all about?

19

The themes within this area are:

God Speaks in Man's Search for Meaning Beyond Himself
The Living God Seeks Man
The Gracious God Judges and Redeems
The Sovereign God Dwells with Man
God Speaks to Man Through the Scriptures
God Acts Through the Church to Make Himself Known
God Speaks to Man Through the Natural Order

20

SONSHIP: THE MEANING AND EXPERIENCE OF REDEMPTION

The focus, or vantage point, of this area of curriculum is man's personal response to God's self-disclosure—accepting God's redemptive love and experiencing the meaning of sonship; the inner witness and the life of faith, or being the Christian.

Comprehended in this area of curriculum is such content from Christian thought and life as: alienation of man from God; God's redemptive love for man; man's acceptance of his sonship relationship to God; interpretation of the new man in Christ; the Christian view of interpersonal relationships within the church and beyond; the meaning of the Christian hope.

In order to have educational value as an area of curriculum, this content must be viewed in terms of its pertinence to the persistent issues of man's life. Some of these issues are: What does it mean to be saved? What does it mean to sin? How can I relate to others? What does God expect of me? What can I expect from God? What difference does God make in my life? What does it mean to be a Christian? To what shall I commit my life? What does it mean to mature as a son of God?

The themes within this area are:

God's Redeeming Love for Man
Man's Responding to God's Redemptive Action
Becoming a New Person in Christ

Growing Up in Christ
Finding Identity in the Christian Community
The Christian's Hope Rests in the Triumphant God

VOCATION: THE MEANING AND EXPERIENCE OF DISCIPLESHIP

The focus, or vantage point, of this area of curriculum is the ethical, service, and social aspects of the Christian life, that is, acting in the Christian way in all relationships, the outward witness of faithful discipleship to Jesus Christ.

Comprehended in this area of curriculum is such content of Christian thought and life as: the concept of the kingdom of God; explication of Christian ethics and Christian social relations; the concept of vocation to the Christian; the Christian view of work; interpretation of the fruits of the Spirit; the church's role and task in the world; Christian stewardship in the natural and social realm.

In order to have educational value as an area of curriculum, this content must be viewed in terms of its pertinence to the persistent issues of man's life. Some of these issues are: For what cause is life best invested? What is the relation of Christianity to society? How may issues between church and state be resolved? What is the political responsibility of the Christian? How shall I choose and perform my life work? How do I know what is right? What values can I live by? How can I meet failure?

21

The themes within this area are:

God's Call to Responsible Decision
Called to Serve One's Neighbor
The Stewardship of Life and Work
Discipline in the Christian Life
Joined in Discipleship in the World
Toward the Kingdom of God

THE CHURCH: THE MEANING AND EXPERIENCE OF CHRISTIAN COMMUNITY

The focus, or vantage point, of this area of curriculum is the nature, the history, and the mission of the church; belonging to the church and participating in its life and work.

Comprehended in the area of curriculum is such content of Christian thought and life as: the doctrine of the church; the meaning of church membership; the history of the church; Christian mission and the missionary enterprise; skills of church-manship; worship and the ministries of the church—teaching, preaching, outreach, service, healing; interpretation of the church triumphant; the history and use of the Bible.

In order to have educational value as an area of curriculum, this content must be viewed in terms of its pertinence to the persistent issues of man's life. Some of these issues are: What can I do about feelings of alienation? Where can I belong? Why is Christianity exported? What is the basis of Christian evangelism? How did the church come to be? Why are there so many denominations? Can't I be a good Christian outside the church? What is the business of the church? Where can I find support for my Christian aspirations and witness? What difference does the church make?

The themes within this area are:

Christians Are Bound Together in God's Love
God's Continuing Action in and Through His People
The Church Permeating Society
Extending Reconciliation and Redemption
The Church Lives by Worship
The Christian Community Mobilizing for Mission
Preparing and Equipping for Ministry

The Context of the Curriculum

The context of the curriculum for Christian education basically is the Christian community—the church, the fellowship of persons who owe allegiance to Jesus Christ. The curriculum becomes a reality through the action of the worshiping, witnessing, nurturing community. This community has a life, a message, a mission, and a heritage to communicate which are best communicated within the Christian fellowship of love. The community includes the Christian home where much of Christian education, formal and informal, takes place.

The context of the curriculum cannot be overemphasized since it is here that the person experiences the learning transaction. Nor can the Christian dimension of this context be minimized since it is this dimension that is at the heart of the nurturing process. The more nearly a Christian community can approximate the given nature of the church, the more effective its witness and nurture become. This community has a faith to communicate—a faith rooted in a gospel with power to encounter and redeem the person in his field of relationships.

Within the church, education is carried on as one of the church's ministries, a ministry that is integrally related to the church's entire life and work expressed in such varied ways as social action, evangelism and other forms of outreach, the missionary enterprise, Christian service, healing, worship. The curriculum implements this teaching ministry which undergirds all of the church's ministries in and to the world.

The person for whom the curriculum is designed is both affected by and has an effect on the context as he is involved in the curriculum. He is at the heart of the communicating process. The effort to communicate is made in order that the person may undertake his task of achieving the objective of Christian education. As he enters the context of the curriculum and engages in the learning tasks which help him master the scope of Christian education, he brings with him his entire field of relationships.

23

When the witnessing and nurturing functions of the church are dynamically related to the person's life situations, the resulting encounter enables that person to realize significant outcomes, and to grow toward Christian maturity as he engages in the five Learning Tasks. The learner is thus enabled to work and witness with the meanings and values of the gospel as the basis for his relationships. The Learning Tasks are identified on page 33.

With this emphasis upon the Christian community as the context of the curriculum it must also be borne in mind that the nurturing work of God through the Holy Spirit is not confined to this community. The church witnesses to the Holy Spirit and the Spirit works in and through the church. The church cannot limit nor direct the work of the Spirit but can obstruct or facilitate the response man makes to the Holy Spirit.

Learning Tasks in Christian Education

The learning process in Christian education is analyzed in terms of Learning Tasks which indicate the way intended learning can be undertaken within the curriculum of the church and the way the process of becoming can be nurtured.

When a person enters into the curriculum of the church, he works towards the realization of the Objective of that curriculum by becoming involved in these lifelong Learning Tasks. The Learning Tasks are undertaken within the Context of the Christian fellowship, reflecting the concerns of the church with the whole field of relationships: God, man, natural world, history.

The Learning Tasks in Christian education are based on the assumption that learning is a process of human change which can be ascribed to experience in the whole field of relationships. The process whereby the learner makes real in his life the Objective of Christian education may be identified as the process of human becoming. Learning is the process of life changing. The process of becoming involves the process of change, or learning, in which the personality is restructured in major and/or minor ways.

Various theories of learning have been advanced to interpret the accumulating research data related to the whys and wherefores of human changing. But as yet there is still no one generally accepted theory of learning capable of satisfying all the necessary considerations introduced by the evidence. There are, however, many practical views about the learning process which are widely supported by most learning theorists. Such views are capable of clarifying how learning takes place and how the curriculum of the church may be organized to involve the learner in appropriate learning tasks within the curriculum. Some of these views and insights are summarized below together with their significance for the educational ministry of the church.

Changes in life charcteristics are attributable both to physical maturation and to experience. The changes that come about through experiences may be identified as learning, although life characteristics are dependent on both types of change. The changes effected in life characteristics may be evidenced in altered concepts, skills, attitudes, appreciations, which may occur singly, all together, or in combination. These changes, in turn, may be reflected in overt behavior.

25

Life changing comes about as the person interacts with, or responds to his environment. Environment is taken to mean persons (human and divine), things, and past experience of the individual and of the race. There is a sense in which the environment may be identified as the field of relationships—God, man, natural world, history. Learning involves exploration of the field of relationships and the consequent discovery of meaning and value which are internalized and appropriated within the life of the person and may lead to the assuming of responsibility in light of the objective of the educational ministry of the church.

How Learning Takes Place

What is known about learning in general is applicable to the teaching ministry of the church. The way in which learning comes about or change is effected can be described but partially. There is much about the way people learn that is not yet understood. The complexity of the learner and the unending variety and interrelatedness of his ever-changing environment contribute to the complexity of the learning process itself. The change effected in any aspect of personality contributes in some way to the change of the whole self. One may observe an infinite variety of behavioral changes in a learner, or one may seek to foster a specific learning at a particular time, and recognize all the while that a whole complex of forces, in addition to those than can be observed, will be at work.

Not all learning which results from one's experience, therefore, is planned learning. Since human responding is to one's total environment, a continuing stream of response is elicted and the person therefore often learns what is unplanned along with that which is intended to be learned. The learner acquires, along with desirable learnings, those which may be considered undesirable from his own or his teacher's point of view. Not all human changes are constructive, progressive, or forward moving. Learning is also involved in the changes in thought, feeling, and behavior which obstruct and stultify one's further development or which negate one's potential for additional achieving.

Not all changes are intentional. Unplanned, unsought, and sometimes unwelcome experiences also foster significant learnings. In the rise and fall of ongoing life, experience, tragedy or catastrophe, or sudden illumination may force the person to respond in changed ways with new attitudes. The orderly procedures of planned learning seem to be in abeyance. Old patterns are shattered, new responses are demanded.

Sometimes such responding leads to learned fears, anxieties, aversions, self-destroying habits. Sometimes such responding leads to profound insights into one's own nature, to new awareness of God and his purposes, to fresh understanding of the worth of one's fellows. Such learnings may thus be deeply significant and permanent, though they are unintended. They take place as one responds to the demands and the ever-changing experiences of one's life.

Not everything that is learned is of equal significance to the learner. Much changing is only peripheral and insignificant as it relates to the major patterns of one's living. The principle is valid that the more central and intentional learning is, the more costly it is. The more significant any learning is, the more likely it is to cause pain and struggle and to bring basic satisfaction. The converse is also true, for the less effort or struggle involved, the less central and more peripheral the change is likely to be. The less energy or readjustment required to realize any specific learning, the less likely the change is to endure as a permanent personality feature.

Not all changes in external, observable behavior necessarily reflect corollary changes in feelings and intellectual commitments. Some observable changes are the learner's reactions to some external demands or expectation placed upon him which he satisfies without any adjustments in his basic commitments, insights, or purposes. The opposite is also true. Not all internal changes necessarily result in adjusted, observable skills or external behavior. While radical learnings are likely to be reflected in appropriately readjusted activities, abilities, preferences, and associations, the more peripheral learnings may appear to be so insignificant to the learner that in fact he may find little utility, if any, for what he has acquired.

The learner has a certain readiness to change when previous learning has not been consolidated. The changing edge of personality is often associated with the individual's quest for meaning and fulfillment or efforts to solve problems, to resolve uncertainty, insecurity, dissatisfaction, or pain. The learner is likely to be eager to change (learn) in those areas of his personality

27

where unresolved issues are troubling him, or challenging goals are beckoning him. When the learner recognizes the relevance of his learning opportunities to his persistent life problems, the resultant learnings are likely to have central value. The more radical the potential learnings are, the more likely it is that the learner will need support and encouragement to sustain his effort.

As a person perceives his problem, or becomes aware of some suitable way it might be solved, or desires to change his condition or state of affairs, or identifies a goal sufficiently desirable to put forth the energy and effort required to achieve it, learning takes place. Learning is usually in direct proportion to learning effort invested, and internally accepted goals issue in intrinsic motivation and a higher level of energy output in goal striving.

Another useful view in regard to learning is that the learner tends to seek to repeat those experiences which are meaningful and satisfying to him and sustain those states which are rewarded commensurate with the effort invested. When a learner perceives the tasks set before him as unrelated to his own real interests or personal goals, the motivation may be said to be extrinsic. The level of energy willingly invested in response to extrinsic motivations is likely to be of moderate strength but at least sufficient to avoid punishment and satisfy whatever external prevailing authority is enforced. Changes acquired under such external pressures tend to fade or to be dissipated under the pressing personal quest for intrinsic values growing out of the learner's intrinsic motivations. Essential to understanding learning, therefore, is an understanding of motivation.

Other useful views of learning point up the widely varying readiness and capacity of individuals to learn. Not all individuals learn equally well or with equal ease. Not all individuals are ready to learn at the same time. Therefore in teaching, individual learning opportunities are often the most valuable when planned in light of the readiness and the ability of the individual learner. Past experience, as well as ability, attitudes, aptitudes, and interests, affects the level of learning that issues from any particular learning challenge. There is an optimal time for learning. When readiness influenced by need or interest prevails, related learnings are enhanced and accelerated. When the degree of difficulty or problem solving related to any learning activity is within the achievable realm for the learner, the potential for striving to achieve is increased. This does not mean that the learner may be left without extrinsic guidance and stimulation. The experience of the human race and the demand of society determine goals with which each individual learner must come to terms. The way in which these goals become relevant and meaningful—intrinsic goals—for each learner is a basic consideration in planned learning opportunities.

In planned learning opportunities, the learner learns to the degree that he perceives learning goals as meaningful and desirable for himself. In undertaking the tasks required to reach his own goals, changes in his personality result. The more responsibility the learner is willing to assume for his own learning, the more likely the learning is to be optimum.

To be sustained, learning requires reinforcement. Reinforcement is effected by repetition, practice, success, and reward. Repetition and practice tend to strengthen learning. Success and reward realized through such learning efforts lead to further practice, which in turn leads to further reinforcement of the achievement. The reverse is also true. Failure and punishment for honest efforts put forth may discourage and inhibit further efforts necessary to achievement. On the other hand, it is sometimes possible for the learner so to respond to his failure that he actually gains positive and desirable learnings from it. Or he may be stimulated by the failure itself to make more determined learning efforts which may then lead to the achievement of the desired goals. Of all failures, that failure which is experienced against a sufficient background of success tends to fall into proper perspective for the learner and to be least inhibitive of further learning efforts. Incentive for learning depends on challenge, and success can be sweeter when contrasted with

29

failure. Thus, the positive learnings potential in failure are highly important.

Goals which the learner is helped to set for himself should be realistic. That is, they should be realizable with a reasonable expenditure of effort and within a reasonable length of time. Otherwise, for lack of the motivation born of the reward of success, further exploration of the risk-taking required for significant life discoveries may not be pursued. Any projected learning opportunity should be sufficiently difficult to challenge the learner to establish vigorous learning efforts and it should be sufficiently within his capacity to learn that it may lead eventually to the degree of success that will encourage further investment of learning effort.

Learning is one complex process. Persons learn through their perceptions, through problem solving, through practice, and through identification. However, it is not to be construed that learning is divisible into tasks or sequences when any change is actually being experienced.

Perception is used in two senses. In its more limited sense, it means the picking up of clues to new or revised ideas, understandings, apprehensions, insights. Also involved in this sense of perception is reflection upon experience and testing the results of reflection. In its broader sense perception means the way a person sees the phenomena of experience and the way he feels about them. As between these two meanings, it may be said that the former is one of the methods by which a learning task is engaged in, whereas the latter is the background from which it is approached. It may also be pointed out that perception in the more limited sense is one of the factors that contributes to learning by perception in the broader sense.

Problem solving has to do with the making of choices and decisions. It includes assessing a situation in terms of goals to be achieved, surveying possible courses of action to achieve the goals together with the predicted consequences of each one, deciding upon a particular course of action and carrying it out (i.e, assuming responsibility), evaluating the consequences after the event in terms of the goals previously determined.

Practice is learning by repetition, drill, and rote. Practice involves engaging in an activity with appropriate frequency. Improvement does not depend directly on the amount of repetition but depends upon a complex of amount, schedule, readiness, and the environmental circumstance within which the practice is performed.

Identification is learning through a relationship. The learner may find change desired or desirable and is supported in change through identifying himself with another person or a group in which he appropriates the values and goals of the person or group. Learning by identification is often unconscious.

Any experience of learning may involve change through all these ways. It would be a rare or very simple type of learning that would be limited to one of these ways. It is also highly important to recognize that learning, while usually a gradual process, may sometimes be sudden and cataclysmic. Furthermore, it must be realized that some learning is so drastic and powerful in its effects upon personality as to mean the radical reorientation of the learner's life goals.

Learning and Christian Education   *31*

What is said thus far about learning in general is accepted as valid for learning the Christian faith. From the Christian perspective, the capacity for learning is God-given, and as God is continuously active in the life of a person, so he is active in the person's processes of learning. These learning processes involve the learner's perceiving an insight into what he might become and taking for himself suitable goals to move him in the direction of God's will as he perceives it. As he does this, God through his Holy Spirit is at work within the life of the learner and within the sustaining fellowship of his church to call the learner and to bring to fruition the promise resident in him as a child of God.

When a person becomes newly aware of God and moves in repentance to be reconciled to God, the life forces involved in his awareness, perception, and response (a part of the learning process) are operative in any consequent change. When a person acquires a new way of responding to other persons in need or feels injustice more keenly or has come to love someone more deeply or has risen to risk personal loss to fulfill what has come to be seen as God's will or has come to a new awareness and appreciation of himself as a person, the process of learning—becoming—is at work in the perfecting of faith. Likewise, faith is being perfected through learning when a person achieves new understandings with verbal skills in the interpretation of Christian principles.

All changes in life characteristics that result from experience may be properly referred to as learning. Experience in the whole field of relationships is the arena in which the learning process is undertaken and the work of redemption begun. God is at work in the learning process to bring his children from darkness into light, from falsehood into truth, from hate into love, from isolation into fellowship, from doubt into faith, from fear into trust, from sin into righteousness, from alienation into reconciliation.

The Learning Tasks

A person's motivations have a significant bearing on the learning process because they are determinative of his assuming responsibility for the Learning Tasks. Persons become involved in the Learning Tasks as they seek to satisfy for themselves felt or unfelt needs, or as they cooperate with others in undertaking specific work toward a group goal. Engagement in any one of the Learning Tasks may cause a person to abandon previously set goals, and to set new goals toward the Objective. Indeed, each Learning Task may be the leverage point for raising sights for new goals. Thus the Learning Tasks are seen together in one dynamic process.

This view of the Learning Tasks reflects the way in which the needs and experiences of persons and the great concerns of the Christian faith are tied together in the curriculum of Christian education.

For clarity and concreteness, learning in Christian education is described in terms of Learning Tasks. They offer practical handles for analyzing the experiences of the learner in any teaching-learning situation.

Five Learning Tasks have been identified:

Listening with growing alertness to the gospel and responding in faith and love

Exploring the whole field of relationships in light of the gosepel

Discovering meaning and value in the field of relationships in light of the gospel

Appropriating personally the meaning and value discovered in the field of relationships in light of the gospel

Assuming personal and social responsibility in light of the gospel

These tasks describe a single process and are not regarded as sequential. They are related to one another in the following manner: "Listening with growing alertness . . . and responding in faith and love," comprehends the other four tasks. These four describe what is involved in "listening and responding."

33

The primacy of "listening with growing alertness" recognizes the transforming power of God's Holy Spirit in the learning experience, thus giving the Christian dimension to all the learning tasks. "Listening" means becoming engrossed with the gospel, experiencing and knowing it. Listening is, therefore, not to be construed as passive.

As he listens to God's Word, the learner explores his field of relationships, discovers and appropriates meaning and value.

This appropriation is evidenced by his response, and issues in assuming personal and social responsibility. The task of assuming personal and social responsibility flows from and feeds into the other tasks.

The task of listening which penetrates all the other tasks, identifies the centrality of the gospel in learning in Christian education. The "responding" implied in all the learning tasks is a corollary task undertaken by the learner under the influence and the activating power of the Holy Spirit.

34

Organizing Principle of the Curriculum

Each of the other components of the Design for a curriculum of Christian education has been isolated for purposes of description and analysis. In operation as living curriculum, however, the several components of the Design cannot be separated. The Design is translated from theory into curriculum reality as it comes within the learner's experience. The curriculum of Christian education becomes dynamic within the learner himself. The several components of the Curriculum Design must be organized in a plan that will bring them into meaningful relationship within the experience of the learner himself as the plan is implemented. To this end, the curriculum is designed for the learner. The curriculum is projected in the last analysis so that the learner may be aware of God and respond to him in faith and love.

The Objective of the church's teaching ministry cannot be realized unless the learner accepts it as his own life objective and undertakes for himself the Learning Tasks. Nor can the learner "be aware of God through his self-disclosure, especially his redeeming love as revealed in Jesus Christ," without considering seriously the content of the curriculum. This is so, for in the gospel God has made himself known to man, and in the knowledge of this revelation the learner is able to appropriate Christian meaning and value for all his relationships. Further, the learner cannot be drawn fully into the fellowship of love and service, where in fact his relationships may be redeemed, if he only listens to the gospel. He must listen, but he listens in order that he may respond to God's initiative and relate effectively in light of the gospel throughout the whole field of his relationships.

The proper Context for education in the Christian faith and life, then, is the church of Christ. The church is the people of God related to him and to one another in Christ. This dynamic relationship has precedence over and gives meaning and vitality to all other relationships. The church provides the congenial environment within the world in which both the witness of the gospel and its implications for all of life can be explored, understood, and undertaken.

Within this Context for Christian education, the great concerns of the gospel as they are relevant to man in his situation (scope) become vital curriculum experience. This experience may foster Christian understanding, Christian discipleship, meaningful participation in the Christian fellowship, and the assurance of the Christian hope.

Objective, Scope, Context, and Learning Tasks, then, are not only components of a theoretical design for curriculum. In a dynamic Christian teaching-learning situation they all come to focus in a unified process within the learner where the operation of each component is dependent on the other and all contribute vitally to the outcome of the process itself.

35

As curriculum planners work to bring together these components of Design, they must keep foremost the principle by which the five components of the curriculum may be organized for blending into the one dynamic process.

Therefore, the organizing principle is a proper fifth component of the Design itself. Its function is to identify the interrelatedness, the interdependence, the basic oneness of all the aspects of the Design and to insure that no one component is given an undue priority or an independent place as the curriculum Design is implemented in teaching-learning.

Organizing Principle

The learner

"becomes aware of God through his self-disclosure . . . and responds in faith and love."	Objective

when

through involvement in the Christian community	Context

he comes face to face with

the great concerns of Christian faith and life as they are relevant to him in his situation	Scope

by

"listening with growing alertness to the gospel and responding in faith and love."	Learning Tasks

PART II

*The Scope
of the Curriculum*

PREFACE TO PART II

In this Curriculum Plan, Part II deals with one component of the Design, Scope of the curriculum, that is, the whole field of relationships in light of the gospel. This section analyzes and organizes the Scope in a manageable form so that it may make its appropriate contribution to the total curriculum plan in relation to the other components of the Design.

The entire Scope has been organized into five areas of curriculum that are in turn subdivided into themes. Each area reflects one aspect of the objective so that when taken together the areas of curriculum present a well-rounded whole intimately related to the objective. Each area, then, provides for appropriate content with which the learner must be engaged in order to fulfill the Objective. In this way a principle of integration is at work between the Objective and the whole field of relationships in light of the gospel.

Furthermore, in addition to its relation to the Objective, each area of curriculum provides a particular perspective on the total Scope. Together they display the full spectrum of the Scope, seen in detail in the themes constituent to each area. Thus, this analysis and organization of Scope provides a means of checking the comprehensiveness of the Curriculum Plan. Also, it provides a ready and well-organized basis for exploring the richness of the church's ministry of education. It may, therefore, enhance the church's view of its educational task and educational resources.

It is in the component of Scope that one may discover most clearly the place of the Bible and history in the Curriculum Plan. It is described below.

39

The Bible in the Curriculum Plan

The Bible is unique as a source to which man may turn in his attempts to understand how God in love chooses to both relate to his creation and declare his intentions for it. The Bible is the library of written accounts of God's acts and man's responses in history; hence, the Bible is the normative source of the church's message and ministry of reconciliation.

As the library of revelation, the Bible not only is a record of how God has revealed himself in the past and how man has responded in the past, it is also a present instrument of revelation for any who are enabled to see themselves as part of the historical community addressed by God. For many who seek him, "God's word to man" as revealed in the Bible has exhibited the power to become "God's word to me." Because of this power the Christian Scriptures are given a central and unique position in the church's educational ministry.

The scriptural foundation of this Curriculum Plan is evidenced in the way in which both the areas and themes are rooted in the Bible. In this Plan the Bible has been used to define the fundamental concerns of the Christian community and to identify the basic issues of human life, along with the persistent needs of man. These definitions and identifications are recognized in the area and theme titles, the delineation of area, and the themes delineated.

The use of areas and themes in the Curriculum Plan assure dependence upon the Bible for the selecting of content, a part of Scope, to be included in the church's teaching ministry. This is true, first, because the areas and themes are an explicating of the Scope of Christian education—man's experience with the divine, human, and natural dimensions of reality in light of the gospel; and, second, because the Bible is recognized within the Curriculum Plan as the source and norm for any understanding of the Christian gospel.

The Bible as the source and norm for understanding and com-

40

municating the gospel makes clear that God is not limited to the Scriptures as the sole means of revealing himself to man. God is active directly in the life and affairs of men, individually and corporately. But the Bible as the source and norm for understanding and communicating the gospel is the essential foundation for any curriculum plan whose scope is the whole field of relationships in light of the gospel. Within this Curriculum Plan the Bible is the ground and guide for all concerns in the Scope and influences the choice of content in every aspect of the church's educational ministry.

History in the Curriculum Plan

The role of history in the Curriculum Plan may be placed in two categories. In one category history provides the arena of man's present encounter with God's continuing revelation; the current events of human existence have the purposes of God resident in them and can become revelatory when viewed with the eyes of faith. In a second category, history provides the record and interpretation of past events, events that yield data from which men derive insights for interpreting their present experiences and for making prognoses of what are God's purposes for his people in their imminent experiences.

41

As the record and interpretation of past events, history can be used to gain an understanding of the ontology of those whose writings are the Scriptures of the church, an understanding which enriches the meaning and interpretation of the biblical record. Therefore, to view the historical ontology of the authors and the relationship of their writings to analogous events of current human existence is consistent with the gospel and guards against the dangers of separating the gospel from reality and/or withdrawing from the world.

History as a tool for understanding how God's people have responded or might respond to him provides an important source for content in the Curriculum Plan. These responses of the people of God are in the form of ecclesiastical decisions, creedal statements, poetry, treatises, annals, drama, visual arts, music. These deposits of history, which might be called the church's heritage, provide not only rich resources for understanding and identifying with God's people over the ages; they also are suggestive of appropriate modes by which God's people today may express their response to his revelation in both their immediate and pending life situations.

42
History offers to every curriculum area and theme a contribution of continuity and of perspective for awareness of God and response to his redemptive love.

Place of Part II in the Curriculum Plan

Part II contributes together with other components of the Design to Part III, *Source for the Development of Teaching-Learning Opportunities.* As a part of *Source,* Scope displays meanings and value for man's whole field of relationships; it identifies and emphasizes the reality of God's immanence in the life of man; it lifts up the inescapable relevance of the gospel to the present condition and need of man and society.

The Curriculum Areas

LIFE AND ITS SETTING: THE MEANING AND EX-PERIENCE OF EXISTENCE

The themes within this area are:

Man Discovering and Accepting Himself
Man Living in Relationship with Others
Man's Relation to the Natural Order
Man's Involvement in Social Forces
Man's Coping with Change and the Absolute
Man's Creativity within Life's Daily Routines

Description of Curriculum Area

The focus, or vantage point, of this area is the significance and purpose of life; what it means to be a human being; the origin, meaning, and destiny of the natural order; the import of history.

Comprehended in this area of curriculum is such content from Christian thought and life as: the doctrine of creation; the doctrine of man including his relation to the natural world; interpretation of personal and social development; struggle and conflict; the concept of eternal life; interpretation of world view including human history and eschatology.

43

In order to have educational value as an area of curriculum this content must be viewed in the terms of its pertinence to the persistent issues of man's life. Some of these issues are: What can I make of the universe? Does it have significance and purpose? Who am I? In what way, if any, does my life have meaning? What is my destiny and that of the world? Does the past tell me anything of value about the present and the future?[1]

---

[1] These three paragraphs are repeated here as necessary background.

Delineation of Area

This curriculum area deals with human life itself and with all that gives it significance and purpose: creation, the nature of man, the contemporary natural and social setting—including institutions and the history and destiny of man and creation. The area encompasses the self, society, nature, religion, and all of man's approaches to truth and falsehood, beauty and ugliness, and good and evil, thus focusing upon "the meaning and experience of existence." Life and its setting gain significance and purpose for persons:

44

As they understand and experience, in Christian faith, what it means to be human.

As they understand and experience, in Christian faith, the origin, meaning, and destiny of the natural order.

As they understand and experience, in Christian faith, the meaning of history.

What It Means to Be Human

In the drive to discover life's meaning and significance, the human quest has taken many forms. Illustrative of the formal, organized expressions of the human quest are the enterprises of philosophy, religion, the life sciences, the behavioral sciences, the social sciences, literature, the fine arts, the practical arts, and technology. These combine to try to help with answers to man's questions about himself: Who am I? Why am I here? Where did I come from? Where am I going? What shall I do? What do I have? What are my relationships? What are my responsibilities? What must I do to have life to the full? What is my situation?

The significance of human life and the human situation is indicated even in the fact of man's being rooted in and dependent upon the natural order. He is created with basic animal needs and drives. Yet human life is distinct in many ways from other forms of creation.

The human creature uses his powers often in different ways from other creatures, and possesses higher powers, such as distinctive potentials for intellectual, social, and spiritual growth. The factors of experience and memory enable man to see meaning in events and in himself, leading to a highly developed sense of selfhood (including an image of what he is and what he can be) and to a power of conceptualization that enables him to discriminate between objective and subjective knowledge, reflected in all his thought and literature. Coupled with these factors are his capacity for self-acceptance, self-determination, and choice. Related to the emotions of hate, fear, joy, and the like is man's capacity for humor and tragedy. His whole emotional life emphasizes his need to give and to receive love. Climaxing his human nature are his capacities for valuing, for moral responsibility, and for communion with God.

Human development seems to be characterized by a kind of continual, yet patterned, change: there is a never-completed process of "putting life together," as interests and concerns grow, as habits are altered, and as the individual tries to define and achieve the good life, to discover the meaning of his life and the direction of his future. Yet the discoveries, achievements, and patterns are likely to give way when man finds himself inadequate to deal with all the problems of existence. Sometimes in ignorance, sometimes involuntarily, sometimes by choice, streams of action and interaction are set flowing which engulf the members of the human family. Man finds himself driven by the limitations of his human capacities to an unanswered "why?"

Man finds sin and evil ever present in himself and in the social and political order, sometimes explicable but often defying comprehension and escape. Although a child of God, man discovers that his predicament is a consequence of his own humanity and he may be driven to discover the divine intervention ex-

45

pressed through God's saving love in Jesus Christ or he may turn to such alternatives as stoicism, practical atheism, and life without purpose.

In a sense, man reaches both the heights and the depths of his being in the dilemmas of success and failure, decision and indecision, freedom and determinism, hope and despair, courage and cowardice, planning and rash action, sickness and health, and joy and suffering. Man lives in a world where suffering and struggle seem unavoidable. In the light of the gospel, suffering and struggle may become means toward deeper insight, richer relationships, and more genuine creativity.

Man may come to rejoice in the knowledge that he is a child of God, created in his image; in the knowledge that though he is a sinner, yet he may respond to God's seeking and redeeming love and receive his forgiveness. He may know himself as a creature for whom Christ died, and in that knowledge understand himself as disobedient, rebellious against God and under God's judgment. Nevertheless he may know he is loved and accepted by God who redeems, calls, remakes, offers him a role in life, and guides him by his Spirit.

Man may learn to value and accept himself and others because God values and accepts them, despite their sin and imperfection. If one values himself in this way, he cannot despise or reject himself or others, or try to make others in his own image. He points to God and to what God has done for man, rather than to himself.

Human beings find meaning in life not merely on an individual basis, but in contact with other human beings in various ways. Human life is a combination of independence of and interdependence with others. There is a consciousness of others, a dependence upon them, and an impulse to be in communication with them. A significant aspect of the human quest at the present time is the study of communication and of the behavior of groups.

Man's prime relationships are those of a person-to-person kind: his relationships with those with whom he lives, whom he sees, with whom he communicates face-to-face, such as members of his family, neighborhood, school, local church, civic groups, and the like. Here he comes to know how people feel, what they need, the similarities and differences among them, how groups work and behave, and other subtleties of human relations. Person-to-person relationships in the realm of sex and marriage, rearing children, and intimate family give-and-take with those older and younger are known both to destroy and to fulfill human life. With person-to-person relationships the meaning of friendship and forgiveness, alienation and rejection, denial and separation may be discovered and deepened. As the gospel is brought to bear on his relationships, a person discovers a quality of give and take that helps him know who he really is. He comes to know himself as a "person" when others accept him as a person, not treat him as a "thing." At the same time, such relationships reveal others to him as *they* are—persons, not things. As his social relationships come to take on this quality of true person-to-personness, the Christian may find that his response to God's revelation of himself as a person moves to a deeper level of experience.

Man is also related to persons whom he does not see or know. These relationships are the result of his inevitable involvement in such institutions as government, property, law, and education. Man may be involved as a participant in institutions that touch the lives of thousands of persons through a church denomination and its outreach, the United Nations, a labor union, a professional society, or a benevolent association. Many relationships that were formerly on a rather personal basis have today become institutionalized; medicine and the healing arts, and education of children and youth provide good examples of this; the gaining and exercising of political power and the power of the legal system may be instances of the same type of development.

Man also sustains intergroup, interfaith, and intercultural relationships; relationships with a social class, a vocational group,

47

a race, an age group, a religious group, and the like. He also, as a person in each group, carries relationships to other groups. Today he is gaining new insight into the forces operating in intergroup, interreligious, and intercultural relationships. He is aware that group pride and group prejudice as well as group solidarity and group values are forces to be recognized. Man is discovering what he can do with both the positive and negative forces operating between and within groups, to use them to create closer and more constructive bonds among people or to use them for socially destructive ends.

Man is related in significant and formative ways to all other human beings through what are sometimes called the "structures" or "orders" of society. By "structures" is meant the habits, the customs, the traditions of a culture or civilization. Every civilization organizes or "orders" the interaction of persons as they seek to meet their needs. These structures or orders can be identified as "the way we do things here" in regard to: relationship of the sexes; family and marriage traditions and customs; "ingroup-outgroup" designations; acceptable ways of getting food, shelter, and clothing; ways of relating to what is accepted as sacred; the basis of personal authority and power. Each person comes at birth into a social matrix made up of the influences of these structures. His values, his perspective, and his purposes, at any age, are the result of his interaction with the particular structures of his environment. God having made man to live in society, has purposes to be fulfilled in and through the social expressions of man's life.

In his social setting, whether it be person-to-person, institutional, intergroup, or societal, man discovers himself in a setting fraught with conflict and tension. Conflict characterizes human life, within the person, within the group relationships, and between groups. The Christian faith sometimes gives rise to conflict within the person, or between persons and the prevailing culture. Conflict, unfortunately, sometimes is expressed in the use of coercion and war, and reveals the desperate need of the

48

world and all human beings to work mutually for reconciliation. Conflict may result in alienation, withdrawal, a disintegration of social life, or it may be resolved in bringing together creatively the diverse elements in new relationships and values.

Man faces continuous change in new knowledge, new inventions, new human situations, new social structures; for example, new concepts of space-time. Such changes make demands on man, both to adjust and to resist. In the midst of change, however, man seeks stability and security which he finds only in centering his life in God.

Even though human life has tremendous significance when viewed individually and socially, it gains its greatest significance when considered in the light of eternity. God is the source of life and the guarantor of life eternal. Man finds himself fully only in trusting in God and in responding in worship and service.

The discussion of life implies the question of death. Man's question is likely to be that of personal identity: Will *I* be *I* after death? Against the desire for a comfortable continuation of life, the Christian faith asserts a vigorous and triumphant resurrection faith: judgment, eternal life, *fulfillment,* and personal responsibility.

New concepts of longer time spans for this universe, penetration of new worlds in space, questions about life on other planets challenge prior assumptions that apparently had long since been settled for good. There is a need to discover the eternal implications in the concrete situations in which man finds himself, including institutional and cultural situations, so that he may come to know what God requires of him and respond in faith, love, and obedience, to his grace.

49

To see the concrete situation man faces in the light of eternity is to understand himself in his human predicament, and thus to accept his finiteness, to know that he is not God, and to be led to explore how he may work with God in spite of human limitations. In this light, he may be able to see the relevance of God's purpose to all the relationships of life and seek God's guidance in making decisions with regard to the problems and circumstances of life, testing his actions in the light of God's will and purpose. God is God; ultimately his will prevails; man's divine destiny and eternal life are God's gifts.

The Meaning of the Natural Order

The setting for man's life consists not only of society, but the natural order as well. In one way, man stands in the presence of nature in awe and wonder at its majesty and mystery. In another way, he sees nature as an order to be understood, mastered, and used to sustain or destroy life. The immediate future promises an encounter with the universe on a scale unprecedented in the life and experience of mankind. Life will take on added significance and purpose for persons as they understand and experience in Christian faith, the origin, meaning, and destiny of the natural order. Man's quests through the physical sciences, the life sciences, and technology thus take on direct relevance to the meaning of human life.

The study of the physical and the life sciences produces such ideas as: concepts of space-time; quantities of energy in motion; laws of probability; multiple galaxies in the universe as theoretical and observable realities. As man's capacity to observe natural phenomena and to predict their performance with greater accuracy increases, he is able to envision many more of the possibilities of life. What is being observed is not nature itself but natural phenomena that are being exposed to a certain method of inquiry. As man continues to learn more and more about the natural world, he discovers ways of relating to it that either sustain or destroy life.

Man needs desperately to discover the purposes of God that are life sustaining and to become involved in making them his purposes. In this way he may become a worker in God's process of bringing his purposes to fruition and fulfillment. Man is both dependent upon and to a certain extent in control of the physical universe. At the same time, the universe remains a mystery, but viewed in light of the gospel, it is seen as moving toward ultimate ends under the control of God. God's creative providence pervades the universe and all of human life.

God is creator of all that exists and all that will exist. All that has been made or will be made is within his care, control, and concern. Man needs to understand and accept the universe about him as coming from and continuing in the will and purposes of God so that man may take his place creatively and responsibly in the world, cooperate with God's plan and purpose, and live in a way that fulfills that for which the world was created.

The Meaning of History

In addition to the personal, the social, and the natural, there is a historical dimension to this curriculum area. Human life on the earth has a continuity which we call history—past, present, and future. Man hears about the past, lives and experiences in the present, and wonders about, anticipates, and plans for the future. He notices life's continuities and its differences; he speculates about the threads of meaning in history and about his own place in the historical processes of the present; he confronts the idea of a God with a purpose for history and the possibility of trusting and hoping in him. Life has significance and purpose for persons as they understand and experience, in Christian faith, the influence and import of history as reflective of life's meaning.

The human quests of science, philosophy, art, and the rest all have their historical aspect and significance. Out of their aspirations and needs persons have developed modes of existence that reflect certain values in life. The values result in religion, art, customs, and social, political, economic, and ethical systems. These systems, expressing the values man finds, contain man's heritage: religious, cultural, racial, national, biological, psychological, sociological, technological, genealogical, and intellectual.

51

Man's heritage consists of everything from his highest insights and aspirations to his prejudices and fears.

A key to history is that God's self-disclosure in history is not only past, but also continuous and contemporary. The gospel is the continuous and contemporary witness to God's redemptive action in Jesus Christ. God's will and acts may be discerned in the events that take place in the world in which God is at work in those events to redeem, uplift, and preserve, through judgment and salvation, through destruction and reconstruction. In this divine-human dialogue, man confronts many contemporary issues with which he must come to terms in the light of God's revelation. These issues are suggested in the following current phrases descriptive of Western life:

Unremitting conflict in ideas, groups, and nations on a global scale; communism, fascism, and democracy; the drive toward freedom and self-government; a new emphasis upon racial and religious groups in the international scene

Faster communication around the globe, increased speed of transportation, and a growing anonymity in travel; mobility of populations within nations and between nations

The knowledge explosion

The new cosmology

Space and space travel

Urbanization and suburbanization

A growing culture of comfort and conformity

Automation; planned obsolescence; a new self-image on the part of workers

Subliminal influencing

New uses for time: a sense of the temporariness of existence; imminent threat of universal destruction; busyness; social pressures; no time for contemplation; overorganization, over-direction, overstimulation; the urgency of the use of the "new leisure"; mothers working; persons holding two jobs

Relaxation of social controls; sex mores; alcohol; divorce; delinquency

Relativity of values; the widening gap between the generations; early maturing of youth; early marriages; youth with their own income and cars; success cult

Continuing education

Experimentation with nonviolent action for social justice and reconciliation; establishment of new causes like the Peace Corps

Such factors and their resulting tensions, problems, and possibilities variously threaten, degrade, and enrich human life. The way in which persons are able to meet them, in light of the Christian faith, gives life significance and purpose.

God is in and beyond history; he is active in history as eternal Creator and Lord from the beginning throughout eternity, from everlasting to everlasting. God's continuing work in history is through creation, judgment, destruction, deliverance, redemption, reformation, renewal, and calling. History is a dialogue between God and man. God takes the initiative and, as man participates, he is held accountable. Man is part of the continuing stream of history past, present, and future, which is dependent upon and subject to God's purpose. He can look at the sweep of history and enter its stream to influence it. Persons are not creatures of fate. They can transcend and participate in history under God, who is its Lord. Because God is the Lord of history, his purpose is bigger than man's purpose. He may overrule man's action, and ultimately will exercise sovereign rule over men and nations. This Christian message of hope enables man to place his primary trust in God in the midst of the turmoil of history, confident that God will realize his will in and beyond history.

Themes Delineated

1. Man Discovering and Accepting Himself[1]

STATEMENT OF THEME

When faced with the enigma of himself, man needs to understand and accept his human nature (including personal limitations and capacities) in order that he may live meaningfully and purposefully as God wills for him.

54

DESCRIPTION OF THEME

When man becomes aware of his own existence, he is already a complex being. He has not made himself, and typically may wish to be quite other than he is. He is not even effectively in control of his own actions, and may never fully be. His initial state of awareness is a heteronomous one, in that his outward being is not a clear consequence and expression of an inner principle, but is given to him, as in the whole of his world, from without. In the Christian view, God is the Giver of this outside world, the setting in which a person develops an awareness of who he is. The person's perception of his whole field of relationships, especially the way others relate to him and accept or reject him, greatly influences his capacity for self-acceptance. This self-acceptance, in turn, becomes a key factor in his capacity to be outgoing in his relationships with others and with God, his Creator.

This basic condition of human existence—that man is not the first cause of who he is, what he is, when or where he is, why he is—constitutes the primary issues of existence and causes man lifelong concern. This human state is interpreted by the biblical metaphor of the creature. Man is made, or created. His existence is not necessary; he might not have been, and again might not be. He is profoundly dependent upon the Creator for

---

[1]Numbering of themes is for convenience of identification and does not indicate rank or sequence.

his continued existence. Man comes to realize his creaturehood in experiences of limitation, every one of which is a reminder of his dependency, and of his potentially or actually broken relationship to the Source of being. Every experience of limitation is likewise a challenge and opportunity whereby, under God's power and leading, man may find meaning and live purposefully. Thus the limitations encountered by the self, that is man's finitude, while still frustrating and truly limiting, are transformed.

Discovery of Limitation

The character of the self is discovered through its interaction with limiting conditions. The limiting conditions of creation make it possible for a human being to become a self-conscious person. Through interaction with these limitations man takes account of that in reality which is important to his own existence. The whole of reality, as thus selectively apprehended, is the world of each individual. Reality, for the individual, is divided into the not-self and the self, according as it either thwarts, or serves as an organ of, the will. Even within the reality of the self, its organs serve ambiguously or faultily; that is, the self is sometimes unable to perceive truly and to apprehend distinctly the reality of the world. Thus the identification of the self over against the world is imperfect and leads to an anxious self-awareness, in that the not-self has gained entrance, with power to subvert the self. This is the experience of not being sure who you are.

The self thus exists by imposing order upon a limited portion of reality which is continuous with the not-self. The self must walk upon, eat, drink, breathe, and assimilate the not-self. But the walker is continuous with what he walks on and the eater with the eaten. This relation is expressed by the biblical (genesis) description of man as made "from the dust of the earth."

The existence of the self, thus dependent on its interaction with its world, requires instrumentation through a body with its systems, organs, and capacities, which imperfectly serve (and thus imperfectly manifest) the essence and will of the self.

55

The body of every organism has systems for food-getting, metabolism, and reproduction. Air-breathing organisms have systems for the assimilation of oxygen. Many animals have systems of locomotion, and all have ways of achieving appropriate survival responses to environment. These responses may be instinctive or intelligent. In man, the intelligent form of response is clearly preferred in that he possesses a specially developed brain through which he may subordinate whatever is instinctive to the rule of intelligent process.

The totality of systems and organs of a living creature is its biological organization, or organism. In man, there is in addition a personal organization, described in psychological terms. This is based upon, but not reducible to, the biological organization. Other aspects of man's capacity for response to reality are his affective and volitional behavior. They are factors (emotion and will) of his personal organization and are related to but distinct from intelligence. To a large extent they account for man's ability to love, to do justly, to make ethical choices; equally they account for the perversion of these properties in man's behavior.

The enormous generality of man's response capacity makes possible not only appropriate survival responses, but also inappropriate and self-destructive ones. Moreover, it makes possible inquiry, learning, imagination, and intellectual construction which are only remotely related to physical survival, if at all. This means, on the one hand, there is no such thing as "human nature" comparable to the nature of another animal species; on the other, that man has practically unlimited freedom to define, through his perceptions of significance, what is to be the human world.

To summarize, the self as it comes to awareness encounters the limiting conditions of life. In interaction with these limitations, the self experiences the rest of the created world (the not-self) and discovers the self's own identity and capacities for coping with life.

Symbols of Limitation

Man is naturally, as a creature, limited with respect to every form of his relation to environment. But he may perceive such limitation as a threat. Some of the symbols of this threat are described here.

🖌 Particularity—Given the great range of human perceptions and valuation, one wonders why the experiences of his life should be only those in which he does in fact take part. Should not an adequate self-realization mean going everywhere, having every conceivable kind of experience? One fancies himself as scholar, poet, athlete, adventurer, builder, etc., and rebels at the limitation of existence that requires the closing of some doors even as others are opened. Man's imagination leads him to desire universality, while the experiences and decisions of every day seal his particularity. The experience of particularity expresses the limitation that the self can be functionally and practically related to no more than a portion of its world.

🖌 Futility—Even within the range of purposes which choice or destiny gives him to pursue, man often lives to see his cherished projects fail or his successes lose their value through the turning of history. Man wonders why he cannot build reliably; why he cannot secure at least a limited range of results free from the threat of loss or change. The "utterly vain" of Ecclesiastes expresses the apprehension that man's responses to environment, no matter how appropriately conceived, are doomed to eventual failure in their aim. The experience of futility expresses the limitation that man alters his world only marginally, and superficially, never fundamentally at the center.

🖌 Death—Every biological organism comprises processes which, after a limited time, result in the disintegration and dissolution

57

of the organism. Each is also vulnerable to accidental destruction or to attack by other organisms. Physical death thus shows that the physical world is prior to, and substantive to, the organisms that live in it. Humanly speaking, death is experienced as a symbol of the limitation that the self cannot sustain the existence of its world, and therefore of itself, but must receive the power to be from beyond itself.

Each of the above experiences of limitation falls naturally to man in his created existence in the world. Each is made a threat by man's desire and effort to escape limitation itself—that is, to escape his created state. In the Christian view these experiences of limitation need not be threatening. Although the Christian faith affirms man's finitude as a created being and takes into account man's desire to escape his created state (that is, to be not man but God), it provides ways of looking at the living with particularity, futility, and death. The good news of the gospel proclaims that man, however particular and limited, is beloved of God and of intrinsic worth; that however futile man's efforts on the human scale, they are blessed by God when directed toward his purposes and may be used by God in the long reaches of history; that Jesus Christ has through his own death and resurrection made it possible for man to transcend his finite existence in eternal life. In short, the Christian places his ultimate trust not in his own being, his own efforts, or his own existence, but in God. It is this trustful relationship which enables man to accept the limitations of finitude, accept himself, and to live meaningfully and purposefully.

For the Christian, the power to transform the forms of experienced limitation is received in Jesus Christ. "The Son of Man" as applied to Jesus interprets the facts that Jesus was born at a certain time and place; that he lived in a particular historical situation which colored both his words and his actions; that his life and death were conditioned by understandable historical causes; and that he is, nonetheless, of universal and timeless significance because of the embodiment of the eternal in him.

This Theme in the Bible

A principal and classical source for the interpretation of the creation of man and the world is Genesis 1 through 3.

Man's self-questioning, his awareness of limitation and divine purpose woven together in his life, is expressed by Psalm 8 ("What is man that thou art mindful of him . . . ?"). The entire Book of Psalms contains numerous examples of reflection upon the state of man and his world as he confronts God.

The Book of Ecclesiastes shows how the categories of time, space, cause, and substance may become static, empty, futile, and "utterly vain" when cut off from the presence of God.

Paul, writing to the Romans, again and again makes reference to both the capacities and limitations of man, who may capitalize on them under God.

2. Man Living in Relationship with Others

STATEMENT OF THEME

Man's optimum development involves his understanding of and living with others as God's beloved children.

DESCRIPTION OF THEME

This theme interprets the existence of man as a moral-social being—that is, one whose being is mutually constituted with and mutually reflects the relationships which he sustains toward other persons. The development of the theme rests upon a conception, drawn from modern sociology, that of the personal-social field (which might be called the moral field).

In this context the concept of "field" means that personal existence is centered in the human being himself (not in any social unit of which he is a part), and that at the same time he lives in a field of interaction with other human beings. The personal center and the field in which it is related to other persons is defined in mutuality, that is to say, mutuality is the norm

59

which characterizes the interaction (or interpersonal relationships) within the field. This concept provides the basis for understanding how man may experience moral claim upon himself (his relation to the rights and necessities of others) without necessarily regarding it as alien and irrational. The force of this concept is to describe the way in which the personal center of an individual lies within himself and does not by that make the person autonomous respecting every other person. The interpersonal relationships within the field are dynamic and have something of the quality of magnetism—therefore, "field."

60

The Social Personality

Anthropological studies have shown that the modern conception of the individual person is a quite recent innovation. Even now, this interpretation of individual worth is not accepted in many parts of the world. In early societies, even some highly developed and stable ones, personality was an attribute of the group, clan, or totem. The moral force of the community was absolute for the not-yet individual. To disobey was to break from the community and was psychologically equivalent to death. More typically, it did not even occur to a member to deviate from the customary or accepted (the original meaning of "moral") way of acting. It is not quite true to say that the individual was seen as without value or being; more precisely, his value and being resided in the moral field of the group, which remained accessible to him so long as he was united with it. This denial of individuality persists in modern dictatorships where the individual is considered to be a dispensable part of the mass.

In despotic societies, such as those of ancient Egypt or Babylonia, the monarch received individuation from the group and personality came to reside in him. Other members of the society had moral existence as extensions of the monarch—his fingers or toes, as it were—a relation made vivid in the colossal memorials of the Pharaohs.

From such beginnings of the concept of the personhood of individuals, the moral history of man can be regarded as a successive extension of personality to more and more persons—in turn leaping over the barriers of dynasty and nobility, kinship, nationality, economic class, race and color, and culminating in a society in which every member will be legally and socially a person in his own right. With each leap that brought individuality and status to persons, there came an enlarged participation in group life, culminating in the conception of "mankind" as the universal group, counterpart of universal individuality. The support and encouragement of this conception has been and continues to be one of Christianity's greatest contributions to society.

The conception of man as such a moral-personal being developed remarkably early in the Old Testament Jewish community; equally remarkable was the fidelity with which it was maintained in Jewish-Christian tradition, though the practical realization is even yet far from complete.

The whole "human" world of institutions and conventions—religion, law, politics, economics, science, art, philosophy—reflects the dynamics of the personal-social field. The institutions and conventions originated as instruments for conserving and transmitting the being and values of the limited human group. All of them have developed toward more universal human forms and at the same time have allowed for increased status and power to the individual.

61

The experiences of persons as they are engaged and live their lives in their personal-social fields produce reactions in attitudes and behavior of several kinds. Some persons react against the personal-social field. Reactions against the personal-social field are of two kinds: "individualistic" reactions seek to collapse the field leaving the individual who is self-contained and unrelated to others; "collectivist" reactions seek to dissolve the field so that once again there are no personal centers (indeed, no clan or totemic centers either).

Even when there is no overt reaction against the personal-social field, persons do not easily or naturally move into creative and constructive relationships with others. They experience various forms of alienation from other persons. These experiences are described in the first section below. The biblical metaphor "beloved children of God" points to the meaning of personhood and individuality as affirmed in the Christian faith; furthermore "living as God's beloved children" indicates the way in which persons may transcend or overcome experiences of alienation. Thus the Christian has clues in the gospel for living in his personal-social field, and for incorporating into his life Christian moral values. The counter to alienation in the Christian view will be called "communication." Experiences of "communication" in the Christian sense are described in the second section below.

The Experience of Alienation

To conceive of oneself as an individual makes it possible to experience group life as foreign and contrary to one's life as an individual. "Morality" is then perceived as self-denying (i.e. for the sake of the group) rather than as self-fulfilling, and as irrational unless sanctions are added to restore the moral balance by making disobedience to the group more self-destructive than obedience. In either case, the self and the moral field are experienced not as mutually supportive, but as mutually antagonistic or alienated. The individual feels separated from and perhaps hostile to other people. This experience of alienation may take several forms, as described below.

Solipsism—A person may refuse to perceive or acknowledge that the moral field claims him. Other persons are then not perceived as beings comparable to the self, but simply as data of consciousness. Their existence, being denied in its most significant aspect, becomes altogether doubtful, and the self-contained individual is reduced to almost total skepticism about the reality even of himself.

☙ Stress—One may achieve a tolerably satisfactory balance between the needs of the self and the claim of the moral field by rigorous effort. Morality is then guiltily experienced as law, perceived through the primary sanction of group disapproval and the secondary sanction of the fear of punishment. The self is experienced as a battleground of conflicting forces; one is permanently required to choose between them, but permanently denied the right to choose in accordance with the inner dynamics of the self.

☙ Conflict—One may choose to oppose to the claim of the moral field a counter claim of the self—an alternative morality. Sundered from the field, however, the self can point to no value except whim and no being beyond the momentary internal state as the basis for its claim. The alternative morality thus degenerates into a chaotic, wanton protest, or into the negative image of the claim that is rejected.

☙ Reserve—One may choose to separate his public from his private life, responding dutifully to the claim of the moral field but withholding himself from complete involvement. That is, he may respond peripherally but not from the center. The self is then experienced as unacceptable, and the moral field as undesirable. Personal openness gives way to formal politeness, and dignity to spurious honor and meaningless protocol.

63

All of these forms of alienation are present to some degree and simultaneously, all the time and in all relationships. They are experienced externally as broken relationships to persons, groups, institutions, and situations; inwardly as distortions of one's personality organization. For example, one who experiences alienation as a broken relationship to his family may feel self-doubt (solipsism), guilt, fear, paralysis of action (stress), rebellion and destruction (conflict), and coldness and lack of intimacy with other persons (reserve).

Communication

The Christian faith supports the view that alienation and its experienced forms are deep in the moral existence of persons, and therefore cannot be overcome by simple, pragmatic strategies. One cannot negate solipsism by cultivating friendships or by eager social activity; one cannot eliminate moral stress by conforming, or resolve conflict by yielding his own interests; one cannot achieve intimacy by abandoning reserve.

The term "communication," as used here, is the opposite of alienation; restored communication cannot be, for the Christian, reduced to a technical matter of persuasion through language, manipulative skill, or motivation. It is a personal-moral achievement that requires the saving power of Jesus Christ. Alienation is sin; restored communication is grace received in faith. The moral values supported by restored communication have their origin in the character of God whose seeking love for his children is revealed preeminently in Jesus Christ.

Further, communication is used here in the root sense "to make common" rather than the derived and usual sense of conveying or publishing information. Information plays an important part in communication, but speech, writing, and rational thought are only a part of the capacities available to persons for use in expressing or building relationships to and with others.

One's affectional capacity, for example, plays a large part in communication in the family or other small groups. The human body and its physiological processes are similarly of use in sexual communication. The rational, affectional, and physical powers are typically united (in varying proportions) in complex acts of communication such as poetry, painting, music, or dancing. The paragraphs that follow, analyzing the dynamics of communication, presuppose the definition of communication as an act of the whole person involving the unity of his expressive and rational powers.

Communication begins with the acknowledgment of the other person. Physically, this means seeing him, noticing him, welcoming him, making room for him. Many of the conventional acts of courtesy such as shaking hands or opening doors facilitate communication in this way. Affectionally, it means hearing, paying attention, being receptive and appreciative of his responses and being responsive to his overtures. Rationally, it means "speaking his language"—making an accommodation to the forms of language and thought which he prefers and in which he finds meaning. As an act of the whole person, acknowledgment helps to overcome solipsism by expressing the personal-moral quality of the self and the other.

Communication is further understood as dialogue—the alternating of initiation and response by the self and the other. Dialogue presupposes moral tension, and provides the ways and means for overcoming it. Stress, as used above, describes a contradiction between the moral claims of the self and the other (or the group). In dialogue, each person accepts the claim of the other without abandoning or mitigating his own. Thus, while remaining in contradiction, both persons are united in commitment to the task of finding a creative solution that will satisfy both claims. (Or, failing that, of continuing the dialogue with full acceptance of tension and mutual responsibility.) Physically, dialogue implies a balance between speaking and listening and a voluntary restraint upon outtalking or outremembering the other. Affectionally, it suggests mutual support, even in disagreement; patience; and complete abstinence from threat, wearing down, manipulation, and emotional blackmail. Rationally, dialogue suggests the avoidance of merely verbal compromise accompanied by mental reservations.

A third aspect of communication is reconciliation, which is the overcoming of conflict between persons and groups. In conflict the moral field is acknowledged, but with disagreement as to the objectives to be achieved in it. Reconciliation begins with acceptance of the other's freedom and right to pursue moral

65

objectives that are repugnant to one's self; it differs from dialogue in that the specific content of these objectives is not accepted, even in a state of tension. Reconciliation may mean "agreeing to disagree," but it opens the door for dialogue and perhaps for ultimate agreement. Physically, reconciliation implies abstinence from war or violent coercion of the other, beyond what is required for self-preservation. It may mean feeding, clothing, and healing "the enemy" even though this contributes to his ability, under conditions of conflict, to pursue morally repugnant aims. Affectionally, it means seeing the opponent as a human being or group and seeking to feel what health there is in his attitudes, however firmly one rejects these attitudes. Rationally, it means searching for whatever agreement is possible on provisional and pragmatic grounds, however peripheral this may be to the main conflict. (Much of our law has emerged, in this way, from the profound conflict of the courts—precedents leading to principles and principles to more comprehensive moral agreements.)

Finally, in communication, the separation of persons through reserve is overcome by mutual intimacy and respect. Intimacy is the positive value, but intimacy alone makes persons vulnerable and evokes reserve as a defense. In profound personal communication, the burden of protection passes from the self to the other; mutual respect provides the guarantee that the self's openness will not be used to injure him. Physically, this relationship is seen clearly in sexual intimacy, which is qualitatively most intense when the partners respect the need of the other to be free from pain or from excessive unfulfilled desire. In the family, true intimacy requires respect for children, who are physically at a disadvantage. Affectionally, intimacy requires that one's openness not be made a subject for gossip or ridicule. Even good-natured kidding or quiet private amusement at the other's expense may discourage profound self-disclosure. Rationally, it means respect for the variety of ways in which reality is perceived and a willingness to learn from the other what he alone can know, because of his unique place in the personal field.

In the achievement of intimacy, the personal-social character of man is seen in its most nearly pure manifestation; that is, the relationship between persons reflects to each, and reveals to each other, the innermost character of the self. The consequent openness and freedom of relationship is interpreted by the Christian faith through the biblical metaphor of "children of God"—freedom and openness being childlike qualities of the self. Such an achievement is in practice limited to the privileged and protected relationships of marriage, the family, or a small circle of friends. There it serves as a promise that the whole moral field is potentially open to the same qualities.

This Theme in the Bible

Personality as an attribute of the group is illustrated in the narrative portions of the Pentateuch, particularly Genesis and Exodus, where the names of Abraham, Isaac, Jacob, and the sons of Jacob are used to denote either the individual so named, or the tribe of which he was the ancestor. In Exodus the covenant of God is with the whole people, who experience collective rather than individual guilt and punishment.

The beginnings of individuation can be seen in the remarkable figure of Moses in the Pentateuch, and the human portrayals of Hebrew kings, notably Saul, David, and Solomon in the Books of Samuel and Kings.

67

The transition to a more individual basis of moral freedom and responsibility is seen in Jeremiah's description of the New Covenant (31:27-34). However, the vivid call to responsible individual morality is seen in Amos and Micah.

Ezekiel 18 pictures the righteous man as an individual whose behavior prefigures the qualities of acknowledgment, dialogue, reconciliation, intimacy, and respect.

The idea of finding restored communication with others

through becoming children of God is found in Romans 8, and in a brief but climactic form in the words of Jesus in Matthew 18:2-3 and parallels. Ways of living as beloved children of God expressing the Christian concept of "communication" (restoration) are described in Matthew 5 and 6 (the Sermon on the Mount). Descriptions of the relationship among Christians and between Christians and nonbelievers are developed in the epistles of John and of Paul (especially Ephesians, Corinthians, and Romans).

68

3. Man's Relation to the Natural Order

STATEMENT OF THEME

Within man's unending quest for knowledge of the natural order are the challenge and the opportunity to relate to it more nearly as God has intended.

DESCRIPTION OF THEME

The theme interprets man's relation to the natural order as a reflection both of its created goodness and wholeness for him, and of the distortion (real and perceived) introduced by man's alienation from God. It points to the conflict between the purposes of God for his creation and the expectations of man which causes the Cross to appear to him as foolishness, stumbling block, or paradox.

Man's Kinship with the Created World

The natural world, as interpreted by the Christian faith, is a rational structure which evokes in man an answering awareness of his own structural kinship with it. He recognizes the world as his—not primarily at the psychological level where he may regard it as unfriendly, but at the level of knowing that his existence is bound up with the existence of the world.

The rationality of the natural order appears under several aspects. The first is that of order—symmetry, balance, congruence, regularity of relationship, integrity, beauty. The inclusive Greek and Christian term for this appearance of order is *logos*—the creative principle which lends reality to phenomena which in their separateness would be as nothing or unreal. A second aspect of rationality is that of moral order, the perception that the created order favors some types of human action and discourages others. A third aspect is that of mystery and majesty in nature. "Mystery" means that the simplest relationships hold enveloped within them a complex order which may be infinitely articulated. "Majesty" similarly ascribes to the moral order profound depths of meaning. Mystery and majesty in nature remind us that God's thoughts are not our thoughts, nor are his ways our ways (cf. Isaiah 55:6-9).

A note of irrationality is introduced by important experiences of adversities suffered from natural causes: disasters such as floods, earthquakes, fires, storms, and the like; disease that attacks man's health and wholeness; accidents in dealing with the forces of nature. Man is subject to such adversities because he is a part of the natural order. Some of them are due to his own carelessness and insensitivity. However, man can use his capacities to avoid, avert, mitigate the results of such experiences.

In the Christian faith God created the world, is still creatively active respecting the world, and continues to rule it. Man's "dominion" over it is a conditional and limited gift from God. Man is expected to live in the world and make use of it including coping with natural catastrophe in accordance with God's purposes for all mankind; he is not free to exploit and despoil nature and natural resources to attain selfish advantage over others nor is he free to behave irresponsibly toward the natural world. His relationship to the created world is expressed in the Christian term "stewardship."

This means that the world is essentially for man and is to be joyously accepted. However, man in his sin comes to be alienated from the world as well as from God. He becomes a sojourner

69

and an exile, a stranger in his own land. The world in its beauty and fulness becomes for him arid and barren, unable to provide for his hunger and thirst. This may be illustrated in the fact that modern man's technological achievements have sometimes made more hostile and inhuman the conditions under which men live. The human species, unlike many living things, does not always improve for its own use the environment it lives in. Man is often not good for the things that are good for him. He spoils, wastes, scars, and pollutes his world. To live, he must evade the homeostatic balance of nature with an "expanding economy" which stays ahead of its own destructive effects only by an ever-widening and accelerating consumption of the world that remains. Genesis 3:17-19 expresses this relationship:

> cursed is the ground because of you;
>> in toil you shall eat of it [the tree] all the days of your
>> life;
> thorns and thistles it shall bring forth to you; . . .

Man's alienation from nature requires of him work and suffering; but it also calls forth his creativity by which the fruitfulness of nature is restored, especially as this creativity, through a repentant response to the love of God, is united with the essential creativity of nature.

The background and part of the source of man's alienation from nature, seen in his abuse of its resources and his subversion of the meaning of the created world, lies in the view of nature taken by modern science, especially modern physics. We have called this view the materialization of the universe as it is described below.

Materialization of the Universe

In the early Greek view (representative of many primitive and of many religious cultures) the word *phusis* or "nature" denoted without differentiation what would now be called the material, the living, and the divine dimensions of reality. This concept of nature had the virtue of respecting and giving expression to the "togetherness" of many aspects of concrete reality. Modern physics, on the other hand, has refined *phusis* by abstracting from it the material aspect and abandoning the living and divine aspects. In this sense materialization of the universe is used here. The result of this materialization is an enormous gain in precision and technical virtuosity; but it should be emphasized that the world described by physics is a radically abstract one. To view the modern physical world as the "real world" has been aptly characterized by Whitehead as "the fallacy of misplaced concreteness."

One of the motives in the materialization of physics was to give man more powerful instruments of practical control over the world, reduced to technique and divorced from a personal-moral relationship to reality. Materialization suited the needs of the industrial revolution in robbing objects (and ultimately, for some, persons) of intrinsic value, mystery, or unique character. Materialization looks for uniformity and interchangeability; differences and deviations are "averaged out" or otherwise disregarded. The only value is use value, and an object after use may be discarded or salvaged—but not treasured. This means essentially that the universe is not a living, creative, nourishing setting for man's existence but an aggregate of dead objects in space-time which can be manipulated in primitive or sophisticated ways without any feeling of responsibility or moral obligation. This means that modern physics, and those sciences which have been guided in their development by the splendid successes of physics, provide little or no rationale for looking upon the world with love, awe, reverence, or mystery. (The fact that many scientists do display these attitudes is accidental, so far as the general trend of physics is concerned.) In short, the Christian view of the natural world has been not so much disavowed as bypassed and ignored.

It should be stressed that the negative implications of the

71

materialization of the universe are psychologically rather than logically derived. Materialized physics does not say that the world is dead; it only confines its attention to questions to which the living or divine qualities of nature are indifferent. Materialism is only methodological in physics. However, as man lives under the condition of alienation, materialism answers his compulsion to find power without repentance and motivates him to view the natural world—and man as part of it—as object rather than subject.

Such diverse experiences as natural catastrophe, traffic and industrial accidents, infections by microorganisms or viruses, and genetic damage from radiation, all serve to threaten man in his material existence. Man experiences such vulnerability as an offense to his moral sense; he feels that it is not fair for a promising talent to be destroyed by an automobile, or the lives of children cut short by disease. For man to be killed by the hatred of an enemy has a kind of terrible moral fitness that is lacking from the quiet subversion, without malice, of his chemistry by cancer.

The aggressiveness of human personality, in combination with the material fraility and vulnerability of the human being, provides a severe temptation in relation to one's brother under the condition of alienation. This is the temptation to avoid reconciliation and dialogue by striking at the brother's weakness. The brother is violated by concentrating the force of relationship, not upon his personal center, but upon his parts. Such violence is physically illustrated by Cain slaying Abel, and by his counterparts in every generation. But violence is not confined to physical assault; persuasion, manipulation, or advertising which by-passes the personal center to directly loose the springs of motivation is equally violent, in that it turns the human organism from its proper subordination to the self. Brainwashing—psychological war—is real war. And "mental cruelty" can be far more real than merely a trumped-up argument in a divorce action.

True and Spurious Effects of Science

The possibility of a creative relation between man and nature depends largely upon the way nature is perceived. For this reason, science has a profound and direct effect upon the religious possibilities for man in nature. In general, science has had the effect of strengthening man's technical mastery of nature, but diminishing his attitudes of love, awe, or mystery toward it.

Several of the major innovations of twentieth-century science have been regarded hopefully as encouraging a restoration of these attitudes. There is some ground for these hopes, but they will be realized better if the scientific "evidence" for religion is used discriminatingly.

For example, the special and general theories of relativity have made possible a new appreciation of mystery in nature—not only by opening up some of its complexities, but even more by making clear the abstract character of time-space continuum and thus upsetting the complacent materialism which preceded. Relativity theory has been widely (and mistakenly) thought to establish that "everything is relative" and thus to introduce a subjective element in the interpretation of nature. Actually the relativities with which these theories deal concern clocks and measuring rods, not human beings; moreover the theories provide a way of discounting these relativities to arrive at a description of time and space which is true for every observer, whatever his position, velocity, acceleration, etc. Relativity does support the view that the universe is finite, thus returning to the realm of deity, where it belongs, the attribute of infinity.

73

Similarly, the uncertainty principle in quantum mechanics has often been interpreted to make moral freedom possible by showing that the universe does not, as a famous nineteenth-century argument had it, run like clockwork. It is mistakenly held that very small particles are shown by this principle to possess the freedom to act spontaneously, in uncaused ways— that at least a component of their behavior is unconditioned—

and that these small deviations are cumulated and magnified by the neural mechanisms of human beings, creating a gap in an otherwise determined world for the exercise of unconditional moral freedom. There are two good arguments against this. One, an unconditioned freedom is not moral but merely random. From the Christian perspective the freedom of man has moral significance precisely in that it accepts and transcends the conditioning factors. Two, the uncertainty principle has not been established that particles act spontaneously, in the first place. What it has shown is that while the individual particle cannot be predicted (because of its interactions with any conceivable measuring instrument), the collective behavior of particles is statistically predictable enough, given a large enough number—and a large number is still a very small portion of the environment of man.

Three recent scientific interests have conspired to renew the ancient art of speculation about cosmogony—the origins of the universe. These are: relativity; the expanding universe; the observation of the "red shift" in the spectra of distant galaxies, indicating their recession from the earth at rates proportional to their distances; and hypotheses concerning stellar evolution. Two main "New Cosmologies" have emerged to unite these theories and observations. Continuous creation is the doctrine of a "steady-state" universe in which the large-scale uniformity of matter in the universe is replenished, as galaxies recede, by the creation of new hydrogen atoms in the emptiest parts. Cosmic explosion is the theory that at one point of time some billions of years ago all the matter of the universe was tightly compressed in one place; the subsequent expansion imparted the great motion to the most distant parts. According to the variations, this expansion will either continue indefinitely, resulting in final "heat death" of the universe, or it will be followed by a phase of implosion and the beginning of a new cycle. Christianity has no clear preference among these theories; all have theologically respectable ancestry in such persons as Origen and Augustine, but their application to Christian belief is indirect and imaginative rather than of direct theoretical consequence.

Space exploration is, in its visible aspects, mostly of technical engineering rather than purely scientific interest. However, the "space age" symbolizes something that is potentially urgent for Christian education—the coming of age of the first generation to be primarily scientifically oriented including all of its members, not just selected ones, and science taught not as a subject in isolation but with scientific attitudes pervading the curriculum.

Foolishness of the Cross

Scientific thought, and modern thought generally, is optimistic about the control and exploitation of nature. Power without repentance or moral obligation is not only a temptation and a hope; it is a program of action. Such a view and life style is not only sub-Christian with respect to the created world; it strikes at the central meaning of the Christian gospel as expressed and witnessed to in the crucifixion. What can modern man make of the cross of Jesus Christ—success achieved through failure, power through submission, a life saved by losing it?

As science searches for greater theoretical and practical competence in dealing with the very large and very small, its models become more and more difficult to visualize or comprehend in human terms. The probabilistic and relativistic worlds are increasingly alien and psychologically hostile to man—to put it precisely, inhuman. As they depart from human scale, they find less and less human quality.

From this point of view, the cross is seen as a decisive point at which human integrity is successfully maintained. This does not argue the relative parts played by God and man in the cross, but points out that, in the divine-human unity of Jesus Christ, the world is conquered and restored to man, along with his own life.

75

This Theme in the Bible

God's creation of nature, man's dominion over it, and his alienation from it (in the curses laid on Adam and Cain) may be found in Genesis 1 through 3.

The Gospel of John, particularly chapter 1, expresses the paradox of Jesus' overcoming of the world in the midst of alienation from it.

Psalms 8, 19, and 24 express the mystery and majesty of nature and of man in relation to nature.

The last chapters of Job (beginning at 38) describe the relative impotence of man when compared with the creative power of God in nature.

The late chapters of Isaiah contain many illustrative uses of nature to express the relationship of God to his people.

Romans 8:18-25 expresses the conviction that man's sin involves his relationship to the creation, and not only to God and to himself.

4. Man's Involvement in Social Forces

STATEMENT OF THEME

Related to life's setting and to God's purpose are social forces, units, structures, and systems with potential for both good and evil, with which man must learn to live in light of the Christian view of history and of the social order.

DESCRIPTION OF THEME

This theme deals with the Christian way of understanding history and society by seeing Jesus Christ as the center of history and the foundation of social order. It interprets the lifelong human concern to participate fully in the structures to which one belongs or which impinge on one's experience.

The Self and Society

The modern understanding of personality has been illuminated by psychology and psychiatry, particularly by the theory and practice of psychoanalysis. Unfortunately, psychoanalysis seems to have long rested upon the assumption that the human being can be completely understood from an internal viewpoint, taking account of his external relationships only as data of his perception. This in turn has raised the problem: Can a man, perhaps, be psychologically "healthy" or self-actualized while violating or ignoring his brother, and being alienated from his social context? Another way to put the question is to ask whether conscience, as the internal reflection of broken relationship outwardly, has objective reality, or is merely a psychic state. Is the wicked man really guilty? Or might he not achieve self-actualization or fulfillment without repentance by means of suitable strategies to relieve him of guilt?

Jewish and Christian tradition has a clear preference in this matter. It gives a clear affirmative answer to the question, "Am I my brother's keeper?" It holds that any psychology which might conceivably describe the sociopath, one who is unable to distinguish right from wrong, as happy or self-actualized because of his deficient experience of guilt, would be inadequate to the religious understanding of the human being. Christian tradition does not absolutize the will of the group; it regards any effort to do so as idolatry. But it does stress the continuity of existence between the person and the group from which he springs, and urges the individual to consider the group's identity, health, and survival as a moral claim comparable in force to his own identity, health, and survival.

77

Tragedy and Transcendence

Tragedy, on its human side, expresses the relationship that a person is bound up with such social structure as family, church, nation, etc., even when he is most acutely alienated from it. Socrates, refusing to leave Athens and thus save his life when the way was open to him, proved himself a better Athenian than those who condemned him to death in the name of Athens. He affirmed the sanctity and validity of Athenian law at the time when its power was most perversely arrayed against him. The law, he said in effect, is more important than its particular applications.

The question of what is the true identity of a group and hence its embodiment in law, custom, morality, cultural tradition, and institutions, inevitably enters such a conflict. Was Socrates supporting the true inner genius of Athens and his enemies? Or were they the bona fide defenders of tradition against a dangerous innovator? Because of the difficulty in knowing what the innermost identity of a group is, man's involvement in social forces can never be reduced to a simple compliance with what seems to be the prevailing will. Socrates denied that the charges which prevailed against him were true or that they were in the spirit and intention of Athenian law. What he affirmed was his moral continuity with the life of Athens, and his will and duty to maintain that continuity even to his death.

The Christian's regarding of Jesus Christ as the center of history rests upon similar considerations. Jesus came preaching a certain interpretation of the character and identity of his people, the nation of Israel. Their genius was to repent, to have faith, to love, to serve, to seek the kingdom. The lines were sharply drawn when the leaders of the prevailing groups, the Pharisees and Sadducees, determined to put him to death. Had he then fled to safety, he would have yielded to their interpretation of Israel's life as the true one. Instead he chose to affirm his oneness with the innermost principle of the community by suffering punishment from it: reviling, trial, scourging, and crucifixion. Hence, his transcendence over tragedy.

As community turned away from Jesus and rejected him—first the religious parties, then the people, and finally his own disciples down to the innermost circle and to the last man—the wholeness of community was not maintained against him, but in him. The messianic community was reduced to the messiah-suffering servant and victim of the cross. His own faithful identification with the community was perfected, his own self-actualization completed. At the same time, there came with bold clarity the judgment that the community, humanly speaking, had failed itself by failing to perceive, in faith, the consequences of its own identity. This judgment is concisely expressed in the Gospel of John: "He was in the world [read: "social order"], and the world was made through him, yet the world knew him not. He came to his own home, and his own people received him not." (John 1:10-11)

The utter failure of the human community to find and express its own existence as it had been ordained by God is symbolized by the defenders of society who crucified, in Jesus, their own humanity. On the other hand, the perfect success of Jesus Christ, in finding and expressing his own and the community's true existence, commends to all time the faithful union of God and man in him as the only basis for social order. The self-actualization of man cannot be achieved apart from the actualization of a social order, but Jesus has shown that this requires union with God as the source.

The principle to be drawn from this is that the social order, like the individual, must lose its life in order to save it. Every institution has its reason for being, its vocation. It must live out the consequences of its own identity and leave to God the question of survival.

79

The Direction of History

It is clear that a social order has a moral as well as physical power over its members since its existence is vital to each of theirs. A group may betray itself, leaving its members the tragic duty of remaining true to it even though it destroys them. Chris-

tians of the first few centuries were faced with exactly this requirement as the Roman Empire plunged into decadence and
self-destruction and left to the despised and persecuted Christians the task of holding together the social fabric. This raised
for them, in acute forms, the question whether the religious
centrality of Jesus could restore the health of the social order; or
whether Jesus did not, instead, serve as the promise that at the
end of the process of degeneration the age would close and a
perfected society be newly created. For most Christians, there
is no finally conclusive answer to this question. Did the loss and
restoration of social order take place in principle with the death
and resurrection of Jesus, and proceed steadily forward like
mustard or leaven? Or did Jesus' suffering only initiate a
process which will reverberate steadily until a final climax?
Jesus at the center of history does not give a clear answer; but
the Christian is called to live in history the consequences of his
faith: to repent, to love, to serve, to seek the kingdom.

Implications for Contemporary Life

The foregoing sections deal with fundamental Christian principles by which the social order with its complex of institutions
and structures should be organized and guided. These principles
seem to give clues as to the way the Christian in the contemporary world may live in and be related to family, church, nation, and also the way he may sustain relationship with economic,
political, military, and cultural units of society. Furthermore,
these principles furnish guidance for the relationship of group
vis-à-vis group, and for both individuals and groups who would
change or direct the development of society.

Building on the Christian principle of mutuality, that is, that
the individual and the group sustain a common life (or vocation), that each is dependent on and responsible for the other,
it may be said that the Christian may not contract out of society nor may a Christian society exile its members in the sense

of denying responsibility for them. It would seem also that the Christian is obligated to witness by word and deed to the true existence of any group or unit of society to which he belongs or with which he is involved. This witness is expressed through his selection of groups (where selection is possible) as well as his activity within groups, both voluntary and involuntary. Jesus Christ in the event of the crucifixion has denied that the social order is amoral and that institutions and structures of society (the home, the economic order, political units, the church) are not subject to the same ethical demands as the individual. The crucifixion confronts society with the imperative to face up to its true genius as ordained by God and to order its life and fulfill its vocation accordingly.

This Theme in the Bible

A triumphant view of the outcome of history is seen in Psalms 77—78 and 105—106 and in Isaiah, Joel, and other prophets as well as in Paul's writings on law and freedom.

The individual's involvement in social fabric and his responsibility for social weal are motifs in Exodus, Deuteronomy, and Judges.

A classical description of the interrelationship between the individual and his social order (in this case the church) is that of Paul in 1 Corinthians 12.

Each of the Gospels provides a slightly differing interpretation of Jesus' self-consciousness about his messiahship. Perhaps Matthew is most illustrative of his continuity with Israel as a potentially messianic community, and of his efforts to recall his countrymen to the religious and vocational basis of their nationhood. The passion stories in Matthew 26 and 27, and parallels, describe the successive abandonment of Jesus concluding with his final cry, "My God, why hast thou forsaken me?"

The letters of Peter, John, and Jude, and the Book of Revelation may be studied for the various forms of expectation about the end of history (eschatology) which grew from the Christian commitment to Jesus as the center and from the experience of persecution.

5. Man's Coping with Change and the Absolute

STATEMENT OF THEME

Man's search for the permanent and at the same time his longing for change are answered by God as ultimate reality and absolute value.

DESCRIPTION OF THEME

This theme expresses the Christian's belief in the eternal being of God in relation to the lifelong human concern for finding enduring meaning and value; and man's wish for stability and security as well as his wish for change and variety in the circumstances and experiences of life.

Man's imagination leads him to see that the potential reality of everything he experiences is only partially actualized. He perceives himself and the world as incomplete; the promise and symbol of eternity, not the full reality of it. This awareness leads man to a religious concern: How may he get hold of the reality which he finds presented obscurely, mixed with the unreality of his ordinary experience?

Threats to Existence

As a human phenomenon, religion represents man's way of dealing with the personal threat involved in his separation from eternal being. These threats take several forms. The reality of man's experience is threatened by impermanence, uncertainty, and indetermination. The value of man's experience is threatened by contradiction, conflict, and ambiguity.

Impermanence describes man's experience that something perceived as real may come into existence and go out of existence.

The objects, relationships, institutions, and persons which make up the world of man do not possess in themselves the quality of permanence; they are made and can be destroyed.

Uncertainty describes the fact that man's imagination wavers between perceiving significant objects as real and as unreal. He cannot make up his mind whether or not to trust the appearance of things. He has many experiences of illusion, which suggest to him that perhaps his important experiences, those to which he commits his life and energy, are also illusion.

Indeterminacy describes man's experience that something perceived as real does not display a clear character. Its meaning and implications cannot be clearly and exactly drawn from it because it is not sufficiently marked off from the context of its appearance. The threat of indeterminacy affects particularly the structural elements of reality which presents many alternative structures and raises the question as to which of these is most nearly the way things really are.

Of the threats of value, contradiction describes man's experience that an object or relationship, when approached in different ways, may be perceived as of both positive and negative value. It suggests an element of arbitrary decision in existence; and insinuates, further, that value perhaps represents no more than the wish or whim of the perceiver.

Conflict of value describes man's experience that positive values often stand in the way of the realization of one another, that man in his relation to reality is required by nature to fall short of the full achievement of which he is capable.

Ambiguity of value describes man's experience that an aspect of reality is perceived as being important, therefore as entering into a valuing relationship to the perceiver, without the possibility of separating the positive and negative aspects of its value. Thus ambiguity suggests that the realization of positive value inseparably carries with it the realization of negative value—a relationship expressed in Jesus' parable of the wheat and the weeds (Matthew 13:24-30).

The Eternal Here and Now

There are two main religious avenues for dealing with threats to existence and value. Both of them are displayed in the picture of Jesus Christ in the Gospels. The first is by participating through mystery in God's transcendence of the world. The Gospel of John expresses the union of Christ with the Father through which eternal reality breaks as a light upon the transitory and doubtful existence of man. Eternal life is a present possibility. The lordship and messiahship of Jesus penetrates existence, transforming it without any external change into the actuality of eternal life.

The second religious answer to the threats is to work and suffer within existence to change into the outward, visible actualization of what is perceived as eternal. In the Synoptic Gospels, the lordship and messiahship of Jesus have this character, that the kingdom is to be seen within history through signs such as that which he gave to John the Baptist: " 'the blind receive their sight and the lame walk, lepers are cleansed and the deaf hear, and the dead are raised up, and the poor have good news preached to them.' " (Matthew 11:4-5)

The first of these religious answers corresponds to the transcendence of God. The eternal is not subject to change and the changing and transitory character of experience is negated as a threat to the person who participates in the eternal. The second corresponds to the immanence of God. God works within change and man, too, may work within change, joining with God to unite changing reality with the eternal reality upon which it rests. Man finds himself in tension between a desire for maintaining the security of the status quo and yearning for a new and different way of life which carries the potential of disappointment and failure as well as satisfaction and meaning. Man feels impelled to break with the past and to align himself with God because of his longing for change, his healthy discontent with things as they are, his desire to actualize in the temporal the values he senses in the eternal. Thus man may participate responsibly in creation and therefore contribute to change and be a part of it.

Freedom and Determination

The Christian understanding of moral freedom has been plagued by a false polarity between the belief that man has freedom and the belief that God is the sovereign ruler of the world. The argument has assumed that for freedom to be possible it must be undetermined and unconditional.

Christian belief distinguishes between freedom as an experience, and freedom as a hypothesis. No one can rob the human being, who has experienced himself as a person, of his moral freedom; but he realizes it precisely at the moment when the determining conditions that press upon existence are heaviest—that is to say, when his decisions matter. (When his decisions do not matter, his hypothetical freedom does not matter either.) Moral freedom therefore does not mean the absence of determination, but it means that the determining factors—the experiences and relationships which make the person what he is—are integrated in his personal center, so that the outward expression in decision and action represents a determination controlled by the character of the personal center. The person's moral freedom is thus expressed not as absence of determination, but as self-determination.

In the Christian faith such self-determination is made possible through personal identification with God and through discipleship to Jesus Christ. This is the paradox of bondage and freedom which is expressed by Paul in Galatians 4 and 5.

85

Authority and Eternal Value

At some points in Christian history eternal value has been assumed to reside in authoritarian church or in received doctrine because these seem relatively unchanging as compared with the caprice of the individual person serving his own will. In general, Protestantism has rejected such an equation, holding that the mere fact of historical endurance and stability is not to be equated with eternity. Specifically, Protestants have been prepared to see eternal value and meaning in that which changes as well as in that which does not change. We serve a "living God"—in whom permanence and change are united and transcended. The ultimate authority for Protestantism is fidelity in relationship with the living God, expressed through discipleship to Jesus Christ. The moral discipline of man which follows is not so much a matter of accommodating his behavior to unchanging norms as it is one of celebrating and glorifying God in whatever is real, and actualizing the divine-human quality of life wherever man participates in the determination of change. Ultimate reality and absolute value cannot be perceived by man. They are a part of his faith and rest in his trust in the kingdom of God.

This Theme in the Bible

The definitive source of Christian belief about bondage, freedom, and authority is found in the Roman and Galatian correspondence of Paul.

Psalm 90 (and many others) expresses the transitory character of man's existence and his need to be united with an enduring, unchanging reality which is attributed to God.

The Gospel of John, especially the prologue and the sections interpreting the messiahship and "glory" of Jesus, and the letters of John provide a source for the interpretation of the eternal as entering actuality at every moment, as a transformation of its inner meaning. (The Synoptics also have this interpretation but less prominently.)

The Synoptics provide a source for interpreting the eternal as in a process of realization through change, in the work and suffering of man and especially of Jesus as the Messiah.

The Remnant theme in the Old Testament identifies the participation of man in the eternity of God's purpose.

The contrast of the permanent and the vaporous is vivid in Ecclesiastes.

6. Man's Creativity within Life's Daily Routines

STATEMENT OF THEME

The lives of all persons involve experiences of daily routine. Routine offers security but it may lead to boredom and meaninglessness. Motivation and direction for daily existence can be found in the purposes of God. Herein are the springs of man's creative attitude toward an engagement in the rhythm of work, leisure, and rest.

DESCRIPTION OF THEME

Most of a person's life is experienced through habitual and regular activities (the daily routines) not in crises of heightened awareness and significance. Modern man, doing specialized work, having regular relationships to his neighbors, routinely receiving satisfactions of his wants, is threatened with failure to see any meaning at all in the experiences that are his. This theme, therefore, interprets the way in which man's relationship to ultimate reality may be expressed creatively in the routines of daily life. Man is creative in terms of bringing things into rightness (the ethical side) and also in terms of bringing into consciousness the reality that already exists (the onotological side). These two expressions of creativity are analyzed below in "creativity as change" and "creativity as celebration."

87

Creativity as Change

On the ethical side of his response to God, man projects in imagination an improved existence for himself and his neighbor. He sees himself as sharing in responsibility for the achievement of such improved existence. The whole range of human work may be interpreted in terms of this response.

Work is thus directed to such diverse ends as the provision of food, clothing, and shelter to make life more comfortable, pleasant, and healthful; the curing of illness; the regulation and ordering of relations between people; and services such as transportation, mass media, distribution of goods and other services ministering to human wants and needs, including the improvement of persons themselves in their character and competence.

Creativity that is manifested through change in existence involves several phases. The first of these is imagination, to understand what are the human needs which may be met by work and effort, and to project the general outlines of a solution for them.

A second phase is that of invention and discovery. Through scientific research, planning, gathering useful knowledge, and putting it together in the form of theories, instruments, and devices, the inventor takes a necessary middle step between imagining a solution and actually bringing it to pass.

A third phase is production. If the need may be met by material goods, this means the production of such goods; but an equally typical form of human work is the production of certain desirable social conditions and services by giving attention to all of the factors, human and otherwise, which must be brought together in order that the desired objective may be achieved.

A fourth phase of creative work is management—the acceptance of responsibility for the achievement of desirable objectives and the marshalling of intermediate steps so as to come out at the right place. This includes financing, organizing, trouble-shooting, gathering necessary support, and otherwise turning to account the opportunities that exist to bring a desired improvement into being.

In all these phases there is a real scope for creative action by man within the limits of his existence. In each the opportunity exists for multiple decisions, and the skillful performance of many tasks, which will be reflected in the quality and usefulness of the final product of labor. In all these phases, also, conflict and struggle are likely to be present. To be truly creative means to struggle with the intransigent forces (human and nonhuman) involved in the tasks described above. Agony of mind and spirit are often required of the person who assumes a creative role in his work. Such agony may be no more (or no less) than is involved in the effort to transcend the boredom and drudgery of monotonous operations by seeing them in the larger framework where their purpose and eventual significance are apparent. Conflict may arise and have to be resolved within oneself in the finding of an occupation that seems to call forth one's creativity. Conflict may also arise among persons in work relationships that require for solution truly creative approaches and insights. The exercise of creativity is never easy nor automatic; it always demands reference to God's purposes for man in order to be valid.

Creativity as Celebration

On its ontological side, man's religious response to God is concerned not so much with changing reality as with perceiving, bringing into consciousness, and enjoying the reality that already exists. Man finds opportunity to hallow his existence by regarding it as a form of praise offered to God. In contrast to man's work, his nonutilitarian activities may be interpreted in terms of this kind of response.

The celebration of reality involves several distinct kinds of activity that are broadly characteristic of man's being. The first of these is play. Play is a spontaneous human response with which persons (often unconsciously) embellish nearly everything they do. Such manifestations as doodling and foot-tapping, even in the midst of hard work, show how universal it is to play. Play as such has no utilitarian value, and therefore is not directed to any future. It is essentially timeless, expressing with great immediacy the fact of being able to move and to act.

The second form of celebration is reverie, which may be defined as mental play. Reverie is the undirected activity of the mind when not confronted with a problem or task. It is probably purposive in the life of the human being, but not consciously so. It leads nowhere in particular, and does not seek to arrive at useful conclusions or to evaluate in relation to each other the images which the mind calls up. Reverie is closely related to the religious activity of contemplation. Contemplation may begin with much self-consciousness about the purpose of finding communication with God, but in its practical form has much spontaneity and joy, directed not so much by the will of the person as by his free response to perceived reality.

A third form of celebration is affection—the enhancement and appreciation of relationship between persons through immediate expressions of love and enjoyment, where the object of such expression is not to secure an advantage or alter the relationship, but simply to increase the awareness of the shared reality in which persons participate. Like play, affection is not directed to any future or improved state, but to the enjoyment of the present.

The fourth form of nonutilitarian response to God is worship. Worship also has an ethical side directed toward improvement without which it becomes idolatrous. But this aspect is secondary to the character of worship as pure expression of joy and adoration to the Creator and Father, and an elevation of the worshiper through awareness that eternity is united with the present moment.

In all of these forms of activity, a creative opportunity exists for finding, in whatever presents itself to consciousness (however commonplace it may be), the representation of infinite and eternal being.

The Materialization of Play

At our own time in history the nonutilitarian functions of life, which belong to the essential nature of man, tend to be transformed into work which belongs to the existence of man under the condition of alienation. Play is turned into something useful, as if this were required to justify it, and is then "worked at" with all the joylessness which that term suggests. In such a process, play (and to some extent reverie, affection, and worship) loses its timeless character. The special sense of transcendence which goes with it becomes an expression not of spontaneity, but of necessity; not of joyous freedom, but of duty. The enhancement of the present moment is reduced to the expectation that somehow what is happening now will permit one to relax and have fun later on, but later on never arrives because the devotion of work to change and futurity does not permit the wasting of time in building the present. It is the future that must be built; the present can be sacrificed for that.

This Theme in the Bible

Two illustrations from the Gospels will indicate something of the relative values which Jesus placed upon change and upon celebration. In the story of Mary and Martha (Luke 10:38-42) Jesus clearly preferred the nonutilitarian activity of conversation to the useful but distracting function of serving the household. In the story of the anointing at Bethany (Mark 14:3-9) the disciples of Jesus reproached the woman for the waste of a costly ointment in an impractical, useless act of affection. But Jesus said, " 'Let her alone; Why do you trouble her? She has done a beautiful thing to me.' "

Matthew 6:25-34 gives further evidence of Jesus' view about present-oriented values.

Jesus' calling of his disciples (Mark 1 and parallels), several of whom were fishermen or tradesmen, illustrates his attitudes toward working people and, by implication, the dignity and creativity of labor. Paul, too, was a tradesman, as shown in Acts 18:3.

The New Testament figure of steward clearly implies men's creative responsibility in the affairs of life and existence.

Several of the Psalms in their joy and celebration illustrate this theme, and the Song of Solomon uniquely celebrates one of the basic experiences in man's life—love.

REVELATION: THE MEANING AND EXPERIENCE OF GOD'S SELF-DISCLOSURE

The themes within this area are:

God Speaks in Man's Search for Meaning Beyond Himself
The Living God Seeks Man
The Gracious God Judges and Redeems
The Sovereign God Dwells with Man
God Speaks to Man Through the Scriptures
God Acts Through the Church to Make Himself Known
God Speaks to Man through the Natural Order

Description of Curriculum Area

The focus, or vantage point, of this area of curriculum is the character of God and his work, the nature and significance of God's self-disclosure—the modes of God's action, and the way he has spoken and still speaks to man's search and man's need.

Comprehended in this area of curriculum is such content from Christian thought and life as: the doctrine of God; the doctrine of the Trinity; interpretation of the person, teaching, and work of Jesus Christ; interpretation of the work of the Holy Spirit; the relation of revelation to reason; interpretation of the nature and meaning of the gospel.

93

In order to have educational value as an area of curriculum this content must be viewed in terms of its pertinence to the persistent issues of man's life. Some of these issues are: Is there a God? Does God speak? If so, how? Does this tell me what I can live for? Does God disclose himself? If so, how? How is God known? What is the Bible all about?[1]

---

[1] These three paragraphs are repeated here as necessary background.

Delineation of Area

The term "revelation" refers to the character of God and his work, the nature and significance of his self-disclosure, the way he has spoken and still speaks to man's need. Though God is always speaking and acting, his being and ultimate purpose are clothed in mystery beyond man's finite capacities. This curriculum area focuses upon God's will to make himself known to all men for their redemption, and the ways in which man may experience God's self-disclosure. The center is thus upon the meaning and experience of the Word of God.

Some of the concerns that are dealt with in this curriculum area include: what revelation is; how the claims of revelation are tested; what God has revealed about himself; how God reveals himself; what light his revelation throws on man's existence and destiny; man's capacity to perceive God's revelation; man's capacity to respond to God's revelation in acceptance and rejection; the guidance that is given for man's response.

How God Makes Himself Known

God's self-disclosure is his communication of himself—his judgment, love, and will—to those whom he has created and called to be his people. The Bible is a record of and continuing means of God's self-disclosure in that it testifies definitively to God's self-revelation of his judgment, love, and gracious acts in history as Father, Son, and Holy Spirit—as Creator, Redeemer, and Sanctifier in his relationship with man, his creature. "The word of the Lord" is God's message, given to his prophets to communicate to his people through the medium of human language. "The Word made flesh," which dwelt among men in the person of Jesus Christ, is the incarnate revelation of God's just love and his climactic way of speaking to man through the Son. The Word of God is also the gospel, the good news of what God has done in reconciling man to himself. Since the days when the

94

gospel was first experienced by men under the power of the Holy Spirit, the Word of God has been experienced, proclaimed, preached, and taught among men. The Living Word continues to be experienced and witnessed to by Christians as they are empowered and guided by the Holy Spirit.

The Christian apprehends God's self-disclosure through his creation. He perceives the witness to God in the natural order. He recognizes his image in humanity and acknowledges his activities in society.

He encounters God's self-disclosure as he listens to the Bible, explores its meaning, discovers its truth, appropriates the eternal life it promises, and assumes the responsibilities that it demands.

The Christian experiences God's self-disclosure in Jesus Christ as he hears his teachings and obeys them, as he comes to know who Christ is and what he has done on our behalf, as he accepts the new life in Christ, and as he lives in love in society.

God's self-disclosure comes to man in the life of the church. In God's presence, he hears the Word read and preached, grows in his understanding of it, shares in Christ's suffering, death, and resurrection, participates in the sacraments, works within the fellowship of faith, and is guided in the Christian life.

One may perceive God's self-disclosure at any time or anywhere as he comes to terms with truth, as he submits to the judgment of the Word, as he proclaims the Word to others, as he worships, as he undertakes mission on behalf of Jesus Christ, and as he finds his particular ministry.

95

In the experience of God's self-disclosure, the Christian is called, confronted, challenged, condemned, cleansed, chastened, corrected, renewed, strengthened, clarified, guided, checked, controlled, and fulfilled.

Revelation Answers Man's Persistent Questions

Revelation makes known that God is one, and is known as Father, Son, and Holy Spirit. Life's persistent questions concerning the "whence" of human life, its "whither," and its "how" find their answer in God. The question "whence," dealing with origins, is answered in knowing God as the Father. The question "whither," dealing with direction and destiny, is answered in knowing God as Son. The question "how," dealing with means and resources, is answered by knowing God as Holy Spirit.

Some of man's persistent questions center upon the reality and mystery of God. Who is God? What is he like? How may I know him? When may I know him? What has he done? What does he do? What difference does he make? What should I know about him? What must I do because of him? How does he reveal himself? How may I search after him? Why does he remain cloaked in mystery? What clues to his nature and existence are there? What tests are there that God himself is being known? Revelation answers man's persistent questions about God's reality and mystery by indicating that God is and that he is one, by showing the essential nature of God's character and work expressed and experienced as the Trinity, and by meeting man's quest to understand God through religious faith. Man's quest and man's needs are met by the revelation of God's reality, his oneness, his mystery, his character, and his work.

Some of man's persistent questions center upon the "whence" of human life. Whence have we come? Whence has the universe come? Why does the universe exist? What was the beginning? What can one know of God from the study of time and space? Why is God high and lifted up? Why has such rich provision been made for the process of time, space, and life? Is impersonal nature or man the final arbiter of destiny? Is there direction, meaning, and purpose in history? What is beyond history—last things? Why does conscience exist? Are there moral and ethical laws? Is morality a social invention or a direction from God? Is there a relation between moral law and natural law? What is the basis of the concept of "law" itself? How can the incalculable order of judgment and justice that man experiences be explained?

Revelation answers man's persistent questions about "whence" by indicating that God is Father, and that he is Creator (the first cause, the innovator, revealing himself in the created world), righteous Lord (holy, transcendent, personal, intelligent, ultimate), Provider (sustainer and continuer), Supreme Ruler (Lord and controller of the universe, Lord and controller of life, and ultimate determiner of destiny, omnipotent), Lord of history (a God who works out his purposive will through men and nations and gives direction and meaning to the affairs of men), Lawgiver and Judge (revealing and administering as well as establishing the moral and natural law), and loving Father (having the characters of love, compassion, forgiveness, acceptance, and fellowship).

Some of man's persistent questions center upon the "whither" of human life. Where ought I to head? In whose likeness ought I to grow? Who is Jesus Christ? What of his early life and ministry? Who did he say that he was? What did he say and teach? What was the import of his life, ministry, death, and resurrection? How do I know about him? What can he mean to me? What has he done for me? What is expected of me because of him? What could he do for me that I could not do for myself? Where is Christ today? How could man and God be one? What record is there of the historical Jesus? What weight is to be given to the record? What is the church's faith in Christ? What evidences and witnesses may be examined to support the church's faith and claim about Christ? What does it mean that Christ continues his earthly life and ministry through the church? What does it mean that he is Lord of heaven and earth? What does it mean to be saved? Are all men ultimately saved? What becomes of those who are adherents of other religions?

Revelation answers man's persistent questions about "whither" by indicating that God is known as Son and that God in Jesus Christ is brother, master, and friend (perfect humanity revealed in love, and in sinlessness, in a human life and ministry of redemption); teacher (a giver of truth and grace, important for

97

his teachings and important as a teacher); redeemer and savior (his death a vicarious sacrifice for the sins of men); living Lord (his resurrection and ascension indicating that he is the Lord of life, the conqueror of death, and the opener of eternity).

Some of man's persistent questions center upon the "how" of human life. Will God speak to me? How does he speak? How has he spoken in the past? What does it mean to experience God as Holy Spirit? What may I expect from the Holy Spirit? What must I do for myself? How does God deal with sin in my life? How does the Holy Spirit assist me in my growth and development? Am I really free? How free am I to follow my own will? How can God come to me when I am in sorrow, pain, sickness, and fear? How does God through the Holy Spirit make restoration and effect reconciliation when I am lost, alienated, and apart? What does it mean to repent? What is "the still small voice"? Where does it come from? How may I hear it? Is conscience the voice of God or the human superego? Is conscience dependable in questions of it and when? Where do moments of insight and inspiration come from? Is there source the genius of the self or the guidance of God? Are effort and action necessary before knowledge and truth can come? How can I come to know the truth? How may I recognize truth? Is there any way that God can act through man's corporate life? What does God will for me, for my family, for my church, for my nation, for my enemies, and for others? How does God fulfill his will among peoples and nations?

Revelation answers man's persistent questions about "how" by indicating that the indwelling God experienced as Holy Spirit is active in the Christian community and in individual human life (he is omnipresent and reveals himself as the inner light, as an inner voice, as witness, as companion, and as the indwelling God); he is sanctifier (the convictor of sin, the purifier, the perfector, and the enabler); he is comforter (counselor, helper, sustainer, and restorer); he is revealer of truth (the indwelling teacher for individuals and for groups, the innovator, the clari-

98

fier, using men and events, leading, convicting of sin, enlightening the mind, quickening man's inquiry after truth); and he is at work within the affairs of men, groups, and nations (immanent and witnessing to truth, beauty, justice, and grace within the social order, nations, the church, and men in the world).

Themes Delineated

1. God Speaks in Man's Search for Meaning Beyond Himself

STATEMENT OF THEME

God's revelation of himself in part in the nature of the human personality explains man's persistent yearnings to worship some God, to know more, to do better, to be in relationship.

DESCRIPTION OF THEME

God discloses something of himself in the character of man, his creature, as one who must see the sense of things, and find the objective source of that sense outside of his own self. Moreover God capitalizes on this very search of man for meaning as the scene for showing something of himself to man.

In this theme there is the dynamic interplay between man's characteristic necessity to know, to choose, to rationalize, to find meaning, to relate to others significantly, and God's readiness to be known, to give life abundant, to offer fellowship, to show truth.

The Nature of Human Personality

God has shown his hand by creating man in his own image. God's very nature is reflected in his creature, man, although reflected brokenly and incompletely. This fact of creation explains man's capacity to apprehend God's self-disclosure and it explains his search for significance, meanings, rationalizations that lodge

99

outside his own being. Man continues to make discoveries about the nature of human personality, and the very urgency of his felt need to know more is a significant characteristic of man's humanity.

Though a creature, man is distinctive from other animals of creation. Clearly he is a particular kind of animal set apart from other creatures, and having capacities, freedoms, attributes, mystery that belong to no other creature. Man's nature is a more dominant motif in themes of the area, "Life and Its Setting: the Meaning and Experience of Existence." This theme picks up some particularities of man's life and being as they relate to God's self-disclosure.

100

The God of Truth

God's self-disclosure as perfect wisdom and truth itself provides man the framework for all his discoveries of truth in the realms of the physical universe, the nature of humanity, the arts, philosophy. Herein also is the root of man's quest to know, his insistence on rational explanations for phenomena, his pursuit of what truth is, his necessity to distinguish truth from error.

God created man with a mind capable of thought, capable of discovery of truth, capable of reason. Creation provided not only these capacities but also the persistent urge to exercise them. Man finds himself invited to think God's thoughts after him, to come and reason with him, to know the truth, to use all the gifts with which God has endowed him as a human being. Moreover God reveals himself to man as truth at the same time he provides for man's discovery of truths.

God, Transcendent Yet Immanent

God who reveals himself as perfect, holy, omnipotent, omniscient, righteous, has implanted in man the necessity to subordinate himself to some higher being or authority to whom he may give devotion and loyalty. This persistent search may express itself in man's vaporous, anxious superstitions, or in unceasing efforts to placate a feared deity, or in the most genuine spiritual communion in response to a loving God. Man's search for an object of his worship and devotion has resulted in many religions. These very expressions confirm the reality of God who calls forth from man some effort toward communion and worship.

This search provides the arena for God's contact with man, and at the same time finds its end in God who is fully worth man's deepest and richest devotion, his unwavering loyalty, and complete surrender. God, moreover, makes himself readily available to man's worship by revealing himself and by providing the means for communion with him.

The God of Righteousness

God has created man with a capacity akin to his—the capacity to discern right from wrong. This capacity does not guarantee man's behavior, nor even the values by which he judges right from wrong. Man's necessity to make such decisions and live by some values is met by God's consistent righteousness, his moral demands on those who affirm loyalty to him, by his promise to be to man the Way.

Man's conscience is something of an enigma. That he has one is not doubted; what it is, where its authority rests, how reliable it is as a guide, and its amenity to education are questions which focus man's inquiry. God shows himself to be the Righteous One, who both endows man with a sense of right and wrong, and also provides for man a dependable content of morality. Perhaps even more significant is his self-revelation in providing man with power to live rightly.

101

The Intimate God

God pours himself out to draw man into his fellowship. He shows himself not as one who stands aloof from man; rather as one who created man for fellowship and at great cost works to bring about the fullest fellowship with and among men. Man's very humanity is endangered without the nourishment of relationship with others. As man fulfills his individuality by his interaction with others, he truly finds himself as he is in fellowship with God and in Godlike fellowship with fellow men. Man's search for selfhood is both a channel for God's communication of himself and a quest fulfilled in God's fellowship.

The Lord of History

God's self-disclosure in his lordship in and over history gives man his surest answer to questions of his own destiny and that of other men and of society.

God, the designer and controller of history, implanted in man his hunger for purposiveness, his longing for significance on the scene of human affairs, his search for assurance that life goes somewhere and means something. These are characteristics of man made in the image of a purposeful God, who controls the destiny of man and society, who will bring to fruition his intent for creation.

God's eloquent self-disclosure in his giving himself for the saving of man forever answers any man's conjecture on the worth of human personality. Man's questions of his own worth and significance never need go unanswered in face of the self-sacrifice of the omnipotent Lord of history for the sake of showing his love for man and his poignant longing for restored relationship.

This Theme in the Bible

The classic Old Testament passage on man's seeking meaning beyond himself is the Book of Job. Ecclesiastes and Proverbs are relevant as are several of the Psalms: 8; 73; 92; 139.

Man's responsibility is celebrated in such passages as Genesis 3 and 4; Romans 1 and 2.

Man's search for something or someone to worship finds rootage in such passages as Isaiah 55:8; 1 Chronicles 16:26; Isaiah 45:20; Psalms 96, 97, 135; Acts 17, 18, 19.

Passages basic to man's search for the meaning in his destiny includes the latter part of Isaiah, the kingdom passages in the Gospels, the Revelation of John, writings of Paul, notably Romans 8:12-25.

2. The Living God Seeks Man

STATEMENT OF THEME

The eternal God (Father, Son, and Holy Spirit) has acted and continues to act in the life and affairs of man, disclosing himself and his redeeming love to man, and drawing man into fellowship with himself. Thus God makes possible man's acceptance of his (man's) significance.

DESCRIPTION OF THEME

The action in this theme centers in God's continuous reaching out to man regardless of man's response to him and in the eternal, transcendent living God centering so much costly attention on finite, temporal, self-interested man. Fulfillment of man's potential for fellowship with the divine satisfies his nagging questions of his own significance. The completion of his search for something or someone to whom he may give devotion is encompassed by God's voluntary exposure of himself as one who, rather than being aloof or disdainful is on the contrary, openly, constantly trying to reach man to draw him willingly into the richest fulfillment of life.

103

This persistent pursuit of man by God has been evident in his dealings with individuals and with people in the past. It is most vivid in the life of Jesus Christ, and continues ceaselessly as it is expressed through individuals and groups who now give themselves to extending God's loving invitation to man everywhere.

The Eternal God and Temporal Man

One of the most awesome convictions in the Christian faith is that the eternal God, Creator of the universe, Lord of history, the perfectly Holy One has focused his love and concern on one of his creatures, man, in spite of man's rebellion, willfulness, independence and transience. Yet this conviction is born of the witness of men in the past and the experience of men of today, showing most transparently in God's emptying himself and taking on human form and living among men.

In God's revelation of his eternal being, man finds lodgment and security in face of his brief span of life and his grasp for continuity.

The eternal God extends himself toward man, with seeking love as evidence in the Bible's creation stories, Elijah's account of the still small voice, the stories of Job and Jonah, the Suffering Servant passages, the testimony of Hosea, the Gospel accounts, and John's vision of the new heaven and the new earth.

God's Continuous and Costly Offer

Though the all-powerful God has control over all his creation, he exercises restraint in seeking man's response to his offer of fellowship. He respects the freedom and integrity of man, and will not coerce man's love. His Spirit is at work within man to illumine the revelation, but man's love must be freely given to be genuine.

In his persistent approach to man, God has many times worked through unwilling channels as well as willing. The actions of kings, pharaohs, warriors, have been used by God to reveal his desire and purpose for man. Through the poignant witness and words of prophets, servants, priests, scribes, God has called and called again to man. And where men and women are responsive to God's outreaching love, he uses them to extend further his open, yet personal, invitation to fellowship.

God's Vulnerability

Revelation, self-disclosure is costly, for it involves the exposure of one's self to others. It means becoming vulnerable to the response of the other. This is the more so when one seeks the free and frank response of the other. God has made himself vulnerable for man's sake as he has revealed himself for man to know and to react in response. He has been hurt by the idolatry, the harlotry, the ritualism, the greed, the self-centeredness of his people. He has been ignored, refused, rebuffed, crucified, yet he seeks man still.

Self-disclosure demands vulnerability because the substance of revelation is not primarily information about God, but essentially the person of God. Knowledge about God is available to man by his own experience with God and by the witness of other men who know him. But the central characteristic of revelation is that it lays bare the person and makes possible personal encounter and intimate relationship.

The Aim and End of God's Seeking

Temporal man finds his eternal significance as he understands the motive and object of God's search for him. God seeks man not to exploit him nor to satisfy and desire for control over him but rather that God may be in mutual self-giving fellowship with man. The end of God's seeking is that man may have abundant life and be brought into fellowship with him and with all men. Such an offer can come only from the living, eternal God who gives himself to man's fulfillment simply because he loves him.

105

This Theme in the Bible

In addition to passages already cited above in the theme development, biblical material from which this theme springs spans the Old and New Testaments: from God's "Where are you?" to Adam to the high point in the Gospels in the life and teaching of Jesus (cf. Matthew 9:12; Luke 12; 15; 19) and on through the witness of the early disciples through their epistles—Hebrews, John's epistles, Philippians.

The biblical witness to God as a living God and not an idol or a past God is found in such passages as Joshua and Judges, where the people of God were meeting with the pagan people of Canaan and their god; the "contest" between the LORD and Baal; passages that ridicule the making of and dependence on idols (Isaiah 45, 46, 48; Deuteronomy 29; Hosea; Habakkuk); the Gospels, with their account of the living God incarnate among men.

3. The Gracious God Judges and Redeems

STATEMENT OF THEME

The grace of God seen in both his holiness and his redemptive love as revealed supremely in Jesus Christ answers man's need for judgment, forgiveness, and renewal.

DESCRIPTION OF THEME

In this theme are found the interlocking realities of the altogether holy, omniscient, righteous, and just God and of man, who knows that right differs from wrong yet cannot of himself know what makes the difference. Inherent in the theme are on the one hand, man's life necessity for being accepted and forgiven, as well as his yearning for rightness within himself; and on the other hand God's dealing with man justly yet forgivingly without regard to man's merit for forgiveness and at great cost to himself repeatedly offering man forgiveness, redemption, renewal.

God's Holiness and Man's Perfection

God—immutable, righteous, holy, just, true—is the fulfillment of man's necessity for stability, integrity, acceptance. God's absolute holiness is a dominant characteristic in his self-disclosure—both in the record of Scripture and in the insistence of his people. His holiness and justness are companion attributes. In face of his holiness, no sin can stand unjudged, whether it be greed to harvest the grain even in corners of the field (Deuteronomy), dishonest sale of shoes to the poor (Amos), hidden hate (David), chicanery in the courts of the land (Micah), adultery and prostitution, self-dependent pride and arrogance (Malachi, Gospels), religiosity among the leaders of worship (New Testament). To be the peculiar people of the holy God calls for perfect obedience to him, having his mind—being perfect as he is perfect—in mind and heart, as well as in word and deed.

Such a God, if he be only holy, confronts men with a despairing situation. God, if only holy, is utterly out of reach and relevance to man, who must find security and stability to live. The situation in which man lives demands of him decisions and actions in the face of conflicting values. Every decision he makes is the result of his judgment of priorities among these values. Man, free and responsible, must make choices of expediency in terms of his estimate of values to be conserved. Every decision presents a temptation to compromise. How, then, can man come into mutual relationship with a holy God?

God's Costly Grace

God's self-disclosure, however, safeguards the impression of hopelessness. In his holiness and justice which demands righteousness and must reject evil and imperfection, he himself provides for man's acceptability in offering his own righteousness to man.

The cost at which God extends his own righteousness to man is related to the accompanying freedom he insists man have in accepting or rejecting his offer, though the use of this freedom is inevitably liable of judgment. The record of God's disclosure to man is threaded through with rejection by man: deceit while seeking the benefits of God's favor, harlotry while claiming to be faithful. The Jacobs, the Gomers, the Peters, the Judases, the Ananiases in the community of God's people testify eloquently to the cost God suffers in his gracious acceptance of man.

God's self-disclosure has always been costly—how costly is revealed in the crucifixion of Jesus Christ, in whom God climac-

107

tically displays his holiness, justness, and grace in the face of man's enmity, rebellion, and sin.

God Redeems Adjudged Man

Man has the capacity to discriminate between right and wrong. He works at making things right as he sees it. In God he finds revealed the accurate plumbline of righteousness, and the power for doing the right which he cannot find dependably in himself (Paul). Man's search for acceptability, for new beginnings is ended in God. God makes him acceptable by making it possible for man through a response in faith and obedience to gain something of God's own righteousness. God empowers him for right living and inner renewal and radical change by giving him—if he will only receive it—new life and by continuing to make his Spirit readily available for righteousness. This is redemption—illustrated in the Exodus, in the return from Exile, and supremely in the life and work of Jesus Christ.

This Theme in the Bible

The biblical interpretation of the purpose of the law of God forms the basis of this theme. This is implicit in the Exodus, Leviticus, and Deuteronomy records of the law, as well as in writings of Paul, James, Peter, and the Gospels. God's purifying or redemptive purpose in judgment is a recurring theme in the Exodus event as well as in the prophets. See also Revelation 6—8. The story of Jacob eloquently illustrates the graciousness and justness of God in his redemptive and forgiving activity with man. Hosea is probably the highest point of Old Testament writing focused on God's grace in forgiveness and redemption. The Psalms again and again extol God's grace, his justness, his redemptive forgiveness.

The life of Jesus as well as his teachings gives foundation to this theme. See especially such passages as Matthew 18:23ff.; Luke 7:36ff.; Luke 19.

The preaching of John the Baptist and, more important, the early preaching in the New Testament churches (Acts) carries the note of judgment and redemption by a gracious God.

In the epistles, notable passages include Romans 1—8; Galatians 3—6; Hebrews 3—12.

4. The Sovereign God Dwells with Man

STATEMENT OF THEME

The infinite God (Father, Son, and Holy Spirit) deigns to live and work with man, quickening, purifying, and empowering.

DESCRIPTION OF THEME

God, though omnipotent, transcendent, Lord of all creation, is forever at work with man in all the experiences of life. He makes himself accessible to man in his loneliness, in his impatience to achieve lofty goals, in his necessity to make decisions and carry them out, in his joy and sorrow, in his efforts to communicate and have fellowship with one worthy of his devotion and allegiance.

Man today can have the assurance of God's presence with him as well as with men of other times and places. He can have the assurance of God's presence under every circumstance of his life, regardless of whether or not he discerns it. Moreover God is not simply at hand—static and passive, but is active and concerned in man's life and affairs.

109

Sovereign Yet Not Aloof

The biblical and Christian witness to God affirms his self-disclosure as supreme Lord of all creation. He has no peer. He alone is God and all creation is under his rule. This is true now; it was true from the beginning; it will be obvious at the close of history when " 'The kingdom of the world has become the kingdom of our Lord and of his Christ" (Revelation 11:15).

110

At the same time God shows himself as Sovereign; he announces an invitation to an intimate covenant relationship (the Exodus, the Incarnation, the Revelation of John). He gives his people evidence of his "tabernacling" among them. He enters into a binding covenant with them, renews it again and again when they break it, reaffirms his presence among them when they doubt. The ultimate disclosure of his offer of intimacy is his appearance in history, incarnate in Jesus Christ, "who, though he was in the form of God, . . . emptied himself, . . . being born in the likeness of men" (Phil. 2:6-7).

The tender answer of God to man's loneliness and insecurity is eloquent in the imagery used to describe the relationship the Lord desires with men: father—children; husband—wife; mother—baby; friend—friend; shepherd—sheep; hen—chicks.

There is another facet of the type of relationship the Sovereign God desires with man. Though God is King of creation and Lord of history, yet, in creating man free, responsible, thinking, inventive, he invites him to share in the shaping of history and the maintenance and development of enhancement of creation. It is the experience of the people of God that he has not created a mechanical world, with an inevitable history, but a dynamic order within which man shares responsibility in the unfolding of history and in the creative use and development of his environment. (See area: "Life and Its Setting: The Meaning and Experience of Existence.")

Omnipotent, Yet Self-Limiting

The human mind thinks in terms of cause and effect; cause must be adequate for and greater than the effect. Men have concluded there must be at least an "Intelligent Cause" behind what is observed. God has not left man simply to wonder if there is a power greater than man: he has revealed himself. God's omnipotence is apparent not only in creation, but also in what seems to man to be miracles, and perhaps most of all within the altered lives of rebellious or indifferent persons.

In his omnipotence, however, God does not violate man's freedom, responsibility, and potentiality. He invites man to think his thoughts after him, to share his purposes with him, to enter into creative and redemptive work with him. This is by invitation; he does not need man for fulfilling his purposes. He will not coerce man to share fellowship and work. He does offer man a covenant of promise and challenge, guaranteeing security rooted not in transient sources of human contriving, but in the very eternal, sovereign, omnipotent God. In making this offer, God does not stand on the sidelines of man's decision; he is found at work within man, encouraging and enabling him to accept the invitation—but only with man's allowing him that influence. And even when man refuses him, God does not depart from him.

Gifts of an Immanent God

The resources of the Sovereign God himself are available to the people who espouse his purpose, who give themselves to him.

Man's slightest genuine response of acceptance opens a wealth of gifts from God to confirm, nurture, strengthen, correct, guide that response and fulfill that commitment (Matthew 7; Luke 15; Philippians 3).

It is the biblical witness that the Holy Spirit dwells with man to provide him keener insight to God's message and will; clearer perception of sin and evil; confirmation of right; comfort in the face of difficulties; sorrow and loneliness; strength for trials, failure, hard duties; guidance for pursuit of godly aims and purposes. The witness is confirmed by the experiences in the Christian community, both among individuals and also in the life of the church.

God may disclose his presence to an individual or a group through Scripture as he illumines its meaning. His presence is real in the communion of prayer and the sacraments. There are no limits to how God manifests himself to man. He moves whenever, wherever, and however he will. But this variety of evidence of God implies no caprice, rather an omnipotence and a sure promise, whose guarantee is rooted in God, that he will be with man in the present and future just as surely as he has been with man in the past.

This Theme in the Bible

From the affirmation of God's purpose in the creation of man for fellowship with him, the Bible carries a major motif of God's presence among men. This has both an individual and a corporate dimension. The evidence and assurance of God's presence with Abraham as he answered God's call is echoed throughout the experience of Moses, of Elijah, of the disciples of Jesus. The cloud and pillar of fire of the Exodus, the tabernacle and the ark all bore witness to God's presence among his people. The Psalms (e.g. 139) and the postexilic writings reflect the discovery of God's presence regardless of buildings of worship; and God's most eloquent proclamation of his intent to dwell with man comes in Jesus Christ. Moreover, his assurance of the presence of the Holy Spirit finds confirmation in the life of the New Testament church and the disciples. See also such passages as Hebrews 1; Philippians 3; John 16; 1 John 4; Revelation 7.

5. God Speaks to Man Through the Scriptures

STATEMENT OF THEME

As man reads the Bible seeking the guidance of the Holy Spirit, he finds there the definitive answers to his urgent questions: Who is God? What is my responsibility to him? How may I know him?

DESCRIPTION OF THEME

This theme involves man's attitude toward the Bible in face of the central position accorded it by the Christian community.

The message of the Bible with its concomitant demands interplay with man's questions about its relevance and authority. Man's eagerness to have guidelines for his life comes up against questions of the function and nature of Scripture, as well as questions of how men of the twentieth century can get at the meaning of such ancient writings. A major motif of this theme is how this written word is related to God's self-revelation, especially in Jesus Christ.

The Nature of the Bible

The critical fact of the nature of the Bible is that it is at the same time divine and human, both in its creation and in its preservation.

Devout scholarship has increasingly unfolded the story of the development of writings that now appear in the canon of Scripture. This story includes both the gradual reduction to writing of the heritage of God's people, and the history of decisions faced by God's people concerning what writings hold authority. The role God himself has played in the way in which Scripture has been written and canonized is intertwined with the role of insightful, dedicated men who put into human language God's message, and those who later made selection of such writings as should be central to the life of the community of the faithful. God's Spirit was active in the collection of the Scriptures as he was active in the writing of them.

The paradox of divine and human mixture continues in the experience of God's people as they have sought to preserve and distribute the Scriptures, and as they have continuously tried to delve through language barriers to mine out the accurate meaning of the original writings.

The Relation of Scripture to Revelation

The church and its antecedent community of God's people have always accorded a special role to Scripture in the process of God's self-disclosure. Christians have argued, indeed have sadly

113

severed relations, over whether the Bible *is* God's Word or *contains* God's Word. But they have agreed that it both records God's acts of self-disclosure to people in the past and at the same time reveals God to man now. It is an important issue to a man to know if every word of Scripture is equally revelatory or if some parts of the Bible are more crucial than others for man's perception of God.

In the Bible, truths of revelation have been put into the language of men. Here is the record of God's acts in history as he made himself known to a people whom he had chosen to be the special instrument of his redemptive purpose for man.

The Bible is the source of all that man actually knows today concerning God's revelation of himself in Jesus Christ. At the heart of Protestant faith there is the conviction that all Christian teaching must be judged in the light of the Scripture. Moreover, the Christian community holds that in the climactic revelation of God in Jesus Christ is the norm for testing any perception of God's self-disclosure that comes to man—whether from Scripture, from the natural order, from a private inner voice, from the community of God's people.

Though a man be convinced that God revealed himself to men of old as reflected in Scripture, he still may question whether the ancient words of Scripture are instrumental in presently revealing God. Or do they simply report the past action of God toward others long dead? The Christian community affirms both the conviction and the experience that God speaks to man today through the words of Scripture.

The Authority of the Bible

The matter of what authority the Bible has in the revelation of God and in the response of his people is not an academic question. If Scripture has any role in the revelation of God, then its relation to the authority of an individual's insight or to the Christian community's corporate judgment or to writings of contemporary devout persons is important. Christendom differs sharply over the relative authority of church and Bible. History shows more than one watershed in the controversy. Protestant Christians hold the Bible as the foremost authority in their effort to know God and his will, recognizing the activity of God's spirit in the church and in individual lives as men seek to understand the Bible and the fallibility of man in his efforts to comprehend or even communicate with God.

From an early period in the life of the people of God, the judgments, the message, the patterns of response of the community were judged by the plumbline of Scripture—from "Moses and the prophets" the "teachings of the apostles," to the reformers' insistence of the explicit teachings of Scripture as the criteria for doctrine and practice.

The Message of the Bible

Effectual revelation involves both disclosure and response; Scripture provides a record not only of God's redemptive actions toward man, but also of man's response in thought and deed to God or of man's perception of God's action and intent.

To the query of man, What does Scripture have to say? the Christian community affirms the conviction that the Bible speaks of man's most significant needs—to his radical predicament. The Scriptures present the story of God's unceasing actions among and toward men to the end that man may be made whole, that his life may be fulfilled, that he may enjoy the full fellowship of his righteous, holy, loving, perfect Father. This composite record of events is understood best when seen as "holy history"—the presentation of events accompanied by their interpretation by the believing community, together with man's response to those events.

The message of the Bible pivots on the events of the incarnation of God in Jesus Christ—his birth, life, ministry, teachings, death, resurrection, ascension. In him God's Word is made

115

flesh to dwell among man. In him the intent of God is made plain. Because of him, all God's actions toward man have a vivid, authoritative point of reference for understanding: "He who has seen me has seen the father." He is God's fullest Word to man. All Scripture finds its interpretation in him.

The Function of the Bible

116

In the search for the clear firm solutions to all enigmas in life, many people have hoped for the Bible to be a treasure chest of answers—and have treated it as such. It is not the function of the Bible to provide a catalogue of answers for all of man's questions or dilemmas but to disclose God to man, and to serve as a means of enlightening man's response to God. It is a book of faith whose main character is God and whose "plot" is the interaction of God—man. History and the natural order are its backdrop, but these always are interpreted by faith for the purpose of illumining the person of God in whom and under whom life makes sense and gains direction, purpose, and destiny.

How Man May Hear God Speak Through the Bible

To have before him a source for hearing and knowing God himself, Creator, King, Redeemer, Lord, man is encouraged and tantalized to inquire how he may hear God speak through words written by men and called Scripture.

The same God who spoke through the prophets, priests, and the community of the faithful, who inspired those who wrote, preserved, and selected Scripture, is present in the contemporary man even as that man seeks to hear God speak through Scripture. The illumination of the reader of Scripture is a companion conviction to the inspiration of the writer of Scripture. The God of truth who discloses himself in the Bible is also and at the same time the Spirit of truth interpreting Scripture to the reader in his search.

Distortion of the message is possible as man takes with him to Scripture preconceived ideas of what it says. One who reads to hear God's message is assured, however, that God's spirit is actively at work to facilitate encounter with the living God. Moreover the community of Christians is used by God as his Spirit works in the church to correct, to enrich, to round out the individual's understanding of Scripture. Acceptance of the Lord of Scripture brings with it increasing understanding of the words of Scripture.

Man's creator endowed him not only with the capacity for faith, but also with capacity for reason. Both have a place in man's attempt to know and hear the God revealed in Scripture. The role of reason is displayed in the diligent work of scholars, archaeologists, linguists in illuminating meanings and contexts of the human language of the Bible, but the use of the mind is no less imperative for the individual Christian as he approaches the Bible. Reason is the companion of faith, not the competitor. In fact, faith and reason discipline one another in man's effort to hear God.

In the church's continuous endeavor to hear God through the reading and study of the Bible, dependable principles have been developed to help man hear God speak through the Scriptures. These include, for example, the necessity of understanding the context of specific passages or books, and the circumstances under which they were written. The apparent meaning of one passage must be evaluated in light of other passages and in light of the whole message of Scripture. The supreme revelation of God is in the person of Jesus Christ, and the clearest disclosure of God's will for man is in his life. Therefore the message of God in the words of Scripture finds its best interpretation in the Word of God incarnate. The message of Scripture must be interpreted in terms of the type of writings carrying the message; parable, poetry, narrative, letter, vision convey truth each in a different way. The cumulative experience of the church has invaluable help for the individual who seeks the God of Scripture.

117

This Theme in the Bible

It is primarily in the experience of the believing community that this theme is based. However, this experience is from time to time alluded to in the Bible itself. The importance of "the law and the Prophets" is reflected in the reform of Josiah, based on the recovered Book of the Law (2 Kings 22ff.) and in the place accorded the Book of Moses in the restored temple of Nehemiah (Ezra 6, 7). The importance of the law and the prophets was especially apparent among the scribes and Pharisees of Jesus' day, though its proper understanding was seriously distorted. Jesus related passages from the Old Testament to himself (Luke 4:16-21; 24:13-27). Paul was conscious that his teaching had come to him under the inspiration of the Holy Spirit (1 Corinthians 2:12-13). In 2 Peter 1:20-21 there is the affirmation that the teachings of Scripture are not matters of personal interpretation but come by the impulse of the Holy Spirit moving men.

Jesus himself bore testimony that in him the Scriptures are fulfilled, and in him lies the test of all Scripture (John 5:30-47; Luke 16:19-31). The sermons of the early church also witness to this conviction (Acts 13:26ff.; 8:35ff.; Acts 2, 3). See also 2 Timothy 3; 1 Corinthians 2:6-13.

6. God Acts Through the Church to Make Himself Known

STATEMENT OF THEME

The church meets man's need to hear the gospel proclaimed, to experience God's presence in group worship, and to have the corrective guidance of a collective Christian conscience.

DESCRIPTION OF THEME

The fellowship of Christians has the God-rooted potential for facilitating encounter with God himself both by those within that fellowship and by those not members of that community. But the testimony of Scripture and of the church through history points to God's action among the community of his people to make himself known more clearly both to the community and to those outside the fellowship. His action is apparent among the Hebrew nation, among Christians, climactically expressed in his incarnation in Jesus. To the extent that the community of Christians is faithful to its commitment to the Lord, it affords the opportunity to meet one of man's most basic needs—for belonging and acceptance in a group significant to him.

God's Continuous Action Through His People

The church is the result of God's redemption of man, and the resultant fellowship is bound together by God's Spirit and the Christian's common debt of love.

The Christian community has its roots in the community of God's people whose history reaches back through the centuries to Abraham, to the people who "once . . . were not people" (1 Peter 2:10) but were made to be "a kingdom of priests and a holy nation" (Exodus 19:6), through whom all nations are to be brought to know him.

It was God's disclosure of himself to Abraham, to Moses, to the people of Israel and his involvement in their life and affairs that brought into being a "chosen" people. Even amid their rebellions, failure, and disobedience he disclosed himself and his purposes to them. Though they were dispersed by defect, capture, and slavery, he reestablished them as a people. When they drew their bounds tight, intending to be a people of privilege rather than servants, he broke their bounds and revealed anew his intention to bring others into his people. His radical re-creation of the community was inherent in the dramatic disclosure of himself in Jesus Christ and in the community of disciples enlivened and empowered by his Spirit, of whose continuing action the Christian community today is the result.

Throughout this long history, God's people and their life together have repeatedly been an arena of God's self-disclosing

119

action. This does not mean that only through what men call the church does God reveal himself. God is not confined to one means or to one identifiable group for his self-disclosure. Indeed, sensitive men see God's action in a variety of places and groups. It is the conviction of Christians that he reveals himself when and how and to whom he will. It is equally their conviction that he has and does reveal himself to those who have committed themselves to him and find themselves to be his people.

120

To know God's revelation through the community of God's people does not negate the reality of his making himself known to an individual. Nor is "the church" intended to signify only the gathered community of God's people. God does make himself known to individuals; the revelation of God to the community provides a context within which the individual may perceive God's revelation to him. Sometimes an individual's distorted perception of God may be corrected by the corporate perception though the community is not immune to distorted perception and may be corrected by an individual. The validity of both individual and corporate perception of God's revelation is not based on majority approval, but rather on consistency with God's revelation in Jesus Christ and confirmation by God's Spirit for the individual and for the community.

God's Revelation to the Church

The community of God's people is at the same time a divine and a human community. This fact explains its paradoxical strength and weakness—its potential for clear apprehension of God's revelation and for distortion of that revelation.

Both the experience and the conviction of the church emphasize the need for God's continuing self-disclosure to his people. It is also the church's experience and conviction that God does act through his church to make himself known more fully to the church as well as to reveal himself to the world.

As both the receiver and channel for communication of God's self-disclosure, the church stands in continuing need of correction, judgment, purification, empowering redemption by God's Spirit.

Because God is living and active, and because man is finite, fallible, and sinful, both the Christian individual and the Christian community need continual contact with God in order to know him and his will.

Whenever God's people have assumed they were out of the reach of error and beyond the need of God, they have become flagrant violators of their own nature. To be the people of God does carry blessings with it, but to be the people of God also carries the demand of being "holy as I am holy," of being "perfect as I am perfect." This demand inevitably brings judgment on a community of fallible men. But God's judgment of the church is as necessary in his self-disclosure as is his empowering of the church. God's revelation of himself to the church is full-orbed, including his gracious forgiveness, his justness, his righteousness, his power, and his majesty.

The church must be alert to God's leading, discerning his will and his judgment not only within its own life but also in the world. Events, attitudes, insights in the life of the world may very well be the modes of God's judging the church or awakening it anew to its real nature and business or challenging it to fulfill neglected duties. It is true for the church as for the individual that whom the Lord loveth he chasteneth. Judgment is for the purpose of putting right, not for condemning.

121

God's Revelation Through the Church

In the course of the life and work of the church—as individuals and as a corporate body, gathered and dispersed—God acts to make himself apparent to men.

The people of God have always been under the double commission of knowing God and making him known to others.

God's call has even been to be a special people "that you may declare the wonderful deeds of him who called you out of darkness into his marvelous light" (1 Peter 2:9), God's invitation to fellowship is not one to be grasped but to be extended. God's action among his people discloses him not only to that people, but also to those outside the Christian community. For this purpose, indeed, the church is empowered by the Holy Spirit to be witnesses so that all men may be drawn unto God.

A major role the church has played in God's revelation has to do with the Scriptures. The People of God whose origin is recorded in the Scriptures is the same people who have by God's guidance written, gathered, preserved, dispersed the biblical record of God's redemptive offer to all men. God acting through his people has made provision for this continuing testimony to his interaction with man in the past and to his urgent invitation to man in the present. The role of the Christian community as custodian and distributor of the Scriptures is a continuous evidence of God's use of the church in his self-disclosure.

The organized life of the Christian community offers both witness to God's revelation and opportunity for the people to gather in his presence. In the preaching and teaching ministries, particularly in the sacraments, in acts of mercy and attacks on causes of social evil, the church both proclaims what God has done and offers to man a personal knowledge of God. In occasions and resources for worship, the church provides for intimate communion with God. Through the active loving concern of his people, and the suffering of faithful Christians persecuted for Christ's sake, God makes evident his own love and concern for all men.

The aim of his self-disclosure is toward *all* men. God's action through the church to make himself known is hardly separable into that which discloses him further to the believing community and that which proclaims him to unbelievers. All the life and activities of the Christian community gathered or dispersed may be useful in bringing both believers and unbelievers into a closer relationship with God.

God's use of the church is not limited to its gathered expression. He makes himself known through the words and actions of individuals as they, led by the Spirit, live obedient lives in their homes, in their civic relationship, at work, in personal relations, by word, deed, and prayer.

This Theme in the Bible

The classical passage on God's activity among his people to make himself known is the Epistle to the Ephesians. Many of the "practical" passages of Paul's epistles demonstrate the conviction that God works through his people to make himself known. These passages reflect the imperative for the inward renewal of the church as well as for the church to witness to God's revelation.

The entire history of the people of Israel emphasizes their role as a servant people for the accomplishment of God's purpose. Isaiah especially, but also Jeremiah and the other prophets, enjoin this people to let God work through them this way. First Peter 2:9 echoes this theme carried throughout the Old Testament.

God's judgment of his people is reflected in Amos, Obadiah, and Habakkuk.

The so-called "high priestly prayer" of Jesus recorded in John 17 may be understood as a prayer based on the mission of the church to serve as a channel of God's self-disclosure.

In Acts and the epistles of the New Testament we see the struggle of the church both to apprehend God's self-disclosure and to serve the further illumination of revelation to those outside.

See especially such passages as Acts 11, 15; Acts 20:17ff.; Romans 6:9—11, chapters 14 and 15; 1 Corinthians 10, 12, 13; Philippians; 1 and 2 Timothy. See also Romans 12ff.; 2 Corinthians 4; 1 Peter 2, 3.

123

7. God Speaks to Man Through the Natural Order

STATEMENT OF THEME

The handiwork of God as Creator and Sustainer is revealed in the universe, which is mysterious and yet yields to man's search for understanding it. As man discovers God's laws in the natural order, he is able to be at home in it and to use these laws creatively.

DESCRIPTION OF THEME

124

Man, a part of the created natural order, may through that order discover much about God, its Creator. Man has never been without evidence of God, and his curiosity and his intelligence encourage him in his efforts to perceive what God reveals of himself through the natural order, which is man's habitation.

Man's involvement with the natural order itself is the focus of a theme in another area—Life and Its Setting: the Meaning and Experience of Existence. In the theme "God speaks to man through the natural order" the action centers on God's self-disclosure to man through this mode of his activity—the creation and sustaining of the natural order.

In God's disclosure of himself through the natural order in which man lives, man finds response to his demands for explanations of his observations in the natural order.

It is the conviction of the believing community that nowhere is God without witness; nowhere can man be outside the possibility of encounter with God. God is the purposeful Sovereign Creator and Sustainer not only of man but also of the whole system of life of which man is a part.

Through the natural order God reveals himself to those isolated from the community of his people or from the biblical witness to him.

Clues to God's Self-Disclosure

Although the natural order seems impersonal and abstract, it provides clues to the character of its Creator. Some of these clues are:

ORDER AND DESIGN

The natural order divulges to man's observation and search systems of order, interrelatedness within the order, design and symmetry. This balance and complexity disclose a Creator of an orderly, organized, purposeful character. Such order within complexity echoes the character of its Maker.

POWER

The tremendous power operative in the universe gives evidence of One able to create, control, and override power. Man's inquiry has continuously uncovered power heretofore latent—from fire to water to electricity to nuclear power and beyond. This is power man has unleashed and harnessed, not made. It portends a maker of power beyond man.

PROVIDENCE

In the complexity of the universe, in the interdependence of the animate and inanimate, and in the balance of chemical composition in earth, air, and sea, there is evidence of provision for life that cannot be accounted for by capricious accident. This is the work of One who makes provision for the sustaining of a planned order. This is the result of knowledge and wisdom unbound by earth's time schedule. Evidence of such overarching intelligence and providence are all around man—atmosphere that sustains human and plant life, weather that is tolerable and beneficial to life, force of gravity adequate to maintain stability, minerals in the earth adequate for plant and animal life, characteristics of plants and animals that perpetuate and propagate life.

125

TRANSCENDENCE

Man's capacity for exploring the natural order and discovering its laws and its latent powers is accompanied by his capacity for controlling much in the natural order and for participating in its development. For all his *increasing* dominance over the natural order, there is yet *much* more beyond his control. The edges of the universe have yet to be found. Discoveries in science proclaim a creation still expanding. Man has not exhausted the knowable. Beyond human discovery is the Creator and Sustainer of man's environment. Neither the Creator, nor his creation, can be contained or commanded by man.

KNOWABLENESS

126

The Creator and Sustainer of this complex natural order exposes a crucial aspect of his character in the inquiring and inventive character of man. He apparently is not content to be alone in his relation to the natural order. He has so created man that he is able to share in the control and direction of forces in the natural order. He provides for man's exercise of that capacity, leaving him free yet also responsible in his use of the natural order.

Moreover, this human part of the natural order seems to be accorded special privileges of probing into the design, purpose, and possibilities of the natural order. This exploration discloses repeated patterns, called natural laws, which add to his sense of security in his environment. Yet new discoveries open up new vistas of enigmas to be explained, and man is drawn into further exploration and efforts toward explanation. Observable consistencies inspire man to look for explanations of apparent inconsistencies. Control achieved and design discovered impel man to wrestle further with what is yet uncontrolled and to examine more closely what appears to be chaos.

Such power trusted to man discloses One who would share creation with man, One who is willing to be known, to have his work questioned, scrutinized, uncovered.

MYSTERY

Almost as dominant as its observability is the mystery inherent in the natural order. The universe yields many of its secrets to scientific investigation and to the man of faith. Yet there is much about the universe which is inexplicable, contradictory, unfathomable. So also there is much that is unknown about the Maker of the natural order. The Creator of the unfathomable complexity of the universe is himself beyond the comprehension of man. Though self-revealing, he does not wholly disclose himself to man. Though he relates himself to his creation, he will not be encompassed by it.

Moreover, there is an awe and mystery surrounding God that is of a different order from that of the universe: the mystery characteristic of the Maker of the universe centers in the quality of his character—his otherness, his omnipotence, omniscience, perfection, holiness. Though man were to uncover all the secrets of the natural order, he cannot dispel the cloud of mystery characteristic of God Almighty, Maker of heaven and earth.

Confirmation of God's Self-Disclosure

Confronted by the natural order alone, man has an unclear perception of the God of the natural order. He cannot be sure which of the characteristics of the natural order are reflections of the Creator and which are distortions. He yet needs a norm by which to sort out the true from the spurious in the evidence he sees. He finds his answer in the fullest disclosure God has offered, Jesus Christ. In him, God makes available the vivid revelation of himself by which man can test his perception of God in the natural order. The general, abstract, contradictory, impersonal character of that revelation is set in context by the specific, concrete, consistent, intimate revelation in the Incarnation.

He who dwelt on this earth within the confines of the natural order, who yet did marvels apparently contradicting natural laws and who clearly was Lord of matter as well as of men, confirms the conviction of the believing community that the Creator and Sustainer of the universe is the loving Father whose intent for all creation is good.

This Theme in the Bible

The biblical passages in which this theme is rooted present a faith-oriented view of the natural order. This is consistent with the character of the Bible as a book of faith. The Book of Job is peppered with relevant inferences regarding the God of Creation (12, 26, 28, 36—42). Many of the Psalms echo man's wonder and awareness of the God of nature (8, 18, 19, 93, 104). See also Jeremiah 10:11ff. See Genesis 1—3.

New Testament affirmations include especially Romans 1:18-24; Acts 14:15-17; Matthew 6:25-30; 10:29-33.

SONSHIP: THE MEANING AND EXPERIENCE OF REDEMPTION

The themes within this area are:

God's Redeeming Love for Man
Man's Responding to God's Redemptive Action
Becoming a New Person in Christ
Growing Up in Christ
Finding Identity in the Christian Community
The Christian's Hope Rests in the Triumphant God

Description of Curriculum Area

The focus or vantage point of this area of curriculum is man's personal response to God's self-disclosure—accepting God's redemptive love and experiencing the meaning of sonship; the inner witness and the life of faith, or *being* the Christian.

Comprehended in this area of curriculum is such content from Christian thought and life as: alienation of man from God; God's redemptive love for man; man's acceptance of his sonship relationship to God; interpretation of the new man in Christ; the Christian view of interpersonal relationships within the church and beyond; the meaning of the Christian hope.

In order to have educational value as an area of curriculum, this content must be viewed in terms of its pertinence to the persistent issues of man's life. Some of these issues are: What does it mean to be saved? What does it mean to sin? How can I relate to others? What does God expect of me? What can I expect from God? What difference does God make in my life? What does it mean to be a Christian? To what shall I commit my life? What does it mean to mature as a son of God?[1]

---

[1]These three paragraphs are repeated here as necessary background.

Delineation of Area

This area of the curriculum recognizes that God has created man as his son, and also that man's sin results in denial of his sonship and in estrangement. God out of his love and grace has acted and continues to act to restore man to faithful sonship. The nature of the restored relationship, the whole meaning and experience of redemption as a dynamic, living, and continuous process and event, is emphasized in this area of curriculum. In developing the area guide, the term "sonship" is used for convenience and for the concept it embodies, namely, the filial relationship of man to God made possible by God in Jesus Christ.

130

"Sonship," then, refers to the relationship that God intends between his children and himself, a relationship which he has made possible and which he invites persons to accept. Sonship refers to the new life in Christ. God leads man to understand the reality and power of sin and his state of rejection of God, which has resulted in bondage to self and inability to escape that bondage. God acts decisively on behalf of man in Jesus Christ in order that man can accept himself as created in the image of God, as dependent upon God, and as a free, responsible creature, able to respond to his father as a son.

This area relates to the other curriculum areas in that it reflects that God has created man and the world and that God continuously reveals himself to man; moreover, the realization of the sonship relationship through redemption undergirds the social and outward expressions of discipleship and makes possible the corporate reality of Christian community.

Integrally involved in "Sonship: the Meaning and Experience of Redemption," as a curriculum area are: the nature of the unredeemed man; God's act in Christ to redeem man; man's response—positive and negative—to God's action; the relation of man's freedom to God's initiative; the relation of the individual to the Christian community in the process of redemption; the nature of the new being in Christ; man's life as son living in faith and growing in grace; the lordship of Christ in the world (society, culture, nations, and institutions); the meaning of the Christian hope.

Unredeemed Man

On the one hand, man is created in the image of God, part of an order that is created good. He belongs to God and is dependent upon him. He is free and responsible. His life is valuable and has meaning. He is creative, able to apprehend truth, to search and work for goodness. He has the capacity to enter into fellowship with man and with God. He is destined to have a measure of responsibility over himself and the created order. On the other hand, sin enters human life as rebellion, rejection of dependence upon God, and misuse of freedom. Sin is characterized by broken relationships between God and man, between man and man. It is both individual and corporate and involves all mankind, pervading history, society, culture, and insitutions. The results of sin for the individual are many: pride and bondage to self, lack or loss of clear self-identity and purpose, broken human relationships, social blindness and ineffectiveness, hardening of the heart, spiritual death, negation of the image of God, broken relationship with God, the sense of guilt, and the restless search for meaning. Results of sin can never be confined to individual expression but are also evident in the actions, attitudes, and policies of social institutions: exploitation of persons, war, corporate selfishness, idolatry of various forms, corrupt power structures, irresponsible use of natural resources.

Man is never an isolated human being in sin or in redemption. What he is and who he is can never be defined apart from other people, society, culture, and institutions. His redemption, while involving an act of his own will, has far-reaching social consequences and is, therefore, never merely an individual experience. His act of will is part of a community, the family, the neighborhood, the labor union, the business community, and the Christian community. No decision, therefore, whether an

131

act of faith, an act of rejection, or an act of moral choice is ever completely individual.

God's Action and Man's Response

God created man for life with him in fellowship and communion. Man's sin estranges him from God. God in his seeking love continuously acts to redeem man.

God's action in the life, death, and resurrection of Christ is decisive in redemption. God does for man what man cannot do for himself. The power of sin is such that man cannot save himself. All of his own efforts, however noble and constructive in terms of the well-being of individuals and society, cannot ultimately save him. As God forgives him, frees him from bondage to sin, renews the broken relationship, man is restored in faithful sonship.

In Christ, God acts decisively on behalf of man, judging him, forgiving his sin, freeing him from the slavery to sin and guilt, restoring him to right relation with God thus enabling man to accept himself and his neighbor and to live boldly and courageously in the world, confident that in both life and death he is secure in God.

God's offer of redemption has two possible responses, and man by God's creation has the responsibility to choose. He may accept God's act on his behalf or he may reject it. Involved in man's choice is the God-given sensitivity to his own need, and the capacity for accepting. Nevertheless, God does not coerce man into redemption, man's choice is a real one. Some men accept and others reject God's offer of new life. Many factors both in the individual and in the milieu of society play a part in such a decision: pride, wilfulness, inertia, isolation, self-deprecation and other emotional blocks, disintegration of life's relationships; awareness of God's offer; awareness of one's guilt and need; responsiveness to love; witness of those who profess redemption; quality of nurture offered by the Christian community.

God's intention is that all shall fulfill their sonship—those who are unaware of their sonship, those who are aware but who have rejected him, those who have acknowledged sonship but failed to fulfill its promise, and those who are aware and who are continually striving to be obedient sons. A faithful son of God has responded to God's self-disclosure affirmatively, is open to his continuing direction and guidance, and is therefore deepening his insight into the meaning and experience of redemption.

Man's Freedom

Because man is created free and responsible, he may either accept or reject God's offer of redemption. All of man's striving and seeking are caught up in his responding to God in repentance, confession, acceptance, commitment, and dedication; man accepts redemption by faith, that is, belief, trust, and obedience.

One claims his sonship when, confronted with the gospel, he responds affirmatively to God's invitation. This experience calls forth a repolarization of the self from a self-centered to a God-centered life. Living in God's grace releases man from bondage to sin, creates him a new being in Christ, inspires in him a sense of identity with the Christian community, and enables him to seek and to yield to the leading of the Holy Spirit.

133

The Individual and the Christian Community

The Christian community functions in redemption as an instrument of God's redeeming work by proclaiming the gospel within and beyond the church; by extending acceptance, love, and forgiveness; by teaching; by nurturing; by bearing witness; and by inviting. The Christian community is a participant in man's response to God's grace by supporting him, encouraging him, accepting him, and providing opportunities for confession, repentance, resolve, worship, and service. The Christian community in this sense is the congregation, the individual member of the church, the Christian home, and any other group in the fellowship.

No person is ever a Christian alone. To be a Christian is to be in the community of those whom God has also called. The Christian participates in the particular community and in the worldwide company of Christians, in the Church Miltant, and in the Church Triumphant. He is involved responsibly in the institutions of the church, even when he feels them to be limited and ineffectual. The son participates in the worship, the sacraments, the nurture, and the witness of the church as it seeks corporately to express the mission and message of God in the world.

The nature and significance of the church is interpreted in the area, "The Church: the Meaning and Experience of Christian Community."

The New Being in Christ

The event of God's-action—man's response—creates a new being. It establishes a new relationship with God. God restores man to the original state intended for him in creation. God's acceptance of man enables him to accept and love God, accept and love himself, and accept and love others. No longer is man bound by the power of his own sin and guilt. He is free to respond to God and to his neighbor in love and dedication. God becomes the new center for his life. The motivation for his decisions begins to move from his own self-interest and rebellion toward a motivation centered in loyalty to the loving, judging, sacrificing God. Man in awareness of his sonship aspires to maturity in these qualities of his new being.

There are many ways in which the contrast of the old and the new man in Christ can be expressed. When one is restored to his right relationship with God, he passes from death to life, that is, he need no longer live in the realm of continual frustration, hopelessness, and despair, but may live in confidence, hope, and affirmation. He passes from the despair of guilt to the freedom of forgiveness. His sin has been forgiven. He need no longer fear death nor be overwhelmed by the human situation because he acknowledges God as the Lord both of life and death.

The change that takes place in man does not separate him from his involvement in corporate sin. He is a new creation in the midst of the same society, the same culture, and the same institutions of which he was a part. What has changed is the stance he takes in relation to that in which he is involved. His stance is one that is controlled and empowered by God, leading him to affirm in his involvement in these institutions and in culture the faith that God is the Lord of life and death, the judge of human finitude and sin, and the source by which the society is transformed and redeemed.

As a new being in Christ, then, man is made aware of his relationship as a son of God. He enters a new life so radical that it has been contrasted as moving from death to life and of "being born again." A new birth does take place, a birth which makes him acknowledge and accept himself as a child of God.

Man's Life as Son

The son of God is open to new insights into God's purposes. There is an increasing realization of sonship through progressive personal experiences of growth in the meaning of being redeemed. Sonship is the essence of humanity in that self-realization in the fullest sense is possible to the person who accepts God's reconciling grace and grows in the life of redemption. One of the evidences of redemption is the reorientation of values. Conversion is an "about face" in life, a response to God's call to acceptance of sonship. The new being evidences a sense of stewardship under the conviction that his particular and personal powers and endowments are gifts of God to be used in his service and in the interest of his children. This sense of stewardship is closely allied to the sense of vocation, the calling to God's work in the world.

The son of God is continually open to God and to the deepen-

135

ing of insights into the Christian faith and life. He lives his son-ship through obedience, commitment, discipleship, and love of God and his neighbor. He is open to Christian nurture and spiritual growth, seeking to discover the will of his Father and the power to do that will in his life.

He responds to the leading of the Holy Spirit, endeavoring always to know and understand more fully the nature of God and his work in the world, through prayer, worship, meditation, and participation in the community of Christians, the Body of Christ. In all of his life he is guided and controlled by the faith that nothing in all creation, whether life or death, whether pressures of society or events of his own creation, can ultimately separate him from the love of God in Jesus Christ. Thus, the Christian can abide in Christian hope in confident assurance of the fulfillment of his redemption in Christ.

136

The Lordship of Christ

The son lives in obedience to and dependence upon Christ as Lord. His lordship is acknowledged by the son not only over his own life and affairs, but also over the temporal order. This conviction is the foundation of the son's radical security and his creative involvement in the transformation of the culture and institutions of society in their local, national, and international expressions. The son recognizes and accepts a dual citizenship, but only one Lord. His sonship gives a new perspective to all decisions and relationships as they are viewed under the Lordship of Christ. History gains new perspective as the son views it as the scene of God's certain victory. Far from removing the son from the world and its affairs, the acknowledgment of Christ as Lord involves the son more deeply and responsibly in society—often in conflict. Yet within temporal values and events, the son lives in confidence under God's rule and in expectation of the ultimate realization of the Christian hope in the consummation of the kingdom of God.

Themes Delineated

1. God's Redeeming Love for Man

STATEMENT OF THEME

Through God's changeless and seeking love for man, supremely manifested in Jesus Christ (his life, death, resurrection, and ascension) redemption is made possible whereby man's alienation from God is overcome and the way is opened for him to be reconciled with God. Thus man's persistent need for reconciliation, meaning, acceptance, integrity, security, and freedom is adequately met.

DESCRIPTION OF THEME

God, the loving Creator and Father, created man as the object of his love and intended that man would love him in return. Man has been created free and with the capacity to act responsibly in freedom and love. But man, in spite of his capacities to respond positively to God, has rebelled and alienated himself from God. In spite of man's sin, God continues to love him and has acted decisively in human history to redeem man. Because that love is redemptive, man can be reconciled to his Maker and fulfill the divine purpose for his life.

God's Purpose for Man

137

Man has been created in the image of God. Inherent in God's image in man is man's capacity for God. That is, man is capable of enjoying fellowship with his Creator. Man was made for fellowship with God and finds his highest fulfillment in a filial relationship with him. The Christian faith declares that the nature of this father-son relationship is one of love, for God created man as the supreme object of his love and intended that man should live in love and obedience to him. In this way man affirms his sonship. Apart from this, man's life lacks meaning and integrity, it lacks freedom and fulfillment, it lacks security and peace.

Not only did God intend man to enjoy a filial relationship with his Father but he also intended him to enjoy a fraternal relationship with his fellowmen. These two facets of man's life can never be divorced; they are integral parts of the same thing. Both creation and redemption envision a harmonious man-to-God relationship and a harmonious man-to-man relationship. These are essential in God's purpose for man.

Man's Rebellion Against God

138

Even though God has intended man to live in obedience to him, he has created man with a certain measure of freedom and responsibility. Man is free to determine his own relationship to God. When man rebels against God, he alienates himself from his Maker. This is the meaning of sin. Sin has its origin in man's willfulness, his tendency to serve his own selfish interests, and his susceptibility to the negative influences about him.

In a mistaken notion of freedom, he has preferred to be his own master rather than to acknowledge the rightful sovereignty of a loving God. Like the prodigal son in Jesus' parable, he has left his Father. As a consequence, he who was made for fellowship with God now lives in separation from him. Though for a time he may think he is enjoying true life in the far country of sin, he realizes, when he comes to himself, that life apart from God can never satisfy his deepest longings.

The effects of sin in man's life are evident in a number of ways: a restless search for meaning, enslavement to unwanted personal and social attitudes and habits, ruptured or strained human relationships, moral insensitivity, a gnawing sense of guilt, an absence of a clear purpose and self-identity, and finally, spiritual death.

Rebellion against God often results in man's living in separation from his fellowmen. This does not mean that he actually divorces himself from the society of other people, although even this may at times be the result of his reconciled attitudes; but it does mean that his human relationships at their best may lack the integrity, the purposiveness, the creativity, the satisfying quality, and the freedom which give meaning to his association with others. At worst, suspicion, fear, hatred, jealousy, and prejudice erect walls of separation which keep men who are apart from God apart from each other also.

However, sin cannot be confined to personal and interpersonal relationships. All men are involved in and are a part of a society which is affected by sin in various ways. Evidences of sin in the social order are seen in the violation of human rights; exploitation of persons; corrupt power structures; outbreaks of violence in war, riots, and civil-rights struggles; abortive and wasteful use of natural resources.

Even though the individual may attempt to deny his participation in corporate sin, it is next to impossible to do so. A man is the sum total of the many emotional, social, cultural, economic, political, and religious relations which he maintains. They are a part of his life and he is a part of them. The sin which is embedded in them is of the same order as the sin which is within his own life.

Man may strive to save himself from his sin but he cannot succeed. Through rejecting God's love man has caused the alienation and, as long as he continues to rebel, he forfeits his claim upon his Creator but cannot place himself outside the love of God. Redemption and reconciliation are among the needs which he is unable to meet solely through his own efforts.

139

God Has Acted

To all of these needs there is but one answer—God's redeeming love. God's love is eternal. God has loved man through all the long centuries of human struggle. Even though man has repeatedly turned away from God, he has never been abandoned by God. God is with man now and will be forever. The writer of the prophecy of Hosea caught something of this when he wrote of the patient love Hosea maintained for Gomer despite her ingratitude and sin. God's love has never been withdrawn from man even though man has often rejected it.

What is more, that love is a seeking love. In man's sinfulness, God's love reaches out to him. In man's forgetfulness, God's love remembers him. In man's weakness, God's love surrounds, lifts, restores, renews, and transforms him. The psalmist declared that none of the experiences of life could take him beyond the reach of God. Man may attempt to flee from the presence of God, as did Jonah, but God is there to remind him of his inescapable responsibility.

140

In the Old Testament God's redeeming love is revealed, though not exclusively, in the history of Israel. The people of Israel came to believe that the mighty act of God that first made Israel a nation was the Exodus and that that act was one of redeeming love. The long history of Israel, with its many vicissitudes, including obedience and disobedience, worthy worship and idolatry, prosperity and adversity, captivity and restoration, is to be understood only in the light of a living, redeeming God seeking the highest good for his people.

Even though there are many profound insights into the nature of God's redemptive action which have been recorded in the Old Testament the Christian believes that God's redeeming love was supremely manifested in Jesus Christ—in his birth, life, death, resurrection, and ascension. Jesus Christ not only spoke the word but was the Word in the flesh. He was both the Son of God and the Son of man. On one hand, God was at work in Christ, judging, convicting, healing, forgiving, redeeming, restoring, and reconciling man. On the other hand, Jesus is an example of the perfect love and obedience the Father desires in all of his sons.

In Christ's death for the sins of the world God revealed in the midst of time his intention for all mankind through eternity. For the Christian the cross is at the center of his faith. In the cross God acted to redeem his people. When man was unable to redeem himself, God in Christ identified himself with man and offered himself on the cross in order that man might be redeemed.

The cross cannot be seen apart from the resurrection. The reality, validity, and efficacy of the life and death of Christ as revealing God's redemptive love for man were vindicated in Christ's resurrection and ascension. The fact of the resurrection was the basis of New Testament witness and faith.

God continues to reveal his unceasing concern for man. His redeeming love is more than a matter of past history or theoretical theology. It is a matter of current events, of personal, life-changing experience, as persons today respond to the gospel and discover the power of God's grace, made real in the lives of men by the work of the Holy Spirit.

When man becomes aware of and responds to God's love in Christ, not only is his alienation from God and man overcome, but he finds the most significant acceptance. He finds meaning in life, he finds integrity, true security, and freedom. Thus God's redeeming love meets basic, persistent, human, life needs.

This Theme in the Bible

God's love for man is implied in the account of creation and God's original intention for his highest creature (Genesis 1—3). The beginning of the outworking of God's redemptive purpose through a chosen people is found in the call of Abram and the promise of blessing to and through him and his descendants (Genesis 12:1-3). That purpose of life is traceable throughout the story of Israel in the Old Testament (a summary of which is found in the New Testament in Acts 7). God's mighty act of deliverance in the exodus of Israel from Egypt with its attendant events (Exodus 12—15) made the nation conscious of its special covenant relationship with the God of love and grace. All of the covenant passages of the Old Testament express God's love (e.g. to Abraham—Genesis 15 and 17; to Isaac—Genesis 26:3-4; to Jacob—Genesis 28:13-15; to the nation of Israel—Exodus 6 and 19; and to David—2 Samuel 7). That love is also

141

brought out in some of the psalms (Psalms 103, 105, 106, 107, 118, 136, 145, 146) and in the prophets (e.g. Hosea 11:1-9; 14:1-7; Jeremiah 1—30, describing man's broken state in sin, and chapter 31, dealing with the "new covenant"; Isaiah 25— 26, and the "book of comfort" Isaiah 40—66). Many of the messianic prophecies speak eloquently of God's redemptive love (e.g. Isaiah 35; 42:1-12; 49:1-13; 52:13—53:12; 61:1-11; Ezekiel 34:11-21).

142

In the New Testament the promise comes to fulfillment as God's love is perfectly revealed in the birth, life, death, and resurrection of Jesus Christ (Matthew, Mark, Luke, John). Particular Gospel passages interpret the significance of redemptive love (e.g. Luke 14 and John 3:16-17). Romans 5:8 is a key verse: "God shows his love for us in that while we were yet sinners Christ died for us." In Christ God was reconciling the world to himself (2 Corinthians 5:19). God's gift through Christ is full redemption (Ephesians 1:3-14). The significance of Christ's ministry and resurrection is affirmed in 1 Corinthians 15. Furthermore, in Christ, God has made all men one (Ephesians 2:1-10). In 1 John that love is set forth as conferring on us the unspeakable privilege of sonship to God (3:1-3) and the relationship of brothers to one another (4:7-12).

2. Man's Responding to God's Redemptive Action

STATEMENT OF THEME

God's offer of redemption demands decision with its inevitable consequences either toward life or death. Man is free to accept or reject God's action on his behalf. The active, positive response which God desires and which brings forgiveness and the awareness and acceptance of sonship is that of confession, repentance, faith, and obedience. Through such response man experiences the ultimate answer to his basic need to be loved and accepted.

DESCRIPTION OF THEME

God's action in Christ has confronted man with an unavoidable decision respecting the ultimate commitment of his life. A number of influential factors are present in the divine-human encounter, yet man is free to make the choice. Man's negative response perpetuates continued alienation and leads to death. Through positive response in faith and love, man affirms his sonship and experiences forgiveness, acceptance, and love.

Man and His Decision

Because God has acted decisively in Jesus Christ, man is confronted with a decision he cannot avoid. God has given every man the freedom to make the final decision concerning the kind of relationship he shall have with his Creator. He cannot remain neutral nor can he avoid his responsibility for the consequences of his choice. The choice is real and the consequences are real. Yet, God does not coerce or force man to make the right decision.

Man's decision is influenced by many factors. These may include previous training; the views, attitudes, and expectations of friends and loved ones; the verbal (and visual) proclamation of the gospel; the testimony of others who profess a relationship with God and the Christian community; a God-given sensitivity to personal need and a capacity to respond to God; an awareness of one's sin and God's acts of redemption; and a realization of the consequences of rejecting God or responding positively to him.

143

The decision man makes concerning his response to God has inevitable consequences: life or death—life if he accepts Christ, death if he rejects him. The tragedy is that by rejecting the grace of God man perpetuates his alienation and rebellion. But the glory of redemption is that man, by the grace of God and the work of the Holy Spirit, can respond in faith and love to what God in Christ has done for him.

When man decides to accept God as revealed in Jesus Christ, his response is one of faith and love. He acknowledges that which

God has done in his behalf and he opens his life to the guidance and direction of the Holy Spirit. In so doing, the light of the gospel is thrown upon his life and all his relationships. He becomes aware of his need for confession, repentance, obedience, and faith.

Man further discovers that even though his response to God's redemptive action might begin at a given point in time, it never ends for the Christian. He is involved in a continual lifelong process of struggle and growth as he seeks to fulfill his role as a son of God. This process will be explicated in the treatment of other themes in this area of curriculum.

Just as man's response to many of the deepest experiences of life cannot be clearly delineated, so his response in faith and love to his Creator may also issue in many forms of expression. These may occur separately or simultaneously and repeatedly. Man's primary concern is that of reestablishing a broken relationship and his response will be conditioned by that which he believes will meet his deepest need.

When a man who has alienated himself from God sees himself in the light of the gospel, he knows that he stands under judgment in his sin. It is then that he becomes aware of his need to confess his sin, to seek God's forgiveness, and to throw himself upon God's mercy.

As man opens his life to the guidance and direction of the Holy Spirit through his response in faith and love, he begins to abdicate his self-centered will and submits to the sovereign will of the Father. Through acknowledging the will of the Father and relationship to him, man affirms his sonship and enters into a faithful and obedient relationship with his Creator.

Through responding in faith and love man also becomes aware of his need to change his stance with reference to those forms of rebellion which produce alienation between himself and God and his fellowmen. An example of this is the story of Zaccheus. (Luke 19:1-19)

To respond actively and positively to God's redeeming love is thus the answer to man's basic and persistent need to be loved and accepted.

This Theme in the Bible

The necessity for decision on the part of man confronted by the redeeeming love of God is evident in the Pentateuch. Repeatedly the people of Israel are called on to affirm their faith and obedience to Jehovah, or admit that their loyalty is elsewhere (Exodus 19; 20; 32; Deuteronomy 4; 6—7; Joshua 1:24; 1 Kings 18; Amos).

In Jesus' parables and in his relationship with persons, some sort of response to God's redemptive offer is inescapably elicited (see Matthew 8; 22; Mark 10; Luke 10; 15; 19; John 1; 3; 4).

Jesus in the parable of the soils made it plain that varying responses to the gospel are to be expected (Matthew 13:1-9; 18—23; Mark 4:1-20; Luke 8:4-15). Paul summed up the right response as being repentance to God and faith in the Lord Jesus Christ (Acts 20:21). The consequences of accepting Christ are life (John 1:11-13) but of rejecting him, death (John 3:16-18; 36; Matthew 11:20-24; 25:31-46). The work of the Holy Spirit in applying the gospel is set forth in John 16:8-11 and illustrated in Acts 2:37-42.

Many of the experiences recorded in the Bible illustrating man's response to God's redemptive action may be mentioned: Nicodemus (John 3:1-15); the Samaritan woman (John 4:1-30); Zacchaeus (Luke 19:1-10); thief on the cross (Luke 23:39); the three thousand at Pentecost (Acts 2:37-42); the Ethiopian eunuch (Acts 8:26-38); Saul of Tarsus (Acts 9; 22; 26); the Philippian jailer (Acts 16:25-34). The story of the prodigal son (Luke 15:11-24) is a beautiful parabolic presentation of the experience of forgiveness and restoration.

Examples of the other responses are the rich young ruler (Matthew 19:16-22; Mark 10:17-22; Luke 18:18-23) and the prodigal son's older brother (Luke 15:25-32).

145

The humble acknowledgement of spiritual need as leading to acceptance with God is illustrated in Psalm 51 and the parable of the Pharisee and the publican (Luke 18:9-14).

The nature of repentance is indicated in Luke 15:17-21; Luke 19:1-19; Acts 26:18; 1 Thessalonians 1:9; 2 Corinthians 7:10. The need of it is stated in Luke 13:3; Acts 17:30-31; 20:21.

The New Testament teaches that faith justifies the believer in the sight of God (Romans 5:1). It also teaches that faith brings the believer forgiveness (Acts 10:43; Ephesians 1:7); peace with God (Romans 5:1); hope (Galatians 5:5); joy (John 15:11); confidence (Ephesians 3:12); sonship (John 1:12; Galatians 3:26); heirship (Romans 8:17); eternal life (John 3:36).

146

Many passages indicate that the forgiven son should live and will live in loving, brotherly relationships with others (e.g. Matthew 22:39; Mark 12:31; Luke 19; John 13:34-35; Romans 12:10; 13:8-10; 1 Corinthians 13; Galatians 5:13-14; 6:1-2; Ephesians 2:14; 4:32; Colossians 3:12-14; 1 Thessalonians 4:9; 1 John 2:9-11; 4:7-8; 11-12, 20-21).

The metaphorical use of terms is as follows: redemption, Romans 3:24; Colossians 1:14; justification, Romans 3:24; 4:25; 5:1; Galatians 2:16; reconciliation, Romans 5:10ff.; 2 Corinthians 5:18-20.

References related to the place of obedience in the life of the sons of God may be found in Acts 5:29; Philippians 2:8; Romans 8. Hebrews 11 also illustrates the interrelationship between faith and obedience.

The first eight chapters of Romans have particular relevance for this theme.

3. Becoming a New Person in Christ

STATEMENT OF THEME

Man's continual need and yearning for wholeness is met by his acceptance of Christ as Lord. This commitment to God in Christ

enables him to become a whole person by overcoming the frag-
mentizing pull of his own selfishness and of the culture in which
he lives. The new person in Christ knows through his own ex-
perience the meaning of freedom, integration of personality,
trust in God, and a reorientation of his purposes.

DESCRIPTION OF THEME

When man becomes a new person in Christ, he begins to realize and experience his sonship with God and all that it entails.
He experiences a new kind of wholeness as his new relationship
with God revealed in Jesus Christ becomes the integrating force
in his life. Life moves in the direction of new purposes. A new
kind of freedom is found in obedience to the lordship of Christ.
In a word, the acceptance of Christ as the Lord of life results
in a new nature.

Becoming Whole

Twentieth-century man in his natural state may be frag-
mentized, pulled in many directions by his own self-centeredness,
by the peculiar pressures of the contemporary culture, by those
who would help him and by those who would use him. This experience of the lack of an adequate central purpose in life brings
a sense of frustration, meaninglessness, and defeat that often
leads to despair. Man needs wholeness but he cannot produce it
in or for himself. He may yearn for wholeness, though in many
instances he may be quite unaware of that for which he yearns.

147

Man's need and yearning for wholeness is met by the central
reality of the gospel, the fact of Christ. Christ is God's answer
to man's dire predicament. This is the central affirmation of the
Christian faith, namely, that Jesus Christ is Lord. It is as the
sovereign Lord of life that Jesus Christ becomes the clue to the
solution of man's need for wholeness. When a man accepts
Christ as the Lord of his life, he is no longer dealing with information or dogma about God, or with a series of legalist commandments, but he enters into a dynamic living relationship that

becomes the center of his life. The disjointed, often conflicting drives and attractions of his life find a new polarization. Self-centered drives and numerous pressures within life are influenced by the new power which is released within the person who accepts Christ as the Lord of his life. He who thus realizes his sonship to God benefits by the integrating power of a central life-purpose large enough to be significant.

To make such statements is not to say that Jesus Christ is the only possible integrating center of life. Personality can be, and often is, integrated by some other master motive on lower levels in the moral and spiritual scale. It is, in fact, possible for personality to be organized around a center so unworthy that the person becomes the embodiment of evil rather than good. Even on the higher levels, personality can be dominated, for example, by a passion for morality or service which, though admirable as far as it goes, falls short of true Christian motivation growing out of commitment and obedience to God in Christ. The point is not that Christ alone can integrate personality, but that Christ alone can integrate personality so that life becomes abundant and eternal.

Becoming New

When a man accepts Christ as the Lord of his life, he enters into a new relationship with God which initiates a lifelong transformation process. Basic radical changes begin to occur in the structure of his life; often these are accompanied by intense spiritual struggle. These changes are characterized by new motivations, attitudes, goals, and aspirations. Many different terms are used to describe this transformation which produces such changes in the lives of persons. Regardless of how this transformation may be described, Christians are agreed that it is an evidence of the power of God at work in human life to create a new being in Christ.

In accepting Jesus Christ as the Lord of his life, man evidences his trust in God. Man may be awed by the mystery of

God and his ways and may be prone to resist those demands which are placed upon him, yet because of the transformation which God has wrought in his life, he will endeavor to entrust himself even more completely to that which he believes to be God's will for him. When difficult experiences come, he does not ask or expect God to help him escape them, but he does believe that God through the work of the Holy Spirit will enable him to live triumphantly in the midst of that which would defeat him. He knows that he is not completely transformed and therefore there are things about his life which are not as they should be, yet, he dares to believe that God who began the transformation process in his life will continue it so long as man is faithful.

The new person in Christ submits himself to a new kind of servitude. He offers himself as a servant of Jesus Christ. In that servitude he discovers the meaning of freedom. In this freedom he is less subject to the power of sin, frustration, despair, and haunting fears. He discovers that he is able to transcend the negative influences and pressures of the society and culture about him as he realizes that the Lord of his life is at work with him in transforming that same society and culture.

Man further discovers that his freedom imposes certain new responsibilities upon him. He was given freedom in order that he might become the person God intended him to be. He is now free to respond more fully to God through faith and love. He is free to accept and serve his neighbor in love and dedication. He is now free to live more consistently as a son of God.

149

This Theme in the Bible

The experience of the symbol of becoming a new person is reflected in the Old Testament as well as in the New. Abram's change in name to Abraham and Jacob's to Israel are illustrative (Genesis 15—16; 32). Jeremiah writes of newness in individuals and also the whole people.

In the Sermon on the Mount, Jesus vividly portrayed the

characteristics of the redeemed person (Matthew 5—7). In other of his teachings he stressed the qualities of humility and forgiveness (Matthew 18). To Nicodemus he spoke of the experience of redemption as a divine impartation of life "from above" (John 3:1-15). He told the Jews that his truth would give them real freedom and enable them to realize true sonship to God (John 8:31-36). He said he had come to give men life abundant (John 10:10) and eternal (John 10:28).

150

In Paul's writings there are many basic passages: Romans 5; 6; 8 and 1 Thessalonians 4. Especially pertinent are Romans 6; Ephesians 4; and Colossians 3.

4. Growing Up in Christ

STATEMENT OF THEME

The faithful son cultivates his relationship of faith, love, and obedience toward God; he also cultivates love for his fellowmen. In the power of the Holy Spirit he grows in grace and develops toward Christian maturity. His quest for personal significance and for a richly satisfying life is answered with increasing meaning.

DESCRIPTION OF THEME

Every human being craves a sense of personal significance. He longs for a satisfying life. God made him so. But his agelong quest for a meaningful existence has become exceedingly baffling in today's world. Automation, depersonalization, fragmentation, group conformity, conflicting value patterns, uncertainty in the world situation, and rapidity of change inevitably alter and color man's life. The gospel, however, still holds the answer to his need. That answer lies in the continuing personal relationship of faith, love, and obedience which the Christian has with God through Jesus Christ. This relationship is fostered both by individual discipline and by life in the Christian community. Although individual believers may differ greatly from one another in their racial, mental, physical, emotional, cultural, and historical backgrounds and endowments, the way is open for all to realize in personal experience the abundant life which Jesus promised.

Cultivating the Christian Life

The Christian's filial relationship with God is not one to be presumed upon; it must constantly be cultivated and developed. Growing up in Christ is not automatic. The faithful son recognizes the fact that his relationship with God involves obligations. One of them is to cultivate that relationship. Desiring to grow as a child of God, he bends his faithful efforts to that end.

He comes to see that faith is important not only at the beginning of his life of fellowship with God but throughout every stage of its continuance. As he continues to live out his sonship, he becomes aware of many occasions which call forth new measures of faith. These may be brought to his attention by new insights into his own life and personality, through study and worship, by circumstances of life—tragic or otherwise, through new relationships with others, or by the reorientation of old values. Each such experience provides a new opportunity for him to exercise his faith and thus grow in his relationship to the Father. Faith means counting on God, living in conscious dependence upon him, constantly drawing on him for spiritual renewal.

151

The Christian's relationship is also one of love for God. For the son of God, love is of the very nature of his relationship with the Father. The early Christians used the term *agape* to describe the unique love relationship which exists in the family of God. It is a self-giving sacrificial kind of love which knows no limitations. That love, as it is cultivated, becomes deeper, richer, purer, and stronger. Outwardly it may become less demonstrative with time, but inwardly it grows more meaningful, more life-transforming, more all-embracing.

The relationship is also one of obedience to God which is the natural outgrowth of man's love for God. Jesus declared that there is a direct correlation between them, for those who love the Father keep the commandments, while those who do not love do not obey (John 14:15, 21, 23-24). The Christian's obedience will occur in wider areas and on deeper levels, as increasingly he comes to realize the implications of his commitment to Christ as Lord. Furthermore, experience will teach him the adequacy of the Holy Spirit to enable him to be and do whatever God is asking of him.

The faithful child of God also cultivates his love for his fellowmen. The Christian life is not lived in isolation. Even as the filial relationship is one of love, so also is the fraternal relationship. Jesus indicated that the badge by which sons of God are identified is their love for one another. (John 14:34-35) Yet, the love for fellowman cannot be confined only to those who are seeking to live as sons of God. It is of such a universal indiscriminate nature that it is all-inclusive.

One cannot read the New Testament or the history of the Christian church, both past and contemporary, without being keenly aware of the work of God in human lives through the power of the Holy Spirit. As man responds to the leadership of the Holy Spirit within his own life and engages in those exercises of faith, obedience and love, he grows in grace. That is, as he cultivates the gifts of Christ to him, he becomes more mature in his spiritual life and personality. This growth depends on divine grace, but that grace must be appropriated.

Growing: a Process

Thus the faithful son develops toward Christian maturity. His relationship to God is never static but always dynamic. His present spiritual stature is not an end but a becoming. Like Paul, he does not claim to have reached the goal, but he presses on, forgetting what lies behind and straining forward to what lies

152

ahead. Having come into freedom, he is prepared to grow into responsible use of freedom. Having begun to learn the secret of trust in God, he continues to grow in his confidence toward God. He also develops such confidence in his Christian brethren that the basis of true Christian community is established. Furthermore, having experienced God's forgiveness, he grows both in the acceptance of forgiveness and in the practice of forgiveness. He also grows in obedience to God and in love to God, as indeed also in love to others and to self.

Growing up in Christ involves assuming a Christlike attitude toward all of life's experiences, relationships, duties, and problems, and living and serving daily in the spirit of Jesus.

There are certain aids to growth which the faithful child of God will utilize to foster and accelerate his reach toward full spiritual maturity in Christ. Such aids include worship, Christian education, Bible study, prayer, church attendance, Christian fellowship, and Christian service. In Bible study the believer gains increasingly clear and meaningful insights into the nature of God and his will for human life. Through prayer he enjoys fellowship with God and receives power for living. In fellowship with other Christians he receives encouragement and guidance. In Christian service he gains experience and understanding that strengthen and bless. Every means of grace which God has provided moves man forward toward the full, Christian life.

153

In this process of growth in grace, the Christian's quest for personal significance is answered with increasing meaning. He comes to know by experience that the secret of personal significance and the meaning of life are found in the vital relationship with God, and his fellowman. He has a sense of oneness with the Eternal that lifts him above the trivial, the sordid, the humdrum, and the temporal. He finds in his growing experience with God in Christ that which satisfies the deepest longings of his soul.

This Theme in the Bible

Though the perspective must be New Testament, this theme is rooted in the Old Testament as well as the New. The Law (Exodus, Leviticus, Deuteronomy) is best understood as God's guidance to his people for their growth in obedience toward holiness. This same interpretation may be placed on writings of the prophets exhorting the people to proper worship and obedience.

154

The Psalms reflect the measure of godliness and its absence in God's people.

Growth in Christ is set forth in the New Testament as both an expectation and an obligation (2 Corinthians 3:18; Ephesians 4:1-16; 2 Peter 3:18).

Marks of Christian maturity are love John 13:34-35; 1 Corinthians 13; 1 Thessalonians 3:12-13); unselfish humility (Philippians 2:1-13); and every other quality of Christlike character (Galatians 5:22-25; Colossians 3:1-17; 2 Peter 1:5-8). The Christian is in a continuous, if uneven, process of refusal to be conformed to this world and the necessity for renewing his mind so as to express in every relationship of life the meaning of his fellowship with God (Romans 12—15). His entire life is characterized by faith, love, and obedience (1 John). The relationship of love and obedience are described in John 14:15-35. He never glories over past achievements but keeps pressing on to the further heights of spiritual attainment (Philippians 3:12-16).

The Holy Spirit is the chief agent of Christian growth and sanctification (John 16:12-15; Galatians 5:22-24; 2 Corinthians 3:18).

5. Finding Identity in the Christian Community

STATEMENT OF THEME

Man's persistent need for meaningful belonging is met when, as God's child, he accepts his role and relationships in the Chris-

tian community, the church. The reconciled son takes his place in the fellowship of Christians, vitally related to his brothers in Christ.

DESCRIPTION OF THEME

The son of God experiences a meaningful relationship with fellow Christians in the Christian community, the church. This aspect of his experience is directly related to the fact that man is by nature a social being. His social nature calls for interpersonal relationships. No one can live in isolation from others and remain a normal human being. Many of man's significant experiences come to him because he must live with other people. He craves association. He wishes to be identified with groups that seem important to him. This is one of man's deepest and most persistent needs.

The Christian, by virtue of his relationship to God, is a member of God's family. One of the values of the life in the Christian community is that it may help the individual see clearly the implications of this relationship.

The nature and significance of the church is interpreted in "The Church: the Meaning and Experience of Christian Community." This theme delineation is concerned with the ways in which man accepts and fulfills his role and relationships as a son of God in the Christian community.

155

The Church in the Home

For many the Christian home provides the primary setting in which persons find identity in the Christian community. This is particularly true with respect to children. In a very real sense, the Christian family may be thought of as the church in microcosm, and as such, it is of the greatest importance to the Christian experience and growth of its members. When parents have wholesome understanding and attitudes with reference to those of the larger Christian community, and when the family circle is a fellowship of Christian love, then it is easy for children to find their identity in the Christian community while they are still in their early years. The Christian family is usually a significant factor in the spiritual growth and development of its children as it provides a setting for the nurture, worship, witness, and service of all its members.

The members of a Christian family are likely to be concerned about finding their identity in the larger Christian community. They are likely to have a high appreciation for the responsibilities, opportunities, and experiences which are theirs as members and participants.

156

When the Christian family is considered to be the setting for many of the primary contacts persons have with the Christian community, questions arise about those who live in non-Christian homes, on the fringes of, or completely outside that community. However, in order for anyone to find identity in the fellowship of believers there must be an evident atmosphere of acceptance and concern. This suggests that those now in the Christian fellowship have an obligation to discover ways which will encourage and help all persons to appropriate the highest meaning possible within their cultural and socioeconomic settings, as well as within one or more expressions of the church.

Members One of Another

Through finding and accepting his rightful place in the body of believers, the Christian experiences that meaningful belonging which is the birthright of every son of God. The oneness and unity in Christ which may be experienced by the fellowship of Christians in their mutual association in the local church may provide the most meaningful belonging possible. Here man can find the answer to his craving to be a part of a highly significant group. The church at its best provides a linking of interests at life's deepest level. In the Christian community man may become aware of a relationship that transcends time and space. Here he can identify himself with all Christians as they seek to fulfill their role as sons of God through ministry to one another, through service to the immediate neighborhood, and through mission in the world. Here he may find identity with the national and world outreach of the Christian community.

Through experiences of worship, giving, study, service, witnessing, and intimate fellowship with others he can discover what it means for Christians to be "members one of another." Here in mutual experiences of struggle, learning, encouragement, joy, confession, repentance, witnessing, service, and sorrow, he may discover the kind of support and acceptance which will enable him to live more faithfully as a "son of God rooted in the Christian community."

This Theme in the Bible

Much of the Book of Acts is a commentary on the life of God's children in the fellowship of the Christian community. Of particular significance is the second chapter as showing the relation of converts to the church and portraying the community of believers. In chapter 4 the community of possessions is described, indicating the spirit of mutual concern of the members (Acts 4:32-37).

Paul, in discussing the varieties of spiritual gifts among members, stresses the importance of unity in diversity in the body of Christ and goes on to point out the supremacy of Christian love (1 Corinthians 12—13; Romans 12). He also sets forth the union of Jew and Gentile in God's household (Ephesians 2:11-22). Further, he appeals to members to seek earnestly to maintain the unity of the Spirit in the church, even as they make it their aim to grow toward the goal of spiritual maturity through mutual service (Ephesians 4). The analogy of family and church (Ephesians 5:21—6:4) and the spirit of love in both church and family (Colossians 3:12-21) are also important aspects of the apostle's teaching. First John stresses brotherly love as a great distinguishing mark of the true Christian (3:11-24).

Some insights into the struggles inherent in the process of becoming identified with the people of God are portrayed in the

157

prophecies of Isaiah and Jeremiah. The New Testament epistles to the Thessalonians, Timothy, and Titus deal with some of the issues relative to this theme.

6. The Christian's Hope Rests in the Triumphant God

STATEMENT OF THEME

Man's tendency to be dissatisfied with the present, his uncertainty about the future, and his need to be vitally related to the eternally significant are addressed through the experience of the Christian hope in God's ultimate triumph in and over history. This hope includes the assurance of eternal life and the consummation of the kingdom of God.

158

DESCRIPTION OF THEME

Man by his very nature is restless and dissatisfied with much of his daily existence. As he looks ahead, he projects much of his restlessness and grows very uncertain about the future, both in the present world and in the world beyond death. In the midst of this uncertainty, he yearns for a relationship with that which is eternally significant. The answer lies in the Christian affirmation, which declares that God is the Lord of history and will ultimately triumph in and over it.

The full meaning of Christian hope is many sided. Essentially, however, it rests on the conviction that God's divine purpose is operative in the course of history. Furthermore, man through faith and love can enter into an eternal relationship with God and can move with God toward the consummation of his kingdom.

Man's Uncertainty

Many experiences cause man to be dissatisfied with the present. He is vaguely aware of a restlessness deep within himself which produces discontent. Even as he longs for perfection he is aware of the imperfection in his own life which ever judges him.

In his saner moments, he becomes aware of the frailty of much of his life and that of the society in which he lives.

The dissatisfaction is not limited to the day by day experiences of life. Man is endowed with the capacity to project his thoughts into the future and thus he can anticipate some of the experiences which await him. However, past experiences have taught him that he cannot accurately predict the future. When he anticipates the unknown future and that which it might bring to him, his dissatisfaction often turns into uncertainty and fear.

What is more, the daily experiences of life serve to remind man of his mortality. Even though he knows that death is an unavoidable event which comes to every one, he tries to avoid thinking about it. Death appears to be so final. Yet, it is ever a part of man's being, and its undertone penetrates all of life.

There is that within man which cries out in protest. Death cannot end all. Life must continue. To assure its continuance it must somehow become vitally and significantly related to that which is eternal. This has been part of the objective and purpose of man's religious quest for generations. In the midst of his uncertainty about the future, he has desperately striven to lay hold on that which is everlasting.

The Basis of the Christian's Hope

The basis of the Christian's hope is the eternal character of God whose kingdom of love stands both within and beyond history. The Bible is a record of God's acting within history, the arena where the ultimate and the temporal meet. Not only has God created the world and all that is within it; his Word has never ceased to move in the human spirit to bring forth a new creation—a creation rooted in the eternal nature of God, developing as a present reality, with a focus on the consummation beyond time when the purposes of God for his creation will be fully realized.

159

Throughout the history of the church the Christian's hope rests in his conviction that, by God's grace, life in the world under all conditions is an intrinsic part of the inexorable movement of God's rule toward the fulfillment of his ultimate purpose.

Eternal Life

When man relates himself to the Eternal through faith in Jesus Christ, he claims the promise and receives the assurance of eternal life. The words of Christ declare that "he who believes has eternal life" (John 6:47).

Eternal life stands for a distinctive kind of life, not just endless existence. The New Testament presents eternal life as a present, growing experience. It is a divine life, imparted by the Holy Spirit in the experience of regeneration. It is life from, and life like, the eternal God's.

The New Testament affirms the basis for hope in the eternal life and declares that the Christian may live triumphantly in this hope. Thus his fears about his future state are alleviated. He may know that he has been accepted and that nothing shall ever separate him from God's love in Christ. Because Christ in the resurrection triumphed over sin and death, the believer has life and hope—hope that reaches like an anchor into the unseen world.

The Consummation of the Kingdom of God

Man's collective yearnings for a better world and his hope for the consummation of the kingdom of God find their ground in the eternal nature of God and his work in the world. His declared purpose in sending his Son was that of redeeming the world, bringing it under his dominion.

Jesus did not argue the existence of the kingdom of God—he assumed it. The kingdom of God may be identified with God's presence, activity, and rule in the world. The reality of the kingdom becomes evident wherever man accepts the sovereignty of God.

The Christian believes that the eternal God whose purpose gives meaning and direction to history will bring evil to judg-

160

ment and righteousness to triumph in his own time and way. The nature of the kingdom of God is yet to be revealed.

The hope of eternal life and the triumph of God's kingdom provide assurance and undergird the Christian. He believes that he can be more than conqueror through faith in him who loved him. To be an heir of God and a joint heir with Christ is to be so related to the eternally significant that one of the deepest and most persistent of all life's needs is met.

Such an experience and such a hope give real point to the whole meaning of the Christian's sonship. He knows that already he is a son of God. Though he does not know all that the future realization of his hope in Christ will mean for him, he does know that he shall be like him, for he shall see him as he is and will live in perfect fellowship with him and his own.

This Theme in the Bible

The assurance of the triumph of God is dominant from "I am that I am" of Genesis to the climactic hallelujah of Revelation. God's lordship over all the nations is the message of Judges, the historical books, the prophets, as well as in the Psalms and in Job.

This assurance is personified in Jesus, both in his life and his teachings (Matthew 4; 6; 10; 22 and parallels; the passion passages in the Gospels; Mark 13; Luke 13; 21; John 7; 8; 10; 12; and the farewell discourses).

Romans 8 is basic here, as are also Colossians; 1 Corinthians 15. Paul's benedictions resound with hope as do John's letters.

161

VOCATION: THE MEANING AND EXPERIENCE OF DISCIPLESHIP

The themes within this area are:

God's Call to Responsible Decision
Called to Serve One's Neighbor
The Stewardship of Life and Work
Discipline in the Christian Life
Joined in Discipleship in the World
Toward the Kingdom of God

Description of Curriculum Area

The focus, or vantage point, of this area of curriculum is the ethical, service, and social aspects of the Christian life, that is, *doing* in the Christian way in all relationships, the outward witness of faithful discipleship to Jesus Christ.

Comprehended in this area of curriculum is such content of Christian thought and life as: the concept of the kingdom of God; explication of Christian ethics and Christian social relations; the concept of vocation to the Christian; the Christian view of works; interpretation of the fruits of the Spirit; the church's role and task in the world; Christian stewardship in the natural and social realm.

In order to have educational value as an area of curriculum, this content must be viewed in terms of its pertinence to the persistent issues of man's life. Some of these issues are: For what causes is life best invested? What is the relation of Christianity to society? How may issues between church and state be resolved? What is the political responsibility of the Christian? How shall I choose and perform my life work? How do I know what is right? What values can I live by? How can I meet failure?[1]

---

[1]These three paragraphs are repeated here as necessary background.

Delineation of Area

Vocation is based upon the conviction that God in Jesus Christ continually calls man to discipleship. The vocation of the Christian is to work out in the ethical, social, and service aspects of life the implications of this call. As man acknowledges God's call to vocation, he undertakes the fulfillment of the responsibilities of discipleship.

Discipleship: in All Relationships

The matter of becoming and being a faithful son of God is the essence of the curriculum area, "Sonship: the Meaning and Experience of Redemption." This curriculum area, "Vocation: the Meaning and Experience of Discipleship," is concerned with the style of life which issues when man, as a faithful son of God, seeks to live in the spirit of God in every relationship. Comprehended in this area of curriculum are experiences and meanings of Christian thought and life such as these: the kingdom of God; situations of choice as in personal ethical decisions, Christian social relations, and Christian citizenship; the concept of vocation to the Christian; the Christian view of work; the guidance and gift of the Spirit in the exercise of vocation; the church's mission as corporate vocation and response.

God's call to the Christian is no ordinary call. It is an imperative one which demands that he bring all his being and potentialities under the will of God, fulfilling his stewardship in the biological, social, intellectual, material, and cosmic realms. The Christian is called to trust God, to accept his "yoke" or discipline willingly, to strive to be at his disposal without reservation at all times and in every situation, to listen to his word of instruction, command, or direction, and to be faithful even when the ends of action are hidden. The man who responds to God's call needs no other reason for acting, nor will he have any reason for not acting.

In the fulfillment of his discipleship the Christian is constantly

163

confronted, as are all men, with persistent pressures to make decisions. For the Christian, there is no distinction between secular and religious choices. Rather, he must seek to perceive God's will in every occasion and situation whether in successful achievement or failure, ease or opposition, sickness or health, trial or temptation in order that he may respond in the light of God's will. He then makes his decisions accordingly, knowing that he is ultimately responsible to God. Thus, the personal ethic of the Christian disciple is always determined by his perception of God's call in each particular situation.

164

In order that a person may respond fully to his vocation, the various occasions of calling and responding must be drawn together into a pattern of continuing discipleship in all significant relationships. Among these relationships are: the biological, the psychosocial, the political, the economic, the social, the intellectual, the cosmic. Evidence of these relationships may be seen in roles such as learner, student, neighbor, family member, worker, consumer, spouse, parent, citizen, and church member. The Christian's discipleship becomes the basis of his personal organization, identity, and fulfillment.

One concrete expression of discipleship is the way the Christian chooses to invest his life. For most persons this is chiefly through their occupations, whatever they may be. This involves the kind of job or occupation accepted and the quality of work done in fulfilling the requirements of the task.

Discipleship: in the Christian Community

God's call to vocation comes not only to the individual but also to the corporate body. Discipleship is expressed not only individually but also corporately in the mission of the church, involving mutual discipline, trust, love, and self-restraint. Corporate discipleship requires a faithful performance of interpersonal obligations which do not violate personal integrity, but allow for its fulfillment.

Interpersonal relationships are expressions of values which are consistently acted upon in concrete occasions. When related to a total pattern, these constitute ethics. To the extent that ethics are in harmony with the gospel they are adequate. However, ethical norms do not relieve the disciple of the continuing need and obligation to "listen with growing alertness to the gospel." He must listen if he is to have increasing understanding.

The disciple has responsibility to understand and respond to God's call, and to labor in the corporate group's efforts to understand and respond. When there is tension in the group, all must work together in faith and love to move closer to the truth. This means that the church may be enlightened by individual members and they, in turn, may be enlightened by the church.

Those who respond to God's call and become disciples begin their "growth as sons of God, rooted in the Christian community." They receive strength from Christ through the Holy Spirit, to be faithful in vocation. At times of crucial decision they bring together their best understandings of their individual and corporate vocations, but they wait upon the Lord for the renewal of their calling, believing all issues to be in his hands. They strengthen each other in times of stress, temptation, and failure and look to each other for love and understanding as they seek to leaven every life situation with the leaven of the kingdom. They acknowledge their responsibility, though they cannot always control or predict the ends of action. Just as the disciple's vocation becomes the basis of his personal organization, identity, and fulfillment, so the corporate discipleship of the body of Christians is the basis for its organization, identity, and fulfillment.

The lifelong task of discipleship involves the learner in seeking an ever-fuller understanding of the meaning of being "called of God" and of what discipleship entails: seeking a deeper commitment to God in discipleship; being involved wholeheartedly with fellow disciples in the life and work of the church; living out his discipleship in all aspects of his life in the world.

165

Discipleship: for the Kingdom of God

The gospel affirms that God is the Lord of the world, and not merely of an ecclesiastical segment within the world. The disciple is called from aimless struggle in the world to be transformed in order that he may recognize the purpose of God and be empowered to take a place in the world where he can be vitally involved wherever God's work is being done. Then, demonstrating the fruits of the Spirit in his whole field of relationships and responsibilities, he bears witness to the fact that God is in the world reconciling the world to himself.

All Christian action in the world is directed to this reconciliation. Among appropriate forms of individual and corporate action for disciples are: witnessing to the gospel in politics, education, business, and industry; loving the world in the light of the gospel to the end that it may be transformed; and supporting those forms of order in the family, local community, nation, and international life that sustain justice, harmony, and good.

The disciple is convinced that God is at work in the world and that the ultimate goal to which he calls man is a single one—the kingdom of God. The kingdom of God is both in existence and is becoming. It is in existence to the extent that God's rule is in effect. The kingdom of God is becoming as men continue to respond to his call according to their growing understanding of it and thus "fulfill their common discipleship in the world" through obedient and purposive witness and action.

The disciple learns that his citizenship in the kingdom of God and life in the world places him in the middle of an inescapable tension. The disciple, therefore, does not seek to avoid the tension because he knows that the kingdom of God by its very nature is in conflict with the principalities and powers of the world. He feels instead that he must put on the whole armor of God and participate actively and sacrificially in the redemptive purpose of God on earth. He acts responsibly and redemptively as a disciple, willingly bearing his own cross and sustained by the strength and companionship of the living Lord.

Theme Development

To live is to choose between alternative actions. There is a persistent pressure to decide what forces thoughtful persons, even while in one process of choosing and acting, to project possible alternatives and consequences for subsequent situations.

The framework of personal belief and sense of order that forms the screen against which one projects the alternatives and consequences of his acts gives meaning to day-by-day life in a world conditioned by human forced choices. For some persons the constant necessity to choose reflects the meaninglessness and caprice of human experience. For others, who see their lives and the world as a part of the purview and concern of their Creator, both the capacity to choose and the pressures to choose testify to the dignity and stature that has been given them through an investment of authority and responsibility, commissioning them stewards of their Creator's universe. The ability and vested authority men possess to choose for themselves, coupled with the corollary responsibility, establishes for human beings an ethical, moral world. In this world each person, by virtue of his being created, must either accept willingly or deign condescendingly to live; and ethics, the science of moral values and duties, becomes a practical discipline for all.

Within ethics, some of the motives and values that affect choice are universal, at least they are very broadly shared. These comprise the realms of natural law, positive (or legally certified) law, and morality. General ethics is the comprehensive, academic study of these realms. There are other motives and values that belong to a community which voluntarily acknowledges them, even, in the extreme examples, to a small group or to a single person. Christian ethics is of this latter type.

Christian ethics derives its value judgments from the nature of God as revealed through Jesus Christ and the witness of the Holy Spirit. Christian ethics is as concerned to provide help in making decisions as it is to understand theoretically how persons make decisions. Therefore Christian ethics includes the real motivations that actually operate, as well as the ideal values or ends that the decisions serve.

Beyond this, Christian ethics involves the common ground of being and meaning for all persons, God. No choice can be made "abstractly" or in isolation from this existential condition. God's nature and therefore his demands are always prior to the moment and condition of choice. God's existence is man's call to respond responsibly, examining alternatives and accepting consequences. Christian ethics is therefore vocational; it is always an answer of action to a call from God.

Seen as an explanation of "an answer of action to a call from God," the themes in the curriculum area of Vocation: the Meaning and Experience of Discipleship can be developed in terms of the various aspects of Christian ethics each theme exhibits. The several themes in this area are developed by examining in turn the aspect of responsibility, the relational or contextual aspect, the economic aspect, the aspect of obedience to norms, the socially purposive aspect, and the self-transcendent aspect in Christian ethics. In this way both the ideational (conceptual) and the existential (practical) sides of vocation can be treated as the human response to God's call to discipleship.

Themes Delineated

1. God's Call to Responsible Decision

STATEMENT OF THEME

The Christian interprets the persistent pressure to make decisions as a call from God, made clear in the demands of the gospel, and seeks to perceive God's call in the factors affecting decision.

DESCRIPTION OF THEME

Christian ethics in its aspect of reponsibility is the motif of this theme. It faces up to the universal human experience of being required to make decisions and to live with the results of action.

Factors in Decision-Making

The ethical situation, reduced to its barest outlines, is that every person is required by his relation to reality, at a particular time and place, to do something—to make a decision—and that even his refusal to do so turns out to be a way of acting or deciding. Vocation is a biblical metaphor by which Christian ethics brings light to this situation.

Ethics, under the vocation of a Christian, implies that the very process of making decisions and weighing values may open up insights into the will of God and into an understanding of one's self. This interpretation of ethics through vocation implies a commitment to the view that the subject of ethics is persons, acting freely and responsibly, rather than abstract rights and wrongs. The consideration of values in the process of making a decision may open up for the respondent some insight into the will of God. Further, in whatever decision results, these values are incorporated only as they correspond with the real motivations of the persons freely in an act that is an expression of his whole self. Thus, action that is truly vocational may be expected to result in a heightened self-awareness and an improved self-understanding. Vocational action reveals not only the God who calls but also the self who responds, and the personal reality of both is affirmed.

In contrast to the academically systematic and abstract nature of the general ethics, Christian ethics is vocational, particular, and concrete. Christian ethics is concerned that individual lives lived in concrete situations be in concord with the will of God in light of the circumstances. In Christian ethics the motives and values are of equal importance to the overt act and, to be con-

169

sidered acceptable, both motive and act must be an answer of faith to God's love and desire for man. In contrast, general ethics is concerned with the logical ordering and balance of its idea system; for it, motives and values are exceptional and are therefore forbidden to the system. Thus vocational ethics is more comprehensive than general ethics, since it includes the calculation of personal and voluntary factors with which general ethics, as an academic discipline, cannot deal. Among such factors are these:

170

🖚 Talents—Many situations of choice involve possible responses which could be made successfully by one person, but not by another, because of differences in their native abilities. In some choices, particularly those having to do with employment or education, the best use of talent may be the foremost consideration. However, persons described in the Bible were sometimes called to pursuits for which they were apparently unsuited, and believed themselves unsuited.

🖚 Opportunities—Having a job, holding office, possessing the required education, having a chance to become educated, being free of contradictory obligations, being married (or single), having enough money, being at the right place at the right time—all these represent forms of opportunity. A decision would be made differently by a person who has the opportunity for a proposed response, and one who has not. However, the Christian should not underestimate the freedom that he possesses, under the grace and providence of God, to find opportunities for those responses to which he is genuinely called.

🖚 Perceptions—Christian ethics can set forth the values which Christian decision should serve, and the human needs which it should meet. The Christian must perceive and accept such values before they can serve as real motives in decision-making. In deciding, the Christian must not be emotionally indifferent to the results of his choice. The perception of need is peculiar to the individual, varying with his own emotional history and its extension, through imagination, into the field of relationships. A person who is predisposed to perceive one kind of need will respond differently in a situation of choice from one who perceives another kind of need. However, the Christian should continually strive to broaden and refine his perceptions, and permit himself to be guided in them by the great symbols of the Christian faith.

⛋ Commitments—Decisions which are not merely random are based upon the acknowledgment of real relationships to God, man, and the created world, and the projection of certain future values to be achieved in these relationships. The Christian faith is profoundly historical in that it judges the integrity of a decision not merely upon the instantaneous purpose, but also upon faithful adherence to this purpose through time. In other words, Christianity acknowledges the ethical reality of time. The claim which the Christian finds in the field of relationships includes the requirement that he, in faith, acknowledge and celebrate the past and commit the future.

Thus the calculation of any choice confronting the Christian includes the questions of whether he is able (so choosing) to be faithful to past commitments and whether he is willing to be faithful to those which now begin. Commitment is of particular significance in decisions affecting livelihood, marriage, and family. However, especially in the area of lifework, one's commitment may fall into the service of pride and stand against the receiving of God's contemporary will, which is ever new. The most radical commitment of Christians, profoundly influencing all their decisions, is to be sons of the Father, in response to his call. "Sonship" fully developed in another area, interprets the fundamental commitment of the Christian life.

171

Talents, opportunities, perceptions, and commitments—these are not so much limitations upon the scope of free choice, as they are a description of how free choice may be a rational expression of the person. These are the elements of decision-making that are most singularly and appropriately the subject's own, in the unique combination of his created nature and his personal history. They are a check upon randomness, whim, and irrationality, and a clue to the ethical identification of the self.

Response to the Call to Decision May Be Ecstatic

Vocation may be meaningfully applied to the learner's growth in ethical self-awareness. With such growth, the learner is made open to the mysteriousness of human decision—the combination of freedom and constraint, of determination by the self and by the not-self. He may thus be led into a singular, unexpected, and even lonely course of action characterized by a very strong sense of personal call. His conviction may be attested to him by signs, voices, or visions—a psychologically ecstatic state. Christian faith does not require these psychological manifestations for a valid calling. One's calling may rest on a quite calm, rational reading of his situation, the resources that he brings to it, the values to which he is committed. But "calling" is not an empty figure of speech; the Christian should be prepared to acknowledge that God is free to make his will known in states that are psychologically and ethically exceptional. Vocation stresses the fact that even the best ethics or the wisest human judgment should not stand in place of God.

This Theme in the Bible

The call of God, extended to individuals and through them to the whole people, is one of the major motifs of the Bible and there is a great deal of material available.

God's call to Adam (Genesis 3) sets the pattern for the inescapable and universal necessity of response to the call of God.

God's call to Abraham to go out from his country (beginning Genesis 12) and later to sacrifice his son Isaac (Genesis 22) illustrates the ethically exceptional character of God's call. (The latter passage is explained from this point of view by Kierkegaard in *Fear and Trembling*.)

The call of Moses (Exodus 3ff.) illustrates the potentially ecstatic character of the call, a sense of being unworthy or unsuitable on the part of the recipient, and the power of God to supply whatever is deficient.

Other individual calls include those of Samuel (1 Samuel 3), Isaiah (6), Job (out of the whirlwind, 38ff.), Jeremiah (1), Jonah (the Book of Jonah describes his attempts to evade the call and his failure to do so); and Paul (Acts 9; Galatians 1:11—2:21) whose call describes the radical changes that are possible as a follower of God comes to a true awareness of his vocation.

The necessity to make decision for or against God is evident frequently in the history of the people of Israel. The covenant-making and renewing illustrate this. Also Joshua 24 dramatically sets the necessity for choice.

The beginning of the ministry of Jesus (Matthew 3 and 4) can be regarded as his vocation, though not described as a literal call. Jesus' actions and sayings are filled with a sense of vocation that touches all aspects of life; his call of the four (Matthew 4:18-22; Mark 1:16-20; Luke 5:1-11) and his choosing of the twelve (Mark 3:13-19*a*; Luke 6:12-16) reflect in his ministry the sense of God's call mediated to men through him; likewise his sayings reflect a continual call to responsible decisions, as in Matthew 12:48-50; Luke 9:57-62; 14:25-33; and John 12:47-50.

173

2. Called to Serve One's Neighbor

STATEMENT OF THEME

The Christian perceives God's call in the give and take of interpersonal relationships in which he is constantly involved. He expresses his vocation in face-to-face relationships with his neighbor in every area of life, by expressing love, understanding, acceptance, helpfulness, and service.

DESCRIPTION OF THEME

Christian ethics in its relational or contextual aspect is the motif of this theme. It faces up to the lifelong human concern of having duty or obligation to a wide variety of persons whose claims take forms that correspond closely to one's roles in relation to them.

The Claim of the Neighbor

In the New Testament, the term "neighbor" is used as the most general conception for interpreting the Christian's relationship to other persons. Neighbor is used in the Old Testament, but there are also strangers, foreigners, and enemies. One of the clear purposes of Jesus' teaching is to universalize neighbor by extending it to every imaginable person. This is the force of the parable of the good Samaritan, for example.

Further, the New Testament tries to draw as close as possible a connection between the religious duty of serving God and the ethical duty of serving the neighbor. Jesus linked together as the two greatest commandments those enjoining the love of God (Deuteronomy 6:4-9, a high-water mark in Old Testament thought), and the love of neighbor (Leviticus 19:17-18, which had no comparable importance to the Jews, his contemporaries). He said further that behavior toward the least neighbor was equivalent to the same behavior toward himself.

The kind of service required is that which fits the neighbor's need; if he is thirsty, a cup of water; if hungry, food; if sick, healing; if in prison, a visit; if outcast, to receive good news of the kingdom. Thus the analysis of the many roles played by the decision-maker provides a tool for understanding the neighbor's need. If neighbor means husband or wife, the ethical response to this relationship includes the free giving of conjugal love, companionship, and support. If neighbor is child, the response is affection, nurture, and discipline. The decision-maker may take to himself these and many other roles simultaneously; his duties will vary according to the aspect of relationship that is his. The landlord's duties differ from the tenant's, but both may be interpreted under the claim of the neighbor. Other relationships include producer-consumer, employer-employee, teacher-learner, governor-citizen, leader-follower, sponsor-protégé, doctor-patient, and friend-enemy, as well as the more symmetrical relationships between peers.

The neighbor is always more than employee, teacher, tenant, doctor. The use of such categories is useful as a tool of analysis for determining the neighbor's needs or attributes, but it becomes idolatrous if used to block his claim for consideration as a whole person. Further, the analysis of relationships permits the extension of ethics to institutions, traditions, and conventions—aspects of culture which, though they are not persons, represent social investments in which persons have much at stake.

The interpretation of all these relationships under the concept "neighbor" provides the clue to some constant qualities which should be present in them. The neighbor must be acknowledged and respected personally; he must never be made an object of even the most benevolently conceived action. In a qualified but real way, the Christian will extend the same respect to human history, culture, and institutions. Thus the call to serve one's neighbor, primarily in face-to-face relationships, also includes indirect forms of service; and the qualities of loving and serving, described below, apply broadly so that the Christian is ethically related to the whole field of relationships and not only to individual persons in it.

175

Qualities of Relationship—Love and Service

▶ Love—To love one's neighbor means, first of all, to accept him. Accepting one's neighbor is ethically the foundation of any attempt to provide the context for encounter wherein he may be changed or influenced by the stimulus of Christ. To "love" the neighbor only provisionally while trying to minister to him is to love something which only closely resembles him, but which he is not. Acceptance as a part of the call to serve expresses the conviction that the neighbor's claim upon one springs from his being, and does not have to be earned by his accommodating himself to one's wishes.

Love further requires as an active expression the effort to know the neighbor (whether an individual person, or anything else in reality to which one is ethically related). This effort will include not only investigation and observation, to get knowledge of a practical kind, but a patient acquaintanceship and "living with" the neighbor in order to receive his self-disclosure of his inwardness. Such knowledge helps not only to strengthen the relationship, but also to ensure that any action undertaken in the interest of the neighbor will not miss the mark through failure to perceive his true needs and interests.

A further dimension of love for the neighbor is understanding and forgiving. What the neighbor is and does, what he loves and hates, must be granted by the decision-maker as a reality if love is to be genuine. Either one shares a common scale of values with the neighbor, or one must at least be able to conceive the possibility of a framework of values which transcends both. This is particularly true in relationship to the enemy as neighbor; his values are directly perceived as false and wrong, but unless they are believed to be at least human, the enemy becomes a monster to be destroyed utterly, and no love or forgiveness is possible.

Perhaps the purest expression of love (because it has no utilitarian value) is that of celebration. Celebration means the pure enjoyment of the neighbor—indeed of anything that is real—enhanced with words, physical attention, courtesy, ceremony, art, and gratuitous care. The celebration of the neighbor and the love relationship with the neighbor enlist the whole range of symbolic communications carried out in a spirit that is at once playful and deeply concerned. In its highest expressions—for example, in the Lord's Supper—celebration provides an avenue for the entrance of profound ethical concern into worship.

🖐 Service—To serve the neighbor means to act in his true interest. On occasion this may mean acting in ways contrary to his desire, by denying him, punishing him, constraining or restraining him. Such action may be a valid expression of love, but should be done repentantly and with thought given to the temptation of power, whether one is a parent, friend, administrator, policeman, magistrate, or military officer.

Fortunately, service to the neighbor is often in forms more directly expressive of good will. One may often give what is required in money, material, or service to meet the neighbor's need. If one has at his disposal what is required to meet a need, then the call to serve the neighbor may mean simply a call to give it.

Often, however, a gift is not effective, even if sufficient means are available. The neighbor's need may be one that cannot be met except from within himself through learning, growing, or achieving a better personal organization. (Similar processes may be required for meeting nonindividual needs in the field of relationships.) Here service to the neighbor may be thought of as actions of a nourishing kind—cultivating the relationship, giving support and encouragement; aiding the processes through teaching, counseling, healing (as a physician), offering friendship, and standing by to help; and praying as an intercessor for the neighbor.

177

A third form of service is analogous to giving, in that the server possesses adequacy for the need. One may act for the neighbor—either as his delegate or representative, or on one's own initiative because of a responsibility for him. A parent, for example, acts for the child who is not yet able to do so himself.

A fourth service is analogous to nourishing, in that the neighbor's need must be met essentially from within himself. This service is helping—bringing one's personal competencies to bear upon the neighbor's problems in concert with his own. This is the form of service most commonly associated with the idea of neighborliness—perhaps because there is hardly any relationship, from the most casual to the most intimate, in which the opportunity for helping is not present.

A fifth service is complementary to those mentioned above. This service is receiving, developing, and fostering the grace of accepting beneficence from one's neighbor. To be a true service, receiving from one's neighbor must be performed in a spirit that avoids superciliousness and feelings of superiority in regard to the one offering the beneficence. *There must be an honest willingness to permit one's self to be in the debt of another. Moreover there must be an honest willingness to recognize oneself as being in debt to another.* The ministry of receiving requires that one honestly analyze his needs so that he may, with full awareness, receive that which will be true benefit to him, a valid gift of worth in light of the natures of his neighbor, the giver, and himself, the receiver.

178

Dynamics of Relationship

"Called to serve the neighbor," as analyzed above, expresses in religious terms the content of Christian ethical responsibility to individual persons and to nonindividual realities that are part of the personal world. The neighbor is anyone or anything to which one is ethically related. One may ask, "How do these relationships come to be perceived and acknowledged, especially as they involve a claim upon the decision-maker?" This process is by no means automatic, but the Christian faith offers help according to the following principle: "We love, because he first loved us." Because of God's forgiveness, the Christian can forgive himself and his neighbor.

In loving and serving the neighbor, the Christian is aided in meeting the ethical claim of the neighbor through:

⚑ Overcoming isolation—The reality of others is in doubt when the self is in doubt. Others may then be regarded as unreal figures in the stream of a doubtful consciousness. The Christian, receiving God's assurance of his (the Christian's) own reality and value, is able to acknowledge others and thus become open to their claims as neighbors.

☙ Exercising personal freedom—One cannot feel himself claimed by the neighbor's need unless he has the power to act to meet the need. If one effectively lacks freedom, the neighbor's need may evoke pathos but will not evoke action. The Christian faith, by stressing the spirit or motive of action (Christian love), leaves free the form. The Christian may choose from all possible responses those which best express and implement the purpose of loving and serving the neighbor.

☙ Achieving effective personal organization—Faced with competing and conflicting claims and having inadequate resources, how may one deal with all of them? Unless one is to respond aimlessly to the flow of pressures, he must have a way of acknowledging claims, balancing them, giving priority to some and deferring others. This cannot be a machinelike function, however, because this would mean that all possible contingencies were accounted for in advance. The Christian acknowledges the moral force of all claims, but is conscious that he cannot meet all of them—perhaps not fully meet any of them. The Christian's vocation sets the priority among the claims upon him, identifying those that are paramount, and organizes his life for the achievement of these paramount claims.

179

☙ Achieving a satisfactory life-style—Although the Christian faith refutes or transforms all popular notions of success or satisfaction, it does not call forth an ethic of frustration or ultimate failure. To do so would be an offense to rationality. The Christian faith does deeply admonish that the self-in-isolation is unreal, and its satisfactions therefore are unsatisfying. Christianity offers, instead, the self-in-relationship-to-others and defines the satisfaction of this self as the success of Christian love. Only as one has a "whole heart" and a "single eye" healed by the grace of God can he so live that the satisfaction of the neighbor's claim and the satisfaction of his own inner need are one and the same.

This Theme in the Bible

The principal biblical material for this theme is Luke 10:25-37 which contains the question about the great commandment (in a slightly different form) linked to the parable of the good Samaritan as a way of defining the neighbor. The parallels include Matthew 22:34-39; Mark 12:28-31; and the sources of the two commandments, Deuteronomy 6:4-9 and Leviticus 19:17-18; other Old Testament material would be the Ten Commandments in Exodus 20 together with their interpretation in Leviticus and Deuteronomy and the writings of some of the prophets, as Zechariah 8:16ff. Other biblical passages suitable to this theme are Genesis 24:15-30; Exodus 23:6-11; Isaiah 1:10-17; 5:1-23; Ezekiel 33:1-16; Amos 5:10, 12, 21-24; Acts 10; 1 Corinthians 13; Colossians 3:12-17; Hebrews 13:1-6; 1 John 3—4.

Additional material appropriate to the theme centers in the gospel accounts of Jesus' interpretation by his own word and deeds of what love and service for neighbor is and involves. His discourse interpreting the law and the new law—"You have heard it said . . . but I say"—is central (Matthew 5). His teaching on the centrality of service in the life of the disciple is relevant (Mark 10:35-45; Matthew 20:20-28; Luke 22:24-27), as is also the parable of the last judgment (Matthew 25).

The epistles include Paul's theology of moral freedom and grace, found in Romans and Galatians; James's admonishment on the royal law in chapter 2; John's exposition in his first epistle of the source and nature of law.

3. The Stewardship of Life and Work

STATEMENT OF THEME

Every decision is a choice among values that are often compet-
ing and contradictory. The disciple decides in light of his calling
as a Christian how he will enjoy his time, energies, money,
talents, and interests so as to achieve the most important or
necessary ends. This choice is especially seen, because of the
specialization involved, in the choice of an occupation.

DESCRIPTION OF THEME

Christian ethics in its economic aspect—the weighing of alternative uses for limited means—is the motif of this theme. It
faces up to the lifelong human concern that arises from being
limited in time and resources, and of having to choose to concentrate on certain ends in preference to others.

Stewardship of Resources

Though the Christian tends to want an ideal ordering of the
material world, he recognizes that because of his limitations this
condition will never prevail. He acknowledges his limitations not
as malevolent but as a fact of his creaturehood. This is the way
God has created mankind and the world; and in making all but
the most trivial decisions, the Christian is aware that he must
ask about any proposed action whether or not he possesses the
resources to see it through successfully. He may often proceed
when the answer is doubtful, but his decision will be less than
fully ethical if he has failed to consider this question. The New
Testament metaphor of the steward suggests the qualities required for the ethical deployment of resources; foresight (in providing), frugality (in conserving), prudence (in dispensing),
and good judgment (in weighing alternative uses). What, then,
are some of the resources which the good steward must select
and employ in meeting the claims upon him?

181

▶ Personal assets—These we may mention in passing, since the stewardship of personal endowment is fully dealt with in the area of "Sonship: the Meaning and Experience of Redemption." Personal assets include a person's talents and intelligence; his interests and concerns, including a willingness to sacrifice, to endure, and to pay the price of fatigue or suffering; his physical and emotional energy; and that quality of the organized self known as "personality."

182

▶ Intellectual assets—The use of these, too, is more fully developed in the area of "Sonship: the Meaning and Experience of Redemption." They include knowledge; skill in thinking and in developing relationships; perceptions, understandings; and the mastery of certain subjects. Intellectual assets become most useful as they are enriched by experience.

▶ Social assets—These include influence and reputation; authority (i.e. to make decisions or judgments affecting others, by virtue of an office or position held); one's job (the power to produce certain results in the course of earning a livelihood) and other relational roles; one's credit; and one's educational credentials (degrees, etc.).

▶ Extrinsic assets—These include one's time; such natural resources (materials) as he owns or may use; tools and equipment; and money which, though it is a social artifact, is best thought of as representing the power to command through the marketplace, the use of personal services and material goods including tools.

The Economy of Christian Decision

The economic aspect of ethics is the weighing of alternative uses for limited means. Human beings cannot find ideal solutions to their problems because of their limitations. Limitations as a characteristic of human experience is fully developed in the area of "Life and Its Setting: the Meaning and Experience of Existence." This section deals with two particular forms of limitation. One form of limitation is that most resources have a general rather than a particular usefulness, i.e. are raw materials. Man must choose which of several "forms of use" he will impose upon any given material. In adapting the material for one use he will, at the same time, most likely make it unusable for other purposes. For example, in building a house a board cut to become a doorsill becomes unusable for flooring, stair tread, or roof sheathing.

The idea of general usefulness is broadened when one considers that, for most purposes, any given material is never uniquely necessary. The doorsill mentioned above could be formed from plastic, aluminum, fiberglass, or composition board as well as from wood. Today, any given material is more or less necessary according to its relative cost and convenience of use. The economic effect of this form of limitation is primarily seen in the problems of supply and demand.

Another form of limitation is that any given resource can be used but for one purpose at a time. For example, a bar of iron can be worked into one long bolt, or can be cut up to form several nuts, but it cannot at the same moment be both a long bolt and several nuts. Or, investment funds may be used to purchase a unit of stock or a unit of bonds or debentures or time certificates, but a given dollar sum for only one like unit at a time. Though a resource may later be reformed, converted, or transformed to be used for a different purpose, this can be done only successively; it cannot be used in two or more different ways simultaneously. Therefore, the cost of using a resource in a certain way must include the calculation of how long it is required to be used in this certain way, being thus kept from alternative uses, and what its yield might have been in the best alternate uses. This form of limitation impinges upon economics primarily in the interest rate, and in other time-related statistics such as depreciation, obsolescense, and depletion rates, growth rates, efficiency-of-investment rates, time lags, and the like.

Considering the nature of these limitations, one may define

183

economy as the prudent deployment of limited means among alternative ends to secure maximum total welfare. Under the condition of limitation in human existence, every decision is to some degree an economic one. Thus Christian ethics is economic in more than the obvious sense that the Christian must decide how to use his own money, materials, and time. Every decision involves a weighing of alternative values and an implicit (or explicit) calculation of the relative efficiency of using one's available resources to achieve these values.

184

The choice of an occupation is sometimes spoken of as "investing one's life"—a phrase highly expressive of the ethical calculation that is a part of this decision. An investment is not justified only on the basis that it may produce a desired result; to this must be added the probability that it will thus be more efficient (weighing all the assets used and the time required) than if applied to another end of equal value.

Economic judgment, that is, the relating of alternate uses and limited means, can most easily take into account only those values which are comparable in terms of "more or less." In money economics, all values are strictly and precisely comparable in terms of price. The description of Christian ethics as "economic" is intended metaphorically, of course, and does not mean that all values can or should be reduced to money values. What it does mean is that ordinary decision-making involves a rather careful weighing of preferences and the relinquishing or deferring of certain values in favor of others.

Economic ethics, that is, the weighing of alternative uses for limited means, is unable to deal with "absolutes"—those value-judgments, laws, or commandments, which cannot be fitted into a preferential scale. There are many aspects of Christian life which one may choose to interpret as absolute, but reflection should suggest the dangers of this. Choices reflecting an absolute preference may signal fanaticism or idolatry. And, if many values are considered absolute, then which one shall prevail? Which is the more, or most, absolute? The effort to escape making relative judgments of value may be interpreted as a prideful hope of escaping the condition of human existence.

Specialization and Lifework

The term vocation is sometimes used to mean only an occupation or lifework. Actually the biblical concept of vocation is useful for interpreting all the decisions encountered in the Christian life; but it has an important reference to lifework because much of any person's time, energies, and other resources is employed in earning a living.

In money economics, where values are compared in terms of price, one of the chief means for increasing the efficiency of an economy as a whole is specialization. Historically, specialization is as old as civilization and has increased in proportion to the progress of technology. This increase of specialization may very well tend to characterize the future as it has the past; it remains to be seen whether automation will at least reverse the trend to specialization as some persons have predicted.

It follows that one of the most far-reaching of all decisions which any person must make is that which specializes or limits his field of likely future employment, for example, continuing in school, electing certain school courses, enrolling for further education, acquiring special skills through apprenticeship, training or professional education, accepting a job or position, beginning a practice. All these choices are important "vocational" decisions and apply just as much to the blue-collar worker or white-collar worker as to the professional person. A person who enters a profession usually does so with considerable deliberation, and it may occur to him more often than to persons in some other occupations to interpret his choice as vocational; but there is no valid reason to limit the use of this term to such decisions. The choice of occupation for a nonprofessional worker can be equally as climactic as that for the professional.

185

The concept of vocation is often confused with the essentially secular idea of a career. The term "career" may mean nothing more than "occupation," but in its origin and roots it describes a projection of personal pride and ambition. Outwardly a career may counterfeit one's vocation; the motives, however, are different. A vocational choice of occupation, though it may involve a lifelong commitment, is immediately responsive to the will of God and the ethical duty of serving the neighbor. It is this sense of dedicating one's occupation as his Christian vocation (finding in it opportunities of service and ministry) that can redeem a routine, even monotonous, form of labor by viewing it in its larger setting of the end product of which it is directed, and of the way this end product can serve mankind as neighbor. Furthermore, the activities of one's leisure may compensate or round out a monotonous occupation. See the theme "Man and Creativity Within Life's Daily Routines" in the area, "Life and Its Setting: the Meaning and Experience of Existence."

186

There are two other kinds of vocational specialization. One may choose, at a given point in history, to act as a corrective to destructive trends. The vocation of a prophet may be of this kind—his is not a balanced message, but a particular message for his time. The witness of the vocational pacifist or the political activist may also be a corrective to the conditions of the times. Still another significant specialization is that of seeking excellence or perfection by undertaking a limited task of unusual difficulty. Such diverse vocations as those of the poet, the artistic performer, the scholarly researcher, the experimentalist—works of genius or special talent—may be limited in output or in immediate effect, but serve to extend the total range of possible human expression.

This Theme in the Bible

In the Old Testament Abraham is the epic character typifying the best of the dedicated stewardship of life and work (Genesis 12—18, 20—25:10); Joseph is an eloquent example of the vocational steward (Genesis 37-50). The stewardship of position illustrated (both positively and negatively) in kings and other leaders of Israel should not be overlooked (David, Solomon, Hezekiah, Josiah, Ezra, Nehemiah, Esther). The sabbatical laws in Leviticus for the use of land are rooted in the concept of God as owner, man as steward. In the New Testament there are several parables on stewardship contained in the Gospels which, taken together, provide the basis for this theme. These include Matthew 20 (laborers in the vineyard), Luke 12:13-21 (the foolish rich man), Luke 12:35-48 (responsibility of the steward to deal justly and prudently and be able to give an account of himself), and Luke 16:1-13 (making friends with unrighteous mammon).

4. Discipline in the Christian Life

STATEMENT OF THEME

The Christian learns to cope with the difficult demands of decision-making situations under the disciplines of the Christian faith.

DESCRIPTION OF THEME

Christian ethics in its aspect of obedience to certain norms, which may be regarded as given or discoverable in Christian tradition, is the motif of this theme. It faces up to the lifelong human concern for achieving competence by receiving help from the experience or wisdom of others when making difficult decisions.

187

The Basis for Discipline

Every historical religion has a particular ethical tradition which, in some measure, controls the choices of its adherents. This tradition may take the impersonal form of law, as in the Old Testament where certain forms of behavior are prescribed or prohibited in great detail. At the opposite pole this tradition may take the form of a highly personal commitment to the guidance of a wise and trusted leader. Such a tradition, found in the New Testament and in the continuing life of the church, is interpreted through the biblical conception of discipleship. This term describes the relationship between a disciple (learner) and his master (teacher). The form of this relationship is discipline.

Historically, discipleship is a fairly common disciplinary relationship, having been practiced in the Old Testament and by religious leaders such as John the Baptist and perhaps Paul in the New Testament. It was, in fact, common for a religious teacher to have a group of disciples. There were not merely casual listeners, however; their relationship to the master was a practiced and voluntary one. It sometimes involved practical problems of feeding or housing the group, and economic arrangements for making this possible—perhaps the pooling of resources and the election of a treasurer. Duties to family or livelihood might have to be set aside, as by the disciples of Jesus who left their nets to follow him. The duty of trusting obedience was part of the relationship; the Gospels have numerous incidents in which Jesus "commanded" his disciples. Through trusting obedience, the disciple would come to possess the saving knowledge which the master could not communicate directly (but only by example, or hiddenly in parables or occult sayings, and also by personal qualities of the master). The disciple would come to be like the master. The master, in turn, would entrust to the disciple the keeping and proclaiming of his message. The description of the Christian life as "discipleship" points to a similar relationship to Jesus Christ—voluntary, practiced, obedient, disciplined—which provides the source for Christian ethical norms.

The discipleship of the modern Christian is partly a mystical relationship as a son directly to God through commitment to Jesus Christ as Savior and Lord; it is also partly a practical relationship in which the dual aspects of discipleship—learning and obedience—are continued in the Christian community as a whole. The community not only acknowledges the sonship of the

Christian to God as Father but also provides the disciple support in his learning and obedience so that he may clarify his perceptions, define the causes to which he commits himself, and harness his energies to action. The disciple, in relationship to his fellow disciples, both is corrected by and corrects the Christian community (the church) of which he is a part.

Discipline Inherent in Sonship

On the mystical side, the Christian's relationship to Jesus Christ as master is intimately tied up with his relationship to Jesus Christ as savior. Sonship involves being "conformed to the image of his Son" (Romans 8:29)—becoming inwardly like Christ, accepting the disciplines of that relationship. See "Sonship: the Meaning and Experience of Redemption."

Discipleship on its mystical side is the work of the Holy Spirit, as Paul makes clear in Romans 8. Those who "live according to the Spirit" and "set their minds on the things of the Spirit" (Romans 8:5) have Jesus Christ present in them, for the Holy Spirit is "the Spirit of Christ." (Romans 8:9) The Spirit helps and intercedes (8:26-27); moreover its influence gives rise to the fruit of the Spirit—"love, joy, peace, patience, kindness, goodness, faithfulness, gentleness, self-control. . . ." (Galatians 5:22-23) These words describe the personal qualities which should characterize the Christian and be evident in his ethical decisions.

189

The Disciplines of Learning and Obedience

On the practical side, the fact of commitment to Jesus Christ calls for undertaking the disciplines of learning and obedience.

In the Christian discipline of learning the Bible occupies a special place. The Christian is not much concerned about the religious authority of the Bible, for authority means only the power to compel a reluctant assent and is chiefly useful in religious controversy. The Christian disciple is not a reluctant student; he is eager to learn of Jesus, whose "yoke is easy," and is grateful for the acquaintance with him which the Bible uniquely makes possible. A wish to accept only so much of the Bible's witness as can be incontrovertibly proved is foreign to the spirit of discipleship.

The disciple's eagerness to search and listen profoundly affects his manner of use of the Bible. His purpose is to be sensitive to all of its meaning, with a heightened awareness to be ready for God's disclosure of himself through the word or the Spirit. His approach to the Bible is one of scholarly recovery—a reverent, searching, critical, methodically faithful willingness to use every method of study which may open to him some unexpected find of knowledge and meaning. His study will include the parallel disciplines of theology and history. The scholarship of the Christian will not be a prideful attempt to prove one's view, but an offering of trustful obedience to the Master in the hope or receiving his self-disclosure.

The methodical practice of prayer, worship, and reflection will be a part of the search for Christlikeness in the Christian's learning. These practices provide the frame of reference for the Christian that makes the result of learning joyous and wondrous rather than dreadful or menacing.

The Christian discipline of obedience opens the way to new truth and help the learner become like the teacher. For the Christian, obedience means doing one's duty whenever it becomes clear, no matter what the cost is. The person who refuses his clear duty (upon both religious and psychological grounds) incurs guilt that will muddy his future moral perceptions. This process is described in the Bible as "hardening the heart"—the seat of intelligence and judgment. But one who knows what his discipleship requires, and does it, has his heart made clear and his eyes and ears opened.

Obedience is both practical and voluntary, that is, it involves a deliberate decision to be methodical and faithful in attending the duties prescribed by the teacher. The significant forms of obedience to discipline for the modern Christian include private and public worship, study, and devotions; witnessing to the gospel in politics, education, business, and industry; loving the world in light of the gospel to the end that it may be transformed; and supporting those forms of order in the family, local community, national and international life that sustain justice, harmony, and good.

The Christian who seeks to grow in discipleship by undertaking Christian disciplines will be appreciative of the opportunity for mutual correction and restraint among Christians. As a corrective to whim or pride, and as he copes with failure and success and with trial and temptation, he will frequently seek the counsel and support of others. He will also call upon the recorded wisdom of the past in a conscious effort to make his decisions, as fully as possible, Christian ones. In seeking the help of others, he will not try to shirk his freedom or evade responsibility for his decisions; but he will try to make every decision a potential occasion for growth in Christlikeness and in the awareness of his vocation through his having been a diligent learner. Used in this way, the disciple's obedience is not a negation of his moral freedom. It is not a slavish and unknowing submission to a will that is foreign to him; it is rather the practice of trust in the will of a person to whom he is voluntarily related. In this obedience the moral quality of decision is not obscured, but is brought fully into consciousness.

191

This Theme in the Bible

The personal relationship germane to discipleship is emphasized by the prophets as they reinterpret the laws of religious ceremony (Micah, Amos, Hosea). The entire wilderness experience of Israel can be viewed as discipline in the ways of the Lord. All Four Gospels describe throughout the relationship of Jesus to his disciples; and many passages in the epistles elaborate that relationship as the determinative factor in discipleship (Ephesians 4; 1 Corinthians 3).

Many of the didactic passages of the Gospels elucidate the

duties of Christian discipleship. The promise of the Holy Spirit (John 14) emphasizes the necessity to continue learning discipleship. Paul's discourses on being "in Christ" and his admonitions to observe disciplines—worship, prayer, study of Scriptures, fasting—reflect this theme. Psalms 119 and other Psalms in praise of the law together with much of Proverbs will be relevant.

Specific reflection of disciplines as needful in the church is found in 1 Timothy 4, Galatians 5, 6, and Ephesians 6.

192

5. Joined in Discipleship in the World

STATEMENT OF THEME

Those who are Christ's disciples are united in the task of making their vocation visible, interpreting it to the world, and bringing it to effect in the world. In this way the Christian is strengthened and aided in meeting the obligation to live out his discipleship among men.

DESCRIPTION OF THEME

Christian ethics in its socially purposive aspect—the projection of coherent goals and the use of a united effort to attain these goals—is the motif of this theme. It faces up to the lifelong human concern of mutual help among persons who have common interests or who may benefit from projects undertaken in common.

The vocation of the Christian is lived out in an interpersonal and social world where others are pursuing diverse vocations with all different degrees of faithfulness. Persons acting from the most varied and contradictory motives give evidence of believing themselves to be just and right. But the many occupations of Christians can be interpreted as one vocation with respect to their common discipleship to Jesus Christ. Moreover, Christians believe, their common vocation receives organized and visible form in the community of Christian disciples.

Forms of Shared Discipleship in the World

In Christian witness, Christians unite to make their vocations visible to the world through the proclamation of the gospel of Christ and through service to persons "in the name of Christ." A person becomes identified as a witness for Christ through such acts as bearing personal testimony of the power of the gospel to those met in daily occupations, making the public profession of faith required for church members, receiving baptism and uniting with the church, holding offices of leadership in the church, attending worship, participating in the Lord's Supper, serving as a minister, and serving as a lay speaker or evangelist. These activities signal one's willingness to be identified and judged by the community at large as a Christian disciple. A person so identified testifies through his daily decisions in all his relationships, "These, the things I do daily are the acts of a Christian, one who learns from Jesus Christ and who is moved and enabled by the gracious love of God."

Along with their witness, Christians help educate the world through the united interpretation of their vocation to the world. Their preaching, in addition to its prime function of proclaiming the gospel, has a function of explaining where realities referred to in religious language have their daily manifestation. Thus, Christians educate their community when they interpret reality and history so that the urgent duty of serving God makes sense. In this way the individual disciple's vocation, which in isolation may appear erratic or futile, can be seen in the context of the whole people of God, part of a purposive movement toward a historical fulfillment of the will of God.

193

Christians also unite in social action and outreach to bring their vocations to effect in the world. The moral freedom of each Christian to choose the means by which he will function encourages concerted action for extending the influence of the gospel, both geographically (spreading the gospel in places remote from his local community) and in penetrating his local community with the "leaven of the gospel." Christians work in voluntary groups and through political channels for persuasion and legislation to bring about needed social changes.

The ministries of witness, education, and social outreach may be carried out in ways that require effective instrumental activity —associating for common action; communicating purposes through speech, writing, teaching, and debate; administering or planning for one's own work and that of others; recruiting others; and supporting collective action by financing, litigating, lobbying, or by being identified with such actions by the community. Christians are called upon to perform all of these activities in the course of fulfilling their common vocation through their diverse occupations. Though each Christian disciple may have the talent or enabling grace to perform but one of these activities, others are equipped to perform many or all of them. The balance in the community of disciples is reflected when each disciple functions in accord with the spiritual gifts entrusted to him by God, being aware of the reality of the support which that community gives to him in his ministry even when he is physically absent from them.

The Church, Congregational Communities penetrating the World Community

Recent theological attention has shown that the church does not disappear when it adjourns worship to go about the business of daily living. In the fulfilling of their vocations, Christians are conscious of the several degrees of their association. These range from the occasions when the congregation is gathered in its dedicated place for sharing services of worship and praise to the associations formed when disciples from various congregations become a community of cooperative Christian action in their neighborhood or in the larger community of the world.

Each Christian group acts on behalf of all its members and with their consent creates structures for the fulfillment of common discipleship. These include local and denominational boards, agencies, and commissions, and also include the inter-denominational ones such as the American Bible Society and the world, national, state, and local councils of churches. These agencies take positions and promote ends which they believe to be broadly representative of qualified Christian opinion among their constituencies, while respecting the right of any persons so represented to dissent and to disagree.

Christians working together as the community of faith also pioneer in the development of programs for education, witness, social action, and outreach which may be adopted for use by local congregations or by regional governing or associational bodies, both denominational and interdenominational.

Finally, these Christian bodies, both local and national, denominational and interdenominational, undertake to influence public action in ways that represent the wishes of the Christian community as expressed by their governing bodies or their representative, or that may be inferred from their history and doctrine, or that are derived by a local congregation. In particular, both denominational boards and church councils make representations to government in matters affecting the immediate interest of the churches and involving the legal relationships between church and state, as well as matters expressing the concern of the church for the general welfare in all of its dimensions affected by government.

195

The Church, an Intimate Community

Christians have discovered that the sense of institution and movement can often obscure the sense of the community for the individual. Much recent effort has been directed toward the recovery of the small group as a valid and integral expression of the church's life. Such groups would not be casual gatherings but, in keeping with the character of discipleship, practiced and voluntary associations, acknowledged to be acting as an arm of the whole Christian community. Intimate groups can aid the discipleship of the members by offering mutual support on a personal level, correction, restraint, and intercession. This, what could be called the pastoral function, belongs to the whole church, and should be so exercised.

Small groups can provide formal and informal learning experiences for their members. Christian educators are conscious of the need for the family (for example) to be aware of its opportunity to further the learning of its members. Small groups can also be effective in making a collective witness to the community. They can quietly persuade local leadership of the need of change, and may work to create a climate of goodwill for the reduction of tensions accompanying change. They have particularly good opportunities for dealing with the problems of prejudice and injustice on account of race, social class, or economic class.

The basic component of the small group and of the larger congregational community is the individual disciple. He is the person who has publicly identified himself as a Christian, being fully aware that before the eyes of the world community his daily decisions reflect credit or discredit upon those with whom he has identified himself (his fellow disciples) and upon their service to the one who is their master—Jesus Christ. Therefore, the individual disciple will try to be sure that his choices and actions are not only just and fair, but spring from worthy motives; he will try to interpret his actions to the community in terms appropriate to his discipleship.

The disciple will continually attempt to be conscious of his duty of obedience to God as he considers the factors involved in making his decisions. His decisions should display the character of Christ's church in whose name he acts; it is *holy* (set apart, devoted to God) and *apostolic* (under orders, and representing Christ). When the disciple must take recourse to guide or to correct others in the particular Christian community of which he is a part, this recourse should display his conviction that the church is *one*.

Discipleship in the World

The Christian's vocation is to work to bring about an effect in the world which may very well oppose or frustrate his private desires. Therefore his decisions cannot be once for all; the Christian must take account of the countermoves of the opponent, and project endeavors toward the ultimate achieving of his purpose. Such endeavors will include evangelism, the enlistment of persons in conscious discipleship to Christ; and the bringing of Christian standards to bear on culture and morality. The New Testament figure of the Christian community as a "colony of heaven" expresses this twofold task. When governed by a sense of his true vocation, the disciple's decisions in the world will display a conviction that no part of the world has been abandoned to lawlessness and sin; they will testify to the fact that the church of Jesus Christ is, at least in potential, universal (catholic).

This Theme in the Bible

The principal biblical source for this theme will be the letters of Paul that deal with matters of church discipline and the duties of discipleship—particularly the Corinthian correspondence, which provides an insight into the very knotty and difficult problem of the church's making an effective witness to the community around it while torn with dissensions within. In the Old Testament there are few references that can be considered directly related to this theme, "Joined in Discipleship in the World." One might, however, attend to such writings as Isaiah 49 to gain insight into concept of the Jews of the nature of their responsibility as disciples in the world; and also to the work of reformers such as Hezekiah and Josiah under the influence of the prophets.

The duty of the Christian community to penetrate society is reflected in the parable of the leaven, the lamp, and the salt.

197

6. Toward the Kingdom of God

STATEMENT OF THEME

The conviction that the decisions to which God calls men are ultimately directed to a single goal, the kingdom of God, gives purpose and structure to man's life, and brings into a meaningful whole the separate vocations of men.

DESCRIPTION OF THEME

198

This theme faces up to the lifelong concern of Christians struggling toward objectives that are only partially achieved, and loving and valuing realities with which they may not come directly into contact or directly possess. Accordingly this theme stresses that aspect of Christian ethics which transcends the self of the decision-maker.

In making decisions, the Christian can neither have recourse to a blind obedience nor to assured success through perfect knowledge. "We walk by waith, not by sight." (2 Corinthians 5:7) But the Christian's decision must be an intelligent and purposive one, not merely a response to the pressures of the moment. It will reflect not only his hopes for his own life, but also the way he views his relationships to other persons and to their common history.

The kingdom of God is a biblical metaphor which recognizes the sovereignty of God and interprets for Christians the end toward which history moves. The degree to which this metaphor is applied either within or beyond history and the form of its culmination is developed in the area "Life and Its Setting: the Meaning and Experience of Existence." The concept of the kingdom of God gives completeness to the partial and special vocations of men, and unites them in a total view of life and history.

The ethical significance of the kingdom makes possible the evaluation of suprapersonal structures in the world: economic systems and arrangements, political states and constitutions, social organizations, corporations, laws, and military power. In each of these areas, the Christian must constantly make decisions whether he will support, oppose, or accommodate himself to the existing order. Has he any standard for judging other than his immediate self-interest? Can any spirit be manifest in these institutions other than a raw contest of will and power? The Christian will seek to be guided by the overarching purpose of the kingdom and to have the kingdom reflected in the forms of these social structures.

At every turn, the Christian will confront partial success and partial failure. The kingdom is called a transcendent objective, to express the belief that the full realization of the kingdom is unattainable under the condition of history as we know it. The transcendence of the kingdom reflects the transcendence of God. Just as the Christian both speaks through and stands in judgment upon every idolatrous representation of himself (which is to say, upon everything that humanly can be said about him), so also the kingdom both renews and reforms every human institution. Both renewal and reform are clearly seen in the history of the church. The church's existence is always radically threatened by the saying of Jesus to the Pharisees, " 'Bear fruit that befits repentance, and do not presume to say to yourselves, "We have Abraham as our father"; for I tell you, God is able from these stones to raise up children to Abraham. Even now the ax is laid to the root of the trees; every tree therefore that does not bear good fruit is cut down and thrown into the fire.' " (Matthew 3:8-10) Under this threat, the kingdom's power of renewal enables the church to save its life by losing it.

199

Modes of Discipleship in Light of the Kingdom

The Christian's vocation toward the kingdom is that he live in the kingdom of God though in this world. By acknowledging his spiritual citizenship he bears a testimony to the reality of the kingdom, and makes this reality more evident; it is God, not man, who brings his kingdom into being. Man is called to enter it, and to live in it as harmoniously as his limitations allow.

Though his creatureliness makes perfect justice impossible under the conditions of existence, man's organizations can regulate their relationships on the basis of approximate justice. Though every human institution is a mixture of love and pride, of equity and exploitation, condemned under the standard of the kingdom as unjust, approximate justice can become a workable compromise offered to God in the spirit of the unworthy servants who say, " ' "We have only done what was our duty." ' " (Luke 17:10) An approximate justice is characterized by repentance, and its achievement is one way in which Christians may "bear fruit that befits repentance." For example, laws for punishment of crime should be merciful, not only out of a regard for persons convicted but also as the state's acknowledgment that the community and its laws share his guilt through their injustice.

Strategies for the achievement of approximate justice include the individual and corporate witness of Christians, who confess on behalf of the community the guilt of all. In order that it may remain free to perform this function, the church should seek to preserve its freedom from either control by the state or obligation to it on account of favors. Moreover, Christians may perform a corrective or restorative function in aiding poor or disadvantaged persons, or through favoring legislation to maintain the balance of power between conflicting groups. Christians may express repentance for society's wrongs by taking initiative as citizens to reduce racial and religious tensions and to protect the rights of minorities. Christians may seek to hold injustice in check through the support of law and order, and in particular they may seek peace and world order through a world rule of law, and the strengthening of international institutions aimed toward reducing world tensions.

The kingdom of God is presently realized through the signs or symbols by which the disciple believes or infers its reality.

Because the kingdom has not been actualized in history, the disciple must live as a citizen of two worlds: the present, temporal world and the coming, eternal kingdom in which he is a present partial participant. This dual relationship demonstrates the impinging of the kingdom upon the present world order; through the participation of some of its persons in the eternal kingdom the present world order is being renewed and reformed. Christians witness to this relationship between the world and the kingdom of God through the use of a variety of symbols.

The Christian's use of language may describe in imaginative terms the forms of a heavenly community. For many persons, the language of the biblical apocalypses or the popular reflection about heaven have this function—they describe a condition of being in which moral and human qualities are preserved, but free of accident and sin. Modern religious thought has, however, developed the idea of the heavenly community in a more realistic and this-worldly form—the study of Christian social ethics and the analysis of social structures from the standpoint of the Christian faith. This modern tradition will be of value to the disciple as he seeks to make his decisions in light of the meaning of the kingdom.

The Christian's use of art can symbolize the kingdom's penetration of the world by elicting from the audience a heightened awareness of the reality and value of the world. By celebrating the world in imagination, Christians show forth its potential for change and transformation.

201

Christians may symbolize Christ's concern for the total redemption of the world through associating themselves with groups or institutions in the world dedicated to the betterment of the common life. This identification of Christian disciples with unpopular causes may have greater effect symbolically, by stirring the conscience of the world, than the same persons could have through direct action, attempting to make their personal influence sway the decisions of those in positions of civil authority. The influence of Christian disciples upon the choice of forms used in organizing governments and institutions can have both tangible and symbolic effects. As an example, the trial procedures defined as "due process of law" in both English and American courts offer real protection to accused individuals. These procedures are a powerful symbol of the value attached to the life and person of the citizen in countries where the hertage of leadership has included men who acknowledge personal Christian responsibility for their society and the world.

The entrance of the kingdom of God into the world is symbolized through worship as the disciples, representing the entire community, gather to offer repentance, seek forgiveness, and rejoice in praise and adoration—returning to their daily tasks with a fresh resolution to live as followers of Christ.

The church itself is the chief symbol of the kingdom in that it lives in the world without any guarantee or advantage except that secured to it by its faithful witness and obedience to Christ. The church lives by its discipleship; like the individual disciple, its obedience opens the way to saving truth. To the extent that the church's obedience is genuine and faithful, it will realize in its own life the heavenly community and thus point toward a similar achievement in society as a whole.

Power from the Kingdom to Overcome Uncertainty

The importance of the symbolical realization of the kingdom for ethics is this: it keeps alive for the decision-maker an ethical relationship to reality in the extremes of hopelessness and futility. All moral choice is shrouded in uncertainty. One cannot know for sure whether the future results of even the most noble act will be more good than evil. Why act at all? One's lifework may be wiped away by war or catastrophe; surely it will be wiped away by time. One's children are born to die, and one's fortunes to be dissipated. It is at least questionable whether the world makes any moral progress with time.

Faced with experiences so conducive to moral skepticism as are profound failure and the awareness of one's own ultimate death, how can a man remain ethical in his attitudes or care very much about the effects of his choices? The answer must be: he can remain ethical through the transcendence of the self in a faithful relationship to a reality that is imperishable. The kingdom offers such a reality. Its symbolical realization elicits the effect in the life of the decision maker, of which Jesus spoke when he said, " 'But seek first his kingdom and his righteousness, and all these things shall be yours as well.' " (Matthew 6:33) He was not offering a materialistic reward for faith, but promising to those who are united with the kingdom freedom from anxiety about the world and the self.

Such a self-transcendent faith makes possible for the decision maker a practical tranquility about the ultimate result of his choices, combined with a profound ethical involvement and the willingness to exert himself rigorously for the goals he seeks. Ultimately the choices of the Christian disciple rest not upon his own power to assess and control the situation in which he finds himself, but upon belief in the God who does all things well.

This Theme in the Bible

The mission to which God calls his people is independent of earth's time schedule: it is toward his eternal purpose, both in and beyond earth's time. This is seen in the historical books of the Old Testament. Among the prophets, Jeremiah stands out as one who saw the role of the people of God in eternal perspective, though the messianic passages in the writings of others have this major theme. This theme also draws upon the remnant passages in the Old Testament.

Hebrews 11 describes the qualities of faith in those who act in obedience to God without being able to see the fruit of their action. This passage is valuable because of the sweep of its perception of this relationship in human life and in the religious history of Israel.

The parables of the kingdom, found at various places in the Gospels, provide a series of analogies to show how the kingdom

203

ingresses into the world—silently, unseen, and undetected, but with ultimately overwhelming force. John 16 proclaims the assured victory with triumph.

In the epistles, Peter's discussion of the Christians' relations to human institutions (1 Peter 2:11ff.; see also Romans 15), Paul's description of the Christians' perspective on suffering (Romans 8; 2 Corinthians 4, 5) are roots of this theme.

204

THE CHURCH: THE MEANING AND EXPERIENCE OF CHRISTIAN COMMUNITY

The themes within this area are:

Christians Are Bound Together in God's Love
God's Continuing Action in and Through His People
The Church Permeating Society
Extending Reconciliation and Redemption
The Church Lives by Worship
The Christian Community Mobilizing for Mission
Preparing and Equipping for Ministry

Description of Curriculum Area

The focus, or vantage point, of this area of curriculum is the nature, the history, and the mission of the church; belonging to the church and participating in its life and work.

Comprehended in the area of curriculum is such content of Christian thought and life as: the doctrine of the church; the meaning of church membership; the history of the church; Christian mission and the missionary enterprise; skills of church-manship; worship and the ministries of the church—teaching, preaching, outreach, service, healing; interpretation of the church triumphant; the history and use of the Bible.

205

In order to have educational value as an area of curriculum, this content must be viewed in terms of its pertinence to the persistent issues of man's life. Some of these issues are: What can I do about feelings of alienation? Where can I belong? Why is Christianity exported? What is the basis of Christian evangelism? How did the church come to be? Why are there so many denominations? Can't I be a good Christian outside the church? What is the business of the church? Where can I find support for my

Christian aspirations and witness? What difference does the church make?[1]

Delineation of Area

206

"The church" refers to the fellowship of persons who own allegiance to Jesus Christ, who have found new life in him, and who are seeking in their particular time and place to perform his ministry and fulfill his mission. To deal with the curriculum area of the church is thus to deal with the whole meaning and experience of the Christian community.

The focus of this area of curriculum is the nature, the history, the mission, and the message of the church, viewed from the vantage point of those who belong to and participate in the life and work of the Christian community. As the Christian approaches the church from within it and views it from the perspective of the organizing principle of the curriculum, "involvement in the life and work of the Christian community," he becomes a part of it and not a passive spectator. The church may be regarded as the instrument through which the curriculum of Christian education comes to life and through which its objective is sought and achieved. The history of the church is experienced through participation in the relevance and meaning of baptism and the Lord's Supper. The focus of this curriculum area should help to bring the objective history of the church together with the experience of the Christian community.

The Nature of the Church

From a biblical perspective certain significant names have been associated with or used to describe the church. These represent specific points of view or emphasis and all contribute to an understanding of the nature of the church. They are: The Body of Christ (with Christ as head), the people of God (stressing the church's divine origin and relationship), the Israel of God

---

[1] These three paragraphs are repeated here as necessary background.

(stressing the connection between the experience of Israel in the Old Testament and the doctrine of the church in the New Testament, between the "people of God" and the "church of God"), the covenant community, the redemptive community, the community of faith, the *koinonia,* the ecclesia, the bride of Christ, God's flock, the kingdom of God, the pillar and ground of truth.

Reflection upon these names given to the church leads to descriptions of the nature of the church, such as: one, holy, catholic, apostolic, visible and invisible, militant and triumphant, gathered and dispersed, empirical and ideal, spiritual, charismatic, and authoritative and fallible.

Still further reflection leads to a delineation of various aspects of the life and work of the church, such as:

Studying and proclaiming the Word of God (including providing a context for study, interpretation, and application of the Scriptures)

Administering the sacraments

Providing a context for the worshiping community

Providing a context for the witnessing community

Providing a context for the prophetic community

Providing a context for the community of faith doing its work in the world (the church in mission, political responsibility, and social action)

Providing a context for encounter between God and man and man and man

Being the guardian and transmitter of a living tradition and heritage

Following an orderly discipline for its life and work

Following the example of its servant Lord by being a servant church

Encouraging and providing a base for the priesthood of believers, the ministry of the laity

207

Living and speaking within and to the culture

Living with the state and yet loyal to the kingdom of God

Looking for the coming of a new age and a new order

The Message of the Church

The message of the church is always the gospel, the good news of man's condition, God's judgment and his requirement of righteousness and love, his concern for all men, his reconciling acts and Word, the enfleshment of the Word of God in Jesus Christ, Christ's life, his teachings, his proclamation of the new day, his healing work, his suffering and dying for the sins of all men, his rising again in triumph over sin and death, his living lordship, the proclamation of his reconciling ministry, and the whole continuous activity of God in history and in concern for history.

The message of the church must be delivered to the world in such terms that the church and the world will both see its relevance, cutting edge, and promise. Today this means that the message of the gospel must be seen in its bearing on the problems of war and international relations, the mutual interdependence and responsibility of the nations, the demands for justice and freedom around the world, the ways in which men may see and work with each other, the relations of the races, personal insecurity and anxiety, personal morality and the good life, and the intellectual and aesthetic quests. From time to time, as the situation demands and as insight is forthcoming, the church must speak on these and like issues. The church must speak locally, personally, regionally, nationally, and internationally. Its delivering of its message may be the stimulus for discussion and dialogue between the church and the world. Only so can the church become relevant to its situation and times.

The church's message has to be couched and delivered in language that can be understood by those to whom it is addressed. The function of preaching is to see to it that the Word

208

of God, the message of the Christian community, is clear and intelligible to the members of the community itself and to those not members of the community who may nevertheless be induced to listen. The translation of the Bible has recently taken on new dimensions, it being put not only in the tongues of many hundreds of persons around the world ("a thousand—and more—tongues") but also translated into the vernacular English of the man in the street so that changes in language will not dull its impact. The church needs to experiment with the use of the idiom of philosophy, science, the arts, politics, economics, and the like, to see how far it can use this idiom for the delivering of its message. In doing so it must also discover the irreducibles of its own theological language and learn how to teach their meaning to those unfamiliar with the language.

The couching of the message of the gospel for any particular time is the responsibility of the discipline of theology. The technical theologian needs to work at the solution of these problems, without forgetting to instruct those around him in what he is learning. The lay theologian, i.e., the whole laity, needs to be alerted to the depth and urgency of the theological task, helped to grasp its essentials, and assisted in the practical aspects of delivering the message to the world.

The Mission of the Church

209

The mission of the church is to proclaim the gospel of God's self-disclosure in Jesus Christ. The church is called to worship, preach, teach, serve, heal, and thus to declare the sovereignty of God.

The church is called to respond in faith and obedience. It is sent into the world to exercise its discipleship with passion and zeal. As it heeds the voice of its Lord, even as it stands under its Lord's judgment, the judgment of the world, and its own self-criticism, the church is continually being formed and re-formed in a continuing action of renewal.

To be faithful to its mission, the church is required to enter into dialogue with the world. While being judged, the church as servant is itself in judgment upon the world. The church is in the world for the sake of the world. Its encounter with the world may be the moment for the encounter with its risen Lord. The dialogue with the world exacts a demand from the church that it seriously examine its apologetic and dogmatic presentation. In this dialogue with the world the Christian church also has the opportunity for conversation with the non-Christian religions.

As the church in reality becomes the redemptive community, it has the awesome responsibility of serving as the instrument of God's gracious activity of reconciling man to God, man to self, and men to one another. To do this the church has to be willing to identify itself with sinful men. The service to which the church is called by its servant Lord is for the church to be the suffering servant in the world. As the church enables the world to see itself as it is, God's creation and yet rebellious, as the church communicates God's seeking and inviting love, the church may be able to comfort the afflicted and afflict the comfortable.

The church must permeate the social structures of the community and world in response to God's redemptive work. As Jesus taught, Christians are to be leaven, salt, and light. The church has to be active in influencing the world of man's activities, willing to enter the conflict with the present-day kingdoms of evil.

The mission of the church is also to nurture persons toward maturity in Christ. The church must both establish the convert and guide its own children into mature manhood in Jesus Christ. For this the church is guardian, translator, and transmitter of its heritage. The church nurtures as it encourages worship and devotion, provides for strengthening the home, makes possible experiments in Christian community life, and creates a proper setting for Christian education.

All this the church is called to do in order that it might witness to the eternal purpose of God. Called to be witness to God's redemptive work in Christ, the church abides in the hope made manifest in its risen Lord. Partaker of the resurrection world of God, the church is conscious that ultimately it is not of this world but that it participates in the eschatological mission of its Lord, a victory in history which fulfills all of history.

The Church's History

The story of the church as a phenomenon in history forms one definite segment or constituent part of the curriculum area, "The Church: the Meaning and Experience of Christian Community." The logic of the church's history may be put this way:

The appearance of the New Testament church in history— This is the result of God's self-disclosure, a fulfillment of divine intention. The New Testament itself came out of the life and thought of this new people of Israel. The events recorded in the Acts, the story of conflict with the Roman Empire, the biographical materials, and the teachings of the epistles all form part of the content and meaning of the church's life.

The antecedents of the New Testament church—The history of Israel indicates the emergence of a people of God as a witness to revelation. This "people of God" was in conflict with other cultures in which it lived, a type of conflict destined to be a part of the life and meaning of the church in every age from its birth to the present time. The Old Testament is to be seen as integral to "holy history," the story of salvation, the events by which God made himself known and prepared for the appearance of the "new people of God" in history.

The church through the ages—Through the ages there are key events, the story of changing thought and interpretation, the story of relationships between the church and the world, and emerging movements such as the Reformation. Included are such elements as the story of the development of the text and canon of the New Testament, monasticism, the development of creeds, the history of the spread of the church into new countries,

211

missionary biography, the story of the persecutions, the growth of the liturgy and the history of worship, hymnody, and the church's whole heritage and tradition.

☙ The church in the contemporary scene—The church is creating history through its interaction with men, movements, and crises at the present time. Some of the conflicts now are with secularism, communism, and facism. The whole missionary enterprise is having to be rethought and recast in order to provide a fitting medium for the church's basic mission. The ecumenical movement is an outstanding contemporary development. There is a rediscovery of and new emphasis upon the nature of the New Testament church.

212

Themes Delineated

1. Christians Are Bound Together in God's Love

STATEMENT OF THEME

The special nature of koinonia *that makes it different from other community or fellowship is the love relationship of man to man and man to God which supports man's authentic being as a person. This fellowship meets man's primary needs to love and be loved.*

DESCRIPTION OF THEME

The Unifying Love of God

The love of the universal Father God is the binding force that brings all Christians together as his children and as brothers in Christ. This is not a love which is deserved by the church. The church has no claim upon the affection of God. But he has declared his affection and through Jesus Christ has once and for all revealed it. This love is outpoured without regard to human distinctions, and through it all persons may realize themselves as the children of the divine and as a part of the great family of God.

The binding love of God evokes a response from its recipients. It calls for mutual concern, a sense of responsibility for one another, and loving acceptance of all men. This unity is not merely a task. It cannot be performed. It is rather a gift from God which is to be experienced, actualized, and shown forth in human relationships. Thus it may become vital and significant.

The Body of Christ

The church is a believing fellowship of all who respond to God's activity in repentance, faith, obedience, and open acknowledgment of Jesus Christ as Lord. This fellowship of response cuts across all lines which would alienate persons from each other and makes them one in Christ. A common recognition of the love of God for all men—whatever their race, class, or nation— challenges the church to respond in kind in all its relationships with persons.

As the body of Christ, the church possesses a unique quality of community which answers the deepest yearnings of man. This is the distinctive Christian *koinonia* which not only consists of an empathetic love relationship of man to man, but further partakes of the divine element in the relationship of man to God. This latter dimension helps man to perceive his authentic being as a person before his Creator and his fellows.

213

Thus the church offers man the ultimate fulfillment of his need to belong, to love and to be loved, to communicate and to commune with others. These experiences exist at the deepest levels of interpersonal relationships when they take place under a sense of the presence of God.

The aspiration of man to feel himself a part of universal mankind is realized in the universality of *koinonia*. The Christian church is not limited to time or space—it has its roots in eternity, and its destiny in a kingdom without end. It is the Church Universal—obedient to one Lord—declaring one gospel. Thus Christians may participate in the *koinonia* which spans the centuries and which girds the continents. Man's longing for participation in that which is ongoing and for contribution to some kind of permanence finds fulfillment through meaningful identity with "a kingdom which cannot be shaken."

The Shared Fellowship

The oneness of the church is founded upon the conviction of the church since its beginnings that "Jesus Christ is Lord." The New Testament clearly affirms that Jesus Christ is the head of the body—and that the church is this Body of Christ. This body must be one since its Lord is one. Furthermore, this concept of oneness is rooted in an Old Testament heritage which speaks of the "people of God" as a cohesive and divinely created community through which a prophetic witness should be revealed. This witness was designed not only for members of the community itself but, at its best, was also destined for the blessing of the world at large. The ecumenical movement may be viewed as an overt expression of the Christian's search for the unity which he senses is God's ultimate purpose for his church. In common enterprises that cut across denominational distinctions, the church rediscovers its essential unity in spite of the diversities and even cleavages of thought and practice. The various communions bring to bear on common obligations their distinctive contributions and become aware of and learn to transcend the limitations of understanding that are only denominational or confessional. At the same time, a denomination may by its obedience and insight in its life as a denomination provide a witness to the rest of the Christian community. The common faith in and commitment to one Lord unite Christians in essential areas of religious life and deepen acceptance and appreciation of one for another.

This Theme in the Bible

God's love as the determining factor of relationships among his people is emphasized at various points in the Bible. The laws among the early people of Israel were rooted in God's steadfast love which had created them a people (Exodus, Leviticus, Deuteronomy). The stories in Jonah and Ruth give further evidence of the critical factor in relations among those who are God's people. The latter chapters of Isaiah proclaim the love of God as binding together for all those who respond to him.

Israel's indifference to this rule of relationship is the root of the hostility between Jew and Samaritan; between the Pharisees and "sinners." The ministry of Jesus proclaims the love of God as cementing the fellowship among persons, both by his teaching and his example. The Lord's Supper, and his intimate discourses following (John 15 notably) poignantly give expression to this love.

In the early chapters of the Book of Acts, the unique fellowship of the believers is described in terms such as "with one accord" and "they had everything in common." Christians ate together, talked together, lived together, and shared all phases of their life in common. They were a fellowship under their common debt of God's love (Colossians 4).

The letters of the New Testament also reflect the theme of Christian unity based on God's gift of love. Paul, in the earlier part of the Epistle to the Romans, presents weighty arguments for the universal scope of God's grace. Later in the letter he urges his readers to practical Christian living upon this basis: "so we, though many, are one body in Christ, and individually members one of another." (Romans 12:5) This same figure, "the body of Christ," is used effectively in 1 Corinthians, Ephesians, and Colossians.

215

The Johannine literature of the New Testament stresses the importance of love as a quality of life in the believer. It is a love which binds him inevitably to his brother. It is a love which originates wholly in the love of God. This love is seen as personal in its particularity and universal in its comprehensiveness.

The impartiality of God's love, to be imitated among the brethren, is a matter both of controversy and of admonition in the life of the early church. Peter's experience with Cornelius, accompanied by the whole Judaizing debate, is recorded in Acts 10ff. and Galatians. The epistles not only of John but also of Paul call for love of the brethren as a response to God's love of each.

2. God's Continuing Action in and Through His People

STATEMENT OF THEME

God has established his church within the world and through its life he is active on behalf of man in fulfilling his righteous purposes. The Christian community has been and continues to be used of God and so its members find meaning, direction, and assurance for their corporate and individual lives in God's promise of his ultimate victory within history.

DESCRIPTION OF THEME

Being a part of the Christian community raises questions in the minds of participants about its beginnings. Christians are conscious of the significance of the church in their own experience, and this leads them to inquire, "How did the church come to be?" Man's search for a sense of ultimate purpose moving through human history is answered in his discovery of a historic perspective of the activity of God through the church.

Old Testament Antecedents of the Church

Investigation of the genesis of the church reveals that it is not a phenomenon originating in the first century without relatedness to any previous religious experience of man. On the contrary, the faith that God has called the church into being, that it is divine in its origin, leads naturally to investigation of "the chosen people" as a theme in the Old Testament.

The church finds meaning in a conviction that God has worked in and through a chosen people beginning with Abraham, and that it was in the subsequent "mighty acts of God" by which this people became a nation. The church may see foreshadowings of itself in the disciplines of the exile in which the "chosen people" became a "suffering servant." The church develops an awareness of the divine use of Assyria, Babylon, and Persia as the instruments of discipline just as the church today has been chastened by social forces. The church beholds Israel's saving remnant and is reminded of the rigors that attend earnest Christian commitment, together with the enrichment that the church has received because of those who have been "faithful unto death." The church listens to the denunciations of the prophets against that shallow religion which prides itself upon external displays and does not require inward righteousness. The church discovers in Jesus Christ the fulfillment of all that Israel anticipated—the "chosen one" through whom all men may become among "the chosen." Thus, the church continually finds a relatedness to the history of Israel as a "called community" through which God has acted within history.

The Church in the New Testament

The sense of the movement of God's purpose in history continues in a study of the New Testament church. Here, the church is seen as a creation of God and as the fulfillment of the divine intention. In the New Testament, the church centers in a person: Jesus Christ as Lord. The message which that early Christian community risked death to proclaim affirmed: "God was in Christ reconciling the world to himself." The New Testament church was convinced that it did not exist for itself alone; it was sure that it was called into being to fulfill a divine mission.

In the New Testament the church believes that God is with them. He has been with them in Jesus Christ, and now he is in their midst in the Holy Spirit. The works of God among them are done in the life and power of the Spirit of God. Since this is their faith, no power on earth can defeat them. They are the "called out" ones who are "called into" the service of God and into fellowship with one another. God's will ultimately must

217

triumph. Therefore, any defeat for the church is only temporary. Hardships, persecution, even threats of death are endurable, for God is the Lord of history and his church cannot be overcome.

The Church in History

As the church looks at its history through the ages, it senses the hand of the God who created it, leading it in accordance with his purposes. Key events of history include the following: early persecutions and conflicts; church councils and creeds; the formation of the biblical canon; worldly acceptance of the church; the Holy Roman Empire; conflict with Islam; East-West schism; the Crusades; the Renaissance; the Reformation and the Counter-Reformation; the Enlightenment, proliferation of denominations; concern about Christian education; the ecumenical movement; scientific terrors and the doctrine of eschatism. In all of these historical situations, God is seen as acting in and through his people to accomplish his purposes in the world. History displays not only the faithlessness of the church but instances of the church's rising to its mission with relevance.

God's Present Activity in his Church

The human longing to be sustained by meaningful relationship in a community which cherishes abiding values may achieve fulfillment in the church as it expresses its faith that God is still at work in human life. This conviction speaks to the question: What difference does the church make in the world? A view of history may reinforce the conviction that the God who has acted still acts.

God may be seen at work in *faith and personality*. The significance of redemption, the meaning of becoming recipients of God's great salvation through Jesus Christ, the purpose that comes to men through God's forgiveness and their repentance, man's conversion from lesser aims to the fulfillment of the will

218

of God—here may be seen the activity of God within human personality.

One may also consider God at work in *faith and learning*. The church believes that God is at work in the educational process whether within the institution of the church or in any other occasions of learning. These may serve to help persons be aware of God and his seeking love, leading them to respond to him in faith and love.

In the area of *faith and healing,* God is at work in his church through concern for the well-being of the total man, through development of hospitals, through the administration of medicine and the offering of psychotherapy, through the healing power of love expressed in lives first touched by divine love.

God is at work through *faith and world community*. Christians align themselves with the purposes of God as individually and corporately they work for the realization of justice and freedom in the world. The church in part fulfills its mission as it aids in the quest for an effective international body to lead the way to peace and understanding among all men. The movement in world missions toward the erasure of distinctions between "sending" and "receiving" churches reveals the divine intent finding realization within the worldwide church.

The Future of the Church   *219*

As man considers the life of the church in the past and in the contemporary world, he finds assurance that the God who has acted is acting and will continue to act. God will act as in the past to bring his judgment on the church when it departs from his ways and purposes; but also man may have confidence that when the church turns again to God in repentance and obedience, God will act to reform and transform the church. Man's fear of modern scientific terrors of annihilation are given perspective in light of the God whose purpose has been carried out in history through his dealings with his people Israel, through his Son, Jesus Christ, and through the church which is his body.

This Theme in the Bible

Rather than in occasional reference, the Bible in its entirety treats this theme as a central affirmation. The Pentateuch recounts the story of the calling of Abraham, the beginnings of the nation which emerged from his descendants, their deliverance from bondage through the hand of God, and their establishment in "the promised land." The historical books describe the fluctuations of Israel's faith and the persistent call of God which followed these "chosen people." The prophets seek for the refinement of Israel's faith and interpret God's call as one involving special responsibility.

In the Gospels, the New Testament church has not yet come into being. However, the nucleus of the church is in the disciples. Their faith in Jesus Christ is to become the foundation of the church. Jesus responds to Peter's great confession of faith by saying, "You are Peter, and on this rock I will build my church."

The Book of Acts provides the vital data on God's creation of the Christian community. It describes the small and devoted band of followers who gathered for prayer in the upper room in Jerusalem. It testifies to the power of the Holy Spirit poured out upon the church at Pentecost. It describes how under God's guidance and power the church branched out from its Judaistic roots into Gentile soil, penetrating even to the seat of imperial power at Rome. It witnesses the development of organized activity and the phenomenal growth of the Christian fellowship under God's blessing. Throughout the Book of Acts, the clear emphasis is upon the power of the Spirit of God working in and through the church to fulfill its mission in the world.

The letters of Paul unfailingly evidence his conviction that God had acted, was acting, and would continue to act in his church. To be sure, Paul was aware of the ethical problems in which the church was involved and the doctrinal misapprehensions that plagued it (witness the Corinthian epistles). But he was not dismayed because he was certain that the foundation of God stands sure.

In Ephesians, the church is pictured as the "bride of Christ," the "body of Christ," and the "temple of the Spirit." The classic Ephesian passage on the catholicity and unity of the church (4:1-16) also affirms the continuing activity of God in the church to carry out his will in the many members that make up the body. The ultimate triumph and eternal glory of the church is declared in Ephesians 2:1-10.

The Book of Revelation focuses its message upon the final consummation toward which the whole biblical message of redemption is directed. Beginning with messages to seven churches of Asia Minor, this apocalyptic literary work moves to the triumphs of God and his people over every enemy. The theme of conflict with evil and the ultimate victory of God in his church may be found repeatedly throughout the book.

3. The Church Permeating Society

STATEMENT OF THEME

Such biblical figures as salt, light, leaven suggest and point to the church's responsibility in and to society as it confronts, engages, and permeates all the social structures. The church carries out this responsibility both as a corporate body and through its individual members, who thus fulfill their need to relate significantly to social groupings and to act upon their Christian commitment in community with other Christians.

221

DESCRIPTION OF THEME

The Basis of the Church's Concern to Influence Culture

This theme speaks to the church's responsibility to the society in which it lives. It is associated with man's urge to identify himself with the larger social units within which he finds himself, his longing to find relatedness with his fellowmen. It speaks to man's need to feel himself a significant part of the community in which he lives.

Man naturally desires to influence the social order. This drive for self-expression may be rooted in a complex of motivations, but it is a general characteristic of all kinds of men. At best, a person will wish to influence society out of altruism, but often self-interest also is a dominant motive.

The church cannot live in isolation. This would be contrary to its very nature and would contradict its mission. As the church encounters the world, it finds its opportunity to witness to its faith. And the witness that it bears has within its objective the welfare of the social order in which the church exists.

The Hebrew concern for social justice was strongly reflected in the New Testament church. This tradition persists in the church to this day. There have been dark days in the history of the church when little social concern was evident. There have been other dismal periods when the church by dint of temporal power enforced its will upon society in autocratic fashion. But the church has risen to its greatest glories when it has become strongly involved in society, exerting a positive influence for transformation, cleansing itself of its sins, and through witness, in example, and in action has sought to bring a Christian perspective to the social order.

The Corporate Church and Society

The church is usually recognized as a "gathered community" of believers. There is much that the church in its "gatheredness" can do to challenge the world in which it lives. It can hold up the values of truth and justice. It can clearly denounce the evils which bring disruption and decay to men and their institutions. Too often, the church has been satisfied to address itself to individuals, and has not spoken out to society as a whole or to segments of the surrounding culture. But the gathered community that is the church must also speak to the business community (both management and labor), to the professional community, to the social community, to the political community challenging them to ethical practices and honorable conduct; urging them to consider whether their goals are worthy, their demands justified, and to consider the effect of their community decisions and actions upon the lives of others.

The gathered church speaks to the family, to government, to educators, and to every block of power and influence which must be reckoned with in the world. Its statements of conviction are most meaningful, however, when the expressed concerns of the church grow out of dialogue within itself. Pronouncements of church bodies upon social situations need the validity of consensus which grows out of rigorous investigation and soul-searching through open dialogue by both laymen and clergy. When the Christian community speaks, it should bear its witness with conviction.

The Dispersed Church and Society

It must be recognized, however, that the "gathered" church does not represent all of the life of the church. Indeed, the church is in dispersion far more than it is collected together. Therefore, a significant part of the church's task to permeate the social order is accomplished only in its existence as the "scattered" church. The gathered church reveals its validity only as it remains the church when scattered (dispersed) in the common life (experience) of its individual members. It follows that the church must infiltrate the social institutions which surround it. This infiltration takes place as individual Christians make their witness felt in every relationship of their lives. This is part of their ministry as disciples.

223

One obstruction to an effective church strategy to infiltrate society with Christian values is that the corporate church and its individual members are themselves in peril of becoming infiltrated by the values of the world. Rather than the church permeating the social order with Christian principles, the church often finds that its membership is being permeated with sub-

Christian standards, values, and goals. But this is an inevitable risk which the church must take and with which it must always struggle. As the gathered church stands in vital relationship to Jesus Christ, it is best able to challenge the scattered church to find its real mission in all of the relationships of daily life.

Corporate and Individual Action

Although the church as a community of faith has often sought to exert social pressure to bring about social reform, this method has not always achieved lasting results. Often, however, as the scattered church, individual Christians have suffered "for righteousness' sake," and the result has been significant social improvement. As Christians become willing to follow their servant Lord in vicarious suffering, a powerful witness is released and the world is influenced toward good rather than evil.

Thus the church as a corporate body may identify social concerns, lift them up for scrutiny by the entire fellowship, suggest possible courses of action, and point to what seem to be responsible Christian ways of dealing with the situation. Such procedures make it possible for individual Christians to enjoy the enrichment of experiences and information from other Christians not available to them as individuals. In the sharing of these insights, new understandings come together with new concepts of appropriate actions for Christians to take corporately and individually. Also, renewed alertness is developed by the church as it faces social issues in the normal routines of life.

This Theme in the Bible

The Old Testament records strong concern for social justice at many times in the history of the Hebrew nation. This concern was a characteristic of patriarchs such as Abraham and Joseph (Genesis 12—23; 37—50). Many of the laws recorded in Leviticus clearly forbid injustice and attempt to enforce right relationships among men. When the monarchy was established in Israel, even the king could be challenged for wrongs against society (e.g., Elijah facing Ahab, 1 Kings 21). Proverbs abounds in wisdom which upholds social as well as personal ethics. Some of the prophets are keenly discerning in their denunciations of national and personal sins of the men of Israel. This is especially true of the latter part of Isaiah and the prophecies of Jeremiah, Amos, and Micah.

In the New Testament the Sermon on the Mount (Matthew 5—7) gives support for the view that followers of Christ must be active in their witness to the world. The figures used here are especially pertinent. "You are the salt of the earth," indicates that Christ's followers are to season the world with righteousness. "You are the light of the world," indicates that the good works of Christian disciples enlighten society and honor the name of God. The penetrating power of the kingdom of heaven is illustrated in the parable of the leaven (Matthew 13:33).

In his ministry, Jesus spoke out against the abuse of religion which resulted in social injustice. His act in cleansing the temple demonstrated his holy judgment upon those who would profiteer from divine service and profane the worship of God. Jesus did not inveigh against the evils of totalitarian Rome or suggest specific ways to improve the social order. But in Jesus' teachings are the principles by which every social evil is judged and every worthy value for the good of man is elevated.

225

In the Book of Acts, the church is characterized by an all-consuming passion to proclaim the gospel. However, social concerns were not overlooked, as witness the provisions for widows and orphans. Paul's letters reveal his concern that pagan culture might penetrate the church rather than the witness of the church penetrate society. This, in part, had taken place at Corinth, and the letters written to this church were intended to correct this situation. Similar situations in other churches are also treated in the practical section of the Pauline epistles. Paul speaks directly of the church's participation in government in Romans

13 and his letter to Philemon illustrates the constraint to transform social institutions in which one is involved. See also 1 Peter 2:11ff.

The Epistle of James deals with many practical matters of ethical behavior. The church is challenged to take care in its speech, to avoid inconsistency of witness and of life, to avoid acquiring riches by underpaying one's workers. The pastoral epistles are directed to individual church leaders, but express similar social concerns for ethical behavior in the Christian community as an inherent part of the Christian faith and life.

4. Extending Reconciliation and Redemption

STATEMENT OF THEME

Brought into being by God's gracious redemption, the Christian community is a servant people of a servant Lord, to whom is committed the message of reconciliation between God and man and among men. This involvement gathers up man's need to give himself in loyalty and to make a significant contribution by his life.

DESCRIPTION OF THEME

This theme deals with the church's role in making known the reconciliation and redemption which men may have through Jesus Christ. The very heart of the message and work of the church is that God in Christ is reconciling men to himself and to each other, enabling them to live as children of God.

Men's Need for Reconciliation and Redemption

The persistent need of man for reconciliation is everywhere apparent. He suffers from estrangement (man-God relationship). He experiences hostility (man-man relationship). He tastes the bitterness of frustration (man-self relationship). Man's estrangement from God is related to his feeling of self-sufficiency and his idolatry of power, riches, and the pleasures of life. His hostility for his fellowmen is expressed through broken homes, criminal acts, racial and cultural prejudices, strife among economic groups, conflicts of nations. Man's inner frustrations are revealed in his evident unhappiness even in the midst of material bounty, in his neurotic tendencies and psychosomatic illnesses, and in his inability to find any measure of abiding contentment. Man finds that he is inadequate to come to terms with his estrangement, his hostilities, his frustrations. He needs help beyond himself to be extricated from his dilemma.

The God Who Reconciles

The church's faith is centered in a God of reconciling love. He has taken the initiative through Jesus Christ in reconciling the world to himself. This reconciliation has been costly. In the incarnation and the atonement, God reveals himself as the God of suffering love. By his redemptive acts, God is at work to remove estrangement, break down hostility, and erase frustration.

The Church Reconciling and Being Reconciled

The church is called to respond in faith and love in view of what God has done for men in Jesus Christ. This call speaks to man's need to be reconciled, but also this relates to man's need to become a reconciler. As a part of the servant people who follow their servant Lord, persons may sense that they make contributions to life that have continuing significance.

227

The church does not see itself as redeemer. Rather it is the agent and instrument of the redemption which only its Lord can impart. It can make no valid claim to virtue. It has not achieved reconciliation and redemption through any effort of its own. The church constantly stands under the judgment of its Lord and is first the object of reconciliation before it may become agent of reconciliation. Only as the church is being redeemed can it offer to the world the redemption which it is receiving in Christ.

The Church as Servant

The church seeks to discover the meaning of servanthood in its nature as a reconciled fellowship. Even as Jesus Christ came into the world to minister, so the church exists to serve, to wash feet, to engage in the humble task. The church follows the example of its servant Lord out of concern for the needs of men (rather than the projection of a benevolent "image" for public-relations purposes). This will mean that the congregation will suit its ministry to meet the needs of the persons for whom it is responsible whether in the inner city, in the suburbs, or in rural areas. It may involve the church's stand for international peace during times of war hysteria. It may require that the church will take the unpopular side of a burning social issue because it sees its role as an agent of ministry, not as a recipient of the ministry of others.

Bearing the Cross

The church extends reconciliation and redemption as it takes up its own cross and follows its Lord. It does this voluntarily, not out of a neurotic compulsion to endure suffering. This is not the same kind of suffering which the church endures justly as the result of its own sins and wrongs. It is only as the church is willing to bear undeserved suffering (see 1 Peter) that it takes up its cross in discipleship to follow the example of Jesus Christ. This is far different from the insignificant self-denials that many Christians regard as real sacrifices. The true spirit of Christ demands a willingness to give all for others, to extend one's self, hazarding one's very life for the sake of others.

Identification with the World

If the church is to be effective in its ministry of reconciliation and redemption in the world, it must identify itself with the world. It feels the pain, the anxiety, the despair which the world experiences. It travels the same paths that other men walk. It knows what men in general are feeling. It is not unaware of the temptations that daily confront persons in all walks of life. Rather than remaining aloof and unrelated to the hard problems of everyday life, the church is fulfilling its mission in redemptively sharing the human struggle and in creatively communicating the message of reconciliation by word and deed. When the church is most aware of its need of redemption, it may become most effective as an instrument of redemption.

The church is that segment of the world which recognizes the redeeming work of God in Christ and accepts the gift of costly grace and lives in the world in obedience to its Lord. The church remains in the world, yet refuses to give dominance to the lesser loyalties of the world. It is in this environment that the church, created in the redeeming work of God, pours forth its life in reconciling men to God. This is strategically related to the mission of the church in the world, for, as the church thus identifies itself with the world in its need, the church is also able to introduce the divine dimension of God's love into human experience.

The Church as Example of Reconciliation

The church in its work of extending reconciliation and redemption to the world is called to demonstrate this reconciliation within its own being. This involves its structures, its treatment of persons, its official pronouncements and its unofficial attitudes, its programs of activity, and its methods of operation. The church which lifts up the ethic of love among all men is disloyal to its mission when hostility characterizes attitudes within its own structures. In the Johannine epistles, the position is taken that hatred for one's brothers contradicts any profession of one's love for God.

The gospel impinges on the basic aggressive drives of man who exists in a tension between the urge to express his hostility and the desire to become reconciled to others. The love of God working through the life of his church overcomes the hostility and enables Christians to live as the children of God. The church is called upon to exhibit forgiveness not only within its

229

own being, but also toward parts of the world itself which often sin grievously against the church. Thus God's redemption is manifest in human relationship.

The God-Man Encounter

In extending reconciliation and redemption, the church helps prepare the way for an encounter between God and man. It cannot create the God-man encounter, but the church has a role in leading men to readiness for this encounter to take place. This is the evangelistic responsibility of the church. It summons men to respond to God in faith and love in light of what he has done for them in Jesus Christ.

The proclamation of the gospel through preaching and teaching centers in the redeeming love of God as revealed in Jesus Christ reconciling the world to himself. Thus, through the church, men are made aware of the gospel and are prepared for encounter with the God who has created them and is now seeking them.

The Body of Christ

The church is called to be the body of Christ, revealing to the world the spirit of its Lord. As Jesus Christ brought reconciliation into the world in his life on earth, so the church becomes an instrument of reconciliation. The church as the body of Christ in this sense becomes an extension of the incarnation into the history of the world, manifesting its Lord's spirit of concern and willingness to give up life. Since the term "body" denotes a unity and an interrelatedness, it may be assumed that the church most effectively extends the reconciliation and redemption of God when it is united in the spirit of love and dedication.

This Theme in the Bible

The Old Testament antecedents of the church in the Judaistic tradition make reference to the work of atonement as a reconciliation between God and man (see Leviticus). The law also seems to make clear that a part of its objective is the reconciliation of men to one another. In fact the nature of the relationship God established with his people through Abraham and Moses, and to which he repeatedly recalled them was a relationship not only of blessing to them, but of mission to extend that blessing to all men (Genesis 12, 26, 28). Several of the Psalms reflect the necessary outreach by his people (Psalms 22, 67, 72, 96). Isaiah and Jeremiah reminded the people of God—not only of their blessing but also of their obligation to extend God's reconciling offer.

The "suffering servant" idea of Isaiah is especially relevant to this role of the church. Jonah illustrates the burden on God's people to extend God's offer of redemption beyond Israel.

The total thrust of Jesus' earthly mission has to do with the work of redemption, therefore, the Four Gospels provide significant background for this theme as they treat the teachings and the works of Jesus Christ. The Book of Acts records the continual witness of the early church to the redemption in Christ. Many of the New Testament letters are appropriate to the theme, particularly Romans, Ephesians, and Colossians. The Book of Revelation indicates the final triumph of God and his church in the redemption of man.

231

5. The Church Lives by Worship

STATEMENT OF THEME

Adoration, praise, thanksgiving, confession, acceptance of pardon, reexamination of life in all its relationships, dedication in obedience to God's will sustain, nurture, and inspire the church in its life of love and service. The Christian community renews its faith and life in Christ and finds strength and help for every need through corporate and individual worship including the sacraments.

DESCRIPTION OF THEME

One of the basic characteristics of the Christian church is its worship. The New Testament bears clear witness to the fact that worship was the center of life in the ancient church. To be sure, there are many forms of worship which may vary widely from one another. But the fact remains that wherever there is a church, there is some kind of worship that is at the heart of its life.

Man is concerned about worship because he is concerned about the ultimate. In worship he may develop a sense of awe, a feeling of dependence, a reverence in the presence of the *mysterium tremendum*. Men of all religions seem to be seeking to become related to an object of worship to which they turn in praise and adoration and from which they seek forgiveness, cleansing, guidance, and approval. Worship is a way by which man may assert his faith in an absolute and confess his own finitude.

However significant may be some of the persistent life concerns of men relating to worship, the focus is not upon man. In worship the primary theme is the glory of God rather than the edification of man.

God Is Central in Worship

The fact of God is the basis for all Christian worship. Worship may include elements of aesthetic appeal, instruction, and plans for action; but it is more than these. Only the centrality of God can make for true worship. The nature of Christian worship is determined by the nature of the God who is worshiped. This God has revealed himself through Jesus Christ as the God of suffering love who graciously redeems sinful men. Thus Christian worship becomes much more than something man does for his God. Rather it is the response man makes to the God who has already acted in mercy and grace toward him.

In much modern worship, a great deal is made of what happens to the worshiper. The focus is upon what "inspires" or "lifts up" man and upon methods of heightening the emotions. But worship cannot become a device to manipulate divine things in order to evoke the intended reaction from man. This makes man, not God, the center of worship. The objective for worship is the glory of God, not the delight of man.

Thus worship is considered at the heart of the Christian's life. It is not a means for religious entertainment, or even for a better social order. Worship is an end in itself; it is not to be used for the purpose of achieving certain personal benefits or to turn persons in upon themselves. Man worships in order to acknowledge God to be God and himself as under his lordship; he worships in order to offer himself as an instrument of God's justice and peace. In the life of the church and of every member of the Christian community, worship has a place that is central and inalienable.

The Church Worships Corporately

The church is often called "a worshiping community." At worship the church experiences its deepest and most basic level of existence as a Christian community. Christian worship is essentially corporate. A worshiping congregation is not a collection of individuals praying individually as best they can. There is a wholeness of the group of worshipers that makes it a community.

233

The corporate nature of the church in worship does not cancel out the fact that religion is also intensely personal. The encounter which man has with God takes place within the very essence of his personal being. But it is also true that to be reconciled to God in Christ inevitably brings one into relationship with persons in the household of faith. Corporate worship brings the family of God together in the presence of God to worship him. In such gathering of the body of Christ, individual believers may come to realize their oneness as the people of God. To be in Christ is to be in Christ's body, which is the church. One cannot at the same time fail to worship with the people of God and profess with integrity that he is a Christian. One of the earliest descriptions of the church is its enduring characteristic through the centuries: "All who believed were together" (Acts 2:44).

The corporate experience of the church in worship is one in which all Christians are to participate. The priesthood of all believers does not mean that all believers have identical tasks. It does mean that there is an essential equality of believers in responsibility to serve God. Implications for this in worship of the church point to active participation by each church member in all of the corporate worship expressions of the church in which he is involved. The modern proclivity toward becoming a passive spectator is inappropriate to corporate worship. When the experience is genuine, all of the congregation is involved in meaningful worship of God.

God's Initiative in Worship

In the Protestant tradition, worship centers in the preaching of the word of God and the sacraments. These are not to be understood as the works of man, but rather as the mighty acts of God. God has taken the initiative in the life of man, and worship must communicate this priority. The word of God is the act of God in revealing himself, in giving himself to man. This has supremely taken place in Jesus Christ. True worship, therefore, faces man with God's act in Jesus Christ and elicits a response upon the part of man. The word of God and the sacraments thus become those "means of grace" which help create and sustain the church of God on earth.

Within the church the Bible has had a particular role in the communication of God's word to man, both in preaching and teaching. The New Testament contains the record of what the early church proclaimed about Jesus Christ. Therefore, the Bible is recognized as the prior authority concerning the nature of the word of God. This is not an externally imposed authority. Rather it is intrinsic and self-authenticating. Since the Bible has been found effective in confronting men with the redemptive acts of

God, it has become a fundamental part of the church's worship. It is to be read, preached and taught, for through it God speaks to man. The proclamation of God's acts may also take place as the church lives through events in the life of Christ, such as in the Christian year.

The sacraments are also regarded as "means of grace," through which the church and its members become partakers of God's agape in Christ. Both baptism and the Lord's Supper dramatize the word of God. The redemptive work of God through which man becomes a member of Christ and of one another is proclaimed in baptism. This is the confirmation of the believer's participation in the household of faith. Rather than merely a "dedication" on man's part, baptism is a proclamation that God has acted in man's redemption. Man is baptized into the corporate life of the church so that he prays and works toward the reconciliation of all men with God and with one another. Baptism enlists him with other believers under the banner of God.

In the Lord's Supper, the attention of the worshiper is focused on the suffering love of Christ offered for redemption. Here Christ fulfills his promise to meet his church in the bread and wine of the Holy Supper, taking them into communion with himself so that they may share in the salvation that he offers. This is the visible act which speaks continually of God's self-giving love and the final triumph of his kingdom.

235

Man's Response in Worship

In the word of God coming through preaching, the reading of the Bible, and the ministering of the sacraments, God confronts man and offers himself to man in grace and love. In all of this, God has acted and acts. He has taken the initiative. But worship also involves the response of man. This response is made in light of the majesty, holiness, fatherhood, and redemptive love of God.

The individual and the church at worship respond to God

through prayer. Prayers may be in the form of praise to God, adoration of God, thanksgiving to God, confession of sins to God, or renewal of vows to God. These are all responses common to the worship expression of the Christian community and of its individual members. Prayer may also take the form of intercession for those within and without the Christian community as well as petitions for blessings from God. Worship sounds profound depths when it evokes joyful response to God through the medium of prayer.

236

The church at worship sits at once under the judgment and mercy of God. It cannot evade responding to God through decision. As the revelation of God's activity and purpose unfolds, persons must choose the ways of life that they will follow. The worshiping spirit is an obedient spirit. In a sense, the church in worship offers itself to God in penitence and in praise seeking to find God's will for its life now and in the days to come, to renew its commitment to live in obedience to God and in fulfillment of his purpose.

Service is also a part of worship. The Greek word *leitourgia,* from which our word "liturgy" comes, is derived from words which mean "public work." In the New Testament the word is translated "service." This suggests that worship, the liturgical experience of the church, must issue in service to men. Surely the offering of material gifts to God, which is a part of most services of worship, is appropriate to the occasion to which it is related. But the worship of the church in public work continues after the last prayers have been uttered. The church as a scattered community of God is under obligation to make its continuing response of love to God manifest through its service to God and men. If the church is to be saved from being irrelevant, it must activate the relationship between liturgy and life.

This Theme in the Bible

In the worship of the Hebrews, acts of the ceremonials were engaged in by the worshipers as a response to what God had already done for them. This contrasted with the pagan practices which were designed to gain divine favor. Such approaches prepare the way for the New Testament emphasis upon worship as the response to the mighty acts of God in Christ. The development of worship practices of the Hebrew nation held central the purpose of worship. (See Leviticus, and also the kinds of worship led by David and by Solomon in 1 and 2 Samuel.) Repeatedly the prophets attempted to reform rituals of worship and interpret them against a holy life among God's people. (See Micah 6; Isaiah 1; Hosea 2; Amos 5.)

Many of the Psalms provide an illuminating background for the worship of the church. To this day, many of these are used as hymns of praise and petition. The Sermon on the Mount (Matthew 5, 6, and 7) gives Jesus' teaching concerning the essence of true religion, including its outer expression in worship. His rebukes toward the temple worship of the Pharisees are relevant to the Christian's worship. Other significant passages relating to worship may be found in Luke 4, 11, 18, 20, 22; and in John 4 and 17.

The worship of the early church is described in this fashion: "they devoted themselves to the apostles' teaching and fellowship, to the breaking of bread and the prayers" (Acts 2:42). Other passages refer to confession and singing of hymns. Thus the content of worship in the early church seems to have centered in the gospel, in the apostolic proclamation (see the sermons in Acts), and in the Lord's Supper, accompanied by hymns of praise, prayer, and confession.

Almost all of the New Testament letters are helpful in describing something of the nature of worship in the church. Of particular relevance are the Corinthian and Ephesian letters and 1 Timothy. The Revelation of John makes numerous references to the worship of God by his people in the final consummation of the age.

237

6. The Christian Community Mobilizing for Mission

STATEMENT OF THEME

In order to carry out its mission in the world, the church under the leading of the Holy Spirit calls up its people, organizes its life, plans its work, and finds appropriate means. In this mobilization, the Christian discovers orderly and corporate channels of expression for the deepest concerns and convictions of his life.

DESCRIPTION OF THEME

238

Wherever man has lived in groups, he has developed some kinds of social frameworks within which to live. Even the most primitive societies have their taboos and their hierarchal systems. Seemingly, one of the universal urges of man is to live within some kind of organizational social pattern which he can understand and accept for his own. It is not strange then that the Christian church has developed operational procedures and structures to carry on its work. The church has sought to attain its goals through the development of orderly and corporate channels of expression.

The Church's Mission Demands Organization

The church has a mission in the world. The church finds that bound up in this mission are some of the profoundest areas of its beliefs. These have to do with God, his redemption in Christ, the purpose of God's creative work, and other concerns basic to the Christian faith. The church is under the orders of its Lord to proclaim the gospel in the world. It is charged to communicate the good news of God to all men everywhere. This task cannot be attempted by any disorganized approach. It demands the best skills that the church can devote to it. It requires the best strategies that the church can devise.

The church must function in the world of time and space. It must employ earthly means to accomplish spiritual ends. As the body of Christ, it is the incarnate instrument through which his spirit may now be evidenced to the world. Thus this theme must deal with the institutional aspect of the church as it seeks to create the necessary earthly structures through which the spiritual ministries of the church may be channeled.

Mission is not just one more of many concerns to be assigned to some board of the church for implementation. It is the total church in action. "The church exists by mission as the fire exists by burning." Without mission, it has no excuse for existence. This is the people of God expressing God's loving concern for all men everywhere, calling all men also to become a part of the people of God. In order to carry out effectively such a mission, the church must organize its life and work for that purpose.

The mission of the church requires *proclamation*. How is the gospel to be declared, by whom, to whom, with what preparation, and in what manner? The church's mission implies *education*. What educational forms does the church provide, for whom, led by what persons, organized upon what principles? To fulfill its mission, the church is involved in *communication*. What media of communication are to be used, by whom, in what manner, with what preparation, and for what purpose? The mission of the church leads to *acts of service*. What decision-making groups in society should be identified and worked with in order that basic needs of persons might be met and God's intention for the world more readily achieved? How should the church work with and influence these groups without being accused of ecclesiastical aspirations of domination, and what other ministries of service of a more personal nature should be provided through the church's structure for persons in immediate need? All of the foregoing concerns, and more, are involved in the mission of the church. It is clear that patterns, plans, structures, institutions, and organizations are necessary to the church in fulfilling its mission in the world.

239

Forms of Church Organization

The church has carried out its mission on earth under many different kinds of organization. Jesus left no pattern for his disciples to use, and the New Testament provides no detailed code of regulations which govern the church. There are some general principles, however, which are found in the New Testament church. Jesus Christ is the supreme authority and all church government is exercised in his name and in his spirit. This means that the humility of Jesus is the pattern for those who minister in his name. The highest earthly authority centers in church councils rather than in an exalted leader. Ruling the church is closely associated with teaching in the church. Some of the believers are assigned to administrative responsibilities to assist those whose main task is the proclamation of the gospel.

There are three general classifications of church government. One is the *episcopal* type of organization. In this, bishops (*episkopoi*) become the overseers of the church who are the guardians of its tradition and the supervisors of its work. A second category is the *presbyterial (presbuteros)* form of organization. In this, authority is vested in elders (laymen and ministers) who are chosen by the congregation. The third type of church government is *congregational (ecclesia)*. In this system, authority does not lie in the bishops or in the elders, but rather directly in the local congregation. Each congregation is autonomous.

Each of these systems of government has its strengths; each has its problems. From a historical perspective, it may be said that the church has carried on its mission under all of these forms of government and under combinations of them. The Holy Spirit has blessed and empowered the people of God to make their witness known through many kinds of structures. The church is in the world to serve the purposes of its Lord. Therefore, it needs to be flexible enough to use whatever form may best serve the mission to which it has been called. It must not seek to imprison God's Spirit within a rigid man-made mold, but rather permit that same Spirit to re-create the church after that pattern which will cause the work of God to progress best in each locale and during each period of history. The forms of church government always stand under the judgment of Christ.

They are under his rule as the Lord of the church, and they must serve his purposes or stand condemned.

Mobilization of Manpower

One of the responsibilities of church polity is to organize the life of the church for the mobilization of the manpower within the church. This means that the church will strive for maximum effectiveness in the development of its members' skills which can be used in the accomplishment of the church's mission. It also means the wise deployment of forces in strategic ways to carry on the church's ministry. In realizing this, the church will at times lay aside programs and institutions of long standing which have become almost sacrosanct in the eyes of many persons. The leaders of the church must be prepared to endure the criticism of those who are shortsighted enough to mistake the form of church activity for the life of the church itself. They must also dare to use the church's manpower in new ways which are created by new circumstances and opportunities which present themselves in the surrounding culture.

In fulfilling its ministry the church is dependent upon all of those within it. Within the body itself each one is to make his contribution to its growth and in its service. In life within society each one is responsible for witness, service, and mission in the name and spirit of Christ. Therefore, in the effective use of its manpower, the church will take seriously the biblical doctrine of the priesthood of believers and will help each member recognize opportunities of effective service. The concept of the priesthood of believers involves both the right of each individual to appropriate directly the message of the forgiveness of sin as proclaimed in the gospel and his responsibility to witness to others of the availability for them of the salvation he has received. Every part of the body of Christ has its distinctive function, and every Christian has his responsible work in the life of the church of Christ. The discovery of what this work may be for each member is a task which should be of major concern to the church.

241

Its organization must provide a framework in which maximum participation in the mission of the church in the world is encouraged in the life of each member.

Mobilization of Material Resources

In its institutional aspect, the church like every other organization is involved in financial concerns. It exists in the world and therefore in carrying out its work it must pay for products and services which it finds necessary to employ. It obtains property for uses related to its mission, and it experiences expenses in maintaining that property for its intended purposes. When it calls persons into church-related occupations, it must provide adequate financial support for life, and their ministry.

The specific manner of support for the church may vary widely according to different situations, customs, and times. However, universally the church has expected its members to offer it material support in one fashion or another. The Hebrews gave their tithes and offerings. In the beginning the Christians in Jerusalem were described as holding all things in common. They felt a deep responsibility for the care of all members of the believing community. (Acts 2:44) At other times the church was urged to "put something aside" (1 Corinthians 16:2) each week for an offering. The usual emphasis has now become to ask members to give voluntarily to the church and to give proportionately, according to their ability.

In its handling of material resources, the church is concerned to emphasize that all the gifts of life come from God. What is devoted to the church and its mission is not a "payment" to God for his blessings. Rather it is the free response of a child of God who gives in the recognition that all he has has come from God, belongs to God, and, however used by him, is devoted to the service of God.

As the material possessions of the church grow and its involvements in financial matters increase, there are subtle temptations that the church must face. The General Board of the National Council of Churches recently stated:

The churches themselves own property, invest funds, and employ labor. Often their policies have been no better than those which the church condemns in the secular world. Its divisions often reflect and seem to give a religious sanction to the social divisions that are characteristic of society at large. In all these matters judgment should "begin at the house of God."

This places serious responsibility upon the church in its mobilization and utilization of material resources to act in accordance with the principles which lie at the very heart of its redemptive mission in the world.

Renewal of Structures

The structures of the church are always under the judgment of God. These exist so that orderly procedures and appropriate institutions may be provided for the work of God to take place. There is always danger that the church may lose sight of the original purpose of structures and institutions and allow them to become ends in themselves. When this takes place, structures tend to circumscribe rather than further the Christian mission. History has demonstrated that God has at times set aside the approved channels of the institutional church and has accomplished his purposes by other means.

243

Such events constitute a warning to the church that it must ever reexamine how it attempts to do the work of God. Earnest study of the church's organizational patterns may from time to time lead to a renewal of structures, a redesigning of methods, a conversion of institutions. The church must always be concerned to provide a framework in which maximum growth, guidance in the life of the Spirit, and the fulfillment of Christian discipleship may take place in the lives of all who are a part of the church. It must also be concerned to provide the best possible means by which it may fulfill Christ's purpose for it in the world.

This Theme in the Bible

The roots of the church's necessity to organize for its mission are seen in Moses' organizing the children of Israel. The later elaboration of the duties of priests, Levites, and scribes can be traced through the historical books of the Old Testament.

244

The Gospels record something of the organization of the Twelve during the earthly life of Jesus. He chose them to be with him and later appointed them to be his witnesses. The Gospels indicate that some of them assumed special responsibilities. The Book of Acts tells of the primitive kinds of structures which began to be developed in the early church; appointment of seven assistants to the apostles to administer the church's charity (6:1-6); the setting apart of Paul and Barnabas to be sent as missionaries; the appointment of elders on Paul's missionary journeys (Acts 14:21-23); the Jerusalem Conference (Acts 15); Paul's meeting with elders at Miletus (20:17-38).

In the New Testament epistles, organization seems to have developed even further. References are made to various functions in the church including elders, pastors, prophets, evangelists, teachers, bishops, and others with special responsibilities. The Corinthian and Ephesian epistles make reference to various roles which persons assumed in the church according to their gifts. They and the letters to the Thessalonians also make several references to the church's obligation to provide financial support for the ministry of the church. The pastoral epistles in particular give insight into some of the specific functions within the early church. However, it must be admitted that the New Testament does not carry explicit and detailed information concerning church organization, and it would appear that the forms of church government may have varied somewhat from place to place.

7. Preparing and Equipping for Ministry

STATEMENT OF THEME

In order to fulfill its mission, the Christian community provides its members training, guidance, admonition, support. As they accept the significance of their personal involvement in the body of Christ and of their mission, they find that their ministries are enriched, informed, and empowered by the Holy Spirit.

DESCRIPTION OF THEME

This theme speaks to the need of man to grow, to continue to develop in his understandings and his skills. It relates to man's need to belong meaningfully to a community in which he is challenged to develop his capacities to the full and to use them in service to others in such a way that shall give his life dimensions of significance before unrealized. In the context of the Christian community this involves the development of the potential Christian faith, life, and service of each church member so that he can participate fully and meaningfully in the ministry of the church.

Christian Nurture and the Church's Mission

The church is concerned to teach, both to enrich the lives of its members and ultimately to equip them to carry on their ministry in the world. The church's teaching must be biblical, treating the revelation of God and his acts among men as found in the Holy Scriptures. The church's teaching must be theological, dealing with the meanings of things having to do with God, man, and the natural order. The church's teaching must be historical, investigating the course of human events and trying to discover their significance. The church's teaching must be practical, embracing various methods in the church's expression of its witness.

In addition, such disciplines as the humanities and the sciences will have their influence upon the teaching of the church. Not only will the Christian community derive perspective from these

245

disciplines but in its ministry of nurture will give perspective to those who work in these fields. In attempting to extend the rule of God over the whole life of man, all of the probings of the mind of man may be viewed in light of the gospel as a legitimate part of the continuing educational concern of the church. Thus learning tasks in the Christian community reflect the concerns of the church with human experience in the whole field of relationships.

Learning takes place best within the church when the church experiences true *koinonia*. The person is not exploited, rather he is welcomed sincerely, offered security and fulfillment, and given that acceptance in Christian love that helps him to become a participant in the fellowship, not just a spectator. Small groups lend themselves effectively for such kinds of creative encounters among persons, but the technique alone is insufficient. The small group must be in the truest sense the church, offering *koinonia* as the redemptive community of God.

Equipping the Laity for Ministry

Every member of the church has a responsible place in the total ministry of the church. It is foreign to the biblical emphasis to consider the church as having active and passive sections. All persons who have responded to the call to become a part of the family of God have thereby assumed the privileges and obligations of ministry. Some Christians feel that the laity has an insignificant place in the life of the church. Witness the disclaimer: "I'm only a layman." Such a feeling contradicts the New Testament emphasis where the word *laïkos,* from which "layman" is derived, is used to refer to the "people of God." Manifestly, no higher privilege than this is possible to any man. In this sense, the clergy are honored to be called "laymen," for they too are a part of the "people of God."

In the United States the laity has played a vital role in church history. Indeed, Christian education, missions, and the very planting of the church in American can be attributed to the

246

efforts of devoted laymen. Every Christian is a minister of Christ and in the priesthood of believers is responsible to render that ministry faithfully on behalf of his Lord. Whenever the church has lost sight of the ministry which is the birthright of every Christian, it has become subject to the danger of bureaucracy in its structures. If the church would fulfill its mission, every member will accept his responsibility as a minister of Christ and will participate in such training and guidance as the church can offer him in effectively carrying on his work of ministry.

If the church would prepare itself for its ministry in the world, it should place primary emphasis upon exploration and discovery by laymen of what is meant by the church's mission. The church will be concerned to impart to its members vital insight into the significance of that mission and their personal involvement in it. Laymen must come to realize more realistically that their church schools or study groups are not just "meetings to attend." These and other church programs are seen as occasions for development as literate Christians and therefore are opportunities to become better skilled as communicators of the gospel. It is this latter objective which is too often forgotten or overlooked. All of the enrichment of the individual Christian's experience in the "gathered" community is not merely for his personal edification. More properly, this is for his increased efficiency as a witness—as a minister of Jesus Christ to his family, his friends, his associates, his community, and his world.

247

In light of this, the church provides a context for continued evaluation and restudy of individual and group ministries, providing opportunities for the development of skills of evaluation. It offers a community of faith in which each member may develop as a minister of Christ. It becomes the supportive family of God, assisting each person to carry on his ministry in the world. It develops the necessary curriculum, offers the essential training experiences, and provides standards of evaluation—all for the purpose of helping all of its members to carry out their responsibilities in the mission of the church on earth.

The Role of the Clergy

The question naturally arises: if all members of the church are to be ministers, what is the particular responsibility of the clergy? One of the prominent biblical figures is that of the shepherd. A clergyman is to be seen as charged with a shepherd office. The authority of his office is not an authority of itself. Its authority is in the Lord of the church, and its wisdom is in his word. The clergyman is a servant of the "means of grace." His distinctive role is to take initiative in preparing and equipping the congregation for its ministry.

The clergy is charged with responsibility to help all members see their obligation and fulfill it as effective ministers of Christ. The clergy realizes that only when the church in dispersion understands itself to be as fully the church as it is in the Sunday worship service can this ministry to the world be accomplished. Therefore, the pastor bends his efforts toward helping the congregation understand the purpose for the church in the world.

The clergyman's office is fulfilled through preaching, evangelizing, teaching, counseling, helping persons in times of crisis and distress, administering the sacraments, and leading in worship.

The Power of the Holy Spirit

In the experience of the early church, the basic preparation and equipping of the church for its ministry came through the empowering of the Holy Spirit. The church today can become effective in its witness only through the same source of spiritual power. As men are possessed by the Spirit of God, the compassion of Christ is manifest through them. The ministry of the church is not of itself or for itself. It is of God, and it is for the glory of God. Under the leadership of the Holy Spirit, the church seeks to provide training, guidance, and admonition for all of its members so that they may be fully fitted for the ministry which has been committed to them.

This Theme in the Bible

The biblical concept of the church is one that involves the vital participation of all members in the ministry of the church. There is never any division into "active" and "inactive" members. Jesus sent out all of his disciples to proclaim the kingdom of God. Perhaps his poignant charge to Peter to "feed my flock" can be interpreted as the awareness he had of the utter necessity for continued guidance and nurture. Certainly his promise of the Holy Spirit (John 16) evidences his concern for his disciples to continue to grow in understanding and power for their calling. In the Book of Acts, the early church is seen as a witnessing community in which every member was expected to be equally responsible.

The New Testament letters call for the churches to respond to God's love by showing forth this holy love in their own relationships among men. In Romans 12, and again in 1 Corinthians 12 —14, Paul uses the figure of the body to convey the significance of the many members of the church with various gifts and functions, but all one and all ministering in Christ's name. A similar emphasis is found in Ephesians where it is stated that gifts of leadership are granted to some in the church "for the equipment of the saints for the gift of ministry" (4:1-16). This epistle also reminds the church that the equipping of the saints is the work of the Holy Spirit. Philippians stresses the joy of service, calling for the church to "shine as lights in the world." In Colossians, Paul speaks of becoming a minister for the church, the body of Christ, as well as his concern that they guard against becoming "prey . . . to empty deceit" (See Chapters 2, 3).

249

The pastoral epistles have numerous exhortations to the readers to make full proof of the ministry to which God has called them. The letters addressed to Timothy in particular contain specific references to responsibilities of several church officials. The "train the trainers" technique is found in this: "What you have heard from me before many witnesses entrust to faithful men who will be able to teach others also." (2 Timothy 2:2) The Epistles of Peter are concerned to enjoin, "Tend the flock of God," in the contemporary times of persecution. First John is well known as "the epistle of love," calling for the ministry of love as the supreme evidence of the church's redemptive relation to God.

250

PART III

Source for Teaching-Learning Opportunities

The Function of Part III in the Curriculum Plan

Part III of the Curriculum Plan functions as a primary source to be used by denominational bodies in the development of teaching-learning opportunities for the curriculum for the educational ministry of the church. It is not a description of specific teaching-learning units for particular groups or settings. Rather, this Part relates Objective, Scope, and Learning Tasks to one another according to the Organizing Principle and takes account of the capacities, motivations, needs of the learner at successive stages in his life, in terms of effective modes for communicating meanings and experiences.

Part III is built upon and reflects the understandings and interpretations which are set forth in the preceding Parts of the Curriculum Plan. Part I consists of a comprehensive description of the Curriculum Design and an analysis of each of its five basic components—Objective, Scope, Context, Learning Tasks, and the Organizing Principle. In Part II, the Scope of the Curriculum Design is analyzed in terms of the five curriculum areas which in turn are further explicated by themes.

253

The Organization of Part III

In Part III every theme is treated at each of four life periods so as to make clear the significance of the theme for the person, the way in which the theme may be communicated, and what learnings within the theme may result from a person's engaging in the learning tasks. Four life periods have been selected in recognition of the graduated levels of communication which are possible across the life span. Early childhood refers to preschool children. Elementary years are inclusive of those in elementary school or roughly between the ages of six and twelve years. Youth includes young people through senior high school. All those beyond senior high school or senior-high-school age are considered in the adult life period in this Curriculum Plan. Because this Curriculum Plan is concerned with the entire life-span and the unity of content, Part III is organized so as to display the life-span dimension of each theme.

254

A theme treatment provides an analysis consisting of three major sections for each of the four life periods. Such a framework makes clear the interrelation of the components of the Design within each theme with reference to the learner, thereby forming the basis for teaching-learning units or opportunities.

For each life period the first section sets forth the significance of the theme for the learner by identifying those meanings and experiences within the theme (a selected part of Scope) which are relevant for him during the particular life period. The second section shows how these meanings and experiences may be communicated as the learner engages in the learning tasks. The third section points to the Objective by identifying the range of learnings which may result from the learner's involvement in the theme. Thus the three sections show the result of relating Objective, Scope, and Learning Tasks with reference to the learner and in accordance with the Organizing Principle.

A word about the relation of Context, the remaining component of the Design, to Part III is appropriate. The Design affirms the importance of the Context to the educational ministry. (See page 23.) The Context, Christian community, is a quality that resides among persons in live situations; and the stage at which Context makes its contribution to education is the operational stage, that is, in the local situation as curriculum comes alive and learning is engaged in by specific people. Context, therefore, cannot be written into this part of the Curriculum Plan. Its influence, however, is a factor in Part

III, in the description of modes and procedures of communication. The Context, Christian community, is characteristically the facilitator of communication in the Christian faith. Context and how it is pertinent to teaching-learning experience is further dealt with in the Afterword, "Using this Curriculum Plan to Derive Teaching-Learning Units."

The Structure of Theme Treatments

It will be helpful to look more closely at a description of each of the three sections of the theme treatment, noting their nature and function in this Curriculum Plan.

The first section of a theme treatment for each life period identifies the meanings and experiences within that theme which have particular relevance for the learner at that period of life. This section has two dimensions in order that the meanings and experiences (or content) of the theme and the readiness of the learner for the theme, might be seen apart from one another yet in relation to one another.

The first part (1-a) of section one identifies those specific meanings within the theme which may be experienced by the learner. These find their source in the gospel and the Christian faith. This is not to say that the gospel is seen in a segmented manner and that only what is identified in 1-a is significant for the learner. Rather, it is to say that the whole gospel is relevant at every stage of life and within this theme there are certain great concerns of the Christian faith which have heightened significance and relevance for the learner at his particular stage of development.

The other part of the first section (1-b) focuses on the readiness of the learner. This has its source in the Christian view of man and the understandings about man which have come from the humanities and the social sciences. Here are identified those factors within the learner which suggest his readiness to enter

255

into the meanings and experiences within the theme through the learning situation.

Readiness involves motivation, interests, capacities, basic needs and developmental tasks. Any or all of these factors may be major contributors or deterrents to the learning process. The description which appears under 1-b includes both factors of which the learner may be aware and those of which he may not be aware.

In the second section the theme treatment displays the contribution of two more components of the Design: Context and Learning Tasks. This section of the theme treatment indicates how the meanings and experiences identified in the first section may be communicated as the learner engages in the Learning Tasks. Communication is seen as a two-way process which may occur between the learner and the teacher, the learner and fellow learners, and the learner and God. It is never considered to be a one-way operation. Moreover, it is within the Context— Christian community—that communication of meanings and experiences takes place.

It is recognized throughout this Plan that the educational ministry of the church is being carried out whenever and wherever learning in the Christian faith and life takes place. Much of this is not and cannot be planned for or organized. The theme treatments deal only with those modes of communication which are planned for and organized.

The modes of communication listed in section two have been selected because of their appropriateness to that which was identified in section one. The suggestions include both methods and procedures designed to encourage and assist the learner as he engages in the Learning Tasks.

The third section of the theme treatment identifies the possible range of learnings which may be achieved within this theme by the learner. The range of learnings includes changes in understandings, habits, values, skills, concepts, perceptions which may be anticipated as the learner engages in the curriculum.

These three sections of the theme treatment for each of the four life periods comprise the source for developing teaching-learning units.

The Basis in Part III for Development of Leadership

All Christians as members of the body of Christ, are called to assume responsibilities in the ministry of reconciliation in the world and within the Christian community. Assuming appropriate responsibilities involves a Christian in functions of leadership, sometimes as a responsible member of a group, sometimes as the head of a group. When the church seeks to move toward its objective, it is confronted with the obligation to help equip each Christian for carrying such responsibilities. In the Foreword of this book, the point is made that this Curriculum Plan encompasses the educational opportunities necessary for preparing persons for responsibilities of leadership. This assumption implies three expectations of the Plan: that it will alert persons to their responsibility for ministering to persons in the world; that it will provide opportunities for educational experiences which will equip each for assuming leadership within the church and the community at large; and that it will develop in the congregation an understanding of the nature of leadership with an emphasis upon a concerned leadership witnessing and serving in the world in obedience to Christ. If a church is to carry out its mission, the members must acquire skills of leadership for engaging in a ministry of reconciliation.

257

Part III makes explicit how the Curriculum Plan provides for developing concern and skill for such leadership. The treatment of several themes points out this provision: Man's Involvement in Social Forces, God Acts Through the Church to Make Himself Known, Growing Up in Christ, God's Call to

Responsible Decision, Called to Serve One's Neighbor, Joined in Discipleship in the World, The Church Permeating Society, Extending Reconciliation and Redemption, The Christian Community Mobilizing for Mission, Preparing and Equipping for Ministry.

This Curriculum Plan also recognizes that a function of the educational ministry is to equip persons to carry designated responsibilities within the life and work of the church, in such roles as chairman, officer, teacher, and the like. Duties related to the motivation, selection, and training of persons for such responsibilities are properly seen as administrative services related to the implementation of the Curriculum Plan. Part IV, "The Relation of Administration to the Curriculum Plan," therefore, deals with leadership in this perspective.

Source for
Teaching-Learning
Opportunities

LIFE AND ITS SETTING:
THE MEANING AND EXPERIENCE OF EXISTENCE

The themes within this area are:

1. *Man Discovering and Accepting Himself*
2. *Man Living in Relationship with Others*
3. *Man's Relation to the Natural Order*
4. *Man's Involvement in Social Forces*
5. *Man's Coping with Change and the Absolute*
6. *Man's Creativity Within Life's Daily Routines*

Statement of the Area

The focus, or vantage point, of this area is the significance and purpose of life; what it means to be a human being; the origin, meaning, and destiny of the natural order; the import of history.

Comprehended in this area of curriculum is such content from Christian thought and life as: the doctrine of creation; the doctrine of man including his relation to the natural world; interpretation of personal and social development; struggle and conflict; the concept of eternal life; interpretation of world view including human history and eschatology.

259

In order to have educational value as an area of curriculum this content must be viewed in the terms of its pertinence to the persistent issues of man's life. Some of these issues are: What can I make of the universe? Does it have significance and purpose? Who am I? In what way, if any, does my life have meaning? What is my destiny and that of the world? Does the past tell me anything of value about the present and the future?[1]

[1]Repeated here as necessary background.

1. Man Discovering and Accepting Himself

STATEMENT OF THEME

When faced with the enigma of himself, man needs to understand and accept his human nature (including personal limitations and capacities) in order that he may live meaningfully and purposefully as God wills for him.

EARLY CHILDHOOD

260

1. Significance of the theme for this age level

a. Meanings and experiences within this theme relevant for this age level. This is content, a selected part of Scope.

Although my body can do all sorts of things, there are some things I cannot make it do yet.

God wants me to take care of my body and use it to do good things.

I am a boy (girl) and my body is like my father's (mother's) and some day I may be a father (mother).

God has planned for each person to be unique, differing from others in appearance, capacities, and characteristics.

God made human beings distinct from animals and things.

All persons are of value and are important to themselves, to one another, and to God.

God continues to love persons even when they make mistakes or do wrong and he is willing to forgive them when they seek his forgiveness.

Living in God's world involves limitations of time, space, ability, skill, including separation and death. Some of these limitations are within the person, some are imposed by the nature of the universe, or by other persons.

It is part of God's plan for persons to use their minds as fully as possible; to learn all they can about themselves and the world in which they live.

1. **Significance of the theme for this age level**

   b. **Readiness of the learner for this theme in terms of basic needs, interests, motivations, capacities, developmental tasks**

The young child is curious about the various aspects, functions, and capacities of his physical body, and how he can control his body.

The young child begins to recognize himself as a person—one who is different from other persons, animals and things.

The fulfillment of physical needs and desires, together with a sense of being loved and secure, is essential for the young child's well-being.

The young child is predominantly self-centered, putting first his own needs and desires, so that he is often in conflict with his peers and with adults.

The young child needs constant love and acceptance from those around him, including the receiving of loving discipline for his mistakes and wrongdoing.

New motor skills and exploration of his environment make it necessary for the young child to have acceptance and encouragement from adults.

The young child is able to recognize the limitations of his physical world and to learn to live within these limitations.

261

The young child understands primarily through his relationship with other persons rather than through words.

2. **How may this content be communicated as the learner engages in the Learning Tasks? What are the methods and procedures by which the learner may explore the meanings and experiences within this theme (1-a) in the light of his readiness (1-b) in order to discover significance and value?**

By having relationships with adults who love and accept him as a person of worth.

By exploring his environment to discover the ways in which he is different from others and from inanimate objects.

Through firsthand experiences with and observation of animals, the young child finds that he and the animals have different characteristics.

By receiving discipline in an atmosphere of love and forbearance.

Through associating with persons who have experienced and demonstrate the love of God in their relationships.

By doing things for himself, and using his capacities.

By exploring and identifying the parts of his body and how they work.

By being cared for by those who treat his body as a good gift from God.

By observing those about him who acknowledge God as the Source of all life and demonstrate in their own attitude and behavior that God's provisions for life are good.

By exploring and enjoying the interesting sights and sounds of God's out-of-doors.

By talking about, play acting, his sex role.

3. **What may the learner achieve within this theme in the fulfillment of the Learning Tasks? What are possible changes or learnings on the part of the learner that may result from his appropriation of the significance and value discovered? These changes or learnings may be associated with skills, attitudes, motivations, perceptions including understandings and appreciations.**

The young child may accept his body and its functions as good, because it has been created by God.

The young child may recognize himself as distinct from other persons because God has made persons different from each other.

The young child may appreciate that he is a boy (she is a girl) according to God's intent and accept his male role (her female role) as good.

The young child may understand that mistakes, failures, and wrongdoings are not to be ignored, but that through them he may learn how to do better and what is acceptable behavior.

The young child may be willing to admit his wrongdoing and to seek the forgiveness of those he has hurt.

The young child may begin to appreciate that he is beloved by God.

The young child may sense he is not sufficient unto himself but dependent upon a Source beyond his parents for provisions for his needs.

The young child may begin to discover his natural capacities and abilities and sense their importance for his life.

The young child may develop control over his body appropriate to his level of growth and development and thus discover that he is an entity created by God.

1. Man Discovering and Accepting Himself

STATEMENT OF THEME

When faced with the enigma of himself, man needs to understand and accept his human nature (including personal limitations and capacities) in order that he may live meaningfully and purposefully as God wills for him.

263

ELEMENTARY YEARS

1. Significance of the theme for this age level

a. Meanings and experiences within this theme relevant for this age level. This is content, a selected part of Scope.

Physical health, growth, and development are part of God's plan for each person.

It is part of God's plan for persons to use their minds as fully as possible; to learn all they can about themselves and the world in which they live.

God loves all persons and he wants them to know what it means to be his children.

God has planned that persons be different from one another in appearance, skills, capacities, and characteristics.

There are limitations in God's world which help persons but also puzzle and frustrate them. Some of the limitations are time, space, physical capacities, death.

Even though each person has times when he selfishly insists on doing as he pleases without limitations, God continues to love him and offer forgiveness.

God has made persons with minds with which to remember, reason, and work out solutions to their problems and they are accountable to God for how they develop their mental capacities.

God is ready to forgive persons who acknowledge wrongdoing and ask his forgiveness.

1. Significance of the theme for this age level

b. Readiness of the learner for this theme in terms of basic needs, interests, motivations, capacities, developmental tasks.

The elementary child has periods of rapid physical growth alternating with periods of development or maturation. Each period is marked by its own particular problems.

The elementary child's mental faculties are expanding rapidly, and he is thrust into situations apart from adult supervision where he must attempt to think and reason on his own.

The elementary child's expanding contacts with persons provide him with opportunities to experience acceptance of himself as a person, indifference, or outright rejection.

The elementary child wonders about who he is, why he is on

this earth, where he came from, where he is going, and the abilities and skills that he may be able to develop.

As the elementary child becomes increasingly able to assume responsibility for making his own decisions, he wants to be assured that he is loved and accepted by his parents, teachers, and peers, and that God loves him and accepts him for himself.

The elementary child needs guidance in overcoming temptation, in learning from his mistakes, and in rising above his failures.

The elementary child needs to increase his understanding of the differences between the sexes and to accept his role as a boy (as a girl) while acknowledging and accepting the role of the opposite sex.

The elementary child tends to fancy himself in many different roles and is ready to accept behavior patterns of those whom he admires.

The elementary child desires someone he can trust and in whom he can confide his innermost thoughts.

The elementary child tends to become frustrated and rebellious over the limitations of time and space and in his ability to achieve what he sets out to do.

Many elementary children have a sense of foreboding, a sense of being threatened by the unknown. Sometimes such threats are undefined, sometimes they stem from actually being lost, from being alone in the dark, from personal sickness, or from the death of someone close to them.

265

The elementary child has a need to find his own pattern of behavior amid the pressures to conform to the standards of the groups of which he is a part, such as the family, his peers, the school, and the church.

Most elementary children have a deep urge to excel in competition. They need opportunities to measure their abilities and achievements against their potential, as well as against the abilities and skills of their peers, at the same time learning how to handle achievements and failures.

Each elementary child needs the satisfaction of accomplishing some achievement on his own.

The elementary child needs experiences in making constructive use of his emotions. He needs to learn to use words instead of actions to express anger, sorrow, disappointment, frustration, fear, and enthusiasm. He needs to know what to do when he is teased, when he is afraid. He needs to learn how to express affection so that it is acceptable to others and satisfying to himself.

2. **How may this content be communicated as the learner engages in the Learning Tasks? What are the methods and procedures by which the learner may explore the meanings and experiences within this theme (1-a) in the light of his readiness (1-b) in order to discover significance and value?**

By studying what the Bible tells of God as the Creator of man and of God's great love and concern for man in that he sent Jesus into the world.

By reading books about the structure of his physical body and how to maintain good health habits, and about men who tried to live as beings made in God's likeness.

By viewing and discussing filmstrips which depict the nature of man and what individuals have achieved when they have developed their potentials to the fullest.

By participating in physical exercise and health classes, viewing and discussing filmstrips on physical development.

By reading and studying the biographies and the lives of persons who have succeeded despite handicaps.

By studying and discussing the Christian attitude toward prosperity, adversity, and the Christian interpretation of life and death.

By participating in family worship and celebrations.

By assuming leadership or being willing to follow a leader in groups of his peers.

By studying how God worked through persons in Bible times.

By observing the rhythm of work, play, and rest and how these are affected by time, space, his abilities, and the society in which he lives.

By comparing what society expects of him (her) as a boy (girl) and his (her) understanding of the Christian concept of God's intent in creating male and female.

3. **What may the learner achieve within this theme in the fulfillment of the Learning Tasks? What are possible changes or learnings on the part of the learner that may result from his appropriation of the significance and value discovered? These changes or learnings may be associated with skills, attitudes, motivations, perceptions including understandings and appreciations.**

The elementary child may accept responsibility for his increased independence as a part of growing up.

The elementary child may gain confidence in his own ability to do for himself and to reach right decisions, coming to be less dependent upon adults.

The elementary child may begin to accept himself as a person, made in the likeness of God, who is called to live in harmony with this likeness.

267

The elementary child may develop the ability to assume a task in a responsible way and may carry it through to satisfactory completion.

The elementary child may begin to accept himself as a child of God, recognizing the potential this gives him as well as the responsibility to live as a child of God.

The elementary child may begin to accept his sex as a part of God's plan for himself and the world and assume responsibility for fulfilling his role.

The elementary child may understand that God has endowed him with particular talents, capacities, and abilities and that he is responsible for the highest development of these talents, capacities, and abilities.

The elementary child may begin to respond in love and faith to God's love for him.

The elementary child may begin to understand the limitations of time space, and his own finiteness and begin to accept them as the way God has ordered the universe, rather than as capricious or arbitary bounds.

The elementary child may begin to understand that he can learn better ways of doing things if he is willing to learn from his mistakes and failures.

The elementary child may begin to realize that when he does wrong he can repent and God will forgive him.

1. Man Discovering and Accepting Himself

STATEMENT OF THEME

When faced with the enigma of himself, man needs to understand and accept his human nature (including personal limitations and capacities) in order that he may live meaningfully and purposefully as God wills for him.

YOUTH

1. Significance of the theme for this age level

a. Meanings and experiences within this theme relevant for this age level. This is content, a selected part of Scope.

God is the source of the youth's physical body with all its capacities, potentialities and limitations; youth is responsible for the mastery of his physical powers.

God made persons male and female; youth is responsible for choosing to use sexuality for self-gratification or for self-fulfillment, as a power for good or for evil.

God has endowed persons with minds and spirits which distinguish them from animals; youth is responsible for developing his mental powers to the fullest and for the cultivation of his spiritual capacities so that he is aware of the universe and sensitive to the feelings and desires of other persons.

In accord with God's plan man is finite, a created being who is born, faces limitations to his will and action, and finally dies. At the same time, God offers him eternal life which enables him to face, and, to some extent, transcend the finiteness of human life.

Young people share with all men the tendency to rebel against God. Recognition of oneself as a sinner is essential to acceptance of one's finiteness and God's infiniteness.

Each person is of worth because he is made in the likeness of the Creator.

Recognition of God's redeeming love as shown especially in the life, death, and resurrection of Jesus Christ is essential to a firm basis for accepting oneself as a person of worth and for accepting others, too, as having worth.

Within the limitations of the material universe, each youth is free to make his own particular choices. When these are in harmony with God's purposes, the youth reaches the highest fulfillment of his selfhood.

Each person has the capacity to live as God's son.

Death is inevitable as the end of finite life yet for the Christian this is an incident in eternal life.

269

1. **Significance of the theme for this age level**

    b. **Readiness of the learner for this theme in terms of basic needs, interests, motivations, capacities, developmental tasks.**

The physiological development coupled with the mental and emotional changes which occur in adolescence frequently cause contradictions in the youth's image of himself and frustrations in his dealings with other persons. He may fluctuate between being on top of the world and feeling completely forsaken.

Youth is acutely self-conscious, causing him to need reassurance that he is accepted by his peers and by the adults in his world. He is able to respond wholeheartedly to the assurance that he is of significance and worth to God.

Youth needs to understand and adjust to his own sexual maturation and to that of the opposite sex.

Youth needs to establish and maintain appropriate relationships with persons of the opposite sex.

Youth longs to find security among his peers. He wants to be loved, accepted, and to be popular with his peers.

Youth is torn between wanting to conform to the standards and expectations of individuals and groups beyond himself and wanting to be himself, having an individuality of his own.

With youth's emotional volatility, every temptation, failure, mistake, or enthusiasm is intensified.

Oftentimes youth is frustrated by limitations, such as time, space, personal ability to reach his goals, and restrictions of his parents, society, and religion.

Youth is sharply aware of the threat of particularity, futility, and the prospect of death.

Youth is capable of thinking abstractly, and needs to learn how to harness his imagination.

Youth has the capacity for idealism, and seeks a cause around which he can focus his life.

One of youth's developmental tasks is assuming responsibility for maintaining good health habits.

2. **How may this content be communicated as the learner engages in the Learning Tasks? What are the methods and procedures by which the learner may explore the meanings and experiences within this theme (1-a) in the light of his readiness (1-b) in order to discover significance and value?**

By relating what the sciences divulge about man's capacities to the concept of man's stewardship under his Creator.

By exploring and testing his capacities and limitations under appropriate guidance.

By making efforts to develop his capacities to their fullest extent.

By considering with Christians the meaning of sexuality as basic to God's purpose for man.

By studying the biblical concept of the nature of man.

By associating with Christians who have accepted themselves, appreciative of their capacities and limitations and of their responsibility for their development as a mature person under God.

By associating with persons who appreciate him in his uniqueness of personality and in his significance as a person.

By observing and discussing with others how Christians face death as an incident in, rather than an end to, life.

By participating with others in identifying and confessing failures, shortcomings, transgressions, and rebellion.

By reading about and studying the lives of persons who found the meaning of life and of self that results from commitment to God.

By trying to cope with himself and with his relation to others in light of his understanding of man created in God's image.

271

3. **What may the learner achieve within this theme in the fulfillment of the Learning Tasks? What are possible changes or learnings on the part of the learner that may result from his appropriation of the significance and value discovered? These changes or learnings may be associated with skills, attitudes, motivations, perceptions including understandings and appreciations.**

Youth may understand and appreciate that the self has been endowed upon him by God.

Youth may accept God as infinite and himself as finite.

Youth may increasingly succeed in assuming a task in a responsible way and carrying it through to fulfillment.

Youth may accept himself as a child of God with the privileges and responsibilities resulting from this view of his personhood.

Youth may become sensitive to the will of God and assume responsibility for making his choices in light of God's will.

Youth may accept his sex as a part of God's intention that human beings be male and female, each with his own particular role.

Youth may develop ability to direct his sexual desires into wholesome, creative relationships with those of his own sex and with those of the opposite sex.

Youth may accept his body as created by God and assume responsibility for developing his physical capacities and maintaining health as his Christian stewardship.

Youth may gain a less fearful view of death.

Youth may gain an appreciation of intellectual ability—his own and that of others.

Youth may gain in his ability to be honest with himself and with God about his rebellion and his sins.

Youth may increase in self-respect and self-expectations.

Youth may be increasingly able to relate scientific truth to religious truth.

1. Man Discovering and Accepting Himself

STATEMENT OF THEME

When faced with the enigma of himself, man needs to understand and accept his human nature (including personal limitations and capacities) in order that he may live meaningfully and purposefully as God wills for him.

ADULTHOOD

1. Significance of the theme for this age level

a. Meanings and experiences within this theme relevant for this age level. This is content, a selected part of Scope.

The infinite God has created man a finite creature, limited by time, space, physical strength, futility, and death.

Because of his finite limitations, each person has the potential to become conscious of his selfhood and individuality.

In the incarnation man has the fullest expression of human nature and personality.

God's gift of eternal life opens the way for each person to transcend his finite existence, in time and eternity.

God creates human personality with intrinsic worth; selfhood is a gift from God, its potential for living meaningfully, purposefully realized under the lordship of Christ.

God has created each person with the ability to make his own particular choices and decisions, within the limitations imposed by his capacities and his environment.

Recognition of oneself as a sinner—in rebellion against God —is necessary to understand one's human situation.

Appropriation of God's redeeming love gives significance and purpose to one's life.

Maleness or femaleness is a gift of God which involves fulfilling one's role as man or woman in general and in the procreative process in particular.

273

The adult is accountable to God and his fellows in the development and expression of his sexual nature.

God has created persons as complex beings of individualities, emotions, and will.

Human health and well-being depend upon understanding mental, physical, and emotional needs and meeting these in accordance with God's purposes.

Man's self-acceptance as a creature of God is a key factor in his ability to relate to others and to God.

The source for the meaning of man's life is not his being, efforts, or span of years, but God.

1. Significance of the theme for this age level

b. Readiness of the learner for this theme in terms of basic needs, interests, motivations, capacities, developmental tasks.

Adults, amid the changing conditions of their lives, wonder who they are, are driven in search of answers to the questions of where they are going, what is the purpose of life.

Adults have a natural concern about relationships with their own and with the opposite sex.

Each adult needs to accept his sex, and acknowledge and accept persons of the opposite sex.

The adult needs to adjust to being married, or to being single.

Frequently adults are caught by conflicting patterns of relationships between the sexes involving their own desires, the pattern of behavior sanctioned in contrast to the behavior practiced by society, and the teachings of religion.

Oftentime the adult feels loneliness and alienation from his peers and at odds with his society.

The adult needs the assurance that he is beloved by God, and the feeling that he is of worth and significance because he is God's creature.

The adult seeks the security of being accepted by his fellows, and a sense of belonging with other persons.

The adult learns to deal constructively with the temptation to do less than his best, to go contrary to his own principles, to break the rules of society, or succumbs to the temptations.

The adult has the need to learn how to accept achievement and good fortune without "resting on his laurels" or lording over his fellows.

The adult may become frustrated by the limitations of time, space, and his own abilities which, themselves, could be the framework of his security.

Each adult longs to have someone he can trust implicitly

and someone in whom he can confide with confidence.

The adult struggles to remain a person of worth in the face of the depersonalizing forces in society arising from urbanization and automation.

In adult life one experiences continuous challenge by accepted value patterns, requiring reassessment of values and a deeper understanding of the will of God.

The adult faces the task of appropriately relating society's demands for conformity and personal desires to act according to his own ideas and principles.

Adults are capable of thinking abstractly.

Adults have the capacity to search for solutions to problems by reasoning, and to project and test possible solutions.

Adults have lived long enough to be somewhat aware of their tendency to rebel against God and to become estranged from him.

Adults have peculiarly interpersonal developmental tasks such as assuming the responsibilities of singleness or marriage, adjusting to a life partner, accepting the responsibilities of parenthood and grandparenthood, adjusting to widowhood or possibly to separation and divorce.

2. **How may this content be communicated as the learner engages in the Learning Tasks? What are the methods and procedures by which the learner may explore the meanings and experiences within this theme (1-a) in the light of his readiness (1-b) in order to discover significance and value?**

275

By studying the biblical concepts of the nature of man.

By relating what the sciences have reported about man's capacities to the concept of man's stewardship under his Creator.

By working to develop fully his talents and capacities.

By examining his abilities in relation to his occupation to look for ways of greater efficiency in this work, and/or ways of changing the nature of his work to bring about higher correlation between it and his abilities.

By considering with Christians the meaning of sexuality as basic to God's purpose for man.

By associating with Christians who have accepted themselves and appreciate their capacities, their limitations, and their responsibility to develop as mature persons under God.

By associating with persons who appreciate his uniqueness and significance as an individual.

By observing and discussing with others how Christians take death as an incident in, rather than an end to, life.

By sharing meaningfully with others in identifying and confessing failures, shortcomings, transgressions, and rebellion.

By reading about and studying the lives of persons who have found the meaning of life and of self that results from commitment to God.

By having to cope with himself in relation to others in light of his understanding of man created in God's image and dependent upon God's forgiveness.

By exploring and testing his capacities and limitations in an atmosphere of empathetic acceptance.

By studying what scholars of various faiths have written about the nature of the image of God in man.

By exploring, cataloging, and using the variety of spiritual disciplines observed by Christians to know better themselves and God.

3. **What may the learner achieve within this theme in the fulfillment of the Learning Tasks? What are possible changes or learnings on the part of the learner that may result from his appropriation of the significance and value discovered? These changes or learnings may be associated with skills, attitudes, motivations, perceptions including understandings and appreciations.**

The adult may make a realistic appraisal of his personality in light of the gospel and learn to live with his particular limitations.

The adult may assume the responsibility for more fully developing and utilizing his capacities.

The adult may accept his own physical body and the limitations brought on by maturation, illness, and advancing age.

The adult may accept his sex as a part of God's plan for humans and assume responsibility for fulfilling his sex role.

The adult may perceive more clearly the image of God in himself with the potential and the responsibility this implies.

The adult may accept himself as finite and God as infinite, recognizing that man tends to rebel against God, seeking to become god himself.

The adult may recognize that mistakes and failures can become learning opportunities.

The adult may develop a greater ability to cope with success, mediocrity, and failure.

The adult may have a sense of freedom that stimulates creative living under the lordship of Jesus Christ.

The adult may develop a deeper conviction that he can transcend his finite experience and share in eternal life with God.

The adult may regard his body as created by God and assume responsibility for developing his physical capacities and maintaining health as his Christian stewardship.

The adult may develop a greater ability to accept and value others, both those more generously and those less generously endowed with talents and abilities than he.

277

2. Man Living in Relationship with Others

STATEMENT OF THE THEME

Man's optimum development involves his understanding of and living with others as God's beloved children.

EARLY CHILDHOOD

1. Significance of the theme for this age level

a. Meanings and experiences within this theme relevant for this age level. This is content, a selected part of Scope.

Each young child is of infinite worth because he is a person, made in God's likeness.

God wants each young child to recognize other persons and respect them as persons having worth and significance.

God wants young children to love one another.

God wants young children to forgive one another readily.

Young children who love God worship, work, and fellowship with other persons in the church.

Each young child is distinctive yet with needs, interests, desires, and capacities similar to those of every other person.

God expects a young child to settle his conflicts without harming others.

Each young child has a right to possess things which belong to him alone and which others are not to take from him.

God wants each young child to recognize and respect the rights of others to possess things which are theirs alone and which he is not to damage or take from them against their will.

God expects each young child to be friendly toward others even when others do not return this friendliness.

God wants each young child to accept every other member of his family as having worth and importance.

God expects each young child to love the others in his family despite their faults and shortcomings.

Young children are boys or girls and they are different from one another. They live in a world of men and women. Both sexes are essential to God's plan for mankind.

1. Significance of the theme for this age level

> **b. Readiness of the learner for this theme in terms of basic needs, interests, motivations, capacities, developmental tasks.**

The young child's capacity and need for love and affection cause him to look for satisfaction in his relationships with others.

The need for physical care and his inability to care for his own physical needs, makes the young child dependent upon other persons.

The young child needs loving, training, and guidance from other persons in many areas of behavior.

The young child is basically self-centered and he seeks to express himself and to gain the attention of other persons.

Until the young child has developed the capacity to learn through verbal communication, he is dependent upon relationship with others for much of his learning.

The young child's interest in people begins to expand and go beyond the small circle of his family.

The process of learning motor skills and language motivates the young child to relate to others.

The source of a young child's security is found in his relationships with others.

A natural capacity for love and forgiveness enables the young child to relate to others openly.

A developing conscience in the young child readies him to affect changes in the way he lives with others.

The young child has an increasing capacity to distinguish between persons and things.

The young child needs to recognize that persons are male and female and both sexes are important.

The young child needs to receive equal acceptance in relating to persons of both sexes.

279

2. **How may this content be communicated as the learner engages in the Learning Tasks? What are the methods and procedures by which the learner may explore the meanings and experiences within this theme (1-a) in the light of his readiness (1-b) in order to discover significance and value?**

By having face-to-face experiences with other children, under adult guidance, to discover satisfactory ways of relating to his peers.

By working with another child to achieve a common purpose.

By associating with children from other racial and social backgrounds.

By associating with adults who are consistent in their behavior toward him and in the verbal guidance given him concerning the boundaries of his freedom in relation to the rights and responsibilities of others.

By associating with persons who treat him as a person having worth and significance.

By associating with persons who regard all persons as children of God and treat them as persons of worth and significance.

By listening to and dramatizing Bible stories and frequently repeating Bible verses which set forth man's relation to his fellowmen.

By vicarious experiences of the lives of people beyond his immediate environment gained from television, radio, pictures, picture books, and stories.

By observing a person exercising a particular skill, by imitating him, failing, and being encouraged to try again.

By experiencing expressions of love and friendliness himself and by noting how others respond to his expressions of love and friendship.

By experiencing forgiveness of others for his own wrongdoings and by recognizing the occasions when he needs to seek the forgiveness of another.

By participating in family worship at home and by observing and participating in some occasions of congregational worship.

By participating in activities which express loving concern for others—visiting shut-ins or the elderly, preparing gifts for another, giving money to aid persons in need.

By observing the attitude of adults as demonstrated in their conversation, their actions, as well as in direct instruction concerning the acceptance of an appropriate sex role as part of God's plan.

3. **What may the learner achieve within this theme in the fulfillment of the Learning Tasks? What are possible changes or learnings on the part of the learner that may result from his appropriation of the significance and value discovered? These changes or learnings may be associated with skills, attitudes, motivations, perceptions including understandings and appreciations.**

The young child may become aware that others are persons of worth and significance.

The young child may be willing to play fair, wait turns, and share toys.

The young child may seek forgiveness when he offends others and may be willing to forgive those who offend him.

The young child may begin to respect the ownership rights of others.

The young child may accept the authority of those who have responsibility for his welfare—the older brother or sister, parents, or other adults.

The young child may recognize that telling the truth in every relationship regardless of the consequences is of first importance.

The young child may begin to feel a part of the Christian fellowship within the church.

The young child may distinguish truth from falsehood, reality from fancy.

281

The young child may begin to be aware that the Bible is a book from which he can learn how to get along with other persons as God desires him to do.

The young child may recognize that persons are created by God, male and female, and that it is good to be a boy, good to be a girl.

The young child may begin to distinguish within the scope of his experience what is right and what is wrong in light of the gospel.

A young child may begin to know what he can do on his own

and when he must accept the help of another.

The child may begin to sense his own importance to others.

The young child may discover he can rely upon others to teach him skills he needs to master.

The young child may begin to discover acceptable ways of being affectionate and friendly with other persons.

The young child may begin to develop concern for others and assume responsibility for expressing his concern in practical ways.

282

2. Man Living in Relationship with Others

STATEMENT OF THE THEME

Man's optimum development involves his understanding of and living with others as God's beloved children.

ELEMENTARY YEARS

1. Significance of the theme for this age level

a. Meanings and experiences within this theme relevant for this age level. This is content, a selected part of Scope.

Every member of the family is a person of worth and importance.

Boys and girls should accept and have affection for younger children, their peers, and adults as fellow members of the Christian community.

God planned for persons to be boys and girls, men and women, and to live together in families.

Both males and females are essential in God's plan for life on the earth.

For the Christian, the basis for right relationships is in the moral values set forth in the gospel.

Boys and girls should accept and maintain a balance of dependence upon and independence from others.

Each boy or girl has human qualities in common with every other person. These and his individual differences form a basis for creative interpersonal relationships.

Each boy or girl is individually responsible (accountable to God) for his interpersonal relationships.

Intentional and even unintentional harm to another person damages relationships. Such offenses require deliberate effort on the part of the offender and the offended to mend the relationship.

Tensions in interpersonal relationships are eased when a person seeks what is best for his opponent.

Knowing God's love and forgiveness helps persons to express love and forgiveness in their relations with others.

Love and concern for others are not limited to persons the boy or girl knows and meets face to face but are reflected in the elementary child's understanding of and attitude toward persons beyond his immediate experience.

Boys and girls are responsible to God and to their fellowmen of the present and the future for the use they make of natural resources.

1. Significance of the theme for this age level

b. Readiness of the learner for this theme in terms of basic needs, interests, motivations, capacities, developmental tasks.

The child needs to be related to persons he can trust and on whom he can safely depend.

The child needs to be related to persons with whom he can join in mutual expressions of affection.

The child needs to be recognized and accepted as a person in his own right.

The child increasingly seeks approval and/or self-fulfillment in relationships with other persons.

The child spends increasingly more time outside the home and apart from parents and siblings, extending the field of personal relationships.

The wider experience with persons makes the child curious as to why persons act as they act, why they think as they think, why they feel as they feel.

The child needs to discover appropriate limits and likely consequences of his self-assertion.

The child needs to discover a satisfactory balance between his increasing capacity and opportunity for independence and his continuing need to depend upon other persons.

The child has a need and a desire to belong to a group(s) in which he finds personal fulfillment through personal relationships.

In a mobile society, the child needs to develop skill in making friends quickly and adjusting to the loss of friends.

The child has a natural desire to dominate and control a group or another person, which is likely to be tempered by experiences in which he feels disapproval, rejection, or suffers physical injury.

Developing language and motor skills tend to engage the child in complex activities involving other persons. These activities present occasions for conflict between viewpoints, ideas, and ways of working.

Conflict in relationships may motivate the child to seek new skills in maintaining relationships, or may make him sullen, combative, or withdrawn.

The child has a growing curiosity about people, particularly those who are different from him in appearance, in customs, in ideas, in desires, and in objectives or motivations.

The child is increasingly aware of others as persons with feelings like his own.

The child is eager to experiment with cause and effect in personal relationships. He knows what he does that teases another, that angers his parents or teachers, that delights a friend.

A growing sense of responsibility leads the child to take the initiative in making and keeping friends.

The child has the capacity to anticipate and choose those relationships in which he finds satisfaction and to avoid those which make him uneasy or interfere with the achievement of his own task.

The child is curious about sex.

The child needs relationships with persons of both sexes.

2. **How may this content be communicated as the learner engages in the Learning Tasks? What are the methods and procedures by which the learner may explore the meanings and experiences within this theme (1-a) in the light of his readiness (1-b) in order to discover significance and value?**

By studying and discussing what the Bible teaches as right relationships among persons.

By articulating his own ideas of how a Christian lives with others.

By assaying on his own, or with adult guidance, his own relationships with others in light of the gospel.

By pursuing his interest in and concern for people beyond his own immediate community through vicarious experience such as reading books, viewing television and movies, listening to radio and to travelers talk of their experiences.

By participating in groups of his peers.

By attempting to hear and understand what another says and trying to judge what the actions of another person may mean.

By associating with Christian men and women who demonstrate through precept and behavior toward one another and toward the child their understanding of sex and the acceptance of appropriate sex roles as a part of God's plan for man.

By participating in family worship and group worship in the church.

By engaging in common activities with persons of other social classes, races, and creeds.

285

By attempting to articulate and apply his own Christian understanding in resolving conflicts.

By observing or participating in groups where Christian concepts are followed.

By examining the reasons for conflicts, attitudes, and behavior which handicap the solution of conflicts in groups he observes or to which he may belong.

3. What may the learner achieve within this theme in the fulfillment of the Learning Tasks? What are possible changes or learnings on the part of the learner that may result from his appropriation of the significance and value discovered? These changes or learnings may be associated with skills, attitudes, motivations, perceptions including understandings and appreciations.

The child may recognize the Bible as a source of guidance in establishing and maintaining right relationships among persons.

The child may have some ability to deal with differences without breaking relationship with another.

The child may be willing to try to restore broken relationships, to seek and accept forgiveness from one he has offended, and may willingly forgive those who offend him.

The child may accept his maleness, or her femaleness, as God-given and recognize that though boys are different from girls, and men are different from women, all are important in God's plan.

The child may assume personal responsibility for getting along well with other persons.

The child may maintain a relationship with each member of the family based on his understanding that each is a person of significance and worth and each has a contribution to make to the whole family.

The child may have a sense of belonging to a family and that it is good to belong.

The child may have a feeling of belonging to the church fellowship.

The child may be interested in and concerned for the welfare of persons outside his own immediate group.

The child's concern for the welfare of others may give him responsibility for the conservation of natural resources.

The child may respect the property rights of others.

The child may be sensitive to the feelings of others, rejoicing with them when they are happy and sympathizing with them when they are disappointed or in physical pain.

The child may measure the values of others as demonstrated by what they say and do against his own values and the values the church teaches.

The child may be able to reason why he fails and falls short of his goal, and he may tolerate his failures and shortcomings by renewed effort to do better.

The child may recognize and appreciate the physical and cultural differences among persons.

The child may respect authority of those who exercise authority over him, and may responsibly exercise his authority over others.

The child may accept every person as a child of God having worth and significance.

The child's genuine concern for the well-being of others may lead him to intercessory prayer on their behalf.

287

2. Man Living in Relationship with Others

STATEMENT OF THE THEME

Man's optimum development involves his understanding of and living with others as God's beloved children.

YOUTH

1. Significance of the theme for this age level

a. Meanings and experiences within this theme relevant for this age level. This is content, a selected part of Scope.

Significant interpersonal relationships for the Christian are based on acceptance of others as persons of worth in the sight of God.

Persons have a commonality which finds its source in God who has created them in his image.

Youth are faced with many complex relationships with authority figures, with members of their peer group, with members of their family, with those of the opposite sex.

The moral law of God provides the criterion for evaluating the appropriateness of social behavior.

Every person has a God-given measure of responsibility for the kind of relationships he maintains with others.

The boundaries of independance and freedom in interpersonal relationships are determined by a number of factors including God's supreme authority, the rights of other persons, the nature of man.

God created persons male and female and has assigned a unique function to those of each sex.

Every person is accountable to God for the fulfillment of his sex role and how he, or she, relates to the opposite sex.

The masculine and feminine roles which prevail in society are evaluated in the light of Christian values.

Understanding and empathy are essential for sustaining right relationships with others.

Every person is responsible to God for attempting to renew or mend broken human relationships regardless of who is to blame for breaking them.

Conflicts between persons and groups may be resolved and tensions relaxed through love and forgiveness.

Christian relationships within the family call for mutual respect, appreciation, and love.

Every person has been created as an individual who has

unique desires, needs, and rights and should not be manipulated or used by another to his own advantage.

1. Significance of the theme for this age level

b. Readiness of the learner for this theme in terms of basic needs, interests, motivations, capacities, developmental tasks.

Most youth are basically gregarious and have the urge to associate with others.

Physical and mental maturation, cultural expectations, and social patterns ready youth for new relationships between those of the opposite sex.

Youth have a growing capacity for making decisions and assuming responsibility for relationships with other persons.

Youth are seeking for solutions to many conflicts they find within themselves in their relationships with others.

Youth actively seek social approval from others and especially from those in their peer group.

Youth have developing sensitivity to the effect attitudes and actions have upon interpersonal relationships.

Youth have the capacity to appreciate the significance of mutual respect and love or lack of the same in family relationships, both their own and those of their friends.

Youth have a desire to join with others in causes involving altruistic service.

289

Youth are often disillusioned as they become aware of sham, inconsistencies, and deceit in others whom they have trusted and respected and they are seeking for new bases upon which to maintain old or build new relationships.

Youth have the capacity for entering into friendships and significant relationships with others.

Youth need to love and be loved.

The young person longs to be accepted by peers and adults as a person in his own right.

The young person is seeking to discover his own worth and his potential significance in a world of people.

Youth are struggling to understand their maleness and femaleness as a part of God's creation and to accept their responsibility for the use they make of their sex.

Youth are attracted to those of the opposite sex.

Youth are seeking a moral basis upon which they might resolve the conflicts which arise between what society expects of them or condones and what their parents and others have told them.

The young person searches for the boundaries within which he might experience freedom in his relationship with others.

2. **How may this content be communicated as the learner engages in the Learning Tasks? What are the methods and procedures by which the learner may explore the meanings and experiences within this theme (1-a) in the light of his readiness (1-b) in order to discover significance and value.**

By associating with peers and with adults who accept and relate to him as a person who has significance and worth.

By associating with Christian adult leaders who are willing to become learners with youth and who are able to transcend the dividing line between youth and the world of adults.

By assuming leadership in the youth program of the church, planning, executing, and evaluating in cooperation with other youth and adults.

By associating with Christian adults whose relationships with others give evidence of their Christian faith.

By consciously attempting to identify with and undertake common endeavors with persons in the congregation who are outside his own peer group.

By discussing interpersonal problems in light of the gospel with peers, parents, and other adults.

By engaging in depth Bible studies which focus on relationships between persons and groups.

By considering in light of the gospel what history teaches about human relationships, the causes for conflicts among individuals, groups, and nations, and the solutions man has attempted.

By discussing ways to relate to each member of the family in ways which will contribute to his growth as a Christian.

By giving consideration to sex as a part of God's plan, the place of sex in life, and the effect of one's attitude toward sex in relationships with persons of his (or her) sex and persons of the opposite sex.

By getting acquainted with persons of other racial, ethnic, cultural, religious, social, and economic backgrounds, by having opportunity to deal with them as persons of worth and importance in the sight of God.

By comparing Christian values with one's own values and those of his peers and the relationship of values to patterns of conformity and nonconformity in social relationships.

By studying about the meaning of man's common relationship due to the fact that all have been created in the image of God.

By practicing the art of accepting and forgiving others.

By exploring the meaning of freedom in the light of the gospel and relating it to interpersonal relationships.

By seeking the forgiveness of God and others for wrongs which have been committed.

291

3. **What may the learner achieve within this theme in the ful-fillment of the Learning Tasks? What are possible changes or learnings on the part of the learner that may result from his appropriation of the significance and value discovered? These changes or learnings may be associated with skills, attitudes, motivations, perceptions including understandings and appreciations.**

Youth may develop a workable Christian faith and value system on which he may base his attitudes and behavior toward other persons.

Youth may accept each person as a child of God with infinite worth and significance.

Youth may develop a sense of social responsibility in light of the gospel that affects all his choices in everyday living.

Youth may recognize his own failures and mistakes in inter-personal relationships and may seek the forgiveness of those he has offended.

Youth may become more willing to forgive those who offend him.

292

Youth may develop his ability to use his expanding freedom responsibly, without violating the rights of others.

Youth may have the courage to stand for his convictions against the pressure of the group, without despising or bemean-ing members within the group.

Youth may develop ability to live in wholesome relationships with members of his family, understanding and accepting each member as a person who has rights, needs and interests of his own.

Youth may accept his sex as God-given, and may recognize that sex is a significant factor among the complex of factors which constitute a person's life.

Youth may identify with the fellowship of the church in which he may be brought into relationship with God and others.

Youth may develop capacity to worship God wholeheartedly and to appreciate the experience of worship with others.

Youth may become more sensitive to the rights and feelings of others and may develop understanding about his response to them and their response to him.

He may learn how to get along with others so that he is ac-cepted and wanted without violating his own integrity.

Youth may develop more respect for law and authority, both human and divine, and may willingly obey laws and accept the authority others exercise over him.

Youth may accept the responsibility of authority over others and learn to exercise such authority wisely.

Youth may learn to be more at ease with others with whom there is mutual appreciation and acceptance based upon common Christian experiences and understandings.

Youth may become more aware of the impact which the Christian faith has upon interpersonal relationships.

Youth may develop a greater appreciation for and willingness to accept those of other racial, ethnic, cultural, religious, social, and economic groups.

2. Man Living in Relationship with Others

STATEMENT OF THE THEME

Man's optimum development involves his understanding of and living with others as God's beloved children.

ADULTHOOD

1. Significance of the theme for this age level

a. Meanings and experiences within this theme relevant for this age level. This is content, a selected part of Scope.

All persons are created by God and therefore bear a kinship to one another.

Each individual is accountable to God for how he treats another person.

In every human relationship each person is of infinite worth without regard to his origin, cultural background, economic standing, religious beliefs and practices.

Living together within the Christian fellowship is characterized by each person's understanding of and compassion for the other.

Sensitivity to the needs of others and a willingness to serve them is characteristic of those who are committed to the lordship of Christ.

God expects his people to resolve their differences within a mutuality of love and understanding.

293

God calls a person to ask and accept forgiveness of anyone he has offended and to stand ready to forgive those who have offended him.

A person is unable to receive God's forgiveness for sin except as he forgives those who have offended him.

God created man for fellowship with him and with one another.

God has created male and female, and has given each sex a unique function. Each person is responsible to the Creator for the fulfillment of his sex role in accord with God's intent and his relationship with the opposite sex.

Parents within the Christian community have the responsibility of living with their children so as to nurture them in the Christian faith.

Within the Christian fellowship adults are responsible not only for establishing open communicative relations with others within the fellowship but also for working to establish this kind of relation with all persons everywhere.

One of the Christian community's major contributions to society as a whole has been its assertion, support, and encouragement of the concept that every individual is legally and socially a person in his own right.

God calls the Christian church to become a community of open communication among men, involving acknowledgment of others, alternating initiative and response (speaking and listening), overcoming conflict between persons and groups (by whatever agreement is possible on provisional and pragmatic grounds), and cultivation of mutual intimacy and respect (acknowledging a variety of ways in which reality is perceived).

God calls man to understand and work to overcome human experiences of alienation: solipsism, stress, conflict, reserve.

1. Significance of the theme for this age level

b. Readiness of the learner for this theme in terms of basic

needs, interests, motivations, capacities, developmental tasks.

The adult's urge to "succeed" in a highly competitive society frequently leads to interpersonal conflicts, the disregard of the other persons's needs, desires and rights, and to broken relationships.

Adult egocentricity can become a barrier to creative relationships with other persons.

The adult's feelings of guilt, anxiety, frustration, and hostility frequently hamper or distort efforts to reestablish relationships with others.

The adult has need for the self-fulfillment, acceptance, and love found in interpersonal relationships of depth, and integrity.

The adult faces the necessity to make adjustments in his personal relationships as changes occur in his health, employment, financial position, marriage status, mobility, and age.

The adult seeks ways of handling interpersonal tensions.

Adults have often acquired a sense of religious indignation about the unfortunate, the outcast, the handicapped which provides motivation for working to bring about wider relationships with these persons within their community.

The adult tends to crystallize his opinions and attitudes about a person, group, or segment of society from one particular experience.

295

The adult is motivated to attain status in the eyes of those whose personal appraisal of him he values.

The adult is motivated by the expectations of society to enter into and maintain a variety of personal relationships.

The adult finds within himself such conflicting tendencies as the desire to help others and the desire to thwart them; the urge to forgive and the desire for revenge; the urge toward conformity to mass opinion and the desire for independence.

The adult is often disillusioned as he comes to grips with evil in himself and others.

The adult needs to discover modes of celebrating his sex, relating to members of his own sex and of the opposite sex in a salubrious manner.

The adult needs to reassess his own attitudes and behavior in terms of the church's assertion of the infinite worth and significance of every other person.

The adult tends to soften the reality of his own shortcomings and the evils of society by engaging in rationalizations: "no one is perfect," "compromise is better than strife," "man is only human."

296

2. **How may this content be communicated as the learner engages in the Learning Tasks? What are the methods and procedures by which the learner may explore the meanings and experiences within this theme (1-a) in the light of his readiness (1-b) in order to discover significance and value?**

By analyzing present interpersonal relationships to discover why tensions among persons occur and what insights are provided by the gospel as to ways of relieving tensions.

By testing in actual situations ways of dealing with interpersonal tensions in the light of the gospel and evaluating the results, looking for clues for further exploration.

By participating in group worship and discussion to look for ways of identifying with others in the worship and in common aspirations to make the worship meaningful in daily living.

By working with persons to achieve a common goal regardless of differences in racial, ethnic, social, economic, and religous backgrounds.

By taking part in small groups engaged in the task of looking for the nature of the relationships which may be established among adults who know and understand one another.

By making deliberate attempts to become acquainted with persons outside the field of their present associations, attitudes, and behavior patterns.

By studying and discussing biblical incidents and precepts dealing with human relationships.

By attempting reconciliation through dialogue when sharp differences of opinion disturb interpersonal relationships.

By analyzing the roles of each person in one's family and defining the needs and rights of each member and his significance to the family's life.

By exploring the implications of the assumption that each person is a child of God, with needs and rights of his own and defining a life style which takes into account the needs and rights of others.

By exploring within an empathetic group in the Christian community the meaning and responsibility of one's sexual role as male or female.

By evaluating, in light of the gospel, one's experiences of being under authority or exerting authority over others within the socio-economic milieu.

3. **What may the learner achieve within this theme in the fulfillment of the Learning Tasks? What are possible changes or learnings on the part of the learner that may result from his appropriation of the significance and value discovered? These changes or learnings may be associated with skills, attitudes, motivations, perceptions including understandings and appreciations.**

297

The adult may understand the Bible as a source from which he can learn of God's intent for all his interpersonal relationships.

The adult may gain greater ability to perceive when conformity to the group or to society is consistent with or violates Christian principles.

The adult may better maintain personal identity and integrity in the face of pressures arising from within the group and from his wider social environment.

The adult may become better able to live altruistically.

The adult may feel more deeply compassion for those who suffer and set about finding ways of alleviating this suffering.

The adult may be led to accept every person as a child of God, having worth and significance.

The adult may come to see God's requirement for treating each person as a beloved brother, regardless of function, race, class, occupation, or social or economic status.

The adult may gain a deeper respect for law and authority, both human and divine, as he deems them essential for wholesome interpersonal relationships.

The adult may accept his (her) sex role within the family and society as God-given, distinguishing between society's interpretation of the masculine and feminine roles and the Christian perspective.

The adult may become more sensitive to the rights and feelings of others and may respond to others so as to foster their own growth as persons created by God.

The adult may develop a Christian faith and value system which enables him to enter into and maintain right relations with others.

The adult may recognize his own failures and mistakes and seek and accept the forgiveness of those he offends.

The adult may try to maintain a readiness to forgive those who offend him.

The adult may assume responsibility for maintaining or reestablishing right relationships within the family.

The adult may accept the responsibility of authority and endeavor to use it wisely.

The adult may discover that all men are children of God, and that God intends them to live together in brotherly love.

The adult may discover how to fulfill his responsibility when in the role of authority without violating his basic respect for the individual and how to submit to authority without denying his own rights as a person.

3. Man's Relation to the Natural Order

Within man's unending quest for knowledge of the natural order are the challenge and the opportunity to relate to it more nearly as God has intended.

EARLY CHILDHOOD

1. Significance of the theme for this age level

a. Meanings and experiences within this theme relevant for this age level. This is content, a selected part of Scope.

God has created everything, all that we can see, taste, smell, hear, and touch. What God has created is good.

God has created all living creatures that walk or crawl upon the earth, fly through the air, swim in the waters.

God has created the sun, moon, and stars and has set them in paths so that there is day and night, cycles of days, weeks, months, years.

God has provided for all living things to grow and to die; this means to change from day to day. Plants grow from seeds, produce new fruit and seeds, then die. Animals are born, grow, produce new animals, and eventually die.

God is still at work in the world. He is the Creator and Sustainer of everything.

299

God has so made the earth that within its natural resources we have food to eat, materials for houses and clothing for our comfort and protection.

God has created the world for us to live in and enjoy.

God intends for us to use the resources of the natural order to supply our needs and to give us pleasure, but he intends for us to take care of these resources, using them wisely and not wastefully.

God expects us to learn about the world and to enjoy it.

Floods, hurricanes, earthquakes, tornadoes, accidents, sickness occur, and persons seek to understand why they happen.

God makes certain things happen at regular intervals, such as day and night, summer and winter, and this influences when we do certain things.

We don't always like all the things that happen in the natural world (if we fall on a stone, we skin our knees) but must learn to live in it as God wants us to live (watching where we run).

1. Significance of the theme for this age level
b. Readiness of the learner for this theme in terms of basic needs, interests, motivations, capacities, developmental tasks

300

The young child is curious about the world around him; he asks questions about everything he sees, touches, tastes, smells, and hears.

The young child is involved in learning that he must balance the variety of foods he eats; he tries new foods, gains a general impression of why certain foods are to be eaten.

The young child is confronted with the need to guard against wasting food: taking small helpings, eating all that is on his plate, avoiding spilling foods.

The young child is confronted with adapting to weather changes: certain clothing is used for rain, cold weather, very warm days.

The young child is able to have some understanding of why playing outdoors is healthful, why he needs light when holding a book or looking at something closely.

The young child has the ability for a general concept of time, such as to distinguish now from yesterday and tomorrow, to learn how far to jump to reach his mark, and to aim his throw so the ball goes where he intended.

The young child has some sense of caution in approaching strange animals, handling unfamiliar objects, and moving over unexplored land.

The young child has the ability to distinguish objects by color, texture, and temperature, such as the orange color of an orange, the smooth fur of a kitten, the cold smoothness of an ice cube.

The young child wants to become acquainted with the beauties and wonders of the natural world, such as the stars, moon, and sun, birds and animals, rocks and shells, the fragrance of flowers, the songs of birds.

Unpleasant experiences in exploring the unknown may create an unreadiness which may be overcome by satisfactory experiences so that the young child's ability to explore is increased in relation to caution against unknown dangers.

2. How may this content be communicated as the learner engages in the Learning Tasks? What are the methods and procedures by which the learner may explore the meanings and experiences within this theme (1-a) in the light of his readiness (1-b) in order to discover significance and value?

By enjoying some of the natural phenomena which God has provided.

By observing how living matter—plants, animals, and persons —changes in keeping with God's plan for growth. (This may be done through planting seeds, tending plants, gathering fruit, periodically measuring and recording the young child's height and weight, noting the growth of a pet, and distinguishing pictures of baby animals and grown animals.)

By observing orderliness and dependability in natural processes such as the rising and setting of the sun, the coming of day and night, and the changes in seasons of the year.

By conversing about God as Creator and Sustainer of the universe, its beauties and wonders, and about God's provision for food, clothing, shelter.

By caring for clothing and possessions, tending pets and plants, wearing the proper clothing or not being wasteful of food, and by having opportunities to converse about some of the reasons for these actions.

301

By looking for beauty in the natural order. (This may be done through listening and imitating the song of a bird; through observing the colors in a sunset; through watching cloud formations; through smelling the fragrances of flowers; through painting pictures of the outdoors.)

By relating the occurrences of natural phenomena to the Christian concept of God.

By exploring ways God shows his creative power in the natural order. (This may be done through examining rocks, coal, minerals, insects, and plants; through simple demonstrations to tell the direction the wind is blowing; field trips and excursions to see waterfalls and rivers, plants, animals and birds, mountains, valleys, plains and the sea; through looking at pictures of natural phenomena; through painting pictures.)

By observing how Christian adults and older children react to the death of a member of the family or of a close friend.

By observing and imitating the actions of adults in conserving natural resources.

By hearing the conversations of adults which reflect their belief in God as the Creator and Sustainer of the universe and themselves as God's stewards of natural resources.

By hearing Bible stories and selected passages concerning God as Creator and Sustainer of the universe.

3. What may the learner achieve within this theme in the fulfillment of the Learning Tasks? What are possible changes or learnings on the part of the learner that may result from his appropriation of the significance and value discovered? These changes or learnings may be associated with skills, attitudes, motivations, perceptions including understandings and appreciations.

The young child may begin to identify aspects of the natural order which surround him daily, and to sense God as the Source.

The young child may achieve feelings of comfort and security within his physical environment.

The young child may desire to give thanks and praise to God for those aspects of the natural order that he can identify such as food, rain, sunshine, wind, flowers, birds.

The young child may begin to assume some responsibility for caring for things God has provided or that man working with God makes available—flowers, toys, pets, plants, clothing.

The young child may begin to express simple concepts in his own words about God as the Creator and Sustainer of the natural order and his own relation to it.

The young child may begin to recognize and appreciate the dependableness of the natural order as found in such phenomena as the regularity of night following day or the rotation of the seasons.

The young child may begin to accept and appreciate that growth and other life changes are a part of God's plan.

The young child may begin to realize that death is a part of the natural order which God created and sustains.

3. Man's Relation to the Natural Order

STATEMENT OF THE THEME

Within man's unending quest for knowledge of the natural order are the challenge and the opportunity to relate it more nearly as God has intended.

ELEMENTARY YEARS

1. Significance of the theme for this age level

a. Meanings and experiences within this theme relevant for this age level. This is content, a selected part of Scope.

God has created the universe, all its vastness, its minute intricacies, and the orderly yet complex relatedness of the parts to the whole.

God has made it so that the natural order supplies man with

303

all the resources he needs for food, shelter, and clothing, but man has to do his part in the growth, development, and distribution of these resources.

The natural order operates on a sequence of cause and effect that persons can recognize. (The sun rises in the east each morning and sets in the west each evening. Seeds planted in the soil, with sunshine and moisture to make them germinate, will develop into full-grown plants like the ones from which the seeds came. The new plants will produce seeds, then wither and die.)

304

God's plan for the life cycle of all living creatures is seen in man's physical development. (He is born, grows to maturity, becomes old, and dies.)

Although man recognizes the natural order as basically dependable, he is not yet able to predict accurately every occurrence.

The beauty, majesty, and wonder of the natural order calls persons to praise the Creator and Sustainer of the universe. God makes evident his greatness and wonder in all that man discovers about the natural order.

Natural disasters, such as earthquakes, storms, and disease, occur and God expects man to seek to understand why they happen and what God's intent may be, and to use man's understanding in beneficial ways.

Persons are responsible to God for the use they make of natural resources and of what they are learning about these resources.

God continues as Creator and Sustainer of the universe and is still at work in it.

God intends for persons to explore the universe and discover better ways of living within it.

Time and distance are essential aspects of the natural order and persons live within the bounds of time and space.

The universe operates within a well-defined order which man can recognize in part and for his well-being he must live in harmony with this order.

God as Creator is the Source and Sustainer of all life and gives meaning to all of life.

1. Significance of the theme for this age level

b. Readiness of the learner for this theme in terms of basic needs, interests, motivations, capacities, developmental tasks.

The elementary child is curious about the world in which he lives and desires opportunities to explore the natural world.

The child is filled with awe and wonder at the mystery of the universe—its vastness and its minuteness as discovered by the telescope and microscope.

The child has a measure of security in his own relationship to the natural order. He experiences being lost, falling down stairways and steep inclines, stumbling and falling, fear from strange sights and sounds and unexplained noises and phenomena, and he reads and hears of or sees movies or television depicting fearsome beasts or happenings in the physical universe.

The child hears about or experiences hurricanes, tornadoes, floods, drouths, storms, and disease and wonders why God permits such to occur.

The child has some opportunities to choose what he eats with awareness of its relationship to health.

The child is able to consider the food needs of all persons and to develop concern that all have enough to eat.

The child can recognize the relationship of fresh air, adequate rest, and proper clothing to good health.

The child is able to assume much responsibility for his own health routines.

The child needs to develop survival skills in protecting himself from hazards, such as learning how to ride a bicycle safely in traffic, taking precautions around fire and in the use of tools, recognizing poisonous plants and dangerous animals.

The child has the ability to select and combine colors and to

305

create designs out of the basic forms in the natural order.

The child is able to relate much that he hears and sees about space exploration to an interpretation of the natural order God has created and sustains.

The child has ability to appreciate the beauty, majesty, and grandeur of the physical world in which he lives.

The child is interested in why plants and animals grow, mature, then die. He is interested in how infants grow into children, why adults grow old, why persons die, and what happens after death.

The elementary child is aware that a creative force in the natural order sustains it and he can understand that for the Christian this force is God.

The elementary child is capable of assuming responsibility for much of his use of natural resources and he can understand the need for and participates in wholehearted conservation of natural resources.

2. How may this content be communicated as the learner engages in the Learning Tasks? What are the methods and procedures by which the learner may explore the meanings and experiences within this theme (1-a) in the light of his readiness (1-b) in order to discover significance and value?

By exploring what God has revealed about man's relation to the natural order through study of selected biblical records of man's relation to the natural order and affirmations of faith in God who cares for man and has given him the capacity to know his world and use its resources for his own benefit.

By exploring predictable and unpredictable natural phenomena with adults concerned to provide a Christian orientation. (This may include observing the stars; gathering and identifying a collection of rocks, butterflies and moths, leaves, wildflowers, and minerals; making field trips to observe natural phenomena, including visits to farms, marine laboratories, zoos, and aquariums; tending a pet and planting and tending plants; studying the nutritional values of the foods eaten regularly; observing the relation of cause and effect as in weather prediction—all in light of the Christian point of view.)

By relating Christian faith in God as Creator and Sustainer to scientific understandings about the natural order. (This may be achieved through study of the Bible and reading and listening to how Christians today are interpreting space exploration, atomic and nuclear action, discoveries in animal husbandry, agriculture, and similar fields.)

By experiencing beauty, awe, and wonder at the splendor, intricacies, and vastness of the natural order. (This may come about through nature hikes, through movies, filmstrips, and photographs of natural phenomena; through the child's own efforts to reproduce in painting and modeling what he has seen in the natural order; through preparing worship materials that center on God as Creator and Sustainer of the universe.)

By exploring personal responsibility and ways a person may assume responsibility for preserving and conserving natural resources and for using them as God's steward. (The child may note the natural resources he uses in daily living, then plan ways a Christian should use these sources. This may include the use of the natural resources of the nation. Viewing and discussing movies, filmstrips, and written reports may aid in this study. The child may also study the Scriptures which set forth the concept that man is accountable to the Creator and Sustainer of the universe for the use he makes of natural resources.)

307

3. **What may the learner achieve within this theme in the fulfillment of the Learning Tasks? What are possible changes or learnings on the part of the learner that may result from his appropriation of the significance and value discovered? These changes or learnings may be associated with skills, attitudes, motivations, perceptions including understandings and appreciations.**

The child may recognize that God is the Creator and Sustainer of all the child sees, hears, smells, tastes, and feels.

The child may gain a sense of security through an awareness of the dependableness of the natural order and the ability to foresee the effects to be expected when particular conditions exist.

The child may recognize that the universe is vast and intricate.

The child may recognize the beauty and wonder in the universe.

The child may assume responsibility for his own use of natural resources as God's steward.

The child may gain ability to articulate his belief in God as the Creator and Sustainer of the universe and himself as God's steward.

The child may recognize God as the Source of the natural order and develop a desire to offer praise and thanksgiving to the Creator.

The child may develop confidence in the basic dependableness of the natural order and a willingness to explore the unknown, to adapt himself to the limitations of time and space, to live in accord with the orderly processes of nature.

The child may accept the principle of change as inherent in the natural order God created and as manifested in the life cycle of all living matter, including birth and death.

The child may recognize that mankind has not discovered all there is to know and understand about the natural order and how it operates, but that God intends for man to continue exploring the universe and making use of its resources.

3. Man's Relation to the Natural Order

STATEMENT OF THE THEME

Within man's unending quest for knowledge of the natural order are the challenge and the opportunity to relate it more nearly as God has intended.

YOUTH

1. **Significance of the theme for this age level**

   a. **Meanings and experiences within this theme relevant for this age level. This is content, a selected part of Scope.**

God is Creator and Sustainer of the universe. He continues to work in the natural order.

God made man an integral part of the natural order and his physical life depends upon the natural world for sustenance.

God has given man intelligence to explore the natural order and to learn how to live in harmony with natural law.

The order, beauty, majesty, and mystery of the universe are evidences of God's creative and sustaining power.

Man, as part of the created natural order, is to praise and worship the Creator and Sustainer of that order.

The natural order is dynamic; this means continuous change. When seen in the life span of a plant, an animal, even man himself, this involves birth, growth, maturity, death.

God has endowed man with the rights and responsibilities of a steward of the natural world. Therefore man is accountable to God for the knowledge and skills he acquires as well as the uses he makes of natural resources.

309

The universe operates within a well-defined order which man can recognize in part and for his well-being he is to live in harmony with natural law.

Natural disasters, such as earthquakes, storms and disease, occur and God expects man to seek to understand why they happen and what God's intent may be, and to use man's understanding in beneficial ways.

Time and space are essential dimensions of the natural order and persons must live within these limitations.

The ultimate meaning of life for man is to be found in the Creator rather than in the created.

1. Significance of the theme for this age level

b. Readiness of the learner for this theme in terms of basic needs, interests, motivations, capacities, developmental tasks.

The youth's curiosity and increased capacity to reason enhance his readiness to learn about the origin of all life, especially the Christian concept of the natural order.

The youth's capacity to comprehend the vastness and intricacies of the universe makes him eager to explore the natural order and his relation to it.

The youth's awareness of technological achievements and scientific discoveries creates an interest in knowing more about the natural order.

The language of technology and science and some persons engaged in these fields seem at variance with the language of Christian faith and positions taken by church members. This tends to create confusion in the minds of youth, open rebellion against Christianity, or an eagerness to explore the issues.

Increased perception and intensity of feeling tend to make youth more aware and appreciative of the beauty, grandeur, and mystery of the natural world, which may result in moments of deep spiritual insight into the nature of God, Creator and Sustainer of the universe.

Sensitive to sharp distinctions between right and wrong, good and evil, youth tend to question why such natural phenomena as earthquakes, tornadoes, floods, drouths, hurricanes, and disease exist in a world created and sustained by God.

Youth has the ability to understand his own limitations and responsibilities in exploring the natural order and in using natural resources.

The youth has the capacity to realize the relation to health and physical stamina of the use of foods and other natural resources and has the ability to exercise control over his personal selection of them.

The youth is able to recognize the time-space dimensions of the natural order and to make creative and constructive use of them.

The youth seeks an understanding of the creative force in the universe.

The youth often ponders and reflects upon the meaning of the changes which take place in the life cycle of all living matter.

2. **How may this content be communicated as the learner engages in the Learning Tasks? What are the methods and procedures by which the learner may explore the meanings and experiences within this theme (1-a) in the light of his readiness (1-b) in order to discover significance and value?**

By exploring the natural order in light of the purposes of God as Creator and Sustainer of the universe. (This exploration may include the selection, reading, and discussion of appropriate scripture to discover what the Bible has to say about the origin, nature, and purposes of the natural order.)

By exploring what present-day scientists who are Christian believe about God's creative activity in and through the natural order. (This may be done through study of the writings of such persons, listening to them tell their beliefs, or engaging in dialogue with them, viewing movies and filmstrips which set forth their concepts.)

By studying the scriptures which deal with man's relation to the natural order to discover the role God intends man to have in the natural order.

By analyzing learnings from science which throw new light on man's understanding of the natural order and his ability to control the forces of nature or accommodate himself to these forces so that he can make wider use of them. (Youth may demonstrate his scientific knowledge through his own interpretation of these findings in the light of God as Creator and Sustainer of the universe. Youth may explore ways mankind is being and can be

311

benefited by present-day knowledge of the universe.

By preparing worship materials that focus upon the dynamic and orderly, the majestic and unfinished, the known and the mysterious aspects of the universe, and the significant role God intends for man to have within the natural order.

By participating with other Christians in activities and the use of resources that enable youth to gain increased understanding of the activity of God in the natural order which he has created.

By exploring the Christian and the scientific approaches to the natural order. (One procedure is to examine and study materials which interpret the view of each and comparing or contrasting these viewpoints.)

Studying the scriptures and scientific disciplines to discover man's limitations and responsibilities in the care and use of natural resources.

By using art media—drawing, painting, preparation of models, music, poetry and descriptive prose—by which youth may express feelings toward the Creator and Sustainer of the natural order.

By exploring with Christian adults the meaning of life and death as inherent in God's plan for the universe—conception, birth, development, maturity, death. This might include the analyzing of man's fears and uncertainties about life and death and evaluating these in the light of biblical teaching and affirmations of the Christian faith.

By exploring the significance of being a steward of the natural order, accountable to God for the use made of natural resources.

3. **What may the learner achieve within this theme in the fulfillment of the Learning Tasks? What are possible changes or learnings on the part of the learner that may result from his appropriation of the significance and value discovered? These changes or learnings may be associated with skills, attitudes, motivations, perceptions including understandings and appreciations.**

Youth may accept that God is Creator and Sustainer of the natural order and that man is his steward in the use of natural resources.

Youth may acquire ability to articulate faith in God as Creator and Sustainer of the natural order.

Youth may assume responsibility for personal and corporate worship of God as Creator and Sustainer.

Youth may recognize his own dependence upon the natural order for sustenance and gain ability to use natural resources as God intended.

Youth's appreciation of the orderliness and dependableness of the natural order may lead him to adapt his way of life to be in harmony with them.

Youth's appreciation of the beauty and majesty within the natural order may lead youth to have a more meaningful sense of awe and wonder of the Creator and Sustainer of the universe, to preserve and enhance this beauty and majesty, and to create new beauty.

Youth may discover the various points of view concerning the natural order and youth's relation to it, and gain ability in evaluating these theories in the light of the gospel.

Youth may come to expect new discoveries concerning the operation and processes of the natural order and evaluate them in terms of man's responsibility as God's steward.

313

Youth assumes responsibility for the care and use of what God has made available in the natural order.

Youth may develop awareness that the natural order was created and is sustained for the benefit of man, at the same time acknowledging that man is not free to exploit and despoil natural resources.

Youth may accept the principle of change in living matter as inherent in the natural order God created—conception, birth, maturity, death.

Youth may believe that, in light of the gospel, the physical death of man is not his ultimate destiny.

3. Man's Relation to the Natural Order

STATEMENT OF THE THEME

Within man's unending quest for knowledge of the natural order are the challenge and the opportunity to relate it more nearly as God has intended.

ADULTHOOD

1. **Significance of the theme for this age level**

   a. **Meanings and experiences within this theme relevant for this age level. This is content, a selected part of Scope.**

God is the Creator and Sustainer of the universe of which man himself is a part and continues to work in it.

God intends the natural order, with the help of man, to supply man with all he needs for physical sustenance.

God has given man the intelligence to explore the universe and discover how it operates and expects man to use that intelligence in responsible ways.

God has given man the ability to find ways of using natural resources for his own good.

God expects man to act as a steward of the natural order, therefore man is accountable to God for the knowledge and skills he acquires as well as the use he makes of natural resources.

Because God alone is omniscient, there is an element of mystery in the universe. The more man discovers about the natural order, the more he finds is unknown to him.

Not only is there mystery in the universe, there is mystery in God's intent in the natural order and man's relation to the natural order. A part of the mystery is God's intent in such occurrences as storm, earthquakes, tornadoes, hurricanes, and disease.

Man, as part of the created natural order, is to worship and praise the Creator and Sustainer of that order.

God's plan for the life cycle in the natural order, including man himself, involves birth, growth, maturity, and death.

The ultimate meaning of life for man is to be found in the Creator rather than in the created.

1. Significance of the theme for this age level

b. Readiness of the learner for this theme in terms of basic needs, interests, motivations, capacities, developmental tasks.

The adult has a need to strengthen the relationship that exists between him and the natural order by exploring and using the materials around him.

The adult has the capacity to reflect on the origin of all life and to differentiate as well as to see the relationship between human life and other life in the natural order.

The adult yearns to understand the mysteries of the universe and his relation to the natural order.

The adult is motivated by his own physical needs to explore his environment in order that he may find ways of meeting his needs.

The adult's persistent quest for knowledge, his desire to see the relation between cause and effect and to control natural forces motivate him to explore the natural order.

The adult's concern for health and well-being lead him to experiment with ways of using natural elements.

The more the adult comprehends of the vastness and intricacy of the universe, the more he wants to understand.

The adult is curious about his ultimate destiny: he may look upon death with fear and dread of the unknown, he may rebel against death as the ultimate deterrent to fulfillment of his destiny, or he may view death as a basic aspect in God's plan for all living matter.

The adult may have tension between his concepts of God as

315

Creator and Sustainer and the rapidly expanding knowledge of the created universe.

The adult has the capacity to recognize that God is still creatively active and rules the universe, and to accept responsibility as God's steward of the natural order.

The adult, confronted with natural disasters, such as hurricanes, floods drouths, tornadoes, earthquakes, and disease, seeks an explanation consistent with his understanding of the Creator.

316

2. **How may this content be communicated as the learner engages in the Learning Tasks? What are the methods and procedures by which the learner may explore the meanings and experiences within this theme (1-a) in the light of his readiness (1-b) in order to discover significance and value?**

By exploring the natural order in light of the purposes of God as Creator and Sustainer of the universe. (This exploration may include the selection, reading, and discussion of appropriate scripture to discover what the Bible has to say about the origin, nature, and purposes of the natural order.)

By exploring what present-day scientists who are Christian believe about God's creative activity in and through the natural order. (This may be done through study of the writings of such persons, listening to them tell their beliefs, or engaging in dialogue with them, viewing movies and filmstrips which set forth their concepts.)

By studying the scriptures which deal with man's relation to the natural order to discover the role God intends man to have in the natural order.

By analyzing learnings from science which throw new light on man's understanding of the natural order and his ability to control the forces of nature or accommodate himself to these forces so that he can make wider use of them. (The adult may demonstrate his scientific knowledge through his own interpretation of these findings in light of God as Creator and Sustainer of the universe. He may explore ways mankind is being and can be benefited by present-day knowledge of the universe.)

By preparing worship materials that focus upon the dynamic and orderly, the majestic and unfinished, the known and the mysterious aspects of the universe, and the significant role God intends for man to have within the natural order.

By participating with other Christians in activities and the use of resources that enable adults to gain increased understanding of the activity of God in the natural order which he has created.

By exploring the Christian and the scientific approaches to the natural order. (One procedure is to examine and study materials which interpret the view of each and comparing or contrasting these viewpoints.)

By studying the scriptures and scientific disciplines to discover man's limitations and responsibilities in the care and use of natural resources.

By using art media—drawing, painting, preparation of models, music, poetry and descriptive prose—by which adults may express feelings toward the Creator and Sustainer of the natural order.

By exploring with other Christians the meaning of life and death as inherent in God's plan for the universe—conception, birth, development, maturity, death. This might include the analyzing of man's fears and uncertainties about life and death and evaluating these in the light of biblical teaching and affirmations of the Christian faith.

By exploring the significance of being a steward of the natural order, accountable to God for the use made of natural resources.

317

3. **What may the learner achieve within this theme in the fulfillment of the Learning Tasks? What are possible changes or learnings on the part of the learner that may result from his appropriation of the significance and value discovered?**

These changes or learnings may be associated with skills, attitudes, motivations, perceptions including understandings and appreciations.

The adult may grow in the Christian belief that God is Creator and Sustainer of the natural order.

The adult may understand the tenets of the Christian faith, especially as stated in scripture, about man's relation to the natural order.

The adult's appreciation of the orderliness and dependableness of the natural order may lead him to adapt his way of life to be in harmony with them.

The adult's awareness of his dependence upon the natural order for sustenance may lead him to work within the principles operative in the natural order to secure the material resources he needs.

The adult's appreciation of the beauty and majesty within the natural order may lead the adult to have a more meaningful sense of awe and wonder of the Creator and Sustainer of the universe, to preserve and enhance this beauty and majesty, and to create new beauty.

The adult may accept responsibility for the care and use of what God has given in the natural order.

The adult's acceptance of the mysteries within the natural order may challenge the adult to probe them and to discover more about the processes and operation of the natural order as the ways in which God works.

The adult may recognize the implications of the principle of change in all living organisms of the natural order God has created, and grow in his ability to accept changes in his own cycle of life.

The adult may entrust his life to God, believing that God does not intend physical death as the ultimate destiny of man.

4. Man's Involvement in Social Forces

STATEMENT OF THE THEME

Related to life's setting and to God's purpose are social forces, units, structures, and systems with potential for both good and evil, which man must learn to live with in light of the Christian view of history and of the social order.

EARLY CHILDHOOD

1. Significance of the theme for this age level

a. Meanings and experiences within this theme relevant for this age level. This is content, a selected part of Scope.

God is the Creator of everyone and cares about each person.
God intends for us to love one another and to live together happily.
God has planned for us to live in families.
We show our love for members of our family by being thoughtful and helpful.
We show our love for persons outside the family circle by being thoughtful and helpful.
We show love and concern for others by letting them play with our toys.
God made persons different from one another.
People in the church care about me and I like to be with them.

319

1. Significance of the theme for this age level

b. Readiness of the learner for this theme in terms of basic needs, interests, motivations, capacities, developmental tasks

The young child is constantly facing situations involving other persons in which he needs to know what is expected of him and how he is to act. He wants to know: what is the acceptable response when a stranger smiles at him, when another person cries, when the other person is angry, when he is being teased.

The young child seeks ways of showing affection which are acceptable to others.

The young child becomes aware of differences among persons: boys and girls, men and women, persons with different colored skin, older children and younger children, older persons, persons who live in his neighborhood and those who live beyond his neighborhood.

The young child demands reasons for behaving in a particular way. Sometimes he is comfortable in familiar patterns and sometimes he is frustrated when he must conform.

The young child learns that there are ways of acting which bring the approval of the other members of his family and there are other ways of acting which bring disapproval, even punishment. He must learn how to distinguish these ways of acting and understand why some behavior is acceptable and other behavior is rejected.

The young child is discovering that acceptable behavior patterns differ. What is acceptable at home may not be acceptable at church, or at a home in which he is a visitor.

The young child is eager for opportunities to act independently of others, but he wants to continue to be supported by his family and/or friends.

Oftentimes the young child runs into conflict between what he wants to do and what another wants. He must learn to give and take in relationships with others.

2. **How may this content be communicated as the learner engages in the Learning Tasks? What are the methods and procedures by which the learner may explore the meanings and experiences within this theme (1-a) in the light of his readiness (1-b) in order to discover significance and value?**

By being with adult Christians who by their behavior reflect their respect for the worth and significance of every person as being created by God.

By having opportunities under the guidance of adult Christians to work and play with others in his home and elsewhere.

By having opportunities under the guidance of adult Christians for experiences with others in which he may have help in handling problems of relationships.

By hearing simple Bible (and other) stories and having conversations about God's plan for families and how this plan is carried out in a variety of ways.

By having opportunities to do small acts of service for parents or others he can do by himself or with little guidance, such as doing easy errands or performing easy tasks, making simple gifts, or otherwise showing kindnesses.

By having opportunities for play with other children during which he lets them play with his toys or they play with one another's toys without undue pressure from adults.

By being with Christian adults who in their conversation reflect their willingness to help others and by the way they live show their concern for others.

By having experiences in his local congregation in which he feels love and concern for him as a person.

By hearing simple stories about the church and his place in it.

By being with persons of various ages, races, sizes, and color and having opportunity to talk with Christian adults about any of his experiences with various persons.

By doing helpful acts for others in company with those older or younger than he is.

By becoming aware of participation of his parents in groups that are serving and helping others.

3. **What may the learner achieve within this theme in the fulfillment of the Learning Tasks? What are possible changes or learnings on the part of the learner that may result from his appropriation of the significance and value discovered?**

321

These changes or learnings may be associated with skills, attitudes, motivations, perceptions including understandings and appreciations.

The young child may become aware of love for God who loves him and for groups of persons, such as his family.

The young child may develop as a cooperative member of his family and other groups of which he is a part.

The young child may find satisfaction in simple work which he does with others.

322

The young child may develop some ability to deal with tensions and frustrations in the family and in other groups of which he is a part.

The young child may begin to develop ability to make choices based on his own understanding of right and wrong, or on his parents' standards of right and wrong, rather than on pressures from a group such as a play group.

The young child may develop beginning awareness that some groups serve and help others, for example, the church, the family, the kindergarten group.

The young child may begin to identify with groups beyond his family.

4. Man's Involvement in Social Forces

STATEMENT OF THE THEME

Related to life's setting and to God's purpose are social forces, units, structures, and systems with potential for both good and evil, which man must learn to live with in light of the Christian view of history and of the social order.

ELEMENTARY YEARS

1. Significance of the theme for this age level

a. **Meanings and experiences within this theme relevant for this age level. This is content, a selected part of Scope.**

God acts in the relationships and events of everyday life.

Each person lives in social settings that help shape his attitudes, values, and behavior patterns. Such settings include the family, school, community, and church, each with its traditions and mores which the child is to judge in light of his understanding of the gospel.

God intends for persons to live together.

God expects persons to live in accord with his purposes even when this causes them to act contrary to the will of the group.

The elementary child is dependent on the groups of which he is a part and they are dependent upon him.

Each person is a creature of God and has worth and significance.

The child is responsible as a member of his family and of any other group to which he belongs. This responsibility includes upholding the mores, traditions, and purposes of the group when it is endeavoring to live within the purposes of God.

God intends for each individual to be unique, therefore persons do not think, feel, and act alike.

The Christian church is a unique social force which nurtures the child in the Christian faith and provides him opportunities to develop his ability to evaluate all other experiences with social forces in light of the gospel.

323

1. **Significance of the theme for this age level**

b. **Readiness of the learner for this theme in terms of basic needs, interests, motivations, capacities, developmental tasks.**

The elementary-age child is discovering that he lives in an ever-enlarging world of persons and that he is interrelated with them in many different ways.

The child finds that his relationships with persons requires obedience or conformity to laws, mores, and behavior patterns which often have little meaning to him.

The child is adjusting to the ways in which his family functions—its traditions, customs, and its authority structure.

The child identifies himself with various groups outside his family—neighborhood groups, both peers and adults; school groups, both pupils and teachers; and church groups including peers, teachers, clergy, and officers of the church.

As the child develops ability to formulate his own ideas and his own patterns of behavior, he tends to assert himself. Sometimes this brings him into conflict with established authority and group pressures at home, school, church, and community.

The child begins to distinguish social forces, in which he may or may not be directly involved, as being constructive or destructive.

The child makes decisions in events or within group activities—decisions that may not always conform to the group's will. This may cause the group to reject the child, or may cause a new grouping to form around him which, in turn, may give the child an inflated sense of importance and power.

The child is becoming aware of the unique role of the church as a social force in relation to other social forces.

The child has the capacity to respond creatively to changing social forces.

The child is discovering that the support of family and other groups is essential for his self-realization.

2. **How may this content be communicated as the learner engages in the Learning Tasks? What are the methods and procedures by which the learner may explore the meanings and experiences within this theme (1-a) in the light of his readiness (1-b) in order to discover significance and value.**

By studying customs, ordinances, or laws of his community,

such as those dealing with traffic, that affect his life and conduct, to determine to what extent they are consistent with Christian teachings regarding the worth of persons.

By reading biographies of Christian leaders who have worked for the rights of every person.

By evaluating with Christian adults various group experiences in the church, school, and community, and discussing the influence members of the groups had on these experiences as well as the ways the group experiences influenced the members.

By engaging in Bible study dealing with the significance and worth of persons and by considering, under the leadership of Christian adults, the implications this study has for the child's life in school, church, or elsewhere.

By exploring the history and customs of his immediate community to discover ways God has worked in its history and continues to work in this community.

By hearing, reading, and studying Bible (and other) stories that show some of the ways God has acted and continues to act through persons and especially through the church and its leaders.

By analyzing some of the social forces, including school, home, groups, and friends, which help shape his own ideas and determine his choices.

By identifying some of the problems and failures and successes in dealing with these problems in social units in which he is involved—family, neighbor groups, school groups, church groups—and by seeking for improved ways to deal with these problems to the end that he may better cope with them and become a more responsible and useful member of the group and of society.

325

3. **What may the learner achieve within this theme in the fulfillment of the Learning Tasks? What are possible changes or learnings on the part of the learner that may result from his appropriation of the significance and value discovered?**

These changes or learnings may be associated with skills, attitudes, motivations, perceptions including understandings and appreciations.

The child may develop awareness that God works through groups to influence daily events.

The child may realize the value of being part of a family and what the support of a Christian family means.

The child may share in groups trying to exert a Christian force.

The child may be able to withstand group pressures of a social unit which do not conform to Christian standards as he is beginning to understand them.

The child may be aware that some social forces are harmful to individuals and to groups of persons.

The child may increasingly respect and obey the social pressure of law and order in relation to Christian citizenship.

The child may understand something of the uniqueness of the church as a social force among other social forces.

The child may become a more responsible member of the social unit to which he belongs.

The child may develop some skill in helping relieve tensions and solve disagreements in a group.

4. Man's Involvement in Social Forces

STATEMENT OF THE THEME

Related to life's setting and to God's purpose are social forces, units, structures, and systems with potential for both good and evil, which man must learn to live with in light of the Christian view of history and of the social order.

YOUTH

1. Significance of the theme for this age level

a. Meanings and experiences within this theme relevant for this age level. This is content, a selected part of Scope.

God acts purposefully in history—calling, choosing, shattering, covenanting and judging—through social structures, events, institutions, units, and systems.

Man, as created by God, is a social being. In his living with other persons his potential selfhood is actualized.

Each person is born into a particular social order and lives in a society which exerts formative influences upon him. The Christian youth evaluates, accepts, or rejects these influences in light of the gospel.

Each youth is responsible for cooperating with and working constructively in and through social forces to enable the life of man to come more nearly in line with God's will.

Sometimes, to be consistent with God's purposes, youth has to resist what a group (or social force) would require him to think or do. When he acts contrary to the ways of the group, he risks disapproval and/or rejection.

The Christian church is a unique social force providing youth opportunities to understand the gospel, to evaluate other social forces in the light of that gospel, and to act in accord with the requirements of this evaluation, confident that he is working within the purposes of God.

Youth is responsible to his family, upholding its traditions and purposes and at the same time evaluating them and helping the family evaluate them in light of the gospel.

1. Significance of the theme for this age level

b. Readiness of the learner for this theme in terms of basic needs, interests, motivations, capacities, developmental tasks.

Youth desires to relate his Christian faith to the social forces operating in his world.

327

Youth has the capacity to see that his actions and those of the groups to which he belongs have consequences for society and for himself.

Youth needs to be challenged by a goal or a cause that demands his best efforts and to which he may be committed.

Youth questions traditions, cultural practices, and values society expects him to accept without questioning.

Youth faces threats to his security when his peers or persons he respects reject him or find fault with him; when his values are tested and found inadequate by the values of other persons and groups; when he loses confidence in parents, teachers, national and world heroes, and his peers; when he is confronted with the fact that men today have the know-how to destroy themselves and the earth.

Youth is continually coping with pressures to conform to behavior patterns which evolve outside himself, especially those related to his being accepted by peer groups.

Youth is aware of the church as a social force. (Some find it effective; others may find it ineffective in today's world; and still others may find it effective within its own area but unrelated to other social forces and meaningless for the individual's own daily life.)

Youth tends to strive for leader roles especially among his peers and when the role allows him to demonstrate his abilities before adults.

Youth is often caught between his need to establish his own unique identity and his desire to be accepted by other persons and groups.

Youth is able to suffer for his Christian faith when, because of his faith, he goes counter to the mores or norms of social forces in which he is involved.

2. **How may this content be communicated as the learner engages in the Learning Tasks? What are the methods and procedures by which the learner may explore the meanings**

and experiences within this theme (1-a) in the light of his readiness (1-b) in order to discover significance and value?

By exploring ways in which God has worked and is working in history through social forces. (Procedures for this exploration are selecting, studying, and discussing appropriate scripture passages and views from religious literature; and evaluating events in secular history to discover how moral decisions have given the direction to events.)

By evaluating in light of the gospel his involvement in various groups and the social forces operating within them. (Some procedures are studying biblical passages and sociological literature that give insights on the nature and the operation of social forces and their effects upon youth; engaging in individual and group actions which later are evaluated in terms of the interdependence of the youth and the social units; and analyzing art, theater, TV, and other mass communication media which reflect social forces at work.)

By examining social forces to discover their potentialities for good or for evil. (Procedures for this examination are selecting, analyzing and discussing relevant source materials; using observations, field trips and projects that reveal social forces at work.)

By exploring opportunities to cooperate with and work constructively in and through social forces in ways consistent with God's will. (Some procedures are developing and/or using projects in social action, community service, and world outreach as forms of Christian witness.)

329

By exploring how God expects him to act when confronted with social forces contrary to his convictions. (Procedures are examining biblical and biographical literature; evaluating case studies involving tensions with social forces, and illustrating ways in which persons have obeyed God without counting the cost.)

By exploring ways in which persons, though the victims of unjust social forces, have been forgiving and have witnessed to

God's love and will. (Procedures are studying the Bible and religious literature; analyzing studies of the lives of the prophets, apostles, missionaries, social and political reformers.)

By exploring the unique role of the Christian church as a social force. (Procedures are selecting, studying, and discussing the purposes and functions of the church as presented in the New Testament, as shown in church history, and as reflected in present-day writings about the church's responsibility to society; and discovering society's view of the church's role and comparing this with the church's view.)

3. What may the learner achieve within this theme in the fulfillment of the Learning Tasks? What are possible changes or learnings on the part of the learner that may result from his appropriation of the significance and value discovered? These changes or learnings may be associated with skills, attitudes, motivations, perceptions including understandings and appreciations.

Youth may recognize that God acts in and through social forces to achieve his purpose in history.

Youth may discover the force of Christian cultural practices and social values.

Youth may become creatively concerned for the rights and welfare of all peoples and risk discomfort, rejection, and antagonism to help those whose rights are in jeopardy.

Youth may assume responsibility to cooperate with and work constructively in and through social forces in ways consistent with God's will.

Youth may develop the ability to deal with inner conflicts on Christian bases when the will of a social unit in which he is involved is counter to the will of God.

Youth may develop skill in resolving conflicts which arise within his social groups.

Youth may discover the unique role of the church among other social forces.

4. Man's Involvement in Social Forces

STATEMENT OF THE THEME

Related to life's setting and to God's purpose are social forces, units, structures, and systems with potential for both good and evil, which man must learn to live with in light of the Christian view of history and of the social order.

ADULTHOOD

1. Significance of the theme for this age level

a. Meanings and experiences within this theme relevant for this age level. This is content, a selected part of Scope.

God acts purposefully in history—calling, choosing, shattering, covenanting, and judging—in social structures, events, institutions, units, and systems.

Man, as created by God, is a social being. In his living with other persons his potential selfhood is actualized.

Each person is born into a particular social order and the society in which he lives influences what he thinks, feels, and does. The Christian evaluates these influences in light of the gospel, then chooses to submit to those influences which are in accord with the will of God and resists those which are contrary to his will.

331

The social institutions, units, structures, events, and systems in which the adult is involved are necessary for his proper functioning as a human being, at the same time they are worthy of his involvement only if they enable him to fulfill the purposes of God.

The adult is responsible to each social group in which he

participates, to help it evaluate its life in light of the gospel, and to make changes in its life consistent with God's will.

The Christian church is a unique social force, providing the Christian adult opportunities to understand the gospel and evaluate all other social forces in the light of that gospel, confident that he is working within the purposes of God.

Sometimes, to be consistent with God's will, the adult has to resist what a group (or social force) would require him to think or do. When he acts contrary to the ways of the group, he risks disapproval and/or rejection.

332

The adult is responsible to his family, for upholding its traditions and purposes and helping establish new practices and purposes, and at the same time for evaluating these traditions, purposes, and practices and helping others in the family evaluate them in light of the gospel.

1. Significance of the theme for this age level

b. Readiness of the learner for this theme in terms of basic needs, interests, motivations, capacities, developmental tasks.

The adult desires to see the relevance of his Christian faith in all his involvements with social forces.

When the adult comes into conflict with a social force, he must weigh his position, or his group's position, in light of the purposes of the social force. He may find himself the victim in a clash between two opposing social forces, and as a consequence thrust into establishing his own Christian viewpoint on the issue.

The adult's deep allegiance and responsibility to himself and to his family inclines him to interpret the influences of social forces in the light of their effect upon him and/or his family.

The adult responds to the requirements of laws, behavior patterns, mores in his society with varying degrees of willingness. He has the capacity to become involved in social action and to work aggressively to change his society.

The adult is aware that broad social changes usually require group action as well as individual. He has the capacity to associate himself with those groups which will support him and enlarge his influence in social action.

The adult has the capacity to reappraise and challenge opinions, traditions, systems, and institutions, and to follow through with appropriate action to effect change.

The adult has the capacity for awareness of his dependence for health and welfare upon units within the social order over which he has little control.

The adult has the capacity to work for the redemption of society.

The adult is able to count the cost of going counter to the established social forces to maintain his own integrity in the Christian faith, and he is capable of suffering the consequences.

2. How may this content be communicated as the learner engages in the Learning Tasks? What are the methods and procedures by which the learner may explore the meanings and experiences within this theme (1-a) in the light of his readiness (1-b) in order to discover significance and value?

By exploring ways in which God acts in and through man's institutions, laws, structures and other social units, forces, and events. (This may be done through studying the Bible, through a Christian interpretation of history, contemporary literature, art and other media of expression.)

By examining the social aspects of his nature as created by God and the influence of social forces upon his life. (This may be done through studying biblical material on God's expectations for man; through investigating scientific theories and findings about man as a social being; through expressions of man's relationships with his fellows as reflected in the theatre, the arts, and literature.)

By investigating how man, through his social structures, may either thwart or support the purposes of God. (This may be

333

done through studying the Bible passages which deal with social forces and their relation to God's purposes for man; engaging in studies (course) in the social sciences or other disciplines which throw light upon man's need for and use of social forces; and organizing and/or participating in Christian social action.)

By exploring what it means to obey God's call to act responsibly in and through social forces in which he is or may become involved. (This may be done through a study of social forces, structures, units, and traditions within the community in order to discover what the Christian does in obedience to God; through appraising previously unchallenged opinions, traditions, systems, and institutions in light of the gospel.)

By seeking to discover the uniqueness of the church as a social force in providing the adult an opportunity to develop a Christian perspective toward all other social forces. (This may be done through research into the purposes and functions of the church as set forth in the New Testament and in writings about the church's relation to other social forces; through becoming informed about the church's current role in social issues; through participating in a variety of projects in Christian action and community service; through worshiping with the congregation.)

By exploring the Christian principle of mutuality (i.e., the individual and the group are dependent upon and responsible for each other) and its role in the adult's self-actualization. (This may be done through selecting, examining, and discussing relevant Bible passages; analyzing local social units for evidence of the mutuality principle and its results; testing the mutuality principle in one's own primary social groups; examining scientific findings and/or engaging in studies or projects which show how the adult finds fulfillment in responsible group relationships.)

3. **What may the learner achieve within this theme in the fulfillment of the Learning Tasks? What are possible changes or learnings on the part of the learner that may result from his appropriation of the significance and value discovered?**

These changes or learnings may be associated with skills, attitudes, motivations, perceptions including understandings and appreciations.

The adult may become increasingly able to withstand pressures of social forces to conform when this is contrary to his own will and/or contrary to what he believes to be the will of God.

The adult may commit himself to participate constructively in social forces in the community and world around him, being especially sensitive to his responsibility to those mistreated or hurt by social forces.

The adult may have a high degree of understanding of and skill in using Christian principles for analyzing social forces—units, events, institutions, structures, and systems.

The adult may develop sensitivity to the gap between Christian principles and social injustice, inequity, prejudice, with maturing ability to live creatively within this tension.

The adult may become fully aware of what social forces provide for man's life, and increase his ability to recognize and utilize those provisions which help man and reject those that bemean man.

The adult may assess the life of the organized church in light of the gospel and attempt needed reforms of social injustices within the church.

335

The adult may participate responsibly in church groups which are attempting to bring social forces more nearly in accord with God's will.

The adult may recognize the unique role of the church, as a social force, among community, national, and international structures and systems, and take a responsible part in the fulfillment of this role.

The adult may realize that God works in and through social forces to benefit mankind and to achieve his purpose in history, and may assume responsibility for helping in the fulfillment of this purpose.

5. Man's Coping with Change and the Absolute

STATEMENT OF THE THEME

Man's search for the permanent and at the same time his longing for change are answered by God as ultimate reality and absolute value.

EARLY CHILDHOOD

1. Significance of the theme for this age level

    a. Meanings and experiences within this theme relevant for this age level. This is content, a selected part of Scope.

God's love for us is permanent and unchanging.

God is the Creator, Sustainer, and Ruler of the universe. This is the Father's universe.

The natural order which God created and sustains is dependable.

No two days, no two happenings are exactly alike; change is a part of God's plan for daily life. Change can be a source of excitement, eager anticipation, and surprise, and need not be threatening as the familiar and precious are replaced by the new and untried.

The body grows from day to day, and use of my body increases from day to day. God planned change as essential to life. The growth of our bodies from day to day shows this.

God has made us so that each person must choose how he will respond to his changing situation. His choices have consequences.

God's love can be depended on, even in catacylsmic change, such as an earthquake, hurricane, flood, separation and divorce of parents, and death.

1. Significance of the theme for this age level

    b. Readiness of the learner for this theme in terms of basic

needs, interests, motivations, capacities, developmental tasks

The young child has a basic need for physical and emotional security.

The young child is beginning to have experiences of change in his life. Some are with persons outside his family who may or may not be friendly and trustworthy.

The young child needs to be loved and to love.

The young child has capacity to learn where the bounds are on what he can do, what is acceptable behavior, how these change, and where authority rests.

The young child's curiosity about the unknown leads him to explore the unknown. At the same time he may be aware that there are limits beyond which he cannot explore on his own.

The young child's security is enhanced by simple explanations of what is happening or about to happen in changes that affect him.

The young child has the capacity to become increasingly aware of the dependableness of God's universe.

The young child has the capacity to recognize to an increasing degree that adults about him accept God as the ultimate authority and determine right and wrong in the light of God's will.

337

The young child may experience catastrophic changes in his life such as earthquake, hurricane, flood, separation and divorce of parents, or death of loved ones, and his resultant sense of loss may especially ready him for the assurance of God's continuing love.

The young child is curious about the changes in his own growth and his mastery of basic skills such as walking, talking, dressing himself, and managing his own food, and has increasing capacity to identify these changes as part of God's plan for his development.

2. **How may this content be communicated as the learner engages in the Learning Tasks? What are the methods and procedures by which the learner may explore the meanings and experiences within this theme (1-a) in the light of his readiness (1-b) in order to discover significance and value?**

Through associating with Christian adults who are themselves dependable.

Through associating with Christians who articulate their love of God and others and reflect his love in their relationships.

Through experiences in the physical universe in the company of persons who have found it dependable and a good home that God has provided man.

Through hearing Bible stories and verses which tell of God as Creator and Sovereign Ruler of the universe.

Through observing and talking with Christian adults or youth, about his own physical growth.

Through observing the growth of animals and plants, the change of seasons, the withering of a plant, the harvesting of crops, the birth or death of a pet.

Through hearing Bible stories or verses that tell about God's gifts.

Through acknowledging God in prayer and song as the Source of daily food and of all that the child has.

Through observing adults who, by their behavior, acknowledge God as Ruler of their lives.

Through being with adults whose attitudes and behavior toward cataclysmic events reflect their faith in God.

Through being with Christian adults who help him to know what is right and wrong behavior.

3. **What may the learner achieve within this theme in the fulfillment of the Learning Tasks? What are possible changes or learnings on the part of the learner that may result from his appropriation of the significance and value discovered?**

These changes or learnings may be associated with skills, attitudes, motivations, perceptions including understandings and appreciations.

The young child may understand that God is his loving Father who cares for him at all times.

The young child may think of God as dependable and trust him.

The young child may discover that certain natural phenomena in God's world are dependable and that they occur over and over again.

The young child may have beginning understanding of God as having power over all the universe.

The young child may have beginning knowledge that right and wrong are related to God's will and may endeavor to do what God would want.

The young child may recognize that authority outside himself sets bounds to his freedom and he may accept this authority and live within its bounds.

5. Man's Coping with Change and the Absolute

STATEMENT OF THE THEME

Man's search for the permanent and at the same time his longing for change are answered by God as ultimate reality and absolute value.

339

ELEMENTARY YEARS

1. Significance of the theme for this age level

 a. Meanings and experiences within this theme relevant for this age level. This is content, a selected part of Scope.

God's love for the elementary child is steadfast and unchanging.

God is dependable and unchanging. He does not change his mind from day to day, but is always the same.

In God's plan life is continually changing—no two days are alike, and the person changes from day to day.

The child's relationship with God may be continuous from today and forever and may grow and deepen with new experiences.

God is always available to the person. If the relationship is broken, the person breaks it.

340

God has created each person free but responsible for his choices. Each person makes choices within the limitations of his finiteness, within the boundaries set by his family and by the society in which he lives, and in light of the meanings and values God has disclosed. Each person is responsible for the consequences of his choices as they affect his own life and the lives of those about him.

God has made known that he is Absolute Value, and that responsible use of freedom depends upon acceptance of God as Lord (Absolute Value).

Right and wrong are determined in light of the righteousness and justice of God who is the Supreme Authority.

In the midst of catastrophic changes in a child's life such as hurricane, earthquake, flood, separation or divorce of parents, and death, God's steadfast love never wanes or falters.

1. **Significance of the theme for this age level**
   b. **Readiness of the learner for this theme in terms of basic needs, interests, motivations, capacities, developmental tasks.**

The child has a basic need for physical and emotional security in a world that is rapidly changing.

The child seeks security in the face of rapidly widening personal relationships.

The child needs to love and be loved.

The child has the ability to know and to live within the bounds for acceptable behavior in his family, in his neighborhood, in his school, and at church.

The child has many questions about changes taking place around him and seeks interpretation of these changes, with assurance of stability in spite of them.

The child is capable of recognizing God as the source of Ultimate Authority.

The child is aware of conflicting cultural standards of right and wrong and of realizing that to the Christian God is Ultimate Authority.

The child is curious about the processes of growth in all living matter, including himself, and has the capacity to recognize that they are normal in God's plan for change.

When confronted with catastrophic events such as earthquakes, hurricanes, separation or divorce of parents, or death of loved ones, the child may develop doubts about why such catastrophes occur in the universe God made and sustains, at the same time the child may yearn for something stable and dependable in his life.

The child frequently is afraid of the unknown in his world and holds on to childish or uninformed ideas that influence his attitudes toward change.

The child is aware that the physical universe is more than he can see, smell, taste, touch, and hear. The unknown in it may be a challenge to him or a great fear.

The child ponders about what happens after death.

The child has a rapidly expanding concept of community, nation, world, universe due to exposure to mass communications media, school, and association with adults, which enables him to observe change and to accept it as a part of life.

The child is increasingly aware of threats to his existence: disruption in the home, illness, war and the threat of war, the uncertainty of how atomic energy may be used for man's benefit or destruction.

341

2. How may this content be communicated as the learner engages in the Learning Tasks? What are the methods and procedures by which the learner may explore the meanings and experiences within this theme (1-a) in the light of his readiness (1-b) in order to discover significance and value?

Through exploring the natural law and principles upon which the universe operates.

Through studying Bible passages that depict God as Creator and Supreme Ruler of the universe and that reflect his unchanging and unalterably dependable love.

Through studying excerpts from history and reading biographies which illustrate how men have interpreted history in terms of God as the Absolute Value and Supreme Ruler in the lives of man.

Through identifying and evaluating the value systems of the society in which he lives in light of his learnings about God as the Absolute Value.

Through discovering in interviews with teachers and school administrators what the school expects of the pupils and comparing this with what is being learned about what God requires of man.

Through studying what the Bible says about God as Supreme Authority and how he expects persons to live as compared with some commonly accepted behavior in school and community.

Through studying ways biblical characters have faced cataclysmic events and disasters.

Through exploring the areas of life where change is essential.

Through studying what the church and Christians throughout the ages have believed and taught about God as Absolute Value and Supreme Authority, unchanging even in the face of great change.

Through discussing with Christian adults the child's immediate choices involving right and wrong and the child's personal freedom if God is Supreme Authority.

3. **What may the learner achieve within this theme in the fulfillment of the Learning Tasks? What are possible changes or learnings on the part of the learner that may result from his appropriation of the significance and value discovered? These changes or learnings may be associated with skills, attitudes, motivations, perceptions including understandings and appreciations.**

The child may accept God as unchanging, dependable, and Ultimate Authority.

The child may accept the impermanence of life as a part of God's plan for man.

The child may identify the choices he is free to make within the limitations set by his parents, the laws and ordinances of the community, the rules and practices set by school authorities, the customs and practices of his peer group, and the standards set by his church.

The child may be aware that there are ultimate values and these are related to God as Supreme Ruler of the universe.

The child may believe that God is the loving Father who cares for him and for every person through all kinds of changes occurring in and around the person.

The child may evaluate right and wrong as viewed by his family, his neighbors, his school, his community, in light of Christian teaching about right and wrong.

The child may recognize that the concepts of right and wrong of his home, and his culture, may not be identical with what the church teaches as right and wrong and may make up his own mind regarding his own bases for his conduct.

The child may sense that faith in God as Absolute Authority and Eternal Value can help him overcome his fear of the changes which come in his relationships with family and friends, in his being uprooted from his community, in his uncertainty about what he wants to do and be, in his inability to achieve the goals he sets for himself and his discontent over failure.

343

The child may experience security and at-homeness in the fellowship of the church.

The child may comprehend the changes which persons and groups should make in light of God's purpose for man as revealed in Jesus Christ and may participate in activities directed toward bringing about such changes.

5. Man's Coping with Change and the Absolute

STATEMENT OF THE THEME

Man's search for the permanent and at the same time his longing for change are answered by God as ultimate reality and absolute value.

YOUTH

1. Significance of the theme for this age level

    a. Meanings and experiences within this theme relevant for this age level. This is content, a selected part of Scope.

God is unchanging, dependable, and offers steadfast love at a time when youth is finding impermanence and uncertainty within his daily life.

God's unlimited love remains steady in spite of the confusion of personal and cultural values and in it God reveals himself as Ultimate Reality and Absolute Value.

God who is Ultimate Reality and Absolute Value is the author of change and works within change.

God calls youth to work with him in bringing about change in the existential situation to the end that society may more nearly fulfill God's purpose.

God is the Sovereign Ruler of the universe and thereby determines the bounds of man's existence. Yet within these boundaries, God has given man freedom.

In exercising the freedom God has given him youth is accountable to God and must accept the consequences of his choices.

When youth superimposes or substitutes a lesser value system for Absolute Value, relation with God is distorted and broken. The relationship can be restored only as the youth recognizes the break, seeks God's forgiveness, and, depending on God's help, changes his value system, whatever the cost.

Youth's relationship with God is continually threatened by the impossibility of living in accord with Ultimate Value, or by open rebellion against Ultimate Value. Relationship can be restored and youth can be reconciled through God's grace and by the assurance that God's love is ever present with youth in spite of his finiteness.

God acts in many ways to the end that persons bring their value systems into harmony with his will. He calls persons to be his sons, to take upon themselves his nature and his purposes, he judges men, he brings the unrighteousness of men into sharp focus when seen in the light of God's uprightness.

God makes it inevitable that man must respond to him but leaves man free to choose the nature of his response whether he will accept or reject God.

The fellowship of Christians, the church, as it reflects the will of God, supports youth in the midst of change in his struggles between his own desires and God's purpose.

345

God as ultimate reality offers youth eternal life as a present possibility and a future reality.

Youth's moral freedom does not mean an absence of any external values but rather that these values are so internalized that youth acts from a center within himself in which these values are integrated and distinctly his own.

Ultimate authority for Protestant youth is faith in a living relation with God who reveals his unchanging love in Jesus Christ.

1. Significance of the theme for this age level

b. Readiness of the learner for this theme in terms of basic needs, interests, motivations, capacities, developmental tasks.

Youth needs to love and to be loved.

Youth is concerned with and involved in conflicts of value systems: his own vs. his family's, his family's vs. the peer group's, his peer's vs. what the church teaches, the accepted values in the culture vs. the will of God.

Youth desires to accept responsibility for his own actions, but in moments of stress may negate or reveal his inability to handle this responsibility.

Youth has a great desire to be accepted by his peers.

Youth is susceptible to group pressures; sometimes he lacks the skill to withstand family and adult pressures; sometimes his desire for acceptance blinds him to his own value system.

Youth rebels against authority while still desiring to live within the bounds which are set by the culture, the family, the church.

Youth has an increasing capacity for self-discipline.

Youth is aware of his failures and may have a sense of guilt.

Youth, confronted with conflicting evidence out of his experience, doubts precepts and concepts he has been taught.

Youth is capable of wholehearted commitment to a great cause.

Youth wants his life to count.

Youth is capable of rendering selfless service to his fellowmen.

Youth tends to identify with national and international crises and may view them as threats to his existence.

Youth is capable of and takes pleasure in thinking abstractly, symbolically.

Youth searches for the meaning of suffering and death and desires assurance of life after death.

Youth seeks a sustaining faith and a dependable value system; he seeks a philosophy of life to live by.

2. **How may this content be communicated as the learner engages in the Learning Tasks? What are the methods and procedures by which the learner may explore the meanings and experiences within this theme (1-a) in the light of his readiness (1-b) in order to discover significance and value?**

By exploring, analyzing, and testing the value systems lived in his home, taught in the church, and practiced in society, using Bible study, studies in church history, review of present-day teachings and practices of the church and a survey of his community's laws and ordinances that affect his life and practices.

By studying with peers and Christian adults current writings on today's problems and threats to existence.

By studying biblical and present-day writings which provide background for the Christian belief in God as Absolute Value and Ultimate Reality.

By contrasting commonly accepted concepts of life, death, and eternity as reflected in current literature, the theater, art, and the behavior of youth with the Christian interpretation as reflected in the Bible and through the witness of the church.

By articulating a philosophy of life which the youth can accept as his own and which includes his beliefs about change and about God as Absolute Value and Ultimate Reality.

By exploring bases of the Christian faith in God by which youth can live and by cultivating disciplines of faith: prayer, worship, meditation, individual or group service projects, study, dialogue with persons of faith.

347

By analyzing and evaluating reactions to authority in an effort to discover how to be free at the same time he is under the authority of God.

By studying the biographies of Christians who felt themselves to be free yet lived under rigid self-determination because of their relation to God.

By determining youth's own definition of freedom and evaluating this in light of his understanding of God as Ultimate Authority.

By talking with qualified Christian adults about the physical and emotional changes experienced in adolescence and their effect on youth's ideas and behavior, by studying literature in this field, and by examining behavior that may result from these changes in the light of God's will and purpose as revealed in Jesus Christ.

3. What may the learner achieve within this theme in the fulfillment of the Learning Tasks? What are possible changes or learnings on the part of the learner that may result from his appropriation of the significance and value discovered? These changes or learnings may be associated with skills, attitudes, motivations, perceptions including understandings and appreciations.

Youth may be aware of and appreciate eternal values, and may commit himself to these values regardless of the cost.

Youth may understand the basic nature of sin and forgiveness.

Youth may recognize his own sin and his participation in corporate sin.

Youth may seek and accept God's forgiveness.

Youth may broaden his concept of God and of God's activity in the universe.

Youth may acquire confidence in his ability to cope with change.

Youth may recognize that his freedom does not mean license but demands responsible action in terms of his own value system.

Youth may accept the Supreme Sovereignty of God.

Youth may be motivated to try to change society in keeping with the will of God as revealed in Jesus Christ and to participate in action that tends to bring about such change.

Youth may distinguish various systems of right and wrong and choose that value system which comes nearest to Ultimate Value.

Youth may recognize support given him by the fellowship of the church and feel at home in the Christian community.

Youth may act upon his understanding of what is right regardless of the cost.

Youth may accept the dependableness of the natural order, while at the same time recognizing that change is a part of this dependableness.

Youth may adjust to the physical and emotional changes within himself in light of his commitment to God as Ultimate Value.

Youth may understand his changing role in society and may act responsibly in education, courtship, marriage, vocational choice.

Youth may develop a philosophy of life which enables him to interpret cataclysmic and all other changes in light of the gospel.

Youth may understand the meaning and value of eternal life, and may act and live in light of this understanding.

Youth may understand and experience the transcendental strength and power that Christian celebration of worship and praise can give him in his struggle to center his life in values that reflect the Absolute Authority of God.

5. Man's Coping with Change and the Absolute 349

STATEMENT OF THE THEME

Man's search for the permanent and at the same time his longing for change are answered by God as ultimate reality and absolute value.

ADULTHOOD

1. **Significance of the theme for this age level**

   a. **Meanings and experiences within this theme relevant for this age level. This is content, a selected part of Scope.**

God, unchanging and absolute, is the ground of man's hope for permanence and worth in the face of the impermancy and uncertainties of human existence.

The nature of God's unlimited and steadfast love for each person removes the threat of God's withdrawal, leaving the person alone and insecure amid the uncertainties of human existence.

The kingdom (reign) of God is a present and transcendent reality in which adults may actively participate.

God transcends the finite and transient values of human existence and offers all men eternal life as a present possibility and a future reality.

God works within change—men and women are called to work with him in bringing about change in their existential situation that it may be more nearly one with God's purposes.

The foundation for understanding the dependability of God is laid when an adult is dependable in his relations with his fellows, especially with children and youth.

God is the Sovereign Ruler of the world, determining the bounds of human existence and giving man freedom within these bounds to make his own choices.

God calls man to live with the consequences of his choices, both those which affect him as a decision-maker, and those which affect persons beyond himself.

Man lives with the threat of separating himself from God, with the hope of a renewed relationship by God's unmerited favor; and with the assurance that God works always to bring good out of evil.

Man alienates himself from God when without intent he denies God as Absolute, when he attempts to substitute human values for Ultimate Value and calls these human values God's will, when he fails to do God's will as well as he knows, or when he rebels against God.

God acts in many ways to guide persons in establishing their value systems in accord with his will.

God has so created man that man must respond to him, but man is free to choose the kind of response he will make.

Christian fellowship gives support and security to individuals in the midst of life change, helping them deal with the conflicts between God's design and man's desires.

Man's moral freedom does not mean an absence of determinism, but means that determining factors are integrated in an individual's personal center, with consequent decisions and actions representing a determination controlled by the character of the center.

Ultimate authority for Protestantism is faith in a living relationship with God expressed through discipleship to Jesus Christ.

Each adult seeks a value system in terms of which he may confidently build his life style.

1. Significance of the theme for this age level

b. Readiness of the learner for this theme in terms of basic needs, interests, motivations, capacities, developmental tasks.

Each adult is recurringly involved in searching for, finding, and maintaining his place in the adult society.

The adult experiences economic insecurity as a threat to his existence.

351

The adult is confronted with competing value systems and with pressures to compromise his own system in favor of one or more of the others.

The adult faces sequential changes in the makeup of his home and family.

Married adults face the need for congruency or accommodation in value systems between husband and wife.

Each adult unconsciously builds his life style around some value system.

The adult faces decision-making as a process of continual engagement between his immediate desires and his overall value system.

The adult longs for the support of a sustaining fellowship which can foster his personal commitment to values.

The adult has the capacity to focus on Ultimate Value even when the pressures of life force him to immediate decision.

The adult is plagued by his finitude confirmed by the threat of death which tends to produce a sense of futility.

The adult longs for assurance that death will not diminish him as a self-conscious personality.

The adult has entered the period of life wherein he is reaching his greatest capacity to comprehend God as the Absolute and to make his own value system consistent with God's will as he understands it.

Adults have the capacity to realize that their decisions may have far-reaching effects on themselves and others.

Adults need to love and be loved.

2. **How may this content be communicated as the learner engages in the Learning Tasks? What are the methods and procedures by which the learner may explore the meanings and experiences within this theme (1-a) in the light of his readiness (1-b) in order to discover significance and value?**

By exploring how commitment to God as the Absolute can influence a person's life.

By participating in the fellowship and mission of the church.

By studying and testing the value systems operative in society and testing these against the values revealed by God in Jesus Christ.

By articulating in terms of God's love for man the Christian's view of existence, death, and eternal life.

By reading, studying, and discussing the biblical passages which point up God's authority and man's freedom.

By identifying and analyzing the threats to human existence, and evaluating them in the light of God as the Absolute.

By examining one's own reactions to authority and analyzing the reactions of others to authority in relation to belief in God.

By reading, studying, and discussing the contemporary art forms on man's search for freedom, the distinction between freedom and license, the nature of true freedom under God.

By exploring in the light of God's will and purpose how the physical and emotional changes in adulthood influence attitudes and behavior.

By evaluating in light of the gospel contemporary value systems reflected in current literature, the theater, art, and music.

By exploring ways of living creatively within the changes and limitations (physical, social, mental, economic) brought on by advancing age.

3. **What may the learner achieve within this theme in the fulfillment of the Learning Tasks? What are possible changes or learnings on the part of the learner that may result from his appropriation of the significance and value discovered? These changes or learnings may be associated with skills, attitudes, motivations, perceptions including understandings and appreciations.**

The adult may become more aware of and appreciative of eternal values.

353

The adult may commit himself to live in accord with eternal values as revealed in Jesus Christ.

The adult may understand the basic nature of sin and forgiveness.

The adult may recognize his own sin and his participation in corporate sin, and may seek God's forgiveness.

The adult may accept God's forgiveness and attempt to live a more disciplined life.

The adult may broaden his concept of God and of God's activity in the universe.

The adult may accept his dependency upon God as the source of his values.

The adult may accept the call to Christian vocation to help provide both stability and ferment or change in his society.

The adult may live with his physical, emotional changes and his sex role in the light of eternal values.

The adult may develop a philosophy of life that enables him to interpret suffering and death in light of the gospel.

354 The adult may define a system of values for himself that is consistent with eternal values.

The adult may recognize the trustworthiness of the natural order which God creates and sustains.

The adult may show proper respect for authority and be able to live creatively under authority.

The adult may experience increased confidence in his ability to cope with change.

The adult may appreciate the joys and responsibilities of his freedom.

The adult may understand better the nature of human freedom and its relation to God's will as revealed in Jesus Christ.

The adult may long to change the world in keeping with the purposes of God; he participates eagerly in activities designed to bring about that change.

The adult may cope with changing roles in society (marital status, parenthood, childlessness, "empty nest," automation, job security or lack of it, retirement, death).

The adult may make decisions in light of the gospel even when faced by pressures to conform to conflicting values.

Adults may understand and experience the transcendental strength and power that Christian celebration of worship and praise can give him in his struggle to center his life in values that reflect the Absolute Authority of God.

6. Man's Creativity Within Life's Daily Routines

STATEMENT OF THE THEME

The lives of all persons involve experiences of daily routine. Routine offers security but it may lead to boredom and meaninglessness. Motivation and direction for daily existence can be found in the purposes of God. Herein are the springs of man's creative attitude toward and engagement in the rhythm of work, leisure, and rest.

EARLY CHILDHOOD

1. Significance of the theme for this age level

a. Meanings and experiences within this theme relevant for this age level. This is content, a selected part of Scope.

God has created an orderly world in which there is day and night, a time for work and play, and a time for rest.

Routines are necessary in my life: sleeping, eating, going to nursery school at a particular time.

God has planned for us to sleep at night, waken in the morning, alternate play and rest.

God intends for us to do what we can to care for ourselves and to help others.

God has made the world full of wonder and expects us to enjoy and use creatively the beauty of colors, sounds, design, and their various combinations.

355

1. Significance of the theme for this age level

b. Readiness of the learner for this theme in terms of basic needs, interests, motivations, capacities, developmental tasks

The young child experiences routine and rhythm within his life: day and night, sleeping and waking, rest and activity.

The young child's developing ability to coordinate the movement of arms and legs, to manipulate objects makes it increasingly possible for him to engage in simple, creative activities.

The young child who has experienced the love of those about him is likely to be ready to understand that God cares for him at all times: in his eating, sleeping, playing, and other routines.

The young child has increasing ability to make choices within the routines of daily life.

356

The young child is increasingly able to distinguish different colors, musical sounds, shapes and sizes, to draw and paint, to sing simple melodies, to play musical instruments (rhythm band), to compose melodies and to build simple objects, especially when he is left free to create what he desires to create and to do it in his own way.

The young child finds security in routines and has the satisfaction of doing routine tasks well and efficiently, but at times he may rebel against doing the same thing over and over again.

The young child is full of "whys" about the routines of life.

The young child has capacity to use imagination in dealing with his routines.

To the limit of his skills, the young child wants to do routine things for himself—he wants to feed himself, to handle his own toys, to dress himself, to walk alone.

In the instant of a happy experience, even in routine, the young child is capable of spontaneously expressing affection for another and of expressing joy and adoration of God, the Creator and Father.

2. How may this content be communicated as the learner engages in the Learning Tasks? What are the methods and procedures by which the learner may explore the meanings and experiences within this theme (1-a) in the light of his readiness (1-b) in order to discover significance and value?

Through exploring simple natural phenomena to discover the routine processes of certain aspects of the natural order, such as day following night, the rising and setting of the sun, the change of the seasons.

Through exploring the daily routines of the young child's own life to discover why such routines are necessary.

Through participating in situations which use various media to express his creative urge, such as crayons, finger paints, modeling clay, chalk, scissors and paper, and making up songs.

Through sensing from the attitudes and behavior of those about him that routine and creative aspects of living are a part of God's plan.

Through Bible stories and verses that illustrate God's plan for orderly processes and creativity in the midst of daily routines.

Through play, as part of a program under the guidance of Christian adults, in which the child has opportunity to play out some of the routines of daily living of his own life and that of adults.

3. **What may the learner achieve within this theme in the fulfillment of the Learning Tasks? What are possible changes or learnings on the part of the learner that may result from his appropriation of the significance and value discovered? These changes or learnings may be associated with skills, attitudes, motivations, perceptions including understandings and appreciations.**

357

The young child may recognize routine as a part of God's plan.

The young child may recognize that God as Creator has given him his ability to create.

The young child may experience the presence and love of God in his daily routines.

The child may give expression to his feelings and attitudes

in singing, making up songs, drawing and painting, and constructing simple objects.

The young child may identify activities within his daily life which are harmful to himself and others and/or destructive of property.

The young child may learn to follow certain routines as a means of satisfying his own immediate needs.

The young child may express affection as an immediate response to persons whom he recognizes as helpers with his daily routines and as providers of opportunities for creative play.

6. Man's Creativity Within Life's Daily Routines

STATEMENT OF THE THEME

The lives of all persons involve experiences of daily routine. Routine offers security but it may lead to boredom and meaninglessness. Motivation and direction for daily existence can be found in the purposes of God. Herein are the springs of man's creative attitude toward and engagement in the rhythm of work, leisure, and rest.

ELEMENTARY YEARS

1. Significance of the theme for this age level

    a. Meanings and experiences within this theme relevant for this age level. This is content, a selected part of Scope.

God created and sustains the universe and all living things with order, pattern, rhythm, and yet with infinite variety.

God is the Lord of all that exists, therefore all experiences, both routine and creative, can be meaningful.

God, the Creator, has created each child in his own image and expects all persons to use the capacity he has given them to create.

God has endowed each person with a variety of gifts which are uniquely his own and expects each person to use his gifts in his own way.

In God's Creation, routine is a necessary and desirable part of the child's life and of the world in which he lives, and provides a dependable structure for daily activity.

The Creator has endowed the child with imagination and intends him to use it to look ahead and identify his needs and desires and devise ways of meeting these needs and achieving these desires.

It is God's intent that as his abilities develop, the child assume increasing responsibility for satisfying many of his own daily needs and those of others.

God has given the child play as a spontaneous, joyous response to and release from daily routine.

It is God's intent that the child's capacity to create is to be used constructively.

1. Significance of the theme for this age level

b. Readiness of the learner for this theme in terms of basic needs, interests, motivations, capacities, developmental tasks.

As the child's relationships widen, he seeks more opportunities to develop and use his creative skills.

As the child becomes involved in a wider range of social units, he has more routines to deal with. He is called upon to manage his time and his energy so that these routines expedite his activities rather than hamper them.

Widening experiences and increased conceptional and language skills enable the child increasingly to engage creatively in certain routines.

The child can discern patterns of order and routine in his own life, and in his experiences with nature and with other persons, and may reflect upon their meaning.

359

The child has the capacity to realize that the mastery of routines is part of self-discipline and essential to his development.

The child's development is somewhat dependent on having his creative activities approved and appreciated by others, particularly his parents, teachers, and persons who represent authority in his life.

The child may often be ready for opportunities for spontaneous worship within his daily routines when in moments of joy he can offer adoration and praise to God, the Creator and Father.

The child uses his imagination to dream of what he might do and be and, at the same time, he is increasingly able to distinguish fantasy from reality.

The child's development is dependent on his assuming responsibility for maintaining his own routines.

The child is exploring and discovering his world; he has the capacity to improve the products of his creativity and to enjoy them.

The child longs for security, some of which comes from following routines, and is motivated by the satisfaction and approval that may come from doing them well and efficiently.

2. How may this content be communicated as the learner engages in the Learning Tasks? What are the methods and procedures by which the learner may explore the meanings and experiences within this theme (1-a) in the light of his readiness (1-b) in order to discover significance and value?

Through exploring under Christian adult guidance the cycles of nature, such as day and night, the rising and setting of the stars, the phases of the moon, the changing seasons, the cycles of growth and decay and of birth and death in plant and animal life to discover patterns of natural order and routine.

Through investigating with a Christian adult the routines of his own life (in sleeping and waking, in work and play, in study and relaxation, in schooltime and vacationtime, in workdays and holidays) to see how these human patterns reflect and fit into the larger patterns and rhythms of life as God made it to be.

Through participating in groups where God is regarded as the Lord of all of life which have discovered meaning and purpose in the routines of work and play.

Through participating in local church and other groups which give opportunity and support for creative expression in daily living.

Through analysis of experiences under the leadership of a Christian adult to discover the extent to which life is organized around recurring routines, such as in his own daily and weekly activities; in the activities of one or more adults (father, mother, or other adult whose pattern of life would be familiar); or in the activities of a professional, business, or factory worker as observed in a visit that takes into account the contribution this routine is making to the world; and through imagining how life would be without these various routines.

Through opportunities to consider ways in which routines may help him become the kind of person God intends him to be.

By listening to the testimony of older children or young people who have achieved significant skills (as in vocal or instrumental music, arts, sports, home economics, 4-H contests) in which they indicate the relation of their success to their faithfulness within the routine of practice or experimentation and considering what this means in the development and use of skills that God has given him.

Through looking at, discussing, and/or evaluating episodes on film—biblical or nonbiblical in subject matter—which portray persons expressing themselves creatively to see whether the creativity was beneficial or harmful to other persons, the natural order, community life and why.

Through sharing his creative expressions with other persons such as shut-ins, other children, youth, or adults who want to learn the routines of a particular creative skill.

361

Through studying Bible stories, verses, or passages which portray routine as created by God, and which illustrate creative ways of approaching daily routines and of responsible use of God-given gifts.

Through reading and studying biographies of Christian leaders who have been faithful to routines of Christian disciplines and who have used their creative abilities to serve God and benefit people.

By using role play, story play, creative dramatics, and other arts to express ways God intends man to follow routines in daily living, to be creative within them, and to depart from them when departure seems beneficial to others and/or to self.

3. **What may the learner achieve within this theme in the fulfillment of the Learning Tasks? What are possible changes or learnings on the part of the learner that may result from his appropriation of the significance and value discovered? These changes or learnings may be associated with skills, attitudes, motivations, perceptions including understandings and appreciations.**

The child may begin to comprehend that what he does in his daily activities is a way of responding to and serving God.

The child may develop a desire to reexamine what he does so that he may better serve and obey God.

The child may begin to view routines as a necessary and useful part of his daily life.

The child may increasingly realize that God is the Source of his talents and creative urge, and that these are God's gifts to him.

The child may begin to cherish his talents and accept the necessary disciplines to cultivate them as a part of his stewardship routines.

The child may distinguish between self-expression that is creative and beneficial and that which is detrimental.

The child may use his creative capacities constructively and find satisfaction in doing so.

The child may understand the Christian basis for and accept responsibility for his own routines in such areas as regular family chores, bedtime, care of his person, study for exploring of new situations and opportunities, and in the seeking of new truths.

The child may come to see the pattern of his own life, with its routines and freedoms, in relation to the larger patterns and routines within which God has set life.

The child may appreciate and find joy in the rich variety of God-endowed gifts and talents possessed by himself and/or by other persons.

The child may spontaneously respond to God through creative routines of praise and adoration.

6. Man's Creativity Within Life's Daily Routines

STATEMENT OF THE THEME

The lives of all persons involve experiences of daily routine. Routine offers security but it may lead to boredom and meaninglessness. Motivation and direction for daily existence can be found in the purposes of God. Herein are the springs of man's creative attitude toward and engagement in the rhythm of work, leisure, and rest.

363

YOUTH

1. **Significance of the theme for this age level**

   a. **Meanings and experiences within this theme relevant for this age level. This is content, a selected part of Scope.**

God has created life with order, pattern, rhythm, and yet with infinite variety.

God has created youth in his own image and endowed him with the creative urge.

Through God's graciousness, youth participates in God's continuing creativity.

God is the Lord of all life and has endowed all aspects of living, both creativity and routine, with meaning and purpose.

God has created routine as an integral and desirable part of youth's existence with elements of it in the everyday business of living, in school, in every occupation, in marriage and parenthood.

Routine may threaten with sameness and monotony but it also provides security, efficiency, freedom, and a challenge to creativity.

God has given youth a variety of gifts through which he may express creativity within life's routines and that God expects the adult to use creatively.

In keeping with God's will, youth's creativity is to be used constructively.

God has created youth so that he requires many rhythms in his life; such as work and play, involvement and withdrawal, activity and rest.

God has endowed the youth with inventive capacities by which he can bring into existence what he sees in imagination, and thereby change or give new dimensions to daily routines.

1. Significance of the theme for this age level

b. Readiness of the learner for this theme in terms of basic needs, interests, motivations, capacities, developmental tasks.

Youth longs for periodic release from the monotony and frustration he feels when pressured by the routine of class schedules, homework for school, home tasks, and responsibilities for his personal care.

Youth rebels against routines which seem meaningless to him and recognizes the value of meaningful routines, therefore it is important for him to find valid reasons for the routines which are essential for his daily living.

Youth requires assurance that what he is doing is useful or meaningful.

Youth has the capacity for creative imagination in dealing with routines.

Youth has the capacity to employ inventiveness in dealing with his routines.

Youth is able to assume responsibility for making his dreams come true, even to running the risk of failure and jeers from his peers.

Youth is capable of reverie (undirected activity of the mind when not confronted with a problem) which can produce true creativity.

Youth has the capacity to appreciate and enjoy others with whom he engages in creative experiences within daily routines.

Youth has the capacity to pause amid pressures of daily living to respond to God in worship with joy, adoration, and thanksgiving.

2. **How may this content be communicated as the learner engages in the Learning Tasks? What are the methods and procedures by which the learner may explore the meanings and experiences within this theme (1-a) in the light of his readiness (1-b) in order to discover significance and value?**

Through exploring the order, pattern, rhythm, and routine which God made and sustains as part of the created order, using the Bible, examining the natural order, investigating the insights of psychology and sociology, and analyzing what life would be like if there were no order or pattern to it.

Through participating in groups which give opportunity and support for creative expression as a part of daily life, which recognize God as the source of man's creativity, and which provide for reflection upon and discussion of ways in which man

365

gives evidence of this creative urge; for study of Bible passages that illustrate man's creative nature in dealing with daily life and that reflect how persons have shared in God's continuing creation; and for exploration of ways in which daily routines may be relieved through the creative use of art, literature, crafts, hobbies.

By comparing biblical passages with the similarities and differences in meanings given to daily routines and the result and effects upon the lives of people.

366

Through observing and discussing the effect of the growing mechanical and technological nature of our industrial society and the monotonous routines that this development inevitably brings, through examining the responsibility this condition places upon the church in helping men live creatively in the face of these routines, and through working with his group to undertake its share of this responsibility.

Through examining and evaluating routines of family and neighborhood life in light of what Christians believe to be God's intent for home and community to discover those routines that have value in the lives of persons as well as any that are destructive or inadequate and that should be changed.

Through sharing and discussing the boredom and frustrations he experiences because of the repetitiousness and monotony of his routines and considering ways Christians have learned to cope with these frustrations.

Through considering the relation of routines and freedom and their relative place in the Christian's use of time.

Through joining with others in providing community opportunities for creative activities as a part of daily living.

Through appraising in a group the routines of daily life in light of his understanding of the purposes of God as Lord of life, and expressing his feelings and attitudes in petition and praise.

3. What may the learner achieve within this theme in the fulfillment of the Learning Tasks? What are possible changes

or learnings on the part of the learner that may result from his appropriation of the significance and value discovered? These changes or learnings may be associated with skills, attitudes, motivations, perceptions including understandings and appreciations.

The youth may come to know God as Lord of all of life.

The youth may understand God to be present in every sphere or area of life.

The youth may discover, understand, and recognize anew his talents and abilities as God-given.

The youth may assume responsibility for developing his talents and abilities and practice the disciplines necessary to explore and develop them as a steward of God.

The youth may accept routine as necessary and useful and may find within routine the purposes of God.

The youth may see the necessity and usefulness of being selective in the choice of routines that make up his life and of providing for some freedom from routines.

The youth may become aware of the values of and accept responsibilities for the routines involved in Christian family life and the maintenance of a home.

The youth may become better equipped to handle illness, death, and other drastic changes in life's routine in ways that are creative and motivated by Christian understandings.

367

The youth may see and act upon opportunities to witness to his faith that God is present and at work in the midst of life's daily routines.

The youth may seek continually to cultivate an attitude of curiosity, inquisitiveness, wonder, and awe.

The youth may appreciate and find joy in the rich variety of God-endowed gifts and talents possessed by himself and other persons.

The youth may find that self-expression which is beneficial has value for him, but that expression which is destructive or hurtful is destructive to him.

The youth may accept, with faith in God's wisdom, what he cannot change in the routines of his daily life.

The youth may develop compensations for boredom in routine by enjoying satisfying experiences in other areas of life, i.e., recreation, service, creative arts, hobbies.

The youth may seek ways to make his leisure time more creative and productive for the improvement of society.

6. Man's Creativity Within Life's Daily Routines

STATEMENT OF THE THEME

The lives of all persons involve experiences of daily routine. Routine offers security but it may lead to boredom and meaninglessness. Motivation and direction for daily existence can be found in the purposes of God. Herein are the springs of man's creative attitude toward and engagement in the rhythm of work, leisure, and rest.

ADULTHOOD

1. Significance of the theme for this age level

a. Meanings and experiences within this theme relevant for this age level. This is content, a selected part of Scope.

God has created life with order, pattern, rhythm, and yet with infinite variety.

God has created the adult in his own image and has endowed him with the creative urge.

Through God's graciousness, the adult participates in God's continuing creativity.

God is the Lord of all life and has endowed all of life, both creativity and routine, with meaning.

God has created routine as an integral and desirable part of the adult's existence.

Routine may threaten with sameness and monotony but it also provides security, efficiency, and freedom, and a challenge to creativity.

God has endowed the adult with imagination with which he can dream a better life for himself and his fellows, a way to change routines.

God has endowed the adult with inventive capacities by which he can bring into existence what he sees in imagination, and thereby change or give new dimensions to daily routines.

God's intent is that the adult use his creativity constructively within God's purposes.

God has created the adult so that he requires many rhythms in his life; such as work and play, involvement and withdrawal, activity and rest.

God has given the adult a variety of gifts through which he may express creativity within life's routines and God expects the adult to use them creatively.

1. **Significance of the theme for this age level**

369

    b. **Readiness of the learner for this theme in terms of basic needs, interests, motivations, capacities, developmental tasks.**

The adult has had much experience with monotomy and frustration within daily routine and longs for creative release from such monotony and frustration.

The adult is able to assume responsibility for making his dreams come true, even to running the risk of failure and jeers from his peers.

The adult finds security in routine and satisfaction in efficiently caring for the business of daily living.

The adult is capable and often desires to live within well-defined routine.

The adult has some capacity to be creative in the dailyness of life and may long to express this creativity.

The adult requires assurance that what he is doing is useful or meaningful to himself.

370 The adult may be stimulated to use his imagination, his inventiveness, and to keep on working at creating better routines for old ones.

The adult has the capacity to pause amid pressures of daily living to respond to God in worship with joy, adoration, and thanksgiving.

2. **How may this content be communicated as the learner engages in the Learning Tasks? What are the methods and procedures by which the learner may explore the meanings and experiences within this theme (1-a) in the light of his readiness (1-b) in order to discover significance and value?**

Through exploring the order, pattern, rhythm, and routine which God made and sustains as part of the created order, using the Bible, examining the natural order, investigating the insights of psychology and sociology, and analyzing what life would be like if there were no order or pattern to it.

Through participating in groups which give opportunity and support for creative expression as a part of daily life, which recognize God as the source of man's creativity and which provide for reflection upon and discussion of ways in which man gives evidence of this creative urge; for study of Bible passages that illustrate man's creative nature in dealing with daily life and that reflect how persons have shared in God's continuing creation; and for exploration of ways in which daily routines may be relieved through the creative use of art, literature, crafts, hobbies.

By comparing biblical passages with the similarities and differences in meanings given to daily routines and the result and effects upon the lives of people.

Through observing and discussing the effect of the growing mechanical and technological nature of our industrial society and the monotonous routines that this development inevitably brings, through examining the responsibility this condition places upon the church in helping men live creatively in the face of these routines, and through working with his group to undertake its share of this responsibility.

Through examining and evaluating routines of family and neighborhood life in light of what Christians believe to be God's intent for home and community to discover those routines that have value in the lives of persons as well as any that are destructive or inadequate and that should be changed.

Through sharing and discussing the boredom and frustrations he experiences because of the repetitiousness and monotony of his routines and considering ways Christians have learned to cope with these frustrations.

Through considering the relation of routines and freedom and their relative place in the Christian's use of time.

Through joining with others in providing community opportunities for creative activities as a part of daily living.

Through appraising in a group the routines of daily life in light of his understanding of the purposes of God as Lord of life, and expressing his feelings and attitudes in petition and praise.

3. **What may the learner achieve within this theme in the fulfillment of the Learning Tasks? What are possible changes or learnings on the part of the learner that may result from his appropriation of the significance and value discovered? These changes or learnings may be associated with skills,**

371

attitudes, motivations, perceptions including understandings and appreciations.

The adult may come to know God as Lord of all of life.

The adult may understand God to be present in every sphere or area of life.

The adult may discover, understand, and recognize anew his talents and abilities as God-given.

The adult may assume responsibility for developing his talents and abilities and practice the disciplines necessary to explore and develop them as a steward of God.

The adult may accept routines as necessary and useful and may find within them the purposes of God.

The adult may see the necessity and usefulness of being selective in the choice of routines that make up his life and of providing for some freedom from routines.

The adult may become aware of the values of and accept responsibilities for the routines involved in Christian family life and the maintenance of a home.

The adult may become better equipped to handle illness, death, and other drastic changes in life's routine in ways that are creative and motivated by Christian understandings.

The adult may see and act upon opportunities to witness to his faith that God is present and at work in the midst of life's daily routines.

The adult may seek continually to cultivate an attitude of curiosity, inquisitiveness, wonder, and awe.

The adult may appreciate and find joy in the rich variety of God-endowed gifts and talents possessed by himself and other persons.

The adult may find that self-expression which is beneficial has value for him, but that expression which is destructive or hurtful is destructive to him.

The adult may accept, with faith in God's wisdom, what he cannot change in the routines of his daily life.

The adult may develop compensations for boredom in routine by enjoying satisfying experiences in other areas of life, i.e., recreation, service, creative arts, hobbies.

The adult may seek ways to find greater meaning and creativity in his daily work and its routines, even to the extent of changing his job.

373

REVELATION: THE MEANING AND EXPERIENCE OF GOD'S SELF-DISCLOSURE

The themes within this area are:

1. *God Speaks in Man's Search for Meaning Beyond Himself*
2. *The Living God Seeks Man*
3. *The Gracious God Judges and Redeems*
4. *The Sovereign God Dwells with Man*
5. *God Speaks to Man Through the Scriptures*
6. *God Acts Through the Church to Make Himself Known*
7. *God Speaks to Man Through the Natural Order*

Statement of the Area

The focus, or vantage point, of this area of curriculum is the character of God and his work, the nature and significance of God's self-disclosure—the modes of God's action, and the way he has spoken and still speaks to man's search and man's need.

Comprehended in this area of curriculum is such content from Christian thought and life as: the doctrine of God; the doctrine of the Trinity; interpretation of the person, teaching, and work of Jesus Christ; interpretation of the work of the Holy Spirit; the relation of revelation to reason; interpretation of the nature and meaning of the gospel.

In order to have educational value as an area of curriculum this content must be viewed in terms of its pertinence to the persistent issues of man's life. Some of these issues are: Is there a God? Does God speak? If so, how? Does this tell me what I can live for? Does God disclose himself? If so, how? How is God known? What is the Bible all about?[1]

---

[1] Repeated here as necessary background.

1. God Speaks in Man's Search for Meaning Beyond Himself

STATEMENT OF THE THEME

God's revelation of himself in part in the nature of the human personality explains man's persistent yearnings to worship some god, to know more, to do better, to be in relationship.

EARLY CHILDHOOD

1. Significance of the theme for this age level

a. Meanings and experiences within this theme relevant for this age level. This is content, a selected part of Scope.

Parents and other adults pray and worship God and we can praise and worship him also.

God is always near us and whenever we feel like it we can pray to him and ask him to help us.

God has made me able to learn.

God knows everything, he has planned for me to learn and he helps me to learn.

God is good. He is holy and wants me to worship and praise him.

God is dependable.

People who know God help me to know what is right and wrong. God always knows and does what is right and can help me to make the many choices I must make for myself.

God is always near me, no matter where I am, how I feel and act, or if I am alone or with others. One way he is near me and that I know he is near is through persons who love him and who love me. I want to be loved.

God plans for me to have birthdays. He has put me in a family with persons in it who are older (or younger) than I am. Life in my family is not always the same as in my friends'

375

families. I remember some people and some events that are important to me, and to my life.

1. Significance of the theme for this age level

b. Readiness of the learner for this theme in terms of basic needs, interests, motivations, capacities, developmental tasks

The young child is struggling to become an individual.

The young child is beginning to talk, to sing, and develop a language for worshiping and talking about God.

The young child seeks and needs approval.

The young child seeks and needs acceptance.

The young child seeks and needs security for his life to have meaning.

The young child needs to receive and give love.

The young child is inquisitive about his environment and its meaning for him.

The young child's ease of accepting mystery frees him to accept God's majesty.

The young child is increasingly discovering an expanding world reaching beyond himself, his needs, and his activities.

2. How may this content be communicated as the learner engages in the Learning Tasks? What are the methods and procedures by which the learner may explore the meanings and experiences within this theme (1-a) in the light of his readiness (1-b) in order to discover significance and value?

By engaging in play experiences with others with whom he may identify.

By participating in simple family duties and projects.

By receiving the love and acceptance of adults around him.

By hearing about Bible personalities and others into whose lives God has brought meaning.

By receiving approval and correction from those he knows love him.

3. **What may the learner achieve within this theme in the fulfillment of the Learning Tasks? What are possible changes or learnings on the part of the learner that may result from his appropriation of the significance and value discovered? These changes or learnings may be associated with skills, attitudes, motivations, perceptions including understandings and appreciations.**

The young child may find meaningful relationships with other persons which may begin to give him some indication of a meaningful relationship with God.

The young child may enjoy simple worship experiences.

The young child may experience something of God's love and care for him.

The young child may have a growing security in discipline of love.

The young child may grow in understanding of himself as an individual.

The young child may have a sense of thrill in learning.

The young child may begin to appreciate the joy others feel in being in God's family.

The young child may have a beginning perspective of time as part of God's concern and under his control.

The young child may have an awareness that right and wrong are basically related to God.

The young child may have a developing desire and ability to talk with God in prayer.

377

1. God Speaks in Man's Search for Meaning Beyond Himself

STATEMENT OF THE THEME

God's revelation of himself in part in the nature of the human personality explains man's persistent yearnings to worship some god, to know more, to do better, to be in relationship.

ELEMENTARY YEARS

378

1. Significance of the theme for this age level

a. Meanings and experiences within this theme relevant for this age level. This is content, a selected part of Scope.

God is always available anytime, anywhere for help and strength to those who seek him.

God speaks to persons in their desire to seek his guidance and to draw near to him in worship.

God has made man in his own image and many of man's deepest thoughts and feelings come from the desire to be in fellowship with God.

God speaks to man in many of his deep thoughts and feelings and in his longing to understand many things he thinks and wonders about.

There will always be much that only God knows and understands but he has given man desire and ability to know more and more about many things and in his search to draw closer to God as the source of all truth.

God is holy. He is perfect. He is righteous. He is worthy of loyalty and devotion and answers one's longing for someone to turn to in perfect confidence and with supreme loyalty.

God is righteous and speaks to persons in many ways if they will listen as they make decisions and choices.

As persons learn more of God's ways and what he expects of them, and how to live as he expects, he answers many of their questions about what is right and wrong and how they know which is which.

In Jesus Christ, God shows man the perfect way to live.

God made each person to be an individual but he implanted in each man a desire to be with others in relationship with them. He makes man more of a person through these relationships with others and with him.

Man's deep desire to be with others and to be like them, at the same time each person wanting to be himself, is one of God's ways of showing man what God expects of him.

God works and has worked in many ways through the people and events in each local community, in the state, in the nation, in the world.

God has revealed and is now revealing to man God's works and his way of working in man's longing and search to discover and open up new nations, new territories, new frontiers in the universe.

God has planted in man a desire to explore new realms of thought, to work out his problems of living together and to find answers to many questions. In these desires and in man's search to satisfy them, God reveals himself and his truth.

Life has meaning because God is at work in it.

379

The sending of his Son is God's supreme act in history, by which he reveals himself and his purpose for all mankind. He is the fulfillment of man's longing.

1. Significance of the theme for this age level

b. Readiness of the learner for this theme in terms of basic needs, interests, motivations, capacities, developmental tasks.

The elementary child has a growing self-awareness and self-identity.

The elementary child has a growing sense of identity with others whom he admires as persons whom he would like to imitate and follow.

The elementary child has a growing inquisitiveness along with a demand for rational explanation.

The elementary child seeks and needs acceptance of peers and adults.

The elementary child seeks and needs approval of peers and adults.

The elementary child is able to relate freely to more persons.

The elementary child needs to receive and give love.

The elementary child has a growing awareness of forces beyond himself.

The elementary child has a developing capacity to discern right from wrong.

The elementary child has a growing ability to assume responsibility for his actions.

The elementary child has a developing sense of justice.

The intellectual capacity of the elementary child has matured to the extent that he can begin to think symbolically, for example he can begin to conceptualize history and the relation of space and time.

The elementary child has developed basic reading skills.

The elementary child has a growing capacity to participate in worship.

2. How may this content be communicated as the learner engages in the Learning Tasks? What are the methods and procedures by which the learner may explore the meanings and experiences within this theme (1-a) in the light of his readiness (1-b) in order to discover significance and value.

By participating in family projects and family celebrations

and by hearing how other families assume their responsibilities to each other and celebrate happy occasions.

By participating in worship.

By studying Bible personalities through whom God has revealed something of himself.

By studying Christian personalities.

By reading and studying selected Bible passages and Bible stories.

By exploring aspects and consequences of right and wrong behavior.

By having contacts with persons of other races, cultures, and nationalities.

By enjoying loving, by understanding and accepting relationships.

By exploring how information and theological interpretation are related to each other.

By exploring what science says about human personalities.

By opportunities for creative expressions such as drawing and writing.

By planning and carrying out simple service projects.

By building on the relationships developed through resident and day camping.

381

By participating in field trips to Christian centers and other places where he can widen his relationships.

By attempting to express through the creative and performing arts meanings they are beginning to grasp.

3. **What may the learner achieve within this theme in the fulfillment of the Learning Tasks? What are possible changes or learnings on the part of the learner that may result from his appropriation of the significance and value discovered? These changes or learnings may be associated with skills,**

attitudes, motivations, perceptions including understandings and appreciations.

The child may develop a growing appreciation of self and his potential as created by God.

The child may face fears with the confidence of God's help and care.

The child may sense in worship the presence of God, as revealed in Jesus Christ.

The child may participate in worship to the full extent of his ability.

The child may realize that God is concerned for all people.

The child may recognize his responsibility to accept all persons.

The child may develop elementary criteria for determining right and wrong.

The child may assume increasing responsibility for right behavior.

The child may discover in his unfolding abilities that God has purpose for his life.

The child may begin to see that God is at work in history and in the affairs of men.

The child may begin to find some answers to some of his questions about God, about the world, and about himself.

The child may come to some realization of a meaningful relationship with God.

The child may develop skills for getting information from various sources.

1. God Speaks in Man's Search for Meaning Beyond Himself

STATEMENT OF THE THEME

God's revelation of himself in part in the nature of the human personality explains man's persistent yearnings to worship some god, to know more, to do better, to be in relationship.

YOUTH

1. **Significance of the theme for this age level**

   a. **Meanings and experiences within this theme relevant for this age level. This is content, a selected part of Scope.**

God is worthy to receive youth's full devotion and loyalty.

To search for knowledge and truth is obligatory for man created in the image of God.

Truth in every realm of knowledge is compatable with God who is the source of truth.

God provides dependable guidance for distinguishing between truth and error, right and wrong.

Human personality is an imperfect but meaningful reflection of God's personhood.

God's love is worthy to receive youth's full devotion and loyalty.

God who desires man's fellowship perfectly fulfills youth's quest for relationship.

God, the Lord of history, assures the significance of one's own destiny and that of society.

God responds with gifts of insight and assurance to man's brooding questions, to his wrestling with doubt, to his pursuit of imponderables.

Man's rapidly expanding achievements of power and knowledge will never comprehend and outdate God.

God gives individual and corporate life its most satisfactory meaning and its largest perspective.

In the incarnation God shows the meaning of abundant life and offers the means of living abundantly.

Many of man's deepest thoughts and feelings come from the desire to be in fellowship with God, since he has created man in his own image.

383

God speaks to persons in their desire to seek his guidance and to draw near to him in worship.

Jesus Christ calls youth into fellowship and identity with him and his cause.

1. Significance of the theme for this age level

b. Readiness of the learner for this theme in terms of basic needs, interests, motivations, capacities, developmental tasks.

Youth's ability to think abstractly encourages his search for meaning beyond himself.

Youth's intensifying need for acceptance by his peer group hastens his search for abiding relationships.

Youth, in the tension between independence and dependence, searches for a source of integrity.

Youth's capacity to make his own value judgments opens him to a variety of sources of guidance.

Youth has the capacity and desire to accept responsibility for his actions.

Youth begins to make, on his own, many of the major decisions of his life.

Youth needs to receive and give love.

Youth questions the adequacy of the explanations and practices of childhood and seeks for answers commensurate with his growing intellectual capacities.

Youth is capable of entering fully into corporate and private worship experiences.

Youth is developing heterosexual interests which widen his search for meaning.

The ability of youth to project enables him to gather from his own self-awareness insights into personality whether of God or others.

2. **How may this content be communicated as the learner engages in the Learning Tasks? What are the methods and procedures by which the learner may explore the meanings and experiences within this theme (1-a) in the light of his readiness (1-b) in order to discover significance and value.**

By participating in corporate and private worship in which youth are confronted by and respond to God.

By exploring what the Bible says about the purposes of life.

By exploring what the Bible says about the nature of human personality.

By exploring what the sciences say about the nature of human personality.

By becoming personally involved with others, listening, perceiving, and sharing insights about self in meaningful relationships to God and to man.

By exploring criteria for making decisions concerning right and wrong.

By observing human behavior for evidences of God's influence and revelation—noting changes such as from hate to love, retaliation to forgiveness, fear to courage.

By exploring what the Bible says about God's action in history.

By searching for meaning in current happenings whether personal, local or worldwide.

By using commentaries and books in the course of studying doctrine.

By considering and trying out value judgments and moral decisions in the company of fellow Christians.

By becoming acquainted with persons expert in their field of knowledge who relate their faith to their occupation.

3. **What may the learner achieve within this theme in the fulfillment of the Learning Tasks? What are possible changes or learnings on the part of the learner that may result from**

385

his appropriation of the significance and value discovered? These changes or learnings may be associated with skills, attitudes, motivations, perceptions including understandings and appreciations.

Youth may gain knowledge of God as Person and as Spirit.

Youth may develop acceptance of himself and others as created in God's image.

Youth may increasingly take God's revelation into consideration as he makes moral judgments and choices.

Youth may find in the God of truth the source of a framework for discovering and appropriating truth.

In the midst of insecurity youth may increasingly depend on God who is in control of history and one's destiny.

Youth may come to a recognition of others as persons of worth—to be served, not exploited.

Youth may have experiences of meaningful worship of God as he is revealed in Jesus Christ and the Scriptures.

Youth may express commitment to God (as revealed in Jesus Christ) as Lord of life.

Youth, in the presence of his increasing knowledge of the world around him, may develop a growing concept of the majesty of God and his omnipotence.

Youth may develop increasing ease in the presence of doubt.

1. God Speaks in Man's Search for Meaning Beyond Himself

STATEMENT OF THE THEME

God's revelation of himself in part in the nature of the human personality explains man's persistent yearnings to worship some god, to know more, to do better, to be in relationship.

ADULTHOOD

1. **Significance of the theme for this age level**

   a. **Meanings and experiences within this theme relevant for this age level. This is content, a selected part of Scope.**

God's personhood is reflected imperfectly but meaningfully in human personality.

As adults search for truth (accuracy, system, stability) within their world, God discloses himself as the ground, being, and framework of wisdom and truth.

God's readiness to be known is reflected in his implanting in adults a restless desire to find meaning beyond themselves.

God shows his constant righteousness in the adult's struggle to understand human conscience and its relation to external codes of right and wrong.

God shows himself controller of history—man's source necessary for purposiveness and significance.

God has implanted in man a drive to discover his own individuality and identity in relation to his fellowman, his world, and God.

The variety of religious expressions among the cultures of the world forms the reality of God who calls men to communion and worship.

387

God has created man with capacities for thought, reason, and discovery that make possible common foci of interest and concern between God and man and among men.

God provides to those who seek it power for living in accord with God's desires for man.

Truth in every realm of knowledge is compatible with God who is the source of truth.

God, the Lord of history, assures the significance of one's own destiny and that of society.

God who desires man's fellowship perfectly fulfills the adult's quest for relationship.

Man's quest for relationship is satisfied in God's availability for fellowship.

Jesus Christ calls man into fellowship and identity with him and his cause.

God speaks to persons in their desire to seek his guidance and to draw near to him in worship.

God is worthy to receive man's full devotion and loyalty.

388

1. Significance of the theme for this age level

b. Readiness of the learner for this theme in terms of basic needs, interests, motivations, capacities, developmental tasks.

Adults need a supreme loyalty that resolves the conflicts of lesser loyalties.

Adults have the capacity to distinguish sufficiently between themselves and their human situation to permit self-evaluation in light of extrinsic values.

Adults have the capacity to distinguish among failure, frustration, and lack of purpose and to admit their reality in his life.

Adults have the capacity to relate meaningfully to a wide range of persons and social situations.

Perceiving his inability to cope alone with the crises of life such as pain, sorrow, war, sin, poverty, and affluence readies the adult to seek for meaning beyond himself.

Adults have the capacity for identifying and evaluating the various competitors for men's allegiance and the commonly accepted sources of security.

Adults have a continuing need to worship a Supreme Being.

Adults are constantly called upon to exercise judgment concerning right and wrong.

Adults have recurring questions about death and their ultimate destiny.

Adults are able to project out of their own self-awareness and experience something of the nature of man's Creator.

2. **How may this content be communicated as the learner engages in the Learning Tasks? What are the methods and procedures by which the learner may explore the meanings and experiences within this theme (1-a) in the light of his readiness (1-b) in order to discover significance and value.**

Through participating in corporate and private worship in which men are confronted by God.

Through studying what the Bible says about the nature of human personality and purpose of life.

Through studying the social and psychological sciences to find out what they say about the nature of personality.

By sharing with others insights about the self in meaningful relationships to God and man.

By becoming acquainted with and weighing various criteria for making decisions concerning right and wrong.

Through personal association with and by biographical study of persons who have found meaning in themselves.

By reflecting on the meaning of events in one's life history.

By expressing through the performing and graphic arts one's concepts and feelings about search and discovery of meaning beyond oneself.

By expressing through speaking and writing one's understandings resulting from his search for meaning beyond himself.

389

3. **What may the learner achieve within this theme in the fulfillment of the Learning Tasks? What are possible changes or learnings on the part of the learner that may result from his appropriation of the significance and value discovered? These changes or learnings may be associated with skills,**

attitudes, motivations, perceptions including understandings and appreciations.

The adult may accept himself and others as persons within whom is resident the image of God.

The adult may enjoy fellowship with God as person with Person.

The adult may experience a sense of awe and adoration of God as he reveals himself in Jesus Christ and the Scriptures.

390

The adult may discover in God's revelation a framework for discerning and appropriating truth.

In making moral judgments and choices the adult may increasingly take into consideration God's will as he understands it.

The adult may confess that Jesus Christ is Lord of his life.

The adult may develop a sense of assurance that God is in control of history and ultimate destiny.

The adult may recognize others to be persons who, like him, experience meaning beyond themselves.

The adult may develop a new perspective for viewing his life and the lives of others as rooted in God.

The adult may develop increasing skill in articulating and communicating his understanding of God as discovered in his own experience.

2. The Living God Seeks Man

STATEMENT OF THE THEME

The eternal God (Father, Son, and Holy Spirit) has acted and continues to act in the life and affairs of man, disclosing himself and his redeeming love to man, and drawing man into fellowship with him. Thus God makes possible man's acceptance of his ultimate significance.

EARLY CHILDHOOD

1. Significance of the theme for this age level

    a. Meanings and experiences within this theme relevant for this age level. This is content, a selected part of Scope.

God's love for the young child makes possible the child's loving response to him.

God's love for the young child is constant regardless of the child's behavior.

God's seeking and forgiving love is experienced by the young child in the events and relationships of daily life.

God's love, as expressed through Jesus Christ, gives the young child an awareness of God's concern for him and a sense of his own worth.

1. Significance of the theme for this age level

    b. Readiness of the learner for this theme in terms of basic needs, interests, motivations, capacities, developmental tasks

The young child has a readiness and capacity to understand some things about God (related to the theme) as seen in the life and teachings of Jesus.

391

The need for a sense of belonging and acceptance readies a young child to respond to the fellowship of the family and the larger Christian community in which God's seeking love is demonstrated.

The young child's capacity to learn some things through analogy makes possible the use of daily experience with others, especially parents, to convey the nature of God's seeking love, for example, the anxiety of a young child when he feels the disfavor or reproof of a person he loves and the ensuing experience of accepting love and forgiveness, readies him to sense something of the nature of God's forgiving love.

2. **How may this content be communicated as the learner engages in the Learning Tasks? What are the methods and procedures by which the learner may explore the meanings and experiences within this theme (1-a) in the light of his readiness (1-b) in order to discover significance and value?**

By listening to the gospel of God's acts of seeking love for men.

By hearing biblical stories, parables, and events which illustrate God's seeking love.

By experiencing something of the love of God through association with and discipline by persons who love and care for him.

By becoming involved with his peers within the fellowship of the Christian community which by its nature reflects God's seeking, loving action.

By being accepted by a teacher or adult in the Christian fellowship who takes initiative in helping the child feel sought out and accepted.

Through opportunities for association with other adults in the church.

3. **What may the learner achieve within this theme in the fulfillment of the Learning Tasks? What are possible changes or learnings on the part of the learner that may result from his appropriation of the significance and value discovered? These changes or learnings may be associated with skills, attitudes, motivations, perceptions including understandings and appreciations.**

The young child may recognize that he is loved even when disciplined.

The young child may become aware that God is always present, loving him.

The young child may develop a sense of self-acceptance and personal worth.

The young child may develop a sense of belonging to the family of God.

The young child responds with love to the love of God.

The young child may help others and share with others as a response to God's love.

The young child may become aware that he is wanted by God who cares about him.

The young child may realize that God loves him as a person.

The young child may experience trust and security because of his awareness of God's love and care.

The young child may become more willing to forgive others as he realizes God forgives his shortcomings.

2. The Living God Seeks Man

STATEMENT OF THE THEME

The eternal God (Father, Son, and Holy Spirit) has acted and continues to act in the life and affairs of man, disclosing himself and his redeeming love to man, and drawing man into fellowship with him. Thus God makes possible man's acceptance of his ultimate significance.

ELEMENTARY YEARS

393

1. **Significance of the theme for this age level**

   a. **Meanings and experiences within this theme relevant for this age level. This is content, a selected part of Scope.**

God is seen at work in the lives of persons who show his love.

God's love for the child opens the way for the child to see himself as a person of significance.

In Jesus Christ God reveals to the child how much he loves him.

God's persistent seeking love is not altered by the child's behavior.

God's continuous, dependable love is revealed in his concern that children experience fellowship with him.

God's seeking and forgiving love is experienced by the elementary child in the events and relationships of daily life.

1. Significance of the theme for this age level

b. Readiness of the learner for this theme in terms of basic needs, interests, motivations, capacities, developmental tasks.

394

The elementary child's need for security and something on which he can depend as he faces precarious situations in his life readies him for the disclosure of God's seeking love for him.

The elementary child's capacity to identify with Godlike persons of whom he learns by reading or personal acquaintances helps him to experience God in his own life.

The elementary child's ability to recognize that when he does wrong he is disciplined but not rejected, prepares him to understand that God's love is not withdrawn when man does wrong.

The elementary child's interest in the lives of persons and his questions about what has influenced them readies him to understand how God reveals himself to men.

The elementary child's need for love and acceptance gives him a readiness for the revelation of God's love.

The elementary child's capacity for doing things on his own for others readies him to appreciate the activity of God in his seeking love for men.

The elementary child's developing sense of history readies him for the conception of God as eternal.

2. How may this content be communicated as the learner engages in the Learning Tasks? What are the methods and procedures by which the learner may explore the meanings

and experiences within this theme (1-a) in the light of his readiness (1-b) in order to discover significance and value?

By exploring how God has acted in the past to make his redeeming love known to man.

By listening to the gospel of God's seeking, loving acts.

By comparing the ways God acted in the lives of men in the past with the ways he acts today.

By participating in a group which accepts responsibility for expressing God's accepting love.

By identifying with persons past and present who evidence response to God in their lives.

By associating with persons who experience and reflect God's seeking love in their lives.

3. **What may the learner achieve within this theme in the fulfillment of the Learning Tasks? What are possible changes or learnings on the part of the learner that may result from his appropriation of the significance and value discovered? These changes or learnings may be associated with skills, attitudes, motivations, perceptions including understandings and appreciations.**

The child may achieve a sense of security in the midst of new perplexing and uncertain situations of life.

395

The child may recognize that discipline can be an expression of love.

The child may experience acceptance by others and by God.

The child may experience a deeper sense of personal worth.

The child may freely accept God's seeking love and consciously decide to live as God requires.

The child may grow in love for God and others.

The child may have deeper fellowship with God in the context of the Christian community.

The child may experience that God is always present and loving him.

The child may serve as a worker with God in his mission of love to all men.

The child may behold God's supreme revelation of seeking love in Jesus Christ.

The child may be more keenly aware of the presence of God in daily events and relationships.

2. The Living God Seeks Man

STATEMENT OF THE THEME

The eternal God (Father, Son, and Holy Spirit) has acted and continues to act in the life and affairs of man, disclosing himself and his redeeming love to man, and drawing man into fellowship with him. Thus God makes possible man's acceptance of his ultimate significance.

YOUTH

1. Significance of the theme for this age level

a. Meanings and experiences within this theme relevant for this age level. This is content, a selected part of Scope.

God's respect for the integrity of each person is seen in the freedom which God has given to man to accept or reject his seeking action.

God's pursuit of every person enables youth to sense the significance of his own being and that of others.

God's persistent effort to draw all men into fellowship with himself reveals the nature of his love.

God's action in history and in the affairs of men forces men to respond to his call to fellowship with himself.

God's gift of himself in Jesus Christ reveals the intensity of his seeking love.

The continuity of God's action from the past to the present helps man to be aware of God's mission in the world.

In Jesus Christ, God supremely reveals to the youth his love, his teachings, his own nature.

God is revealed in the lives of people who show his love, concerns, and carry out his will.

1. Significance of the theme for this age level

b. Readiness of the learner for this theme in terms of basic needs, interests, motivations, capacities, developmental tasks.

Youth's exaggerated reaction to the physical, psychological, and social adjustments experienced in adolescence causes him to search for the kind of sustaining support that may be experienced when he perceives that God is active in his life and affairs.

The unrest and insecurity of the adolescent who needs assurances of love and acceptance in a fellowship of peers provide a readiness for a deeper fellowship and belongingness to God.

Youth's disposition to commit himself in abandonment to great causes prompts him to enter a relationship with God who demands total commitment.

397

Youth's enlarged capacity to reason enables him to recognize God's action in the past and thus to perceive God at work in the present.

Youth's desire for adventure and new experience provide a readiness for a widening awareness of the presence of God in all facets of his life.

Youth's desire for a sense of direction in life as he is confronted with big decisions, such as occupation, marriage, education, ethical and moral problems, social and personal crises may lead to a readiness to accept God's activity in life's affairs and may lead him to seek God's guidance.

Youth's push for independence and his rejection of established authority provide a readiness for discovery of the seeking God who is relevant to the contemporary world.

Youth's growing conception of an eternal God, who pursues temporal man, enables him to see more clearly the ultimate significance of man.

398

2. How may this content be communicated as the learner engages in the Learning Tasks? What are the methods and procedures by which the learner may explore the meanings and experiences within this theme (1-a) in the light of his readiness (1-b) in order to discover significance and value.

By exploring the behavior of man for evidences of freedom to accept or reject God's redeeming acts.

By identifying with persons whose lives exemplify response to God's invitation to fellowship.

By proclaiming the gospel of God's seeking love for all persons.

By studying evidences of God's action in events of history and in the lives of men which point to the ultimate worth of persons.

By participating in a Christian fellowship which reflects the nature of God's loving acts.

By associating with youth and adults whose lives demonstrate the effect of God's seeking action upon them.

By participating in a Christian fellowship whose active outreach expresses God's seeking love.

By sharing experiences and discussion of the meaning of God's seeking love.

By participating in service and evangelism projects.

By research and study of God's actions in history.

By studying biographies relevant to theme.

By studying other religions and their concept of God and history.

3. **What may the learner achieve within this theme in the fulfillment of the Learning Tasks? What are possible changes or learnings on the part of the learner that may result from his appropriation of the significance and value discovered? These changes or learnings may be associated with skills, attitudes, motivations, perceptions including understandings and appreciations.**

Youth may know that God is active in the life of every person.

Youth may accept himself as a person of significance to God.

Youth may become aware that God is continually at work in his life and that he awaits response in faith and love.

Youth may commit himself fully to the seeking God who calls him into fellowship.

Youth may choose and prepare for a life of service as a channel of God's love and purpose.

Youth may participate in witnessing to the seeking love of God for every person.

Youth may relate to others in ways which reflect God's seeking love.

Youth may be aware of God's supreme revelation in Christ.

Youth may recognize that God's seeking love includes discipline ("chastening") of those he loves.

Youth may be more keenly aware of God's presence in daily events and relationships.

Youth may be aware of God's action in the events of history.

399

2. The Living God Seeks Man

STATEMENT OF THE THEME

The eternal God (Father, Son, and Holy Spirit) has acted and continues to act in the life and affairs of man, disclosing himself and his redeeming love to man, and drawing man into fellowship with him. Thus God makes possible man's acceptance of his ultimate significance.

ADULTHOOD

1. Significance of the theme for this age level

a. Meanings and experiences within this theme relevant for this age level. This is content, a selected part of Scope.

God's action in history and the affairs of men reveal that he is continuously calling men to come into fellowship with himself.

God is revealed in the life of people who show his love, concerns, carry out his will.

400

God's persistent pursuit of man, past and present, reveals his redemptive love and enables man to sense something of how God values him.

The continuity of God's persistent action in the life and affairs of men, evident in both history and current events, continuously confronts men with the choice to accept or reject God's fellowship.

God's persistent pursuit of man reveals that he has purpose for each person.

In Jesus Christ God supremely reveals his love, teaching, and nature.

God's exposure of himself in Jesus Christ illumines the depth of his love, concern, and willingness to suffer in order to bring men into fellowship with him.

God has revealed his respect for the integrity of man, giving each person the freedom to accept or reject his love.

God's seeking love, when accepted, calls each man to develop to the fullest his capacities and to fulfill his significance.

God's action in his people in love and suffering for others brings man into fellowship with him and with each other.

God uses those who are responding to his seeking love to make known to others his invitation to fellowship.

The openness and vulnerability God takes on in his revelation of himself calls man to open himself and take on a vulnerability that makes possible a depth of personal encounter and individual relationship with God and others.

God's seeking love establishes a fellowship with persons irrespective of their worthiness but not irrespective of their response.

1. Significance of the theme for this age level

b. Readiness of the learner for this theme in terms of basic needs, interests, motivations, capacities, developmental tasks.

Man's search for something to which he can give himself readies him for openness to God's seeking love.

The adult's acceptance of rebellion, willfulness, hopelessness, temporality, independence, drives him to a search for significance and meaning in his existence.

The adult's longing for sustaining support and security when faced by life's temporality of other social and personal uncertainties readies him to accept the dependability and trustworthiness of God in the affairs of his life.

The adult's ability to relate space and time enables him to recognize God's action in the past and to perceive God at work in the present.

The adult's need for a sense of purpose in life makes him open to divine action.

401

The adult's capacity for empathy makes possible his being willing to share God's vulnerability in the search for fellowship.

2. How may this content be communicated as the learner engages in the Learning Tasks? What are the methods and procedures by which the learner may explore the meanings and experiences within this theme (1-a) in the light of his readiness (1-b) in order to discover significance and value.

By exploring history, both biblical and secular, to discern God's action in it.

By participating in a Christian community whose active outreach is consciously motivated by God's seeking love.

By associating with persons who have confidence in God's seeking action in the affairs of their lives.

By participating in a community whose acceptance of God's seeking love is reflected in respect and concern for all persons and a desire to be in fellowship with them.

By identifying with persons of history whose lives exemplify awareness and response to God's continuous action in their life and affairs.

402

By witnessing to God's seeking love both within and beyond the organized church.

3. **What may the learner achieve within this theme in the fulfillment of the Learning Tasks? What are possible changes or learnings on the part of the learner that may result from his appropriation of the significance and value discovered? These changes or learnings may be associated with skills, attitudes, motivations, perceptions including understandings and appreciations.**

The adult may accept himself as a person of significance in the eyes of God.

The adult may gain a conviction that God is active in persons lives and affairs irrespective of their worthiness, but not irrespective of their response.

The adult may become aware that God is working in his life and awaits response in faith and love.

The adult may experience fellowship with God.

The adult may realize that fellowship with God involves mutual self-giving and leads to the desire that the fellowship include all men.

The adult may commit himself to God and his purposes as a response to God's loving acts.

The adult may participate with others in witnessing to the seeking love of God for all men.

The adult may commit himself to minister as a servant to all persons, as a channel through whom God continues to act.

The adult may gladly accept with thankfulness the chastening of the loving God.

The adult may hear the call of God in the events and relationships of daily life.

The adult may experience new dimensions of God's seeking love, especially in Jesus Christ.

The adult may be more aware of God at work in the affairs and events of daily life.

3. The Gracious God Judges and Redeems

STATEMENT OF THE THEME

The grace of God seen in both his holiness and his redemptive love as revealed supremely in Jesus Christ answers man's need for judgment, forgiveness, and renewal.

EARLY CHILDHOOD

1. Significance of the theme for this age level

a. Meanings and experiences within this theme relevant for this age level. This is content, a selected part of Scope.

Persons who love God expect us to be and do what he would want and help us to know what he desires of us.

Persons who love God and who love us are displeased when we do not do what they believe he desires of us and pleased when we do what he would want us to do.

We know of God's pleasure or displeasure (judgment) through the words and actions of persons who love God and through our own thoughts and feelings.

403

We know of God's forgiveness through the forgiveness of persons who love God and who love us and through our own thoughts and feelings.

God helps persons to do what he wants them to and lets them know when he is pleased or displeased with their behavior.

Because God forgives we can restore our relationship with him and with others even after we have displeased him (known his judgment).

God forgives when persons are sorry for wrongdoings and for not doing what he would want.

Persons who love God are gracious and forgiving and can be trusted to love others regardless of their behavior.

God is loving and good and wants to forgive us. Because he loves us he helps us to do our best.

God's love is unchanging and does not depend on a person's conduct.

We call God holy because he is so loving and knows always what is right for us.

1. Significance of the theme for this age level

b. Readiness of the learner for this theme in terms of basic needs, interests, motivations, capacities, developmental tasks

The young child is experiencing pain when his relationship with a playmate or with his parents is broken and joy when this relationship is restored. This forms the basis for a beginning understanding of divine judgment and forgiveness.

The young child is experiencing approval and disapproval of parents and others and is discovering their attitudes toward right and wrong. This forms a basis for a beginning understanding of God's judgment.

The young child needs the security and support that can come from knowing that God loves him at all times.

The young child is beginning to develop the capacity to distinguish between right and wrong.

The young child is sensitive to and can begin to deal with the various emotions and feelings, the pleasure and displeasure that adults and other children may express in response to his behavior.

2. **How may this content be communicated as the learner engages in the Learning Tasks? What are the methods and procedures by which the learner may explore the meanings and experiences within this theme (1-a) in the light of his readiness (1-b) in order to discover significance and value?**

By living with Christian adults who express the spirit of God's forgiveness in human relationships.

By singing songs and listening to stories which tell about God's unconditional love and care within a context that reflects that love and care.

By living with dependable and trustworthy adults who trust and depend on God.

By being judged with love and acceptance by adults who, out of their relation with God, are gracious in their judgment of themselves and others.

By discovering through various experiences what brings approval or disapproval from others who trust and depend on God.

By having guided experiences at home, nursery school, kindergarten, and church in making right choices and distinguishing between what is acceptable and unacceptable to persons who love and trust God.

By hearing others say, "I'm sorry," and, as a result, experiencing restored relationships that have been broken.

By providing situations in which the preschool child can discover meaning in experiences of discipline with love.

By listening to stories, or looking at pictures which tell of Jesus' love in his dealing with people.

405

3. **What may the learner achieve within this theme in the fulfillment of the Learning Tasks? What are possible changes or learnings on the part of the learner that may result from his appropriation of the significance and value discovered? These changes or learnings may be associated with skills, attitudes, motivations, perceptions including understandings and appreciations.**

406

The young child may begin to learn that God loves him unconditionally and is ready to forgive and help him.

The young child may experience being forgiven and forgiving.

The young child may begin to learn how to express forgiveness.

The young child may begin to learn that in the sight of God and those who love God he has worth under all conditions.

The young child may begin to learn to trust God.

The young child may love others even when their behavior has not been acceptable to him.

The young child may feel some sense of security in his growing awareness of God's love and care for him.

The young child may begin to understand what is right and wrong and assume responsibility for making some of his own choices.

The young child may begin to discover that God wants him to make right choices and will help him do so.

3. The Gracious God Judges and Redeems

STATEMENT OF THE THEME

The grace of God seen in both his holiness and his redemptive love as revealed supremely in Jesus Christ answers man's need for judgment, forgiveness, and renewal.

ELEMENTARY YEARS

1. **Significance of the theme for this age level**

   a. **Meanings and experiences within this theme relevant for this age level. This is content, a selected part of Scope.**

God's judgment is at work in the suffering caused by the harmful consequences of wrong choices or acts.

God's judgment follows rejection of and failure to fulfill life's opportunities and responsibilities.

Relation to God is maintained and restored when opportunities and responsibilities are accepted and fulfilled to the best of one's abilities.

God's revelation of his holiness is the basis of what is right and wrong for the child.

God's judgment and redeeming love provide a guide for certain standards of conduct but at the same time allow freedom of choice in decision-making.

God acts as Redeemer to bring forgiveness for thoughtless or wrong deeds.

God reveals his graciousness in helping anyone who turns to him for forgiveness, seeking help to do his will.

God's forgiveness restores relationships without doing away with the consequences of wrongdoing.

God makes known his graciousness through his love that is not dependent upon one's behavior.

407

1. **Significance of the theme for this age level**

   b. **Readiness of the learner for this theme in terms of basic needs, interests, motivations, capacities, developmental tasks.**

An elementary child looks for firm boundaries for or limitations on his behavior and is able to cope with the fact of judgment.

An elementary child's need for and experience with rules in the home, school, and community prepare him to be aware of God's laws.

An elementary child's high regard for fair play gives him the capacity to understand something of the meaning of God's judgment.

An elementary child can project his thoughts to situations and experiences. This gives him the capacity to understand something of the holiness of God and his complete righteousness.

The elementary child's shock to discover that grown-ups often do not do what they should and often suffer the consequences may provide openness for understanding man's need for redemption.

The younger elementary child is likely to be especially hard on those who do not do what they should, even in little things, but is maturing in his ability to understand and forgive.

The elementary child depends a great deal upon feeling the love and support of his family and group. Such dependence makes him ready to respond to the revelation of God's love and concern for him.

An elementary child has experiences of disobeying his parents and of knowing forgiveness and reconciliation. These experiences enable him to understand God's disappointment when he does wrong and to accept God's forgiveness when he repents.

The elementary child has experiences of needing to forgive others, which can contribute to his understanding of God's forgiveness.

The elementary child knows that adults can give him both support and correction when he attempts a task that is beyond his own strength. This experience gives him readiness to understand and depend upon the help of God's judgment, forgiveness, and redemption.

2. **How may this content be communicated as the learner engages in the Learning Tasks? What are the methods and procedures by which the learner may explore the meanings and experiences within this theme (1-a) in the light of his readiness (1-b) in order to discover significance and value?**

By participating under Christian guidance in a group whose life affords opportunity for planning with others, taking responsibility in carrying out plans, and for reflecting on the experience.

By reading, dramatizing, and discussing stories relevant to the age-group's concerns in which choices involving right and wrong are made in light of the gospel and their consequences explored.

By dramatizing or otherwise exploring Bible teachings relevant to the theme—such as the message of Amos or stories of the ministry of Jesus.

By studying and using in worship Bible passages and hymns extolling God for his holiness and righteousness.

By exploring the parallels and differences between relations of human beings to each other and the relations between man and God.

By participating in prayer and worship, dealing with judgment, forgiveness, and redemption.

By studying the accounts of how Jesus dealt with persons who did wrong.

409

3. **What may the learner achieve within this theme in the fulfillment of the Learning Tasks? What are possible changes or learnings on the part of the learner that may result from his appropriation of the significance and value discovered? These changes or learnings may be associated with skills, attitudes, motivations, perceptions including understandings and appreciations.**

The child may come to a greater realization of God's concern for him and for all people.

The child may understand that discipline can be an expression of love.

The child may respond personally to God's redemptive love.

The child may recognize and understand more of what God expects of him, and be more willing to obey God's laws.

The child may realize that wrongdoing and disobedience result in trouble and suffering to himself, to those he loves, and to God.

410

The child may repent of his wrongdoing.

The child may realize his own need for forgiveness and be more willing to forgive others.

The child may understand in a new way God's holiness and righteousness.

The child may be led to more thoughtful and responsible making of choices.

3. The Gracious God Judges and Redeems

STATEMENT OF THE THEME

The grace of God seen in both his holiness and his redemptive love as revealed supremely in Jesus Christ answers man's need for judgment, forgiveness, and renewal.

YOUTH

1. Significance of the theme for this age level

a. Meanings and experiences within this theme relevant for this age level. This is content, a selected part of Scope.

The holiness of God in contrast to man's sinfulness gives credence to God's judgment upon man as a sinner.

God makes his judgment known in part as youth recognizes and accepts responsibility for making choices.

God reveals his judgment and redemptive love by satisfying man's deep desire for forgiveness and renewal.

The gracious God acts in judgment and redemption within many of the humbling as well as exalting experiences of life.

God's judgment of youth's sin and rebellion often become more apparent in his experiences of suffering, loneliness, isolation, failure, and guilt.

God's disclosure of his holiness is the ultimate criterion by which youth may discern what is right and wrong.

God's grace when experienced provides a basis for Christian hope.

God reveals his grace in redemption as youth discovers in Jesus Christ the source of forgiveness and renewal.

That which God discloses through judgment may be accepted, or rejected to youth's peril.

1. Significance of the theme for this age level

b. Readiness of the learner for this theme in terms of basic needs, interests, motivations, capacities, developmental tasks.

Youth's increasing drive for independence from adult authority readies him to seek for himself an ultimate source of authority in God.

As youth experiences unreliability in human relationships, he has a readiness for the reliability of the gracious God and the relationship that engenders.

In realizing his need for forgiveness in human relationships, youth may sense his need for God's forgiveness.

Those experiences which have a fragmentizing effect upon youth's life accentuate a need for the integration provided in redemption and renewal.

Because of the disparity between what he perceives to be right and his failure to achieve this, youth is prompted to recog-

411

nize his need for forgiveness and renewal which is shared by all human life and institutions.

The increased awakening of the drives brought about by the growth and development pattern of the youth years coupled to the ways in which they are expressed give youth a need to explore the basis of the moral law in his life.

Youth's growing ability to think abstractly enables him to understand more deeply the concepts of grace, forgiveness, judgment, and redemption.

Youth's ability to understand some of the consequences of wrong choices helps him understand the fact of God's judgment.

Youth's experience with wrong choices in his life, and a recognition of the mistakes he has made help him to be aware of his need for God's forgiveness and redemption.

Youth's experiments in relationships with his fellowmen often result in wrong choices that break relationships so that he stands in need of reconciliation.

The quest for acceptance readies youth to seek reconciliation when relationships have been broken.

Youth seeks the ultimate meaning of life which may be found in redemption.

2. **How may this content be communicated as the learner engages in the Learning Tasks? What are the methods and procedures by which the learner may explore the meanings and experiences within this theme (1-a) in the light of his readiness (1-b) in order to discover significance and value.**

By reading, writing, and/or participating in dramas which deal with moral tensions, choices, dilemmas, and problems.

By studying and discussing biblical teachings about sin, judgment, forgiveness, and redemption.

By preparing for and engaging in experiences of worship which lead to conviction, contrition, confession of sin, acceptance of forgiveness, and efforts at restitution.

Reading biographical and devotional literature which reflects experiences of confession and forgiveness and the consequent redeemed life.

By learning about judgment and redemption through one's own acts of forgiving others and being forgiven by others.

By discussing one's problems with trusted Christian persons: parents, teachers, ministers, counselors, and peers.

By utilizing situations of need and related service projects as opportunities for deepening awareness of and response to God's judgment and plan for redemption.

By looking at current events as an arena of God's judgment and redemptive purpose and action.

By facing openly and frankly one's own life and associations as an arena of God's judgment and action, and his grace.

By arranging to go on field trips to social institutions such as mental hospitals, orphanages, prisons, where questions about God's judgment and redemption may be provoked, and afterward discussed.

By learning about God's judgment and redemption in the daily relations of home and school as, for example, in the matter of discipline.

3. **What may the learner achieve within this theme in the fulfillment of the Learning Tasks? What are possible changes or learnings on the part of the learner that may result from his appropriation of the significance and value discovered? These changes or learnings may be associated with skills, attitudes, motivations, perceptions including understandings and appreciations.**

413

Youth may gain a deeper appreciation that every aspect of human life is of supreme concern to the judging and redeeming God.

Youth may grow in appreciation of the righteous character

of God as revealed through the prophets and supremely in Jesus Christ.

Youth may become conscious of his own sin and guilt and through repentance can experience forgiveness and restoration.

Youth may discover God's redemptive mission and appropriate it as a central purpose for his life.

Youth may assume responsibility to God and to man for every aspect of his life.

Youth may recognize that he is being judged by a righteous, impartial judge who loves him.

Youth may realize that God's judgment and redemption are inseparable.

Youth may achieve a deeper understanding of the concepts of the grace, judgment, forgiveness, and redemption of God and experience these in his life.

Youth may recognize and accept himself and others as objects of God's redeeming love in spite of present imperfections.

Youth may discover the basis for Christian hope in his experience of God's redemptive grace.

Youth may discover and adopt the basis for decision-making through his experience of God's judgment and redemptive acts.

Youth may sharpen his discernment between right and wrong through an increased awareness of God's holiness.

3. The Gracious God Judges and Redeems

STATEMENT OF THE THEME

The grace of God seen in both his holiness and his redemptive love as revealed supremely in Jesus Christ answers man's need for judgment, forgiveness, and renewal.

ADULTHOOD

1. Significance of the theme for this age level

a. Meanings and experiences within this theme relevant for this age level. This is content, a selected part of Scope.

In revealing his perfection and righteousness, God helps man find the absolutes which make him aware of right and wrong, obedience and rebellion, holiness and sinfulness.

God reveals his gracious concern for man's life and affairs as he judges man's sin and provides him redemption from the consequences of sin.

God's impartial judgment on human sin is revealed when man senses loneliness, isolation, failure, guilt as the result of rebellion against the divine will.

As God reveals his holiness in the face of man's conflicting values and his human expediency, man realizes his need for redemption from sin and his inability to redeem himself.

God's reconciling love conditions man's own attempts at human reconciliation.

God reveals his justice, goodness, and redemptive purpose by graciously offering his own righteousness to man in the face of man's incapacity to achieve a righteousness of his own.

In Jesus Christ, God reveals his gracious redemption of man, his gift of power over the forces of sin and death.

God's grace is not thwarted by man's recalcitrance; the gracious God stands able tenderly to renew again and again his covenant of judgment and redemption with man.

God's grace rather than man's goodness is the basis of human redemption.

The grace of God in redemption suggests the quality of free and open relationships which should exist among men.

In revealing his graciousness to man, God defers to man's freedom by proffering redemption as a gift that man may either receive or reject.

1. Significance of the theme for this age level

b. Readiness of the learner for this theme in terms of basic

415

needs, interests, motivations, capacities, developmental tasks.

The making of ethical decisions in relation to others for whom adults have responsibility gives them experiences in which indecision and compromise may cause them to develop the ability to be sensitive to the difficulties of judging rightly and doing justly without divine aid.

Realizing the disparity between what they perceive to be right and their achievements, adults may have a readiness for admitting their insufficiency and their need for a redemptive power beyond themselves.

As they experience unreliability in human relationships, adults are torn between a desire for disengagement from others and a drive to establish redemptive relationships which are found in God.

The realization by adults that they violate human relationships and need human forgiveness may provide a basis for acknowledgment of their violation of the divine relationship and their need for God's forgiveness.

As adults experience the fragmentation of their lives, they may be motivated to look for a center around which to become integrated.

As parents experience the necessary judgmental and redemptive events of family living, they may develop readiness to understand the necessity for God's judgment and redemption.

Adults may have experienced the gracious judgment and redemption of God and thus be ready to invest fuller meaning in the biblical descriptions of God's acts of judgment and redemption.

2. **How may this content be communicated as the learner engages in the Learning Tasks? What are the methods and procedures by which the learner may explore the meanings and experiences within this theme (1-a) in the light of his**

416

readiness (1-b) in order to discover significance and value?

By studying and discussing the action of God in history through biblical teachings about sin, judgment, forgiveness, and redemption which comes to a climax in Jesus Christ.

By preparing for and engaging in experiences of worship which lead to conviction, contrition, and confession of sin.

By accepting forgiveness and making efforts at restitution.

By reading biographical and devotional literature which reflects experiences of confession and forgiveness, and the consequent redeemed life.

By asking God for the grace to forgive, and expressing forgiveness when one has been wronged.

By examining redemptive experiences to appreciate more fully God's initiative and action.

By participating in dramatic situations in which adults may identify with others who are experiencing the judgment and redemption of God. (Role playing, films, plays, etc.)

By studying the biblical doctrines of holiness, grace, judgment, and forgiveness.

By examining one's own acts of forgiveness in order to discover more about the cost and results of forgiveness.

By utilizing emergent and often unexpected expressions of need or of strong feelings (affection, aggression, grief) to deepen awareness of and response to God's judgment and redemption in current situations.

417

By examining current events as an arena of God's judgment and redemptive purpose and action.

By facing openly and frankly one's own life and associations as an arena of God's judgment, action, and manifestation of grace.

By listening to sermons on God's holiness, love, judgment, and redemption.

By working to create a climate in small groups within the church in which healthy communication can take place.

3. **What may the learner achieve within this theme in the fulfillment of the Learning Tasks? What are possible changes or learnings on the part of the learner that may result from his appropriation of the significance and value discovered? These changes or learnings may be associated with skills, attitudes, motivations, perceptions including understandings and appreciations.**

The adult may recognize that God's judgment is an expression of his redemptive love.

The adult may recognize and accept his own and other's feelings of guilt.

The adult may understand the concept of God's grace, and honestly recognize his need for grace.

The adult may experience for himself the reality of God's grace.

The adult may recognize and accept the whole range of feelings and emotions both in himself and in others which are a part of the experience of God's judgment and redemption for him.

The adult may seek to understand and to deal with the whole range of emotion in himself and in others, when accepting and responding to God's judgment and redemption.

The adult may reduce barriers between himself and other persons, progressively becoming open to persons in daily life, and may make restitution for wrongs committed.

The adult may learn to receive forgiveness as a condition of becoming able to forgive others.

The adult may increase his awareness of the many kinds of human situations in which it is possible to extend acceptance and love.

The adult may gain a deeper understanding of his own shortcomings and the need for God's grace.

The adult may be willing to listen to others' interpretation of God's judgment and love, especially when it applies to himself.

The adult may develop an expanding appreciation of God's holiness and righteousness as contrasted with man's sin.

The adult may develop a trust in God's goodness as the guarantor of enduring values.

The adult may have a growing conviction that in the long run man cannot get away with sin.

The adult may become able to distinguish between an appropriate regard for himself as a part of God's creation, and the sinful pride which attempts to gain superior status, or act like a god.

4. The Sovereign God Dwells with Man

STATEMENT OF THE THEME

The infinite God (Father, Son, and Holy Spirit) deigns to live and work with man, quickening, purifying, and empowering.

EARLY CHILDHOOD

1. Significance of the theme for this age level

a. Meanings and experiences within this theme relevant for this age level. This is content, a selected part of Scope.

419

God's love and care are with us all the time and in all that we do.

God uses parents and others who love God to help know what God wants us to do.

I can turn to God in times of joy and sorrow.

God is helping me to know for myself what is right and what is wrong.

People who love God pray to him, learn about him from the Bible, and worship him.

We can feel close to God and can talk with him when we are alone as well as when we are with other people.

God will forgive me when I do wrong.

God is great. He has provided for the sun to rise and set, the seasons to come and go.

1. Significance of the theme for this age level

b. Readiness of the learner for this theme in terms of basic needs, interests, motivations, capacities, developmental tasks

The young child has the capacity for beginning awareness of God's presence.

The young child has the capacity for growing awareness of what is right and wrong.

The young child is beginning to be responsible for some decisions concerning his behavior.

The young child has the ability to recognize success and failure as they pertain to himself and to react to them.

The young child needs the immediate availability of someone on whom he can depend.

The young child has a growing sensitiveness to the differences in relationships with others.

The young child experiences feelings of guilt and of wrong-doing.

The young child has the capacity to experience some wonder and awe.

The young child may have an uncritical sense of trust that makes it easy for him to trust God.

2. How may this content be communicated as the learner engages in the Learning Tasks? What are the methods and procedures by which the learner may explore the meanings and experiences within this theme (1-a) in the light of his readiness (1-b) in order to discover significance and value?

By discovering what behavior is approved or disapproved by persons who love him and who love God.

By recognizing with the preschool child God's presence in experiences of joy and sorrow.

By associating with persons who have a consciousness of the presence of the sovereign God.

By providing opportunities for free and creative play experiences within the context of Christian love, acceptance, and guidance.

Through simple experiences of worship in which the preschool child may be aware of God's nearness.

By the use of conversation, stories, and music that may help the child think about and become aware of the presence of God.

Through simple conversations about and observation of God's activity in the world.

By playing stories which interpret how God helps us choose.

Through conversation about how God wants us to live.

3. **What may the learner achieve within this theme in the fulfillment of the Learning Tasks? What are possible changes or learnings on the part of the learner that may result from his appropriation of the significance and value discovered? These changes or learnings may be associated with skills, attitudes, motivations, perceptions including understandings and appreciations.**

421

The young child may develop a beginning awareness of God's love and concern for him at all times.

The young child may begin to associate right with God and to seek God's help.

The young child may realize that God is with him when he is alone as well as at all other times.

The young child may have beginning understanding of how to express his feeling of closeness to God.

4. The Sovereign God Dwells with Man

STATEMENT OF THE THEME

The infinite God (Father, Son, and Holy Spirit) deigns to live and work with man, quickening, purifying, and empowering.

ELEMENTARY YEARS

1. Significance of the theme for this age level

422

   a. Meanings and experiences within this theme relevant for this age level. This is content, a selected part of Scope.

God's presence is revealed by his helping, comforting, and sustaining those in need of such.

God's presence is felt when the elementary child is sorry for wrongdoing or rejoices in decisions or choices in accord with what God would desire.

God helps each child live as his children.

God helps each child know and do what God would desire.

Even as God reveals his greatness, he also reveals something of his love and concern for the elementary child in the midst of the daily round of activities.

God makes himself known as one to whom the child can turn with confidence in times of joy and sorrow.

God discloses his sovereignty and lordship to the elementary child as the basis for daily life and activities.

God invites the elementary child to be aware of him and responsive to him in all of the activities of life.

The sovereign God acts through persons in working out his purposes in the world.

God gives the elementary child freedom to respond to God or reject him and to choose whether or not to live as God desires but the child cannot escape from the consequences of his choices.

1. **Significance of the theme for this age level**

   b. **Readiness of the learner for this theme in terms of basic needs, interests, motivations, capacities, developmental tasks.**

The elementary child's ability to generalize in terms of knowledge and experience enables him to sense God's greatness and his nearness.

The elementary child is able to read and thus to begin to discover for himself in the written testimony of others how God dwells with man.

The elementary child is increasingly able to understand what God has revealed about right and wrong, which may be a guide for his choices.

The elementary child is asking many questions about himself and how he relates to God and others.

The elementary child's capacity for fellowship enables him to seek fellowship with one worthy of his devotion and allegiance.

The elementary child's difficulties with the many decisions he is called upon to make ready him for God's help in making them.

The elementary child's frequent exposure to competition and success or failure increases his need for a constant source of inner strength and stability.

423

2. **How may this content be communicated as the learner engages in the Learning Tasks? What are the methods and procedures by which the learner may explore the meanings and experiences within this theme (1-a) in the light of his readiness (1-b) in order to discover significance and value?**

By providing situations in which the indwelling love of God may be expressed in relationships between teacher and teacher, pupil and teacher, and pupil and pupil.

By acquainting children with resources of the faith which tell about how God's sovereignty and power as well as how God has dwelt and now dwells with man (with Bible, stories, biographies, poetry, films, music, art, etc.).

By providing opportunities through play experiences, dramatization, conversation, study, worship, in which the elementary child may come to have new appreciations and understandings of how the sovereign God dwells with man, in which the child may be free to test these learnings.

424

By guiding the elementary child in thinking through the meaning of commitment of life to God as revealed in Jesus Christ.

By providing opportunities for the elementary child to observe evidences of the presence of God in the lives of others.

By involving the elementary child in experiences of worship which help him be aware of God's presence.

By exploring with the elementary child the meaning of God's presence in experiences of joy, sorrow, or disappointment.

By cultivating devotional disciplines including personal and group Bible reading and prayer which contribute to the elementary child's sense of the indwelling presence of God.

3. **What may the learner achieve within this theme in the fulfillment of the Learning Tasks? What are possible changes or learnings on the part of the learner that may result from his appropriation of the significance and value discovered? These changes or learnings may be associated with skills, attitudes, motivations, perceptions including understandings and appreciations.**

The elementary child may grow in his awareness of the presence of God in all of his activities.

The elementary child may experience the influence of God in behavior.

The elementary child may grow in his understanding of what it means to commit one's life to God and to rely on God's power for living in obedience to him.

The elementary child may grow in his understanding of and appreciation for the greatness of God who is anxious to dwell with him.

The elementary child may grow in his ability to experience God's presence in every aspect of life, in times of joy and sorrow, of failure and success, and of decision.

The elementary child may consciously strive for the awareness of God in his daily life.

The elementary child may realize that God can actually work through him and that his influence on others is important.

The elementary child may become aware of his responsibility for the use of the freedom he is granted and for the consequences of his choices.

4. The Sovereign God Dwells with Man

STATEMENT OF THE THEME

The infinite God (Father, Son, and Holy Spirit) deigns to live and work with man, quickening, purifying, and empowering.

425

YOUTH

1. Significance of the theme for this age level

a. Meanings and experiences within this theme relevant for this age level. This is content, a selected part of Scope.

God's presence in his life enables a person to fulfill God's purpose for it.

God reveals his concern for a youth's life and affairs as the youth depends upon him in decision-making.

God reveals a willingness to be in relationship even though man is sinful and breaks relationships.

Youth experiences God dwelling in his life and affairs as God cleanses him from sin.

God through the Holy Spirit empowers youth to do what is right and quickens him to become the person he is capable of being.

God's presence and power are revealed as youth experiences new birth and life.

426

God invites youth to participate with him in shaping history and in the development or enhancement of creation.

God reveals his involvement in the life and work of persons in manifold ways.

The spirit of God quickens man to believe in God and to work for the purpose of God.

God is active in the forces at work in society.

God penetrates a person's loneliness, impatience, joys, and sorrows to chasten, succor, sustain, and enrich.

The power and majesty of God are seen in the universe which is a sign or symbol of his power and majesty.

God makes his own resources available to those who give themselves to him and espouse his purposes.

God, though sovereign, never violates the freedom of man, nor removes the consequences of his choices from man.

Man's freedom derives from God's gracious self-limitation and makes possible a mutuality of relationship between man and God.

God's indwelling spirit enables man to know the reality of God, to experience his presence and to respond to him.

1. Significance of the theme for this age level

    b. Readiness of the learner for this theme in terms of basic needs, interests, motivations, capacities, developmental tasks.

Youth's need for more stability than he finds within himself may motivate him to respond to God's indwelling presence.

Youth's capacity for self-evaluation in which he sees his shortcomings, incompleteness, and lack of purpose, coupled with the ability to compare himself with those who have experienced God's presence, prepares him for seeking God's power in his life.

Youth's search for meaning for his life makes him open to explore the possibilities of God's dwelling with man.

Youth's felt need for a source of help in decision-making may contribute to his opening of life to the leadership of the Holy Spirit.

Youth is able to sense God's approval or disapproval of behavior.

Youth's experience of loneliness may cause him to desire God's presence.

Youth has the ability to recognize his need for God's empowering and purifying action to assist youth in fulfilling God's purpose for life.

Youth's recognition of his own limitations may lead him to seek for a source of inner strength.

2. **How may this content be communicated as the learner engages in the Learning Tasks? What are the methods and procedures by which the learner may explore the meanings and experiences within this theme (1-a) in the light of his readiness (1-b) in order to discover significance and value?**

427

Through group worship in which he is aware of God's presence.

By contrasting persons whose lives evidence the presence of God with those which do not.

By being confronted by persons in whom commitment to God has given new meaning to life.

By exploring problems of loneliness, guilt, and alienation in the light of God's involvement in the life of men.

By exploring evidences of the presence of God in the lives of men.

By participating in groups in which the reality of God may be evident.

By the development of devotional disciplines, including personal Bible reading, meditation, and prayer, which contribute to the sensing of the indwelling presence of God.

By researching history and/or creation, looking for evidences of a sovereign God and manifestations of his presence in the natural and social orders.

3. **What may the learner achieve within this theme in the fulfillment of the Learning Tasks? What are possible changes or learnings on the part of the learner that may result from his appropriation of the significance and value discovered? These changes or learnings may be associated with skills, attitudes, motivations, perceptions including understandings and appreciations.**

Youth may grow in his experience of the presence of God in his life.

Youth may appraise his own shortcomings and incompleteness and in turn recognize his need for God.

Youth may grow in his understanding of and willingness to accept God's guidance and power in everyday living.

Youth may respond in faith to God who desires to dwell with man and thus experience new life in Christ.

Youth may recognize the need for the cleansing power of God in his life and experience it through repentance and faith.

Youth may gain deeper insights into the living presence of God as expressed in Jesus Christ.

Youth may surrender to the will of God and devote himself to the work of God.

Youth may become increasingly sensitive and responsive to the power and presence of God in his own life and life about him.

Youth may find in the God who dwells with man resources for facing loneliness, joy, sorrow, impatience, disappointment.

Youth may discover that God's presence is often experienced in the fellowship of Christians.

Youth may become aware that God, even though sovereign, has given complete freedom to man to accept or reject him and the youth may also recognize and fulfill the responsibility this places upon him.

The youth may assume responsibility for his part in the shaping of history and the development and enhancement of what God has created.

4. The Sovereign God Dwells with Man

STATEMENT OF THE THEME

The infinite God (Father, Son, and Holy Spirit) deigns to live and work with man, quickening, purifying, and empowering.

ADULTHOOD

1. Significance of the theme for this age level

429

    a. Meanings and experiences within this theme relevant for this age level. This is content, a selected part of Scope.

God discloses his sovereign presence as persons experience his guidance and direction.

God reveals his sovereignty over man's life and affairs as he judges man and provides for cleansing him from sin.

God reveals his power in the lives of men when he enables them to become, to be, and to do that which man could not do apart from divine power.

God reveals his cleansing and power as a man experiences new birth and life in Jesus Christ.

God is active in the midst of forces in society, using them, transforming them, overriding them for his purposes.

God penetrates man's loneliness, impatience, joys, and sorrow to chasten, succor, sustain, and enrich.

God, as Creator and Sovereign Ruler, dwells with man in his daily life and work.

430

God manifests his presence with man in a variety of ways to assure man of God's continuous involvement with man.

The power and majesty of God are seen in the universe which is a sign and symbol of his power and majesty.

The spirit of God quickens man to believe in and work for the purposes of God.

God makes his own resources available to those who give themselves to him and espouse his purposes.

God, though sovereign, never violates the freedom of man nor removes the consequences of his choices from man.

Man's freedom derives from God's gracious self-limitation and makes possible a mutuality of relationship between man and God.

The sovereign God stands over against man and with man, inviting him to share in the shaping of history and in the development or enhancement of creation.

God's indwelling spirit enables man to know the reality of God, to experience his presence and to respond to him.

1. **Significance of the theme for this age level**

    b. **Readiness of the learner for this theme in terms of basic needs, interests, motivations, capacities, developmental tasks.**

The adult's ability to sense his finiteness, shortcomings, lack of wholeness, and inability to achieve purpose makes it possible for him to be open to a God who is infinite, all-powerful, holy, and able to pursue his purposes.

The adult's need to give his full devotion and allegiance to one who is worthy makes him ready to respond to the sovereign God.

The adult's desire for direction and for power to do what is right helps him recognize the necessity of taking account of God in all of human life.

The adult's experiences of broken relationships, loneliness, failure, and disappointment with which he cannot cope become expediencies of God to evoke responses in man to the God who dwells with men.

The adult's ability to accept help in making decisions readies him to accept God's guidance in making decisions.

The adult's ability to identify many evidences of God's presence and direction in the affairs of men enables him to be responsive to God.

2. How may this content be communicated as the learner engages in the Learning Tasks? What are the methods and procedures by which the learner may explore the meanings and experiences within this theme (1-a) in the light of his readiness (1-b) in order to discover significance and value?

431

By engaging in devotional disciplines, including private devotions and use of the Bible, which contribute to sensing the power of God and awareness of his indwelling presence.

Through group worship which helps him become aware of the presence and power of God.

By encouraging participation in fellowship groups in the Christian community where one may experience the presence of God.

By confronting adults with persons (historical or contemporary) whose lives express the indwelling presence of God.

By studying modern-day groups and organizations through which God is quickening, purifying, and empowering the lives of persons.

By witnessing to experiences in which the sovereign presence of God has been perceived.

432

3. What may the learner achieve within this theme in the fulfillment of the Learning Tasks? What are possible changes or learnings on the part of the learner that may result from his appropriation of the significance and value discovered? These changes or learnings may be associated with skills, attitudes, motivations, perceptions including understandings and appreciations.

The adult may experience God's indwelling presence.

The adult may accept his understanding of God's will as the guide for decision-making.

The adult may grow toward Christian maturity as a result of the quickening power of God in his life.

The adult may experience new birth which results in a new person and which may be evidenced by changed attitudes, habits, thoughts, and relationships.

The adult may grow in the ability to rely upon God's power in everyday living.

The adult may find in the God who dwells with man resources for facing loneliness, joy, sorrow, impatience, disappointment.

The adult may realize that God is continually working and is concerned with the lives and affairs of men.

The adult may discover myriad evidences of the presence and workings of God in daily life and in the natural order.

The adult may surrender himself to the sovereign God and devote his life to the mission of God.

The adult may discover that God's presence is often experienced in the fellowship of Christians.

The adult may become aware that God, even though sovereign, has given complete freedom to man to accept or reject him and the adult may also recognize and fulfill the responsibility this places upon him.

The adult may assume responsibility for his part in the shaping of history and the development and enhancement of what God has created.

5. God Speaks to Man Through the Scriptures

STATEMENT OF THE THEME

As man reads the Bible seeking the guidance of the Holy Spirit, he finds there the definitive answers to his urgent questions: Who is God? What is my responsibility to him? How may I know him?

EARLY CHILDHOOD

1. Significance of the theme for this age level

    a. Meanings and experiences within this theme relevant for this age level. This is content, a selected part of Scope.

433

The Bible is a special book that people who love God treat with respect and reverence.

The Bible is a very important book because people turn to it to find out about God and Jesus.

Bible stories about Jesus show us what God is like.

The lives and teaching of the people in the Bible show us how God plans for people to live and act.

It is through the Bible that we come to know that God created us and the universe.

The Bible tells us that God loves us and cares about what happens to us.

The Bible tells us about God who spoke to and helped the people of long ago and who speaks to and helps us.

1. Significance of the theme for this age level

    b. Readiness of the learner for this theme in terms of basic needs, interests, motivations, capacities, developmental tasks

The young child has a capacity for, readiness for, and interest in listening to and acting out Bible stories and verses.

The young child has an interest in and beginning appreciation for the Bible as a special book.

The young child asks questions about ultimate issues (life, death, God) to which the Bible speaks.

The young child has a capacity to relate some biblical teachings to his daily living.

2. How may this content be communicated as the learner engages in the Learning Tasks? What are the methods and procedures by which the learner may explore the meanings and experiences within this theme (1-a) in the light of his readiness (1-b) in order to discover significance and value?

By becoming acquainted with the Bible as a special book—handling it, seeing it used.

By seeing parents and teachers read and study the Bible.

By listening to, illustrating, and acting out stories and verses from the Bible.

By trying out ways of living that the Bible says are ways God plans for children to live.

By associating with persons who exemplify the teachings of the New Testament.

By participating in sharing opportunities as an expression of biblical teachings.

By talking about the Bible and what it says.

3. **What may the learner achieve within this theme in the fulfillment of the Learning Tasks? What are possible changes or learnings on the part of the learner that may result from his appropriation of the significance and value discovered? These changes or learnings may be associated with skills, attitudes, motivations, perceptions including understandings and appreciations.**

The young child may develop an appreciation of the Bible as a special and important book.

The young child may enjoy stories and verses from the Bible.

The young child may begin to understand that the Bible has something to say about the way he should live.

The young child may develop appreciation of the Bible as the book which tells about Jesus, about God, and about his love and care.

The young child may acquire growing knowledge of and love for Jesus as revealed in the Bible.

435

5. God Speaks to Man Through the Scriptures

STATEMENT OF THE THEME

As man reads the Bible seeking the guidance of the Holy Spirit, he finds there the definitive answers to his urgent questions: Who is God? What is my responsibility to him? How may I know him?

ELEMENTARY YEARS

1. **Significance of the theme for this age level**

a. Meanings and experiences within this theme relevant for this age level. This is content, a selected part of Scope.

In the Bible, God makes something of his nature, his will, and his purpose known to the elementary child.

The Bible is a book which deals with people who relate to God in their everyday life situations with which children can identify.

The Bible is a very important book because people turn to it to find out about God and Jesus.

The life, teachings, and significance of Jesus Christ as recorded in the Scriptures are evidences of God's love and care.

God speaks to persons through the Bible which is the writings of men whom he used to put his message into language that others can understand.

In the Bible, God proclaims his love for all men and calls men to love each other.

In the Bible, God makes known something of the nature of relationships he wants us to have with one another and with God.

The Bible is a book that is held in reverence by Christians because it is the record of God's love, concern, and purpose for his people.

1. Significance of the theme for this age level

b. Readiness of the learner for this theme in terms of basic needs, interests, motivations, capacities, developmental tasks.

The elementary child has a capacity for and interest in reading the Bible for himself.

The elementary child has a growing historical and geographical awareness which permits him to put biblical events and places into perspective.

The elementary child has a capacity to explore concrete details regarding how and why the Bible came to be.

The elementary child has a capacity for understanding, memorizing, and dramatizing Bible passages and stories.

The elementary child feels free to ask questions, many of which are basic and are dealt with in the Scriptures.

The elementary child has the ability to relate some biblical teachings to events and situations for his everyday living.

The elementary child attaches importance to things and ideas held to be important by those he loves and trusts.

The genuine faith of an elementary child is adequate to hearing God speak through scripture.

2. **How may this content be communicated as the learner engages in the Learning Tasks? What are the methods and procedures by which the learner may explore the meanings and experiences within this theme (1-a) in the light of his readiness (1-b) in order to discover significance and value.**

By listening to, reading, and studying the Bible individually and in groups.

By tracing the development of the Bible from oral tradition to its present form.

By getting acquainted with personalities of the Bible to discover clues about how God may work in the lives of people today.

By associating with persons who have responded to the message of the Bible.

By discussing everyday situations and ways in which Bible teachings are relevant.

By listening to interpretation of the Bible in worship.

By exploring what the Bible says about Jesus Christ as the one who makes God known.

437

By studying ways in which the Bible has been translated for use around the world.

By associating with persons whose lives exhibit the quality of relationships described in the Bible.

By exploring answers suggested in the Scriptures to the questions of boys and girls about ultimate issues.

By using Bible atlases and reference books, commentaries and concordances in Bible study.

By engaging in drama, AV's, music, art for understanding what God is saying through the Bible.

438

3. **What may the learner achieve within this theme in the fulfillment of the Learning Tasks? What are possible changes or learnings on the part of the learner that may result from his appropriation of the significance and value discovered? These changes or learnings may be associated with skills, attitudes, motivations, perceptions including understandings and appreciations.**

The child may accept the Bible as a unique book which is central to the Christian faith.

The child may develop skill in reading and studying the Bible.

The child may begin to appreciate the sweep of biblical history, including interrelationship of stories, events, and persons.

The child may recognize that the Bible is a record of how God acted in relationship to man and of man's response to God and his ensuing relationships to his fellowmen.

The child may realize that response to the message of the Bible results in changes in his relationships and behavior.

The child may recognize that the Bible's message is for *all* persons throughout the world.

The child may commit himself to God in Christ to the full extent of his ability and understanding of the revelation in the Scriptures.

The child may assume responsibility for making the Bible known to others.

The child may grow in acquaintance with Jesus as revealed in the Scriptures.

The child may understand something of how the Bible came to be and how it was handed down through the ages.

The child realizes that the Bible has clues to the answers to questions about ultimate issues (God, life, death, etc.).

The child may appreciate the value of knowing biblical passages so well as to be able to recall them from memory.

The child may acquire sufficient facility to use memorized passages and knowledge of the general contents of other stories and verses of the Bible.

5. God Speaks to Man Through the Scriptures

STATEMENT OF THE THEME

As man reads the Bible seeking the guidance of the Holy Spirit, he finds there the definitive answers to his urgent questions: Who is God? What is my responsibility to him? How may I know him?

YOUTH 439

1. Significance of the theme for this age level

a. Meanings and experiences within this theme relevant for this age level. This is content, a selected part of Scope.

Scripture is a ready channel for God's message to contemporary man.

The Bible is authoritative for modern man because it is the eternal God who speaks through it.

The Bible has a unique function which does not compete with other sources of truth.

The Scriptures not only reveal God; they set forth what is expected of youth in his relationships to God and man.

The Bible throws light on how God is actively at work in history today.

The Bible deals with basic problems and issues common to everyone's life; and through it God offers youth guidance for coping with the expression of these issues in his life.

The biblical message is to be interpreted in the light of its historical background and development.

440

God's Spirit guides and enlightens any person who in faith seeks God's word in the Bible.

The continuing experience of the church with the message of scripture offers helpful correction for individual interpretation of scripture.

God as revealed by Jesus Christ and made known today by his Spirit is the same God whose revelation is recorded and made available in the Bible.

The meaning of scripture is made more lucid as well-tested principles of interpretation are brought to bear in Bible study.

The biblical message focuses in the incarnation and one derives the most dependable interpretation of scripture from the perspective of the revelation of God in Jesus Christ.

The message and authority of the Bible cannot be damaged by bringing to bear on the Bible findings of genuine scholarship of men of faith.

Perception of God's revelation in scripture is not dependent on specialized skills but rather on a seeking faith.

1. **Significance of the theme for this age level**

    b. **Readiness of the learner for this theme in terms of basic needs, interests, motivations, capacities, developmental tasks.**

Youth's development of intellectual skills opens up possibilities of discovering his capacity for discerning the God of scripture.

Youth needs to challenge secondhand knowledge and interpretations and to arrive at his own.

The urgency in adolescence of facing life-shaping decisions stimulates the quest for authoritative guidance.

Youth has the capacity to think conceptually and symbolically and to understand the deeper meaning of the Scriptures.

Youth's involvement in expanding his scope of knowledge in a variety of fields prompts him to explore and question the biblical record of God's acts in creation and history in the light of scientific discoveries and historical research.

Meeting conflicting standards of right and wrong in peer group and community, precipitates the need for ethical standards as revealed in scripture against which to test behavior.

Youth has the capacity for hearing and responding in personal commitment to God's plan of salvation as revealed in the Scriptures.

2. How may this content be communicated as the learner engages in the Learning Tasks? What are the methods and procedures by which the learner may explore the meanings and experiences within this theme (1-a) in the light of his readiness (1-b) in order to discover significance and value.

441

By participating in Bible study and discussion, using such tools as commentaries, atlases, concordances, dictionaries, word books, and doctrinal resources.

By participating in corporate worship involving reading and listening to Scripture and hearing it interpreted.

By discussing with peers the implications of the Bible message for situations in which they find themselves.

By comparing the Bible's affirmation on man and on the natural order with other views as found in the arts or sciences.

By listening to the testimony of and having fellowship with Christians for whom the Bible is authoritative and relevant.

By agreeing on and practicing a set of disciplines for regular Bible reading and study.

By investigating the sacred books of other religions in order to compare their teachings with those of the Bible, concerning the nature of God and of man.

By becoming acquainted with and practicing the use of dependable principles of biblical interpretation.

By becoming acquainted with the implications of biblical truth as articulated through literary, graphic, or performing arts by Christians of various cultures.

By reading about the experience of individuals and of the church in their attempt to understand the message of the Bible.

By paraphrasing Scripture in contemporary language.

By memorizing Scripture passages and using them.

By knowing adults who accept the validity of doubt about the Bible and its message and who can sympathetically guide them to resources for coping with doubt.

By becoming acquainted with the teachings of Christ on his relationship to the law and the prophets.

By reviewing the process by which the Bible came into being, has been disseminated, retranslated, and preserved through the history of the church.

3. **What may the learner achieve within this theme in the fulfillment of the Learning Tasks? What are possible changes or learnings on the part of the learner that may result from his appropriation of the significance and value discovered? These changes or learnings may be associated with skills, attitudes, motivations, perceptions including understandings and appreciations.**

The youth may understand and come to appreciate the uniqueness of the Bible within all literature, including the sacred books of all faiths.

Youth may accept the message of the Bible as the word of God.

The youth develops skill in interpreting the Bible message and relating it in a valid way to his own life situation.

The youth develops patterns of regular Bible reading and study.

Youth may become concerned about and active in making the Bible known to others.

The youth may discover the unity of the biblical message.

The youth may understand something of the wholeness of the Bible coming to focus and the fullness of meaning in Jesus Christ and begin to develop a Christ-centered perspective on the biblical record.

The youth may develop an awareness that God speaks through the Scriptures to *all men,* despite their differences, and that his understanding of Scripture may be deepened and enriched by the insight of others.

The youth may realize something of the unifying effect which a devoted, intelligent study of the Bible has upon those who participate.

Youth may reach a conviction that the Bible offers clues to some answers to youth's questions about God's nature and man's purpose for being.

443

Youth may find himself represented increasingly in the Bible.

Youth may for the first time become aware of God speaking to him personally through the Scriptures.

Youth may begin to discern wherein various views of man and the universe—scientific or religious—are consistent with or in opposition to the biblical view.

Youth may become acquainted with the Bible well enough to know where in it to look for guidance.

5. God Speaks to Man Through the Scriptures

STATEMENT OF THE THEME

As man reads the Bible seeking the guidance of the Holy Spirit, he finds there the definitive answers to his urgent questions: Who is God? What is my responsibility to him? How may I know him?

ADULTHOOD

444

1. Significance of the theme for this age level

   a. Meanings and experiences within this theme relevant for this age level. This is content, a selected part of Scope.

The Bible is man's normative record of God's self-revelation.

God's desire to be known and to be in relationship with men is demonstrated through his use of insightful, dedicated persons to put his message into human language.

God speaks to the adult when, through the assistance of the Holy Spirit, man reads himself into the biblical story.

The Bible describes the natures of God and man in redemptive engagement.

The Bible is relevant to man's current involvements even though the events it recounts are not contemporary.

God's call to individuals and insights regarding the demands of this call are made known to adults as they search the Scriptures.

The Bible is one story of God's message, making plain his intentions for man.

The Bible presents the events of history in company with their interpretation by the believing community, together with the record of man's response to those events.

In the Scriptures God provides guidance for man in his relationships with God and other men.

Through the Bible, God speaks the same message to all men,

regardless of age, race, or culture.

God calls men to draw both on their faith and on their reason in their attempts to find and know biblical truth.

God works within the community of faith to round out, enrich, and correct the individual's interpretation of scripture.

The Bible is not and should never be used as a treasure chest or catalogue of particular answers to man's incidental or trivial questions.

The adult's authoritative point of reference for understanding the Bible is Jesus Christ as he is revealed by the Holy Spirit.

The Bible is the highest authority to which men can appeal for knowledge of God and his will and for a norm against which they may test their faith and lives.

The biblical message is focused in the story of God's self-disclosure in Jesus Christ.

Both in its creation and in its preservation through history, the Bible has continuously afforded God's people a plumb line of explicit teachings to serve as criteria for doctrine and practice.

That God speaks to man today through the words of the Scriptures is both a conviction and a present experience of the community of faith.

The primary function of the Bible is to help man know God and know how to respond to God.

445

Those who search to find God's message in the Bible may be assured that the Spirit who led in its creation is the Spirit who enlightens them in their search.

1. **Significance of the theme for this age level**
    b. **Readiness of the learner for this theme in terms of basic needs, interests, motivations, capacities, developmental tasks.**

Adults have the capacity to distinguish between timeless truths in the message of the Bible and the assertions that are related specifically to a cultural setting or practice of the past.

As they face their responsibilities, adults need the sense of direction and undergirding support that the Bible message can give.

Adults have the capacity to find in the Scriptures guidance for dealing with the increasing complexity in their ethical decisions; problems of success and failure; illness; conflict; suffering; and bereavement.

446

Adults need a system of values to which the Scriptures speak, against which to test their decisions and actions.

Adults have the capacity to understand the biblical affirmations about God at work in history.

Adults need to have a rational basis for accepting the validity of the Bible.

Adults have the capacity to reexamine their responses to contemporary issues in light of new insights from the Bible.

Adults are able to explore and question the biblical record of God's acts in creation and history in light of scientific discoveries and historical research.

As they become aware of their sin and the reality of their own rebellion against God, adults are motivated to hear the message of reconciliation.

The adult's increasing realization of the brevity of human existence contributes to his need for a message of hope in this life and in the life to come.

Adults are in a position within the Christian community to serve as the normative age group for enriching, correcting and rounding out the congregation's interpretation of Scripture.

Adults have experienced enough of life to be able to empathize with the persons of the Bible, gaining fuller insights into their motives and actions.

2. How may this content be communicated as the learner engages in the Learning Tasks? What are the methods and

procedures by which the learner may explore the meanings and experiences within this theme (1-a) in the light of his readiness (1-b) in order to discover significance and value.

By studying the Bible in occupational groups, such as doctors, salesmen, etc., to interpret the Bible's relevance for daily work.

By discussing with fellow Christians the various convictions of the church throughout history regarding the nature, authority, and interpretation of the Bible.

By examining current ethical and social issues in the light of God's message in the Bible.

By engaging with congregational groups in systematic Bible reading and study.

By listening to the reading of the Bible in corporate worship, and to its exposition in preaching.

By bearing witness by attitude, behavior, words, and actions to their own understanding of the will of God as revealed in the Bible.

By interpreting to others the relevance of the Bible to the twentieth century.

By praying for insight and illumination in Bible reading and study.

By studying the history of the Bible to know its influence on society throughout the centuries, especially as it was translated into the language of the people.

By comparing the biblical world view with that of contemporary ontologies in order to relate appropriately to the cultural expressions which carry the biblical truths.

By exploring the relationship of biblical to scientific views of man and nature.

By testing present moral and ethical standards and behavior against the norms defined in the Scriptures.

By researching the Scriptures to gain help for meeting crisis experiences of life.

447

By trying consciously to identify with personalities in the Bible in order to discover how God called and still calls individuals to commitment and service.

By exploring what the Bible says about Jesus Christ as the perfect revelation of God.

By using tools of Bible study such as various versions and translations of the Bible, Bible atlases, encyclopedias, concordances, biblical maps, etc.

By paraphrasing scripture into contemporary language.

By using devotional books which illustrate the meaning of the Bible.

By tracing particular biblical and theological teachings as presented in various parts of the Bible.

By selecting and using various art forms to illustrate, dramatize, and reinforce biblical teachings.

By memorizing Bible passages.

3. **What may the learner achieve within this theme in the fulfillment of the Learning Tasks? What are possible changes or learnings on the part of the learner that may result from his appropriation of the significance and value discovered? These changes or learnings may be associated with skills, attitudes, motivations, perceptions including understandings and appreciations.**

The adult may commit himself to God's high demands as revealed in Scripture.

The adult may develop love for and appreciation of the Bible, its uniqueness and authority.

The adult may develop skill in relating the message of the Bible to the making of moral and ethical decisions.

The adult may begin to experience a desire for and skill in meaningful reading and study of the Bible.

The adult may more fully grasp the message of the Bible coming to focus and fullness of meaning in Jesus Christ.

The Adult may develop the ability to interpret specific passages of Scripture within their context and in relation to the message of the Bible.

The adult may achieve a comprehensive overview of the content and basic message of the Bible.

The adult may become aware that God speaks through the Scriptures to *all* men.

The adult may develop skill in discussing knowledgeably some basic questions about God, man, and problems of biblical interpretation.

The adult may appropriate the message of the Bible so that it sustains him and helps him sustain others in times of crisis such as illness, catastrophe, and death.

The adult may develop an appreciation of the reasons for the differences between the biblical and contemporary views of man and the universe and what these differences imply for biblical interpretation.

The adult may develop skill in translating the biblical message into everyday personal and social behavior.

The adult may have a deepened appreciation and acceptance of the worth and significance of persons in keeping with the biblical message.

The adult may have a deeper faith that God's promises in the Scripture will be fulfilled.

449

The adult may discover the biblical record to be the revelation of God's acts throughout history.

The adult may commit to memory Bible passages which can be recalled to leaven his thinking and direct his actions.

The adult may participate with other Christians in making the Bible known and available to other persons.

The adult may accept the diagnosis of his own need and of God's redemptive acts as revealed in the Scriptures.

Through the Scriptures the adult may come to know Jesus Christ as his Savior and Lord.

6. God Acts Through the Church to Make Himself Known

STATEMENT OF THE THEME

The church meets man's need to hear the gospel proclaimed, to experience God's presence in group worship, and to have the corrective guidance of a collective Christian conscience.

EARLY CHILDHOOD

450

1. Significance of the theme for this age level

   a. **Meanings and experiences within this theme relevant for this age level. This is content, a selected part of Scope.**

When we go to church, we meet warm, friendly people who are kind to us and care about us.

God wants us to worship him together and, when we do, we begin to feel something of his love, mystery, and omnipresence.

God loves all people everywhere and we can show God's love by helping people in our church who may be in need.

People who love God try to do what is right and help others see that God knows what is right for them.

The Bible is used in church worship and is treated with reverence by people who love God.

God's presence and activity among his people are emphasized in the celebration of sacraments and other special occasions in the life of the church.

1. **Significance of the theme for this age level**

   b. **Readiness of the learner for this theme in terms of basic needs, interests, motivations, capacities, developmental tasks.**

The uncertainty experienced by the young child as he ventures from the home into wider groups intensifies his need for the security and love which members of the church can give as they express God's love.

The increasing desire of the young child to comprehend makes him ready to seek answers to questions beyond his understanding from persons to whom he can talk about God.

The expanding social relationships of the young child cause him to search for acceptance as a person from those beyond the circle of his own family.

The young child is beginning to develop the sense of right and wrong from adult or peer group acceptance or lack of acceptance and this readies him to receive guidance that can come through relationships within church settings.

The young child's sensitivity to the attitudes of others and his ability to learn from these attitudes make possible his acceptance of the values of those with whom he associates in church settings.

The young child's capacity to learn through association with and imitation of adults makes possible growth in the understanding of the values and practices of adults in the Christian community.

The creative imagination of early childhood makes it possible for the young child to comprehend some of intangible as well as tangible nature of the gospel proclaimed by the church.

2. **How may this content be communicated as the learner engages in the Learning Tasks? What are the methods and procedures by which the learner may explore the meanings and experiences within this theme (1-a) in the light of his readiness (1-b) in order to discover significance and value?**

451

By participating in occasions at church where adults accept him as a person and he feels the warmth and friendliness of the Christian community.

By attending church worship services and sharing in them.

By hearing about God's concern for persons and the church's plan to care for needy people and having a share in it.

Through relationships with other children and adults in church school classes or other small groups, observing what God considers to be acceptable or unacceptable behavior.

By seeing the Bible at church used as a book that is respected and treasured by adult church members.

By sharing with the family and other adults in church services; especially festivals of the church, such as Christmas and Easter.

By observing church members participate in the sacraments of the church.

452

3. **What may the learner achieve within this theme in the fulfillment of the Learning Tasks? What are possible changes or learnings on the part of the learner that may result from his appropriation of the significance and value discovered? These changes or learnings may be associated with skills, attitudes, motivations, perceptions including understandings and appreciations.**

As he participates in the Christian community, the young child may develop awareness of God's presence.

Through expressions of love and forgiveness by members of the Christian community, the young child may develop a sense of God's love and forgiveness.

As members of the Christian community express their concern for his well-being, the young child may begin to sense that God is concerned for every individual.

The young child may begin to appreciate the church building as a place where people come who want to know God and have fellowship with him.

The young child may have a sense of being part of the church in ministering to the needs of others for Christ's sake.

The young child may begin to sense that being good is related to God's will for him.

The young child may accept Jesus as a person important to all Christians.

6. God Acts Through the Church to Make Himself Known

STATEMENT OF THE THEME

The church meets man's need to hear the gospel proclaimed, to experience God's presence in group worship, and to have the corrective guidance of a collective Christian conscience.

ELEMENTARY YEARS

1. Significance of the theme for this age level

   a. Meanings and experiences within this theme relevant for this age level. This is content, a selected part of Scope.

God's redemptive love may be experienced through the reconciling fellowship of Christians.

The worship of the church focuses in God's divine nature—his mystery, majesty, presence, love, forgiveness, fatherhood.

God's purposiveness penetrates the church's history and tradition.

God's concern for all persons is revealed as it is expressed in the church's ministries of service, witness, and nurture after the manner of Christ.

God's judgment and power impel the church to proclaim God's will in today's world.

God in his righteousness demands the church to be righteous as well as to call others to be righteous.

453

God has commissioned the church to make the Bible available to every person.

1. Significance of the theme for this age level

   b. Readiness of the learner for this theme in terms of basic needs, interests, motivations, capacities, developmental tasks.

The elementary child's need for social acceptance and his capacity to enter into accepting relationships with others prepare him to experience something of God's concern for him, as expressed by concerned persons within the Christian community.

The elementary child is able and has freedom to make some responsible choices, and needs the guidance and help that is available through the church.

As the elementary child's life orientation expands beyond the circle of his own home, there comes a readiness to respond to the sources of authority, purpose, and discipline of the church.

454

The elementary child's mental capacity to relate things and persons meaningfully to each other and to himself prepares him to derive meaning from relations to and within a redemptive fellowship.

The elementary child chooses and is loyal to personalities who in turn influence his personality and his patterns of conduct. This readies him for the corrective and guiding influence of the persons who are the church.

The innate curiosity and venturesomeness of the elementary child enable him to respond to new experiences, to gain new depths of meaning in discovery, and to be challenged by the accounts of pioneers in every field of life's activity. This readies him to hear and examine the gospel as it is proclaimed by the church.

The elementary child's natural curiosity may interest him in finding out about and participating in the life of the church.

The elementary child's curiosity enhances his capacity to learn new insights.

The elementary child's curiosity about people excites his interest in personalities of the church, current and past.

2. **How may this content be communicated as the learner engages in the Learning Tasks? What are the methods and procedures by which the learner may explore the meanings**

and experiences within this theme (1-a) in the light of his readiness (1-b) in order to discover significance and value?

By participating in the fellowship of the church.

By participating in and talking about the worship of the church.

By associating with persons in the Christian fellowship and becoming acquainted with its history.

By hearing about God's concern for persons and what the church has done and is doing through its ministries to others and participating in the ministries of service, nurture, and witness that are open to him.

By listening to the church proclaim God's will for men in the world and thinking of his own involvement.

By observing and abiding by the discipline by which the fellowship regulates its conduct and makes known the righteousness of God.

By listening to and studying the church's interpretation of the Scriptures to discover the message of the gospel.

By examining the story of the church through the historical accounts in the Bible and the history of the church to discover how God has acted through it to make himself known.

By sharing with the church family in the observance of church festivals such as Christmas, Easter, and Pentecost.

By observing church members participate in the sacraments or ordinances of the church.

455

3. What may the learner achieve within this theme in the fulfillment of the Learning Tasks? What are possible changes or learnings on the part of the learner that may result from his appropriation of the significance and value discovered? These changes or learnings may be associated with skills, attitudes, motivations, perceptions including understandings and appreciations.

The elementary child may become aware of God's reality and presence within the Christian community.

The elementary child may gain knowledge and experience of God's love, forgiveness, and ongoing concern for his people.

The elementary child may experience the mystery of the presence of God.

The elementary child may develop a sense of partnership with God's people ministering to the needs of others.

The elementary child may develop respect for the corrective guidance of the church as an attempt to represent God's will.

The elementary child's life may begin consciously to relate himself to the purposes of God.

The elementary child may begin to see the relation between the ministry of Jesus and the ministry of the church.

The elementary child may begin to appreciate the role of the church in making the Bible available.

The elementary child may begin to accept some responsibility for extending the Bible's availability.

6. God Acts Through the Church to Make Himself Known

STATEMENT OF THE THEME

The church meets man's need to hear the gospel proclaimed, to experience God's presence in group worship, and to have the corrective guidance of a collective Christian conscience.

YOUTH

1. Significance of the theme for this age level

a. Meanings and experiences within this theme relevant for this age level. This is content, a selected part of Scope.

God's redemptive love is made evident as his people live in reconciling fellowship with one another and extend that fellowship to others.

God's will and presence may be made known to the church through individual insight through corporate worship, through group deliberations, or through study.

God expects his people to listen obediently to him and to respond in relevant action and word.

God's concern to meet the needs of all persons is made clear as his people express a like concern through compassion, service, and diligent effort to attach the causes of need.

God may make himself known to his people and to the world as individuals or groups speak and act prophetically in the church and in society.

God's judgment and correction of the church is as necessary as his empowering and blessing if the church is to be a fit instrument for his purposes.

God has laid on the church the responsibility of making the Bible available to men everywhere as a means of his making himself and his will known.

God, who formed his people into a community, is active among them to reform, to guide, to quicken their life together and their ministry in the world.

Events and issues in the common life of the people of God offer opportunity for God's activity among his people to become apparent to them.

Power and wisdom for the Christian to have a lasting influence on society derives from the presence and activity of God within the community and not from the status and morality of the people in the church.

457

1. Significance of the theme for this age level

b. Readiness of the learner for this theme in terms of basic needs, interests, motivations, capacities, developmental tasks.

Youth's tendency to criticize may alert him to God's judgment on the church.

Youth's discontent with inactivity may make him responsive to God's activity among and through his people.

The strange inner stirring of youth which may bring feelings of inadequacy and his response to the apparent turmoil of existence make him sensitive to inadequacies and failures of the church which deserve the judgment and correction of God.

Youth's shift from dependence on arbitrary authority toward dependence on internal authority readies him to be responsive to corporate efforts to identify and respond to guidance from God.

458

Youth is eager to play a part in the shaping of a group to which he belongs.

Youth's developing intellectual and emotional abilities enable him to sense and respond to God's guidance and power in the life of the Christian community.

Youth's desire for dependable criteria of his own provides a readiness to hear the proclamation of the gospel.

Youth has a beginning understanding of the framework and dynamics of groups in society.

Youth is developing skills of listening and of articulation.

Youth needs concrete evidence of God's activity in individual lives, in groups, and in society.

2. **How may this content be communicated as the learner engages in the Learning Tasks? What are the methods and procedures by which the learner may explore the meanings and experiences within this theme (1-a) in the light of his readiness (1-b) in order to discover significance and value?**

By being himself the object of reconciling love in a fellowship of those who acknowledge God's redemptive love for them.

By reflecting on his experiences of worship and considering modes of response based on his insights.

By reading or hearing about occasions throughout the history of the church when by judgment and correction God has redirected or reformed the church.

By becoming acquainted with various communities of Christ to see the variety of ways in which the church is used to make God known.

By studying the biblical and ecclesiastical interpretations of the servant role of the people of God.

By hearing the church's interpretation of God's word and exploring with others in the church the depths of the meaning about the nature and purpose of God.

By participating regularly in worship with the congregation and individually.

By developing skills by which to listen for God's message in preaching, prayer, Bible study, meditation.

By becoming acquainted with religious art and symbols, literature and drama growing out of the church's heritage which shed light on God's revelation of himself.

By studying the biographies of Christians to discover what role the church has had in making God known to them.

By studying the biblical record of God's activity among his people.

By hearing from other Christians their insights and convictions regarding God's action in and through his church.

By participating with other Christians grappling with the tasks of understanding God's will in the face of issues and problems in the church or in society.

By hearing from those engaged in compassionate service or in Christian social action their reasons for such involvement.

3. **What may the learner achieve within this theme in the fulfillment of the Learning Tasks? What are possible changes or learnings on the part of the learner that may result from his appropriation of the significance and value discovered? These changes or learnings may be associated with skills, attitudes, motivations, perceptions including understandings and appreciations.**

459

Youth may discern God's invitation to him and accept him as his Lord and Savior.

Youth may sense God's presence in corporate or private worship.

Youth may gain insight into God's redemptive love by experiencing or witnessing reconciliation between men.

Youth may gain an appreciation for the positive values of judgment and correction.

Youth may commit himself to participation in the varied ministries of the church for making known the gospel and meeting the needs of men.

Youth may identify himself with the Christian community in its failures as well as in its faithfulness to God's will for the church.

Youth may come to an appreciation of the role individual Christians play in making God and his will known to individuals and to the Christian community.

Youth may accept responsibility for constructive criticism and efforts at change in the life and work of the church.

6. God Acts Through the Church to Make Himself Known

STATEMENT OF THE THEME

The church meets man's need to hear the gospel proclaimed, to experience God's presence in group worship, and to have the corrective guidance of a collective Christian conscience.

ADULTHOOD

1. Significance of the theme for this age level

a. Meanings and experiences within this theme relevant for this age level. This is content, a selected part of Scope.

God's redemptive love is made evident as his people live in reconciling fellowship with one another and extend that fellowship to others.

God's will and presence may be made known to the church through individual insight, through corporate worship, through group deliberations or study.

For God to be known in and through his people, the church must genuinely listen to him and respond to him in decision and action obedient to his will and relevant to the current scene.

God's concern to meet the needs of all persons is made clear as his people express a like concern through compassion, service, and diligent effort to attack the causes of need.

God may make himself known to his people and to the world as individuals or groups speak and act prophetically in the church and in society.

God's judgment and correction of the church is as necessary as his empowering and blessing if the church is to be a fit instrument for his purposes.

God speaks to and through his people as the church seriously and responsibly makes the Bible accessible to persons, both by distribution of the Bible and by engagement in Bible study.

God, who formed his people into a community, is active among them to reform, to guide, to quicken their life together and their ministry in the world.

Events and issues in the common life of the people of God offer opportunity for God's activity among his people to become apparent to them.

461

Power and wisdom for the Christian to have a lasting influence on society derive from the presence and activity of God within the community and not from the status and morality of the people in the church.

God is not dependent on the church for making himself known; and it is possible for the church to lose its opportunity as an instrument for God's self-disclosure.

1. Significance of the theme for this age level

    b. Readiness of the learner for this theme in terms of basic

needs, interests, motivations, capacities, developmental tasks.

The pressures of environment, the inner conflicts of family and business interpersonal relationships, the disillusionment which comes in the hard realities of living, the sense of frustration and inadequacy, the tendency toward increasing passivity in the routines of daily life, the sense of loneliness, the unfulfilled ambitions and desires in life and career, as well as the deepening concepts of meaning in religious and spiritual values, all ready the adult to hear the message the church proclaims from God.

The involvements of interpersonal relationships, the temptations toward moral violations, the pressures of secular mores, and the guilt rising out of strained or willfully broken relationships, all evidence man's need for the guidance of a collective Christian conscience which the church may provide.

The adult has an increasing ability to understand and to influence the structure and the nature of groups in which he participates. This puts him in a position to appreciate and to influence the role of the church in God's self-disclosure.

The adult's broadened experience, the scope of relationships, and accumulation of knowledge enhances his capacity for gaining insights from the history of the church for its greater alertness to God's action today.

The adult by his role and responsibilities in the church, in business, in society, in the home is in a position to see and facilitate God's action in and through the church.

The adult has perspective for appreciating the constructive function of judgment and correction.

The adult has the ability to see basic continuity throughout history, which may help him interpret God's current actions in terms of his actions among his people in the past.

The adult's desire to "make his mark" may motivate him to take a responsible part in the church's efforts to make God known in and through its life and ministry.

2. How may this content be communicated as the learner engages in the Learning Tasks? What are the methods and procedures by which the learner may explore the meanings and experiences within this theme (1-a) in the light of his readiness (1-b) in order to discover significance and value?

By becoming involved in and extending the reconciling fellowship of the Christian community.

By exploring the meaning of worship as experienced in the church.

By studying the history of the church to discover how God has revealed himself in it and through it.

By taking part in the church's ministries of service, nurture, witness, and its mission around the world as a conscious effort to communicate God's concern and message.

By hearing the church's proclamation of the gospel and discussing its meaning for knowing God and for extending the knowledge of God.

By joining with others in interpreting the Scriptures to discover the nature of the church and God's purpose for it.

By participating intelligently and feelingly in the worship of the congregation, including the sacraments.

By engaging regularly in prayer and worship by himself and in company with others.

463

By examining various forms and expressions of art which has been inspired by the church for what it discloses of God and his will.

By evaluating the life, work, and worship of the church in terms of its aptness to hear God and to serve as his instrument for making God and his will known.

By sharing in the search for ways of improving the effectiveness of the church.

By participating with other Christians grappling with the tasks of understanding God's will in the face of issues and problems in the church or in society.

By hearing from other Christians their insights and convictions regarding God's action in and through his church.

By studying the biblical record of God's activity among his people.

By becoming acquainted with various communities of Christ to see the variety of ways in which the church is used to make God known.

By experimenting with various forms for individual and corporate communication of God's self-disclosure.

464

By considering the challenge to the church of nonchurch groups, who do a good job of extending fellowship and help.

By studying the biographies of outstanding Christians to discover how God spoke to them through the church or through them to the church.

3. **What may the learner achieve within this theme in the fulfillment of the Learning Tasks? What are possible changes or learnings on the part of the learner that may result from his appropriation of the significance and value discovered? These changes or learnings may be associated with skills, attitudes, motivations, perceptions including understandings and appreciations.**

The adult may develop skills to discern God's will for guiding and reshaping the life and actions of the church.

The adult may find through the church strength to face the pressures of life.

The adult may develop skills for individually and corporately approaching those outside the Christian fellowship to make God known to them.

The adult may experience God's presence in worship.

The adult may through God's people contribute to or experience the undergirding love of God for those facing tragedy, death, illness.

The adult may accept personal responsibility for the sin of the church and its need for God's continued grace, forgiveness, and renewal.

The adult may commit himself to disciplined efforts in study and worship to receive God's self-disclosure and to work out ways of making him known.

The adult may experience and extend reconciling fellowship of God's people.

The adult may take initiative to effect reconciliation among men, both within the Christian fellowship and outside.

7. God Speaks to Man Through the Natural Order

STATEMENT OF THE THEME

The handiwork of God as Creator and Sustainer is revealed in the universe, which is mysterious and yet yields to man's search for understanding of it. As man discovers God's laws in the natural order, man is able to be at home in it and to use these laws creatively.

EARLY CHILDHOOD

1. Significance of the theme for this age level

a. Meanings and experiences within this theme relevant for this age level. This is content, a selected part of Scope.

465

God shows us something of his care by the things the natural world provides for the physical needs of animals and man.

God shows us something of what he is like as we see some of the order and beauty of the natural world.

God shows us something of his power and of his love in the forces of the natural world (storms, wind, sun).

God shows us something of his power and love in processes of growth and healing (plant, animal, and human life, healing after illness or injury).

God shows us something of his love and dependability in the consistency and rhythm of the world of nature.

God shows us something of his greatness in the variety in the world he has made and in the things we cannot understand.

God shows us something of his love and concern for us in his plans for life, growth, birth, and death.

God shows something of his love for us by making a world we can enjoy (sun, wind, rain, food, color, water, etc.).

466

God shows us something of his dependability by providing some things in the physical world that man cannot change (rain when a picnic is planned).

God shows us something of what he is like by always following the same way of working in his world without showing any favoritism.

1. Significance of the theme for this age level

b. Readiness of the learner for this theme in terms of basic needs, interests, motivations, capacities, developmental tasks.

The young child has a need for physical security.

The young child has curiosity and developing ability to handle, to examine, to enjoy what he finds in the natural environment.

The young child has many questions about physical aspects of nature.

The young child has a growing ability to cope with and relate to his physical environment.

The young child may have developing awareness and appreciation of beauty.

The young child may experience awe, wonder, and mystery.

The young child thinks in terms of the concrete such as is found in the natural order rather than in abstract ideas.

2. **How may this content be communicated as the learner engages in the Learning Tasks? What are the methods and procedures by which the learner may explore the meanings and experiences within this theme (1-a) in the light of his readiness (1-b) in order to discover significance and value?**

By finding out about and observing plants and animals, their homes, habits, color, design.

By hearing Bible stories and simple interpretations about God's creation and his concern for the natural world (animals, plants, people, the world).

By observing habits, needs, and growth of animals, plants, people.

By observing germination and growth in seeds and bulbs.

By observing nature and natural objects with persons who see and appreciate them as God's handiwork.

By expressing ideas about God's world of nature through creative activities (art, music, conversation, making things).

By thanking God for meaningful experiences in the natural world.

By exploring the out-of-doors for evidences of God's handiwork.

By enjoying the wind, rain, sun, water, food, cold, warmth and listening to interpretation that these are a part of God's creation.

By recognizing that disappointments and suffering may result from events in the natural world (death, storms, natural disasters), in the company of persons who have a Christian interpretation of the universe.

By conversations about the birth of animals or babies and helping to prepare for the birth of either.

3. **What may the learner achieve within this theme in the fulfillment of the Learning Tasks? What are possible changes or learnings on the part of the learner that may result from**

467

his appropriation of the significance and value discovered? These changes or learnings may be associated with skills, attitudes, motivations, perceptions including understandings and appreciations.

The young child may begin to develop a trust in God as he reveals something of himself in the natural order.

The young child may begin to understand the friendly aspects of the created universe.

468

The young child may begin to accept responsibility for helping to care for God's created things.

The young child may begin to develop an understanding of how man cooperates with God in the use and control of the natural order (keeping warm, watering plants, keeping dry).

The young child may begin to develop a sense of gratitude to God for what he has created and what he continues to do in the natural realm.

The young child may develop a beginning awareness of the wonder of God.

The young child may develop a beginning awareness of the power of God.

The young child may begin to realize that God is the source of beauty, joy, and wonder in the world.

The young child may begin to realize the disappointing experiences within the natural world are inevitable.

The young child may begin to realize that God is the source of all life.

The young child may begin to realize that God is at work in birth and growth.

7. God Speaks to Man Through the Natural Order

STATEMENT OF THE THEME

The handiwork of God as Creator and Sustainer is revealed in the universe, which is mysterious and yet yields to man's search for understanding of it. As man discovers God's laws in the natural order, man is able to be at home in it and to use these laws creatively.

ELEMENTARY YEARS

1. Significance of the theme for this age level

a. Meanings and experiences within this theme relevant for this age level. This is content, a selected part of Scope.

God reveals himself as an intelligent Creator in the beauty and design of the universe.

God's continuing creation is revealed as persons experience growth and change.

God has shown his willingness for man to control some of the elements of the physical world as men come to understand and to use these elements (cultivation and improvement of plants, harnessing water power, wind tunnels, launching of satellites, etc.).

God's awesomeness is revealed in part as man confronts the vastness and magnitude of the universe.

God shows something of his bounteous goodness in the abundance of natural resources he provides for the physical needs of men and animals.

God's trustworthiness is revealed as men experience the dependability of natural laws, even though men may not always understand these laws.

God reveals something of himself as persons discover that God's laws operate consistently even when they result in suffering, disappointment, or death.

God shows something of his fairness and impartiality through natural laws that cannot be disobeyed or broken by men without inevitably leading to disastrous consequences.

God shows his restoring power as men experience and observe

469

healing, such as the healing of broken bones, recovery from illness.

God reveals something of his greatness and power in the vast mysteries of the universe man has not yet fathomed, in spite of all he has discovered.

God shows something of his greatness and power in the discoveries man has made regarding the vastness of the universe and the complexity of its nature.

470 God reveals himself as being active in the universe as new forms of life come into being or as old forms of life change.

1. Significance of the theme for this age level

b. Readiness of the learner for this theme in terms of basic needs, interests, motivations, capacities, developmental tasks.

The elementary child has a conscious need for physical care and sustenance.

The elementary child has the capacity to understand the dependence upon the natural world for existence.

The elementary child has an inquisitiveness about the natural world and his physical environment.

The elementary child has the capacity to explore and is curious about the physical environment, such as changing weather, seasons, and other elements of the world.

The elementary child has the capacity for awareness and appreciation of the importance of law and order in the natural world.

The elementary child has the capacity for appreciation of the beautiful and for recognizing it.

The elementary child has the capacity for understanding and experimenting with natural law (gravitation, changing leaves, etc.).

7. God Speaks to Man Through the Natural Order

STATEMENT OF THE THEME

The handiwork of God as Creator and Sustainer is revealed in the universe, which is mysterious and yet yields to man's search for understanding of it. As man discovers God's laws in the natural order, man is able to be at home in it and to use these laws creatively.

YOUTH

1. **Significance of the theme for this age level**

   a. **Meanings and experiences within this theme relevant for this age level. This is content, a selected part of Scope.**

God reveals himself as a God of order and beauty through the complexity, relatedness, and design in nature.

God reveals his constancy in the consistency of his laws.

God reveals his mystery as well as his dynamic creativity in part as men confront the unpredictable elements in the physical universe.

God reveals his purpose to sustain life through the provisions which have been made to propagate and perpetuate life in the natural order.

God reveals his impartial nature as men break natural laws with inevitable consequences.

473

God reveals his creative and restorative power in part through the healing processes of the natural order.

God reveals his infinite power and creative intelligence through man's expanding exploration and discovery of the universe.

God shows his continuing creativity through productive and mutative processes in plant and animal life, changes in the surfaces of the earth, climate and weather changes.

God reveals something of his transcendence and mystery through the complexities of the universe which are beyond the comprehension of man.

God reveals his intent to perpetuate life through the manner in which men, animals, and plants withstand injury or adversity.

God reveals his intent to propagate or change the forms of life through the manner in which various forms come into existence or are altered.

God has revealed something of himself in that he has placed so much beauty and symmetry in the world and created man with ability to perceive and enjoy it.

God reveals his concern and love for man by giving man a preeminent position within the natural order.

God reveals his greatness in that the magnitude of the universe, with its provision for minuteness and for vastness, shout the glory, majesty, dominion, and power of God.

God reveals something of his own nature as man observes and participates in the creative process.

God declares his concern for man and for all of life through the healing processes of nature.

God communicates his infinite power through the magnitude of the forces of the universe with which man must learn to live.

God reveals more and more of his mystery and omniscience as man goes further and further in exploration and discovery in the universe.

God reveals his intelligence and purposiveness as men discover the orderliness and interrelatedness in the natural order.

God reveals something of the transitoriness of existence in the natural order as men confront the cycle of growth, change, death, and decay.

God reveals his wisdom and providence through the giving of natural resources.

1. **Significance of the theme for this age level**

    b. **Readiness of the learner for this theme in terms of basic needs, interests, motivations, capacities, developmental tasks.**

474

Youth recognizes man's dependence upon the natural order for sustenance.

Youth longs to be close to the natural world and to understand it.

Youth has an urge and some ability to master the elements of nature.

Youth has the capacity to explore and interpret the physical and natural sciences.

Youth has the ability to accept the limits and authority of natural law.

Youth has an increasing ability to think and to reason that prepares him to explore and experiment in the natural order.

Youth has increasing capacity to appreciate beauty, to recognize it, and to create it.

Youth longs to probe the unknown and is eager to act on new discoveries.

Youth is vitally concerned with the creative processes of God in reproduction and all of life.

2. **How may this content be communicated as the learner engages in the Learning Tasks? What are the methods and procedures by which the learner may explore the meanings and experiences within this theme (1-a) in the light of his readiness (1-b) in order to discover significance and value?**

475

By studying the biblical accounts of creation and of God's continuing creative activities through reading selected Bible passages and discussing their meanings.

By exploring the universe from a Christian orientation, through visiting planetariums or observatories, viewing films on astronomy and outer space, examining slices of living tissue under a microscope, viewing films showing the composition of cells and atoms, making field trips to study various aspects of the natural world.

By expressing feelings toward God as Creator and Sustainer through the development and use of music and art in worship centering on God's activity in the natural world, choral reading or singing of biblical expressions of praise—as in the Psalms—composing litanies, hymns, or poems of praise and appreciation which may be used in worship.

By considering God's relation to natural catastrophies such as volcanoes, tornadoes, earthquakes, tidal waves.

By observing the healing and restoring processes of God in the natural order.

476

By considering God's provision for the propagation of life and the meaning this has for human personality.

By observing the way God has revealed his constancy in his natural laws that makes it possible to use these laws for the well-being of all mankind.

By reflecting upon the cycle of life, growth, birth, and death as an evidence of God's orderly process.

3. **What may the learner achieve within this theme in the fulfillment of the Learning Tasks? What are possible changes or learnings on the part of the learner that may result from his appropriation of the significance and value discovered? These changes or learnings may be associated with skills, attitudes, motivations, perceptions including understandings and appreciations.**

Youth may develop a view of the natural order which is in keeping with the eternal truths of the biblical record and consistent with the findings of science.

Youth may achieve a firm confidence in the dependability of God as he reveals himself in the natural order.

Youth may recognize the elements of good in the universe.

Youth may gain the realization that God intends for man to explore and learn about the natural order.

Youth may discover God's natural laws and use them for human betterment.

Youth may develop appreciation and respect for the natural order as God's handiwork.

Youth may become aware of the constant and continuing creation of God.

Youth may achieve a faith which can deal with accidents and catastrophes of the natural world.

Youth may develop a profound respect for the impartial laws of God written into the structure of the universe and endeavor to obey them.

Youth may acquire a sense of gratitude for all the healing, constructive forces in the universe and cooperate with God in the use of them for the welfare of all mankind.

Youth trust in God's care and appreciate the providence of God.

Youth may accept responsibility for increasing man's dominion over nature.

Youth may develop a faith that can accept the transitory nature of physical life (growth, change, death) as a part of God's plan.

Youth may have a deep appreciation for God who speaks to man through the natural order.

477

7. God Speaks to Man Through the Natural Order

STATEMENT OF THE THEME

The handiwork of God as Creator and Sustainer is revealed in the universe, which is mysterious and yet yields to man's search for understanding of it. As man discovers God's laws in the natural order, man is able to be at home in it and to use these laws creatively.

ADULTHOOD

1. Significance of the theme for this age level

a. Meanings and experiences within this theme relevant for this age level. This is content, a selected part of Scope.

God reveals himself as a God of order and beauty through the complexity, relatedness, and design in nature.

God reveals his constancy in the consistency of his laws.

God reveals his mystery as well as his dynamic creativity in part as men confront the unpredictable elements in the physical universe.

God reveals his purpose to sustain life through the provisions which have been made to propagate and perpetuate life in the natural order.

God reveals his impartial nature as men break natural laws with inevitable consequences.

God reveals his creative and restorative power in part through the healing processes of the natural order.

God reveals his infinite power and creative intelligence through man's expanding exploration and discovery of the universe.

God shows his continuing creativity through productive and mutative processes in plant and animal life, changes in the surfaces of the earth, climate and weather changes.

God reveals something of his transcendence and mystery through the complexities of the universe which are beyond the comprehension of man.

God reveals his intent to perpetuate life through the manner in which men, animals, and plants withstand injury or adversity.

God reveals his intent to propagate or change the forms of life through the manner in which various forms come into existence or are altered.

God has revealed something of himself in that he has placed so much beauty and symmetry in the world and created man with ability to perceive and enjoy it.

God reveals his concern and love for man by giving man a preeminent position within the natural order.

478

God reveals his greatness in that the magnitude of the universe, with its provision for minuteness and for vastness, shout the glory, majesty, dominion, and power of God.

God reveals something of his own nature as man observes and participates in the creative process.

God declares his concern for man and for all of life through the healing processes of nature.

God communicates his infinite power through the magnitude of the forces of the universe with which man must learn to live.

God reveals more and more of his mystery and omniscience as man goes further and further in exploration and discovery in the universe.

God reveals his intelligence and purposiveness as men discover the orderliness and interrelatedness in the natural order.

God reveals something of the transitoriness of existence in the natural order as men confront the cycle of growth, change, death, and decay.

God reveals his wisdom and providence through the giving of natural resources.

1. Significance of the theme for this age level

b. Readiness of the learner for this theme in terms of basic needs, interests, motivations, capacities, developmental tasks.

479

The adult has capacity to be at home in the physical universe, and increasing knowledge of it.

The adult has need for physical security.

The adult has concern about survival, sharpened by experience with disappointment and death.

The adult has capacity to understand and accept physical insecurity.

The adult works at controlling and using forces and chemical elements in the physical universe.

The adult has ability to adjust to forces of nature for survival.

The adult has capacity to appreciate beauty.

The adult has capacity to enter into the mystery and awe in the natural processes of creating life.

The adult has need to accept the fact of death.

The adult has concern for survival after death.

The adult is concerned for posterity.

The adult has responsibility for others in his control and use of natural forces and elements.

The adult has capacity for seeing himself as a part of and in relation to the natural order and for grappling with the meaning of life.

The adult has ability to develop perspective in the midst of order and/or change in the natural world.

The adult has capacity to know God and to relate to him.

The adult has capacity to share responsibly in the process of reproduction.

2. **How may this content be communicated as the learner engages in the Learning Tasks? What are the methods and procedures by which the learner may explore the meanings and experiences within this theme (1-a) in the light of his readiness (1-b) in order to discover significance and value?**

By studying the biblical accounts of creation and of God's continuing creative activities through reading selected Bible passages and discussing their meanings.

By exploring the universe from a Christian orientation, through visiting planetariums or observatories, viewing films on astronomy and outer space, examining slices of living tissue under a microscope, viewing films showing the composition of cells and atoms, making field trips to study various aspects of the natural world.

By expressing feelings toward God as creator and sustainer through the development and use of music and art in worship centering on God's activity in the natural world, choral reading or singing of biblical expressions of praise—as in the Psalms—composing litanies, hymns, or poems of praise and appreciation which may be used in worship.

By considering God's relation to natural catastrophies such as volcanoes, tornadoes, earthquakes, tidal waves.

By observing the healing and restoring processes of God in the natural order.

By considering God's provision for the propagation of life and the meaning this has for human personality.

By observing the way God has revealed his constancy in his natural laws that makes it possible to use these laws for the well-being of all mankind.

By reflecting upon the cycle of life, growth, birth, and death as an evidence of God's orderly process.

3. **What may the learner achieve within this theme in the fulfillment of the Learning Tasks? What are possible changes or learnings on the part of the learner that may result from his appropriation of the significance and value discovered? These changes or learnings may be associated with skills, attitudes, motivations, perceptions including understandings and appreciations.**

The adult may develop a view of the natural order which is in keeping with the eternal truths of the biblical record and consistent with the findings of science.

481

The adult may achieve a firm confidence in the dependability of God as he reveals himself in the natural order.

The adult may recognize the elements of good in the universe.

The adult may gain the realization that God intends for man to explore and learn about the natural order.

The adult may discover God's natural laws, and use them for human betterment.

The adult may develop appreciation and respect for the natural order as God's handiwork.

The adult may become aware of the constant and continuing creation of God.

The adult may achieve a faith which can deal with accidents and catastrophes of the natural world.

The adult may develop a profound respect for the impartial laws of God written into the structure of the universe and endeavor to obey them.

The adult may acquire a sense of gratitude for all the healing, contructive forces in the universe and cooperate with God in the use of them for the welfare of all mankind.

482

The adult may trust in God's care and appreciate the providence of God.

The adult may accept responsibility for increasing man's dominion over nature.

The adult may develop a faith that can accept the transitory nature of physical life (growth, change, death) as a part of God's plan.

The adult may have a deep appreciation for God who speaks to man through the natural order.

SONSHIP: THE MEANING AND EXPERIENCE OF REDEMPTION

The themes within this area are:

1. *God's Redeeming Love for Man*
2. *Man's Responding to God's Redemptive Action*
3. *Becoming a New Person in Christ*
4. *Growing Up in Christ*
5. *Finding Identity in the Christian Community*
6. *The Christian's Hope Rests in the Triumphant God*

Statement of the Area

The focus, or vantage point, of this area of curriculum is man's personal response to God's self-disclosure—accepting God's redemptive love and experiencing the meaning of sonship; the inner witness and the life of faith, or being the Christian.

Comprehended in this area of curriculum is such content from Christian thought and life as: sin; the doctrine of grace; the doctrine of salvation; interpretation of the new man in Christ; the Christian view of interpersonal relationships; the stewardship of personal endowment; interpretation of personal growth under the leading of the Holy Spirit—santification.

483

In order to have education value as an area of curriculum, this content must be viewed in terms of its pertinence to the persistent issues of man's life. Some of these issues are: What does it mean to be saved? What does it mean to sin? How can I relate to others? What does God expect of me? What can I expect from God? What difference does God make in my life? What does it mean to be a Christian? To what shall I commit my life? What does it mean to mature as a son of God?[1]

---

[1]Repeated here as necessary background.

1. God's Redeeming Love for Man

STATEMENT OF THEME

Through God's changeless and seeking love for man, supremely manifested in Jesus Christ (his life, death, resurrection, and ascension) redemption is made possible whereby man's alienation from God is overcome and the way is opened for him to be reconciled with God. Thus man's persistent need for reconciliation, meaning, acceptance, integrity, security, and freedom is adequately met.

484

EARLY CHILDHOOD

1. Significance of the theme for this age level

a. Meanings and experiences within this theme relevant for this age level. This is content, a selected part of Scope.

God loves us and wants us to love and obey him.

God loves us, even when we do wrong.

God loves all persons; all are important to him.

Jesus shows us what God's love is like.

Jesus is the example of the kind of person God wants us to be.

The love of a good parent reflects something of God's love.

People who love God love others.

People who love God express this love to others in a variety of ways.

God is forgiving when we make mistakes.

1. Significance of the theme for this age level

b. Readiness of the learner for this theme in terms of basic needs, interests, motivations, capacities, developmental tasks

Dependable, consistent love is absolutely necessary for the young child.

The young child needs to be wanted, approved, and accepted.

The young child needs a sense of security.

The young child has a growing awareness of himself as a person.

The young child has a need for others to recognize him as a person who has value.

The young child has a growing ability to relate to others.

The young child has a developing ability to distinguish between right and wrong.

The young child has a developing ability to distinguish between acceptance and rejection.

The young child has a developing ability to distinguish between approval and disapproval.

The young child's mind requires the demonstration of concepts in concreteness.

The young child is able to perceive something of the love of God through parents and parent-figures who themselves are committed to God.

The young child wants to experiment with freedom within secure protection and boundaries.

2. How may this content be communicated as the learner engages in the Learning Tasks? What are the methods and procedures by which the learner may explore the meanings and experiences within this theme (1-a) in the light of his readiness (1-b) in order to discover significance and value?

485

By experiencing the love of other persons.

By being with people who recognize the worth of each person and being with people who realize that all persons are important to God.

By being with people who reflect in their love of others their own assurance that God never stops loving us.

By experiencing dependable care expressed by significant Christian adults in his life.

Through experiencing forgiveness.

Through hearing the witness to God's love from persons the child has grown to love and appreciate.

By observing the joy, gratitude, and confidence expressed by those who know God's love.

By observing the expression of love toward a variety of persons.

By listening to Bible stories which show God's love.

Through hearing stories about Jesus as one who shows what God's love is like.

Through listening to stories which relate persons and experiences in the family, the church, and the wider community to God's redemptive love.

By engaging in conversations which relate persons and experiences in the family, the church, and the wider community to God's redemptive love.

By participating in play activities which relate persons and experiences in the family, the church, and the wider community to God's redemptive love.

3. **What may the learner achieve within this theme in the fulfillment of the Learning Tasks? What are possible changes or learnings on the part of the learner that may result from his appropriation of the significance and value discovered? These changes or learnings may be associated with skills, attitudes, motivations, perceptions including understandings and appreciations.**

The young child may achieve a beginning awareness that God loves everyone.

The young child may achieve a beginning awareness that God's love does not change, regardless of the way a person behaves.

The young child may achieve a beginning awareness that Jesus shows us what God is like.

The young child may achieve a beginning awareness that God wants us to love and obey him.

The young child may achieve a beginning awareness that persons who love God love others and show that love in various ways.

The young child may achieve a beginning awareness that the Bible is a book that tells of God's love.

The young child may achieve a beginning awareness of desires to be with persons whose lives express God's love.

The young child may achieve a beginning awareness that a growing sense of security comes from the assurance that God loves us.

The young child may achieve a beginning desire to express God's love to others in simple ways.

The young child may achieve a growing consciousness of his own worth as a person as he comes to realize that God loves him.

The young child may achieve a developing ability to accept forgiveness as he comes to know that God loves him and that persons who love God are forgiving.

The young child may achieve a growing consciousness of the worth of other persons as he comes to realize that God loves everyone.

487

1. God's Redeeming Love for Man

STATEMENT OF THE THEME

Through God's changeless and seeking love for man, supremely manifested in Jesus Christ (his life, death, resurrection, and ascension) redemption is made possible whereby man's alienation from God is overcome and the way is opened for him to be reconciled with God. Thus man's persistent need for reconciliation, meaning, acceptance, integrity, security, and freedom is adequately met.

ELEMENTARY YEARS

1. **Significance of the theme for this age level**

    a. **Meanings and experiences within this theme relevant for this age level. This is content, a selected part of Scope.**

God, who created us, loves us and intends that we should love and obey him.

God loves us even when we feel we are unlovely or do not want to be loved.

God in his love wants to forgive us for doing wrong.

God in his love is ready to help and strengthen a person at any time he seeks help and strength.

God has shown us his love for us in the life, death, resurrection, and ascension of Jesus Christ.

God's love is always with us and can be depended on even when we are not loving.

God loves everyone, no matter who he is.

God's love makes it possible for persons to love one another.

God continuously offers his redeeming love to each of us whether we deserve it or not and whether in our freedom we accept or reject it.

It is only through God's love and forgiveness that a person can be fully himself.

God has created persons free to follow or reject the life he purposes for them.

1. **Significance of the theme for this age level**

    b. **Readiness of the learner for this theme in terms of basic needs, interests, motivations, capacities, developmental tasks.**

The elementary child has a need for love and acceptance by adults and peers.

The elementary child has a growing capacity to understand

that God loves us and intends that we should love and obey him.

The elementary child requires the experience of being loved even when he may be unlovely or acts as if he does not want to be loved.

Knowing human love provides and adds to the readiness of the elementary child for understanding God's seeking love.

The elementary child has a developing consciousness of the need to be forgiven for hurts inflicted on others.

The elementary child has experiences of forgiveness and of the refusal of forgiveness together with the resulting effect on relationships.

The elementary child has increasing capacity to identify his feelings of acceptance and rejection; of alienation and reconciliation.

The elementary child has experiences and increasing capacity for conceptualizing which make it possible for him to grasp the ideas of love and forgiveness.

The elementary child has a capacity for beginning comprehension of the love of God as shown in the life, death, and resurrection of Jesus Christ.

The elementary child has a need for security that is met by the understanding that God's love is always with us and dependable.

The elementary child has a desire to affirm his identity by being important to someone.

489

The elementary child has already experienced distortions and deprivations that may affect his readiness and ability to love and to accept love, and may be in need of therapeutic relationship if he is to perceive God's redemptive love. This may be especially true for children of low socio-economic groups, those emotionally deprived in various economic groups, those victimized by discrimination of various kinds, and children in institutions.

2. **How may this content be communicated as the learner engages in the Learning Tasks? What are the methods and procedures by which the learner may explore the meanings**

and experiences within this theme (1-a) in the light of his readiness (1-b) in order to discover significance and value.

By becoming better acquainted with the life, ministry, death, and resurrection of Jesus Christ as the supreme revelation of God's love.

By being with persons who recognize and respond to Jesus Christ as the supreme example of God's love.

By experiencing forgiveness by persons who know God's forgiveness.

By associating with persons he admires whose lives bear witness to God's redemptive love.

By participating in individual and group experiences of adoration and thanksgiving to God.

Through hearing about God's love for all persons without regard to country, culture, or race.

Through exploring the Bible as the source of knowledge of God's reconciling love.

By being in a group that recognizes the worth of each person as an object of God's love.

Through reading, hearing, telling, and acting out Bible stories that show God's love.

Through reading, hearing about, and observing persons whose lives bear witness to God's love.

By participating in groups that include persons of a variety of races, creeds, cultures, who know God's reconciling love.

By becoming familiar with various art forms produced by others to express God's redeeming love.

By participating in the development of various art forms (dramatizations, painting, modeling, poetry, music) as means of expressing God's redemptive love.

3. **What may the learner achieve within this theme in the fulfillment of the Learning Tasks? What are possible changes or learnings on the part of the learner that may result from**

490

his appropriation of the significance and value discovered? These changes or learnings may be associated with skills, attitudes, motivations, perceptions including understandings and appreciations.

The elementary child may achieve an awareness of God's great love for him which calls for love and obedience.

The elementary child may achieve a growing understanding of Jesus Christ as revealing the love of God.

The elementary child may achieve an awareness of the significance of Jesus' life, death, resurrection, and ascension.

The elementary child may achieve a desire for a personal relation with God who expressed his love for him in Christ.

The elementary child may achieve a sense of belonging to God's people and a feeling of God's loving acceptance.

The elementary child may achieve a sense of his own worth in God's sight in spite of any negative pressures of peers.

The elementary child may achieve a sense of security in the vast, mysterious universe based in the assurance that God's love can be depended on.

The elementary child may achieve a realization that God loves everyone.

The elementary child may achieve a desire to help others know God's redeeming love.

491

The elementary child may achieve a growing willingness to forgive and to be forgiven in gratitude for God's love.

The elementary child may achieve skill in expressing forgiveness and support to others.

The elementary child may achieve an appreciation that God's love makes it possible for persons to love one another.

The elementary child may achieve a growing desire to love others as God loves us.

The elementary child may achieve a beginning understanding that each person is involved in the good and in the bad that happens in the world.

1. God's Redeeming Love for Man

STATEMENT OF THE THEME

Through God's changeless and seeking love for man, supremely manifested in Jesus Christ (his life, death, resurrection, and ascension) redemption is made possible whereby man's alienation from God is overcome and the way is opened for him to be reconciled with God. Thus man's persistent need for reconciliation, meaning, acceptance, integrity, security, and freedom is adequately met.

492

YOUTH

1. Significance of the theme for this age level

a. Meanings and experiences within this theme relevant for this age level. This is content, a selected part of Scope.

God has created man as the supreme object of his love and intends that man should live in love and obedience to him.

God in his love is ever reaching out to meet youth where they are and bring them into fellowship with himself.

God's redeeming love for man manifest from creation on is supremely manifested in Jesus Christ (his incarnation, life, crucifixion, resurrection, ascension). In the incarnation, God identified himself with man and offered himself that man might be redeemed.

God in his love offers forgiveness for sin, even when as free persons man rejects his love or forgiveness.

God's redeeming love gives meaning and purpose to life; it shows that all persons have intrinsic undeniable value.

God's redeeming love can overcome man's sense of aloneness in the world and can provide an indestructible sense of security and belonging, regardless of external circumstances.

God's redeeming love is dependable, unchanging, ever present, eternal.

God loves all persons, regardless of their background, culture, race, or moral condition.

God in his redeeming love both purposes and provides the means for man to overcome man's alienation from God and from one another.

Persons who themselves have responded to God's redemptive love in Jesus Christ may be channels of that love to others.

God loves a person even when that person cannot love himself.

God's forgiveness is always available no matter how serious the offense.

It is only through God's love and forgiveness that a person can be fully himself; and it is only through acceptance of God's love and forgiveness that a person becomes fully himself .

In his seeking love God enables man to recognize his need for redemption and to express it through repentance and confession.

In his seeking, redemptive love God suffers for and with man; commitment to God carries with it a willingness to suffer for the sake of his love.

Through God's action the Son knows the joy of reconciliation with God.

In Christ, we see God at work judging, convicting, healing, forgiving, redeeming, restoring, and reconciling man.

God holds man responsible for his choice to accept or reject his redeeming love.

493

1. Significance of the theme for this age level

b. Readiness of the learner for this theme in terms of basic needs, interests, motivations, capacities, developmental tasks.

Youth is struggling to establish a meaningful self-concept and to discover personal significance in an impersonal world.

Youth frequently has a sense of inadequacy, failure, and insecurity.

Youth experiences times of depression, aloneness, and frustration.

The young person is looking for the meaning and purpose of life.

Youth's need for love and acceptance, shown in an intensifying desire to belong, contributes to his readiness to perceive that God loves all persons, unqualified by who they are or by what they have done.

494

Youth is emotionally and intellectually capable of realizing his involvement in personal and corporate sin, and of experiencing resultant guilt.

Youth is at the stage of life where he has the intellectual capacity to recognize that God through his redemptive love manifested in the life, death, and resurrection of Jesus Christ has made forgiveness available to every person.

The young person has a need for, and some experience of, meaningful relationships with persons of the opposite sex, which may enlarge his understanding of love.

The youth experiences emerging feelings of independence coupled with a desire to have his own workable system of beliefs and values.

A young person's keenness to observe consistency and inconsistency between the affirmations and actions of persons provides a backdrop for his perception of God's dependable love.

In his idealism the youth is able to identify positively with the One who so loved him that he was willing to die for him. Youth is beginning to realize his own predicament, and his need for a way for overcoming his separation from his Creator and his fellowmen.

During the youth years a person is assessing his worth—in his own eyes, and in the eyes of others.

Youth's capacity to identify with others may lead him to recognize himself as one for whose redemption Christ died.

Youth has the capacity for comprehending the idea that he

is made in the image of God and that God in his love is seeking a reconciled relationship with him.

Youth has had experiences that affect his readiness and ability to love and to accept love and he may be in need of therapeutic relationship if he is to perceive God's reconciling love.

Youth's capacity for a historical perspective enables him to perceive God's continuous action in history for man's redemption.

2. How may this content be communicated as the learner engages in the Learning Tasks? What are the methods and procedures by which the learner may explore the meanings and experiences within this theme (1-a) in the light of his readiness (1-b) in order to discover significance and value?

Through engaging in Bible study.

Through discussing insights into God's love.

Through reading theological interpretations of that love.

Through studying artistic expressions of God's redemptive love.

By becoming involved directly or vicariously with people and groups who have experienced the redemptive love of God, and who are willing to share their experience with others.

Through interpreting and evaluating the meaning of the Christian heritage and human history as they bear witness to God's redeeming love.

495

Through reflecting on one's personal experiences and observations of God's love, through such means as regular devotional reading, experiences of meditation and prayer, and encounters in depth with other Christians.

By experimenting with ways to express the redemptive love of God through obedience and service.

By taking part in deliberate efforts to demonstrate God's love in actual experiences at home, in school, or wherever one may be.

By observing how other Christians have expressed God's love through their efforts for reconciliation among men.

Through practicing the expression of forgiveness and of the need for forgiveness, e.g., role playing family tensions in the home and discussing ways to practice forgiveness under various circumstances.

By participating in expressions of personal and corporate confession in worship.

By listening to others interpret God's redemptive love.

Through observing persons who by their love of others reflect God's redemptive love for all persons.

496

3. **What may the learner achieve within this theme in the fulfillment of the Learning Tasks? What are possible changes or learnings on the part of the learner that may result from his appropriation of the significance and value discovered? These changes or learnings may be associated with skills, attitudes, motivations, perceptions including understandings and appreciations.**

Youth may achieve a growing understanding of the nature of God's redeeming love as a yearning, seeking love which reaches out to persons where they are and draws them to their Creator.

Youth may achieve an understanding of impartial love, extended to all kinds and conditions of people.

Youth may achieve an understanding of forgiving love, making possible the forgiveness of sin.

Youth may achieve an understanding of sacrificial, self-giving love, supremely manifested in the life, death, resurrection, and ascension of Jesus Christ.

Youth may achieve an understanding of eternal, unchanging, ever-present love which transcends human love and encompasses the entire universe.

Youth may achieve a sense of freedom to be himself, as God made him, even in spite of conflicting pressures.

Youth may achieve the beginning of a realistic concept of himself and his personal worth and integrity, based on his worth in God's sight.

Youth may achieve a realization that God's universal love is particular love for him.

Youth may achieve a confidence that God's redemptive love can make life whole and an acceptance of the fact that God's love brings true meaning and purpose of life.

Youth may achieve a sense of security rooted in the steadfastness of God's love, in the face of evil, death, and possible nuclear destruction.

Youth may achieve a growing appreciation of the dependability of God's love which can sustain man in the disappointments, demands, sorrows, and frustrations characteristic of adolescence.

Youth may achieve a beginning acceptance of imperfect human lives as channels through which God shows his redemptive love.

Youth may achieve a sense of responsibility to God in gratitude for his (God's) redemption through Christ.

Youth may achieve a growing willingness to forgive and be forgiven.

Youth may achieve a feeling of oneness with Christians everywhere.

Youth may achieve a desire to share the good news of God's redemptive love with others.

Youth may achieve an awareness of the continuing warm presence of a loving God, which overcomes a sense of loneliness.

497

Youth may achieve an acceptance of his own responsible involvement in the sin and evil around him.

Youth may achieve knowledge of God's redemptive action throughout history.

1. God's Redeeming Love for Man

STATEMENT OF THE THEME

Through God's changeless and seeking love for man, supremely manifested in Jesus Christ (his life, death, resurrection, and

ascension) redemption is made possible whereby man's aliena-
tion from God is overcome and the way is opened for him to be
reconciled with God. Thus man's persistent need for reconcilia-
tion, meaning, acceptance, integrity, security, and freedom is
adequately met.

ADULTHOOD

1. Significance of the theme for this age level

498

    a. Meanings and experiences within this theme relevant for this age level. This is content, a selected part of Scope.

God has created man as the supreme object of his love, and intends that man should live in love and obedience to him.

God's love is a yearning, seeking love, ever reaching out to bring unreconciled men into fellowship with himself.

In Christ, we see God at work judging, convicting, healing, forgiving, redeeming, restoring, and reconciling man.

God's redeeming love for man manifest from creation on is supremely manifested in Jesus Christ (his incarnation, life, crucifixion, resurrection, ascension). In the incarnation God identified himself with man and offered himself that man might be redeemed.

God in his love offers forgiveness of man's sin, even when man as free rejects his love or forgiveness.

Only God's redeeming love makes possible wholeness and true freedom into man's personality and life.

God's love can overcome man's sense of aloneness in his world and can provide an indestructible sense of security and belonging, regardless of external circumstances.

God's redeeming love is dependable, unchanging, ever present eternal.

God's redemptive love extends without discrimination to all persons, regardless of their background, culture, race, or moral condition and emphasizes the intrinsic, undeniable value of each person.

God in his redemptive love both purposes and provides the means for man to overcome man's alienation from God and from one another.

Jesus is the manifestation of the perfect love and obedience the Father desires in all his sons.

Persons who themselves have responded to God's redemptive love in Jesus Christ may be channels of that love to others.

God's redeeming love and forgiveness are always available to all persons no matter how serious the offense and even when persons do not love or forgive themselves or others.

God holds man responsible for his choice to accept or reject his redeeming love.

In his seeking redemptive love, God suffers for and with man; and to become involved as a channel of God's love is to participate in such suffering.

God's love and forgiveness do not obliterate the inevitable results of sin and evil, but enable man to redirect life in spite of these results.

In his seeking love, God enables man to recognize his need for redemption and to express it through repentance and confession.

Through God's action the Son knows the joy of reconciliation with God.

499

1. **Significance of the theme for this age level**
   b. **Readiness of the learner for this theme in terms of basic needs, interests, motivations, capacities, developmental tasks.**

Much of the attention and energy of the adult is bent toward finding and fulfilling personal significance, which is rooted in God's love for man.

The universal need to be loved provides the adult a base for perceiving God's redeeming love and for understanding that God's love is extended to all people.

The adult's awareness of his own struggles, failures, and inconsistencies give him a readiness for perceiving God's redemptive love and identification with man in Jesus Christ.

An adult's varied and cumulative experiences of needing forgiveness and needing to forgive may sharpen his ability to recognize God's offer of forgiveness and reconciliation in Christ.

A major drive in the adult years is for security which will reach into the future.

500

Adult experiences emphasize the importance of relationships of dependable love.

The adult's need to sustain vital relationships emphasizes the continuing necessity to overcome alienation.

The adult has had experiences that affect his readiness and ability to love and to accept love; he may be in need of therapeutic relationship if he is to perceive God's reconciling love.

The adult is emotionally and intellectually capable of realizing his responsibility for and his entanglement by personal and corporate sins, and of experiencing the guilt and the sense of need for forgiveness and for reconciliation that comes with this realization.

The responsibility for others that comes with adulthood makes the adult open to appreciation of what God has done and is doing for him.

2. How may this content be communicated as the learner engages in the Learning Tasks? What are the methods and procedures by which the learner may explore the meanings and experiences within this theme (1-a) in the light of his readiness (1-b) in order to discover significance and value?

Through studying the message of the Bible for evidences of God's redemptive love.

Through reading about and discussing evidences of God's redemptive love as it is manifested in the Christian heritage, theology, and human history.

Through hearing and reading about the meaning of God's redemptive love revealed in the life and mission of Jesus Christ.

Through associating with persons who have responded to God's love and who bear witness to this love in their personal relationships.

Through participating in the services and the sacraments of the church, which describe or interpret God's redeeming love.

Through sharing in family and fellowship groups the acceptance and forgiveness that express God's love.

Through engaging in encounter with individuals whose sensitivity to God's love expresses confidence in God's abiding presence.

Through sharing in individual and group experiences that praise God for his wonderful gift of redemption.

Through studying and discussing the nature of a maturing relationship with God in Christ that expresses the qualities of obedience and service engendered by God's redeeming love.

By experimenting with ways to express the redemptive love of God through obedience and service.

Through listening to others interpret God's redemptive love.

By becoming involved in actual experiences that can demonstrate God's love at home, at work, or wherever he may be.

By reflecting on one's personal experiences and observations of God's love, through such means as regular devotional reading, experiences in meditation and prayer, and encounters in depth with other Christians.

501

3. **What may the learner achieve within this theme in the fulfillment of the Learning Tasks? What are possible changes or learnings on the part of the learner that may result from his appropriation of the significance and value discovered? These changes or learnings may be associated with skills, attitudes, motivations, perceptions including understandings and appreciations.**

The adult may achieve a growing understanding of and belief in God's redeeming love as being eternal and unchanging, steadfast and dependable.

The adult may achieve a growing understanding of and belief in God's redeeming love as extending to all people and seeking to draw all people to himself.

The adult may achieve a growing understanding of and belief in God's redeeming love as being supremely manifested in Jesus Christ.

502

The adult may achieve a growing understanding of and belief in God's redeeming love as being forgiving and accepting.

The adult may achieve a growing understanding of and belief in God's redeeming love as transcending human love.

The adult may achieve a growing understanding of and belief in God's redeeming love as binding man to man, and man to God.

The adult may achieve a growing understanding of and belief in God's redeeming love as encompassing the entire universe.

The adult may achieve realization of the meaning of redemption and a deepened loyalty to God in gratitude for his redemption in Christ.

The adult may achieve an increasingly vital awareness that a personal relationship to God is based on the love he expressed for man in Christ.

The adult may achieve a sense of joy in being accepted by God in Jesus Christ.

The adult may achieve personal realization of true freedom in God's reconciling love in Christ.

The adult may achieve a sense of security in God's eternal love in the face of evil, death, disaster, and destructive forces under man's control.

The adult may achieve a realization that God's redeeming love is offered regardless of man's sins and failures.

The adult may achieve an understanding that men's imperfect lives can be limited channels of God's love.

The adult may achieve a sense of the warm presence of a loving God.

The adult may achieve an understanding of personal wholeness and significance in God's redemptive love.

The adult may achieve a realization that God's love enables persons to maintain a proper balance between the facts and struggles of daily life and the demands of Christian commitment.

The adult may achieve a sense of oneness with all Christians as he comprehends God's redemptive love for mankind.

The adult may achieve a desire that others may know this good news.

The adult may achieve an ability to forgive and be forgiven.

The adult may achieve an acceptance of his own responsible involvement in the sin and evil around him.

The adult may achieve a knowledge of God's redemptive action throughout history.

2. Man's Responding to God's Redemptive Action

STATEMENT OF THE THEME

God's offer of redemption demands decision with its inevitable consequences either toward life or death. Man is free to accept or reject God's action on his behalf. The active, positive response which God desires and which brings forgiveness and the awareness and acceptance of sonship is that of confession, repentance, faith, and obedience. Through such response man experiences the ultimate answer to his basic need to be loved and accepted.

503

EARLY CHILDHOOD

1. Significance of the theme for this age level

    a. Meanings and experiences within this theme relevant for this age level. This is content, a selected part of Scope.

Experiences with choice and decision-making involving the love of family and friends provide a basis for later, more mature decisions concerning response to God's redeeming love.

The appropriate response of persons to God is one of love.

Many situations in life require choices in which a person must discover response(s) appropriate for a child of God.

When persons show love to others, they are showing God's love and this brings joy to those who love and are loved.

504

Persons often feel unhappy or unsatisfied when they are unfriendly or unkind to others.

When a person has made someone unhappy, it helps him to be sorry and show it. God will help him in this experience.

People are happiest when they are obedient to rightful authority because this is one way of responding to God's love.

1. **Significance of the theme for this age level**
   b. **Readiness of the learner for this theme in terms of basic needs, interests, motivations, capacities, developmental tasks**

The young child makes some of his own decisions and helps determine others. This begins the maturing process which enables him later to make more mature decisions of Christian commitment.

The young child's desire for approval, especially from significant persons, makes him sensitive to reactions reflecting the acceptability or unacceptability of his decisions.

The need for giving and receiving love is crucial in this period of life. Readiness to respond to human love must find expression in early childhood so as to provide for maturing responses to God's redeeming love.

The young child's enthusiasm and spontaneity make him ready to respond to genuine expressions of love and consequently to the love of God.

The young child's ability to imagine himself as various persons in many relationships readies him for experiences of forgiveness, trust, repentance, and obedience.

The young child needs acceptance by others as a person of worth in order to sense his own worth in God's sight.

As the young child experiences forgiveness, he is prepared to seek and accept God's forgiveness.

The young child's readiness to respond to adults who love him makes him ready for a beginning relationship with a loving God.

As the young child accepts appropriate direction and discipline from parents and other more mature persons, his motivation to learn obedience to God is enhanced.

2. **How may this content be communicated as the learner engages in the Learning Tasks? What are the methods and procedures by which the learner may explore the meanings and experiences within this theme (1-a) in the light of his readiness (1-b) in order to discover significance and value?**

By participating in the supportive environment of such groups as families or church groups which reflect God's redemptive action. Within this environment the young child has opportunities to make choices in response to that redemptive action and live with the results of those choices.

By being with adults such as parents, neighbors, church school teachers, the minister, and other church members who accept the young child as a person and give approval to his positive acts, reflecting God's redemptive love. As the young child relates to these adults, he has opportunities to respond to this redemptive love.

By sharing in family and other personal and group relationships including informal play where opportunities are present for giving and receiving love.

Through situations in family life and church school groups which encourage initiative and free response and provide op-

505

portunities for the young child to use his beginning capacity for making free choices which may express his response to God's redemptive action.

Through creative activities where roles are tried out and feelings and ideas such as obedience, forgiveness, and love are expressed to provide young children opportunities to respond to God's redeeming love as they have seen it expressed in the lives of other persons. Dramatic play, finger painting, free play time, and conversation offer such opportunities.

506

Through guidance and support for exploration of a variety of action and behavior patterns provided in play groups, family, church school class, and outdoor activities and in ordinary, everyday informal play activities in church groups, at home, and in the community.

By apprehending the love of God through association with adults whose lives reflect their response to God.

3. **What may the learner achieve within this theme in the fulfillment of the Learning Tasks? What are possible changes or learnings on the part of the learner that may result from his appropriation of the significance and value discovered? These changes or learnings may be associated with skills, attitudes, motivations, perceptions including understandings and appreciations.**

The young child may have a beginning realization that God desires the love of all persons.

The young child may have a growing ability to find satisfaction in showing love to others as a response to God's love.

The young child may have a growing ability to make his own decisions in light of a growing understanding of God's love.

The young child may have a growing capacity to forgive persons who have hurt him, and to be sorry when he has hurt someone else and to show that he is.

The young child may have a growing ability to discern between actions that bring happiness and those that bring unhappiness.

The young child may have a willingness to obey persons in rightful authority.

2. Man's Responding to God's Redemptive Action

STATEMENT OF THE THEME

God's offer of redemption demands decision with its inevitable consequences either toward life or death. Man is free to accept or reject God's action on his behalf. The active, positive response which God desires and which brings forgiveness and the awareness and acceptance of sonship is that of confession, repentance, faith, and obedience. Through such response man experiences the ultimate answer to his basic need to be loved and accepted.

ELEMENTARY YEARS

1. Significance of the theme for this age level

a. Meanings and experiences within this theme relevant for this age level. This is content, a selected part of Scope.

God offers the elementary child his redeeming love which must be either accepted or rejected. The child cannot just ignore it.

507

God will not force him to accept his love, but does require him to abide by the results of rejecting that love.

Through accepting God's love persons are forgiven and may be assured that God has accepted them.

Through refusing to accept God's love, persons are separated from him, yet God continues to love them.

It is appropriate for a child of God to confess and repent his unloving acts for then he realizes that God forgives.

Being a child of God means obeying him, trusting him to lead in the best way.

When persons accept God's love, they love him and serve him by obeying his laws and serving others.

The commitment of life to God is one of the great decisions which persons have opportunity for making; it may be made when the person senses God's call to such commitment.

1. Significance of the theme for this age level

    b. Readiness of the learner for this theme in terms of basic needs, interests, motivations, capacities, developmental tasks.

The inquiring mind and natural curiosity of the child make him concerned about the meaning for him of God's love and action in Jesus Christ.

The child's desire to do things for himself and his emerging ability to select among alternatives enable him to make some decisions on his own about his relationship to God.

The elementary child's sensitivity to approval or disapproval in his relations with significant persons around him causes him to be concerned about his relationship to God.

The elementary child's readiness to forgive enables him to seek and accept God's forgiveness.

The child's quick and unprejudiced acceptance of other people and his faith in their acceptance of him enable him to respond to God's love in trust and obedience.

The child's need for love and acceptance as a person of worth gives him a readiness to respond to the redeeming love of God.

The elementary child's capacity for recognizing wrong in himself prompts him to seek God's forgiveness.

The child's need for security that comes through knowing the limits of his freedom prepares him to be obedient to God.

2. **How may this content be communicated as the learner engages in the Learning Tasks? What are the methods and procedures by which the learner may explore the meanings and experiences within this theme (1-a) in the light of his readiness (1-b) in order to discover significance and value?**

By studying the biblical story of God's redemptive action: Jesus' birth, life, death, resurrection; stories of Jesus' followers and their response to God's redemptive love.

By associating with persons as they witness to and respond to God's love: through participating in services of worship and witness, through observing teachers, parents, church leaders and friends in the Christian community as they meet life situations and respond as redeemed persons.

By interpreting and relating God's redeeming love and man's response to it as they participate in choral readings, drama, role play, festivals, holy days, music, life in the out-of-doors.

By experiencing through worship the presence of God and committing themselves to him to the extent of their capacity. Much of the meaning of the presence of God and of commitment to him may come through the atmosphere created by worshiping adults.

By responding to God's redeeming love, as interpreted in the life of the family in the midst of its experiences: undergirding love and faith, forgiveness, obedience, respect for persons, service, repentance, humility, confidence, reliance on God. Resources may provide guidance for parents on family problems, suggestions for family devotions and worship, suggested opportunities for the whole family to share.

509

By participating in real life situations in which the child may come to realize that appropriate Christian action is an important response to God's love: visiting the sick and aged, giving help to the needy, being friendly to lonely boys and girls, witnessing to loyalty to Christ's way in times of temptation, being kind and thoughtful beyond what is normally expected, doing tasks for which they are responsible with a sense of Christian stewardship.

3. What may the learner achieve within this theme in the fulfillment of the Learning Tasks? What are possible changes or learnings on the part of the learner that may result from his appropriation of the significance and value discovered? These changes or learnings may be associated with skills, attitudes, motivations, perceptions including understandings and appreciations.

510

The child may have a beginning understanding of what is involved in commitment to God through faith, love, and obedience.

The child may have a beginning desire to undertake commitment to God through faith, love, and obedience.

The child may have a response to God's love expressed in specific decisions in concrete life situations, involving active love of and service for others.

The child may have a developing awareness that obedience to God and discipline in living are called for from Christians as they experience the freedom to make their own decisions.

The child may have experiences of God's forgiving love after repentance for wrong decisions and the sense of security that comes with forgiveness.

The child may have a recognition that God never stops loving persons but that a person is not in good relations with God if he has turned away from God's love.

The child may have a realization that accepting and responding to God's love brings joy and security.

2. Man's Responding to God's Redemptive Action

STATEMENT OF THE THEME

God's offer of redemption demands decision with its inevitable consequences either toward life or death. Man is free to accept or reject God's action on his behalf. The active, positive response which God desires and which brings forgiveness and the awareness and acceptance of sonship is that of confession, repentance, faith, and obedience. Through such response man experiences the ultimate answer to his basic need to be loved and accepted.

YOUTH

1. Significance of the theme for this age level
a. Meanings and experiences within this theme relevant for this age level. This is content, a selected part of Scope.

God's redeeming love requires frequent and continuous decisions from all those able to make responsible decisions. Trying to avoid such a response is in reality negative response.

Each person is free to accept or reject God's redemptive actions and must make the decision himself. God does not compel anyone to accept his grace.

A positive response to God's redemptive action brings experience of forgiveness and of acceptance as a child of God.

511

Failure to make a positive response to God's redemptive action perpetuates alienation from God.

To respond to God in faith and love is to accept him as Father, to repent of one's sin, to know the joy of forgiveness and restoration, and to trust God and be obedient to his will in all life's situations.

Acceptance of God's love results in joyous service.

1. Significance of the theme for this age level

b. Readiness of the learner for this theme in terms of basic needs, interests, motivations, capacities, developmental tasks.

Youth is at a stage of development—intellectual, emotional, spiritual and physical—which is conducive to response to God's redeeming love.

Many of the drives, talents, and curiosities make this a crucial period in lifelong response to God's redeeming love.

512 Youth's desire to express his independence and make his own decisions creates a need for him to understand and respond to God's providence.

Youth's growing ability to make considered decisions prepares him for a willing, decisive response to God's redeeming love.

The heightened awareness of himself as a person leads youth to a search for ultimate meaning and value in life.

Youth's questions, "Who am I?" and "Where do I fit in?" make him ready to accept his identity as a son of God.

Youth's need for an experience of meaningful relationships with persons about him creates a readiness for a basic understanding and experience of divine love which relates to all of life.

The need to belong to a peer group and desire for conformity intensify the challenge to make a decision which, in the final analysis, must be an individual one.

Youth are aware of personal sin and guilt—sometimes to an extreme—and thus are not only ready to consider confession, but are often in desperate need of God's forgiveness.

As youth becomes increasingly aware that the authorities in whom he has put his trust (parents, for example) are not perfect, he may be ready to look to God for dependable guidance and trustworthy authority.

As youth encounter life's disappointments and frustrations,

they need to know that responding to God in trust and obedience will bring experiences of fulfillment.

The need for security may lead youth to seek it not only in family and peer group, but also in the redeeming love of God.

2. How may this content be communicated as the learner engages in the Learning Tasks? What are the methods and procedures by which the learner may explore the meanings and experiences within this theme (1-a) in the light of his readiness (1-b) in order to discover significance and value?

By associating with persons whose lives demonstrate response to God's redeeming love. Such association may come through face-to-face contacts, through the Bible and other past and current reading and visual material and biography, through speakers and leaders whom youth meet or hear.

By associating with significant adults and peers who may provide opportunities for observing evidence of response to God's redeeming love. The parents, the church school teacher, the youth advisers and the public school teachers—as the adults with whom youth deals most intimately—have a crucial witness here. Other such associations may take place in the church, the school, the peer group, the athletic team, the club, and the community.

By studying the meaning and experience of redemption (individually and in groups) in the Bible, in theological writings, and in biography.

By participating in worship (individual and group), especially services of worship in which decision is called for.

Through opportunities to witness concerning the meaning and experiences of responding to God's offer of redemption.

Through opportunities to participate in expressing love of God in service to other persons.

By engaging in conversation with older Christians and with other youth about the meaning and experience of redemption.

513

By hearing the word of God preached, especially as it relates to redemption.

By listening to music which sets forth the meaning and experience of redemption and provides a means for youth to be aware of the call of God.

Through drama, creative expression, speech, writing, art, music related to redemption.

3. **What may the learner achieve within this theme in the fulfillment of the Learning Tasks? What are possible changes or learnings on the part of the learner that may result from his appropriation of the significance and value discovered? These changes or learnings may be associated with skills, attitudes, motivations, perceptions including understandings and appreciations.**

Youth may have acknowledgment of sin issuing in wrong decisions and of a need for forgiveness and restoration.

Youth may have an acceptance of God's love and a response expressed in faith and obedience to his will.

Youth may have an acceptance of Jesus Christ as personal Savior and Lord.

Youth may have a growing spiritual union with God through Christ.

Youth may have an awareness and acceptance of sonship to God, with the responsibilities entailed.

Youth may have a desire to continue faithful in his filial relation to God.

Youth may have a new sense of the power that accrues from the exercise of responsible freedom.

Youth may have the realization that the answer to feelings of alienation and guilt lies in a growing relationship with God.

Youth may have a response to the love of God expressed in love of and service to neighbors.

2. Man's Responding to God's Redemptive Action

STATEMENT OF THE THEME

God's offer of redemption demands decision with its inevitable consequences either toward life or death. Man is free to accept or reject God's action on his behalf. The active, positive response which God desires and which brings forgiveness and the awareness and acceptance of sonship is that of confession, repentance, faith, and obedience. Through such response man experiences the ultimate answer to his basic need to be loved and accepted.

ADULTHOOD

1. Significance of the theme for this age level

a. Meanings and experiences within this theme relevant for this age level. This is content, a selected part of Scope.

God's offer of redemption in Christ demands commitment of life and continuing decisions appropriate for a committed person. He cannot remain neutral. To remain uncommitted is to reject God.

Man is free to accept or reject God's redemptive action on his behalf. God does not compel acceptance of his grace, but each one must abide by the consequences of his choice.

Decision brings inevitable consequences: eternal life if one accepts and is faithful to God as revealed in Jesus Christ.

Positive response to God's redemptive action brings experiences of forgiveness and the awareness and acceptance of sonship.

Rejection of God perpetuates alienation and leads to death.

Man, by the grace of God and through the work of the Holy Spirit, can respond in faith and love to what God in Christ has done for him.

To respond to God in faith and love is to accept him as Father, to repent of his sin, to know the joy of forgiveness and

515

restoration, and to trust God and be obedient to his will in all life's situations.

The response in faith, love, and obedience to God's redemptive action is lifelong, not once and for all; it is expressed in a variety of ways depending upon individual circumstances and personality characteristics.

1. Significance of the theme for this age level

516

b. Readiness of the learner for this theme in terms of basic needs, interests, motivations, capacities, developmental tasks.

An adult's basic need to be loved and accepted prepares him to respond in faith and love to what God in Christ has done for him.

The need of the adult to find his true identity—to know who he is in relation to God, to other persons, and to the world about him—may make him ready to accept himself as a son of God.

The continuing need to find significance in life may stimulate in the adult a readiness to respond positively to God's redemptive activity on his behalf. This need may be evidenced in such feelings as lack of fulfillment and dissatisfaction with himself; dissatisfaction with his social environment; loneliness, frustration, and uncertainty because of world events; guilt, boredom, fragmentation; fear and insecurity—in relation to all life's experiences including old age, death, and the world beyond death.

The burdens and responsibilities of adulthood may ready him for becoming aware of the relevance of Christian faith and obedience. Such responsibilities include marriage, parenthood, livelihood, and community service.

The adult's readiness to accept sonship may grow out of his desire for trustworthy principles to use in distinguishing between right and wrong (for himself and his children).

The adult's need for wisdom and strength in facing personal life situations which he cannot handle on his own may prepare him for responding to God's offer of redemption in Christ.

The adult's need to find a source of help in trying to relieve the distress of others may make him ready to respond to God's redeeming love.

The adult's ability to recognize the consequences of rejecting God and the importance of responding positively to him may prepare the adult to accept God's offer of mercy and pardon.

The adult's need for something dependable in which to trust may prepare him to put his trust in God.

Awareness of the adult's developed abilities and personal resources call for their being used in meaningful ways and according to his supreme commitment in his life.

2. How may this content be communicated as the learner engages in the Learning Tasks? What are the methods and procedures by which the learner may explore the meanings and experiences within this theme (1-a) in the light of his readiness (1-b) in order to discover significance and value.

By acquaintance with persons whose lives exemplify sonship. Such acquaintance may come about through personal contacts, the Bible, biography, newspapers, magazines, and other reading and visual materials.

Through association with persons whose lives give evidence of their having responded to God's redeeming love. Such association may take place in the family, the church, the community, working relationships, and personal friendships.

517

Through study of the meaning and experience of redemption (individually and in groups), in the Bible, in theological writings, and in biography.

By worship (individual and group), especially services of worship in which decision is called for.

Through opportunities to witness concerning the meaning and experience of responding to God's offer of redemption through Christ.

Through opportunities to express the love of God in service to other persons.

Through conversations with Christians about the meaning and experience of redemption.

By hearing the word of God preached, especially as it relates to redemption.

By listening to music which sets forth the meaning and experience of redemption.

Through drama, speech, writing, art, music related to redemption.

518

3. **What may the learner achieve within this theme in the fulfillment of the Learning Tasks? What are possible changes or learnings on the part of the learner that may result from his appropriation of the significance and value discovered? These changes or learnings may be associated with skills, attitudes, motivations, perceptions including understandings and appreciations.**

The adult may have an acknowledgment of sin issuing in wrong decisions and of a need for forgiveness and restoration.

The adult may have an acceptance of God's love and a response expressed in faith and obedience to his will.

The adult may have an acceptance of Jesus Christ as personal Savior and Lord.

The adult may have a growing spiritual union with God through Christ.

The adult may have an awareness and acceptance of sonship to God, with the responsibilities entailed.

The adult may have a desire to continue faithful in his filial relation to God.

The adult may have a new sense of the power that accrues from the exercise of responsible freedom.

The adult may have the realization that the answer to feelings of alienation and guilt lies in a growing relationship with God.

The adult may have a response to the love of God expressed in love of and service to neighbors.

The adult may have an acknowledgment that growth in sonship is lifelong and that each Christian expresses his sonship in many individual ways according to his personal circumstances and development.

3. Becoming a New Person in Christ

STATEMENT OF THEME

Man's continual need and yearning for wholeness is met by his acceptance of Christ as Lord. This commitment to God in Christ enables him to become a whole person by overcoming the fragmentizing pull of his own selfishness and of the culture in which he lives. The new person in Christ knows through his own experience the meaning of freedom, integration of personality, trust in God, and reorientation of his purpose.

EARLY CHILDHOOD

1. Significance of the theme for this age level

a. Meanings and experiences within this theme relevant for this age level. This is content, a selected part of Scope.

519

God in his love is ready to help and strengthen a person at any time he seeks help and strength.

God helps persons grow in the direction of his will when they seek his help.

God loves me and wants me to love him.

God's love is experienced through people who know and love him.

Through Jesus Christ we know God's love for all persons, including ourselves.

God is our loving Father who will guide each of us when we seek his help.

One way we know God's will for us is through persons who know and love God.

Persons who are Christians love God.

Persons who are Christians love and serve others.

Knowing and loving Jesus Christ makes a difference in people and in their lives.

Through Jesus Christ we know what God desires of his people.

1. Significance of the theme for this age level

b. Readiness of the learner for this theme in terms of basic needs, interests, motivations, capacities, developmental tasks

The young child is developing a sense of trust or distrust.

The young child is developing a sense of his worth or lack of worth as a person.

The young child is dependent on love as a major factor in development.

The young child needs to become an autonomous person moving from outer to inner direction for personal decisions.

The young child is rapidly developing conscience.

The young child has growing ability to realize the need for forgiveness.

The young child has growing ability to be aware of the healing power of forgiveness.

The young child has increasing ability to comprehend certain portions of the Bible that make known God's love in Jesus Christ.

The young child has increasing ability to recognize some of the ways in which persons influence one another for good or bad.

The young child has increasing ability to love.

The young child has need for consistency in the significant persons in his life.

2. How may this content be communicated as the learner engages in the Learning Tasks? What are the methods and

520

procedures by which the learner may explore the meanings and experiences within this theme (1-a) in the light of his readiness (1-b) in order to discover significance and value?

By receiving love from persons who are committed Christians.

By having physical and emotional needs adequately met when with those who are committed to Christ.

By experiencing relationships that are characterized by love, appreciation, understanding, and forgiveness, with parents, parent substitutes, or a small number of additional persons who are committed Christians.

By taking part in home, church, and community patterns of living characteristic of Christians.

By engaging with peers and adults in play and other planned activities that involve personal interaction, and that provide for recognition of the worth, needs, and contributions of each person.

By worshiping—in ways meaningful to him—with others, particularly those who know themselves to be committed to Christ.

By participating under the guidance of adults who are Christian in activities that encourage him to explore and express his developing selfhood with peers and adults.

By hearing Bible and other stories that tell of the influence of Jesus upon others.

521

By being in an atmosphere that supports changes in relationships and behavior.

By having opportunities to associate with persons who are committed to Christ as Savior and Lord, whose lives exemplify values that reflect this commitment.

3. **What may the learner achieve within this theme in the fulfillment of the Learning Tasks? What are possible changes or learnings on the part of the learner that may result from his appropriation of the significance and value discovered?**

These changes or learnings may be associated with skills, attitudes, motivations, perceptions including understandings and appreciations.

The young child may achieve a sense of security and trust in relation to individuals who are committed Christians.

The young child may achieve a developing awareness of God's love for him as a person.

The young child may achieve a developing dependence on God for help and guidance.

The young child may achieve a developing sense of his worth as a person.

The young child may achieve a developing sense of autonomy and accompanying realization of personal responsibility.

The young child may achieve an awareness that the Bible contains stories of persons who were influenced by Jesus.

The young child may achieve familiarity with some Bible and other stories of persons whose lives were influenced by Jesus.

The young child may achieve a beginning appreciation of prayer as a means of receiving help from God.

The young child may achieve a beginning awareness that change takes place in what one wants to do when one comes to love a person.

The young child may achieve a beginning awareness of the relationships of Jesus of the Bible to us today.

3. Becoming a New Person in Christ

STATEMENT OF THE THEME

Man's continual need and yearning for wholeness is met by his acceptance of Christ as Lord. This commitment to God in Christ enables him to become a whole person by overcoming the fragmentizing pull of his own selfishness and of the culture in which he lives. The new person in Christ knows through his own experience the meaning of freedom, integration of personality, trust in God, and reorientation of his purpose.

ELEMENTARY YEARS

1. Significance of the theme for this age level

a. Meanings and experiences within this theme relevant for this age level. This is content, a selected part of Scope.

Becoming a new person in Christ involves beginning a lifetime of learning how, with God's help, to follow best his plan for our lives.

When a person accepts Jesus Christ as Savior and Lord, the direction of that person's life begins to move from living to please only himself toward living to please God.

Giving one's loyalty to Christ as friend and Lord involves the facing and resolving the conflict of loyalties.

Evidences of individuals' becoming new persons in Christ can be seen in the life of the church from Bible times to the present.

Something of the meaning of "being in Christ" comes to those who participate in the fellowship of Christians in the corporate life of the church.

Response to God's redeeming love expressed in Jesus Christ helps one toward realizing his full potential as a maturing person.

In becoming a new person in Christ the relationship of external structures and rules of a community under the lordship of Christ and personal integrity under the lordship of Christ becomes evident.

523

1. Significance of the theme for this age level

b. Readiness of the learner for this theme in terms of basic needs, interests, motivations, capacities, developmental tasks.

The elementary child has a need for friendships with significant persons to whom he can give his loyalties.

The elementary child has an increasing capacity to give his loyalty in response to friendship.

The elementary child has a capacity to begin assuming increasing responsibility for his own behavior.

The elementary child has capacity to take part with others in acts of sharing and service.

The elementary child has a need for association with persons significant to him with whom he may identify.

The elementary child has the capacity to respond to persons by identification with them.

The elementary child is required to deal with peer group attitudes and relationships, make proper decisions, and take adequate actions, all of which contribute to his readiness to examine and change his life purposes.

2. How may this content be communicated as the learner engages in the Learning Tasks? What are the methods and procedures by which the learner may explore the meanings and experiences within this theme (1-a) in the light of his readiness (1-b) in order to discover significance and value?

By having opportunities to associate with persons who are committed to Christ as Savior and Lord, whose lives exemplify values that reflect this commitment.

By conversing about and reading Bible stories of Jesus and his disciples and followers.

By conversing about and reading the parables of Jesus, such as the parable of the lost son.

By participating in a setting where it is possible to develop close friendship with those who are committed to Christ and actually face the challenge of conflicting loyalties.

By participating in discussions on becoming a new person in Christ led by an adult who reflects his faith in his life and can articulate it.

By exploring within the Christian fellowship the appropriateness of various alternative decisions in terms of one's loyalty to Christ.

By exploring implications of loyalty to Christ in the various areas of life.

By taking part in worship opportunities of congregational confession and rededication to Christ as Savior and Lord.

By hearing and reading about persons in the church past and present whose lives show their commitment to the Lord.

By exploring the rules and structures by which the Christian community lives.

By studying the heritage of the church with reference to the new person in Christ.

By exploring ways land and other resources may be conserved or restored so that their potential may be fulfilled.

3. **What may the learner achieve within this theme in the fulfillment of the Learning Tasks? What are possible changes or learnings on the part of the learner that may result from his appropriation of the significance and value discovered? These changes or learnings may be associated with skills, attitudes, motivations, perceptions including understandings and appreciations.**

The elementary child may achieve an openness to the loyalties that distinguish a person who gives allegiance to God in Christ.

525

The elementary child may achieve a practical, though partial, understanding of what it means to be committed to Jesus Christ as Lord.

The elementary child may achieve a growing dependence on the Holy Spirit for guidance and for strength to obey.

The elementary child may achieve a deepening assurance of availability of God's forgiveness and restoration.

The elementary child may achieve a beginning ability to recognize the decisions a Christian must face.

The elementary child may achieve a beginning system of values by which he will deal with decisions in light of his understanding of the Christian faith.

The elementary child may achieve a deeper discernment of what is involved in the choice of committing his life to Christ and the consequence of such a decision.

The elementary child may achieve an increasing desire to commit his life to Christ as Savior and Lord.

526

The elementary child may achieve a deeper sense of personal worth as one for whom Christ gave himself in sacrifice and promise.

The elementary child may achieve a beginning ability to reflect on the decisions he makes, judging them in light of his developing awareness of God's purposes for him.

The elementary child may achieve a desire to join with those whose lives are committed to Christ as Lord.

3. Becoming a New Person in Christ

STATEMENT OF THE THEME

Man's continual need and yearning for wholeness is met by his acceptance of Christ as Lord. This commitment to God in Christ enables him to become a whole person by overcoming the fragmentizing pull of his own selfishness and of the culture in which he lives. The new person in Christ knows through his own experience the meaning of freedom, integration of personality, trust in God, and reorientation of his purpose.

YOUTH

1. Significance of the theme for this age level

    a. Meanings and experiences within this theme relevant for this age level. This is content, a selected part of Scope.

Acceptance of God's redeeming love expressed in Christ involves one in an experience of transformation toward wholeness.

The transformation and development resulting from commitment to Christ is a lifelong process.

The new being in Christ is given freedom to become the person God intends.

As a new person in Christ, man is involved in a reorientation to decision-making.

To submit to the lordship of Christ integrates personality and so makes possible that quality of life which the New Testament describes as "abundant and eternal."

The new person in Christ has access to the guidance and empowering of God toward consistency in living as a son of God.

One's commitment to God in Christ puts him into a new framework of control which gives new perspective to fears, pressures, frustrations, drives, needs.

One who has committed himself to God in Christ is faced with reassessing former patterns of behavior, former scales of values, former goals and motivations.

Acceptance of Christ as Lord opens to a person new dimensions of freedom from guilt, dependable sources of power for disciplined and purposeful living, new bases for acceptance of one's self and of others.

527

The new person in Christ enters into a deeply based fellowship with fellow Christians.

To be in Christ makes it possible for the person to deal creatively with the tensions between Christ's standards and those of the society and culture so that the new person is set free to be a witness and servant within that society.

The new person in Christ becomes able to accept forgiveness from others and to forgive others.

1. Significance of the theme for this age level

    b. Readiness of the learner for this theme in terms of basic

needs, interests, motivations, capacities, developmental tasks.

The young person has the capacity to identify consistency and inconsistency within himself.

Youth is caught in the paradox of pressures to conformity in the culture around him and of desire for self-direction.

The young person has a readiness to respond to guidance from self-authenticating sources.

Youth is seeking dependable measurements or standards by which the positive and negative forces and experiences of life may be identified and assessed.

The young person frequently senses disappointment with the consequences of selfish decisions.

Youth often recognizes his own internal conflicts of motivations, values, goals, desires.

Youth appreciates consistency in the life of other persons.

The young person wants both freedom and control.

The young person needs to understand and resolve his fears, despair and frustration, which frequently keep him from experiencing wholesome relationships with peers and others.

The young person needs and wants to be recognized and accepted as a person of worth who has the capacity to achieve a respectable status in his group or in society.

The young person needs to embrace goals and values around which to orient his life.

2. How may this content be communicated as the learner engages in the Learning Tasks? What are the methods and procedures by which the learner may explore the meanings and experiences within this theme (1-a) in the light of his readiness (1-b) in order to discover significance and value?

By exploring and studying the biblical record of God's plan to provide for the individual's redemption and new life in Christ.

By studying the historical and contemporary witness of persons who have committed themselves to Christ and are becoming new persons in him.

Studying and discussing culture and society, in light of concepts of freedom within the Christian faith.

By observing, reading about, or getting acquainted with persons who have been able to handle well the decisions of life on the basis of their commitment to Christ.

By studying and analyzing Christianity alongside other religions of the world to see the different implications of commitment within each.

By studying the New Testament to explore the meaning of new life in Christ and the implications of his lordship over a person's life.

By engaging in worship opportunities designed to help persons become aware of the availability of God's power, discipline, wisdom.

By exploration of alternatives within decision-demanding situations in life with an attempt to relate one's commitment to Christ to the alternatives.

By associating with persons whose integrity is rooted in their commitment to Christ.

By joining with fellow Christians in analyzing various external pressures in terms of values derived from commitment to Christ.

By hearing others interpret and describe their sense of freedom under Christ's lordship.

By repeatedly reexamining one's purposes and patterns of life in light of his commitment to Christ.

By studying the bases on which Jesus made decisions and related to persons and to culture.

By taking part in discussing the issues involved in committing oneself to Christ.

3. **What may the learner achieve within this theme in the fulfillment of the Learning Tasks? What are possible changes or learnings on the part of the learner that may result from**

529

his appropriation of the significance and value discovered? These changes or learnings may be associated with skills, attitudes, motivations, perceptions including understandings and appreciations.

Youth may achieve a beginning sense of true freedom in Christ that results from his dependence upon and allegiance to God.

Youth may achieve a growing understanding and acceptance of the fact that commitment to Christ radically influences all the other decisions he makes in his life, and also his response to and involvement in the society and culture of his day.

Youth may achieve the beginnings of a wholeness and integration of his life reflected in his relationship with others.

Youth may achieve a growing ability to accept and live with himself.

Youth may achieve a growing ability to relate to, and work with, his peers and others in the Christian fellowship.

Youth may achieve a growing sense of responsibility to participate in the various phases of the life of the Christian community.

Youth may achieve an increasing recognition of the demands and responsibilities of the Christian as distinguished from those of others in society.

Youth may achieve an increasing ability to accept forgiveness and to forgive others as an expression of new life in Christ.

Youth may achieve a sense of dissatisfaction with sin in his life.

Youth may achieve a growing ability to distinguish values that are consistent with commitment to Christ.

Youth may achieve an increasing ability to see in himself inconsistencies between behavior and commitment.

Youth may achieve a modification of some of his goals, values, and self-assessment in light of his understanding of the Christian faith.

Youth may achieve an increasing self-determination as over

against conformity to cultural patterns in behavior, attitudes, and values.

Youth may achieve an increased ability to tolerate and cope with tension between values and standards growing out of the Christian faith and those from other sources.

Youth may achieve a growing understanding of the Bible concept of redemption.

Youth may achieve a growing disposition to embrace disciplines that will strengthen his obedience to Christ.

3. Becoming a New Person in Christ

STATEMENT OF THE THEME

Man's continual need and yearning for wholeness is met by his acceptance of Christ as Lord. This commitment to God in Christ enables him to become a whole person by overcoming the fragmentizing pull of his own selfishness and of the culture in which he lives. The new person in Christ knows through his own experience the meaning of freedom, integration of personality, trust in God, and reorientation of his purpose.

ADULTHOOD

1. Significance of the theme for this age level

531

a. Meanings and experiences within this theme relevant for this age level. This is content, a selected part of Scope.

The transforming effect of acceptance of God's redeeming love in Christ involves continuing lifelong response to God and is not automatic.

Acceptance of God's redemptive act in Christ opens up to one the possibility of becoming whole, an integrated, disciplined person increasingly sharing God's fellowship and purposes.

The freedom to become the person God intended rests within the framework of Christ's lordship over every realm of one's life.

Becoming a new person in Christ gives one a new perspective on society and a new basis for participation in it.

As a new person in Christ, one is faced with new decisions as well as familiar ones, and all these demand a perspective resulting from his Christian faith.

The lordship of Christ is a radically distinctive basis for integration of personality and life.

Becoming a new person in Christ opens up new dimensions of abundant and eternal life.

532 The new person in Christ has access to the guidance and empowering of God toward consistency in living as a son of God.

One who has committed himself to God in Christ is faced with reassessing former patterns of behavior, former scales of values, former goals and motivations.

Acceptance of Christ as Lord opens up to a person new dimensions of freedom from guilt, dependable sources of power for disciplined and purposeful living, new bases for acceptance of one's self and of others.

Commitment to Christ enables one to see new issues, new conflicts, new inconsistencies in individual and social life.

One's commitment to God in Christ puts him into a new framework of control which gives new perspective to fears, pressures, frustrations, drives, needs.

To become a new person in Christ makes one more susceptible to suffering and at the same time gives one a perspective and motivation for coping with it.

1. Significance of the theme for this age level

b. Readiness of the learner for this theme in terms of basic needs, interests, motivations, capacities, developmental tasks.

The adult is enmeshed in inescapable pressures to conformity to conflicting patterns in life which highlight his need for a dependable internal basis for choices and decisions.

The adult needs to develop a basis for personal integrity which he himself can respect.

The adult is increasingly able to recognize in himself enslaving or debasing habits and patterns of behavior inconsistent with his own sense of rightness.

The adult is able to set long-range goals for himself and for society and to pursue them with some degree of steadiness at the cost of lesser gains.

The adult is capable of willfully bringing various areas of his life under scrutiny and assessing them against accepted goals and standards.

The adult needs an internal freedom which will allow him to cope with the varied ways in which his life is liable to control.

The adult's expanding relationships and responsibilities increase the need for a dependable set of values by which to live.

Many adults are acutely dissatisfied with themselves and their patterns of life, yet frustrated in efforts to make any lasting changes.

2. **How may this content be communicated as the learner engages in the Learning Tasks? What are the methods and procedures by which the learner may explore the meanings and experiences within this theme (1-a) in the light of his readiness (1-b) in order to discover significance and value.**

533

By exploring and studying the biblical record of God's plan to provide for the individual's redemption and new life in Christ.

By studying the historical and contemporary witness of persons who have committed themselves to Christ and are becoming new persons in him.

By observing, reading about, or getting acquainted with persons who have been able to handle well the decisions of life on the basis of their commitment to Christ.

By studying and analyzing Christianity alongside other religions of the world to see the different implications of commitment within each.

By analyzing culture and society in the light of the concepts of Christian freedom in terms of the revised relationships and responsibilities of the new person in Christ.

By studying the bases on which Jesus made decisions and related to persons and to culture.

By studying the New Testament to explore the meaning of new life in Christ and the implications of his lordship over a person's life.

By engaging in worship opportunities designed to help persons become aware of the availability of God's power, discipline, wisdom.

By exploration of alternatives within descision-demanding situations in life with an attempt to relate one's commitment to Christ to the alternatives.

By associating with persons whose integrity is rooted in their commitment to Christ.

By joining with fellow Christians in analyzing various external pressures in terms of values derived from commitment to Christ.

By hearing others interpret and describe their sense of freedom under Christ's lordship.

By repeatedly reexamining one's purposes and patterns of life in light of his commitment to Christ.

By deliberately trying to put into practice some of what one understands to be the results of new life under Christ's lordship.

3. **What may the learner achieve within this theme in the fulfillment of the Learning Tasks? What are possible changes or learnings on the part of the learner that may result from his appropriation of the significance and value discovered? These changes or learnings may be associated with skills, attitudes, motivations, perceptions including understandings and appreciations.**

The adult may achieve a deepened understanding that his decision to find his life in Christ radically influences the other decisions he makes.

The adult may achieve a willingness to scrutinize additional realms of his personality and life in terms of their consistency with his commitment to Christ.

The adult may achieve an appreciation for the contribution of the disciplines of worship and study to living out one's commitment.

The adult may achieve a responsiveness to the guidance and the empowering of the Holy Spirit in his life.

The adult may achieve an acknowledgement of the lifelong character of transformation under Christ.

The adult may achieve an increasing integration of his life around his commitment to Christ rather than to former or lesser loyalties.

The adult may achieve an increasing sense of freedom from social pressures to conform.

The adult may achieve a growing ability to accept himself and others.

The adult may achieve an increasing sensitivity to sin in his life and desire for forgiveness and for God's help to change.

The adult may achieve a deepening sense of fellowship with others who are becoming new persons in Christ.

535

The adult may achieve growth in genuine humility.

The adult may achieve an increased willingness and skill in relating his commitment to personal and corporate decisions and actions.

The adult may achieve modification of some of his life goals in the direction of his transformed value-structure.

The adult may achieve a deepened sense of assurance and confidence in coping with inevitable conflicts of aims and values within the Christian community with those of society and culture in general.

4. Growing Up in Christ

STATEMENT OF THE THEME

The faithful son cultivates his relationship of faith, love, and obedience toward God; he also cultivates love for his fellowmen. In the power of the Holy Spirit, he grows in grace and develops toward Christian maturity. His quest for personal significance and for a richly satisfying life is answered with increasing meaning.

536

EARLY CHILDHOOD

1. Significance of the theme for this age level

a. Meanings and experiences within this theme relevant for this age level. This is content, a selected part of Scope.

God wants each person to love him and to love his fellowman.
The love of other people helps persons grow.
Persons know about the love of God through Jesus.
The choices and decisions which persons make influence their growth.
Appropriate response to the guidance and authority of wise and loving persons—and to the guidance and authority of God as mediated through them—helps persons grow.
To grow in the right ways brings satisfaction and joy to oneself and to others.
Persons love one another because God loves all persons.

1. Significance of the theme for this age level

b. Readiness of the learner for this theme in terms of basic needs, interests, motivations, capacities, developmental tasks.

The young child has a need for supportive love and security.
In early childhood there is the capacity for receiving and giving love.

The young child's struggle to establish his individuality opens the way to the lifelong quest for personal significance.

The young child is growing in his ability to give himself to new ways, new things, and new friends.

The young child displays an increasing awareness of other persons.

The young child is growing in his ability to distinguish among values and is beginning to develop a personal system of values.

The young child's sense of awe and wonder at the world around him fosters an attitude of expectancy towards life.

The young child's normative spontaneity is evidence of an initial capacity for an emerging faith in God through Christ.

2. How may this content be communicated as the learner engages in the Learning Tasks? What are the methods and procedures by which the learner may explore the meanings and experiences within this theme (1-a) in the light of his readiness (1-b) in order to discover significance and value?

Through receiving loving care from family and from other members of the fellowship of the church.

Through opportunities to exercise growing abilities to love and to act responsibly in experiences of play, sharing, and helping.

Through participation in worship and prayer, and in the observance of Christian festivals and special events.

Through observing and being helped to understand growth and change.

Through opportunities to become acquainted with the Bible as a special book which tells of God's love and what he wants him to be.

Through opportunities to make choices and decisions, and to live with their consequences.

Through participating in the use of pictures, stories, music, and conversation relevant to growing in love, understanding, and responsibility.

537

Through engaging in creative activities which help him to explore, express, and release his feelings, and to develop and test his ideas.

3. **What may the learner achieve within this theme in the fulfillment of the Learning Tasks? What are possible changes or learnings on the part of the learner that may result from his appropriation of the significance and value discovered? These changes or learnings may be associated with skills, attitudes, motivations, perceptions including understandings and appreciations.**

The young child may begin to develop a sense of trust in persons and security in living that are basic to Christian maturity.

The young child may discover and accept himself as a worthwhile individual, which helps him respond to his inner urge to grow.

The young child may become aware of and begin to accept other persons as part of a developing concern for their well-being.

The young child may develop the ability to interact with others in ways that are related to growth in Christ.

The young child may develop a beginning awareness of growth according to God's will as something to be desired.

The young child may develop a beginning sense of responsibility for making appropriate decisions and playing one's part as a Christian in his family and in his gradually expanding world.

The young child may become aware of Jesus as a person of special significance.

The young child may develop an awareness of the Bible as an important book in the lives of growing persons who love God.

The young child may begin to have an interest and satisfaction in participating in the relationships and some of the observances and other activities of the Christian community.

4. Growing Up in Christ

STATEMENT OF THE THEME

The faithful son cultivates his relationship of faith, love, and obedience toward God; he also cultivates love for his fellowmen. In the power of the Holy Spirit, he grows in grace and develops toward Christian maturity. His quest for personal significance and for a richly satisfying life is answered with increasing meaning.

ELEMENTARY YEARS

1. Significance of the theme for this age level

   a. Meanings and experiences within this theme relevant for this age level. This is content, a selected part of Scope.

Growing up in Christ is personal, continuing growth in Christlikeness.

Human love and forgiveness are foundations for experiences of God's love.

Growing up in Christ requires involvement in the Christian heritage, including the Bible as a source of meaning for growth in grace and development toward Christian maturity.

To grow up in Christ involves the development of personal value systems in light of the gospel.

Growing as children of God requires the establishing of goals in harmony with his will and the developing of inner disciplines to achieve these goals.

Growing up in Christ requires the relating to other persons according to Christian values.

Growing in sonship includes experiences of prayer and worship.

Persons grow up in Christ in the context of the Christian community which is set in the world.

539

1. Significance of the theme for this age level

b. Readiness of the learner for this theme in terms of basic needs, interests, motivations, capacities, developmental tasks.

The child's tendency to ask why about every new meaning, responsibility, or action evidences his readiness to begin to explore the demand of the Christian life for growth.

The fact that a child is already in the midst of growth toward maturity may indicate his readiness to grow up in Christlike ways which enhance and transform the experience of maturation.

Readiness for growth in the Christian life is evident in the fact that the child is aware that growth is expected of him in all areas of life, e.g., intellectual, social, psychological, and physical.

The child's desire for acceptance, as evidenced in his relationships with his peers, his family, and his adult leaders, enables him to respond to his acceptance by God who enables him to grow in Christ.

The child's desire to be a significant person is evidence of his readiness to develop the spiritual aspects of his life.

The child's sense of anticipation helps him respond favorably to the promises in Christian growth.

A child's readiness for Christian growth is evident in the satisfactions he receives from the various aspects of growth, i.e., mental, physical, and social.

The child's ability to sense the attitudes and feelings of peers and adults of his acquaintance gives evidence of a growing capacity to sense the spirit of God as it is expressed in persons.

The increasing ability of a child to read and study books and to use other resources within his range of understanding witnesses to his readiness to relate to those parts of the Bible which are comprehensible to him, some of which may inspire growth in Christ.

The child's readiness to respond to the love of persons by emulating them is evidence of his readiness to respond to the love of God as expressed in Jesus Christ.

The child's capacity for loyalty to the home, the church, the school and the community gives evidence of his readiness to be loyal to Jesus Christ and respond to his presence in his life with growing obedience.

The growing ability of the child to discern between right and wrong, the capacity to begin formulating his own value system, and an increasing readiness for self-discipline contribute to a readiness to grow in the way of Christ.

2. How may this content be communicated as the learner engages in the Learning Tasks? What are the methods and procedures by which the learner may explore the meanings and experiences within this theme (1-a) in the light of his readiness (1-b) in order to discover significance and value?

Through the child's acquaintance and friendship with persons whose lives exemplify growing up in Christ (personal association, indirect contact with persons portrayed in the Bible, biographies, daily newspapers).

Through the child's association with persons of different races, cultures, and religions by means of travel, contacts in the home, school, and church.

541

By studying (directed and free) the Bible, history and literature in which light is thrown (negatively and/or positively) on this theme, the increasing scientific knowledge about humanity and the universe viewed in the Christian perspective.

Through meaningful group experiences, such as camping, clubs, field trips, hikes in which the Christian disciplines and human relationships associated with growing up in Christ may be tested and practiced.

Through involvement in the life of the church especially in corporate worship and in observances throughout the Christian year.

Through participation in, and conversation about events in the family, such as birthdays, new babies, death.

Through opportunities to express feelings and thoughts about growing up in Christ through the arts and play.

Through opportunities to make decisions in concrete situations and to live with the consequences.

Through experiences with the mass media (TV, newspapers, comic books, radio, movies) as occasions for exploring the meaning of faith in God through Christ.

542

3. **What may the learner achieve within this theme in the fulfillment of the Learning Tasks? What are possible changes or learnings on the part of the learner that may result from his appropriation of the significance and value discovered? These changes or learnings may be associated with skills, attitudes, motivations, perceptions including understandings and appreciations.**

The child may increase his understanding of God as revealed in Jesus Christ, and his sense of dependence upon God.

The child may increase his ability to recognize and sort out values, and to accept and live by those values that are in harmony with the gospel.

The child may develop increasing skill in using the artifacts of the Christian heritage, especially the Bible.

The child may find increased satisfaction in the associations within the Christian community and in his experiences of growing up in Christ.

The child may grow in his respect for persons, in concern for others, and in appreciation for the property and rights of others.

The child may grow in his willingness to assume increasing responsibilities in family, church, community, school, and other groups.

The child may achieve wider knowledge and deeper appreciation of cultures, races, and religions other than his own.

The child may gain an increasing ability to set personal standards and goals, and to follow them, including discrimination in making choices and accepting the consequences of choices.

4. Growing Up in Christ

STATEMENT OF THE THEME

The faithful son cultivates his relationship of faith, love, and obedience toward God; he also cultivates love for his fellowmen. In the power of the Holy Spirit, he grows in grace and develops toward Christian maturity. His quest for personal significance and for a richly satisfying life is answered with increasing meaning.

YOUTH

1. Significance of the theme for this age level

a. Meanings and experiences within this theme relevant for this age level. This is content, a selected part of Scope.

Faith in God through Christ stimulates and informs the experience of becoming a mature person and a mature Christian.

To grow up in Christ is to engage in a lifelong process of transformation and development.

Faith in God through Christ enables persons to find direction and increasing significance in their lives.

Talents and abilities are gifts of God to be used in the service of self and others as a person struggles to become a mature Christian.

Fellowship with others in the Christian community is an essential element in the life of a growing Christian.

The truth revealed in Christ is the foundation for the standards, value systems, and goals of growing Christians.

The spirit of God at work in man creates tension between what he is and what he knows he should be.

543

Sin is separation and estrangement from God and from fellow human beings, therefore it inhibits Christian growth.

The Bible has an important role in Christian growth because it witnesses to the truth of God's purpose for man and his redemptive action in Christ.

Life confronts persons with certain challenges to growth, which can be met only through faith in God through Christ.

Responding to neighbors in light of God's loving concern is an important part of growing up in Christ.

544

The Holy Spirit cultivates growth to mature faith and guides growing persons as they express God's redeeming love for the world.

Persons grow up in Christ in the context of the Christian community which is set in the world.

1. Significance of the theme for this age level

b. Readiness of the learner for this theme in terms of basic needs, interests, motivations, capacities, developmental tasks.

Youth desire maturity and fulfillment.

Youth have the capacity for, and the innate drive toward learning, and live in a culture that expects youth to grow physically, mentally, emotionally, socially, and spiritually.

Youth are inquisitive concerning the nature, meaning, and purpose of life.

Youth are motivated to discover what is true and false, right and wrong.

Youth have a strong desire for selfhood, personal acceptance, and integrity along with the desire for acceptance by their peers and others.

Youth are often eager to identify with outstanding individuals and worthy causes.

Youth desire to discover and develop personal potentialities, talents, and other gifts.

Youth have the capacity to establish meaningful person-to-person relations, both with God and their fellowman.

Youth desire to make their decisions freely and have the capacity to make them responsibly.

Youth are able to recognize their strengths and weaknesses, and deal with them.

Youth have a marked ability to study the Bible as a source of guidance for developing their lives.

Youth have the capacity to think abstractly and to make decisions on the basis of rational judgment.

Youth have a drive to get the most out of life.

2. **How may this content be communicated as the learner engages in the Learning Tasks? What are the methods and procedures by which the learner may explore the meanings and experiences within this theme (1-a) in the light of his readiness (1-b) in order to discover significance and value?**

Through study of the biblical records and other sources of the Christian heritage which reveal the nature of mature sonship and its importance for growing up.

Through personal involvement in the arts—such as paintings, dramas, music, and literature—which treat the meaning and experiences of this theme.

Through opportunities to study the nature of human development and growth as interpreted by the social and behavioral sciences in order to take these into account for Christian growth.

Through association and dialogue with other Christians, individually or in groups.

Through meaningful experiences of personal, family, and corporate worship of which a by-product is inspiration and reinforcement for Christian growth.

Through participation in the fellowship and activities of the church which contribute to Christian growth.

Through opportunities for making individual and group decisions in light of the gospel.

545

By studying the lives and works of Christians through the centuries which reveal their concepts and understandings of growing up in Christ.

Through involvement of persons in attempts to understand the implications of contemporary issues, events, and problems in light of the gospel, which have a bearing on growing up in Christ.

Through opportunities for formal and informal study and discussion with peers and with persons across the life span which contribute to the understanding of maturing in sonship.

Through meaningful relationships with persons of differing cultures, races, nationalities, and creeds which provide opportunity to verbalize and reflect upon concepts of Christian maturity.

3. What may the learner achieve within this theme in the fulfillment of the Learning Tasks? What are possible changes or learnings on the part of the learner that may result from his appropriation of the significance and value discovered? These changes or learnings may be associated with skills, attitudes, motivations, perceptions including understandings and appreciations.

The young person may give evidence of developing maturity as a Christian when he responds to God's love in thanksgiving, repentance, and trust.

Youth may increase in the ability to deal with their powers and limitations in ways that foster growth in sonship.

Youth may become more able and willing to relate to other persons with ever-deepening love and concern and with increasing inclusiveness.

Youth may increasingly make decisions having to do with standards, values, and goals on the basis of their faith in God through Christ.

The young Christian may develop in the willingness and skill required to accept the tensions between what he is and what he knows he should be as stimuli for continued growth in Christ.

Youth may grow in the ability to surmount sin, that is, estrangement from God and man, by faithful acceptance of the forgiveness of God, by reliance upon the Holy Spirit in newness of life, and by ever deepening devotion to Christ.

The young person may accept more consistently and more responsibly his place and role in the Christian community.

The young person may grow in the use of his intellectual powers under the influence of the Holy Spirit to refine his faith in God through Christ.

The young person may grow in his acceptance of the self-disciplines and sacrifice essential for Christian maturity.

The young person may grow in his knowledge of the Christian faith and in his ability to articulate it and act upon it.

Youth may become increasingly aware of his relation as steward to material things and of his obligation to use them in Christian ways.

The young person may become more skillful in developing his personal gifts and in using them responsibly and for the achievement of appropriate Christian purposes.

The young person may become more highly motivated to know the will of God for his life and to commit himself to it.

The young person may become more sensitive to the hurt he inflicts upon others, more willing to offer restitution and to ask and accept forgiveness.

547

Youth may discover with increasing clarity the joys and satisfactions that accrue from the life in Christ.

4. Growing Up in Christ

STATEMENT OF THE THEME

The faithful son cultivates his relationship of faith, love, and obedience toward God; he also cultivates love for his fellowmen. In the power of the Holy Spirit, he grows in grace and develops toward Christian maturity. His quest for personal significance and for a richly satisfying life is answered with increasing meaning.

ADULTHOOD

1. Significance of the theme for this age level

a. **Meanings and experiences within this theme relevant for this age level. This is content, a selected part of Scope.**

Faith in Christ stimulates growth toward mature living.

Christ engages persons in a lifelong process of transformation and development.

Faith in Christ answers the basic questions of human existence thus enabling persons to find increasing significance in their lives.

Talents and abilities are gifts of God to be used in the process of growing up in Christ.

Fellowship with others in the Christian community is an essential element in the life of a growing Christian.

The truth revealed in Christ is the foundation for the standards, value systems, and goals of growing Christians.

The spirit of God at work in man creates tension between what he is and what he knows he should be.

Sin is recognized and dealt with as a hindrance to Christian growth.

The Bible is important to Christian growth because it witnesses to the truth of God's purpose for man and his redemptive action in Christ.

Life confronts persons with challenges to growth which is possible only through faith in Christ.

Seeing neighbors in light of God's loving concern is an important part of growing up in Christ.

The Holy Spirit cultivates growth to mature faith and guides growing persons as they express God's redeeming love for the world.

Persons grow up in Christ in the context of the Christian community which is set in the world.

1. Significance of the theme for this age level

b. Readiness of the learner for this theme in terms of basic needs, interests, motivations, capacities, developmental tasks.

Adults want to be considered mature and seek fulfillment.

Adults recognize that the culture expects persons to improve themselves in a variety of ways.

Adults are concerned about the meaning and end of life.

It is necessary for adults to discover for themselves what is true and false, right and wrong.

Adults have a strong desire for selfhood, self-acceptance, and integrity, along with the desire for acceptance by their peers and others.

Adults have a readiness to be associated with purposeful individuals and with worthy causes.

Adults desire to discover and develop personal potentialities, talents, and other gifts.

Adults have the ability to establish meaningful person-to-person relations, both with God and their fellowman.

During most of their lives, adults are faced with necessity of making rational judgments and of making decisions and abiding by them.

Adults have the ability for self-criticism which is the basis for overcoming inadequacies and enhancing strengths.

2. How may this content be communicated as the learner engages in the Learning Tasks? What are the methods and procedures by which the learner may explore the meanings and experiences within this theme (1-a) in the light of his readiness (1-b) in order to discover significance and value?

549

Through study of the biblical records and other sources of the Christian heritage which disclose the nature of Christlikeness and its importance for maturity and significance in life.

Through personal involvement in the arts—such as painting, drama, music, and literature—which treat the meaning and experiences of this theme.

Through opportunities to study the nature of human development within the adult years as interpreted by the social and behavioral sciences in order to take these into account for Christian maturity.

Through association and dialogue with other Christians, individually or in groups.

Through meaningful experiences of personal, family, and corporate worship of which a by-product is inspiration and reinforcement for Christian growth.

Through participation in the fellowship and activities of the church which contribute to Christian growth.

Through opportunities for making individual and group decisions in light of the gospel.

Through involvement of persons in attempts to understand the implications of contemporary issues, events, and problems in light of the gospel which have a bearing on growing up in Christ.

Through studying the lives and works of Christians through the centuries which reveal their concepts and understandings of growing up in Christ.

Through opportunities for formal and informal study and discussion with peers and with persons across the life span which contribute to the understanding of maturing in sonship.

Through meaningful relationships with persons of differing cultures, races, nationalities, and creeds which provide opportunity to verbalize and reflect upon concepts of Christian maturity.

3. **What may the learner achieve within this theme in the fulfillment of the Learning Tasks? What are possible changes or learnings on the part of the learner that may result from his appropriation of the significance and value discovered? These changes or learnings may be associated with skills, attitudes, motivations, perceptions including understandings and appreciations.**

The growing person gives evidence of developing maturity in his expressions of confession, repentance, trust, thanksgiving, love, forgiveness, and understanding.

Faith in Christ becomes more meaningful as it provides insights into the meaning and purpose of human existence and as it guides each step toward maturity and fulfillment in the Christian life.

The individual deals with his own potentialities and limitations in a creative manner.

The growing Christian relates to other persons with ever-deepening love and concern and with increasing inclusiveness.

Standards, values, and goals derived from knowledge of Christ and faith in him become the basis of decision-making.

The growing Christian accepts the tensions between what he is and what he knows he should be as a stimulus for continued growth.

551

Sin and estrangement are recognized as hindrances to Christian growth which may be surmounted by ever-deepening devotion to Christ, reliance upon the Holy Spirit, and the forgiveness of God.

Active engagement in Bible study, prayer, worship, the practices of church membership, and witness in the world characterize the growing Christian.

Growing Christians meet the challenges of evil in the world with responses based on their Christian faith.

Persons who are growing up in Christ relate to their neighbors with love which is expressed in service.

The faith of growing Christians is being continuously refined in the fires of the human mind under the influence of the Holy Spirit and in the crucible of human relations.

The growing Christian accepts discipline and sacrifice as essential for witness.

The person who is growing up in Christ develops a growing knowledge of the Christian faith and an increasing ability to articulate it and act upon it.

552

The adult may become more sensitive and resolute in using his total resources responsibly and for the achievement of appropriate Christian purposes.

Persons who are growing up in Christ evidence a desire to know the will of God for their lives and a willingness to follow it.

5. Finding Identity in the Christian Community

STATEMENT OF THE THEME

Man's persistent need for meaningful belonging is met when, as God's child, he accepts his role and relationships in the Christian community, the church. The reconciled son takes his place in the family of God, vitally related to his brothers in Christ.

EARLY CHILDHOOD

1. Significance of the theme for this age level

a. Meanings and experiences within this theme relevant for this age level. This is content, a selected part of Scope.

The young child has a place in the Christian community.

The young child is accepted, loved, listened to, and cared for in and by the Christian community.

It is good to be with people who are in the Christian community.

As a part of the Christian community the young child can help and share in the life and work of the church.

The Christian community exists wherever there are Christians, whether in family, or in the congregation.

The Christian community is made up of people of varying ages, races, and nationalities who love Jesus Christ.

1. Significance of the theme for this age level

b. Readiness of the learner for this theme in terms of basic needs, interests, motivations, capacities, developmental tasks.

The young child is completely dependent, physically and emotionally, on those who care for him.

The young child needs to achieve trust and establish himself as an individual in his own right.

The young child is sensitive to approval and to disapproval, to the attitudes and example of others.

The young child is seeking to establish himself as a person capable of having ideas, and of initiating and carrying out activity.

Love, acceptance, and care are necessary to the health and development of a young child.

The young child begins to explore in the world of persons beyond himself and his family.

The young child is increasingly able to make friends and to share ideas and experiences with others.

The young child imitates others.

553

2. How may this content be communicated as the learner engages in the Learning Tasks? What are the methods and procedures by which the learner may explore the meanings and experiences within this theme (1-a) in the light of his readiness (1-b) in order to discover significance and value?

By living in a home in which persons love God and seek to express that love in relationships with other persons.

By entering into the give and take of interpersonal relationships with his peers and others in the church.

By being known individually and by name by persons in the church.

By acting out and talking about the roles he has observed in the life drama of older children and adults.

By taking part in music, sharing toys, games, and refreshments with others in the Christian community.

By assuming responsibilities of which he is capable in the Christian community, e.g., hanging up one's personal effects and putting the toys away after play.

By exploring within the permissive and secure relationship of the Christian fellowship the increasingly wider ranges of life.

By observing and entering into relationships with persons of other ages, races, nationalities within the framework of the church.

By taking part in a Christian community other than the home in which persons love God and seek to express that love in relation to other persons.

3. **What may the learner achieve within this theme in the fulfillment of the Learning Tasks? What are possible changes or learnings on the part of the learner that may result from his appropriation of the significance and value discovered? These changes or learnings may be associated with skills, attitudes, motivations, perceptions including understandings and appreciations.**

The young child may achieve an acquaintance and relationship with persons in the Christian community who love Jesus Christ.

The young child may achieve a developing awareness that he is a person of worth who is loved by his parents and by other significant adults in the Christian community.

The young child may achieve a beginning ability to express love to parents and to other members of his family.

The young child may achieve a beginning awareness that to help and share with others in the Christian community is a means of expressing his belonging to the group.

The young child may achieve a growing desire to see other children have the benefits of the love and care of parents and of God.

The young child may achieve a beginning appreciation for Christian persons of varying races and nationalities.

The young child may achieve a sense of pleasure and joy at being with others in the Christian community.

The young child may achieve a beginning sense of "This is my church."

The young child may achieve a growing sense of at-homeness with others in the Christian community.

5. Finding Identity in the Christian Community

STATEMENT OF THE THEME

Man's persistent need for meaningful belonging is met when, as God's child, he accepts his role and relationships in the Christian community, the church. The reconciled son takes his place in the family of God, vitally related to his brothers in Christ.

555

ELEMENTARY YEARS

1. Significance of the theme for this age level

    a. Meanings and experiences within this theme relevant for this age level. This is content, a selected part of Scope.

Within this theme the meanings and experiences relevant for the elementary child are:

Christians are members of one family by virtue of the commonality of their individual relationships to God through Christ.

A sense of personal involvement with others in the Christian community constitutes a major expression of being a mature Christian.

Finding one's identity in the Christian community means, in part, serving God through serving others, sharing their struggles, sorrows, victories, joys.

556

A person may first find his identity within the Christian community through the home.

The environment of love and acceptance which is the basic nature of the church fosters finding one's identity.

Finding one's identity within the Christian community involves discovering areas of personal responsibility and service.

Making evident an atmosphere of acceptance and concern to those outside the Christian community is possible because God has called Christians so to relate to one another and to the world.

Becoming "members one of another" is fostered through sharing in experiences of worship, study, service, witnessing, fellowship.

Christians of all races and nationalities are called to discover their mutuality as well as their particularity within the Christian community.

Finding one's identity within the Christian community is expedited by a willingness to follow Christ's principles and directives for making choices and determining behavior.

One may find his identity in any expression of the Christian community, regardless of its structure.

Each person, including me, is important in and to the Christian community.

1. Significance of the theme for this age level

b. Readiness of the learner for this theme in terms of basic

needs, interests, motivations, capacities, developmental tasks.

The child has an interest in establishing friendships and sharing ideas and experiences with his peers.

The child has a capacity to distinguish differences in the life styles of persons with whom he is acquainted.

The child has a proclivity toward hero worship, admiring, imitating, and identifying with more mature persons whose characteristics appeal to him.

The child has an increasing perception of historical and geographical realities; he is becoming less dependent on the immediate presence of persons to perceive their reality.

The child's range of personal contacts with others is increasing, providing him opportunities for relating directly to a wider fellowship.

The child's desire to be included as a member of what are to him significant groups gives him a readiness to accept the standards, attitudes, and values of those groups.

The child has a beginning drive to understand for himself who he is, what he should be and do, and why.

2. How may this content be communicated as the learner engages in the Learning Tasks? What are the methods and procedures by which the learner may explore the meanings and experiences within this theme (1-a) in the light of his readiness (1-b) in order to discover significance and value?

557

By having an opportunity to observe a fellowship of persons who love and follow Jesus Christ as Savior and Lord.

By being welcomed by a Christian congregation as a follower of Jesus Christ, being allowed as a person of worth to share all phases of the congregation's life appropriate to his age and level of ability.

By being given opportunities to look for and discover his sequential roles within the church fellowship, supported by a spirit of love and acceptance.

By meeting and becoming acquainted with Christians of other races and nationalities.

By reading and hearing about the Bible, the history, and the heritage of the church with which he is associated.

By having opportunities to discuss what are the demands of the gospel for him and his peer group in terms of his church's ministries.

By making a contribution in worship, commensurate with his age and experience (through music, drama, reading of sections of the service).

By learning about, writing to, meeting with, perhaps actually working with, others who are engaged in specific projects of ministry in the community, nation, or world.

By initiating, taking part in, or leading, worship and service within the home.

3. **What may the learner achieve within this theme in the fulfillment of the Learning Tasks? What are possible changes or learnings on the part of the learner that may result from his appropriation of the significance and value discovered? These changes or learnings may be associated with skills, attitudes, motivations, perceptions including understandings and appreciations.**

The child may achieve an increasing awareness of his family's membership in the family of Christians that is the church.

The child may achieve a beginning recognition that God has a purpose for his life and a desire to fulfill it.

The child may achieve a start at identifying himself with those within the Christian community whose lives reflect a dedication to Christ as Lord.

The child may achieve the beginnings of a conceptual structure, based on the gospel, that can become the foundation for the development of his system of values.

The child may achieve an increasing sense of personal involvement and integration with others within the Christian community.

The child may achieve a maturing view of and appreciation of his parents as servants of Christ.

The child may achieve a deeper appreciation for and support of the home of which he is a part.

The child may achieve the development of relationships with particular persons within the Christian community that tie him into that community.

The child may achieve a willingness to attempt personal roles which exemplify the qualities of life characteristic of a follower of Christ.

The child may achieve an affinity for those in his peer group (school, church, play, work) whose choices are premised mainly on the value system of the Christian community.

The child may achieve a desire to contribute personally to the mending of broken relationships within his group.

The child may achieve a growing willingness and ability to understand and accept as persons those with whom he may come into conflict.

The child may achieve a developing sense of need for and desire to unite formally with the church.

The child may achieve a beginning awareness of the ecumenical nature of the Christian community.

The child may achieve increasing ability to differentiate actions that reflect dedication to Christ as Lord.

559

5. Finding Identity in the Christian Community

STATEMENT OF THE THEME

Man's persistent need for meaningful belonging is met when, as God's child, he accepts his role and relationships in the Christian community, the church. The reconciled son takes his place in the family of God, vitally related to his brothers in Christ.

YOUTH

1. Significance of the theme for this age level

a. Meanings and experiences within this theme relevant for this age level. This is content, a selected part of Scope.

560

The Christian community, embracing all persons who are responding to God's redeeming love, offers relationships at a distinctively significant level.

Identification with the Christian community adds a necessary dimension to one's relationship with the eternal God.

Identification with the Christian community is implied by commitment to God in Christ.

The Christian community is the supportive environment in which youth's growing relationship with Jesus Christ can develop and be nourished.

Identification with the Christian community involves acceptance of some common standards, attitudes, and values in the corporate life and action of the community.

The Christian community is a source from which one may expect guidance and encouragement in Christian living and opportunities for common experiences in growth as a Christian.

Identity with the church universal usually comes through responsible identification with the local Christian community.

Identification with the Christian community implies accepting responsibility for the decisions, the ministries, the failures, the mutual care and support of the members of that community—gathered as family, congregation, denomination, or scattered in the world.

The family or a peer group may be a means by which one initially identifies himself with the Christian community.

Identification with members of the Christian community may help clarify an individual's self-image as a Christian.

Finding identity in the Christian community involves relating to its members on the basis of love and active concern.

1. Significance of the theme for this age level

b. Readiness of the learner for this theme in terms of basic needs, interests, motivations, capacities, developmental tasks.

The young person is seeking to find his own identity—his self-hood—in relation to society as well as individually.

Youth are at the height of the tension between childhood's dependence and adult independence.

Youth are testing to see whether various institutions offer valid guidelines to living—standards, attitudes, and values.

Youth tend to build a self-image with reference to persons and groups significant to them.

Youth like to experiment with various roles and responsibilities.

Youth need help in seeing the relationship between personal commitment to Christ and identity with the corporate Christian community.

Young people are increasingly aware of the world beyond their immediate horizon and the interrelation of various communities of which they are a part.

Youth seek ways to express their idealism.

Young people desperately seek acceptance by others.

Youth need and want to be identified with significant groups.

Parents and parent figures are a strong force in the life of youth.

Youth seek guidance toward actions and attitudes which help them appropriately relate dependence and independence.

Youth yearn for some way to engage in deep and meaningful communication with others.

561

2. How may this content be communicated as the learner engages in the Learning Tasks? What are the methods and procedures by which the learner may explore the meanings and experiences within this theme (1-a) in the light of his readiness (1-b) in order to discover significance and value?

By searching for identity in the Christian community through interpersonal relationships with other Christians.

By engaging in corporate worship, making use of expressions that call for his emotional involvement.

By being encouraged to offer ideas, skills, insights in the life and work of the church.

By study of scripture, theology, history related to the nature of the church and the interrelatedness of Christians.

By getting acquainted with persons in the Christian community from various cultures, nations, confessions.

Through participation in groups in which an atmosphere of acceptance is characteristic.

Through study of the life and setting of the early Christian church as an organism—not just as an organization.

Through study of the life and work of the world church, both in history and in current times.

Through family devotions and decisions of Christians in the family toward all of life.

By participating in making decisions and carrying out responsibilities of the congregation.

By participating with persons of other denominations in dealing at a significant level with subjects relevant to the needs of young people.

By being accepted by others in the Christian community.

By trying out as his own, the patterns of action, standards, attitudes, and values which the Christian community understands to be consistent with the faith.

By observing other members of the Christian community living out their faith in their daily work.

3. **What may the learner achieve within this theme in the fulfillment of the Learning Tasks? What are possible changes or learnings on the part of the learner that may result from his appropriation of the significance and value discovered? These changes or learnings may be associated with skills, attitudes, motivations, perceptions including understandings and appreciations.**

Youth may achieve a discovery that he is a member of something called "the Christian community," in the family, in his city or township, and around the world.

Youth may achieve acceptance of the responsibilities as well as privileges that membership in the Christian community brings.

Youth may achieve a willingness to accept some attitudes, values, and standards seen as consistent with life in the Christian community.

Youth may achieve an increasing desire and ability to accept himself and others.

Youth may achieve increasing freedom to communicate his deepest yearnings to others in the Christian community.

Youth may achieve a sense of support from the Christian community in times of trouble or in his efforts to live out his commitment to Christ.

Youth may achieve deepened concern for other members of the Christian community and a willingness to find ways to express such concern.

Youth may achieve seeing more clearly his goals in life and their relation to the mission of the Christian community in God's plan.

Youth may achieve an awareness that his role in the home, both as a growing child and later as a homemaker, is one of responsibility in the effectiveness of the home as an expression of the Christian community.

Youth may achieve a deepened relationship with God and the people of God.

Youth may achieve a beginning willingness to partake of responsibility for the failures, the decisions, the ministries, the mutual care and support of fellow members in the Christian community.

Youth may achieve an appreciation of the variety of gifts, insights, roles, functions which others contribute in the life and work of the Christian community (home, congregation, denomination, interdenominational community, ecumenical church).

564

Youth may achieve increasingly responsible participation in the life and work of the Christian community.

Youth may achieve new motivation for developing his capacities for carrying out the ministry of the Christian community.

Youth may achieve increased ability and desire to offer support to others in the Christian community.

Youth may achieve an increasing willingness to relate to others in the Christian community at a significant level.

5. Finding Identity in the Christian Community

STATEMENT OF THE THEME

Man's persistent need for meaningful belonging is met when, as God's child, he accepts his role and relationships in the Christian community, the church. The reconciled son takes his place in the family of God, vitally related to his brothers in Christ.

ADULTHOOD

1. Significance of the theme for this age level

a. Meanings and experiences within this theme relevant for this age level. This is content, a selected part of Scope.

Identification with the Christian community is implied by one's acknowledgment of Jesus Christ as Lord and Savior.

One's self-image as a person is put in proper perspective as one finds identity in the Christian community.

The concept of "members one of another" embraces the Christian community in its expression in the home, the congregation, the denomination, the interdenominational community, the ecumenical church.

The mutual love which is the distinguishing quality of fellowship within the church permits honest appraisal of one's role in and contribution to the Christian community.

Christians have responsibility to help and support one another in the search for identity in the Christian community.

Identity in the Christian community finds expression not only in the gathered church but also in the dispersion of Christians in home, community, nation, and world.

Every person in the Christian community has contributions to make, functions to perform necessary to the community's fulfillment of its mission.

An understanding of the nature of the church helps one establish his identity in it.

The Christian community is by nature an organism of complementing members rather than an association of separate persons.

1. Significance of the theme for this age level

a. Meanings and experiences within this theme relevant for this age level. This is content, a selected part of Scope.

A sense of identity is necessary to adequately carry out adult responsibilities.

Identity within groups is a necessary part of the adult's identity as an individual.

The adult needs support from those who hold a philosophy similar to his as he attempts to live out his personal commitment in his relationships with others.

The adult finds satisfaction in discovering and carrying out roles, functions, responsibilities appropriate to him.

Man continues to want to be a part of groups that seem to him significant.

The adult is capable of worldwide extension of the idea of membership one of another.

Adulthood implies a fund of varied experiences which can form the raw material for assessing his abilities and potential contributions to groups.

The experience of aging and withdrawing from activity in the economic and social scene may intensify the need for respect and appreciation as a contributing member of the Christian community.

Adults are in a crucial position to influence the structure and life of the Christian community in its varied expressions so that it may be conducive to person's finding their identity in it.

Many groups and situations in which adults are involved tend to facilitate the loss of identity rather than the establishment of it.

2. How may this content be communicated as the learner engages in the Learning Tasks? What are the methods and procedures by which the learner may explore the meanings and experiences within this theme (1-a) in the light of his readiness (1-b) in order to discover significance and value?

Through interpersonal relationshps with other Christians who are finding their identity in the Christian community.

By participating in family and in corporate worship.

By taking advantage of opportunities for service to others both within and outside the Christian community.

By studying the biblical passages that throw light on the essential relationship among God's people in the life and work of that community.

Through participation in groups open and receptive to all persons.

By receiving support and encouragement from others as one

attempts to assess and carry out his possible contributions to the Christian community.

Through study of the life and setting of the early Christian church, its approximation of true community, and the place of individuals in it.

Through study of the work of the world church, both in history and in current times.

By getting acquainted with and working with Christians of various ages, confessions, nationalities, and cultures.

By being encouraged to carry responsibility appropriate to his abilities in the life of the Christian community.

By taking part in groups dealing with subjects which matter and are relevant to their needs.

By being accepted by others at home, in the congregation, and elsewhere as a person with contributions to make to the life and ministry of the Christian community.

By working out together with others in the Christian community valid patterns of action, standards, attitudes, and values appropriate to the Christian community in its own corporate life and in its witness as a scattered community.

By receiving support and encouragement from others in the Christian community as he attempts to live out his faith in his daily work.

567

By participating in opportunities to express and witness to his Christian commitment through creative arts such as drama, painting, and writing.

By becoming acquainted with the variety of functions, roles, and tasks that are necessary to be carried out for the Christian community to fulfill its mission.

3. **What may the learner achieve within this theme in the fulfillment of the Learning Tasks? What are possible changes or learnings on the part of the learner that may result from his appropriation of the significance and value discovered?**

These changes or learnings may be associated with skills, attitudes, motivations, perceptions including understandings and appreciations.

The adult may achieve a deepened understanding of the mutuality of members in "the Christian community," in the family, in his city or township, and around the world.

The adult may achieve increasing willingness to take initiative in identifying and assuming responsibility for the quality of life and work in the Christian community.

The adult may achieve courage and strength to live by attitudes, values, and standards derived from Christian commitment rather than from society.

The adult may achieve a willingness and ability to accept and bear responsibility for others in the Christian community.

The adult may achieve increased ability and desire to communicate his deepest yearnings to others in the Christian community.

The adult may achieve increased desire and ability to help others find acceptance and identity in the Christian community.

The adult may achieve a sense of support from the Christian community in times of trouble or in his attempt to live out his Christian commitment.

The adult may achieve a wider sphere of loving concern for those in spiritual or physical need, and increased initiative in finding ways to express such concern.

The adult may achieve clearer perception of his goals in life and their relation to the mission of the Christian community in God's plan.

The adult may achieve insight into the role of the home in helping persons find their identity as sons of God.

The adult may achieve a deepening relationship with God and with other Christians which increasingly frees him to be the person God intends him to be.

The adult may achieve a willingness to make available to the

Christian community, locally or ecumenically, contributions he may have for its effective ministry.

The adult may achieve a deepened sense of humility and dependence on God's guidance in individual and corporate discipleship.

The adult may achieve a new sense of joy and purpose in living as one committed to Jesus Christ.

The adult may achieve a greater freedom from legalistic conformity to external patterns of behavior.

6. The Christian's Hope Rests in the Triumphant God

STATEMENT OF THE THEME

Man's tendency to be dissatisfied with the present, his uncertainty about the future, and his need to be vitally related to the eternally significant are addressed through the experience of the Christian hope in God's ultimate triumph in and over history. This hope includes the assurance of eternal life and the consummation of the kingdom of God.

EARLY CHILDHOOD

1. Significance of the theme for this age level

569

a. Meanings and experiences within this theme relevant for this age level. This is content, a selected part of Scope.

It is natural and desirable that all things and all people die. God loves and cares for people when they are alive and also when they die.

Jesus lived and died and lives forever.

Persons who love God do not fear death.

God rules the heavens and the earth.

God rules and blesses the people who love him; he blesses but overrules the people who do not love him.

1. Significance of the theme for this age level

b. Readiness of the learner for this theme in terms of basic needs, interests, motivations, capacities, developmental tasks.

The young child's need for love and for a feeling of security make him ready to learn of God's love and care in life and in death.

The young child's exposure to pictures and events in the public realm related to Jesus' death and resurrection stimulates wonder and questions.

The young child's beginning awareness and curiosity about the fact of death make him ready to learn of God's love in life and in death.

The young child's interest in the natural world helps him in observing God's sovereignty over all of life.

The young child's sense of beauty, awe, and wonder give the young child a readiness for response to God's rule in all of life.

2. How may this content be communicated as the learner engages in the Learning Tasks? What are the methods and procedures by which the learner may explore the meanings and experiences within this theme (1-a) in the light of his readiness (1-b) in order to discover significance and value?

Through hearing Bible stories which illustrate the Christian hope.

Through hearing Bible stories about Jesus which are appropriate to the theme.

Through singing songs which express joy and gratitude for God's never-ending love and care.

Through association with persons and groups whose lives express the Christian hope.

Through conversation about death as a part of God's plan and of God's love and care through life and death.

By participating in experiences of worship which express the Christian hope.

By receiving loving care and acceptance which foster a sense of security from persons whose lives express the Christian hope.

3. **What may the learner achieve within this theme in the fulfillment of the Learning Tasks? What are possible changes or learnings on the part of the learner that may result from his appropriation of the significance and value discovered? These changes or learnings may be associated with skills, attitudes, motivations, perceptions including understandings and appreciations.**

The young child may achieve a beginning realization that God created and cares for all persons and things.

The young child may begin to appreciate the Bible as the special book that tells about God's never-ending love and care, and about Jesus.

The young child may enjoy being with persons whose lives express the Christian hope.

The young child may have a feeling of security in relationship with persons whose lives express the Christian hope.

The young child may feel joy and gratitude for God's love and care.

571

The young child may begin to recognize that death is a part of God's plan.

The child may come to a beginning realization that God rules all he has created with power and love.

6. The Christian's Hope Rests in the Triumphant God

STATEMENT OF THE THEME

Man's tendency to be dissatisfied with the present, his uncertainty about the future, and his need to be vitally related to the eternally significant are addressed through the experience of the Christian hope in God's ultimate triumph in and over history. This hope includes the assurance of eternal life and the consummation of the kingdom of God.

ELEMENTARY YEARS

1. Significance of the theme for this age level

    a. Meanings and experiences within this theme relevant for this age level. This is content, a selected part of Scope.

Jesus' life, death, and resurrection show God's power over life and death.

The power of God revealed in Jesus Christ is present today in the lives of Christians and in the world.

God made persons to be his children now and after death.

Christians are not afraid of death because the resurrection of Christ gives hope in eternal life.

Persons who do not love God are often afraid of life now and of life in the future.

God is in control of all his creation and, even though wrong often seems to win and right often seems to lose, God's purpose will ultimately win.

Eternal life begins now and lasts forever.

1. Significance of the theme for this age level

    b. Readiness of the learner for this theme in terms of basic needs, interests, motivations, capacities, developmental tasks.

The child questions the meaning of the evil and disaster in the world which he observes or experiences personally.

The child desires and needs a feeling of security even beyond that provided by the home.

The child needs love and acceptance which he feels are permanent and unconditional.

Children are curious about death and what happens after death.

The child is motivated to wonder about the "way the world is run" through observing or personally experiencing the triumph of wrong over right.

The child has a beginning capacity for thinking in time-space categories.

The child's interest in the natural world, and his beginning studies in history and science supply motivation for exploration of God's sovereign rule in all of life.

The child's will to live prepares him for responding to the Christian hope.

2. **How may this content be communicated as the learner engages in the Learning Tasks? What are the methods and procedures by which the learner may explore the meanings and experiences within this theme (1-a) in the light of his readiness (1-b) in order to discover significance and value?**

Through reading, listening to, studying, and discussing Bible material that deals with the life, death, and resurrection of Jesus, the kingdom of God, and the future life.

573

Through reading about, hearing about, and discussing persons, past and present, whose lives witness to the power and love of God.

Through study of the Christian belief in God's ultimate triumph in and over history.

Through association with Christians whose lives radiate confidence in the Christian hope.

Through listening to preaching which sets forth the Christian hope.

Through experiences with the arts—especially music and painting appropriate to the theme.

Through studying and singing hymns which express the Christian hope.

Through conversation about death as a part of God's plan and of God's love and care in this life and beyond.

Through opportunities for personal experiences of prayer and worship that enable the child to grow in his trust in God.

Through opportunities for experiences in the natural world that reveal God's sovereign power in his creation.

3. **What may the learner achieve within this theme in the fulfillment of the Learning Tasks? What are possible changes or learnings on the part of the learner that may result from his appropriation of the significance and value discovered? These changes or learnings may be associated with skills, attitudes, motivations, perceptions including understandings and appreciations.**

The child may begin to understand the relation of the resurrection of Christ to the Christian hope.

The child may achieve a fuller understanding that God is in control of the universe and will finally bring the right to victory.

The child may grow in his love for Christ and be ready to acknowledge him as Lord of life.

The child may begin to develop a personal devotional life in which God's never-ending love is experienced.

The child may grow in his appreciation and understanding of the witness of the Bible to the Christian hope.

The child may begin to incorporate into his life the influence of Christians whose lives show the Christian hope.

The child may grow in his ability to be articulate about the Christian hope in conversation and discussion.

The child may enjoy association with persons whose lives express the Christian hope.

The child may feel at home in the natural world as a world under God's sovereign rule.

The child may accept the naturalness of death as a part of life.

6. The Christian's Hope Rests in the Triumphant God

STATEMENT OF THE THEME

Man's tendency to be dissatisfied with the present, his uncertainty about the future, and his need to be vitally related to the eternally significant are addressed through the experience of the Christian hope in God's ultimate triumph in and over history. This hope includes the assurance of eternal life and the consummation of the kingdom of God.

YOUTH

1. Significance of the theme for this age level

a. Meanings and experiences within this theme relevant for this age level. This is content, a selected part of Scope.

The Christian hope is in the triumph of God's redemptive purpose.

God's creativity, sovereign power, and love as revealed in Jesus Christ are the basis of the Christian hope.

575

The resurrection of Christ gives assurance of his triumph over death and of the reality of eternal life.

He who is without hope in Christ often is uncertain and afraid of life now and of the future.

The power of God revealed in the resurrection of Christ is at work in the life of the Christian, giving meaning to his life now and the hope of eternal salvation.

God is sovereign in his universe and, in spite of all that seems to point to the contrary, will triumph in and over history, bringing evil to defeat and righteousness to victory.

Hope in the triumph of God's kingdom upon earth under-girds the Christian's confidence, security, and expectation.

Eternal life is not the same as endless existence. It is a distinctive quality and style of life—life given by God, lived in fellowship with God, and dedicated to the praise of God.

The Christian, although unable to comprehend all that his hope of eternal life means, believes that ultimately he will be conformed to the image of Christ, and live in fellowship with him.

The nature of life enjoyed in fellowship with God is indestructible—a present experience and a future hope.

576

God created men to be his children in this life as well as in the life to come.

1. Significance of the theme for this age level

b. Readiness of the learner for this theme in terms of basic needs, interests, motivations, capacities, developmental tasks.

Youth's maturing concern about the world situation and the meaning of personal and social existence readies him for understanding the sovereignty and triumph of God and the meaning of eternal life.

Youth are ready to identify with a transcendent cause.

Youth's fear about the future of the world suggests a readiness to understand the meaning of the ultimate triumph of God's redemptive purpose.

The uncertainty of life creates an interest on the part of youth about the basis of the Christian hope.

Youth's awareness of the power of evil in today's world stimulates questions about the rulership of God.

Youth's desire to find significance in his existence opens the opportunity to understand the significance of life revealed in the resurrection of Christ.

Youth is concerned to be vitally related to the eternally significant.

Christian's belief in eternal life speaks to youth's yearning for assurance that death does not end it all.

Youth are curious about the meaning of death, the possibility of life beyond, and the Christian's understanding of eternal life.

Youth have a desire for justice to which the authority, power, and rulership of the Sovereign God speaks.

Youth's desire for ultimate personal security is spoken to in the faith of the Christian that eternal life means fellowship with God now and in the future.

Youth are seeking a philosophy of life and a satisfying system of beliefs and values to which eternal life as a distinctive quality and style of life—life given by God, lived in fellowship with God, and dedicated to the praise of God—forcefully speaks.

Youth in coming to terms with life raise questions about the role of God in history.

Youth's maturing interest in history and science conditions him to an inquisitiveness about life now and in the future.

Youth's concern about vocational choice introduces the struggle for meaning in life now.

Youth's capacity for aesthetic appreciation opens the opportunity to deal realistically with certain imagery associated with life after death.

577

Youth's will to live prepares him for responding to the Christian hope.

Youth have the capacity to appreciate the implications of the reality of God's love as revealed in the life, death, and resurrection of Christ.

2. **How may this content be communicated as the learner engages in the Learning Tasks? What are the methods and procedures by which the learner may explore the meanings and experiences within this theme (1-a) in the light of his readiness (1-b) in order to discover significance and value?**

Through opportunities for Bible study (individual and small group) and small group discussion concerning the life, death and resurrection of Christ, the kingdom of God, the Old Testament hope of the Messiah, the New Testament hope of the return of Christ, the prophetic understanding of history, the Pauline teachings of the resurrection of Christ and the resurrection of the body, the nature of eternal life, the character of God revealed in his mighty saving acts, the work of the Holy Spirit as God present with us.

Through reading, study, and conversation about the writings of theological scholars concerning the issues involved in this theme.

Through critical, creative, and constructive discussion of basic affirmations of faith from the perspective of the Christian hope.

Through opportunities for experiences with music, painting, literature, drama, which express feelings, ideas, images related to this theme.

Through study of and participation in hymnody of the church related to this theme.

Through listening to preaching which sets forth the Christian hope.

Through examination of ancient, medieval, and modern history from the perspective of God's role in and beyond history.

Through association with persons whose lives give evidence of the basic security and outlook that are grounded in the Christian hope.

By exposure through study tours, seminars, consultations, and conferences to the realities of life, thereby giving youth an opportunity to examine and make value judgments as to which is meaningful and less meaningful in terms of knowing eternal life now.

Examination and consideration of current social issues and events from the perspective of the role of God in and beyond history.

Through comparative study of the great religions of the world in terms of eschatology.

Through opportunities for personal experiences of prayer and worship that foster trust in God.

Through a consideration of the funeral practices of our culture in light of the Christian understanding of death.

An examination of current "revolutions" (racial, sexual, national, and the revolution in cybernetics) and their relationship to Christian eschatology.

3. **What may the learner achieve within this theme in the fulfillment of the Learning Tasks? What are possible changes or learnings on the part of the learner that may result from his appropriation of the significance and value discovered? These changes or learnings may be associated with skills, attitudes, motivations, perceptions including understandings and appreciations.**

Youth may acknowledge and commit themselves to Jesus Christ as Lord of life.

Youth may achieve the beginning of a quality and style of life which exhibits the security and outlook that are grounded in the Christian hope.

Youth may achieve a fuller understanding of the way the Christian hope rests in the triumphant God.

Youth may gain a fuller understanding of God's sovereignty in and over history.

Youth may express confidence in the ultimate triumph of God, even in the face of current world revolutions and possible world destruction, and assurance that the kingdom of God can never be overthrown.

The youth may achieve a fuller understanding of the relationship of Christ's life, death, and resurrection to the Christian hope.

579

Youth may have a more secure understanding of the meaning of eternal life.

Youth may gain a growing ability to articulate the Christian hope.

Youth may increase in their ability to discern and commit themselves to values which are consistent with the Christian hope in contrast to the false values that often claim men's loyalties.

Youth may develop a deepened devotional life based on appreciation of the rule and love of God.

Youth may become more able to respond to the fact of death in ways that are consistent with the Christian hope.

Youth may begin to develop the ability to face the inevitability of their own death with diminishing fear.

Youth may accept the assurance of the Christian hope in the presence of tragedy and death.

Youth may gain an increasing familiarity with the resources of the faith concerning the Christian hope.

Youth may become increasingly involved in those things which are of the essence of life now, and which have their origin and fulfillment in the kingdom of God.

6. The Christian's Hope Rests in the Triumphant God

STATEMENT OF THE THEME

Man's tendency to be dissatisfied with the present, his uncertainty about the future, and his need to be vitally related to the eternally significant are addressed through the experience of the Christian hope in God's ultimate triumph in and over history. This hope includes the assurance of eternal life and the consummation of the kingdom of God.

ADULTHOOD

1. Significance of the theme for this age level

a. **Meanings and experiences within this theme relevant for this age level. This is content, a selected part of Scope.**

The Christian hope is in the triumph of God's redemptive purpose.

God's creativity, sovereign power, and love as revealed in Jesus Christ are the basis of the Christian hope.

The resurrection of Christ gives assurance of his triumph over death and of the reality of eternal life.

He who is without hope in Christ often is uncertain and afraid of life now and of the future.

The power of God revealed in the resurrection of Christ is at work in the life of the Christian, giving meaning to his life now and the hope of eternal salvation.

God is sovereign in his universe and, in spite of all that seems to point to the contrary, will triumph in and over history, bringing evil to defeat and righteousness to victory.

Hope in the triumph of God's kingdom upon earth undergirds the Christian's confidence, security, and expectation.

Eternal life is not the same as endless existence. It is a distinctive quality and style of life—life given by God, lived in fellowship with God, and dedicated to the praise of God.

The Christian, although unable to comprehend all that his hope of eternal life means, believes that ultimately he will be conformed to the image of Christ and live in fellowship with him.

The nature of life enjoyed in fellowship with God is indestructible—a present experience and a future hope.

God created men to be his children in this life as well as the life to come.

581

1. **Significance of the theme for this age level**

   b. **Readiness of the learner for this theme in terms of basic needs, interests, motivations, capacities, developmental tasks.**

The failure of large numbers of adults to achieve victory in the moral struggles of life may predispose them to give favorable consideration to the gospel which promises them identification with God's own triumph over evil here and hereafter.

Restlessness and dissatisfaction with themselves on the part of adults underline their need for the basic security to be found in the Christian hope.

In addition to the normal awareness of the uncertainty of life and the natural tendency to be afraid of the future, many adults are plagued with concern about the world situation, the power of evil in today's world, and fear about the future of the world.

Adults are curious about death, the likelihood of life beyond death, and the Christian understanding of eternal life.

Adults desire to be vitally related to the eternally significant.

The responsibility which the majority of adults have for the care of loved ones may give them a concern about the eternal welfare of these loved ones.

Adults have a desire for justice to which the authority, power, and rulership of the Sovereign God speaks.

2. **How may this content be communicated as the learner engages in the Learning Tasks? What are the methods and procedures by which the learner may explore the meanings and experiences within this theme (1-a) in the light of his readiness (1-b) in order to discover significance and value?**

Through study and discussion of the following areas of content in the Bible: the resurrection; the kingdom of God; the Old Testament hope of the Messiah; the New Testament hope of the return of Christ; the prophetic understanding of history; the future life; the nature of eternal life; the character of God revealed in his mighty saving acts; the work of the Holy Spirit as God present with us.

Through association with and hearing about persons whose

lives give evidence of the basic security and outlook that are grounded in the Christian hope.

Through study of history from the perspective of God's role in and beyond history.

Through reading, study, and conversation about the writings of theological scholars concerning the issues involved in this theme.

Through opportunities for experiences with music, painting, literature, drama, which express feelings, ideas, images related to this theme.

Through association with persons whose lives give evidence of the basic security and outlook that are grounded in the Christian hope.

Through listening to preaching which sets forth the Christian hope.

Through all the ministries of a church at the time of death, and through funerals or memorial services that are conducted in such a manner as to distinctly express the Christian hope.

Through study and participation in the hymnody of the church related to this theme.

Examination and consideration of current social issues and events from the perspective of the role of God in and beyond history.

Through study of comparative religions in terms of eschatology.

583

Through opportunities for personal experiences of prayer and worship that foster trust in God.

By exposure through study tours, seminars, consultations, and conferences to the realities of life, thereby giving adults an opportunity to examine and make value judgments as to which is meaningful and less meaningful in terms of knowing eternal life now.

Through an examination of current "revolutions" (racial, sexual, national, and the revolution in cybernetics) and their relationship to Christian eschatology.

3. **What may the learner achieve within this theme in the fulfillment of the Learning Tasks? What are possible changes or learnings on the part of the learner that may result from his appropriation of the significance and value discovered? These changes or learnings may be associated with skills, attitudes, motivations, perceptions including understandings and appreciations.**

The adult may gain a more mature understanding of the relationship of Christ's life, death, and resurrection to the Christian hope.

The adult may gain a more resolute confidence in the ultimate victory of God and the establishment of his kingdom.

The adult may become more steadfast in his Christian faith and work because he has appropriated the meaning and value of the Christian hope.

The adult may express confidence in the ultimate triumph of God, even in the face of current world revolutions and possible world destruction, and assurance that the kingdom of God can never be overthrown.

The adult may gain strength to endure with confidence and courage the responsibilities and the buffetings of life.

The adult, especially in declining years, may be delivered from bondage to the false hopes that often claim the loyalties of men.

In many cases adults who have never accepted Christ as their personal Lord and Savior will do so when they discover meaning and value in the hope of eternal life and the triumph of the kingdom of God.

The adult may grow in his love of and trust in God and in his love of other Christians.

The adult may come to the conviction that God is sovereign over history.

The adult may appropriate in his life the confidence that

world history is moving toward its consummation in the kingdom of God.

The adult may develop a quality and style of life which exhibits the security and outlook that are grounded in the Christian hope.

The adult may develop a deepened devotional life based on appreciation of the rule and love of God.

The adult may have a deepening experience of abiding joy resident in the Christian hope.

The adult may become more able to respond to the fact of death in ways that are consistent with the Christian hope.

The adult may face his own death without fear.

The adult may bear genuine witness to the Christian hope in the face of tragedy and death.

The adult may more fully achieve security through his trust in the Christian hope.

The adult Christian with a maturing faith in the triumphant God may work harder for the establishment of justice in today's world.

Confidence in the Christian hope may stimulate adults to earnest, self-giving efforts to spread the gospel.

The adult may become increasingly involved in those things which are of the essence of life now, and which have their origin and fulfillment in the kingdom of God.

585

VOCATION: THE MEANING AND EXPERIENCE OF DISCIPLESHIP

The themes within this area are:

1. *God's Call to Responsible Decision*
2. *Called to Serve One's Neighbor*
3. *The Stewardship of Life and Work*
4. *Discipline in the Christian Life*
5. *Joined in Discipleship in the World*
6. *Toward the Kingdom of God*

Statement of the Area

The focus, or vantage point, of this area of curriculum is the social, ethical, and service aspects of the Christian life, that is, *doing* the Christian way in all relationships, or the outward witness of faithful discipleship to Jesus Christ.

Comprehended in this area of curriculum is such content of Christian thought and life as: the concept of the Kingdom of God; explication of Christian ethics and Christian social relations; the concept of the vocation of the Christian; the Christian view of work; interpretation of the fruits of the Spirit; the church's role and task in the world; stewardship in the natural and social realm.

In order to have educational value as an area of curriculum, this content must be viewed in terms of its pertinence to the persistent issues of man's life. Some of these issues are: For what causes is life best invested? What is the relation of Christianity to society? How resolve issues between church and state? What is the political responsibility of the Christian? How shall I choose and perform my life work? How do I know what is right? What values can I live by? What about meeting failure?[1]

---

[1] Repeated here as necessary background.

1. God's Call to Responsible Decision

STATEMENT OF THE THEME

The Christian interprets the persistent pressure to make decisions as a call from God, made clear in the demands of the gospel, and seeks to perceive God's call in the factors affecting decisions.

EARLY CHILDHOOD

1. Significance of the theme for this age level

a. Meanings and experiences within this theme relevant for this age level. This is content, a selected part of Scope.

God created each one as a free person who must make decisions. On certain occasions a young child is called to make decisions for himself, at other times he has counsel by an older person in making decisions, to some decisions he must submit.

God calls the child to live in a relationship with parents and others in which his acceptance of proper authority is helpful to his experience of freedom and provides a basis for right choices.

God's call to responsible decision may come through Christian parents, teachers, and others.

There is a measure of consistency basic to various decisions made by responsible persons.

God created each one as a free person who must make decisions.

587

1. Significance of the theme for this age level

b. Readiness of the learner for this theme in terms of basic needs, interests, motivations, capacities, developmental tasks.

During early childhood the person is discovering himself as an individual who can make decisions. (The foundational values of this period for lifelong decision-making are crucial.)

In decision-making, the young child has a basic need to be associated with persons more mature than himself who accept him as a person of worth, give him care and freedom, and set limitations for him. The young child needs and in most cases is amenable to guidance in making choices.

The young child is ready to experiment in decision-making within loving, understanding boundaries within which he has freedom to express himself in his own way.

With experience in decision-making the young child needs the assurance that, should he fail, he will continue to receive the love and support of parents, family, and teachers.

In a limited way the young child has the capacity to discern the consequences of decisions. He has expanding capacity to accept the consequences and recognize that some are pleasing or displeasing to others.

The young child has the ability and is open to motivation to hurt another person. This fact impinges on the decisions he makes or participates in.

The young child is ready to perceive in a limited way the relation of God to his decisions and those of his family.

The young child is able in a limited way to recognize some of his abilities and interests which are the beginnings of factors that affect decision-making.

2. **How may this content be communicated as the learner engages in the Learning Tasks? What are the methods and procedures by which the learner may explore the meanings and experiences within this theme (1-a) in the light of his readiness (1-b) in order to discover significance and value?**

By taking part in some group decisions.

By receiving help to live with or rectify the consequences of his unwise decisions.

By being related to responsible persons whose decisions reflect consistency.

By being called on and permitted to make simple choices within a framework of freedom characterized by just and reliable limitations.

By observing more mature Christians in the process of Christian decision-making.

By hearing interpretation and conversation about Christian decision-making.

By hearing Bible stories which illustrate decision-making.

By hearing or participating in prayer that seeks God's guidance in decision-making.

By listening to conversations dealing with decisions.

By engaging in play situations designed to involve the learner in decision-making.

3. **What may the learner achieve (at this age level) within this theme in the fulfillment of the Learning Tasks? What are possible changes or learnings on the part of the learner that may result from his appropriation of the significance and value discovered? These changes or learnings may be associated with skills, attitudes, motivations, perceptions including understandings and appreciations.**

The young child may gain a beginning understanding and experience of the fact that he is free to make decisions.

The young child may gain a beginning sense of his own worth which undergirds decision-making and achieve a measure of competence and self-reliance in making simple decisions.

The young child may perceive that decisions that affect him often affect others.

The young child may gain some understanding of what it means to live with the consequences of decisions, be they pleasant or otherwise. In this connection he may also gain some facility in receiving or extending forgiveness.

The young child may achieve some ability in distinguishing between acceptable and unacceptable behavior, and be guided to this extent in his decision-making.

589

The young child may become aware that there is a God who is concerned about the decisions people make and the resulting consequences.

The young child may grow in his ability to accept at this state of development decisions made for him by others.

The young child may develop a beginning sense of the fact that even adults cannot make all the decisions that affect him.

The young child may recognize the dependability of some persons in the decisions they make.

590

The young child may recognize there are things he cannot decide to do without accepting painful consequences every time.

1. God's Call to Responsible Decision

STATEMENT OF THE THEME

The Christian interprets the persistent pressure to make decisions as a call from God, made clear in the demands of the gospel, and seeks to perceive God's call in the factors affecting decisions.

ELEMENTARY YEARS

1. Significance of the theme for this age level

a. Meanings and experiences within this theme relevant for this age level. This is content, a selected part of Scope.

God created each person as a free individual who must make decisions.

God calls every person to make decisions. This is part of God's plan for living, and God is interested in the kinds of decision a person makes.

Decision-making is not easy and sometimes persons make unwise decisions. God offers his forgiveness for unwise decisions and helps persons make wise decisions.

God calls persons to accept the consequences of decisions.

Many decisions affect other persons. Responsible decision-making requires persons to consider the influence of their decisions on the lives of others.

Responsible decision-making builds on previous decisions with some measure of consistency.

Responsible decisions grow out of one's understanding of and relation to God.

1. Significance of the theme for this age level

b. Readiness of the learner for this theme in terms of basic needs, interests, motivations, capacities, developmental tasks.

The child needs to feel a sense of his own worth and to have confidence in his ability to make responsible decisions. He has a growing desire and capacity to be on his own and to decide things for himself.

The child needs to feel the love and understanding of parents, teachers, and other adults in all of his decision-making—whether wise or unwise.

The child is growing in his ability to reason and is eager to use this capacity in making decisions affecting self.

Because of his growing ability to understand cause and effect, the child is able to foresee the consequences of many of his decisions. He is increasing in his ability to evaluate the results of his decisions in their effect upon himself and others.

The learner is becoming increasingly able to concentrate for several hours or hold a task in mind several days. This enhances his ability to make decisions regarding the use of leisure time and of special talents.

The child is able to initiate, carry out, and do some evaluating of his own projects. This opens up occasions for decision-making.

The child's developing sense of justice and injustice motivates responsible decision-making.

The child's understanding of what is acceptable and unacceptable behavior in his family and some larger circles becomes a factor in decision-making.

Special abilities or talents become evident in elementary years

591

and are factors in his decisions.

A growing sense of personal relationship to God increases the elementary child's readiness to recognize God's relation to decisions.

As the child approaches adolescence he has increased capacity to make decisions relative to Christian commitment.

The growing ability and desire of the elementary child to be in group relationships thrusts him into occasions of participating in group decisions.

592

2. **How may this content be communicated as the learner engages in the Learning Tasks? What are the methods and procedures by which the learner may explore the meanings and experiences within this theme (1-a) in the light of his readiness (1-b) in order to discover significance and value.**

Through being involved in tasks or obligations that call for decisions such as being entrusted with helping younger children, or situations having leadership responsibilities within his capacities, being allowed to declare "fouls" and "out-of-bounds" against self in sports, having responsibility for the care of materials, tools, equipment.

Through participating in activities in which there can be identification with persons making responsible decisions. Such activities may include reading and hearing stories, dramatizing, watching T.V., observing and associating with understanding adults who trust him, conversation about alternatives and possible consequences.

Through studying the life and teachings of Jesus and other portions of scripture which give a foundation for making responsible decisions.

Through having opportunities to make decisions with others and live with the consequences. Some of these decisions may have to do with planning leisure time, taking part in family decision-making, participating in peer-group decisions, spending money, choosing companions, joining organized peer groups.

Through acting out situations in which decision-making is called for and evaluating decisions and consequences.

Through hearing interpretation and conversation about Christian decision-making.

Through hearing or participating in prayer that seeks God's guidance in decision-making.

Through listening to conversations dealing with decisions.

3. **What may the learner achieve within this theme in the fulfillment of the Learning Tasks? What are possible changes or learnings on the part of the learner that may result from his appropriation of the significance and value discovered? These changes or learnings may be associated with skills, attitudes, motivations, perceptions including understandings and appreciations.**

The child may develop an understanding that the way he makes decisions as well as the decisions he makes is a response to God.

The child may realize that he can and is expected to grow in the ability to make responsible decisions, that God does not leave him without guidance.

The child may discern in a limited way when to seek help in decision-making and possibly achieve a growing knowledge of the Bible as a source in decision-making.

593

The child may perceive prayer as an avenue of access to God's guidance in decisions and in living with their consequences.

The child may grow in ability to make decisions according to Christian principles.

The child may develop skill in assessing various factors in a situation, including social pressures, and take them into account in making decisions.

The child may grow in ability to trust his own judgment of value.

The child may develop ability to acknowledge mistakes in decision-making and in willingness to seek and accept forgiveness.

The child may grow in ability to share in group decision-making.

The child may be concerned about and identify with others in decision-making.

The child may recognize the value of being a person who can be trusted to make dependable decisions.

594

The child may grow in willingness to act with courage in decision-making even when it is difficult.

The child may recognize his own special talent and take steps to develop it.

The child may grow in resilience in the face of rejection of peers because of his decisions or those of parents or others, by which he must abide.

1. God's Call to Responsible Decision

STATEMENT OF THE THEME

The Christian interprets the persistent pressure to make decisions as a call from God, made clear in the demands of the gospel, and seeks to perceive God's call in the factors affecting decisions.

YOUTH

1. Significance of the theme for this age level

a. Meanings and experiences within this theme relevant for this age level. This is content, a selected part of Scope.

God created each person as a free individual who must make decisions.

Abilities or talents (the metaphor derived from Jesus' parable of the talents) are gifts from God which help the person identify alternatives within a particular decision.

Opportunities may be understood as constituting a call from God to choose to act in support of his continuing creation by serving creatively in it.

The Christian makes responsible decisions in such areas as voluntary service, military or alternative service, choosing a marriage partner, occupation, in the light of his commitment to Jesus Christ in discipleship.

The form of response to God's call to responsible decision-making varies according to personality and circumstances.

The gospel is the basis of meaning and the source of guidance in decision-making.

The basis for behavioral choice(s) is increasingly rooted within one's commitment rather than in conformity to social custom.

The emancipation from external authority places an increased burden on internal integrity.

Apparent inconsistencies in decision-making may root in the radical ethic of love.

1. Significance of the theme for this age level

b. Readiness of the learner for this theme in terms of basic needs, interests, motivations, capacities, developmental tasks.

During youth years intellectual and physical powers approach maturity, special abilities become apparent, and the person's evaluation of them figures in his decisions.

595

Needing acceptance by others as a responsible person as well as provision of the necessities of life, youth are particularly susceptible to pressures to make life-directing decisions early, especially with reference to dating, marriage, education, occupation, Christian commitment, military or alternative service, which produce inescapable extrinsic motivation for decisions in these areas.

Growing intellectual powers make possible extensive exploration of the factors involved in a decision.

Youth's desire to be self-reliant, daring, and adventurous, thrusts him into a variety of decision-demanding situations.

The continual development of a self-image sharply colors the decisions youth makes.

Youth is engaged extensively in "reality-testing" to determine the validity of their own likes and dislikes and their special preferences. They are often frustrated and bewildered by false and unworthy behavior patterns among adults. Because of youth's special need to belong and have a place in society, they are especially sensitive to peer groups' pressures and feel impelled to make decisions in line with these peer-group pressures.

Youth regard most decisions they make as serious and are frightened by the fact that choices close some doors while opening others. The ability to recognize this fact emphasizes personal limitation in decision-making.

Youth are willing to accept responsibility in decision-making but feel the need of support and acceptance by others as responsible persons.

Youth has a sense of history and is able to experience the past as helpful and meaningful in making decisions.

In decision-making youth are able to tolerate the postponement of satisfactions in the interest of a higher value.

In the tension between dependent childhood and independent adulthood, youth are caught up in the tension caused by decisions they can make for themselves and decisions they are not able or are not allowed to make for themselves.

In decision-making youth are able to accept the fact that decisions in the interest of some values inevitably rule out or delay the realization of other values (values that may have equal or even more weight).

The enhanced powers of youth in making discriminations enable them to relate their decisions to Christian values and to their basic Christian commitment.

To the extent that youth has a maturing sense of relationship to God, together with knowledge and experiences in the Chris-

596

tian community, these set the tone for youth's recognition of God's relation to their decisions.

2. **How may this content be communicated as the learner engages in the Learning Tasks? What are the methods and procedures by which the learner may explore the meanings and experiences within this theme (1-a) in the light of his readiness (1-b) in order to discover significance and value?**

By taking part in a group characterized by frankness and honesty in which deviant opinions are permitted and accorded the right to protest and seek to alter structures and values with which he disagrees.

By role-playing decisions of political and social importance.

By analyzing decisions that have been made by civic and church bodies.

Through engaging in efforts to identify and articulate the relevance of Christian commitment to decisions in such areas as voluntary service, military or alternative service, choosing a marriage partner, occupation.

Through hearing decision-making being engaged in by responsible persons.

Through viewing and criticizing motion pictures and drama, reading and criticizing novels for insight into factors affecting decision-making.

597

Through engaging in systematic study of the Bible in order to explore the biblical base for responsible decision-making.

Through engaging in worship through which he may hear and respond to God's call to responsible decision-making.

Through doing the investigation necessary for some decisions.

Within the framework of a supporting community, by experimenting with decisions made on one's own authority rather than external authorities.

3. **What may the learner achieve within this theme in the fulfillment of the Learning Tasks? What are possible changes**

or learnings on the part of the learner that may result from his appropriation of the significance and value discovered? These changes or learnings may be associated with skills, attitudes, motivations, perceptions including understandings and appreciations.

Youth may recognize that his particular abilities and talents make possible some kinds of decision and cut off others.

Youth may recognize that particular abilities may help in the process of decision-making.

Youth may develop an understanding and skill in using strategies and structures by which significant decisions may be implemented.

Youth may develop skill in projecting consequences of alternative decisions and in analyzing factors inherent in decision-demanding situations.

Youth may gain confidence in the support and guidance of the Christian community in decision-making and recognize his responsibility to share in support and guidance of this community.

Youth may develop in his understanding and acceptance of Christian values in decision-making.

Youth may develop skill in discriminating among values as to their congruence with the Christian faith.

Youth may gain in willingness to accept loneliness or rejection in order to implement his decisions.

Youth may achieve a growing understanding of the implications of commitment to God respecting all decisions; recognize this commitment as issuing in a central life purpose and develop skill in relating purpose to life-directing decisions.

Youth may increasingly rely on his relation to God in decision-making.

Youth may recognize increasingly the necessity to make decisions as a call from God.

Youth may begin to develop a pattern of systematic and responsible decision-making and gain in his awareness of the contribution of such a pattern to personal integrity and a consistent style of life.

Youth may grow in understanding, willingness, and skill in participation in decisions in the public sphere as distinct from those in the private sphere.

Youth may have developing confidence that his inward freedom and relationship to God may be maintained even while he acts from external necessity.

Youth may increase skill in mining out Christian principles as witnessed to in the Bible for a guide in decision-making and appropriating these principles in decision-making.

1. God's Call to Responsible Decision

STATEMENT OF THE THEME

The Christian interprets the persistent pressure to make decisions as a call from God, made clear in the demands of the gospel, and seeks to perceive God's call in the factors affecting decisions.

ADULTHOOD

1. Significance of the theme for this age level

a. Meanings and experiences within this theme relevant for this age level. This is content, a selected part of Scope.

599

God calls man to understand his own nature as a person created in the image of God so as to see responsible decision-making as part of his inherent capacity and obligation.

God's grace in Christ brings a moral quickening and a new capacity for responsible decision-making.

The gospel is the basis of meaning and the source of guidance in responsible decision-making in keeping with commitment to Jesus Christ and under the guidance of the Holy Spirit.

Sharpening and deepening of insights and understandings respecting the gospel and skills in handling factors in decision-making are necessary to moral and ethical maturation.

God calls persons to use the guidance of their experience in the Christian faith and membership in the Christian community in making wise and courageous decisions.

Decisions in all areas of life have a reference to Christian commitment.

God created each one as a free person who must make decisions.

600

1. Significance of the theme for this age level

b. Readiness of the learner for this theme in terms of basic needs, interests, motivations, capacities, developmental tasks.

The adult is often baffled and frustrated by the complexity of the social situation and also the diversity in ethical patterns, and thus needs a dependable base upon which to make responsible decisions.

The adult with a Christian orientation and commitment is faced with the pressure to accept non-Christian patterns of decision-making, and therefore needs the light of the gospel, the support of fellow Christians, and the guidance of the Holy Spirit in making responsible decisions.

Most adults carry responsibility for the future of their lives and are embroiled in decisions that affect not only their own future but that of others and are, therefore, faced with some of those decisions having to do with long-range objectives chiefly concerned with the welfare of other persons. This is particularly true of the young and middle adults who are therefore motivated to attend to God's call to responsible decision-making.

As he makes decisions, the adult experiences the need for forgiveness, both divine and human, and needs forgiveness and sympathetic understanding from God and other persons with respect to failures and betrayed responsibilities.

At intervals during adulthood the person is faced with the necessity to reassess past experiences, his own and others, and evaluate objectives for the future with the possibility of reformulating objectives. At these times he would be especially ready to perceive God's call in decision-making.

The adult member of the Christian community, faced with difficult decisions not only with respect to his participation in the Christian community, but also with respect to the Christian community's fulfillment of its mission, is motivated toward responsible decision-making.

As a person who benefits from being a member of a social, economic, political community, the adult is faced with the necessity of responsible decisions with reference to these communities in the light of his Christian commitment.

2. **How may this content be communicated as the learner engages in the Learning Tasks? What are the methods and procedures by which the learner may explore the meanings and experiences within this theme (1-a) in the light of his readiness (1-b) in order to discover significance and value?**

By reflecting upon, analyzing, and evaluating the bases for decisions.

By engaging in systematic Bible study, prayer, worship (corporate, individual, and family), with a view to deepening insight as to the implication of one's Christian commitment for responsible decision-making.

By engaging in dialogue and purposeful study as to issues, values, guiding principles, and divine resources in responsible decision-making.

By giving and receiving support within the Christian community for decision-making.

By reading works of literature, viewing works of art and drama which interpret life's decision-demanding issues.

By engaging in purposive investigation and using resources for decision-making.

601

By using family-life situations to practice and test responsible decision-making.

By taking advantage of guidance and counsel of competent persons relative to decision-making.

By being associated with persons who relate their Christian commitment to decisions in various areas of life.

When decisions have been questioned, by having to defend and interpret them.

By living with the consequences of irresponsible or unwise decisions.

By using past experiences of wise and responsible decisions as a foundation for subsequent decision-making.

3. **What may the learner achieve within this theme in the fulfillment of the Learning Tasks? What are possible changes or learnings on the part of the learner that may result from his appropriation of the significance and value discovered? These changes or learnings may be associated with skills, attitudes, motivations, perceptions including understandings and appreciations.**

Adults may increasingly recognize the necessity to make decisions as a call from God.

Adults may grow in understanding and acceptance of Christian values in decision-making.

Adults may discover the far-reaching effects of their decisions on the lives of other persons and the wider circles of society, and allow themselves to be influenced by this insight.

Adults may understand increasingly the complex human situation and enhance their ability to take into account the personal and social factors bearing on responsible decision-making.

Adults may achieve a growing understanding of the moral factors and Christian values in social issues requiring decision-making.

Adults may become more skilled in drawing on the available

resources, both divine and human, for responsible decision-making.

Adults may increasingly see themselves as necessarily involved in decisions in the public sphere of life.

Adults may achieve a keen sensitivity to the Christian's role as an ethical catalyst in society.

Adults may become increasingly able to accept unpredictable consequences of responsible decisions because they are assured that they are within God's providence.

Adults may grow in ability to tolerate ridicule or other forms of opposition and hostility resulting from responsible decision.

Adults may become increasingly determined to live by Christian decisions and practice the discipline required for responsibility.

Adults may come to a fuller awareness of the relation between responsible decision-making and self-respect and personal integrity.

Adults may accept the relevance of the gospel to responsible decision-making in all areas of life and make use of Christian values.

Adults may grow in ability to analyze issues, weigh factors, and evaluate consequences in responsible decision-making.

Adults may acknowledge and increasingly seek the guidance of the Holy Spirit in making responsible decisions.

603

Adults may become increasingly skillful in providing guidance and reinforcement to other persons in making and implementing responsible decisions.

Adults may increasingly develop the capacity to make decisions which transcend the limitations of prejudices, selfishness, and fear.

Adults may gain in willingness to recognize and accept the forgiveness of God in the face of unwise or irresponsible decisions and gain in willingness and skills in offering forgiveness to others whose decisions affect them adversely.

Adults may grow in their awareness of their fellowship with

Christ through responsible decision-making.

Adults may grow in ability to follow the insights of the gospel in making decisions in keeping with the implications of their Christian commitment irrespective of results to themselves.

Adults may become increasingly able to maintain balance for decision-making in the face of suffering, misfortune, and tragedy, trusting in God's care.

Adults may participate responsibly in group decision-making that involves interpersonal relations.

604

Adults may, through the learnings related to responsible decision-making, gain a deepening appreciation for their freedom as persons and the responsibility involved in it.

Adults may achieve a deepened and more resolute commitment to God through responding to God's call to responsible decision.

Adults may achieve skills in guiding others in analyzing and taking account of factors in responsible decision-making.

Adults may gain in the ability to identify those decisions that are properly theirs to make.

Adults may gain in the skills of diligent study and investigation of the Bible and other sources and in the use of insights so derived in responsible decision-making.

Adults may have developing confidence that their inward freedom and relationship to God may be maintained even while they act from external necessity.

Adults may increase the intensity of commitment to follow principles of Christian ethics in decisions related to personal and public morality, family and vocational responsibility, and social problems.

2. Called to Serve One's Neighbor

STATEMENT OF THE THEME

The Christian perceives God's call in the give-and-take of interpersonal relationships in which he is constantly involved. He ex-

presses his vocation in face-to-face relationships with his neighbor in every area of life, by expressing love, understanding, acceptance, helpfulness, and service.

EARLY CHILDHOOD

1. Significance of the theme for this age level

a. Meanings and experiences within this theme relevant for this age level. This is content, a selected part of Scope.

The call to the young child to serve his neighbor has its basis in the central realities of the gospel: God's love for man; Christ's mission of redemption and compassionate service; the worth and dignity of all persons; the needs of persons in their human situation; and the vocation of Christians in terms of ministry.

For a person in early childhood, the essence of meaning underlying the call to serve one's neighbor can be summed up in the affirmation: God loves all persons everywhere; he therefore wants the young child to love all persons he meets. God's love is expressed in kindness, care, and forgiveness. "We love, because he first loved us" (1 John 4:19).

1. Significance of the theme for this age level
b. Readiness of the learner for this theme in terms of basic needs, interests, motivations, capacities, developmental tasks.

605

The readiness of the young child for this theme is shown by his dependence on love and care, his openness toward people and acceptance of them, his power to give pleasure or to inflict pain on them, his comparative freedom from prejudice, his curiosity about children his own age and younger, his desire for companionship, his eagerness to help, his desire to achieve.

Quite normally the young child often reacts selfishly in interpersonal relations, but he begins to have the capacity to see that others are persons like himself, with needs like his own. On the basis of this identification he may begin acting in response to needs of others.

The young child's world is enlarging beyond the family to his contact with such persons as guests in the home, neighbors and relatives, community helpers, church school leaders and companions, associates in weekday nursery school and kindergarten, and in child-care centers and play schools. The wider associations increase his need and opportunity to express neighborliness.

In his enlarging world the young child has increasing desire for group approval, which causes him to have more concern for the group.

By the strangeness of his enlarging world, the young child experiences greater need for love, acceptance, and support by parents and others, and at the same time may be motivated to give love and support to others.

2. How may this content be communicated as the learner engages in the Learning Tasks? What are the methods and procedures by which the learner may explore the meanings and experiences within this theme (1-a) in the light of his readiness (1-b) in order to discover significance and value?

Through living in a climate of love and acceptance.

Through such activities as hearing Bible stories and verses expressing neighborly feelings; singing songs about helping and serving; hearing stories about children who were helpful to others; and hearing simple interpretations of acts of love and helpfulness.

By sharing toys, taking turns, making gifts for others and presenting these gifts to them, learning or helping others learn the courtesies of being a guest or host.

By observing acts of helpfulness and service performed by others, by play-acting situations in family life and with playmates which show consideration of others, by meeting visitors in the home, at a family camp, or traveling elsewhere.

3. **What may the learner achieve within the theme in the fulfillment of the Learning Tasks? What are possible changes or learnings on the part of the learner that may result from his appropriation of the significance and value discovered? These changes or learnings may be associated with skills, attitudes, motivations, perceptions including understandings and appreciations.**

The young child may evidence a beginning recognition of others as persons like himself and show willingness to surrender his claim to another person's attention (recognizing that sometimes people want to be alone).

The young child may develop an appreciation of what it means to love and accept love and to act upon this meaning in concrete situations.

The young child may gain appreciation for Bible teaching about love for one another and view this teaching as guidance for his life.

The young child may come to have such attitudes as thoughtfulness toward others, willingness to accept helpfulness without feeling inferior, feeling of responsibility for accepting roles and rules as he plays with other children, and beginning willingness to accept responsibility for acts of neighborliness.

The young child may have sense of satisfaction from having shown neighborliness (sense of being a helpful person) and desire to share good things with others.

607

The young child may grow in ability to be helpful and develop resilience when rebuffed in showing neighborliness.

2. Called to Serve One's Neighbor

STATEMENT OF THE THEME

The Christian perceives God's call in the give and take of interpersonal relationships in which he is constantly involved. He expresses his vocation in face-to-face relationships with his neighbor in every area of life, by expressing love, understanding acceptance, helpfulness, service.

ELEMENTARY YEARS

1. Significance of the theme for this age level

    a. Meanings and experiences within this theme relevant for this age level. This is content, a selected part of Scope.

608

The call to the child to serve his neighbor has its basis in the central realities of the gospel: God's love for man; Christ's mission of redemption and compassionate service; the worth and dignity of all persons; the needs of persons in their human situation; and the vocation of Christians in terms of ministry.

This theme presents the child with certain affirmations whose essence is as follows: God loves all persons irrespective of condition or attitude; our love for God is meant to find expression in love for all persons; love for other persons involves willingness to accept them as persons and calls for active goodwill toward them; love for other persons involves willingness to share one's best things with them, and to do things to help them.

1. Significance of the theme for this age level

    b. Readiness of the learner for this theme in terms of basic needs, interests, motivations, capacities, developmental tasks.

The child has these basic needs: to be loved and to give love; to reach out to other persons; to feel social competence in the presence of the needs of others; to recognize his ability to meet needs; to find outlets for his energy.

The child of elementary years is interested in other people and what they do: he joins groups (clubs) taking different roles; he has growing awareness that some people are deprived and others have much; he is concerned about getting along with other groups. He also has concerns about race, war, and peace.

The child has capacities to feel empathy, to sense the kinship of the human family, to sense needs of neighbor and how to meet them, to use his developing skills in service, to postpone realization of his desires for his neighbor's good. He has a growing ability to understand other persons both in his immediate environment and far away and to appreciate their worth and cultures. He is growing in ability to apply principles of neighborliness to new situations.

The child is motivated by gratitude, love, desire to measure up, and wanting to be like Jesus (if in the Christian community).

The child has a need for help in serving his neighbor when he encounters criticism, prejudice, resentment, and rejection by members of his peer group. Often he finds himself perplexed and frustrated by conflicting culture patterns, un-Christian concepts relative to the meaning of neighbor, and varying attitudes towards neighbors.

The child is meeting more persons who are different from himself and his immediate associates—the handicapped, gifted, foreign, those of varied economic status, the rejected. He is exposed to attitudes in home, school, and playground which may support or deny the teachings of the love of neighbor. He has difficulty reconciling the teaching he receives about serving one's neighbor and the expectations of some of his peers.

2. **How may this content be communicated as the learner engages in the Learning Tasks? What are the methods and procedures by which the learner may explore the meanings and experiences within this theme (1-a) in the light of his readiness (1-b) in order to discover significance and value?**

By carrying out explorations, investigations, discoveries related to serving his neighbor; by using open-ended stories dealing with service to neighbor; by weighing alternative responses needed in showing love to neighbor; by exploring situations which deny the teaching of neighborliness.

By hearing stories or viewing films of Jesus' ministry and the early Christians; by observing persons who are serving their

609

neighbors; by learning through discussion, stories, role play, and observations why persons sometimes act in unneighborly ways; by experiencing situations in which he is not the giver but the receiver; by studying about people of other countries.

By extending friendliness to those who are different—the new child, one of another race or from another country, the slow child, the physically handicapped, the socially unacceptable; by responding to appeals for aid such as UNICEF, Red Cross, CARE; by preparing things for others, such as tray favors for hospitals or baskets for shut-ins; by making scrapbooks of incidents of neighborliness; by collecting toys for mending (by adults) and distributing them to others; by going Christmas and Easter caroling, reading to older people, inviting peers to join clubs, attending church school, and sharing in other activities; by performing volunteer service in the community such as taking part in clean-up drives, collecting newspapers.

By taking field trips as an experience of friendliness to observe the work of social agencies; by hearing stories of human need today; by discussing current events such as floods, fires, tornadoes; by role playing problem situations involving neighborly responses; by discovering similarities among people of different nations, races, customs; through games, art, folklore; by seeing pictures of need; by reading biographies of persons who have served; by preparing an exhibit that shows neighborhood service; by having opportunities to associate with people of all ages and circumstances; by exploring ways of showing neighborliness without any feeling or condescension, patronage, or expectation of reward.

3. **What may the learner achieve within this theme in the fulfillment of the Learning Tasks? What are possible changes or learnings on the part of the learner that may result from his appropriation of the significance and value discovered? These changes or learnings may be associated with skills,**

610

attitudes, motivations, perceptions including understandings and appreciations.

The child may achieve such understandings as: a deepening realization that serving one's neighbor is what Christ expects and that it is pleasing to God; a growing knowledge of what the Bible says about neighborliness; a beginning understanding of the ministry of the laity in the world; a realization that enemies are often won over by love; a realization that neighborliness has broader aspects than in the situation in which it was learned.

The child may achieve such skills as: growing skill in treating a person as a true neighbor regardless of the situation; ability to exercise a wholesome influence in his peer group; increasing ability to break down barriers by helping persons in distress, showing love through kindness to another group, class, or race; learning how to deal with feelings of neighborliness and anti-neighborliness when both are present; increasing ability in finding and applying principles learned from Bible study.

The child may come to have the following attitudes: sensitivity to human need; joy in service irrespective of reward or recognition; more understanding and cooperative attitude toward members of his family; desire to share with all people God's love expressed in Jesus Christ; a feeling of friendliness and forgiveness toward persons who have mistreated him.

The child may develop such appreciations as: emulation of heroes who have lived lives of service; appreciation for the operation of love in human situations; growing realization of the difficulties of serving his neighbor especially when the neighbor is considered an enemy; realization of what it means to be rebuffed and experiencing something of the meaning of the cross; enjoyment of human fellowship with the neighbor, especially older people; beginning appreciation of the meaning of commitment of life to Christ.

The child may realize such commitments as: voluntarily assuming responsibility for the well-being of playmates and

611

associates—especially for the child who may be left out, the rejected child; developing a self-image as a neighborly person; engaging in intercessory prayer for neighbor; acting with courage in being a neighbor; fulfilling the role of peacemaker.

2. Called to Serve One's Neighbor

STATEMENT OF THE THEME

612

The Christian perceives God's call in the give and take of interpersonal relationships in which he is constantly involved. He expresses his vocation in face-to-face relationships with his neighbor in every area of life, by expressing love, understanding acceptance, helpfulness, service.

YOUTH

1. Significance of the theme for this age level

a. Meanings and experiences within this theme relevant for this age level. This is content, a selected part of Scope.

The call to youth to serve his neighbor has its basis in the central realities of the gospel: God's love for man; Christ's mission of redemption and compassionate service; the worth and dignity of all persons; the needs of persons in their human situations.

God calls youth to see human relations in terms of neighborliness. Love for God finds expression in love for neighbor. Jesus demonstrated God's love in attitudes and acts of neighborliness.

God calls youth to widen his concept of neighbor to include all persons everywhere, transcending barriers of nation, race, class, and creed. The implications of this concept are real for international affairs, for social arrangements and policies, for political life.

God calls youth to see that a Christian conception of neighborly concern involves helping others to achieve an abundant life—spiritual, intellectual, and material.

The gospel asks youth to see each neighbor as a whole person and treat him as a person of worth and dignity, never as an object.

The practice of neighborliness in the fullest sense demands the payment of a price and involves youth in the commitment, sacrifice, and suffering of the cross.

1. Significance of the theme for this age level

b. Readiness of the learner for this theme in terms of basic needs, interests, motivations, capacities, developmental tasks.

A person in youth years faces on every hand new and more significant decisions involving the concept of "neighbor" and commitment to Christian neighborliness. The youth years introduce crises with increasingly long-range results, affecting the course of his own life and with increased bearing on the lives of other persons.

Experience in school, church, and community challenge youth to consider seriously his concept of neighbor. Youth is endowed with curiosity and a spirit of adventure which may influence him to widen his world by peering over the walls that divide groups of people.

A growing awareness of his own worth and dignity as an individual makes it possible for youth to realize that each neighbor is similarly endowed. A growing experience with acceptance, rejection, love, and hate makes it possible for him to identify increasingly with people in many human situations. Youth often experiences himself as a person of uncertain identity, neither child or adult. This experience may help youth identify with minorities and others of uncertain identity.

Youth is confronted with the implications of neighborliness in the public world of organizations and institutions, as well as the private world of individuals and with the implications of neighborliness in international affairs in matters economic and

613

political, policies, and culture. The facts of a nuclear and space age, of the population explosion confront youth with radical implications for neighborliness.

In regard to the desired extent and nature of neighborliness, youth is often bewildered by what he observes: procrastination in regard to human rights, persecution of minorities, and prejudices among adults. Youth may be caught in the conflicts between antagonistic concepts of neighborliness.

614

Youth enjoys increasing freedom, with opportunity to form his own opinions and attitudes and increasing ability to act upon them. An adolescent, always sensitive to peer-group pressure, frequently senses and has to deal with conflict between peer opinion and neighborliness.

2. **How may this content be communicated as the learner engages in the Learning Tasks? What are the methods and procedures by which the learner may explore the meanings and experiences within this theme (1-a) in the light of his readiness (1-b) in order to discover significance and value?**

By reading and viewing a variety of resources that emphasize the humaneness of neighborliness; through experiences in which youth may demonstrate neighborliness; by taking trips and making investigations in order to discover conditions and the needs of persons in today's world for food, clothing, shelter, living space, and freedom; by studying the world mission of the church in light of God's call to serve one's neighbor; by exploring the message of the Bible in regard to neighborliness (see the references in 1-a); by analyzing motives which actuate neighborly or unneighborly attitudes and behavior; by having interviews and discussions about systems of values different from his own and considering the right of the other person or group to hold these values; by discussing neighborliness with peers and family, in camps, and in conference groups.

Through role playing related to situations in which it is difficult to think or act as a neighbor; by exploring flagrant violations of neighborliness in our century and analyzing these in the light of Christian teaching; by examining aspects of the world social revolution to acquaint himself with the part of neighborliness in producing the revolution; by discussing the relationship of neighborliness to facts of the nuclear and space age and of the population explosion; by discussing encounters with unfriendly attitudes and actions (analyzing causes, deciding upon a Christian response); by discussing neighborliness to enemies; by exploring and discussing neighborliness to socially undesirable persons or groups of persons, in school or in other contexts; by examining the effects of prejudices on neighborly attitudes and a Christian approach to prejudice.

By reading biographies of good neighbors; regarding or presenting plays which encourage identification with neighbors and their needs; exploring expressions of other peoples concerning their attitudes and aspirations in their literature, art, music, and recreation; participating in worship ,discussion, recreation, service activities; with a variety of persons, especially other age groups; observing and working with people who are responsible neighbors; having opportunities for a growing acquaintance with neighbors of the world; celebrating appropriate occasions with neighbors; carrying on correspondence with persons of other groups.

615

By writing poems, hymns, playlets, essays which represent some aspects of neighborliness; creating drawings, paintings sculpture to express an idea related to neighborliness; experiencing part-time or summer service to others, such as work camps or other voluntary service; having opportunities to discover, evaluate, and employ talents in recognizing, understanding, and serving neighbors; having experiences through which some contribution may be made to and values received from persons of other age groups; participating in activities which cultivate interest and skill in sharing insights with others (exhibits and plays are examples of such activities); engaging in intercessory prayer.

3. **What may the learner achieve within this theme in the fulfillment of the Learning Tasks? What are possible changes or learnings on the part of the learner that may result from his appropriation of the significance and value discovered? These changes or learnings may be associated with skills, attitudes, motivations, perceptions including understandings and appreciations.**

Youth may achieve understandings such as: the Christian concept of the extent and qualities of neighborliness; deepening realization that being a true neighbor demands giving one's best and witnessing to one's faith; the obligation to know and love neighbors everywhere; moral discernment as to the implications of neighborliness in social issues; awareness of sources of help in understanding and implementing neighborliness; the spiritual demands in relation to neighborliness.

Youth may achieve such skills as: increased ability to identify with others and to understand their feelings and needs; capacity to enter into rewarding dialogue with persons of different races, nations, classes; the ability to understand people, to respond to calls for neighborliness, to serve acceptably, to receive graciously; progress toward effective personal organization in regard to the claims of neighborliness, that is, orderliness in choosing priorities demanding time and money; growth in competence to recognize challenges in matters of neighborliness.

Youth may realize development in attitudes such as: growing ability to identify with the remote as well as the near-at-hand and with the spiritual as well as material needs of persons; progress in overcoming selfishness and isolation, acknowledging others and thus becoming open to their claims as neighbors; assurance that Christian community will support neighborly action; expanding sensitivity and concern for persons without regard to age, class, race, or religion; growth in appreciation of the worth and dignity of all human beings; growth in appreciation for the courage to act on the basis of Christian convictions about neighborliness.

Youth may realize such commitments as: the biblical teaching that all men are brothers and should be treated as persons; Christian truth regarding the extent and qualities of neighborliness; the achievement of a self-image as an understanding, concerned, loving, serving neighbor; service, attempting to act in the interest of all neighbors, sharing his Christian faith, the best in his culture, technical information; the practice of intercessory prayer as a means to neighborliness; willingness to dare to accept and fulfill the role of neighbor even though it is costly or involves nonconformity; the acceptance of responsibility for attitudes and actions in school.

2. Called to Serve One's Neighbor

STATEMENT OF THE THEME

The Christian perceives God's call in the give and take of interpersonal relationships in which he is constantly involved. He expresses his vocation in face-to-face relationships with his neighbor in every area of life, by expressing love, understanding acceptance, helpfulness, service.

ADULTHOOD   *617*

1. Significance of the theme for this age level

    a. Meanings and experiences within this theme relevant for this age level. This is content, a selected part of Scope.

The call to the adult to serve his neighbor has its basis in the central realities of the gospel: God's love for man; Christ's mission of redemption and compassionate service; the worth and dignity of all persons, and the needs of persons in their human situation. The explication of this call is a dominant theme of the biblical revelation.

God created man to be a member of society. Man is born for community. In the New Testament sense, the term neighbor best defines the Christian's relations with other persons. The New Testament term is inclusive of all persons, regardless of race or class. This term embraces even one's enemies. It has universal implication or meaning. The implications of the concept of neighborliness are real for international affairs, for social arrangements and policies, for political life.

618

The gospel teaches that there is an inseparable relation between religious duty in terms of love for God and ethical duty in terms of love for neighbor. The Christian pattern of human relations calls for the practice of love in all social relationships. Jesus declared that service done to a neighbor in need, with a sense of Christian commitment, is counted as service to the Lord. Service to one's neighbor demands sacrifice, and suffering of the cross.

1. Significance of the theme for this age level

b. Readiness of the learner for this theme in terms of basic needs, interests, motivations, capacities, developmental tasks.

The adult is a member of social groups—family, neighborhood, church, club, union, trade—and by nature is strongly drawn to other persons through the bonds of their common humanity.

The adult is influenced by the prejudices of his social heritage with its cultural patterns. The relevance of this theme for him arises through the strong pressures his society places upon him to ignore the claims of some of his neighbors. The adult with Christian faith and commitment finds himself in constant tension between antineighbor attitudes and pressures, and the call of the Holy Spirit to bear one another's burdens and fulfill the law of Christ. This tension may lead to desire for better understanding of the gospel and for shared experience in answering the call to serve one's neighbor.

The adult has been exposed directly or vicariously to poverty, sickness, tragedy, maladjustment, cruelty, indifference. He is involved inextricably in the pressures that hinder and destroy neighborliness, some of which reside in his own being. He also experiences the need for neighborliness. All these experiences may equip him to respond to the call to serve his neighbor.

Many adults have resources for accepting and discharging the role of neighbor—money, skills, strength, influence, franchise, knowledge. They possess the legal and social autonomy and often the power to make important decisions. The adult years make possible the mature fulfillment of the role of neighbor for everyone.

The adult has a desire for creative expression, humanitarian contribution, and social improvement.

The adult has adequate maturity for instruction as to the deeper meanings and implications of neighborliness, the full meaning of Christian love, the ethical demands of the gospel, and the impact on himself from accepting or rejecting the call to serve his neighbor. He often desires guidance or training in the skills of neighborliness.

The adult is challenged by cooperative or corporate undertakings in serving his neighbor. He seeks reinforcement and support in efforts to fulfill the demands of loving his neighbor as himself.

619

The Christian adult has the potential for maximum creativity and dedication in discovering the ethical demands of Christian love and in developing ways to implement the goals of neighborliness.

The adult is confronted with the need and opportunity to work vicariously for the values of neighborliness through such means as institutions, political parties, social clubs, and welfare agencies.

The adult is confronted with the facts of the nuclear and space age and the population explosion which make revolutionary demands for new concepts and new approaches to neighborliness.

2. **How may this content be communicated as the learner engages in the Learning Tasks? What are the methods and procedures by which the learner may explore the meanings and experiences within this theme (1-a) in the light of his readiness (1-b) in order to discover significance and value?**

Through personal and group study of the Bible—particularly the teachings of the gospel.

Through serious dialogue and research as to the meaning of Christian love.

Through participation in a reading program designed to acquaint adults with problem areas, Christian approaches, and constructive achievements in interpersonal relations.

Through a variety of media, engaging in group exploration of personal behavior, cultural mores, and social arrangements which militate against neighborliness.

By participating in group projects designed to help persons who need food, protection against exploitation, improvement of economic, cultural, health, or civil status.

Through participation in organized movements which aim at making Christian principles an effective guide in human relations and in service undertakings which aim at translating Christian concern into action.

By being confronted with the necessity to understand the perspective and objectives of his opponents.

3. **What may the learner achieve within this theme in the fulfillment of the Learning Tasks? What are possible changes or learnings on the part of the learner that may result from his appropriation of the significance and value discovered? These changes or learnings may be associated with skills, attitudes, motivations, perceptions including understandings and appreciations.**

The adult may find interesting and fruitful experiences in learning the meaning of neighborliness and fulfilling the role of neighbor.

The adult may overcome to a large degree his prejudice and thus grow in social vision, in Christlike compassion, and in generous attitudes.

The adult may achieve more generous attitudes toward other persons as he receives experiences of neighborliness, unexpected or unwarranted. This experience may enrich both giver and receiver.

The adult may learn some of the deeper meanings of the cross and the satisfaction of Christian discipleship through accepting the role of neighbor.

The adult may experience reconciliation and restoration with former enemies as he commits himself to the demands of Christian love.

The adult may experience a growing sense of fellowship with Christ and of the presence of the Holy Spirit through trying to fulfill the role of neighbor, especially when this role involves a clear-cut departure from accepted social patterns.

The adult may achieve ability to become a dynamic witness to the validity of Jesus' teaching and to the adequacy of this teaching as a guide for all human relations.

The adult may come to a fuller understanding of success measured by the practice of the commandment, "Love your neighbor as yourself." He may develop a deepening commitment to accept the role of neighbor in the full Christian sense, irrespective of the demands made upon him.

621

The adult may grow in respect for persons as persons, and thus find new motivation for neighborliness toward all persons.

The adult may come to a broadened understanding of neighbor in terms of the hungry, the sick, the handicapped, the mistreated, the defeated, the incorrigible, the victims of tragedy and circumstance, the poor, the weak, the lonely, the illiterate, the exploited, members of his own family, and persons in all possible relationships (including capital-labor, landlord-tenant, guard-prisoner, court-criminal).

The adult may achieve a richer experience by using material

resources for those in need.

The adult may develop a growing desire and ability to share his faith, and thus translate witnessing into neighborliness.

The adult may develop a growing desire to pray and give, in order that the world mission of the church may be set forward and the Christian faith spread throughout the whole world.

3. The Stewardship of Life and Work

622

STATEMENT OF THE THEME

Every decision is a choice among values that are often competing and contradictory. The disciple decides in light of his calling as a Christian how he will deploy his time, energies, money, talents, interests so as to achieve the most important or necessary ends. This choice is especially seen because of the specialization involved in the choice of an occupation.

EARLY CHILDHOOD

1. Significance of the theme for this age level

a. Meanings and experiences within this theme relevant for this age level. This is content, a selected part of Scope.

Life is a gift from God.

Growth is a part of God's plan and a gift from God.

God plans for persons to grow physically, mentally, emotionally, and socially.

God has provided the natural world and he has planned for persons to enjoy, develop, use, and conserve it.

People are dependent upon God for the source of food, clothing, water, and other necessities of life.

Everything has been created by God and is his, but in his love he lets his creatures use what he has created.

God wants each person to use abilities and possessions for the well-being of self and others.

Even now I am responsible for some decisions.
Work and play are a part of God's plan.
Things are for use but require care.

1. Significance of the theme for this age level

b. Readiness of the learner for this theme in terms of basic needs, interests, motivations, capacities, developmental tasks

The young child has a basic need to be affirmed as a unique person of value to others and of worth in himself.

The young child is curious about the world of nature and of persons and is beginning to develop attitudes and behavior patterns toward them.

The young child is curious about the adult world of work— that of his mother, father, community helpers—and is beginning to develop attitudes and behavior patterns in regard to work.

The young child has a need to manipulate things and use them successfully.

The young child has a need to relate meaningfully to his total environment.

The young child is beginning to differentiate between his own possessions and those of others and to decide for himself how he will use possessions—selfishly or unselfishly, destructively or creatively.

623

The young child is expanding his relations with persons and things and wants to explore these relations.

The young child is forming habits and developing a conscience, both of which will influence his attitudes and behavior toward things and persons and their worth and value.

2. How may this content be communicated as the learner engages in the Learning Tasks? What are the methods and procedures by which the learner may explore the meanings and experiences within this theme (1-a) in the light of his readiness (1-b) in order to discover significance and value?

By observing persons significant to him in their use of things, money, possessions, and at their work.

By experiencing respect and appreciation by others for his skills, abilities, ideas.

By exploring freely, within safe boundaries, the world of nature and being helped to explore some parts of it.

By engaging in play activities that enable him to identify with the adult world of work.

By having appropriate work responsibilities in the family and his church groups.

By making simple decisions about the use of his own time, energy, and talents.

By participating in helpful experiences of serving others and sharing things with them.

By engaging in individual and group activities suited to his development (conversing, hearing stories, seeing and making pictures, etc.) which interpret his world and the meaning of his participation in it.

By having conversations, hearing selected Bible stories and daily-life stories suitable to the theme.

By manipulating toys and other things and being partially or wholly responsible for their use and care.

3. **What may the learner achieve within this theme in the fulfillment of the Learning Tasks? What are possible changes or learnings on the part of the learner that may result from his appropriation of the significance and value discovered? These changes or learnings may be associated with skills, attitudes, motivations, perceptions including understandings and appreciations.**

The young child may begin to become physically self-reliant, taking some responsibility for self.

The young child may begin to accept himself as a person of worth with specific abilities.

The young child may begin to be aware of the world of work and some work roles.

The young child may begin to choose among various ways he will use his time.

The young child may begin to develop a sense of responsibility for material things, conserving rather than wasting, caring for clothing, toys, and other possessions.

The young child may begin to share with others through the family and the church.

The young child may begin to recognize that God created the world, that it belongs to God, and that it is ours to use, enjoy, and care for.

The young child may begin to recognize himself and others as belonging to God.

The young child may begin to utilize constructively and to share his possessions as expressions of love to others.

The young child may begin to know that he is showing love for God as he shares himself and his possessions with others in love.

The young child may begin to appreciate growth as a part of God's plan and to enjoy growing physically, mentally, emotionally, and socially.

The young child may begin to realize that God is the source of all necessities of life.

625

The young child may begin to accept some responsibility for his own decisions.

3. The Stewardship of Life and Work

STATEMENT OF THE THEME

Every decision is a choice among values that are often competing and contradictory. The disciple decides in light of his calling as a Christian how he will deploy his time, energies, money, talents, interests so as to achieve the most important or necessary ends.

This choice is especially seen because of the specialization involved in the choice of an occupation.

ELEMENTARY YEARS

1. Significance of the theme for this age level

   a. Meanings and experiences within this theme relevant for this age level. This is content, a selected part of Scope.

It is God's will that persons share in the responsible stewardship of helping maintain his world.

A consideration of the use of time is necessary because our length of days is a gift of God to be numbered and used in the service of man to the glory of God.

As one studies at school or works around the house, he is called to serve as a steward of God.

God created the natural world in all its manifestations.

Material possessions are possible because of what God puts in the world, and God calls mankind to acknowledge their stewardship of all that they receive, earn, and possess.

Each person bears a responsibility commensurate with his age and ability for the health and welfare of the community in which he lives and by which he is affected.

Life is a gift from God.

Work and play are a part of God's plan.

Things are for use but require care.

1. Significance of the theme for this age level

   b. Readiness of the learner for this theme in terms of basic needs, interests, motivations, capacities, developmental tasks.

The child has an increasing capacity to take responsibility for the use of his time, possessions, and energies and for the development of his talents.

The elementary child is interested in many aspects of the natural world, its development from prehistoric times, the causes of natural events, and scientific discoveries.

The elementary child is interested in entering into the creative process such as caring for plants and animals.

The elementary child has a basic need for being accepted as a person of worth, as a responsible member of his family, peer group, and community.

The elementary child is curious about the world of work, and "tries on" or imitates the role of many different occupations that he observes.

The elementary child begins to assume ownership of pets and things such as clothing, toys, books, items involved in hobbies and collections. These are considered by him to be "his very own."

2. **How may this content be communicated as the learner engages in the Learning Tasks? What are the methods and procedures by which the learner may explore the meanings and experiences within this theme (1-a) in the light of his readiness (1-b) in order to discover significance and value?**

By assuming responsibility for volunteer or assigned tasks in the home, church, school and/or community as he has freedom and encouragement.

By developing hobbies related to the training of natural endowments.

By observing and thinking about various occupations and associating with persons engaged in them.

By living with adults who demonstrate a mature understanding and a Christian stewardship of time in home, church, school, and community.

By being allowed enough leisure and privacy to experiment with making more of his own time choices.

By being permitted occasions to live with the consequences of his choices.

627

By participating in camping and other experiences in the out-of-doors in which there are opportunities to make economical and safe use of natural resources.

By studying the explorations and findings of scientists, particularly those who specialize in conservation.

By observing persons who appreciate the beauty and bounty of the natural world and who practice the principles of conservation.

By caring for plants and animals.

628

By sharing possessions with others in the home, school, church, community, and other parts of the world.

By giving a portion of his money to the church as a tithe and offering.

By having opportunities to decide what is a wise use of the funds at his disposal, with a recognition of the future potential of his resources.

By living in an atmosphere that affirms the necessity and desirability of some form of social organization which guarantees freedom under law and protects the health and welfare of even the youngest or least of its members.

By investigating the work of various institutions by which society tries to meet the needs of its members by both political and voluntary means.

By organizing with others to meet their needs through committees and other forms of deliberation, decision-making, and action.

By studying the Bible for its message relevant to stewardship and its accounts of personalities who recognized their stewardship of God.

3. **What may the learner achieve within this theme in the fulfillment of the Learning Tasks? What are possible changes or learnings on the part of the learner that may result from his appropriation of the significance and value discovered? These changes or learnings may be associated with skills,**

attitudes, motivations, perceptions including understandings and appreciations.

The elementary child may perceive work as a satisfying element of life.

The elementary child may comprehend work as a sacred thing, participating in it according to his ability.

The elementary child may recognize the value of the work of others.

The elementary child may increasingly make better time choices that will safeguard health, allow for exploration of both study and play, and provide for responsible and balanced participation in home, school, and community.

The elementary child may increasingly acknowledge his limitations of time and ability.

The elementary child may become more aware of his own developing talents and accept the limitations of his talents.

The elementary child may see talents as possible guides to future life of stewardship.

The elementary child may see that talents can be related to worthwhile projects, bringing satisfaction to self and contributing to the welfare of others.

The elementary child may accept personal responsibility in the use of talents (especially as a student).

629

The elementary child may come to understand that God can call for special use of his talents to further God's own work in the world.

The elementary child may become increasingly responsible for the health and welfare of others as part of the stewardship of life.

The elementary child may practice stewardship of money and possessions as a natural response to God's will, with a sense of thanksgiving for what God has done for man.

The elementary child may assume initiative and responsibility in aspects of community life of which he is a part and that have implications for the stewardship of life and work.

3. The Stewardship of Life and Work

STATEMENT OF THE THEME

Every decision is a choice among values that are often competing and contradictory. The disciple decides in light of his calling as a Christian how he will deploy his time, energies, money, talents, interests so as to achieve the most important or necessary ends. This choice is especially seen because of the specialization involved in the choice of an occupation.

630

YOUTH

1. Significance of the theme for this age level

a. Meanings and experiences within this theme relevant for this age level. This is content, a selected part of Scope.

It is the intention of God that youth choose, prepare for, and perform his life's work out of a sense of commitment to God's will and purpose.

Time is a gift from God to be used by youth, both in leisure and in productive activity, according to God's will.

Personal talents and opportunities to develop and use them are endowments from God to be employed for his glory and for the enrichment of others.

As one studies at school, works around the house, or engages in part-time employment, he is called to serve as a steward of God.

The earth is filled with natural resources and man is responsible for the careful use, conservation, and enjoyment of them.

The ability to acquire money and other possessions is God-given. Youth is called to use both the abilities and the possessions as means to glorify God and serve mankind in accordance with the biblical concept of stewardship.

God has placed men in community with other families, nations, and in the whole world and has entrusted to man the responsibility to maintain order and renew life.

Man participates indirectly in work beyond his own; this faces youth with the challenge to witness to his faith through the agencies and businesses he supports with his gifts and purchases.

Life is a gift from God.

Every decision involves a weighing of alternative values and an implicit (or explicit) calculation of the relative efficiency of using one's available resources (money, materials, time) to achieve these values.

It is the intention of God that persons base all of their decisions and subsequent courses of action on a sense of commitment to God's will and purpose.

1. Significance of the theme for this age level

b. Readiness of the learner for this theme in terms of basic needs, interests, motivations, capacities, developmental tasks.

Youth has an increasing necessity and ability to cope with new and more consequential decisions related to the use of time, ability, energy, and money.

Youth has the desire to develop newly discovered talents and to express his creativity.

Youth is eager to know and understand his abilities and capacities.

Youth's self-awareness is accompanied by a desire for self-fulfillment in a life which will make a difference and that will be a constructive force.

Youth needs to be accepted in terms of his own abilities, capacities, skills.

Youth desires to acquire possessions and to be financially secure.

Awakened sensitivities in youth make him alert to needs of persons and society which his skills, abilities, possessions, money, may help alleviate.

From school, home, church, and society, youth experiences an increased demand on his time which forces him to make

631

decisions about the use of his time for leisure, for rest, for solitude, and for friendships.

In youth's increasing associations with peers he encounters competitiveness in abilities, skills, and productivity.

Youth desires to become adult and self-supporting.

Society pushes young people to decide on a life occupation and preparation for it.

A young person often controls a significant amount of money.

Youth wants to be accepted and may seek acceptance by conformity in earning and spending habits, in developing particular skills and abilities.

Youth is keen to observe discrepancy in professed stewardship and overt behavior of others in relation to money, work, and possessions.

Youth can make a valuable contribution to family and society through work, whether or not remunerative.

To achieve personal dignity, worth, and status is important to youth.

In youth years there is a growing awareness of sex and the ability to participate in procreation of life.

The business world views youth as an important economic force and bids for youth's business.

2. How may this content be communicated as the learner engages in the Learning Tasks? What are the methods and procedures by which the learner may explore the meanings and experiences within this theme (1-a) in the light of his readiness (1-b) in order to discover significance and value?

By studying the Scriptures.

By becoming acquainted with persons of any age or country who are themselves good stewards of time, work, abilities, money, possessions. This acquaintance he may achieve through reading, conversing, interviewing, observing persons, viewing films.

By reading, engaging in conversations, lectures, travel, and viewing pictures and films that inform him on the character of the natural world and the results of responsible and irresponsible use of its resources.

By observing and evaluating his present habits in the use of time and experimenting in the conservation and apportionment of it.

By role playing in which the youth examines responsibilities of budget-making in light of the concept of stewardship.

By examining and assessing through tests, interviews, experiments, his own various abilities, interests, and capacities.

By observing and evaluating waste of resources and the consequences.

By participating in creative conservation and development of proper utilization and distribution of resources.

By examining through reading, conversation, listening, stewardship thought and practices among people of various faiths and cultures.

By participating in a variety of summer or part-time occupations or volunteers service to assess occupational opportunities and his own aptness for various fields of work.

By watching and evaluating TV programs dealing with problems and challenges of a variety of work tasks.

By actually handling money of others under supervision.

By earning his own money and making decisions with regard to its use.

633

By participating in decisions affecting the time, possessions, money of the family and of other groups, consciously taking account of youth's stewardship role.

3. **What may the learner achieve within this theme in the fulfillment of the Learning Tasks? What are possible changes or learnings on the part of the learner that may result from his appropriation of the significance and value discovered? These changes or learnings may be associated with skills, attitudes, motivations, perceptions including understandings and appreciations.**

Youth may achieve a deeper understanding of God's ownership and his own position as a steward in relation to his time, talents, money, possessions.

Youth may achieve an acceptance of his own capacities, a greater appreciation of their potential, and a deepening sense of responsibility for their use.

Youth may achieve an appreciative attitude toward work.

Youth may achieve increased skill in the development of talents, the discipline of energies, the use of and the conservation of resources.

634

Youth may achieve a conviction that whatever his work, it will be done as a steward of God.

Youth may achieve a growing ability to recognize and accept his limitations in talent, general ability, and health.

Youth may achieve the ability to rejoice in the achievements of others and help them make the most of their talents.

Youth may achieve a sense of proportion in the use of time and an ability to invest it most significantly.

Youth may achieve an appreciation of the beauty and bounty of the natural world and his understanding that its gifts are for all men.

Youth may achieve a commitment to a course of stewardship regarding money and other material possessions which expresses his acceptance. of God's ownership and his understanding of the claim of various causes.

Youth may achieve appreciation of service to others as a value greater than personal gain or self-aggrandizement.

3. The Stewardship of Life and Work

STATEMENT OF THE THEME

Every decision is a choice among values that are often competing and contradictory. The disciple decides in light of his calling as a Christian how he will deploy his time, energies, money, talents, interests so as to achieve the most important or necessary ends. This choice is especially seen because of the specialization involved in the choice of an occupation.

ADULTHOOD

1. Significance of the theme for this age level

a. Meanings and experiences within this theme relevant for this age level. This is content, a selected part of Scope.

As he earns a living, the adult is called to serve as a steward of God.

Time is a gift of God, the use of which calls for the making of responsible decisions in such areas as education, leisure, family life, occupation, community and world relations, church activities, friendships.

God endows each person with abilities and energy and calls him to use and develop them for creative and effective ministry to mankind and for the glory of God.

God has created a world of varied and abundant natural resources. He has placed men in it to enjoy it and to develop and conserve these resources for the benefit of all, now and in the future.

Money and other possessions and the ability to acquire them are God-given, to be used as means to glorify God and serve mankind.

635

Man participates indirectly in work beyond his own; this faces him with the challenge to witness to his faith through the agencies and businesses he supports with his gifts and purchases.

Life is a gift from God.

Every decision involves a weighing of alternative values and an implicit (or explicit) calculation of the relative efficiency of using one's available resources (money, materials, time) to achieve these values.

It is the intention of God that persons base all of their decisions and subsequent courses of action on a sense of commitment to God's will and purpose.

God has placed man in community with other families, nations and the whole world; and has entrusted to man the responsibility to maintain order and renew life.

It is the intention of God that persons perform their life's work out of a sense of commitment to God's will and purpose.

1. Significance of the theme for this age level

636

    b. Readiness of the learner for this theme in terms of basic needs, interests, motivations, capacities, developmental tasks.

The adult has need for a sense of the importance of the job performed and his value in it.

The adult has a concern to provide adequately for himself, his family, and others.

The adult has a need of establishing his personal integrity and of finding acceptance in his lifework and daily activities and decisions as he relates to other persons and to God.

The adult needs to be able to use his talents creatively in his daily work.

The adult has the desire for enlarging the extent of his creative and beneficial contributions to family, friends, and community.

The adult experiences the pressures of various demands on his time. These pressures come from his occupation, home, church, and society. He is forced to make decisions in the face of these competing demands.

The adult has the desire for satisfying experiences in the use of his "free time."

The adult has a need for both intimacy and separateness in relationships with persons with and for whom he works (acceptance without exploitation) and in relationships established in carrying out the responsibilities he assumes for the well-being of his community and the world.

The adult needs to join with groups in the management of the economy.

The adult is confronted by the growing demands of the world's population explosion upon the limited resources of food and fiber.

The adult is able to understand the dependence of health, education, and welfare upon effective structures for production and distribution of available resources. The adult can distinguish between constructive and destructive uses of resources.

The adult has the need and ability to make decisions based on future needs and values rather than on expediency of the moment.

The adult is able to realize the benefits and values that come with continuing development and use of talents with the discerning deployment of time and with the conservation of energy for useful purposes.

The adult has the ability to assume responsibility for his decisions that affects persons of his own and of the opposite sex and for his part in the procreation of life.

2. **How may this content be communicated as the learner engages in the Learning Tasks? What are the methods and procedures by which the learner may explore the meanings and experiences within this theme (1-a) in the light of his readiness (1-b) in order to discover significance and value?**

637

By participating in occupational seminars, study and work groups, on job-related problems.

By participating in work, study, or service projects involving study, discussion, action regarding personal and social stewardship of life and work.

By exploring the biblical witness to God's word regarding personal responsibility in the use of time and talents in work and recreation such as study of the concepts of "vocation," "creation," "servanthood," "stewardship," and "work."

By being exposed to preaching and counseling.

By entering into discussion and conversation with significant persons who can share insights of stewardship of life and work.

By participating in social, political, educational ventures in community, nation, and world which seek to establish Christian values with respect to human and natural resources.

638

3. **What may the learner achieve within this theme in the fulfillment of the Learning Tasks? What are possible changes or learnings on the part of the learner that may result from his appropriation of the significance and value discovered? These changes or learnings may be associated with skills, attitudes, motivations, perceptions including understandings and appreciations.**

The adult may gain increased knowledge and understanding of resources for testing personal decisions, especially those having to do with the use of skills and energies in earning a living.

The adult may gain skill in examining and evaluating attitudes toward and procedures in the use of his energies and abilities in his job and in his use of leisure.

The adult may establish habits of proportionate and systematic giving.

The adult may gain increasing ability to explore issues related to his job and the community and, where desirable, to use available resources in seeking Christian solutions.

The adult may accumulate knowledge and understanding in the use of available resources in making decisions that contribute to the fullest realization of personal and social potentials.

The adult may become sensitive to the larger world of persons and the issues in the world of work which demand Christian solution.

The adult may increase his skill in the evaluation as a Christian of alternative uses of limited natural resources (in both personal and social responsibility for them).

The adult may come to maturity in decision-making as a Christian in such areas as Christian witness in work and service, in finding new ways to correct destructive trends in society.

The adult may budget his time and talents so that they are used appropriately for work, leisure, and personal or social responsibilities.

The adult may come to an increasing knowledge of the nature and purpose of the Christian community, of Christian love and service as the community delays its energies, monies, abilities.

The adult may develop a growing awareness of the worth of self and other persons in their varied abilities, interests, skills, capacities.

The adult may develop ability in helping young people get launched into the world of work.

The adult may develop ability in interpreting to children by word or example the adult world of work and recreation as the Christian experiences that world.

4. Discipline in the Christian Life

STATEMENT OF THE THEME

The Christian learns to cope with the difficult demands of decision-making situations under the disciplines of the Christian faith.

639

EARLY CHILDHOOD

1. Significance of the theme for this age level

a. Meanings and experiences within this theme relevant for this age level. This is content, a selected part of Scope.

Discipleship requires that the young child love God, trust him, and obey him. The gospel affirms that God is dependable even though the child's experience may be too limited to support him in such a basic trust.

Habits of worship, prayer, and learning experiences within the Christian community are disciplines that provide a basic orientation of reverence for, and trust in God, and encourage growth in the Christian faith.

The message of the gospel is that God is present, giving assurance to the disciple who is open and obedient.

1. Significance of the theme for this age level

640

  b. Readiness of the learner for this theme in terms of basic needs, interests, motivations, capacities, developmental tasks

The young child has a marked urge toward freedom and exploration. Touching and tasting, pushing and pulling, making noises and listening, demanding and helping—all express his urge to discover the world around him even as he discovers himself. In the midst of this freedom and exploration, the child is open to receive tenderness and understanding love, accurate and appropriate information, and consistent counsel and correction by parents and other adults.

The young child early in life may experience love and hate, acceptance and rejection, pleasure and pain, freedom and limitations. As he responds to his world, he experiences both fulfillment and denial of his basic desires and becomes aware of the difficult demands of life. In coping with these demands he needs both human and divine help.

The young child has an inquiring mind, asking questions of what, where, how, and why: Where did I come from? Why must I? What's your name? Do you like me? Where is God? Is this the story of a good man or a bad man? These and many other questions indicate the readiness of the child to engage in Christian learning.

The young child senses the desirability to get along with members of his family, playmates in the neighborhood, and others, and therefore is open to learning the beginnings of Christian discipleship that will help him in human relations.

The young child has an unfolding capacity to begin assuming responsibility for his own behavior, attitudes, and actions toward other persons based on Christian disciplines.

The young child begins to practice discipline as he takes limited responsibility for possessions, for caring for pets and for his own safety and welfare.

The young child discovers his own need for controlling his actions through use of elementary discipline.

2. **How may this content be communicated as the learner engages in the Learning Tasks? What are the methods and procedures by which the learner may explore the meanings and experiences within this theme (1-a) in the light of his readiness (1-b) in order to discover significance and value?**

Through opportunities of creative expression: stories, games, play, music, and other arts.

Through opportunities to engage in prayer and worship, to hear and respond to the Bible.

Through contact with those in the home, playmates in the neighborhood, and those at church. These experiences will sometimes require that the young child must be restricted, denied, even punished. Such experiences, when accompanied by forgiveness, restoration, acceptance, and love, will prepare the child to accept the disciplines of the Christian faith.

641

By observing more mature Christians as they assume Christian disciplines.

3. **What may the learner achieve within this theme in the fulfillment of the Learning Tasks? What are possible changes or learnings on the part of the learner that may result from his appropriation of the significance and value discovered? These changes or learnings may be associated with skills, attitudes, motivations, perceptions including understandings and appreciations.**

A young child may grow in awareness that he is loved by God and by people who care for him.

The young child may develop a sense of security resulting from elementary experiences in the disciplines of the Christian life.

Out of a growing sense of reverence, gratitude, and awe toward God, the young child may develop the beginnings of a desire to enter into Christian discipleship.

The young child in his eagerness to find out more about God's world and its laws may respond to it appropriately.

The young child may increase in his ability to assume responsibility for self and possessions, to abide by fundamental rules, and to cooperate with others.

The young child may more readily enter into experiences of personal evaluation and correction.

The young child may participate with more meaning and understanding in experiences of personal, family, and corporate worship.

4. Discipline in the Christian Life

STATEMENT OF THE THEME

The Christian learns to cope with the difficult demands of decision-making situations under the disciplines of the Christian faith.

ELEMENTARY YEARS

1. **Significance of the theme for this age level**

   a. **Meanings and experiences within this theme relevant for this age level. This is content, a selected part of Scope.**

Discipleship requires of the child a growing knowledge of the foundations of the Christian life.

The Christian responds to Jesus Christ in following his teachings and in obedience to him as Lord.

In the Christian life choices related to one's own growth and the welfare of others are made under the disciplines of the Christian faith.

1. **Significance of the theme for this age level**

    b. **Readiness of the learner for this theme in terms of basic needs, interests, motivations, capacities, developmental tasks.**

In his psycho-physical development and in experimentation with his unfolding capacities, the elementary child has a need for authority and for norms of behavior, self-organization, and a sense of personal worth.

The child is confronted with the task of beginning to achieve self-respect.

As the growing child experiences new freedom, the child is interested in persons who provide models of behavior.

The elementary child has innate curiosity which causes him to inquire, explore, and test.

The child's experiences of disappointments and failures provide a readiness for learning how best to cope with life and to make good decisions.

643

2. **How may this content be communicated as the learner engages in the Learning Tasks? What are the methods and procedures by which the learner may explore the meanings and experiences within this theme (1-a) in the light of his readiness (1-b) in order to discover significance and value?**

By opportunities for the elementary child to make his own decisions in the home, church, school, and community under the disciplines of the Christian life. Also through opportunities to act in positions of trust commensurate with his growing ability.

Through association with adults in whom the elementary child has confidence and who live in obedience to God, practicing the disciplines of the Christian life.

In conversation with peers and knowledgeable adults, the child may explore the purposes and practices of prayer, Bible study, worship, self-denial, service to others, giving and receiving forgiveness, obedience to God, and other disciplines of the Christian life.

By reading biographies or viewing films of Christian men and women who can become models for his life.

644

Through experience in a supportive, loving, trusting community atmosphere which allows him freedom to make mistakes and to learn from them.

3. **What may the learner achieve within this theme in the fulfillment of the Learning Tasks? What are possible changes or learnings on the part of the learner that may result from his appropriation of the significance and value discovered? These changes or learnings may be associated with skills, attitudes, motivations, perceptions including understandings and appreciations.**

The child may develop a growing awareness of Jesus Christ as present, living Lord and Savior, and of the meaning of this relationship for discipleship.

The child may grow in his ability to enter into experiences of worship, private or corporate.

The child may grow in voluntary acceptance of such disciplines as Bible study, stewardship, prayer, attendance at worship.

Out of acceptance of Christian norms of attitude and behavior the child may grow in his ability to judge for himself what is a Christian response in a particular situation.

The child may learn the positive values of self-discipline: postponement of the fulfillment of personal desires, loyalty to friends and groups, and the joy which comes from living under these voluntarily accepted disciplines.

The child may increase in ability to choose creative forms of service to others.

The child may increase in ability to endure rebuffs or disappointments with Christian grace.

The child may grow in ability to take realistic attitudes toward his limitations, to accept responsibility for developing his potentialities, to organize resources, and to establish priorities in life's activities.

The child may increase his desire for and acceptance of counsel from trusted peers and elders.

4. Discipline in the Christian Life

STATEMENT OF THE THEME

The Christian learns to cope with the difficult demands of decision-making situations under the disciplines of the Christian faith.

YOUTH

1. Significance of the theme for this age level

a. Meanings and experiences within this theme relevant for this age level. This is content, a selected part of Scope.

The discipline to which Christian youth is called is that of obedience to the will and purpose of God in the relationship of disciple to his teacher, Jesus Christ. This relationship makes possible the fulfillment of his life and requires responsible use of his growing freedom.

To guide the youth in his growth as a disciple, God has revealed certain norms of attitudes and behavior on which to base his decisions and actions—such norms as love of God and neighbors and the necessity to be forgiving, to seek justice for all men, to be humble, to strive for personal holiness. These are made known in the Scriptures and in the ongoing life of the Christian community.

645

Discipline in the Christian life requires the disciple to take advantage of the Christian means of grace (such as worship, study, and witness), and requires him to use these means regularly and responsibly.

God has promised the disciple the abiding presence of the Holy Spirit as Counselor in decision-making.

1. Significance of the theme for this age level

b. Readiness of the learner for this theme in terms of basic needs, interests, motivations, capacities, developmental tasks.

As the young person matures, he finds himself under the necessity of having to make more and more decisions concerning the disciplines that will help him cope with the issues of life. These decisions relate to disciplines in connection with such matters as: other persons in the home, the neighborhood, the church, the school, the community. Especially must he face questions of discipline with his peers, including members of the opposite sex. Other races and cultural groups demand decisions. Personal concerns demand decisions in relation to discipline—health and conduct, studies, hobbies, choice of and preparation for a lifework, choice of a lifemate. Duties toward family, community, and nation call for decisions regarding discipline. Youth must decide what disciplines he will adopt for himself related to his involvement in the life and work of the church. As he is pressed to make decisions affecting all these areas of life, youth may desire help in formulating and accepting the disciplines of the Christian life.

Increasing tensions may awaken youth to the need of thought about desirable disciplines for his life and a consciousness of his need for help in deciding upon them. Some tensions which increase in intensity during youth years are: (a) tension between the standards his home and church have set before him and the conduct his environment may require of him; (b) tension between his growing desire to be free and live his own life and his eagerness to keep the good opinion and respect of persons who are important to him; (c) tension between the demands that home, school, and community make on his time and energies and his obligations to his church; (d) tension between his desire to make his faith meaningful and the doubts and questions that may arise concerning the validity of his religious experience and of the claims of the gospel; (e) tension between his unhappy experiences of disappointment and rejection and defeat and his effort to be Christian about them and react to them in positive ways; (f) tension between his need to be engaged in productive activity and limitations of job opportunity; (g) tension between his desire for self-fulfillment and the personal limitations and social pressures which seem to hem him in; (h) tension between his desire to gratify physical urges and appetites and his desire for self-control.

Youth's increasing liberty often leads youth to question disciplines in general and may stimulate an interest in a study of the matter, including Christian disciplines.

With some experience of failure, youth may have some uncertainty and even a sense of failure about the disciplines he has been following. Youth may feel the need for deeper probing into the disciplines desirable for Christian discipleship.

647

The youth may desire to live a vital Christian life and yet feel that his religious life is inadequate in itself and in the way his faith carries over into acts of everyday life.

The youth may have questions about disciplines of Bible study, prayer, public worship. He may desire to examine the disciplines of Christian life and gain new interpretations of them. He may have reached the end of one stage of Bible study, feeling that the approach used in elementary years is superficial. He may be asking what the Bible really has to say to him. He may be willing to engage in disciplined Bible study, approaching the Bible from the standpoints of history and theology; to examine the reason for Christian disciplines; and to explore the nature of these disciplines.

The youth is accumulating direct and vicarious experience which permits him to observe ever more widely the results of undisciplined lives. He is forced to compare the quality of life achieved by persons with moral and ethical disciplines with that of persons whose lives do not evidence such disciplines.

The youth often experiences a desire to become a part of the church congregation in every way. He may feel the need to receive counsel regarding Christian disciplines and to share insights of his own. He may desire to accept for himself disciplines which will contribute significantly to the lives of others, to the world mission of the church, and to the progress of worthy causes throughout the world.

The youth may become increasingly aware of the presence of the Holy Spirit and develop a willingness to listen to his guidance.

2. How may this content be communicated as the learner engages in the Learning Tasks? What are the methods and procedures by which the learner may explore the meanings and experiences within this theme (1-a) in the light of his readiness (1-b) in order to discover significance and value?

By exploring the meaning of prayer, worship, and the sacraments of the church.

By sharing in planning for and participating in prayer and worship.

By becoming acquainted with the great devotional classics.

By participating in the ordinances or sacraments of the church.

By becoming involved in seminars, prayer groups, and other activity which encourage the disciplined Christian life.

By sharing with others his discoveries.

By reading biographies and viewing films that clarify perceptions concerning Christian disciplines and that portray the value of faithfulness to the disciplines which are norms of the Christian community. Individuals who have made significant contributions to the life of their age may be chosen as subjects of study.

Through significant Bible study, which stretches his expanding intellectual and spiritual powers and through the study of tested findings of the scholars in various fields.

Through study of the origin and nature of disciplines in general and of Christian disciplines in particular, exploring the difference between slavish disciplines and voluntary ones, in which the youth choses a trusted leader as his guide and willingly learns disciplines in order to obey that leader.

Through opportunities to consult with adults of the church on matters related to the disciplines of the Christian life in which correction and support are exchanged and insights gained that clarify disciplines and their values.

Through conversation, interviews, observation tours, and reading. Youth may see the relation of discipline to Christian witness in the homeland and to the Christian missionary outreach in all the world.

Through sharing insights about and supporting one another in Christian disciplines as they respond to God in obedience.

Through frequent participation in planned opportunities to observe and discover Christian disciplines using such media as stage plays, movies, TV dramas, literature studied in English classes in school, personal reading of drama, fiction, poetry, and essays.

649

By observing, discussing, and practicing disciplines as applied to the arts—painting, music, poetry, etc—where achievement depends upon the acceptance of certain disciplines.

By examining aspects of youth culture in North America and other lands. Youth may discover forces which encourage worthy disciplines in the lives of Christian youth. They may detect forces which discourage such disciplines. They may seek ways in which they may participate in their culture and contribute to it and still be true to the disciplines of the Christian faith.

Through personal interviews, viewing films, and reading books and periodicals, to consider the importance of discipline in the lives of church members as they face such problems of this age as race relations, war, the threat of annihilation, the population explosion, and poverty.

3. **What may the learner achieve within this theme in the fulfillment of the Learning Tasks? What are possible changes or learnings on the part of the learner that may result from his appropriation of the significance and value discovered? These changes or learnings may be associated with skills, attitudes, motivations, perceptions including understandings and appreciations.**

The youth may gain a growing sense of relationship to Jesus Christ as teacher and Lord, a deeper appreciation for the sacraments and the ministries of the church, and discover new depths of meaning in prayer and worship.

The youth may develop a growing capacity for self-control, rejecting un-Christian patterns of behavior and developing standards in keeping with his calling as a disciple of Jesus Christ.

The youth may discover that a life of obedience to Jesus Christ is one of deep satisfaction and joy, enabling him to be at his best and to make his greatest contributions to the lives of other persons and the welfare of the whole society.

The youth may come to know the Bible so as to employ its teachings as a guide in making decisions and its message as a source of inspiration, spiritual strength, and dependable insight into the nature of the human situation.

The youth may experience in a fuller measure the grace of God as God offers him forgiveness in failure and provides new strength to continue the life of obedience and service.

The youth may relate to other persons in new and creative ways, especially in his home, with his peers including members of the opposite sex and of the other races and groups.

The youth may grow in his concern for persons throughout the world and become engaged in ministering to them in significant ways.

The youth may join in the life and mission of the church with new interest and devotion.

4. Discipline in the Christian Life

STATEMENT OF THE THEME

The Christian learns to cope with the difficult demands of decision-making situations under the disciplines of the Christian faith.

ADULTHOOD

1. Significance of the theme for this age level

a. Meanings and experiences within this theme relevant for this age level. This is content, a selected part of Scope.

The discipline to which the Christian is called is that of love for, trust in, and obedience to the will and purpose of God in the relationship of disciple to Jesus Christ.

God has revealed certain norms of attitudes and behavior on which the Christian may base his decisions and actions. Some of these norms are love of God and neighbor, the necessity to forgive, to seek justice for all men, to be humble, to strive for personal holiness as these are made known in the Scriptures and in the ongoing life of the Christian community.

651

God has made available to the Christian the means of grace, such as worship, study, and witness, through which the disciple may discover God's will for his life and find strength to be obedient to it in any and all of life's experiences.

God has promised the disciple the abiding presence of the Holy Spirit that as he remains open and obedient to his leading he may "grow in grace and knowledge" and in the likeness of his Teacher and Lord.

1. Significance of the theme for this age level

   b. Readiness of the learner for this theme in terms of basic needs, interests, motivations, capacities, developmental tasks.

   The readiness of the adult for this theme is seen in the fact that through all of his adult years he is challenged, sustained, opposed, or directed with respect to basic decisions affecting the political, economic, and social concerns of his existence.

652

   The adult is confronted with new and radical changes in the world that shake his established loyalties so that he needs to extend his knowledge and understanding of himself, of others, and of his world.

   The adult is confronted by competing authorities between which he has to choose, and many of his norms of judgment and behavior are now questioned or rejected. The adult is therefore ready for learning new insights into the meaning of Christian discipline.

   The adult has a basic need to acquire essential skills for effective occupational and interpersonal functioning.

   The adult has a concern for establishing and/or maintaining a home and for a fulfilling relationship to spouse and family, to peers, and society, which tends to make him open to supportive disciplines.

   The adult has a desire to find an adequate purpose for his life.

   The adult has a continuing need for clarity about, and confirmation, of, his identity and worth in the world of persons, which may make him responsive to appropriate disciplines.

   The adult has need for norms for judgments and decisions which are not merely prudential or pragmatic, but which are theological sound and ultimately meaningful.

2. How may this content be communicated as the learner engages in the Learning Tasks? What are the methods and

procedures by which the learner may explore the meanings and experiences within this theme (1-a) in the light of his readiness (1-b) in order to discover significance and value?

By adopting or developing a habit of regular worship, study, and witness.

By participating in groups of a supportive nature where there is opportunity for discussion and prayer, and for analytical, constructive reflection upon the nature and purpose of Christian discipline.

By organizing or joining groups where knowledge, understanding, skills, habits, attitudes, and values may be developed, tested, and reshaped. These are such groups as short- and long-term seminars, work-camp projects, night school, graduate study, political action ventures, and social welfare activities.

By seeking or accepting counseling in individual and group situations where disciplines for personal and social concerns are examined. This may be with the pastor, interested and knowledgeable laymen, or vocational groups.

By seeking opportunities for dialogue with persons whose witness has involved them in significant application of Christian discipline. This may involve interviews, retreats, conferences, and seminars. The adult may also engage in conversations with persons from other cultures, comparing accepted Christian disciplines in his culture with accepted Christian disciplines in their culture and examining both of these in light of the Scriptures. As opportunity is afforded, he may also compare the Christian disciplines with those which are demanded by non-Christian faiths.

By participating in witnessing to his faith, individually or in group or team activities.

By utilizing a wide range of printed materials and audio-visuals which are relevant for personal and group preparation in certain disciplines. Textbooks, reprints of articles, tapes and records, movies, filmstrips are examples of these materials.

653

By adapting and disciplining himself to certain habits of life such as personal private prayer, public worship, participation in a regular ongoing group for meaningful study, reading for stimulation and new insights into the meaning of the Christian faith, practicing regular and basic giving such as tithing, maintaining special projects which place demands on his time, energy, and money. These habits may be strengthened if the adult develops and maintains meaningful fellowship with a few Christians who give one another mutual support in living the disciplined life.

3. **What may the learner achieve within this theme in the fulfillment of the Learning Tasks? What are possible changes or learnings on the part of the learner that may result from his appropriation of the significance and value discovered? These changes or learnings may be associated with skills, attitudes, motivations, perceptions including understandings and appreciations.**

The adult may establish or strengthen habits of personal participation in various disciplines of the Christian life.

The adult may find increased meaning and value in the sacraments of the church, and may relate the knowledge and understanding achieved in worship, study, and witness to the everyday decisions of life.

The adult may commit his entire life for service as part of the church in the world through his occupations and beyond it.

The adult may grow in obedience to the lordship of Jesus Christ resulting in personal decisions for responsibility for the well-being of others, in family and community, and for peace and justice in the world.

The adult may grow in effectiveness in personal witnessing in occupation, recreation, and retirement.

The adult may increase his skill in making decisions based on Christian disciplines.

The adult may develop a flexible relationship to the changing dimensions of adult life so that there will be continued relatedness to social groups, constant maturing of faith through the life span, successful acceptance of new roles in advancing age and circumstances, and a deepening sense of gratitude for the resources, opportunities, demands of a dynamic world.

5. Joined in Discipleship in the World

STATEMENT OF THE THEME

Those who are Christ's disciples are united in the task of making their vocation visible, interpreting it to the world, and bringing it to effect in the world. In this way the Christian is strengthened and aided to meet the obligation to live out his discipleship among men.

EARLY CHILDHOOD

1. Significance of the theme for this age level

a. Meanings and experiences within this theme relevant for this age level. This is content, a selected part of Scope.

God made people to enjoy and to help one another.

God wants people to live in loving and trusting relationships with him and with each other.

God wants his people to experience fellowship in the church.

Playing together in helpful ways is an expression of group discipleship.

Followers of Jesus of every culture and race are joined together in fellowship.

Dependence on others and joining with them in play, work, and worship is part of God's plan for life.

God has planned for persons to live together in the family and expects them to help one another in every way they can.

We show our love for God by being thoughtful of others as

655

we work and play with them or engage in acts of service to them in the home, in the church, on the playground, or wherever we are.

Followers of Jesus want others to know of God's love and make it known to them.

1. Significance of the theme for this age level

b. Readiness of the learner for this theme in terms of basic needs, interests, motivations, capacities, developmental tasks

656

The young child encounters many differences among people as his circle of acquaintanceship with others in the Christian community widens and in his relationships must cope with these differences.

The young child is widening his circle of playmates and friends and is becoming increasingly ready for widening group relationships.

The young child is growing in readiness to explore, to move out into new relationships to join with others within the family and church circle in a variety of constructive creative activities (suited to his abilities).

The young child has increasing capacity to enter into exchange of thought and ideas with others.

The young child may be sensitive to some of the apparent needs of others and within the limits of his ability to give help as he senses a need.

The young child has the capacity to reenact through play his feelings and relationships with other persons.

The young child has increasing capacity to enjoy some of the values of giving and receiving love, and of sharing with other persons.

The young child requires security in family and other intimate relationships before he can venture forth to cope with wider relationships in the world.

2. **How may this content be communicated as the learner engages in the Learning Tasks? What are the methods and procedures by which the learner may explore the meanings and experiences within this theme (1-a) in the light of his readiness (1-b) in order to discover significance and value?**

By acting out in play many roles, testing limits and boundaries, and responding to the demands involved in relationships with others.

By observing youth and adults use a limited number of selected symbols, rituals, and activities that are characteristic of discipleship.

By engaging in creative activities that enable him to express his care and concern for other persons and to share with them some of his experiences and learnings.

By observing adults in corporate worship, action, services, and fellowship.

By being related to and observing adults who support him and one another in difficult situations and in witness in the world.

3. **What may the learner achieve within this theme in the fulfillment of the Learning Tasks? What are possible changes or learnings on the part of the learner that may result from his appropriation of the significance and value discovered? These changes or learnings may be associated with skills, attitudes, motivations, perceptions, including understandings and appreciations.**

657

The young child may grow in his ability to join with others in creative, constructure activities.

The young child may grow in his ability to play constructively with his peers.

The young child may grow in his ability to relate to others in wholesome friendships.

The young child may grow in his ability to appreciate his need of others and his dependence on them.

The young child may have a growing sense of fellowship and feeling of confidence in the Christian community.

The young child may realize that he can contribute to the well-being and happiness of others.

The young child may realize that others may depend on him in certain ways.

The young child may grow in his ability to take some responsibility for others and for himself in his relationships with them.

5. Joined in Discipleship in the World

STATEMENT OF THE THEME

Those who are Christ's disciples are united in the task of making their vocation visible, interpreting it to the world, and bringing it to effect in the world. In this way the Christian is strengthened and aided to meet the obligation to live out his discipleship among men.

ELEMENTARY YEARS

1. Significance of the theme for this age level

a. Meanings and experiences within this theme relevant for this age level. This is content, a selected part of Scope.

All of life is under God, and this fact provides a basis for belonging in the world, sharing in the responsibility for the welfare of all in it.

God calls the child to join with others in work that makes visible the church's commitment to God's purposes for the world.

Working together calls for some kind of organization and authority.

God calls the child to see the possible reflection of God's authority in such authority as that of parents and teachers.

God's final authority over life is the measure for the kind of obedience he should give to those who are in authority over him.

The community of the church reaches out to the world.

The church is one organism whose being is expressed through many corporate forms, each a vital part of the whole.

Christians are called by God to a common vocation of mission to the world in the name of Christ.

Each Christian has been given a talent (or talents) which, when combined with those of others in the church, can provide a balance of ministries to serve the world's needs.

The church affects society wherever Christ's disciples function in accord with the spiritual gifts entrusted to them.

Each person who commits himself to follow Christ becomes part of a worldwide fellowship of which his local church is a part, but which is inclusive of all Christians and is involved in working toward the fulfillment of God's will in the world.

1. Significance of the theme for this age level

b. Readiness of the learner for this theme in terms of basic needs, interests, motivations, capacities, developmental tasks.

The child has a need to be with peers and know their support in his efforts in discipleship.

The child's ability to comprehend some literary heritage gives him an opportunity for new learning, for inspiration in discipleship.

The capacity to understand and accumulate knowledge in history and geography enables the child to understand more fully the mission of disciples in the world.

The growing ability and desire to operate in groups and the disposition to take pride in his group relationships may heighten his motivation to join with others in common endeavors.

The elementary child's capacity for allegiance and loyalty helps him strengthen his relationship with other disciples.

The elementary child's capacity and disposition to engage in

659

projects provides an opportunity for learning about and participating in discipleship.

Reading skills enable the elementary child vicariously to move
out into the world.

The ability to read music and liturgy enables the elementary
child to join with other disciples in worship.

The readiness to give and receive love on a more mature basis
makes it possible for the child to grow in his relationship with
his family and others.

660

The child is ready for identification with his peers and for
entering into group decisions and expressions of discipleship.

Curiosity motivates the child to discover and test the values
and avenues of discipleship.

**2. How may this content be communicated as the learner en-
gages in the Learning Tasks? What are the methods and
procedures by which the learner may explore the meanings
and experiences within this theme (1-a) in the light of his
readiness (1-b) in order to discover significance and value?**

By visiting in homes with similar values and commitments.

By sharing beliefs in peer group discussions on discipleship.

Through experiences in groups and situations which differ
from his own and which sharpen the child's ideas of vocation
and intensify his devotion to Christ.

By experimenting with new forms of discipleship under adult
guidance and within reasonable boundaries.

By establishing relationships with persons of other ages and
cultures in ways that provide opportunities for an increased
understanding of others: camping, pen pals, stamp collecting.

By taking field trips into areas of his community about which
his normal daily activities do not give him opportunities to know.

Through participation in peer group relationships with children in need.

By reading and studying the literature of the faith that has
to do with discipleship.

By participating in the corporate worship of the church where he may view adults engaged in a major act of Christian discipleship.

3. **What may the learner achieve within this theme in the fulfillment of the Learning Tasks? What are possible changes or learnings on the part of the learner that may result from his appropriation of the significance and value discovered? These changes or learnings may be associated with skills, attitudes, motivations, perceptions including understandings and appreciations.**

The child may achieve an understanding of some of the meanings of Christian discipleship.

The child may achieve a better perception of what helps or hinders participation in group life.

The child may achieve an ability to assess structures of authority related to acts of corporate discipleship.

The child may achieve awareness of the functional unity that can be achieved in the face of diversity within a group.

The child may achieve an enhanced ability to live with appreciation for all persons.

The child may achieve a beginning understanding that those who uphold good order are ordained of God for the good of man and for the minimizing of evil.

661

The child may achieve an increased sense of personal worth that makes it possible to join with parents and family in discipleship activities.

The child may achieve a beginning awareness of the role his talents call for him to fill in the discipleship activities of the church.

The child may achieve an appreciation of church agencies as an extension of his own discipleship.

The child may achieve awareness that his Christian neighbors are engaged, even as he is, in Christian discipleship throughout the world.

The child may achieve an increased skill in weighing and assessing current "models" and exemplary persons in his life in order to achieve a discipleship style of life.

5. Joined in Discipleship in the World

STATEMENT OF THE THEME

Those who are Christ's disciples are united in the task of making their vocation visible, interpreting it to the world, and bringing it to effect in the world. In this way the Christian is strengthened and aided to meet the obligation to live out his discipleship among men.

662

YOUTH

1. Significance of the theme for this age level

a. Meanings and experiences within this theme relevant for this age level. This is content, a selected part of Scope.

God calls youth to accept responsibility for Christian living within the family group.

Though disciples are set apart for God's purposes, yet their mission calls for identity with the world and involvement in the structures of the world.

With fellow Christians a person may find support for carrying out his discipleship in work, in leisure, in social action.

Christian discipleship has an inescapable corporate dimension.

Christian discipleship calls for accepting responsibility for the welfare of all persons and society.

A Christian disciple confesses his faith openly and identifies with the Christian community.

Responsible corporate discipleship demands study (exercise of the mind), and training (skilled and semiskilled).

Participation in common discipleship involves willingness to be changed in one's expression of discipleship.

The Christian evaluates structures of the church from the perspective of the vocation of the church.

There is no aspect of life exempt from the judgment of the Christian ethic.

God's spirit is active and available for guidance in decisions facing disciples confronting structures which should be changed.

To make one's commitment and vocation visible to the world one must know the world, its needs, its structures, its issues.

All Christians share responsibility for the witness in the world to the validity and relevance of the gospel.

Each person who commits himself to follow Christ becomes a part of a worldwide movement of Christians working toward a historical fulfillment of the divine will.

1. Significance of the theme for this age level

b. Readiness of the learner for this theme in terms of basic needs, interests, motivations, capacities, developmental tasks.

Youth has a basic need to be identified with a peer group as a means of assertion of self vis-à-vis the family and as a source of support in expressing his discipleship.

Youth's expanding knowledge and ability to identify imaginatively and empathically with people of other groups and cultures ready him to become part of ecumenical effort to affect the world.

Youth has a feeling of tolerance and magnanimity toward, or prejudice and enmity against, many other groups not now part of his direct experience which may affect his desire to identify with fellow disciples.

Youth has increased knowledge of and contacts with the world about him, together with areas of independence of judgment, which enable him to make many more individual and corporate decisions about responsible discipleship.

Youth has a responsiveness to social and economic pressures

663

which requires him to make decisions on community and social issues.

Through influence and money youth has some power to affect social structures of which he is a part.

Youth has a basic need to find a place of significance in the communities of which he is a part: the family, the civic unit, the church, the nation, the world.

Youth has an eagerness to venture into the world and participate in new expressions of discipleship.

664

Youth's capacity to probe materials enables him to evaluate old patterns of discipleship and to seek effective ones.

2. How may this content be communicated as the learner engages in the Learning Tasks? What are the methods and procedures by which the learner may explore the meanings and experiences within this theme (1-a) in the light of his readiness (1-b) in order to discover significance and value?

Through participation in and identification with groups in the church.

By examining issues which confront the church and thinking up and testing possible approaches to their resolution.

By studying and discussing information concerning the ecumenical cooperation of Christians as they seek to bring the gospel to bear on the needs, social structures, and problems in the world.

By participating in service projects which match his growing strength and intelligence and are significant in contributing to the welfare of persons.

By participating in group decision and action by Christians as they make visible their vocation in the issues and patterns of society.

By firsthand or vicarious visiting and participating in the institutions of the church at home and abroad to see ways in which Christians band together for effective discipleship in the world.

Through hearing about church-related occupations and how

these occupations can strengthen the corporate witness in the world.

Through studying the Bible, church history, and books which discuss the relationship of the church to today's world.

3. **What may the learner achieve within this theme in the fulfillment of the Learning Tasks? What are possible changes or learnings on the part of the learner that may result from his appropriation of the significance and value discovered? These changes or learnings may be associated with skills, attitudes, motivations, perceptions including understandings and appreciations.**

Youth may achieve an understanding and acceptance of his rightful place in the body of Christ as a responsible member.

Youth may achieve participation in family life as a responsible rather than only a dependent member.

Youth may achieve skill in supporting fellow Christians in their discipleship in the world.

Youth may achieve a sense of support of fellow Christians as he attempts individually to fulfill his discipleship.

Youth may achieve a strong sense of identity with other Christian disciples in the world.

Youth may achieve an awareness of and willingness to participate in acts of Christian discipleship beyond their local church.

Youth may achieve understanding of and commitment to the Christian ethic.

Youth may achieve an ability to withstand non-Christian pressures and temptations.

Youth may achieve skill in influencing change in social structures, habits, and attitudes.

Youth may achieve an increased openness to God's guidance for corporate decisions.

Youth may achieve skill in articulating his faith and its relevance to social issues.

Youth may achieve an understanding of an occupation as an

important means of witnessing to individual and corporate discipleship.

Youth may achieve understanding and appreciation of the need for structures in the church to enable it to witness to and serve the world.

Youth may achieve commitment to the missionary outreach of the church, both to study it and to participate in its work.

666 5. Joined in Discipleship in the World

STATEMENT OF THE THEME

Those who are Christ's disciples are united in the task of making their vocation visible, interpreting it to the world, and bringing it to effect in the world. In this way the Christian is strengthened and aided to meet the obligation to live out his discipleship among men.

ADULTHOOD

1. Significance of the theme for this age level

a. Meanings and experiences within this theme relevant for this age level. This is content, a selected part of Scope.

The individual Christian is called on to join with other Christians to meet the needs of the world and to proclaim God's purposes.

Corporate decisions as well as individual decisions fall under the judgment of the gospel.

The adult is inescapably involved with other disciples in a ministry of reconciliation in the midst of conflicts in the world.

Disciples individually and corporately can and should influence the power structures of society.

The ecumenical work of the church is an expression of the nature and mission of the church.

Corporate discipleship obtains not only within the structures of the church but outside them.

Common discipleship affects decisions of a family as it confronts its responsibilities in the community.

Mutual strength for individual and corporate discipleship can derive from identity with and work with fellow Christians.

Effective corporate discipleship demands sure foundations in the Christian ethic and accurate information on the issues confronting society.

1. Significance of the theme for this age level

b. Readiness of the learner for this theme in terms of basic needs, interests, motivations, capacities, developmental tasks.

The adult Christian participates in a wide variety of communities and has many interlocking circles of influence.

The adult has the capacity and citizenship obligations to participate in responsible decision-making in the community.

The adult's ability to assess his own talents, capacities, and limitations readies him both to see and to appreciate that the variety of talents and capacities among the community of disciples gives that community the necessary equipment for joint discipleship in the church and in the world.

The adult has the capacity to set immediate or future goals and to submerge or control other interests in order to join with others in the realization of such goals.

The adult needs the support of fellow disciples in his attempts to live out his vocation.

The adult disciple inescapably wields major influence among members of the Christian community which spans several generations.

The adult needs to know the relevance of his religion to his life-in-community as he participates in decisions of various groups.

2. How may this content be communicated as the learner engages in the Learning Tasks? What are the methods and

667

procedures by which the learner may explore the meanings and experiences within this theme (1-a) in the light of his readiness (1-b) in order to discover significance and value?

By studying the Bible and other resources of the Christian faith that set forth the demands of discipleship.

By worshiping and studying with fellow Christians who face common decisions and actions.

By sharing the insights of others on discipleship to the world.

668

By participating directly or indirectly in corporate efforts of churches to affect social issues or human needs.

By hearing from fellow Christians what their problems and efforts are in proclaiming the gospel and in living out their discipleship.

By reading or hearing interpretations of the gospel's relevance to issues and events in the world.

By establishing or supporting voluntary associations which include fellow disciples to accomplish needed reforms.

By participating in occupational groups across denominational lines where the Christian ethic may be discussed and implemented in its relation to decisions faced in that occupation.

By reading reports of the efforts of various Christian groups to join in common acts of proclamation and of Christian social action.

By reviewing and evaluating from the Christian ethic with fellow Christians courses of action taken by various groups in which Christians participate, both within the church and outside.

By observing various deliberative bodies of the church in action dealing with questions of corporate proclamation and corporate social action.

By interpreting to others the relation of the Christian ethic to a variety of issues.

3. What may the learner achieve within this theme in the ful-

fillment of the Learning Tasks? What are possible changes or learnings on the part of the learner that may result from his appropriation of the significance and value discovered? These changes or learnings may be associated with skills, attitudes, motivations, perceptions including understandings and appreciations.

The adult may achieve a sense of responsibility for using political authority or influence to express his Christian witness with integrity and effectiveness.

The adult may achieve skill to work together with other disciples with patience and persistence in the midst of difficulty and defeat, leaving the outcome of his discipleship to the will of God.

The adult may achieve a perspective on the role of the Christian family in the shaping of the life of a community.

The adult may achieve sensitivity to hear and see the gospel's relevance to social issues as communicated through the arts.

The adult may achieve a sense of identity with fellow Christians around the world facing similar or common issues and responsibilities.

The adult may achieve understanding of the emerging world-wide ecumenical movement and a commitment to participate actively in it.

The adult may achieve confidence for using his specific abilities and his ordinary opportunities for undergirding the common Christian witness in the world.

669

The adult may achieve skill in mobilizing forces for important social causes.

The adult may achieve a realization of strength and courage to engage effectively with others in important social causes.

The adult may achieve skill in analyzing issues in terms of the Christian ethic.

The adult may achieve a sense of confidence engendered by his increasing awareness that his limitations in discipleship are compensated by the abilities of fellow Christians.

6. Toward the Kingdom of God

STATEMENT OF THE THEME

The conviction that the decisions to which God calls men are ultimately directed to a single goal, the kingdom of God, gives purpose and structure to man's life, and brings into a meaningful whole the separate vocations of men.

EARLY CHILDHOOD

670

1. **Significance of the theme for this age level**

   a. **Meanings and experiences within this theme relevant for this age level. This is content, a selected part of Scope.**

   It is God's will that children find direction for living from the example of those who know themselves to be of his kingdom.

   The young child carries responsibility for his contribution to group living and for simple work tasks.

   The world of nature is created by God and sustained by him; it is dependable and provides for man's physical needs.

   God calls the young child to a life of spontaneity, joy, freedom in the context of his kingdom.

   God rules all that he has made despite some hurtful and evil forces.

   The kingdom of God is evidence of the worth of persons.

1. **Significance of the theme for this age level**

   b. **Readiness of the learner for this theme in terms of basic needs, interests, motivations, capacities, developmental tasks**

   The need for a dependable figure in whom he may place his trust leads the young child to respond openly with spontaneity and guilelessness to the provision God has made for him in the coming of the kingdom.

   As the young child begins to experience selfhood, he begins

to test the demands and structures placed upon him. This leads him occasionally to rebel even in a climate of understanding and support. The experience of testing opens up for him the possibility of choice in regard to the coming of the kingdom.

As growing years endow him with new strength and ability to move about, to explore, to move into new areas, try out new toys, participate in new experiences, the young child is ready to understand something of what is involved in the kingdom's coming through his own new experiences.

As the young child's ability to listen and learn, to inquire and ask questions, to explore and discover begin to develop, he manifests those qualities of childlikeness which Jesus pointed out as essential for entrance into the kingdom.

The young child's interest in family rituals and celebrations, his awareness of family traditions and values as qualities of belonging, enable him to begin to understand and to participate in the large realm of relationships which surround him.

A beginning sense of injustice or fair play, a developing ability to express his feelings and to make choices, constitute a readiness for the young child to enter into an awareness of kingdom purposes and to make choices related to them.

2. **How may this content be communicated as the learner engages in the Learning Tasks? What are the methods and procedures by which the learner may explore the meanings and experiences within this theme (1-a) in the light of his readiness (1-b) in order to discover significance and value?**

671

Through the experience of living in dependable surroundings and relationships in the family and the church.

By receiving love and understanding even in the midst of the young child's rebellions.

Through storytelling and through associating with those who differ in economic class, race, age, handicaps, or exceptional gifts.

By observation of the natural world around him.

3. **What may the learner achieve within this theme in the fulfillment of the Learning Tasks? What are possible changes or learnings on the part of the learner that may result from his appropriation of the significance and value discovered? These changes or learnings may be associated with skills, attitudes, motivations, perceptions, including understandings and appreciations.**

The young child may treat himself and others as persons of worth.

672

The young child may begin to understand the meaning of the kingdom of God and to accept God's rule in life.

The young child may develop a sense of awe and reverence for God as Creator and Provider for life.

The young child may begin to accept the things of the world as gifts from God to be used responsibly and in the interest of man's welfare.

The young child may grow in capacity to give and receive love, to accept love while in rebellion, to express care for others and to recognize that these experiences are in harmony with the kingdom of God.

The young child may begin to distinguish between the real world and fantasy. He may begin to use his imagination to help create the new, the good, and the beautiful.

The young child may begin to appreciate his relation to Jesus in and through the Christian community and Christian friends.

The young child may respond with joy and wonder to the unfolding of life under God's plan and rule.

6. Toward the Kingdom of God

STATEMENT OF THE THEME

The conviction that the decisions to which God calls men are utimately directed to a single goal, the kingdom of God, gives purpose and structure to man's life, and brings into a meaningful whole the separate vocations of men.

ELEMENTARY YEARS

1. Significance of the theme for this age level

a. Meanings and experiences within this theme relevant for this age level. This is content, a selected part of Scope.

God's will extends to the larger relationships of the educational and social experiences as the child moves into school and enlarges his experience of the physical world in which he lives and of which he is a part.

The elementary child carries responsibility for his contribution to group living and for simple work tasks.

Every person has a distinctive role as he participates in the kingdom.

The kingdom of God implies appropriate goals in life which influence attitudes and behavior.

It is God's intention that the child begin to see in Jesus the meanings of the kingdom for himself.

God calls the child to participate in the life of the church as a means of entering the kingdom.

1. Significance of the theme for this age level

b. Readiness of the learner for this theme in terms of basic needs, interests, motivations, capacities, developmental tasks.

673

The readiness of the elementary child for this theme is seen in his growing ability to discern the standards and demands of social groups and to compare them with those of the kingdom. It is discerned in the beginning sense of conscience as the child moves from "you must" demanded of him by outside sources to a sense of "I ought" empowered from within himself.

The child's increasing power to study and to communicate his learning to others, the ability to earn money so that he appropriates some of the world and learns how to use it, the growing competence with which the child can begin to use manipulative skills all portray an increasing ability to relate responsibly to the kingdom of God.

The tendency of the child to identify with persons and with social groups reveals a capacity for developing loyalties and for fulfilling the need to belong.

The readiness of the child to experience some of the meanings of the kingdom can be discerned in the glimpses of developing personhood as he begins to idealize other individuals and works at developing his own capacities.

The child's developing sense of responsibility for making his own decisions, accepting the consequences of them, and living with a sense of integrity for the decisions he has made opens the way for him to see the purpose and the necessity of the kingdom.

2. **How may this content be communicated as the learner engages in the Learning Tasks? What are the methods and procedures by which the learner may explore the meanings and experiences within this theme (1-a) in the light of his readiness (1-b) in order to discover significance and value?**

By identification with individuals and situations through role playing, and through acquaintance with Christians in the community as they carry on their work. This may be done by means of field trips through which the child explores governments, occupations, industry, commerce, and farming.

Through the assessment of experience in the light of values that support the kingdom. Dialogue, observation, and Bible study are media for such assessment.

Through family experiences such as worship, church attendance, and celebrations.

Through participation in an evaluation of family decisions and living patterns.

Through observing adults as they acknowledge with willingness their own limitations, failures, and mistakes and ask for forgiveness and seek to give forgiveness.

674

Through participation in worship, celebrations, service, and outreach.

3. **What may the learner achieve within this theme in the fulfillment of the Learning Tasks? What are possible changes or learnings on the part of the learner that may result from his appropriation of the significance and value discovered? These changes or learnings may be associated with skills, attitudes, motivations, perceptions including understandings and appreciations.**

The child in the elementary years may grow in his ability to make decisions in the light of God's rule, to weigh the demands, and assess the expectations and patterns of his society so that he may discover the reality of the kingdom and begin to try ways of participating in it.

As the child grows in understanding of the physical world of which he is a part, learns how to use its resources, understands nature more completely and learns to relate to it effectively, he may begin to cope with it in the light of kingdom values. As a result of earning money and using material possessions, he may learn to direct his own personal influence in ways that serve the ends of the kingdom of God. Also, he may grow in understanding of the interrelatedness of materials and persons in the world as a part of God's larger economy.

As a result of beginning to accept himself, his potentialities and limits, and his role in the family and community, the child may begin to experience participation and service in the kingdom of God. As he begins to understand his own role, he participates appropriately in the kingdom of God. As he learns to understand, participate in, and sense the joy of fellowship in the church, he may become aware of the mission of the church in the world.

The child may continue to deepen his commitment to Christ as Lord and Savior.

Through a growing awareness of possibilities and demands of the kingdom, and the judgment on life resulting from this grow-

675

ing awareness, the child may have an increasing sense of responsibility for the use of time for his self-development and for his contribution to society and the world of which he is a part.

6. Toward the Kingdom of God

STATEMENT OF THE THEME

The conviction that the decisions to which God calls men are utimately directed to a single goal, the kingdom of God, gives purpose and structure to man's life, and brings into a meaningful whole the separate vocations of men.

676

YOUTH

1. Significance of the theme for this age level

a. Meanings and experiences within this theme relevant for this age level. This is content, a selected part of Scope.

God calls youth to participate in the kingdom by directing his life to a single goal, namely, doing God's will. It is God's will that each youth see his personal destiny in the light of what God has done and is doing for mankind and what God can do through the life of a young person.

God calls the young person to assess the claims of society and its way of functioning in the light of the purposes of the kingdom. God calls the young person to review these social institutions and assess their power structure from the perspective of the kingdom. Likewise, God calls the young person to review the claims of family, friends, and economic groups from the standpoint of kingdom values.

God calls youth to make his choice of occupation in the light of the Christian view of vocation.

God calls youth to view the material world as a part of God's realm over which the youth has responsibility as a steward.

God calls youth to reassess his own role in the church in the light of his growing understanding of the kingdom and to work within the church for reformation and renewal in the light of these kingdom values and purposes.

The youth has responsibility in his social group to witness by his work to his loyalty to the kingdom.

1. Significance of the theme for this age level

b. Readiness of the learner for this theme in terms of basic needs, interests, motivations, capacities, developmental tasks.

The growing ability of youth to cope rationally with demands laid upon him enables him to respond to the higher claims of the kingdom.

Youth's readiness to cut away from parental authority and move out on his own into a broader sphere of situations opens up for him the possibility of seeing his own destiny in the light of the purposes of the kingdom.

The growing readiness of youth to accept responsibility for work prepares him to set goals and work toward them with loyalty and persistence.

Youth's ability to experiment scientifically enlarges the possibility of understanding and appreciating God's rule over the natural world.

The necessity to make choices concerning the youth's occupation and the use of leisure time readies him to find direction and purpose in his life.

The youth's openness to new ideas and new patterns of life, his growing consciousness of persons of other cultures, races, and nations, makes him ready for the radical newness of the kingdom.

Youth's enthusiastic endorsement of values and patterns which call for social justice make him open to the changes which are required in the structures of society as God's purposes are worked out.

Youth's inclination to criticize and evaluate events and persons enables him to see the values and commitments of his own life.

677

2. How may this content be communicated as the learner engages in the Learning Tasks? What are the methods and procedures by which the learner may explore the meanings and experiences within this theme (1-a) in the light of his readiness (1-b) in order to discover significance and value?

Through Bible study in which the findings of scholarship are recognized and the youth have opportunity to probe the biblical message for its meaning and value for them. The techniques of paraphrase and role play may be emphasized.

Through study of the relationship of time-space theories and other subjects of the natural sciences to kingdom concepts.

By means of opportunity for individual reflection and group discussion.

Through conversations, interviews, and work with Christians who can assess their roles and responsibilities in the light of kingdom values.

Through young people's groups in the church in which youth may engage in such activities as planning, testing values, evaluating experiences, by participating in discussion groups, leading in worship, using films and play readings and cuttings from current literature, attending camps and conferences.

In his own home where there is a climate for examining his beliefs and value systems. By counseling with persons in the family, he may examine his own responsibilities. Through conversations with visitors in the home, he may explore some new perspectives.

During leisure-time activities, by participation in sports that teach fair play, by learning the lessons of activity and relaxation, by finding sources of renewal and enrichment of life.

Through free and open discussion about the Christian faith and the cultural system.

Through work projects in the community and world.

3. **What may the learner achieve within this theme in the fulfillment of the Learning Tasks? What are possible changes or learnings on the part of the learner that may result from his appropriation of the significance and value discovered? These changes or learnings may be associated with skills, attitudes, motivations, perceptions including understandings and appreciations.**

Youth may grow in understanding of the meaning of the kingdom of God, develop a capacity to assess realistically many of the power figures in our culture, and appropriate for himself standards of values in the light of kingdom purposes.

Youth may develop a more adequate concept of reality from the perspective of the kingdom which will enable him to look at many of the illusions of our society and to develop a wholesome critique.

Youth may commit his life to Christ as Lord and acknowledge his membership in the community of Christ's faithful followers—the church. Youth may relate this commitment to his choice of occupation and in other areas of his life live more consistently by the values of the kingdom of God.

Youth may discover that the individual and his work are significant because he is a part of God's kingdom in the world. He may relate his choice of occupation to his understanding of God's work in the world.

Youth may gain satisfaction in the fulfillment of his own present vocation as a student as a way of participating in the kingdom.

Youth may accept and use leisure in the light of the kingdom perspective, recognizing the need of the individual for a rhythm of creation (work) and recreation.

Youth may develop an increased ability to deal with the natural world responsibly and with freedom.

Youth may participate as a Christian with increasing responsibilities within the social institutions of the culture.

6. Toward the Kingdom of God

STATEMENT OF THE THEME

The conviction that the decisions to which God calls men are utimately directed to a single goal, the kingdom of God, gives purpose and structure to man's life, and brings into a meaningful whole the separate vocations of men.

ADULTHOOD

680

1. **Significance of the theme for this age level**

   a. **Meanings and experiences within this theme relevant for this age level. This is content, a selected part of Scope.**

The kingdom of God is a dynamic influence in human history to which man has a direct relationship. This relationship involves being aware of the kingdom as present, accepting its purposes, and living creatively in it with confident hope.

The particular occupation of the Christian in the world of work has a meaningful relation to the ultimate purpose of the kingdom of God.

The kingdom is a transcendent point of reference by which the adult is able to assess the power structures (economic, political, social, etc.) in which he must live his daily life. The symbolic and transcendent reference of the kingdom of God in relation to the kingdoms of this world gives ethical purpose and direction to the learner's existence. The adult Christian celebrates in worship the kingdom of God.

To live by the values of the kingdom is to be in touch with a source of faith whereby the Christian is able to cope with failure and anxiety and also with a source of hope when pressures frustrate his best efforts in the present.

The church is called to be a manifestation of the kingdom of God on earth. The church stands under the judgment of God as a body through which the goals of the kingdom move toward realization in history, and as a consequence must reassess its role in the world.

God calls the adult to a recognition of the lordship of Christ over the natural world. It is God's will that man should relate to the natural world in the light of the values and perspectives of the kingdom.

God calls the adult to reassess his own role in the church in the light of his growing understanding of the kingdom and to work within the church for reformation and renewal in the light of these kingdom values and purposes.

In ruling over the natural world man is called to exercise a stewardship consistent with the values and perspectives of the kingdom.

1. **Significance of the theme for this age level**
   b. **Readiness of the learner for this theme in terms of basic needs, interests, motivations, capacities, developmental tasks.**

Some clues to the readiness of the adult for this theme are shown in the tension he experiences between "secular" and "spiritual" values. Similar tension may exist between a desire for significance in his occupation and the futility he feels respecting his work. The pressures to conform to lower group standards, cutting corners, producing inferior products are in tension with an attitude of integrity in work. Tensions are set up by constantly changing demands of family and community. International strife, along with the threat of nuclear warfare, produces widespread and continuing stress.

Discontent over the adult's failure to achieve "a fair share" of this life's goods and dissatisfaction with the personal support given to him as he seeks to serve his fellowman may indicate an openness of the adult to the kingdom of God and a readiness to respond to the demands of the kingdom.

The desire of the adult to spend more time with his family, to improve community and church, to use his acquired wealth or materials in the service of mankind constitute a readiness to reorder value priorities in terms of kingdom values.

681

The necessity to reorder his life may provide the adult with an openness toward change based on the kingdom and its values.

Interest in and capacity for expression in the arts may provide the adult an opportunity for new ideas in relation to the kingdom.

In old age the release from the tension of work, reflection upon the past and envisioning new relationships in the future, the ability to reconstruct his plans and style of life, the inspiration that comes in gathering with other people, and the desire to be a wholesome influence create a readiness in the adult to reorder life in terms of the kingdom of God.

2. How may this content be communicated as the learner engages in the Learning Tasks? What are the methods and procedures by which the learner may explore the meanings and experiences within this theme (1-a) in the light of his readiness (1-b) in order to discover significance and value?

Through study that aims to bring into focus the biblical and theological perspectives of the kingdom of God. Such methods of study as reading, reflecting, discussing, investigating, listening to lectures, viewing films may be used.

Through taking his responsible place as a Christian in occupational groups and in community activities.

By participation in social action groups that seek to realize kingdom goals.

Through reflection and meditation on the relationship of creation, providence, and redemption to the natural and social order in which God's rule determines the direction of life.

Through the use of art as a means of seeing the kingdom's ingression into the world and as a mode of imaginative celebration of the kingdom's power to transform.

By entering into the church, participating in her life and world mission.

Through movies, TV, audio-visuals that convey glimpses of

the ultimate meaning of life in the kingdom of God, and through clarifying these meanings and their implications in discussion groups.

Through field trips, travel, reflection, surveys, community studies which enable the adult to discover the realities of this world, and the relevance of kingdom values for social institutions.

Through study in the family setting, especially when children of several ages are present.

3. **What may the learner achieve within this theme in the fulfillment of the Learning Tasks? What are possible changes or learnings on the part of the learner that may result from his appropriation of the significance and value discovered? These changes or learnings may be associated with skills, attitudes, motivations, perceptions including understandings and appreciations.**

The adult may commit his life in discipleship to Jesus Christ and as a member of the community of the church and relate himself more fully to the kingdom of God.

The adult may acquire clearer awareness of kingdom goals and may increasingly realize in his life the values of the kingdom.

The adult may accept his role of citizen of the kingdom in today's world, seeking its implications for world order, economics, politics, and social relations.

683

The adult may develop an ability to live with partial fulfillment of the purpose of kingdom in the ambiguities of the world.

The adult may develop the capacity to place himself at the tension points of life as a servant of God.

The adult may accept his own limitations and trust in God's power to complete that which he leaves partially incompleted or in which he fails.

The adult may achieve an increasing ability to relate to the natural world in the light of the values and perspectives of the kingdom.

The adult may become more willing to use his resources for service and outreach of the kingdom in both the local community and beyond.

The adult may see new and developing sources of power in the world and use them in the interest of the purposes of the kingdom.

The adult may accept the church as a partial realization of the kingdom and accept the judgment of the kingdom upon its partial achievement, while he relates to it and engages in its work in the world.

The adult may see daily work and rest as related to the kingdom.

The adult may accept the ultimate rule of God as the determinant of human destiny.

The adult may develop a sound, mature hope motivated by kingdom ideals.

The adult may develop skill in being able to create situations of reconciliation.

The adult through worship and arts may experience new insights, new devotion, and a fresh effort regarding the kingdom of God.

The adult may grow in ability to participate in decision-making in community groups and in the family that support movement in the direction of entering into the kingdom.

The adult may discover the personal meaning of the kingdom, finding new purpose and strength for his life, which carry over into his decision-making, his work, and interpersonal relationships.

The adult may develop an increasing ability to view the scientific world from a Christian perspective and to work for the values of the kingdom within this world, thus overcoming escapism and relating to the world as a Christian steward.

The adult may be released from undue striving and frustration by placing his hope in the ultimate triumph of God's rule.

THE CHURCH: THE MEANING AND EXPERIENCE OF CHRISTIAN COMMUNITY

The themes within this area are:

1. *Christians Are Bound Together in God's Love*
2. *God's Continuing Action in and Through His People*
3. *The Church Permeating Society*
4. *Extending Reconciliation and Redemption*
5. *The Church Lives by Worship*
6. *The Christian Community Mobilizing for Mission*
7. *Preparing and Equipping for Ministry*

Statement of the Area

The focus, or vantage point, of this area of curriculum is the nature, the history, and the mission of the church; belonging to the church and participating in its life and work.

Comprehended in the area of curriculum is such content of Christian thought and life as: the doctrine of the church; the meaning of church membership, the history of the church; Christian mission and the missionary enterprise; skills of churchmanship; worship and the ministries of the church—teaching, preaching, outreach, service, healing; interpretation of the church triumphant; the history and use of the Bible.

685

In order to have educational value as an area of curriculum, this content must be viewed in terms of its pertinence to the persistent issues of man's life. Some of these issues are: What can I do about feelings of alienation? Where can I belong? Why is Christianity exported? What is the basis of Christian evangelism? How did the church come to be? Why are there so many denominations? Can't I be a good Christian outside the church? What is the business of the church? Where can I find support for my Christian aspirations and witness? What difference does the church make?[1]

---

[1] Repeated here as necessary background.

1. Christians Are Bound Together in God's Love

STATEMENT OF THE THEME

The special nature of koinonia *that makes it different from other community or fellowship is the love relationship of man to man and man to God which supports man's authentic being as a person. This fellowship meets man's primary needs to love and be loved.*

686

EARLY CHILDHOOD

1. Significance of the theme for this age level

a. Meanings and experiences within this theme relevant for this age level. This is content, a selected part of Scope.

The church is a special place in the community where young children find people who love them and are concerned for their happiness.

Church is a place where we have happy times with friends.

The church is more than a place or building; it is the people who love God and try to do his work.

All around the world there are people who love God and belong to the church.

God loves all people just as he loves us.

The Bible tells us that God loves us and helps us know how to show our love for each other.

God has sent Jesus Christ to show us how God loves us and all people.

1. Significance of the theme for this age level

b. Readiness of the learner for this theme in terms of basic needs, interests, motivations, capacities, developmental tasks

Young children need to receive and give expressions of love.

Young children need to be accepted as persons of worth.

Young children are increasingly able to enjoy activities in company with others.

As they develop, young children expand their circle of relationships in church and neighborhood.

Young children enjoy doing things for others.

Young children readily accept friendly persons without regard to status, culture, or color.

Young children are beginning to relate some to friends outside of their immediate family circle and may feel a rather close relation with some friends, such as a teacher or playmate who is a frequent companion.

2. How may this content be communicated as the learner engages in the Learning Tasks? What are the methods and procedures by which the learner may explore the meanings and experiences within this theme (1-a) in the light of his readiness (1-b) in order to discover significance and value?

By participating in his own group at church.

By having experiences of fellowship across age groups in the Christian community.

By getting acquainted with Christians of different ages, races, and cultures.

By becoming familiar with selected Bible material (stories, verses, and pictures) that tell about God's love and about people's love for each other.

By taking part in suitable group activities in the church.

By planning to help and by helping others in the Christian community.

By hearing the family express appreciation for the church, what it is, and what it does.

By experiencing love in his own family and in the church family.

By receiving from persons in the church respect and concern for him and his family, regardless of the nature of his home life.

687

By having the minister and various other church leaders visit his group as part of the church community.

3. **What may the learner achieve within this theme in the fulfillment of the Learning Tasks? What are possible changes or learnings on the part of the learner that may result from his appropriation of the significance and value discovered? These changes or learnings may be associated with skills, attitudes, motivations, perceptions, including understandings and appreciations.**

688

Young children may develop love for their local church and a sense of being at home there.

Young children may feel joy at being a part of the church.

Young children may come to think of the Bible as a special book which tells of God's love for all and of his plan for his people.

Young children may come to feel that people in the church love them and care what happens to them.

Young children may begin to understand that the church is people who love God and seek to do what God wants them to do.

Young children may begin to feel satisfaction in doing things for others in the Christian community.

Young children may begin to realize that they have a contribution to make to others in the church.

Young children can begin to feel security in the confidence of being loved by people who love God.

Young children may experience a sense of fellowship in the church not experienced elsewhere.

Young children may begin to comprehend that the church is for all people who love God, regardless of who or what they are.

Young children may begin to realize that people in the church are dependent on one another.

1. Christians Are Bound Together in God's Love

STATEMENT OF THE THEME

The special nature of koinonia *that makes it different from other community or fellowship is the love relationship of man to man and man to God which supports man's authentic being as a person. This fellowship meets man's primary needs to love and be loved.*

ELEMENTARY YEARS

1. Significance of the theme for this age level

a. Meanings and experiences within this theme relevant for this age level. This is content, a selected part of Scope.

The church is people who love God and whose commitment is to do his will.

In the church children are included in the bonds of love and are helped to know God and what he would have them do.

The Christian fellowship is not dependent on any special place or building, but is found anywhere that Christians gather together.

It is God's intent that the Christian fellowship be open to people of all races, nationalities, and cultures.

All around the world there are Christians bound together by love for God and for one another.

689

Christians today are part of a fellowship which has existed through the ages since the time of Jesus. Our church today is a part of the church which Jesus began.

The Bible tells the story of God's love and of ways his people have shown their love for one another.

It is God's plan that people who love him should love one another, help one another in time of trouble, and learn to work together.

Each member of the Christian fellowship is responsible for doing his part to maintain that fellowship.

1. Significance of the theme for this age level

b. Readiness of the learner for this theme in terms of basic needs, interests, motivations, capacities, developmental tasks.

Children need to be loved and to love.

Each child needs to be accepted as a person of worth.

Children are able to understand why church people have responsibility for helping one another.

Older elementary children have a beginning historical sense.

Children need the support and security that come from being a part of a small group.

Elementary children are coming to know an enlarging world. They are increasingly conscious of many kinds of people who live in many different situations. They have a lively interest in differences—as in people, churches, ways of worshiping, etc.

Children admire people who do things and want to be like them.

Older elementary children need to feel that the church fellowship is supporting them even when they are questioning hitherto accepted ideas and are struggling for independence.

An increasing capacity for meaningful participation in corporate worship characterizes elementary children.

Elementary children have an increasing ability to understand the distinctiveness of Christian love.

Elementary children are developing study habits and skills and the ability to carry on independent investigations.

2. How may this content be communicated as the learner engages in the Learning Tasks? What are the methods and procedures by which the learner may explore the meanings and experiences within this theme (1-a) in the light of his readiness (1-b) in order to discover significance and value?

Through becoming familiar with worship resources as means

by which Christians express their love of God and of their fellow men.

Through having experiences of meaningful corporate worship with their own age group and with the church congregation.

Through studying and discussing, exploring the distinctiveness of the church in terms of its unity and its expressions of Christian love.

Through getting acquainted with different people, groups, and institutions within the Christian community.

Through studying biblical teachings about the way Christians should act toward one another.

By experimenting with expressions of Christian love.

By exploring the nature of the church by studying the various ways Christians express their love of God and affirm his love of them.

Through forming friendships with peers and other persons who share commitment to Christ and his church.

By supporting members of the group who are facing crises, trouble, or other difficulties.

By carrying out projects of giving and receiving with church groups and with other churches around the world.

Through contributing to the life of their church through the assumption of responsibilities, commensurate with their level of growth and development for the relationships among Christians.

691

By observing and discussing Christian actions and attitudes among Christians, within or across age groups.

3. **What may the learner achieve within this theme in the fulfillment of the Learning Tasks? What are possible changes or learnings on the part of the learner that may result from his appropriation of the significance and value discovered? These changes or learnings may be associated with skills, attitudes, motivations, perceptions including understandings and appreciations.**

The elementary child may achieve a growing feeling of being a part of the church family.

The child may achieve a desire to identify himself with the church by becoming a member.

The child may achieve an increasing sense of responsibility for fellowship within his church.

The child may achieve a greater ability to enter into the joys and sorrows of others, to rejoice in their successes and help in their troubles.

692

The child may achieve a sense of pride in being linked with Christians of all ages who have done great things for the church.

The child may achieve the beginning of an awareness of identification with the church eternal and triumphant.

The child may achieve a greater sensitivity to the value of small as well as large service to the Christian fellowship.

The child may achieve a beginning willingness and ability to subordinate immediate personal goals to the goals of the Christian fellowship.

The child may achieve a growing awareness of the uniqueness of the Christian fellowship.

The child may achieve a beginning willingness to take the initiative in expressing God's love in ways that reflect the oneness of the Christian community.

The child may achieve an experience of realizing the strength, joy, and support that come from being a part of the Christian community.

The child may achieve an awareness that God intends that those who love him should love one another.

1. Christians Are Bound Together in God's Love

STATEMENT OF THE THEME

The special nature of koinonia *that makes it different from other community or fellowship is the love relationship of man to man and man to God which supports man's authentic being as a person. This fellowship meets man's primary needs to love and be loved.*

YOUTH

1. Significance of the theme for this age level

a. Meanings and experiences within this theme relevant for this age level. This is content, a selected part of Scope.

The church is the body of Christ and includes believers of all times and in all places.

The Bible pictures people experiencing *koinonia,* the oneness of the church in love.

The Bible affirms the unity of the Body of Christ.

God's love is a bond among all Christians.

God requires and empowers Christians to love as they have been loved.

Christian fellowship transcends cultural, racial, tribal, economic, national, and other boundaries.

Local congregations, or groupings of Christians, are manifestations of the church universal.

Characteristic of Christian fellowship is concern for others, and support for individual Christians as they face hostilities, misunderstandings, temptations, and other crises.

Throughout the ages, youth have had an important part in the life of the church.

Our love of our fellow Christians is an evidence of our love of God.

The character of fellowship among Christians is different and more important than that of any other group to which we may belong.

693

1. Significance of the theme for this age level

b. Readiness of the learner for this theme in terms of basic

needs, interests, motivations, capacities, developmental tasks.

In youth there is a realization of the need to love and to be loved.

Youth need to find a place in a group or cause that transcends self.

Youth yearn for acceptance and recognition by adults, as well as by peers.

694

Youth want to assume real and not token responsibilities.

In youth there is ambivalence between a desire to be independent and a need for support.

Youth's increased understanding of history makes it possible for them to see the church in its historical setting.

Youth have a capacity for setting high goals and for all-out devotion to a cause that seems worthy to them.

Youth have a strong group-feeling and may have intense loyalty to any group with which they have identified themselves.

Youth are capable of abstract thinking and of building generalized concepts from concrete evidence.

Youth are able to recognize ambivalence in themselves toward other persons.

2. How may this content be communicated as the learner engages in the Learning Tasks? What are the methods and procedures by which the learner may explore the meanings and experiences within this theme (1-a) in the light of his readiness (1-b) in order to discover significance and value?

By observing instances of the force and power resident within the Christian fellowship beyond the power of individuals.

By studying the sweep of the biblical record of God's steadfast love and of the claims it makes on men as part of the Christian fellowship.

By taking part in the ecumenical movement locally, nationally, and in the world through study, encounter, and action.

By hearing or reading reports of ways in which the Christian fellowship has undergirded and impelled action in the world.

By cultivating friendships with Christians of other cultures and races.

By searching in history for the distinctiveness of the various denominations and investigating the relationship of denominations in the light of biblical teachings about unity.

By analyzing factors that make for unity and disunity in the church and evaluating them in the light of the gospel.

By worshiping with fellow Christians within their own congregation, across congregational, denominational, and national lines.

By participating with other members of the church in projects expressing their concern for each other.

Through study, interviews, and discussion, analyzing what it is that makes Christian fellowship unique and therefore different from other groupings which they know.

Through experiencing the support of fellow Christians as he individually tries to be obedient to his commitment.

3. **What may the learner achieve within this theme in the fulfillment of the Learning Tasks? What are possible changes or learnings on the part of the learner that may result from his appropriation of the significance and value discovered? These changes or learnings may be associated with skills, attitudes, motivations, perceptions including understandings and appreciations.**

695

Youth may achieve a sense of strength and vitality from the bond of mutual love among a group of Christians.

Youth may achieve the realization that the Christian fellowship is not an end in itself but exists for a purpose.

Youth may achieve a sense of participation in the Christian fellowship, in which each member is significant.

Youth may achieve skill in expressing concern for developing and restoring mutual care in the Christian community.

Youth may achieve an understanding and appreciation of the biblical account and historical heritage of the unity which Christians around the world have in God's love.

Youth may achieve a heightened desire and ability to assume responsibilities rising out of oneness with God and his people.

Youth may come to recognize that there is vitality and oneness in the church despite human failures.

696

Youth may achieve a consciousness of meaningful identity with a movement which is eternal.

Youth may achieve the realization that the maintenance of the Christian fellowship calls for understanding others and helping them to live at their best, and also accepting such understanding and help from others.

Youth may achieve the ability to tolerate as Christians the ridicule or disdain from some persons or groups because of the greater significance of the Christian fellowship.

Youth may achieve the assurance that the realities that bind Christians together are more important than those that differentiate them from one another.

Youth may achieve the realization that the Christian fellowship provides a model for relationships among all persons.

Youth may achieve insight and skill to express the unity among Christians through various language and art forms.

1. Christians Are Bound Together in God's Love

STATEMENT OF THE THEME

The special nature of koinonia *that makes it different from other community or fellowship is the love relationship of man to man and man to God which supports man's authentic being as a person. This fellowship meets man's primary needs to love and be loved.*

ADULTHOOD

1. Significance of the theme for this age level

a. Meanings and experiences within this theme relevant for this age level. This is content, a selected part of Scope.

The love relationship among Christians makes the church different from a club, a society, or other human associations.

The love relationship in the church is a manifestation of the grace of God.

The Holy Spirit acts within the life of the church to unite it in God's love and to empower it to manifest this love to the world.

Members of the fellowship which is the church are obligated to stir up each other to love and to good works.

Jesus Christ is the head of the church: his body the church is a single organism.

The church incorporates believers of all times and places.

Local congregations, or groupings of Christians, are manifestations of the church universal.

The oneness of all Christians should lead members of each congregation to experience love for other Christians around the world.

In the *koinonia,* the love relationship, which is a wise and active concern for others, gives support to individual Christians as they face temptations, persecutions, and other crises in a non-Christian world.

697

The Christian church is not limited to time or space. It has its roots in the eternity of God himself and its destiny in a kingdom without end.

Within the church there is a variety of gifts and abilities, and each person is important and is under obligation to use his gifts and abilities for the welfare of all.

1. Significance of the theme for this age level

b. Readiness of the learner for this theme in terms of basic needs, interests, motivations, capacities, developmental tasks.

All persons need to love and to be loved.

During young adulthood and the middle years, as one's world becomes larger and more complex, there is the need for sources of support. There also is the need for support as one's world contracts during later life.

Man needs to find a group or groups with which he can identify in a cause which transcends self.

Man has a longing to be a part of movements which have significance.

2. How may this content be communicated as the learner engages in the Learning Tasks? What are the methods and procedures by which the learner may explore the meanings and experiences within this theme (1-a) in the light of his readiness (1-b) in order to discover significance and value?

Through studying the Bible and other literature of the church as the record of God's steadfast love, the claims this love makes on man in his life within the Christian fellowship, and the support this love gives to his life in the world.

Through studying the evidences of oneness and continuity of the church as it is displayed in history and in life today.

Through experiencing in the trials and crises of daily living the support given by others in the Christian fellowship.

By experimenting to discover ways of increasing the sense of *koinonia* within their fellowship.

By worshiping with various groups of Christians.

By planning and carrying out experiences with Christians of other races and cultures.

Through participating with members of the church in service to members of the Christian community.

Through discussing problems in areas of differences within

their congregation in such a way that, even though no common solution is reached, they come through with increased love and concern for one another.

By engaging with other Christians in the proclamation of the gospel by personal and group witnessing and in missionary enterprises.

3. **What may the learner achieve within this theme in the fulfillment of the Learning Tasks? What are possible changes or learnings on the part of the learner that may result from his appropriation of the significance and value discovered? These changes or learnings may be associated with skills, attitudes, motivations, perceptions including understandings and appreciations.**

Adults may achieve a perception of themselves as a part of the *koinonia,* in which each member is significant.

Adults may achieve a maturing understanding of the oneness of God's people around the world.

Adults may achieve an understanding of the meaning of the oneness of the church as recorded in the Bible and in history.

Adults may achieve an awareness of the support of the *koinonia* in the midst of temptations, persecutions, and other crises of daily life.

Adults may achieve an increasing ability to recognize and to assume responsibility in those situations that call for an expression of Christian love and oneness.

Adults may achieve a sense of confidence in the oneness and the mutual love of God's people in spite of failures within the fellowship.

Adults may achieve a greater sense of responsibility for developing, maintaining, and restoring the love relationship in the *koinonia.*

Adults may achieve a feeling of personal repentance for sins of disunity and failure to restore a broken fellowship.

Adults may achieve a consciousness of meaningful identity

699

with a "kingdom which cannot be shaken," a movement which is eternal.

Adults may achieve insight and skill to express the unity among Christians through various language and art forms.

2. God's Continuing Action in and Through His People

STATEMENT OF THE THEME

700

God has established his church within the world and through its life he is active on behalf of man in fulfilling his righteous purposes. The Christian community has been and continues to be used of God and so its members find meaning, direction, and assurance for their corporate and individual lives in God's promise of his ultimate victory within history.

EARLY CHILDHOOD

1. Significance of the theme for this age level

a. Meanings and experiences within this theme relevant for this age level. This is content, a selected part of Scope.

The church is a part of God's plan for his people.

God desires all people to be part of his church—including small children.

The church is more than the local congregation.

God intends his church to be open to all persons who hear and respond to his call.

1. Significance of the theme for this age level

b. Readiness of the learner for this theme in terms of basic needs, interests, motivations, capacities, developmental tasks

The young child is aware of the existence of others and is curious about them. He is ready to relate to the fellowship of the church.

The young child makes accommodations to other people and is ready to accept the sharing atmosphere of the church.

The young child knows himself as part of a group, primarily the family, and therefore is ready for the family of God in the church.

The young child is receptive—open to others—consequently he is open to the influence of the church.

The young child needs to be loved, not judged, and is ready to learn of the love and forgiveness of God.

2. **How may this content be communicated as the learner engages in the Learning Tasks? What are the methods and procedures by which the learner may explore the meanings and experiences within this theme (1-a) in the light of his readiness (1-b) in order to discover significance and value?**

By hearing stories from the Bible and participating in conversations about how God has worked through other Christians.

Through association and identification with other Christians in accepting and loving fellowship of the church, both in and beyond his local congregation.

Through appropriate hymns, pictures, and other materials, which express or point to God's continuing action through his people.

701

3. **What may the learner achieve within this theme in the fulfillment of the Learning Tasks? What are possible changes or learnings on the part of the learner that may result from his appropriation of the significance and value discovered? These changes or learnings may be associated with skills, attitudes, motivations, perceptions, including understandings and appreciations.**

The young child may achieve growth in the ability to join with other children and adults engaged in the life and work of the church.

The young child may achieve a developing assurance of being accepted as a part of the Christian fellowship.

The young child may achieve a growing awareness that the church is more than a building.

The young child may achieve a growing sense of worth and importance as a person in the church fellowship.

The young child may achieve the beginnings of a capacity to accept persons who are "different" as a part of the Christian community.

The young child may achieve a growing understanding of God's continuing action portrayed in stories from the Bible.

The young child may achieve an awareness that he and others need and receive God's help.

2. God's Continuing Action in and Through His People

STATEMENT OF THE THEME

God has established his church within the world and through its life he is active on behalf of man in fulfilling his righteous purposes. The Christian community has been and continues to be used of God and so its members find meaning, direction, and assurance for their corporate and individual lives in God's promise of his ultimate victory within history.

ELEMENTARY YEARS

1. Significance of the theme for this age level

a. Meanings and experiences within this theme relevant for this age level. This is content, a selected part of Scope.

The church has a past and future, as well as a present.

What the church is is known through the teachings of Jesus, the lives of other people past and present, and through its history.

People who make up the church are not perfect, yet God uses them.

The church extends around the world.

God accepts into his church all who hear his call and respond.

God established the church and sustains its life.

1. Significance of the theme for this age level

b. Readiness of the learner for this theme in terms of basic needs, interests, motivations, capacities, developmental tasks.

Children know and experience the reality of rejection and judgment. They are therefore ready for the forgiveness and acceptance of God.

Children are beginning to be aware of a world beyond their immediate experience. Consequently they can begin to comprehend God's activity in the world through the church.

Children tend to identify with heroes and dramatic characters. Therefore they can be challenged by accounts of men and women of great faith.

Children know of the reality of the existence of people in other lands and cultures. They are ready to learn that the people of other lands are members of the body of Christ.

Children have a basic sense of loyalty. They are ready to identify with the various causes of the church.

703

2. How may this content be communicated as the learner engages in the Learning Tasks? What are the methods and procedures by which the learner may explore the meanings and experiences within this theme (1-a) in the light of his readiness (1-b) in order to discover significance and value?

Through study of the Bible to learn of God's action through his people.

Through exploring the work of the church around the world.

Through experiences in which he feels himself to be a part of a community which continually seeks to be led by the Holy Spirit.

Through biographies, filmstrips, movies about significant Christians with whom he may identify.

Through meaningful relationships with God in prayer and worship and through meaningful friendships with persons in the church.

Through engaging with others in the life and work of the church.

3. **What may the learner achieve within this theme in the fulfillment of the Learning Tasks? What are possible changes or learnings on the part of the learner that may result from his appropriation of the significance and value discovered? These changes or learnings may be associated with skills, attitudes, motivations, perceptions including understandings and appreciations.**

The child may achieve an awareness of the nature of the fellowship of the church of which he is a part.

The child may achieve a growing understanding of the life and mission of the church and an increasing participation in it.

The child may achieve a growing knowledge of history in which God's action through the church is seen.

The child may achieve a perception that the church does not exist for itself, but is a means through which God reaches out to others.

The child may achieve an awareness that because God is working through persons they are enabled to do more than is expected in ordinary human effort.

The child may achieve an awareness that he, the person, and others need and receive help from God.

2. God's Continuing Action in and Through His People

STATEMENT OF THE THEME

God has established his church within the world and through its life he is active on behalf of man in fulfilling his righteous purposes. The Christian community has been and continues to be used of God and so its members find meaning, direction, and assurance for their corporate and individual lives in God's promise of his ultimate victory within history.

YOUTH

1. Significance of the theme for this age level

a. Meanings and experiences within this theme relevant for this age level. This is content, a selected part of Scope.

God established his church as a means whereby Christian persons may further his purposes in the world.

God is the source of the life of the church.

God acts in the world through individual Christians, groups of Christians, and the church as a corporate body.

God's church was established in history and, as such, is a vital part of the history of man.

God adds to his church all persons who love and serve him.

God judges the church even as he judges individuals.

God continues to reform and transform his church.

God is stronger than evil and his church has endured and will endure in spite of its own weaknesses, defects, and failures.

God promises ultimate victory for his church in order that his ultimate purposes may be fulfilled.

705

1. Significance of the theme for this age level

b. Readiness of the learner for this theme in terms of basic needs, interests, motivations, capacities, developmental tasks.

Youth seek support, identity, style of life, and values from other youth. They are open for learning about and identifying with Christian youth.

As youth rebel against adult culture, including its institutions and mores, they are ready to learn of new ways to be used of God.

Traditions of family, state, or institutions may mean little to youth as compared to contemporary reality which to them is far more important. They are ready to see the action of God as an event for today.

Youth are developing a sense of the sweep of history. They are ready to consider God as the Lord of history in which his church seeks to fulfill his mission.

Youth live in a tension of conformity versus individuality. They are ready for the life of the church in which the values of both conformity and individuality are conserved and used by God.

Youth respond to the challenge of great causes. They are open to God's action through them and able to recognize his action through others.

2. How may this content be communicated as the learner engages in the Learning Tasks? What are the methods and procedures by which the learner may explore the meanings and experiences within this theme (1-a) in the light of his readiness (1-b) in order to discover significance and value?

Through participating in world mission, sharing in the risks and sacrifices involved.

Through exploring secular history to find where God's actions may be discerned.

Through art forms (music, painting, drama), biographies, filmstrips, movies, biblical study which portray the action of God among and through his people.

Through participating in the total life and work of the church *now*.

3. **What may the learner achieve within this theme in the fulfillment of the Learning Tasks? What are possible changes or learnings on the part of the learner that may result from his appropriation of the significance and value discovered? These changes or learnings may be associated with skills, attitudes, motivations, perceptions including understandings and appreciations.**

Youth may achieve increasing willingness to become involved with other persons, accepting them, and identifying with them in the context of the Christian community.

Youth may achieve increased capacity for self-acceptance and a sense of security through acceptance by and finding a place in the fellowship of the church.

Youth may achieve a greater degree of responsible participation in the life and work of the Christian community.

Youth may achieve a growing ability to test what membership in the Christian community means and to appropriate the meaning and value discovered.

Youth may achieve increased understanding of the activity of God—past, present, and future—in and through his church.

Youth may achieve a fuller understanding of the place of the people of God in history.

Youth may achieve growth in his capacity to accept all persons who love and serve God into the fellowship of the church.

Youth may achieve a heightened consciousness of God's presence and help in experiences within the church and the world.

707

2. God's Continuing Action in and Through His People

STATEMENT OF THE THEME

God has established his church within the world and through its life he is active on behalf of man in fulfilling his righteous purposes. The Christian community has been and continues to be used of God and so its members find meaning, direction, and assurance for their corporate and individual lives in God's promise of his ultimate victory within history.

ADULTHOOD

1. Significance of the theme for this age level

a. Meanings and experiences within this theme relevant for this age level. This is content, a selected part of Scope.

God established his church as a means whereby Christian persons may further his purposes in the world.

God is the source of the life of the church.

God acts in the world through individual Christians, groups of Christians, and the church as a corporate body.

God's church was established in history and, as such, is a vital part of the history of man.

God adds to his church all persons who love and serve.

God judges the church even as he judges individuals.

God continues to reform and transform his church.

God is stronger than evil and his church has endured and will endure in spite of its own weaknesses, defects, and failures.

God promises ultimate victory for his church in order that his ultimate purposes may be fulfilled.

1. Significance of the theme for this age level

b. Readiness of the learner for this theme in terms of basic needs, interests, motivations, capacities, developmental tasks.

Because the adult must establish his own individuality in relation to a largely impersonal society, and in the midst of powers and structures which dehumanize, he is ready to listen to an authentic voice.

The adult desires to establish his identity in terms of personal significance and meaning, and the church offers him an appropriate and supporting arena in which to become such a person.

The adult is dependent upon other human beings; he is ready for the kind of support and direction the fellowship of the church offers.

Because the adult makes adjustments of many kinds to other people, he is ready for the universality of the church and its varied expressions.

Since the adult looks for help which comes from outside himself, he is ready to hear the divine authoritative message of the church.

Since the adult must accept himself as he is without condemnation or rejection, he can welcome through the church the message of the judgment and mercy of God.

2. **How may this content be communicated as the learner engages in the Learning Tasks? What are the methods and procedures by which the learner may explore the meanings and experiences within this theme (1-a) in the light of his readiness (1-b) in order to discover significance and value.**

Through engaging in study of the biblical background of the church and history and present activity of the church.

Through service on behalf of the church and as one in a long line of such servants.

Through participation in group activities in which the quality of Christian relationships can be examined and improved and Christian communities more nearly established.

Through opportunities as a responsible church member to bear witness in society.

By being exposed through the arts to affirmations concerning the action of God in the life of his people.

Through exploring secular history to find where God's action may be discerned.

3. **What may the learner achieve within this theme in the fulfillment of the Learning Tasks? What are possible changes
or learnings on the part of the learner that may result from
his appropriation of the significance and value discovered?
These changes or learnings may be associated with skills,
attitudes, motivations, perceptions including understandings
and appreciations.**

The adult may know and feel a sense of his involvement in
and continuity with history as the arena of God's activity.

The adult may understand and accept his identity in an
impersonal society, yet know that his life is set in God's community.

The adult may take a more responsible part in the life and
mission of the church.

The adult may attach more meaning and value to his individual life as an integral part of the Body of Christ.

The adult may seek new ways of expressing his life in Christian witness through his various involvements and relationships
in the world.

The adult may grow in his capacity to accept all persons who
love and serve God into the fellowship of the church.

The adult may grow in his knowledge and appreciation that
much of God's activity in the world is expressed in the nature,
history, and mission of the church.

The adult may have an increasing awareness that God may
be working through him in the church and the world.

3. The Church Permeating Society

STATEMENT OF THEME

*Such biblical figures as salt, light, leaven, suggest and point to
the church's responsibility in and to society as it confronts,
engages, and permeates all the social structures. The church
carries out this responsibility both as a corporate body and*

through its individual members, who thus fulfill their need to relate significantly to social groupings and to act upon their Christian commitment in community with other Christians.

EARLY CHILDHOOD

1. Significance of the theme for this age level

a. Meanings and experiences within this theme relevant for this age level. This is content, a selected part of Scope.

God loves all young children and is concerned about what happens to them and about what they do.

Jesus Christ is Lord of all people—those inside the church and those outside it.

In God's plan all young children are an important part of the community.

People in the church care about all young children whether they are a part of the church or not.

Christians show love and respect for others at all times.

People who are not Christians may be friendly and loving for many reasons, but it is because they know God's love that Christians love others and try to make the world a better place for everyone.

God cares about how people live and work together both in the church and in the community.

The Bible helps us know how God wants people to live and work together in the world.

1. Significance of the theme for this age level

b. Readiness of the learner for this theme in terms of basic needs, interests, motivations, capacities, developmental tasks.

Young children respond with love to love from adults and from other children.

711

Young children experience both love and hate, often toward the same person and in quick succession.

The young child is the center of his own world but he generally draws other children into it.

Young children have the capacity for "openness" to other people.

Young children have the capacity for sensitive and uninhibited responses of sympathy or hostility.

Young children are curious about other people and respond in various ways to new groups and relationships.

Young children adopt adult values such as acceptance of others or prejudice toward various persons or groups.

Young children may be bewildered by social situations and show the need for help in coping with them in a constructive, creative way.

2. How may this content be communicated as the learner engages in the Learning Tasks? What are the methods and procedures by which the learner may explore the meanings and experiences within this theme (1-a) in the light of his readiness (1-b) in order to discover significance and value?

By being loved and accepted in his church group as a basis for his loving others.

By having opportunities to love and accept others at his level of ability.

By having contacts with persons beyond his usual group of acquaintances—visitors, new members, people of another race or culture.

By taking short trips to interesting parts of the community and meeting people at their accustomed work or in normal life situations.

By having visitors who show or explain their accustomed work or service from which others benefit.

By carrying out helpful acts for persons in his own home or community.

By participating in giving of money or the making of simple gifts as a part of the service of the church to a family or group in the community.

By hearing about Bible people who followed God's way in their relations with others, especially with those who were of another culture or faith.

By hearing about Jesus's loving helpfulness to all persons.

By having opportunities under guidance to resolve in love and goodwill conflict situations that arise in neighborhood and other situations beyond the church.

By having worship experiences which help him realize God's love and concern for all people, whenever and whoever they may be.

By having the disciplined support and guidance his immaturity requires as he copes with destructive behavior patterns in others, or social forces within the society of children.

3. **What may the learner achieve within this theme in the fulfillment of the Learning Tasks? What are possible changes or learnings on the part of the learner that may result from his appropriation of the significance and value discovered? These changes or learnings may be associated with skills, attitudes, motivations, perceptions including understandings and appreciations.**

713

The young child may achieve a sense of security and joy in being accepted as a part of God's people that contributes to his reaching out and accepting others.

The young child may achieve an increasing sense of self-worth that contributes to his realization of the value of others.

The young child may achieve a deepening appreciation for the value of other persons.

The young child may achieve a growing sensitivity for the feelings and needs of others.

The young child may achieve increasing skill in getting along with others and in communicating with them, even when they have different backgrounds and viewpoints.

The young child may achieve a growing willingness to share.

The young child may achieve a growing readiness to resolve childhood conflicts and increasing skill in handling difficulties and manifesting goodwill.

The young child may achieve increasing awareness of his neighborhood and of the people in it as well as a growing at-homeness in it.

The young child may achieve growing awareness and interest in people and places beyond his neighborhood.

The young child may achieve increasing awareness of God's love and care for all persons, within the church or outside it.

The young child may achieve increasing skill in coping with undesirable or destructive behavior patterns of others or social forces within the society of children.

The young child may achieve beginning awareness that the church has a mission to society and endeavors to fulfill that mission.

The young child may achieve beginning appreciation of the Bible as a source of help in knowing how God wants people to live and work together in the world.

3. The Church Permeating Society

STATEMENT OF THE THEME

Such biblical figures as salt, light, leaven suggest and point to the church's responsibility in and to society as it confronts, engages, and permeates all the social structures. The church carries out this responsibility both as a corporate body and through its individual members, who thus fulfill their need to relate significantly to social groupings and to act upon their Christian commitment in community with other Christians.

ELEMENTARY YEARS

1. **Significance of the theme for this age level**

   a. **Meanings and experiences within this theme relevant for this age level. This is content, a selected part of Scope.**

Children are a part of the church in its life and in its work for God in the community and in the world.

The church and its people are a part of the community.

The church makes a difference in its neighborhood and community by what its members do.

God expects his people to serve as Jesus did, in love and helpfulness to others.

God works in the lives of his people at all times—at home, at school, at work, as well as at church.

The Christian way of love, of kindness, of justice, of honesty, is best made known by the way Christians act and speak in their everyday relations.

The church is concerned about all people of the world.

The church has a mission to the community.

God calls every Christian to serve him and to carry out the mission of the church wherever that person may be.

The church may learn from the world and come to understand its mission in a new way as it encounters the world.

715

1. **Significance of the theme for this age level**

   b. **Readiness of the learner for this theme in terms of basic needs, interests, motivations, capacities, developmental tasks.**

Children are responsive to recognition by adults and other children.

Children have a desire to join with others in responsible decisions and acts.

Children's horizons are broadening to include their community and its institutions.

Children live in tension between spontaneity and restraint in their relationships.

Children tend to form judgments about corporate actions and social institutions.

Children are attracted by opportunities for activity and creativity.

Children are curious about and interested in other people and other places.

Children are able to understand with increasing insight and sensitivity various facets of the community and to respond to the demands these make.

Children both make demands on and make adjustments to adults and adult society.

Children desire and need guidance and support as they encounter social situations that are destructive or behavior that is unacceptable to Christians.

2. How may this content be communicated as the learner engages in the Learning Tasks? What are the methods and procedures by which the learner may explore the meanings and experiences within this theme (1-a) in the light of his readiness (1-b) in order to discover significance and value?

By planning within their church groups for ways to show love to persons in need in their community.

By getting acquainted with persons in the community who render public service.

By contributing to outreach and service enterprises of the church in giving, prayer, and service.

By associating with persons of other races, cultures, social and economic groups.

By entertaining visitors and taking trips to meet persons and become acquainted.

By seeing pictures, photos, art, about society, its structures, people, problems.

By studying the biblical account of people who serve God by serving others.

By investigating what the Bible has to say about relations between persons and between man and God.

By interviewing adult leaders to discover how their church has shown its concern for and its outreach to others.

By exploring ways of resolving person-to-person or group conflicts.

By participating in worship which focuses on God's presence and available guidance for living as his children in the world.

By studying how the church has gone about working to influence the social structures in the name of Christ.

3. **What may the learner achieve within this theme in the fulfillment of the Learning Tasks? What are possible changes or learnings on the part of the learner that may result from his appropriation of the significance and value discovered? These changes or learnings may be associated with skills, attitudes, motivations, perceptions including understandings and appreciations.**

The child may achieve a growing sense of individual worth in being accepted as a part of the people of God in the world.

The child may achieve a deepening appreciation for the value of persons.

The child may achieve a growing awareness of the needs of others.

The child may achieve an increasing sense of responsibility for the well-being of others within their community and world.

The child may achieve joy in participating in service for others.

The child may achieve increasing skill in working with others in acts of service.

The child may achieve an increasing sense of being called to assume personal responsibility for practicing kindness, justice,

717

fair play, honesty, truthfulness at home, at play, at school, at church.

The child may achieve a growing ability to meet tension and conflict with forgiveness and goodwill.

The child may achieve a growing realization that God is concerned in all phases of a person's life.

The child may achieve an increasing awareness of and confidence in God's presence and help in daily situations.

The child may achieve a knowledge of how persons of the Bible and in the heritage of the church have individually and in groups wrought changes in the social structures.

3. The Church Permeating Society

STATEMENT OF THE THEME

Such biblical figures as salt, light, leaven suggest and point to the church's responsibility in and to society as it confronts, engages, and permeates all the social structures. The church carries out this responsibility both as a corporate body and through its individual members, who thus fulfill their need to relate significantly to social groupings and to act upon their Christian commitment in community with other Christians.

YOUTH

1. Significance of the theme for this age level

a. Meanings and experiences within this theme relevant for this age level. This is content, a selected part of Scope.

God's purposes for the world include not only personal life but the life and relationships of society.

God is working for social justice through elements in the youth culture.

Concern for youth's relationships and involvement in society is part of the life and work of the church.

Part of the meaning of the church is that youth both as individual Christians and as members of the Christian community can be expected to take responsibility for affecting social structures.

God works through youth to bring about social change.

The church may come to a clearer understanding of its mission in the world through conscious dialogue with various groups in society.

The church is a "called out" people not for isolation from society, but indeed for penetration and service in society for God's purposes.

The church must witness to its faith as it encounters the world.

1. Significance of the theme for this age level

b. Readiness of the learner for this theme in terms of basic needs, interests, motivations, capacities, developmental tasks.

Young people are sensitive to what they perceive as being unjust and want to set injustices right.

Youth want to participate with persons and groups they see as worthy.

Youth are eager to be viewed as able to take full social responsibility—for themselves as well as for their own social structures.

Youth identify with causes or groups they see as having value in enhancing their view of themselves.

719

Decisions young people make about what to belong to, where to go, how to act, are often made for them by others—business enterprises, school authorities, the family, other authority figures —although they would like to be independent.

Generally speaking young people are highly sensitive to what their peers are doing and are most conservative in changing or being different from their social groupings.

Youth seek and need the company of mature adults who see them as worthwhile persons and who will help them find a significant place in the world.

Youth live in tension between desire for independence and for dependable authority, and in tension between isolation and community.

Youth are keen to observe discrepancy in professed belief and enacted values.

Youth are capable of understanding Christian principles of social action derived from biblical study.

2. How may this content be communicated as the learner engages in the Learning Tasks? What are the methods and procedures by which the learner may explore the meanings and experiences within this theme (1-a) in the light of his readiness (1-b) in order to discover significance and value?

By participating with other Christian youth in efforts to affect changes in youth culture.

By becoming involved with the adults of the congregation in social action.

By studying either separately or with adults the issues in responsible community participation as Christians.

By reflecting on and discussing from the Christian perspective, their involvement in youth culture.

By working and studying with persons of other cultures, customs, races, and social and economic groups.

By engaging in voluntary service projects of all kinds, with a consciousness of being the church.

By exploring what the Bible has to say about the people of God and their relation to and mission in society.

By observing and participating in community discussions of issues and problems of concern, taking account of religious dimensions.

By experimenting with and weighing alternative ways of witnessing to their social groups concerning the Christian approach to various social issues and problems.

By participating in ecumenical groups in standing against un-Christian structures and actions in society.

By examining the past and current involvement of the church individually and corporately in its attempts to penetrate society.

By trying out and evaluating in hypothetical situations, different means of penetrating social issues and structures with Christian values.

3. **What may the learner achieve within this theme in the fulfillment of the Learning Tasks? What are possible changes or learnings on the part of the learner that may result from his appropriation of the significance and value discovered? These changes or learnings may be associated with skills, attitudes, motivations, perceptions including understandings and appreciations.**

Youth may achieve a growing awareness of God at work in the social structures throughout the world.

Youth may achieve a greater sensitivity to personal responsibility in the church's penetration of society.

Youth may achieve an emerging sense of participating in the work of God in society.

Youth may achieve a developing ability to be discerning about conflicting value systems in social structures.

Youth may achieve a growing sense of the worth of persons.

Youth may achieve increasing ability to deal creatively with social pressures.

Youth may achieve a deepening reliance upon God in every phase of life.

Youth may achieve a more discerning and responsible outlook toward Christian citizenship.

Youth may achieve the awareness of the work of the Holy Spirit in youth's relationship to the world.

Youth may achieve a deepening sense of caring about persons which leads to responsible action in the community.

Youth may achieve an understanding of society's structures in which the church must work as it witnesses.

721

Youth may achieve an appreciation for the role of Christians, individually and corporately, in the changes effected for good in society.

3. The Church Permeating Society

STATEMENT OF THE THEME

Such biblical figures as salt, light, leaven suggest and point to the church's responsibility in and to society as it confronts, engages, and permeates all the social structures. The church carries out this responsibility both as a corporate body and through its individual members, who thus fulfill their need to relate significantly to social groupings and to act upon their Christian commitment in community with other Christians.

ADULTHOOD

1. Significance of the theme for this age level

a. Meanings and experiences within this theme relevant for this age level. This is content, a selected part of Scope.

God is Lord of all society as well as the church.

The church, corporately and through its individual members, is called to follow its servant Lord in ministry to and transformation of society.

The nature and mission of the church compels a continuing involvement of Christians in their society.

All of society, including the Christian community, is under the judgment of God.

As a responsible social structure, the church has a responsibility to the society in which it lives.

The church is in tension with itself and with the society of which it is a part.

The Holy Spirit empowers and enlightens the people of God for their mission in society.

God speaks through his church to society, its social structures, and persons.

The Christian faith includes within its objective the welfare of the social order in which the church exists.

God uses individual members to call the church to fulfill its responsibility to society.

In order to penetrate society effectively and influence social issues, the church must be knowledgeable about the structures and values of society.

1. Significance of the theme for this age level

b. Readiness of the learner for this theme in terms of basic needs, interests, motivations, capacities, developmental tasks.

Adults are involved in society in many ways.

Adults live in tension between isolation and community, and seek supporting relationships with others.

Adults seek a satisfying place in community life.

Adults inescapably influence society's structures, values, and patterns of life.

Adults have the capacity and opportunity to initiate action in the social order.

Adults consciously or unconsciously make value judgments upon society, its structures, its institutions, and on social issues within society.

Adults want to identify with causes and social groupings which enhance man's view of himself.

Adults need the support of others in taking difficult or unpopular positions and actions in society.

Adults have the mental capacity to derive from biblical study principles for affecting society today.

2. How may this content be communicated as the learner engages in the Learning Tasks? What are the methods and

723

procedures by which the learner may explore the meanings and experiences within this theme (1-a) in the light of his readiness (1-b) in order to discover significance and value?

By getting acquainted with persons of other races, cultures, and social and economic groupings in their community.

By engaging consciously as Christians in volunteer service of all kinds within the life of the community.

By studying what the Bible has to say about the people of God and their responsibility for the quality of the community.

By interviewing persons involved in various social issues and groupings and bringing to bear Christian insights.

By gathering data regarding the past and present efforts of the people of God to affect society and reflecting upon this information.

By involvement with the whole community in discussions of issues and problems of concern to all persons.

By articulating insights into specific relevance of the gospel to current social issues.

By exploring with fellow Christians in similar occupations or common civic groupings the implications of the gospel for that particular occupation or civic group.

By participation in social action and personal ministries with other Christians.

By experimenting with and weighing alternative ways of witnessing to their social groups concerning the Christian approach to various social issues and problems.

By examining the past and current involvement of the church individually and corporately in its attempts to penetrate society.

By participating in ecumenical groups in standing against un-Christian structures and actions in society.

By trying out and evaluating in hypothetical situations different means of penetrating social issues and structures with Christian values.

3. **What may the learner achieve within this theme in the fulfillment of the Learning Tasks? What are possible changes or learnings on the part of the learner that may result from his appropriation of the significance and value discovered? These changes or learnings may be associated with skills, attitudes, motivations, perceptions including understandings and appreciations.**

Adults may achieve a growing joy derived from being the people of God involved in achieving God's purposes in the world.

Adults may achieve an increasing sense of the worth of persons.

Adults may achieve increasing skills in working with others in community relationships.

Adults may achieve a developing awareness of the needs of persons and a concern for persons growing out of empathic understanding of them.

Adults may achieve supporting identification with fellow Christians seeking to penetrate society.

Adults may achieve a growing capacity to accept life and the inevitability of its social tensions and conflicts.

Adults may achieve a knowledge and appreciation of the biblical perspective of the relationship of the people of God to the world.

725

Adults may achieve a growing capacity to deal creatively with social pressures, including persecution and his own and others' desires for power within the social structures.

Adults may achieve an identification with the people of God throughout history in their relationships to society and sensitivity to personal responsibility in the church's penetration of society.

Adults may achieve a growing awareness of God at work in the social structures throughout the world.

Adults may achieve an increasing commitment to Jesus Christ as the dynamic for responsible citizenship, and a developing awareness of the relevance of that commitment.

Adults may achieve ability to be discerning about conflicting values and to cope with the various life values found in church and society.

Adults may achieve awareness of and reliance on the guidance of the Holy Spirit in the church's penetration of society.

4. Extending Reconciliation and Redemption

726

STATEMENT OF THE THEME

Brought into being by God's gracious redemption, the Christian community is a servant people of a servant Lord, to whom is committed the message of reconciliation between God and man and among men. This involvement gathers up man's need to give himself in loyalty and to make a significant contribution by his life.

EARLY CHILDHOOD

1. Significance of the theme for this age level

a. Meanings and experiences within this theme relevant for this age level. This is content, a selected part of Scope.

God loves and cares about every person, and all people belong to God.

God works through people to help other people.

God's love and care are most clearly seen in Jesus.

The people of the church are followers of Jesus and help do God's work in the world. God wants us to learn how to show love and be helpful.

When persons are in conflict with each other, they can be helped to resolve the conflict by remembering and acting upon God's love for all people.

When we fail and do wrong, God is always ready and waiting to forgive us if we ask him.

1. **Significance of the theme for this age level**

   b. **Readiness of the learner for this theme in terms of basic needs, interests, motivations, capacities, developmental tasks.**

   The young child yearns for acceptance and love, but at times has to face hostility in himself and others.

   The young child disregards superficial differences and easily identifies likenesses.

   The young child is often concerned about the hurts of others.

   The young child has a capacity for love and friendly responses. Serious conflict, broken relationships, and disaster that affect him and those he loves may cause anxiety and a sense of rejection. He senses a need for restored fellowship.

2. **How may this content be communicated as the learner engages in the Learning Tasks? What are the methods and procedures by which the learner may explore the meanings and experiences within this theme (1-a) in the light of his readiness (1-b) in order to discover significance and value?**

   By experiencing love and forgiveness in relationships with Christian adults. Such loving relationships are normally experienced first in the family and soon thereafter within the Christian congregation.

   By conversation within the Christian perspective with persons and groups involved in conflict.

   By experiencing the joy and satisfaction of restored fellowship both individually and socially.

   By hearing stories about things Jesus did and taught, and about people who were changed by knowing Jesus.

   By hearing stories of persons who live or have lived as the people of God working for reconciliation and redemption.

   By having a part in showing love to neglected and/or lonely persons in the local community; by making gifts for, and showing appreciation of gifts from, persons for whom the church has

727

concern and love; by showing love to persons of special need and accepting them as a part of the group.

Through experiences with materials that exhibit and interpret the work of the church in extending the message of reconciliation and redemption throughout the world; through opportunities to participate in this work at their level.

Through opportunities to pray for others near and far away.

By joining informally in worship with others in thanksgiving for times when love replaces anger and misunderstanding in human relationships.

3. **What may the learner achieve within this theme in the fulfillment of the Learning Tasks? What are possible changes or learnings on the part of the learner that may result from his appropriation of the signifiance and value discovered? These changes or learnings may be associated with skills, attitudes, motivations, perceptions including understandings and appreciations.**

The young child may achieve ability to be aware of and to accept his part in situations of broken relationships and hurts.

The young child may achieve a growing sympathy for the suffering and unhappiness of those around him and a willingness to share with them in healing.

The young child may achieve increasing satisfaction and ability in establishing and keeping happy relationships with others.

The young child may achieve a growing capacity to enter into the work of the church in sharing the good news of God's love and forgiveness.

4. Extending Reconciliation and Redemption

STATEMENT OF THE THEME

Brought into being by God's gracious redemption, the Christian community is a servant people of a servant Lord, to whom is committed the message of reconciliation between God and man and among men. This involvement gathers up man's need to give himself in loyalty and to make a significant contribution by his life.

ELEMENTARY YEARS

1. Significance of the theme for this age level

a. Meanings and experiences within this theme relevant for this age level. This is content, a selected part of Scope.

Sin breaks one's fellowship with God and alienates the individual from God and from others.

God is always seeking to reclaim and forgive. Therefore, the opportunity is before us to repent, to ask for, and to accept forgiveness.

God expects persons to help others know his forgiveness and redeeming love. God works through Christians in restoring love and power to people.

God works through the church to meet the needs of people who are separated from one another and from God.

The Christian community is not without fault. God expects the church to be aware always of its own failures and shortcomings and to seek forgiveness.

729

1. Significance of the theme for this age level

b. Readiness of the learner for this theme in terms of basic needs, interests, motivations, capacities, developmental tasks.

An elementary child yearns for acceptance (including self-acceptance) and love, but at times experiences hostility within himself and others or rejection by others and even rejection by himself of himself.

An elementary child is sensitive to situations in which fellowship is broken (child to God, child to child, child to adult).

An elementary child is concerned about the situations he sees inside and outside the church where there is conflict and a need for reconciliation.

Elementary children are living with the difficulties arising from differences in religious practices and beliefs and from unbelief.

There is often aggressiveness in groups of elementary children. The child needs guidance in developing ability to deal with the antagonisms created by this aggressiveness.

730

The elementary child experiences pressures in his life, including anxiety, hatred, jealousy, etc.

The elementary child is defensive of his own loyalties, those of his family, and group convictions.

The elementary child may experience feelings of guilt that cause him to feel separation from God. With proper guidance he may be helped to seek reconciliation with God.

Elementary children are keenly aware of and react strongly to injustice.

2. **How may this content be communicated as the learner engages in the Learning Tasks? What are the methods and procedures by which the learner may explore the meanings and experiences within this theme (1-a) in the light of his readiness (1-b) in order to discover significance and value?**

Through opportunities to experience the meaning of reconciliation and redemption in their relation to the child's present situations and observations.

Through opportunities to hear about and view the work of the church as it seeks to proclaim the word of reconciliation and to work for reconciliation and redemption in the world.

By opportunities for meaningful experiences of Bible study related to this theme.

By identifying with persons in their needs (a friend loses a parent, a conflict in sports isolates another), is one way a child may participate in the church's work of extending God's redemptive love to others.

By talking about, reflecting on, and praying about the broken relationships experienced in their groups.

By responding to the imperative of reconciliation through trying different ways of resolving conflicts in their particular situations in life.

Recounting, conversing about, and reflecting on experiences of reconciliation.

Through praying with all Christians for persons in all the world.

3. **What may the learner achieve within this theme in the fulfillment of the Learning Tasks? What are possible changes or learnings on the part of the learner that may result from his appropriation of the significance and value discovered? These changes or learnings may be associated with skills, attitudes, motivations, perceptions including understandings and appreciations.**

The child may achieve ability to recognize one's own need for God's help in maintaining relationships with God and with other persons.

The child may achieve a growing sense of the sufferings and frustrations of those around him and a willingness to enter into these as a part of sharing in the lives of those persons.

The child may achieve an increased courage to venture into more difficult situations where reconciliation is needed and to accept responsibility in the situation.

The child may achieve a growing ability to accept failure in tasks of reconciliation without withdrawing or becoming defensive.

The child may achieve increasing ability in establishing and maintaining satisfying relationships.

The child may achieve an increasing willingness to accept

731

responsibility and take initiative in the areas of broken relationships.

The child may achieve a growing ability to discover the ways of reconciliation and skill in working in the task.

The child may achieve increasing ability to enter into the activity of mission in the local church and an increased desire to enlarge the areas of concern for himself and the church.

The child may achieve a growing ability to be patient and recognize one's dependence upon God to effect the work of reconciliation and redemption.

732

4. Extending Reconciliation and Redemption

STATEMENT OF THE THEME

Brought into being by God's gracious redemption, the Christian community is a servant people of a servant Lord, to whom is committed the message of reconciliation between God and man and among men. This involvement gathers up man's need to give himself in loyalty and to make a significant contribution by his life.

YOUTH

1. Significance of the theme for this age level

a. Meanings and experiences within this theme relevant for this age level. This is content, a selected part of Scope.

Sin breaks fellowship with God and alienates the individual from God and from others. God himself is in Christ seeking to overcome all enmity between man and God and between man and man.

God has committed to the Christian community the "word of reconciliation." The community is to proclaim this word and to work for reconciliation and redemption.

As the church recognizes experiences of alienation within the world, God is able to use it as an instrument in effecting reconciliation and redemption.

The Christian community itself is not without sin and failure. God requires repentance and renewal of the church as part of his continuing reconciliation.

1. Significance of the theme for this age level

b. Readiness of the learner for this theme in terms of basic needs, interests, motivations, capacities, developmental tasks.

Young persons sense a lack of wholeness in themselves. They feel a need for a faith to live by, a supreme loyalty to which they may give themselves, and the understanding that these may be found in God.

Youth often feels alienated from himself, from others, and from God. Young persons find themselves inadequate to come to terms with this estrangement and their hostilities.

The young person is fragmented by conflicting loyalties, demands, pressures, interests, and drives.

The young person is involved in struggle for power within the group.

Every person is involved in situations of human need. The young person is aware of this and reacts to the suffering of others.

733

Young persons express both hostility and a longing for harmony. They are aware of the need for creative relationships with others.

Young persons are keenly aware of and react strongly to injustices in the social, economic, and religious orders.

Young persons seek fulfillment of their goals and ideals, but may be disillusioned by the seeming inertia of the Christian community.

2. How may this content be communicated as the learner engages in the Learning Tasks? What are the methods and procedures by which the learner may explore the meanings and experiences within this theme (1-a) in the light of his readiness (1-b) in order to discover significance and value?

Through involvement in community situations characterized by conflicts or difference of view and those which provide opportunity for study, reflection, and action.

Through serving as mediator in intergroup tensions.

Through recognizing situations where reconciliation is needed and through seeking to remove causes of hostility.

Through frankly facing up to the need for reconciliation between individuals and small groups within their own fellowship.

Through participating creatively and taking full share in the life of the church as it gives itself to be an instrument of reconciliation.

Through studying the Bible with the purpose of learning how reconciliation takes place.

Through studies of examples of successful efforts at reconciliation (man to God and man to man).

Through learning to utilize the findings of psychology, psychiatry, and human relations in the process of reconciliation, with due regard to the gospel and the uniqueness of each person.

Through providing opportunities for youth to accept responsibility for strengthening the Christian community as an agent of reconciliation.

Through helping youth identify with persons who need reconciliation and work with God in efforts toward their reconciliation.

Through experiences of prayer with and for Christians in all lands.

Through opportunities to hear about and view the work of the church as it seeks to proclaim the word of reconciliation and to work for reconciliation and redemption in the world.

734

3. **What may the learner achieve within this theme in the fulfillment of the Learning Tasks? What are possible changes or learnings on the part of the learner that may result from his appropriation of the significance and value discovered? These changes or learnings may be associated with skills, attitudes, motivations, perceptions including understandings and appreciations.**

Youth may achieve recognition that reconciliation and redemption begin with God.

Youth may achieve recognition of his own limitations, willingness to ask for help, and respect for the personality of those in need of reconciliation.

Youth may achieve growing ability to sympathize with the sufferings and frustrations of others and to take initiative in reconciliation.

Youth may achieve increasing capacity to take as his own the sufferings and frustrations of others, and to be used for the purpose of reconciliation.

Youth may achieve increasing courage to enter into more demanding tasks of reconciliation and to join efforts with others in this task.

Youth may achieve a beginning capacity to recognize the need for being expendable, and to venture the risk of failure in the situations needing reconciliation.

735

Youth may achieve a profound and abiding joy through sharing in the tasks of reconciliation.

Youth may achieve growing skill in the discovery and in working at the tasks of reconciliation.

Youth may achieve increasing capacity for patience in the process of reconciliation in order that healing may take place (a good physician waits for nature to take its course after having done all within his human powers).

Youth may achieve a greater participation in all areas of the mission of the church as it finds expression in local and world-wide communities.

Youth may achieve the thrill of discovering the meaning of Jesus when he said, "He who would lose his life for my sake shall find it. . . ."

4. Extending Reconciliation and Redemption

736

STATEMENT OF THE THEME

Brought into being by God's gracious redemption, the Christian community is a servant people of a servant Lord, to whom is committed the message of reconciliation between God and man and among men. This involvement gathers up man's need to give himself in loyalty and to make a significant contribution by his life.

ADULTHOOD

1. Significance of the theme for this age level

a. Meanings and experiences within this theme relevant for this age level. This is content, a selected part of Scope.

Sin causes broken fellowship and estrangement from God and man. Through Christ, God's redemption is available to all men at all times.

In redemption the initiative is with God who is always seeking man.

Reconciliation is accomplished only as man responds to God in repentance, renewed commitment, and obedience.

The Christian, even as the Christian community, is called to be an instrument of God's redemption and reconciliation. God has given the Christian community the "word of reconciliation," and the community is called to proclaim the word and to work for reconciliation and redemption.

God summons the church, not to a life of special privilege but to a life of servanthood to overcome the alienation of the world.

God in Christ calls the church to cross-bearing where required in order to effect reconciliation and redemption.

As the church recognizes experiences of alienation within the world, God is able to use it as an instrument in effecting reconciliation and redemption.

The Christian community itself is not without sin and failure. God requires repentance and renewal of the church as a part of his continuing reconciliation.

1. Significance of the theme for this age level

b. Readiness of the learner for this theme in terms of basic needs, interests, motivations, capacities, developmental tasks.

Adults sense a lack of wholeness in themselves. Adults must have a faith to live by, a supreme loyalty to which they may give themselves, and the understanding that these may be found supremely in God.

An adult often feels alienated from himself, from others, and from God.

Every person is fragmented by conflicting loyalties, demands, pressures, interests, and drives. Such feelings may lead to frustrations and destructive tensions which must be resolved.

Man experiences feelings of guilt arising from his personal and social sins.

Persons involved in situations of human estrangement, both personal and social, cannot escape a sense of obligation to bring about reconciliation.

Man expresses both hostility and a longing for harmony. Adults are aware of the need for creative relationships with others.

Confronted by social injustices, man may be defensive, passive, or redemptive in his response to these conditions.

737

2. How may this content be communicated as the learner engages in the Learning Tasks? What are the methods and procedures by which the learner may explore the meanings and experiences within this theme (1-a) in the light of his readiness (1-b) in order to discover significance and value?

By surrounding persons with evidences of the concern of the Christian community at the point of individual need for reconciliation and redemption.

Through providing opportunities for honest recognition, sympathetic consideration, and radical removal of the hostilities between individuals and groups.

By participation in the ministries of proclamation, nurture, and witness of the church as it seeks to be an instrument of God's redemption.

By hearing about and viewing the socially destructive consequences that sometimes stem from differences among persons.

Through involvement in groups and community situations where reconciliation is needed.

By searching out and analyzing situations in which there is need for reconciliation.

In sharing with others examples of effective reconciliation, current and historical.

By utilizing, in light of the gospel, the advances made in behavioral sciences in the field of reconciliation.

By engaging in Bible study looking for the underlying purposes and meaning of reconciliation and redemption.

Through exploring and utilizing all channels of the church in the task of reconciliation.

Through participating in a church that ministers in a changing community.

Through participation in the life of the church as it bears a faithful witness in social issues, such as racial strife, international tension.

Through engaging in prayer in felt union with Christians

around the world for the reconciliation and redemption of all men.

Through opportunities to hear about and view the work of the church as it seeks to proclaim the word of reconciliation and to work for reconciliation and redemption in the world.

3. **What may the learner achieve within this theme in the fulfillment of the Learning Tasks? What are possible changes or learnings on the part of the learner that may result from his appropriation of the significance and value discovered? These changes or learnings may be associated with skills, attitudes, motivations, perceptions including understandings and appreciations.**

The adult may achieve the recognition that reconciliation and redemption begin with God.

The adult may achieve a growing capacity to sympathize with the sufferings and frustrations of others and to bear these burdens as his own.

The adult may achieve increased ability to recognize and courage to venture, with God's help, into more demanding tasks of reconciliation, even with the recognition of one's own limitations.

The adult may achieve acceptance of the risk of failure and the growing capacity for self-giving and expendability.

The adult may achieve a profound and abiding joy through sharing with others in the tasks of reconciliation.

The adult may achieve growth in the skill of discovery and working at the task of reconciliation.

The adult may achieve increasing participation in the redemptive mission of the church.

The adult may achieve willingness to persist in the process of reconciliation for as long as the need exists.

The adult may achieve awareness of one's being a new person in Christ.

The adult may achieve awareness of personal need for continuing reconciliation.

The adult may achieve recognition of creative value of tension.

5. The Church Lives by Worship

STATEMENT OF THE THEME

Adoration, praise, thanksgiving, confession, acceptance of pardon, reexamination of life in all its relationships, dedication in obedience to God's will, sustain, nurture, and inspire the church in its life of love and service. The Christian community renews its faith and life in Christ and finds strength and help for every need through corporate and individual worship including the sacraments.

EARLY CHILDHOOD

1. Significance of the theme for this age level
   a. Meanings and experiences within this theme relevant for this age level. This is content, a selected part of Scope.

We worship God who is kind and just.

God loves young children and wants them to worship him.

God desires that young children turn to him in worship as a loving Father and as his children.

God is always near and listens to every person as he prays.

God helps us see our mistakes and is willing to forgive us our mistakes when we are truly sorry and turn to him for forgiveness.

God is worshiped by all who are in the church anywhere.

God will help us help others if we seek his help through worship.

People who love God worship him.

There are many forms of worship and these include prayer, Scripture reading, preaching, giving an offering, and other special acts.

We can worship God wherever we are.

740

We have times we set aside for the worship of God.

Worship has a special quality unlike anything else we do.

We can worship God privately, with our families, or with groups in the congregation.

God is greater than persons and gives them strength when they seek it.

We express in worship our feelings of awe and wonder before God in connection with birth and death.

In worship we think of Jesus Christ who especially enables us to know God.

Worship is very important in the life of the church.

1. Significance of the theme for this age level

b. Readiness of the learner for this theme in terms of basic needs, interests, motivations, capacities, developmental tasks

The young child has increasing trust in persons whom he loves and in God.

The young child has increasing capacity to respond with wonder and interest to the Creator as beauty and certain aspects of order in the universe are observed.

The young child has growing capacity to respond with love and appreciation to relationships with people and with God and to the meaning these relationships have for him.

The young child is aware of his parents', teachers', and other adults' love and worship of God.

The young child has curiosity about and interest in himself and his world that makes him wonder about the Creator.

The young child has a need for approval, affection, and companionship and seeks them from parents and from God.

The young child has a need for release from bad feelings and for a sense of forgiveness.

The young child has a need to feel personal worth, significance, security.

741

The young child has a need to talk about and explore his feelings of awe and wonder when birth and death come into his experience.

The young child looks to a source of authority and strength on whom he can depend.

The young child seeks to express love and appreciation in various ways.

The young child imitates significant adults to whom he is related.

742

2. **How may this content be communicated as the learner engages in the Learning Tasks? What are the methods and procedures by which the learner may explore the meanings and experiences within this theme (1-a) in the light of his readiness (1-b) in order to discover significance and value?**

By participating with his family in the regular worship of the church.

By participating with his family in celebration of holy days (such as Christmas and Easter).

By observing and imitating the moods and patterns of behavior of his parents and other adults as they are engaged in worship.

By hearing and participating in family and group prayers of thanksgiving, petition, aspiration, and repentance.

By thinking and talking about ways to express his own thoughts and feelings in prayer.

By relating the love and affection of parents and others in the church who give him time, patience, understanding, and guidance to the love God has for him.

By using many forms of expression in worship, such as prayer, story play, simple role playing, storytelling, music, conversation.

By discussing elementary meanings of worship.

By observing and talking about the order, dependability, beauty in his world.

By talking about the mystery of birth and death as this mystery is experienced and expressed by Christians in worship and as birth and death enter his experience.

By thinking and talking about ways to express gratitude to God for his gifts in the world of persons and of nature.

By thinking and talking about God's goodness and love in sending us Jesus and of ways to express our gratitude for his gift.

By having opportunities for seeking God's help in living as God would desire.

By thinking and talking about feelings of alienation and the value of confession when behavior has been disapproved.

By hearing selected Bible passages and stories that express worship.

By hearing selected Bible passages and stories that tell what God expects of man in worship.

By observing adults worship in the home and at church.

3. **What may the learner achieve within this theme in the fulfillment of the Learning Tasks? What are possible changes or learnings on the part of the learner that may result from his appropriation of the significance and value discovered? These changes or learnings may be associated with skills, attitudes, motivations, perceptions including understandings and appreciations.**

743

A young child may develop a knowledge and practice of simple prayers and table graces.

A young child may have a growing relationship with God in worship that can add meaning and warmth to relationships with others.

A young child may experience an awareness of God's continuing love and justice even when the child is disobedient.

A young child may enter into a warm and personal relationship with God as a loving Father.

A young child may achieve an increasing ability to express his own feelings to God.

A young child may turn increasingly to God for help in distinguishing between right and wrong and in seeking God's help in doing that which he would want.

A young child may achieve a growing development of trustful and responsible relationships with God and with people.

A young child may achieve a beginning recognition that persons are not all-powerful; that there is in God a higher source of power and strength upon which a person can depend.

A young child may achieve increasing assurance in a personal relationship with God.

A young child may achieve and express a growing sense of awe and wonder toward God in worship concerning the meaning about birth and death as they enter his experience.

A young child may achieve an increasing appreciation of the Bible as an important and helpful book in worship.

A young child may develop an increasing dependence on God in dealing with rejection and alienation following disapproval.

A young child may respond to and accept forgiveness and reconciliation, both human and divine.

A young child may achieve an awareness that such words as "God," "Jesus," "Bible," have special meanings in the Christian fellowship.

A young child may realize that God is always ready and willing to hear him and to help him.

A young child may use a variety of expressions in his worship of God.

A young child may increasingly turn to God in private and corporate worship.

5. The Church Lives by Worship

STATEMENT OF THE THEME

Adoration, praise, thanksgiving, confession, acceptance of pardon, reexamination of life in all its relationships, dedication in obedience to God's will sustain, nurture, and inspire the church in its life of love and service. The Christian community renews its faith and life in Christ and finds strength and help for every need through corporate and individual worship including the sacraments.

ELEMENTARY YEARS

1. Significance of the theme for this age level

    a. Meanings and experiences within this theme relevant for this age level. This is content, a selected part of Scope.

God loves all persons everywhere and wishes to have fellowship with them.

Children can be very close to God.

God's purposes can be disclosed through worship.

Worship is responding to the presence of God.

God desires that all persons know him as a loving Father and themselves as his children.

Through worship persons can have personal relationship with God.

Worship is a way in which man offers adoration, praise, thanksgiving, and confession to God.

In worship man asserts his faith in God.

Worship helps us free our creative powers through the dedication of ourselves to God.

Worship helps us view ourselves properly as God's creatures and view him as the Creator of us all.

In worship God helps us see values in life as he defines them.

God helps children face and deal with their alienation and need for forgiveness.

All Christians of other churches worship the same God we do.

Persons can worship God privately, but completeness in worship comes as Christians join together to worship as the family of God.

The nature of Christian worship is determined by the nature of the God who is worshiped.

745

In Christian worship we respond to God who has acted in mercy and grace through Jesus Christ.

Worship is at the center of the church—it is the heart of its life.

In worship we acknowledge that God is Lord of our lives and offer ourselves as instruments of justice and peace.

The worshiping congregation constitutes a community that can be identified as separate and unique in society. Persons belong through worship.

746

Worship develops a sense of awe, wonder, dependence, reverence.

1. Significance of the theme for this age level

b. Readiness of the learner for this theme in terms of basic needs, interests, motivations, capacities, developmental tasks.

Elementary children can sense the nature and cause of broken relationships.

Elementary children are capable of experiencing remorse and sorrow and they need release from these feelings through participation in worship that expresses judgment and forgiveness within a climate of love, acceptance, and trust.

Elementary children are able to sense through worship the difference between the true and the false, right and wrong, good and evil.

Elementary children are ready in worship to look for the eternal source of all true values.

Elementary children have a developing capacity for amazement at the mysteries of the world about, beyond, and within them.

Elementary children can identify with others and are capable of identifying with the biblical personalities in their acts of worship and prayer.

Elementary children are approaching the time of making important life decisions and are becoming ready for participation in the self-commitment of worship.

Elementary children have a beginning capacity to seek in worship for needed help and guidance.

Children have the capacity to enter sympathetically into the experiences of others, and can know through worship the experience of intercession.

The elementary child's increasing capacity to symbolize makes it possible for him to be led in worship to place his faith in the God who is the source of faith for those whom the child loves and trusts.

Elementary children face the fact that sin alienates and need to participate in the confession of worship that is essential to restoration.

2. **How may this content be communicated as the learner engages in the Learning Tasks? What are the methods and procedures by which the learner may explore the meanings and experiences within this theme (1-a) in the light of his readiness (1-b) in order to discover significance and value?**

By participating in worship experiences of his own group and the church congregation.

By discussing the meanings and elements of worship.

By interviewing people (ministers and outstanding laymen) and going to written sources of information (such as the Bible, hymnal, books of prayer) to explore ways in which his church worships or has worshiped.

By planning for worship; helping to carry out plans; preparing prayers, litanies, poems, etc., to be used in worship.

By becoming acquainted with art, music, symbols which contribute to worship experiences.

By studing the prayers, litanies, poems, etc. used in worship.

By joining in the congregational observances of the sacraments, or ordinances, either actually or by observation.

747

By visiting churches that have varying forms of worship.

By participating in directed Bible reading and meditation describing worship situations.

By hiking or camping where his contact with the natural world will engender a sense of awe and wonder at the beauty and order of nature.

By sharing in the intercessory prayers of the church as it reaches out in mission.

By taking part in communicants classes dealing with the nature of worship in the church.

3. **What may the learner achieve within this theme in the fulfillment of the Learning Tasks? What are possible changes or learnings on the part of the learner that may result from his appropriation of the significance and value discovered? These changes or learnings may be associated with skills, attitudes, motivations, perceptions including understandings and appreciations.**

The child may achieve an increased feeling of the importance of worship.

The child may achieve an increased sense of awe in worship.

The child may achieve an increased ability to take an active part in corporate worship.

The child may achieve an enriched understanding of the methods of worship and the various ways of worshiping.

The child may achieve some development of ability in personal devotions.

The child may achieve an increased understanding that worship has vital connection with life's motives.

The child may achieve an increased sense of being part of the "church family" and assuming responsibility for it.

The child may achieve an increased sensitivity to the presence of God in worship and the sacraments (or ordinances).

The child may achieve a deepening sense of the significance of the Bible and skill in the use of it in worship.

The child may achieve an assurance of the presence of God.

The child may achieve changed ideas of what is important in life.

The child may achieve an acceptance of the place of worship in the life of a Christian.

The child may achieve a desire to live up to God's purposes by God's help.

The child may achieve courage to admit when he is wrong and to ask for forgiveness.

The child may achieve an ability to see the basic unity of mankind.

5. The Church Lives by Worship

STATEMENT OF THE THEME

Adoration, praise, thanksgiving, confession, acceptance of pardon, reexamination of life in all its relationships, dedication in obedience to God's will sustain, nurture, and inspire the church in its life of love and service. The Christian community renews its faith and life in Christ and finds strength and help for every need through corporate and individual worship including the sacraments.

YOUTH

749

1. Significance of the theme for this age level

a. Meanings and experiences within this theme relevant for this age level. This is content, a selected part of Scope.

Worship of God gives perspective for life's major decisions.

God is present and can be known in worship.

Worship relates to the whole life of youth as he faces God.

God responds to man's sincere worship.

God reveals himself through the Bible, the sacraments (ordinances), and the ministry of Jesus Christ.

Worship illuminates youth's condition of alienation and God's way of reconciliation.

Through giving himself in worship youth may receive inspiration and guidance.

The purpose of worship is God's praise and exaltation, not man's improvement.

Appropriate expressions of worship to God are characterized by genuineness, sincerity, humility.

Worship of God may take various forms with potential meaning for various people.

750

Participation with fellow Christians in worship contributes to the sense of unity of the church.

In worship man asserts his faith in an Absolute and confesses his own finitude.

In Christian worship man responds to God who has acted in mercy and grace through Jesus Christ.

The worshiping community examines life in all its relationships according to the perspective of God, and makes its decision to live in obedience to God's will and in commitment to God's purposes.

The Word of God and the sacraments are the "means of grace" which communicate God's continuing love and redemption to man.

Worship is at the center of the church—it is the heart of its life.

Corporate worship involves active participation by all persons as "the priesthood of believers" who have a responsibility to serve God.

The worshiping congregation constitutes a community that can be identified as separate and unique in society. Persons belong through worship.

In worship man develops a sense of awe, wonder, dependence, reverence.

Through corporate worship the people of God realize their oneness as members of the body of Christ.

In worship we acknowledge that God is Lord of our lives, and offer ourselves as instruments of justice and peace.

1. Significance of the theme for this age level

b. Readiness of the learner for this theme in terms of basic needs, interests, motivations, capacities, developmental tasks.

Youth know feelings of rebellion and the need for forgiveness.

Youth know feelings of remorse and sorrow for their mistakes and failures, the meaning of grief and broken relationships.

Youth respect and seek truth.

Youth want someone dependable to whom to look for fellowship, guidance, forgiveness, acceptance.

Youth have capacity to feel awe and wonder and often are able to express these feelings.

Youth adopt customs and habits they perceive to be indicative of adulthood.

Youth need to find a personal basis for an operational system of values.

Youth want to give expression to love.

Youth have capacity for empathy.

Youth have ability to articulate their feelings and beliefs.

751

2. How may this content be communicated as the learner engages in the Learning Tasks? What are the methods and procedures by which the learner may explore the meanings and experiences within this theme (1-a) in the light of his readiness (1-b) in order to discover significance and value?

By participating in corporate worship.

By observing and/or participating in the Lord's Supper and baptism.

By searching for and examining the purpose and elements of worship.

By experimenting with and creating expressions and forms of worship.

By listening to and pondering the written Word of God.

By studying the historical developments of worship.

By studying biblical accounts of God's people in worship and its results in their lives.

By hearing about the meaning of prayer in the lives of people.

By making use of expressions of worship by Christians of various ages and cultures.

By reading and hearing about the effects of genuine and of false worship on the lives of other Christians.

By participating in disciplines of prayer and Bible study.

By reflecting on the effect of genuine worship on one's personal life and on the church's life.

By studying the biblical and historical meaning to the church of the sacraments.

3. **What may the learner achieve within this theme in the fulfillment of the Learning Tasks? What are possible changes or learnings on the part of the learner that may result from his appropriation of the significance and value discovered? These changes or learnings may be associated with skills, attitudes, motivations, perceptions including understandings and appreciations.**

The youth may achieve skill in recognizing the guidance of God.

The youth may achieve an ability to become aware of and appropriate God's power for life.

The youth may achieve habits of devotional practices.

The youth may achieve a growing ability to identify with and assume responsibility for the church universal.

The youth may achieve an understanding of the nature of God.

The youth may achieve an understanding of the sacraments (ordinances).

The youth may achieve an orienting of one's attitudes, motives, desires to more nearly conform with those of God.

The youth may achieve an increasing sensitivity to spiritual values.

The youth may achieve the courage to face sin and, in humility, to accept God's forgiving love.

The youth may achieve a perspective on the purpose of worship.

The youth may achieve an openness regarding feelings of alienation and a freedom to deal with them through worship.

The youth may achieve insight in relating worship to life's opportunities and problems.

The youth may achieve understanding of the meaning of worship.

Youth may achieve a desire to enter into or renew one's covenantal relationship with God.

Youth, empowered by God, may achieve a growing knowledge of himself, and a willingness to live with his potentialities and limitations.

Youth may achieve a sense of wholeness and unity among persons who acknowledge God as the Father of all.

Youth may achieve a new and continuing dependence on God.

Youth may achieve insight that man's alienation is dealt with by communion with God and with his people.

753

Youth may achieve expanded knowledge and appreciation of expressions of worship in music, art, language.

5. The Church Lives by Worship

STATEMENT OF THE THEME

Adoration, praise, thanksgiving, confession, acceptance of pardon, reexamination of life in all its relationships, dedication in obedience to God's will sustain, nurture, and inspire the church in its life of love and service. The Christian community renews its faith and life in Christ and finds strength and help for every need through corporate and individual worship including the sacraments.

ADULTHOOD

1. Significance of the theme for this age level

a. Meanings and experiences within this theme relevant for this age level. This is content, a selected part of Scope.

754

In worship God confronts man.

The worship of God is essential to the Christian's life both corporate and individual.

Worship relates the whole life of man as he faces God.

God responds to man's sincere worship.

God reveals himself and his will through the Bible, the sacraments (ordinances), and in the ministry of Jesus Christ.

Worship illuminates man's condition of alienation and God's way of reconciliation.

Through giving himself in worship man may receive inspiration and guidance.

The purpose of worship is God's praise and exaltation, not man's improvement.

Appropriate expressions of worship to God are characterized by genuineness, sincerity, humility.

Worship of God may take various forms with potential meaning for various people.

Participation with fellow Christians in worship contributes to the sense of unity of the church.

Corporate worship involves active participation by all persons as "the priesthood of believers" who have a responsibility to serve God.

Through corporate worship the people of God realize their oneness as members of the body of Christ.

In worship man asserts his faith in an Absolute and confesses his own finitude.

The nature of Christian worship is determined by the nature of the God who is worshiped.

In Christian worship man responds to God who has acted in mercy and grace through Jesus Christ.

In worship man develops a sense of awe, wonder, dependence, reverence.

The worshiping congregation constitutes a community that can be identified as separate and unique in society. Persons belong through worship.

Worship is at the center of the church—it is the heart of its life.

The worshiping community examines life in all its relationships according to the perspective of God, and makes its decision to live in obedience to God's will and in commitment to God's purposes.

In worship we acknowledge that God is Lord of our lives and offer ourselves as instruments of justice and peace.

The Word of God and the sacraments are the "means of grace" which communicate God's continuing love and redemption to man.

1. Significance of the theme for this age level

b. Readiness of the learner for this theme in terms of basic needs, interests, motivations, capacities, developmental tasks.

755

Adults are able to perceive something of God's character.

Adults have the capacity to express awe, wonder, praise, contrition, thanksgiving toward God.

Adults have the capacity to personalize group expressions.

Adults need and desire a firm grounding for purposeful living.

Problems and tensions of contemporary life ready the adult for the perspective Christian worship provides.

Adults desire to participate in a meaningful fellowship, such as worship provides.

The adult has the capacity to see himself as he is and as he may become and so participates in confession and commitment.

2. How may this content be communicated as the learner engages in the Learning Tasks? What are the methods and procedures by which the learner may explore the meanings and experiences within this theme (1-a) in the light of his readiness (1-b) in order to discover significance and value?

756

By attending and participating in corporate worship.

By studying biblical accounts of God's people in worship and its results in their life.

By discussing elements of worship and their relative significance.

By using various forms of worship, creating new expressions, and using new materials in worship.

By listening to and pondering the written word of God.

By examining group and individual life in the light of one's experience in worship.

By expressing spiritual aspiration through extemporary and written prayer.

By studying the history and development of expressions of worship.

By hearing about the meaning of prayer in the lives of people.

By making use of expressions of worship by Christians of various ages and cultures.

By participating in disciplines of prayer and Bible study.

By reflecting on the effect of genuine worship on one's personal life and on the church's life.

By reading and hearing about the effect of genuine and of false worship on the lives of other Christians.

By studying the biblical and historical meaning to the church of the sacraments.

By observing and/or participating in the sacraments (ordinances).

3. **What may the learner achieve within this theme in the fulfillment of the Learning Tasks? What are possible changes or learnings on the part of the learner that may result from his appropriation of the significance and value discovered? These changes or learnings may be associated with skills, attitudes, motivations, perceptions including understandings and appreciations.**

The adult may achieve increased skill in perceiving the guidance of God.

The adult may achieve a new and continuing dependence on God.

The adult may achieve development of skills for one's devotional life—praise, adoration, thanksgiving, confession.

The adult may achieve an ever-growing ability and willingness to assume responsibility for the life of the church universal.

The adult may achieve a mature understanding of the nature of appropriate worship.

The adult may achieve deeper understanding of the significance of baptism and the Lord's Supper.

The adult may achieve increased desire to relate drives and ambitions to the will of God.

The adult may achieve a deepening response of one's whole being to God.

The adult may achieve commitment to live as a servant of God in the world.

The adult may achieve an increasing sensitivity to spiritual values.

The adult may achieve a conviction of sin and a recognition of personal need for God's forgiving love.

The adult may achieve a deepened awareness of personal responsibility in the sight of God.

The adult may achieve an increased sense of worth in the sight of God.

757

The adult may achieve insight that man's alienation is dealt with by communion with God and with his people.

The adult may achieve ability to participate personally in group expressions of worship.

The adult may achieve an increased understanding of the meaning of worship.

The adult may achieve appreciation of a variety of means of expressing worship.

The adult may achieve a desire to enter into or renew one's covenantal relationship with God.

The adult may achieve awareness of personal limitations and need for God.

The adult may achieve a sense of wholeness and unity among worshiping persons.

6. The Christian Community Mobilizing for Mission

STATEMENT OF THE THEME

In order to carry out its mission in the world, the church under the leading of the Holy Spirit calls up its people, organizes its life, plans its work, and finds appropriate means. In this mobilization, the Christian discovers orderly and corporate channels of expression for the deepest concerns and convictions of his life.

EARLY CHILDHOOD

1. Significance of the theme for this age level

a. Meanings and experiences within this theme relevant for this age level. This is content, a selected part of Scope.

God wants all people to share together in the work and worship of the church.

God wants each person to find a place for himself in the life of the church.

God wants his people to work together in the church to help others.

By its ministry to children the church prepares them for participation in the mission of the church, both in the present and the future.

1. Significance of the theme for this age level

b. Readiness of the learner for this theme in terms of basic needs, interests, motivations, capacities, developmental tasks

The young child has a capacity to respond with love and to become a part of a loving fellowship.

The young child has an imitative capacity for actions and attitudes.

The young child has an innate trust and openness to God.

Young children are curious about other people and respond to new groups and relationships.

Young children have the capacity to see that there are needs in their world and that people work together to meet these needs.

2. How may this content be communicated as the learner engages in the Learning Tasks? What are the methods and procedures by which the learner may explore the meanings and experiences within this theme (1-a) in the light of his readiness (1-b) in order to discover significance and value?

759

Through opportunities to be in the presence and fellowship of dedicated persons who are concerned about the church in mission.

Through opportunities to observe and talk about the behavior of persons engaged in mission, and the values such behavior supports.

Through participating in activities of mission such as giving, extending friendship to those outside their immediate circle, offering aid to needy persons in the world.

By seeing pictures and hearing stories related to the mission of the church through a variety of media.

Through opportunity to see, hear, and respond to appropriate portions of Scripture.

3. **What may the learner achieve within this theme in the fulfillment of the Learning Tasks? What are possible changes or learnings on the part of the learner that may result from his appropriation of the significance and value discovered? These changes or learnings may be associated with skills, attitudes, motivations, perceptions, including understandings and appreciations.**

760

The young child may achieve a sense of security and belonging in the Christian fellowship.

The young child may achieve a growing trust in and loving response to God.

The young child may achieve a measure of understanding of the purpose and range of mission of the church in the world.

The young child may achieve an awareness that the Christian community of which he is a part is engaged in meeting the needs of people.

The young child may discover that people work in different ways in the life of the church.

The young child may develop motivation for active participation in the mission of the church.

6. The Christian Community Mobilizing for Mission

STATEMENT OF THE THEME

In order to carry out its mission in the world, the church under the leading of the Holy Spirit calls up its people, organizes its life, plans its work, and finds appropriate means. In this mobilization, the Christian discovers orderly and corporate channels of expression for the deepest concerns and convictions of his life.

ELEMENTARY YEARS

1. **Significance of the theme for this age level**

   a. **Meanings and experiences within this theme relevant for this age level. This is content, a selected part of Scope.**

The mission of the church is to help persons live as the people of God.

The church is a worldwide fellowship open to all persons.

God speaks to children through their group experiences to make them sensitive to their part in achieving his purposes for the world.

Christians plan and work together to do God's will in the world through his church; each group in the church has a contribution to make to the total work of the church.

All persons are an important part of God's church as it mobilizes for mission.

The Holy Spirit leads children in their development toward a growing involvement in the work of the church.

God calls persons to express an adventurous and heroic faith in the present-day tasks of the church's mission.

1. **Significance of the theme for this age level**

   b. **Readiness of the learner for this theme in terms of basic needs, interests, motivations, capacities, developmental tasks.**

761

Children normally develop a group awareness and an increasing ability to work together in groups.

Children possess a developing capacity to understand organization and objectives.

Children understand that people join together in helping needy people at home and around the world.

Children are growing in their ability to recognize and to respond to the needs of persons.

Children have a readiness to identify with "heroes" and with persons engaged in worthwhile activities in their world.

2. **How may this content be communicated as the learner engages in the Learning Tasks? What are the methods and procedures by which the learner may explore the meanings and experiences within this theme (1-a) in the light of his readiness (1-b) in order to discover significance and value?**

762

Through the biblical content dealing with the mission of the church and ways it carried out that mission.

Through historical and biographical accounts of the mission of the church.

Through planning and carrying out projects in the church's mission.

Through participating in experiences of worshipful dedication to the work of the church in the world.

Through experiences with peers and with the congregation which explore the way the church organizes for mission.

Through study of the church in mission throughout the world.

By observing and talking about the value of each person's contribution to the mission of the church.

Through sharing in ecumenical projects and activities related to the mission of the church in the world.

Through opportunities to associate (directly or vicariously) with persons engaged in mission, using field trips, drama, audio-visual and printed resources.

3. **What may the learner achieve within this theme in the fulfillment of the Learning Tasks? What are possible changes or learnings on the part of the learner that may result from his appropriation of the significance and value discovered? These changes or learnings may be associated with skills, attitudes, motivations, perceptions including understandings and appreciations.**

The child may develop motivation for active participation in the mission of the church.

The child may achieve an increased understanding of the Bible as a book dealing with the church's mission.

The child may express an emerging sympathy for persons in need.

The child may begin to perceive the significance of the work of the church in the world.

The child may sense that he is involved with the total congregation in getting ready for the church's mission.

The child may experience joy and satisfaction in seeing some of the results of the work of the church in the world.

The child may become aware of his heritage from the church, especially the story of the way the church has fulfilled its mission, and recognize the value of this heritage for himself.

The child may achieve beginning skills in helping organize for group action.

The child may achieve an understanding of how the church goes about its mission in various parts of the world.

6. The Christian Community Mobilizing for Mission

STATEMENT OF THE THEME

763

In order to carry out its mission in the world, the church under the leading of the Holy Spirit calls up its people, organizes its life, plans its work, and finds appropriate means. In this mobilization, the Christian discovers orderly and corporate channels of expression for the deepest concerns and convictions of his life.

YOUTH

1. **Significance of the theme for this age level**

    a. **Meanings and experiences within this theme relevant for this age level. This is content, a selected part of Scope.**

God calls youth to respond to him in carrying out the mission of the church in the world.

God reveals himself to youth, as he works within groups in which they participate, and calls them to Christian mission.

God's purpose is for youth to be vitally involved in the mission of the church through the mobilizing of their lives and resources.

The Holy Spirit works through the developing potential of youth to accomplish the mission of the church in the world.

God's cause is great enough to call for youth's total commitment.

God works through youth of the church in distinctive ways to make his will known in the world.

The revolutionary character of the church challenges youth to enlist in a dynamic fellowship designed to fulfill God's purpose.

Youth has a vital place of responsibility in the church as it mobilizes for mission.

God through youth may effect changes in the institutions and practices of the church in order that it may more faithfully fulfill its mission.

Preparation for mission requires patience in bringing long-range mission plans to fruition as well as zeal and vigor for immediate tasks.

1. Significance of the theme for this age level

b. Readiness of the learner for this theme in terms of basic needs, interests, motivations, capacities, developmental tasks.

Youth has a readiness to join others in a cause worthy of his total commitment.

Youth has a capacity to express intense loyalty to a cause with other persons.

Youth responds to challenges for adventure in relation to his world.

Youth is challenged by a deep, personal fellowship whose mission is characterized by compassion and empathy.

Youth has the capacity to assimilate the rapidly expanding knowledge in modern times and to apply it to the work of the church in the world.

Youth desires to learn to communicate to others the meaning and significance of existence as he has found it.

Youth has the capacity to develop abilities and skills for functioning in groups.

2. **How may this content be communicated as the learner engages in the Learning Tasks? What are the methods and procedures by which the learner may explore the meanings and experiences within this theme (1-a) in the light of his readiness (1-b) in order to discover significance and value?**

Through exploring the imperative and significance of the mission of the church and ways the early church carried out that mission.

Through study, using drama, printed and audio-visual resources, and through personal contact.

By being confronted with opportunities to give and serve in mission in light of the needs in the world.

By participating in ecumenical projects and activities.

By exploring the significance and value of making decisions about the investment of their lives in light of the mission of the church.

Through participating in a continuing evaluation of the life and work of the church and in the creation of new means to fulfill God's mission in the world.

By participating in corporate worship for the purpose of dedication to and empowering for the mission.

By being involved in planning, administering, and evaluating the specific tasks in mission assumed by the church.

3. **What may the learner achieve within this theme in the ful-**

765

fillment of the Learning Tasks? What are possible changes or learnings on the part of the learner that may result from his appropriation of the significance and value discovered? These changes or learnings may be associated with skills, attitudes, motivations, perceptions including understandings and appreciations.

Youth may grow in appreciation of the Bible as a result of using it to explore the church's mission and ways the early church undertook its mission.

766

Youth may achieve a sense of direction for his life as it relates to the mission of the church in the world.

Youth may achieve a deeper understanding of the demands made upon the Christian community for world mission.

Youth may achieve an understanding of the significance, value, and scope of the mission in world history.

Youth may sense the joy that is possible in sharing in the work of the church in the world.

Youth may achieve an increasing sense of patience and perspective in working in the mission of the church.

Youth may increase in confidence, courage, and skill in working with others redemptively and creatively in the mission of the church.

Youth may increase in devotion and dedication for the mission of the church, preparatory to making an effective witness.

Youth may achieve a growing understanding of the mission of the church in home, community, nation, and the world.

Youth may achieve the ability to criticize constructively and at the same time to work creatively within the structures of the church to carry out God's will.

Youth may achieve increased motivation for active participation in the mission of the church.

Youth may come to a new appreciation of the church as a result of an understanding of the meaning and value of its mission.

6. The Christian Community Mobilizing for Mission

STATEMENT OF THE THEME

In order to carry out its mission in the world, the church under the leading of the Holy Spirit calls up its people, organizes its life, plans its work, and finds appropriate means. In this mobilization, the Christian discovers orderly and corporate channels of expression for the deepest concerns and convictions of his life.

ADULTHOOD

1. Significance of the theme for this age level

a. Meanings and experiences within this theme relevant for this age level. This is content, a selected part of Scope.

The mission of the church is to be the people of God, expressing God's loving concern and reconciliation for all men everywhere, calling all men to become the people of God.

God calls his people to carry out his mission in the world as a servant people.

The church, in responding to God's call, organizes its life, plans, and work, and utilizes its resources.

The Holy Spirit empowers the people of God as they develop the means to carry on their mission in the world.

The mission of the church requires the continuing involvement and total mobilization of the people of God.

Through various kinds of organizations and in orderly and corporate channels of expression the church can seek to fulfill God's purpose in the world.

The power of God is expressed in the revolutionary character of the church and his love in the dynamic fellowship of the Christian community.

As every Christian serves in the "priesthood of believers" he has a responsible place in the total mission of the church.

With the leading of the Holy Spirit the church reexamines

767

its structures and policies, always conscious of standing under the judgment of God.

Preparation for mission requires patience in bringing long-range mission plans to fruition as well as zeal and vigor for immediate tasks.

1. Significance of the theme for this age level

 b. Readiness of the learner for this theme in terms of basic needs, interests, motivations, capacities, developmental tasks.

Man senses the need for some kind of social pattern in living.

In order to achieve his goal man develops procedures and structures to carry on his work.

The adult's sense of dependence on other persons creates a climate for social order.

Adults are aware of the necessity to assume some responsibility in living with other persons.

Man has the capacity to respond to what he perceives as the highest good and to cooperate with others in striving to achieve goals commensurate with this good.

Man has the capacity to respond to human need and to cooperate with others in ministering to those in need.

Man hopes for progress in achieving human betterment.

The adult has marked capacity for sharing skills with other persons in the achievement of meaningful objectives in life.

2. How may this content be communicated as the learner engages in the Learning Tasks? What are the methods and procedures by which the learner may explore the meanings and experiences within this theme (1-a) in the light of his readiness (1-b) in order to discover significance and value.

Through exploring the imperative and significance of the mission of the church and ways the early church carried out that mission.

Through exploring the needs of the world through study, survey, and direct contact with persons and areas of need.

Through opportunities with occupational groups for sharing concerns and experiences in relation to a specific area of mission.

By participating in corporate worship for the purpose of dedication to and empowering for the mission.

By becoming involved in the planning, administration, and evaluation of specific tasks assumed by the church.

By a critical and creative examination of the purposes of organized groups concerning their relationship to the mission of the church.

Through becoming personally acquainted with the projects and tasks related to the work of the church in the world.

3. **What may the learner achieve within this theme in the fulfillment of the Learning Tasks? What are possible changes or learnings on the part of the learner that may result from his appropriation of the significance and value discovered? These changes or learnings may be associated with skills, attitudes, motivations, perceptions including understandings and appreciations.**

Adults may grow in appreciation of the Bible as a result of using it to explore the church's mission and ways the early church undertook that mission.

Adults may achieve confidence, courage and skill to engage in the tasks of mission.

Adults may feel the satisfaction of joining with others in planning the work of the congregation in the local community.

Adults may achieve a contagious enthusiasm and satisfaction from identification with the total mission of the church.

Adults may experience the presence and power of the Holy Spirit as the church girds for mission.

Adults may achieve an increasing ability to utilize all available skills and resources, redemptively and creatively, in the mobilization of the church for mission.

769

Adults may achieve an ability to take account of the possibility of failure or rejection as they organize to carry out specific tasks in mission.

The adult may achieve the flexibility to change organizational structures as needed to fulfill the church's mission.

Adults may achieve an understanding of the mission of the church in the local community and around the world.

The adult may achieve facility in working with others within the structures of the church and in organizing the life of the church and its work so that the church may better fulfill its mission.

Adults may come to a fuller understanding of the meaning of responsible giving and a sustained, compassionate, life-giving response to God's call to mission.

7. Preparing and Equipping for Ministry

STATEMENT OF THE THEME

In order to fulfill its mission, the Christian community provides its members training, guidance, admonition, support. As they accept the significance of their personal involvement in the Body of Christ and of their mission, they find that their ministries are enriched, informed, and empowered by the Holy Spirit.

EARLY CHILDHOOD

1. Significance of the theme for this age level

a. Meanings and experiences within this theme relevant for this age level. This is content, a selected part of Scope.

The church helps persons know how to serve and help others.

The church helps persons grow, learn, and work in their ministry to others.

The church helps persons learn how to tell others about God.

The value of study and worship is that they help persons know and do what God would have them do in ministering to others.

The church helps persons know how to show God's love to others.

Certain persons have responsibilities designated to them by the church.

1. Significance of the theme for this age level

b. Readiness of the learner for this theme in terms of basic needs, interests, motivations, capacities, developmental tasks.

The young child is beginning to realize that each of us can be helpful and useful.

The young child has growing ability to minister to others.

The young child has an increasing interest in what "grown-ups" do.

The young child has an active engagement with and interest in learning.

The young child is interested and surprised to discover that adults must study and learn some things.

The young child is interested in the activities of persons who are significant to him, to his friends, to his family.

The young child has a need for some ordered routines in his life and for knowing what to expect in relation to order and routines.

771

2. How may this content be communicated as the learner engages in the Learning Tasks? What are the methods and procedures by which the learner may explore the meanings and experiences within this theme (1-a) in the light of his readiness (1-b) in order to discover significance and value?

By hearing Bible stories and others stories about people who have studied and learned about how to help in the church.

Through being guided in his participation in any work of the church he is able to undertake, however simple it may be.

By participating with others whom he knows to be in the Christian community in learning situations.

By observing people in the church helping one another.

By receiving encouragement and guidance in completing tasks within his capacity to complete.

By getting acquainted with persons with designated responsibilities he can comprehend.

772

Through dramatizing some of the tasks performed by persons with designated responsibilities of leading others in the church's ministry: teachers, ministers, service activities leaders.

By talking about or playing out ways to tell others about his church.

By joining with others in prayer and worship, seeking God's help in ministering to others.

By playing out teaching-learning situations in the Christian community.

By observing and talking about carrying out the work of the church, beginning in his own group.

3. **What may the learner achieve within this theme in the fulfillment of the Learning Tasks? What are possible changes or learnings on the part of the learner that may result from his appropriation of the significance and value discovered? These changes or learnings may be associated with skills, attitudes, motivations, perceptions including understandings and appreciations.**

The young child may achieve the experience of "belonging" with the people of God in learning together how to work and serve in the church, beginning where he is.

The young child may achieve growing ability accompanied by increasing desire to participate in the life and mission of the church.

The young child may achieve growing realization of the need and desire to learn more about how to carry out the work and mission of the church.

The young child may achieve beginning development of the inner life associated with the seeking of God's guidance in the ministry to others (prayer, meditation, openness, sensitivity to what God wants me to do and be).

The young child may achieve awakening understanding of ways to minister to the needs and hurts of others.

The young child may achieve a developing realization that the church designates certain responsibilities.

The young child may achieve growing awareness that there are orderly ways of carrying out the church's work and ministry.

The young child may achieve increasing ability to work within orderly procedures established by the church.

7. Preparing and Equipping for Ministry

STATEMENT OF THE THEME

In order to fulfill its mission, the Christian community provides its members training, guidance, admonition, support. As they accept the significance of their personal involvement in the Body of Christ and of their mission, they find that their ministries are enriched, informed, and empowered by the Holy Spirit.

773

ELEMENTARY YEARS

1. Significance of the theme for this age level

a. Meanings and experiences within this theme relevant for this age level. This is content, a selected part of Scope.

The essential preparation of the church for ministry is the awareness of and dependence on the guidance of the Holy Spirit.

All persons have ministerial talents to be developed and joined with others in fulfilling the church's mission.

We can become more effective in carrying our share of the church's ministry by participating in training offered by the church.

We can help others in their roles of ministry in the church by giving encouragement, guidance, and assistance.

The gifts and abilities necessary for the church's ministries are resident among the people of God.

An integral part of the full development of the Christian is the discovery and cultivation of the skills and abilities for serving others.

Persons in the church are helped to carry out their individual and corporate ministries by the ordained minister through his preaching, leading in worship, counseling, guidance in the administration of the church's life and work.

Each person in the Christian community needs training and help to fulfill his role in the church's mission.

Preparation for engaging in the ministry of the church involves participation in that ministry along with study of the ministry and of its meaning.

Boys and girls can help one another find and fulfill their roles in the ministry.

Commitment to Christ carries with it the obligation to train for servanthood.

The Christian community provides training for persons specifically authorized by the Christian community to carry specialized functions as volunteers or in church-related occupations.

Training gained outside of the institutional church can frequently contribute to carrying out the mission of the church.

Christian learning takes place within the context of the community of faith and is not merely an academic undertaking.

Every member of the church has a responsible place in the total ministry and the Christian community has the responsibility of providing formal learning for this ministry.

Christian nurture is a vital ministry of the church which equips its members to carry on as the church.

1. **Significance of the theme for this age level**

   b. **Readiness of the learner for this theme in terms of basic needs, interests, motivations, capacities, developmental tasks.**

   The child has a growing capacity to be sensitive to the needs of others, with the realization this brings of the necessity for receiving help in ministering to these needs.

   The child has ability to respond to the challenge of the church's ministry as a task that requires preparation.

   The child has an increasing variety of experiences with persons engaged in ministry accompanied by growing understanding of the training they have engaged in in preparation for ministry.

   The child has a growing response to the claims of Christ and to the demands these claims make for which training is required.

   The child has ability to perceive that persons who live meaningful lives of service have prepared themselves to do so through a variety of kinds of training and experiences.

   The child has ability to realize the implications of the need Jesus had for training for his ministry.

   The child has ability to sense and to realize the significance of the fact that he belongs to a community where preparation for ministry is deemed important.

   The child has a growing conception of the complexity of the world situation and of the difficulties the church faces in coping with some of these complexities.

   The child has expanding experience, however limited, in participating in the church's ministry with evaluation of this participation.

   The child has experiences of failure due to inadequate preparation for a task.

   The child has difficulties encountered in working with peers where there has been inadequate planning and leadership.

   The child has a growing desire to participate effectively in the life and ministry of the church.

775

The child has a desire to be recognized as being a capable person who is able to make a worthy contribution.

The child has ability to learn and to recognize the value of learning.

The child has growing awareness of various occupations and of the demands these make by way of preparation.

The child has growing ability to understand organizational patterns and needs.

The child has growing ability to comprehend and work through established channels.

The child has experiences of training required for various forms of community services.

2. **How may this content be communicated as the learner engages in the Learning Tasks? What are the methods and procedures by which the learner may explore the meanings and experiences within this theme (1-a) in the light of his readiness (1-b) in order to discover significance and value?**

By studying biblical, historical, and cultural materials that highlight the requirements of training for the church's ministry.

By finding out about the way his church organizes and makes preparations to carry out its ministry.

By participating with others in planning, preparing for, and carrying out various tasks and activities in the ministry of the church, including some evaluation.

By talking with various persons in the church about their preparation and the value they put on preparation for carrying out designated responsibilities.

By relating whatever he is studying to preparation for ministry.

By studying the place of prayer and worship together with reasons for engaging in them in preparation for ministry.

By considering the place of Bible study and reasons for engaging in it in preparation for ministry.

By participating in training necessary for certain responsibilities designated to him.

By having assistance in evaluating individual and group efforts in ministry and in seeking ways of improving it.

By working with others in organizing his peer groups.

By having experiences of working within the organizational pattern of the church.

By assessing his personal talents and those of others in carrying out the mission of the church.

3. **What may the learner achieve within this theme in the fulfillment of the Learning Tasks? What are possible changes or learnings on the part of the learner that may result from his appropriation of the significance and value discovered? These changes or learnings may be associated with skills, attitudes, motivations, perceptions including understandings and appreciations.**

The child may achieve growing awareness of dependence on the guidance of the Holy Spirit in fulfilling the ministry of the church.

The child may achieve appreciation of his own talents and those of others in fulfilling the church's mission.

The child may achieve growing ability to help and to encourage others to engage effectively in the church's ministry.

The child may achieve growing realization of the demands of the church by way of preparation for carrying out its mission.

The child may achieve responses to the challenge of the demands of the church for equipping for ministry by training for specific tasks.

The child may achieve recognition of the role of the pastor in preparation of the congregation for ministry.

The child may achieve awareness of the array of talents resident in the congregation that are sufficient for the fulfillment of the mission of the church.

The child may achieve willingness to work with others and to accept graciously their contributions to corporate endeavors.

777

The child may achieve recognition of the value of developing his talents for use in the ministry of the church.

The child may achieve growing ability to work within and to participate in further development of the organizational structure of the church.

The child may achieve growing realization of the value of Bible study as a means for equipping the church for mission.

The child may achieve growing awareness of the place of prayer in equipping the church for mission.

778

7. Preparing and Equipping for Ministry

STATEMENT OF THE THEME

In order to fulfill its mission, the Christian community provides its members training, guidance, admonition, support. As they accept the significance of their personal involvement in the Body of Christ and of their mission, they find that their ministries are enriched, informed, and empowered by the Holy Spirit.

YOUTH

1. Significance of the theme for this age level

   a. Meanings and experiences within this theme relevant for this age level. This is content, a selected part of Scope.

The mutual responsibility for equipping all members of the church for their individual and corporate ministry has its basis in the Bible.

To prepare and train its members for effective ministry, the church must understand the current historical scene.

Insights into communications and advances in technology can enhance the effectiveness of the church's preparation for its ministry.

The obligation to prepare and train for ministry rests on every Christian, no matter what his age or occupation is.

The Christian community has an obligation to help every member discover his role and develop his abilities and skills for the ministry of the church.

The study and training the church offers its people has as a major purpose the preparing and equipping of the people of God for their servant role in the world.

Essential in the church's preparation and equipping for ministry is the awareness that the Holy Spirit is the source of power and guidance for the church's ministry.

In order to serve the needs of the persons and group both in the Christian community and outside it, the church must discover these needs and identify with the persons.

The effective ministry of the church requires the varied skills and varied approaches resident among the members of the Christian community.

Commitment to Christ brings with it obligation to participate responsibly in the servant role of the church.

Individual and corporate worship, study, and training are essential for the people of God to fulfill their ministry.

The Christian community has a continuing responsibility to understand and interpret the functions of ordained and unordained members in the church's work of ministry, and to provide training adequate for carrying out those functions.

779

The servant role of the Christian community calls for the cultivation of skills in individual and in corporate ministry.

Knowledge, skills, abilities gained outside of the Christian community can frequently contribute to a person's effective ministry.

Often preparation for ministry in the world and cultivation of skills for that ministry can be accomplished in a fuller perspective if undertaken in an interdenominational framework.

Christian nurture is a vital ministry of the church, equipping its members to carry on as the church.

Christian learning takes place within the context of the community of faith and is not merely an academic undertaking.

Every member of the church has a responsible place in the total ministry and the Christian community has the responsibility of providing formal learning for this ministry.

1. Significance of the theme for this age level

b. Readiness of the learner for this theme in terms of basic needs, interests, motivations, capacities, developmental tasks.

780

Youth has increasing sensitivity to the complexity of the needs of persons and society.

Youth has the desire to be ready and able for challenges facing him.

Youth has the desire for genuinely effective solutions to problems.

Youth has the desire to be recognized as contributing at a significant level in groups important to him.

Youth has an urgent desire for adult responsibilities.

Youth has recognition of need for guidance from outside himself.

The youth insists on the relevance of knowledge to life in the world.

Youth has increasing knowledge of the church's mission.

Youth has expanding opportunity for influencing persons and groups.

Youth has a desire to be involved in specific action.

Youth has an increasing desire to develop his discovered abilities.

Youth has involvement in a variety of training situations relating his own skills, interest, abilities to society.

Youth has a desire to have his loyalty show itself in action.

Youth has increasing ability to relate principles to concrete situations.

Youth has interest in developing his occupational skills, interests, and abilities.

Youth has admiration of proficiency and skill.

Youth has ability to relate discipline to effective performance.

Youth has respect for authority that stems from knowledge, skill, and experience.

Youth has ability to relate professed belief and overt action.

Youth has sensitivity to feelings of inadequacy in himself and in groups of which he is a part.

Youth has increasing ability to make available to others his own abilities, knowledge, skills, and support.

2. How may this content be communicated as the learner engages in the Learning Tasks? What are the methods and procedures by which the learner may explore the meanings and experiences within this theme (1-a) in the light of his readiness (1-b) in order to discover significance and value?

By studying biblical, theological, and historical resources that interpret the necessity and responsibility of the church's preparing for its servant role as God's people.

By engaging in worthy tasks related to the essential church ministries.

By searching for the relationship between recognition of one's self as a "child of God," and ministering in this world as a member of the Christian community.

By exploring and evaluating the past and present efforts of the Christian community to minister relevantly in the world.

By knowing and associating with persons engaged in church-related occupations.

By participating in opportunities for training, study, and worship offered by the church.

By studying the nature of the Christian's mission in the world.

By exploring the opportunities the Christian community offers for education and training for the various functions its members carry out in its mission.

By participating in worship, study, and training in groups that span different ages and different denominations.

781

By observing and participating with persons in the Christian community who are diligently trying to understand the world in which the church's ministry is offered.

By observing and himself experiencing support and encouragement from others in the Christian community as he attempts to engage in the church's mission.

By investigating the variety of functions necessary to the church's carrying out its ministry both within the Christian community and in the world.

782

Through hearing or reading about experiences of Christians who have learned the necessity for the church to deliberately prepare and equip itself if it is to minister significantly.

By experimenting with applying to the church's ministering task the knowledge and abilities gained elsewhere.

By analyzing the changes throughout the church's history in concepts of the roles and functions within the Christian community as it fulfills its mission.

By relating specific study and training to specific work in the church's ministry in which they are engaged.

3. **What may the learner achieve within this theme in the fulfillment of the Learning Tasks? What are possible changes or learnings on the part of the learner that may result from his appropriation of the significance and value discovered? These changes or learnings may be associated with skills, attitudes, motivations, perceptions including understandings and appreciations.**

Youth may achieve an increasing understanding and acceptance of biblical concept of God's people as ministers in the world.

Youth may achieve appreciation of the necessity of training in order to participate in the ministry of the church responsibly.

Youth may achieve recognition of himself as one possessing skills and abilities useful in the church's mission.

Youth may achieve knowledge of the variety of functions and tasks of the church in mission.

Youth may achieve courage to venture into new and unexplored tasks in church ministry.

Youth may achieve appreciation of persons who have developed their abilities and skills for use by the church in volunteer or occupational work in its ministry.

Youth may achieve increasing skills in fulfilling essential church ministries.

Youth may achieve joy in participating in the church's mission.

Youth may achieve increasing ability in relating his developing skills and knowledge to his responsible participation in the church's ministries.

Youth may achieve identification with and appreciation for the Christian community around the world in its efforts to minister.

Youth may achieve growth in understanding and acceptance of the Christian's responsibility to cultivate his gifts and capacities for the effective ministry of the Christian community.

Youth may achieve growth in identification with other peoples as part of God's family.

Youth may achieve increasing comprehension of and willingness to respond to God's call to the Christian community to serve in the world.

783

Youth may achieve a sense of support from and identity with others engaged in ministry.

Youth may achieve awareness of the need for training in ministry.

Youth may achieve growth in ability to apply training to specific needs.

Youth may achieve willingness to put at the disposal of others in the Christian community his knowledge, skills, insights, abilities.

7. Preparing and Equipping for Ministry

STATEMENT OF THE THEME

In order to fulfill its mission, the Christian community provides its members training, guidance, admonition, support. As they accept the significance of their personal involvement in the Body of Christ and of their mission, they find that their ministries are enriched, informed, and empowered by the Holy Spirit.

784 ADULTHOOD

1. Significance of the theme for this age level

a. Meanings and experiences within this theme relevant for this age level. This is content, a selected part of Scope.

Both the individual and corporate ministries of the people of God have biblical, theological, and historical bases.

God's spirit has been and is moving within the church, guiding its ministries and enabling it to serve.

God calls each person to discover his self-identity and to minister as one of the "servant people of God."

The church has a continuing responsibility to understand and interpret the functions of its ordained and unordained members in the Christian community's work of ministry.

Within its membership the Christian community has available the special talents which, when developed, are equal to the tasks God has for the church in the fulfilling of his purposes.

The servant role of the Christian community calls for skills in individual and corporate ministry.

The Holy Spirit directs each individual as he searches for, discovers, and develops the manner in which he can best minister in the name of Christ.

The Christian community has the responsibility to discover and develop new forms of serving in order to keep its ministry relevant to man's changing needs.

The ministry of the Christian community may be extended through interdenominational and interfaith cooperation.

Christian learning takes place within the context of the community of faith.

In the church the laity are viewed as the "people of God" with ministries to perform as they become deeply involved in the life of the church.

The study and training the church offers its people has as a major purpose the preparing and equipping of the people of God for their servant role in the world.

Many of the ministries of the church are carried out by persons who have been called to full or part-time positions of designated service under a sense of unique calling by the Holy Spirit.

The essential preparation of the church for ministry is the awareness of and dependence on the guidance of the Holy Spirit.

1. Significance of the theme for this age level

b. Readiness of the learner for this theme in terms of basic needs, interests, motivations, capacities, developmental tasks.

The adult has the capacity to respond to the call of God to serve.

The adult has the capacity to perceive the needs of persons in the family, community, church, world.

785

The adult has natural compassion that makes possible responding to the needs of others.

The adult faces the implications of the ultimate concerns that are his source of all values.

The adult has a desire to belong, to gain the sense of community that can come through involvement in the church's mission.

The adult has lived long enough to be aware of his lack of knowledge, lack of skills, and lack of practice in church ministry.

The adult has a need for the support and guidance of the Christian fellowship.

The adult has the capacity to see the relevance of the Christian mission to the needs of the world.

The adult has the capacity to recognize that he has a talent needed in the ministry of the church.

The adult has the capacity to recognize himself as one of the servant people of God.

The adult must face the questions of others concerning the Christian faith and life to which he must respond.

The adult has a sense of loyalty to the church that encourages participation in ministry.

The adult has personal and financial independence that make possible maximum response to God's call to special ministry.

The adult has met and dealt with persons of other denominations and polities whose style of ministry differ from his own.

The adult has a capacity to draw analogies between his being ministered to by others in the name of Christ and his own ability so to minister.

2. How may this content be communicated as the learner engages in the Learning Tasks? What are the methods and procedures by which the learner may explore the meanings and experiences within this theme (1-a) in the light of his readiness (1-b) in order to discover significance and value?

By reading the biblical record to gain understanding of the church's mission and ministries.

By engaging in depth Bible study in small groups to discover patterns of ministry.

By studying the theological bases for the ministries of the church.

By reviewing historical records to gain deeper insight into the meaning of church mission.

By engaging in acts of serving that lead to recognition of himself as one of the "people of God."

By carrying out responsibly the commissions for the ongoing tasks of the church that he has accepted from the congregation.

By exploring the variety of current patterns and styles of church ministry.

By enlisting in worthy community enterprises that support or supplement the church's ministries.

By associating with persons engaged in particular acts of church ministry.

By participating in training opportunities for specific church ministries.

By reading about and giving support to the ministries of the church around the world.

By studying denominational and interdenominational guidance materials related to specific church ministries.

By participation in world citizenship through travel and seminars related to Christian mission.

By practicing the inner disciplines of Christian faith basic to personal involvement in the church's ministry.

By reading and talking about the demands of call to church-related vocation.

By interviewing persons in church-related vocations.

By taking part in and encouraging participation in interdenominational activities of ministry.

By participating in some period of full-time Christian vocation in order to learn more what is the nature of church ministry.

787

3. **What may the learner achieve within this theme in the fulfillment of the Learning Tasks? What are possible changes or learnings on the part of the learner that may result from his appropriation of the significance and value discovered? These changes or learnings may be associated with skills, attitudes, motivations, perceptions including understandings and appreciations.**

The adult may achieve an increased knowledge and understanding of biblical, theological, and historical bases for church mission.

The adult may achieve greater ability to participate in the ministries of the church.

The adult may achieve a deeper recognition of himself as one of the "people of God."

The adult may achieve a willingness to accept as meaningful his personal responsibility for tasks of church ministry.

The adult may achieve a willingness to venture into new, unexplored, and more demanding tasks in church ministry.

The adult may achieve a deeper appreciation of the call and requirements associated with church-related occupations.

The adult may achieve a sense of joy in performing tasks related to the ministries of the church.

The adult may achieve more knowledge about and understanding of the work of the church around the world.

The adult may achieve growth in the understanding of and ability to carry out personal involvement in Christian ministry.

The adult may achieve growth in one's willingness to be identified as a member of the Christian community.

The adult may achieve a deeper comprehension of what constitutes a call to a church-related vocation.

The adult may achieve a willingness to respond to God's call to church-related vocation.

The adult may achieve a willingness to serve for a stated period of time as a full-time worker in a church vocation.

The adult may achieve a deeper awareness of the needs of other persons and a desire to minister to them.

The adult may achieve a fuller awareness of himself as a ministering servant of God.

The adult may achieve a sense of stability engendered by a growing appreciation for the potential talents for ministry resident in the church.

PART IV

The Relation
of Administration
to the Curriculum Plan

This section of the book suggests some considerations that must be faced with reference to the implementation of this Curriculum Plan. It does not attempt to resolve the questions that must be dealt with in administering the church's curriculum; but it does indicate some of the central issues and some principles germane to their resolution. Particular attention is given two functions of administration: leadership and evaluation.

Curriculum has been described as all learning experiences under the guidance of the church toward accomplishing the objective of the church. It follows, then, that the way in which persons are guided in administering this phase of the church's life influences the effect of the educational ministry. Part IV, therefore, points up the role of administration in the educational ministry and points out the relation of administration to the Curriculum Plan.

Part IV will be useful as curriculum planners consider questions of structure and organization, of resources called for by the Curriculum Plan, of appropriate approaches to developing leadership, of means and implementation of evaluation, and of procedures and materials called for to guide and service the church as it administers an educational ministry.

Persons other than curriculum planners may find Part IV helpful as a general statement of the relation of administration to curriculum. Such persons include those in training for church occupations, those charged with responsibility for administering an educational enterprise, those writing resource materials for educational administrators, and some who are actively engaged in carrying out various administrative functions identified in Part IV.

791

The way in which Part IV is related to the other three parts of this book is most clearly seen in the section on "Implications of this Curriculum Plan for Administration." That section identifies basic asumptions in the Design that should form the foundation for administration. It restates the unity of educational ministry which embraces all a church does to equip and train its people for mission, and draws out from this basic characteristic of the Design the implications for structure, the development of leadership, evaluation. Further, the section emphasizes the integral place which is given in the Curriculum Plan to training of persons for designated functions of leadership. Here it especially brings to mind certain of the areas of curriculum and specific themes, as these are elaborated in Part II and also in Part III. Part IV lifts into prominence one of the functions of the Objective of the curriculum as it is described in the Design: "to serve as a means of evaluation of the curriculum. The objective serves also indirectly when educational experiences in the church are being evaluated in the light of short-term goals consistent with the objective." In summary, Part IV sets in proper relationship administrative functions and curriculum plan, displaying the influence of curriculum decisions on the resolution of issues in administration.

The Relation of Administration to the Curriculum Plan

For an effective educational ministry, the church is faced not only with the job of developing effective curriculum for that ministry; it is also faced with the task of developing effective administration of that ministry.

Administration is that service which provides for relating persons and groups to one another and to their available resources in such a way that the church's aim in its educational ministry may be achieved.

Questions Basic to Administration

Administration provides the answers to such necessary questions as the following:

What provision shall be made for formulation of basic policies and plans for the educational work of the church? What provision shall be made for the development of detailed plans within such basic policies?

What framework and structures shall be established to relate persons and groups effectively for carrying out the educational ministry?

How may the church's resources for education—financial, material, human—best be employed?

What provision shall be made for supervising the implementation of the educational ministry? What provision shall be made for evaluating this ministry with reference to its structures, processes, results?

Where are responsibility and authority lodged with reference to all facets of the educational ministry?

Several factors influence the way in which administrative questions are answered by the church with reference to its educational ministry. These include the way a particular congregation perceives the nature and purpose of the church; the polity of the church; the church's available resources; the confessional orientation of the denomination; the proposed program of education.

794

Implications of this Curriculum Plan for Administration

As curriculum is developed on the basis of this Curriculum Plan, some of its basic assumptions and their implications for administering an educational ministry should be noted.

Though all of the ministries together contribute to the achievement of the mission of the church, each has a distinctive function. The educational ministry undergirds all the church's mission. The church's educational ministry, therefore, must be administered as an integral part of the church's total work and vitally related to the other ministries of the church.

"Christian education is construed as related to all opportunities offered to persons primarily for the purpose of education in the Christian faith and education for the Christian mission." (Design, page 3) The various facets of the church's educational ministry, therefore, must be encompassed in the church's structure for education, directed by the church's policies on education, and serviced by the church's resources of money, material, personnel.

The development of leadership among the people and the selection and training of persons with particular responsibility of leadership are integral to the church's educational ministry.

Administrative provisions for education, therefore, must embrace provisions for the motivation, selection, and training of these persons.

The objective of Christian education gives direction to the whole educational enterprise of the church. It is this objective, therefore, by which those responsible for administering the educational ministry are to evaluate not only the various aspects of their own responsibility such as policies, aims, plans, but also the structures, processes, and results of the total educational ministry.

Structure for the educational ministry take the form of particular settings in which particular groups of people under particular circumstances may become engaged in teaching-learning experiences. (See Afterword.) The total number and kind of settings, and the way they are related to one another and to the policy-making bodies of the church comprise the structures of a ministry of education.

In addition to settings, concerns of leadership and evaluation are so important a part of administration and so essential to a well-rounded plan of curriculum that some generalizations on these subjects are given below.

The Development of Leadership

795

The kind of leadership (or responsible participation in groups) appropriately exercised by every Christian in the life of the church and in the world has been embraced in Part III. (See Preface) Here, with reference to Administration, the emphasis is upon that aspect of leadership appropriate to a designated leader such as an officer, staff member, teacher, counselor, supervisor, chairman.

Such designated persons perform a function in the life of the group which might be described as headship. Headship and leadership are not necessarily the same thing although they are not mutually exclusive. It is the spontaneous recognition by the group members of the head's contribution to group goals that enables him to lead as well as head a group. An effective head of the group sees it as his function to encourage others in his group to take leadership roles.

Faith, experience, and knowledge which grow out of a commitment to God through Jesus Christ, an openness to the work of the Holy Spirit, an understanding of the Bible, an acquaintance with theology and ethics rooted in the faith are viewed by Christians and the church as essential in the persons chosen to take places of designated responsibility in the Christian community and in the world. This dimension and way of life result in Christians bringing to their leadership resources beyond those brought by persons not grounded in the Christian faith. This rootage enables them to minister to others and to interpret, participate in, and carry forward the heritage of the Christian faith essential to the life and mission of the church.

Still another valuable characteristic in persons with designated responsibility is the capacity to inspire others in the congregation to commit themselves to Jesus Christ and his will, to live in mission, and to engage in educational experiences within the congregation and the community at large which equip them for providing leadership.

It is important for the congregation to work toward a consensus regarding concepts and principles of leadership which will indicate the stance to be taken as leadership is included in the church's educational curriculum. The concept of leadership espoused should be consistent with the gospel and should take into account the results of study, research, and evaluation by the church at large and by nonchurch agencies.

Those responsible for administration of the educational ministry in each congregation must undertake the following tasks in order to select, maintain, and train an appropriate and skillful staff of designated leaders:

—Diagnose the contemporary situation in terms of its problems and opportunities, assessing the needs for leadership in the church and in the community at large for several years in the future.

—Develop or adapt a design for enlisting and equipping persons to take designated responsibility in the educational ministry.

—Provide experiences of training in the skills and art of leadership for these persons.

—Provide opportunity for in-service experiences in "leadership education" under the supervision and guidance of a mature leader.

—Make possible group support for a person in training through either a group of fellow trainees or a group to whom a person is assigned as a leader-in-training.

—Make sure that training programs are designed so that tasks assigned to a trainee will seem significant to him and tend to draw upon his present interests, abilities, and assets of personality.

—Provide access to and employ appropriately materials and personal resources from *within and beyond* the denomination in the training of designated leaders.

The Contribution of Evaluation to Education 797

If the church takes seriously its educational ministry, it will make every effort to facilitate the achievement of the objective of that ministry. Efforts will be increasingly effective if they are made in light of deliberately planned evaluation.

Evaluation involves the systematic gathering of pertinent information concerning the church's educational ministry, relating it to the objective of Christian education, and using that information to form judgments on how to strengthen that ministry so as to make the fulfillment of the objective more likely.

Such assessment includes focusing on structures for the educa-

798

tional ministry, processes in the educational ministry, and results of the educational ministry. It should be kept clear that the purpose of this evaluation is to upgrade the opportunities the church offers for learning; it is *not* for the purpose of passing judgment on the quality of a person's Christian discipleship. Principles and plans for evaluating the church's educational ministry must be consistent with Christian values and beliefs.

The focus of the church's educational ministry is "all persons." It is for their sake that such a ministry is designed and implemented. This fact provides the foundation for evaluation. The objective of Christian education provides the source of criteria for evaluating the educational ministry. Through administration the church makes provision for evaluation.

There are three major dimensions in which the church should have guidance for evaluation relating to the educational ministry: within the specific learning opportunities themselves; throughout the entire educational program on any given judicatory level of the church; and at the national denominational or interdenominational level of curriculum planning.

Evaluation Within the Learning Opportunity

Inasmuch as learning is the property of the learner himself, the specific setting within which learning opportunities are offered to the learner is a critical locus for evaluation. The learner may be helped to assess his own role in learning and thereby enhance his engagement in learning tasks. The community of learners may take stock of their corporate functioning in the learning enterprise to see how they can together facilitate the educational enterprise. The leader in the educational enterprise may be helped to assess the degree of effectiveness with which he carries out his designated functions and to discover ways of improving his performance in the teaching-learning situation. Out of such evaluation both individuals and groups may consolidate learning, improve skills, and redirect goals in learning.

Evaluation Throughout the Entire Educational Program

A necessary part of administering the church's life in any of its expressions—local, regional, national—is evaluation of the total work of the church toward the fulfillment of its nature and mission. In terms of the educational ministry of the church this means that those who offer an educational ministry must systematically examine that ministry from time to time in order to see how it might be made more effective. That is to say, for instance, that regularly the governing body of a particular church should see to it that the total educational ministry of that church is carefully evaluated in order to determine how that ministry might be strengthened so that persons are more likely to "be aware of God . . . and respond in faith and love." The same obligation rests on the authoritative body responsible for an educational ministry on any level of the church's life beyond the local church, whether denominational or interdenominational.

Whether evaluation shall take place is not an option: it does go on continuously. But systematic use of findings of evaluation to improve the educational ministry is an obligation of good stewardship which the church may not treat lightly.

Evaluation at the Denominational Level of Curriculum Planning

Denominational curriculum planners have a dual responsibility in the realm of evaluation: the evaluation of the functions in the educational ministry for which they are responsible and the provision of guidance and resources whereby those involved in implementing curriculum may evaluate the educational ministry as described above. The first of these two responsibilities involves evaluation of the curriculum plan itself, of curriculum materials provided the church, of field programs offered to support the church in its educational ministry, and of other functions of national curriculum planners. The second responsibility involves offering guidance and resources to help the church carry out its obligation to evaluate the educational ministry against appropriate criteria and in appropriate ways and to make use of their evaluations for the purpose of improving the educational ministry offered.

Denominational curriculum planners should give attention to all three of these dimensions of evaluation in the process of constructing a curriculum plan and producing curriculum materials. Guidance and resources for evaluation within the teaching-learning situation should be integral to the teaching-learning resources for that situation. Guidance and resources for evaluation should be a part of the help provided those who are responsible for administration. Procedures for ongoing improvement of curriculum plans, materials, and services provided by national curriculum planners should be established within the regular structures of national bodies.

800

Basic Principles of Administration

As the church answers administrative questions with reference to its educational work, it must take into account not only the implications of its curriculum plan; it must also take into account basic principles of administration. These include the following:

The Principle of Purpose

The framework for administration is derived from the nature and purpose of the task to be done, both that of the church as a whole, and that of the educational ministry in particular.

The Principle of Authority and Responsibility

Authority and responsibility must be exercised and delegated together. To assign either authority or responsibility without the other is to create an untenable situation.

The Principle of Participation

Administration should provide for those persons who are affected by decisions to share in the making of them. Decisions must be made at a level high enough to represent all those affected, but as near as possible to the individual and the group of which he is a part.

The Principle of Unity

Unity must exist in all policies, structures, and procedures. This unity implies that structures to carry similar functions must have a parallel relationship to the same body in the administrative framework. Policies must be consistently applied across similar structures and procedures must be consistent within similar structures.

The Principle of Coordination

Coordination of responsible groups and individuals is necessary to harmonious and productive work. Coordination depends in part on the establishment of workable relationships by means of an adequate organization and of open channels of communication within the total framework of the church.

The Principle of Consistency

Administration must be performed in a manner consistent with the basic tenets of the Christian faith.

Such principles are valid for any institution in society; for the church to be effective it must take them seriously as it provides for administrative services to accomplish its mission.

Afterword

Using This Curriculum Plan to Derive Teaching-Learning Units

All that is dealt with in a Curriculum Plan is for the sake of helping persons become aware of God's "self-disclosure . . . and respond in faith and love." A Curriculum Plan is devised in order that curriculum may take place; it is for this actual engagement of persons in learning that careful planning is done.

Parts I—IV of this book set forth a Curriculum Plan. There remains the task of making use of this Plan so as to offer persons of every age adequate opportunities for learning through particular educational arrangements. It is the function of the Afterword to indicate how this Plan may be utilized in deriving teaching-learning units to compose a lifelong curriculum for a comprehensive educational ministry.[1]

What a Teaching-Learning Unit Is

A teaching-learning unit is a planned and organized event, providing to particular persons in various groupings occasions for engagement in learning in the Christian faith and life. A

---

[1]Sixteen denominations are engaged in this process, working together through the Cooperative Curriculum Development.

teaching-learning unit is a segment of curriculum; it is one of numerous composite educational events under the church's guidance in a person's lifelong process of becoming. As a segment of curriculum, the teaching-learning unit partakes of the Curriculum Plan; it has focus, content, procedures of communication, form; it is organized according to the principle affirmed by the Design of the Curriculum Plan; and it is actualized within the Christian community.

Units of teaching-learning are derived from a Curriculum Plan. As events, teaching-learning units occur locally. Denominational curriculum planners provide the churches with guidance and resources to support these events. The provision of suitable guidance and resources requires that curriculum planners at the denominational level describe units of teaching-learning which are comprehensive of the educational ministry for which curriculum is envisioned. The procedures suggested here are intended to be useful to denominational curriculum planners in this task.

The Relation of Teaching-Learning Units to the Curriculum Plan

For curriculum to have integrity and to make its strongest contribution to a person's becoming, each teaching-learning unit must consistently reflect the Curriculum Plan. A teaching-learning unit is a microcosm of the Curriculum Plan. Provision should be made so that each unit makes its contribution to a person's fulfillment of the Objective. Each unit should appropriately provide for the engagement of the learner with part of the curriculum's content. All units together should comprehend the composite curriculum which the church offers the learner.

The basic necessity, then, for beginning the derivation of particular units of curriculum from this Curriculum Plan is to affirm the Design and to become thoroughly grounded in the Plan. Denominational curriculum planners must be clear on the Objective of the curriculum. They must agree on the Scope of the curriculum they are planning. They must perceive Learning Tasks and their function in this Plan. They must assimilate the nature and function of Christian community as the Context of learning. They must recognize and accept the Organizing Principle by which these dynamic components of the curriculum Design are brought into relationship in curriculum. Therefore, although Part III is entitled "Source of Development of Teaching-Learning Units," it is evident that a thorough assimilation of Parts I and II is necessary preparation for the derivation of teaching-learning units. Furthermore, as is set forth in Part IV, the functions of administration must be kept in mind as units of curriculum are conceived in order to provide an adequate framework in which curriculum may be operative.

Steps in Deriving Teaching-Learning Units

The procedure described below for utilizing this Curriculum Plan in deriving teaching-learning units takes account of every part of the Curriculum Plan. It is well to highlight one component of the Design which comes into active play in teaching-learning units: Context. Inasmuch as the Context for learning in the Christian faith and life is the Christian community, it is clear that within teaching-learning events among persons, the Context makes its vital contribution to learning. The Context is offered through persons as they express Christian community and engage together in the fulfillment of the church's Objective. Plans for teaching-learning units, then, must alert persons to the contribution of Context to curriculum, and to ways in which that contribution can be realized.

805

The answers to two basic questions form the necessary foundation for the description of teaching-learning units. One is the question, In what settings will the curriculum of the church be offered? The other is the question, What shall be the content of the curriculum offered in the settings? After these two questions are answered to the satisfaction of the denominational curriculum planners, specific teaching-learning units for all educational settings can be described and then ordered in such a way as to undergird the total educational ministry of the church.

Denominational curriculum planners must work on these two questions more or less at the same time, for work done on one will help determine the answer to the other. For the sake of clarity, however, procedures for answering first the one and then the other will be considered.

The Settings in Which the Curriculum of the Church Will Be Offered

The first step in determining the settings for the church's curriculum is to define the total educational ministry of the denomination. The description should embrace both the functions ascribed to the educational ministry and the modes in which the educational ministry is expressed. This description will likely differ from denomination to denomination, for it must take account of various denominational particularities. The extent and character of a church's educational ministry are affected by the polity of that church, its confessional orientation, the available resources for an educational ministry, and the forms and traditions which have obtained within its educational ministry in the past. All these factors, and others, will influence the way in which denominational curriculum planners describe the educational ministry of the church.

Some of the ways the church goes about its educational ministry and some of the experiences to which it pertains may be formulated as follows: worship, academic and informal study, service or work, fellowship, informing and training in the work of the church, recreation, and celebration. The description of the educational ministry would include such varied aspects as education for evangelism, education for stewardship, education for mission, education for an intelligent, firm, and defensible faith.

Following such a comprehensive description of the church's total educational ministry, denominational curriculum planners then face the task of examining these functions and expressions in order to identify those functions of the educational ministry which must be supported and guided by curriculum plans, in view of the denomination's obligations and resources. This decision will lead to a description of educational settings which will be most effective for carrying the curriculum of the church's educational ministry.

The educational settings chosen by this means then should be described in such a way that together they accommodate the priority functions and modes of expression of the educational ministry.

An educational setting is a particular structure, planned and organized to provide teaching-learning opportunities in the educational ministry. It is a construct whose form is determined by the decisions made with reference to the following ten factors:

1. Distinctive contribution to the total educational ministry and its relationship to other settings

   In light of the description of the total educational ministry, what is the assigned purpose of this setting? What is its distinctive contribution? What is its relationship to other settings?

2. Constituency

   What particular population is planned for in the setting?

3. Grouping

   What is to be the mode of delineating or assembling the persons in the population for whom the setting is planned?

4. Duration

   What are the anticipated termini for the setting (How is

the time between the termini to be measured? In minutes? hours? days? weeks? months? years? decades?)

5. Frequency

   What is to be the number and schedule of engagements or meetings to be planned for the setting?

6. Time-span of a gathering

   How long will it take to carry out each meeting or engagement planned for the setting?

7. Location

   What situations or localities are assumed or provided for in the setting?

8. Leadership

   What type of persons, how many persons, and what kind of training are needed for guiding the learning opportunities planned for the setting?

9. Administrative Connection

   What group, board, or agency within the church polity is responsible for sponsoring and supervising the carrying out of plans for the setting?

10. Resources

    What physical objects, printed and projected materials, skilled or knowledgeable persons, community institutions, and forms will be used as references and sources of information and guidance in the setting?

The settings in which curriculum is to be offered should each be described in terms of these factors.

Before teaching-learning units for the various settings of the educational ministry are determined, the other foundational question must have been resolved.

The Content of Curriculum Offered in the Settings of the Educational Ministry

Denominational curriculum planners arrive at the answer to this question by working with Part III of the Curriculum Plan against the background of Parts I and II. In the awareness of the full richness of content represented in the Areas of Curriculum and their respective themes, denominational curriculum planners work at an analysis of Part III, "Source of Development of Teaching-Learning Units." This analysis will make apparent the interrelationships among meanings and experiences, readiness of learners, modes of communication, and ranges of appropriate outcomes resident in the theme treatments. These correlations will lift up clusters of the meanings and experiences across the life-span, together with appropriate procedures for engaging in the learning tasks and suggestions as to what the learner may achieve from personal involvement in the meanings and experiences.

A common procedure can be used for analyzing each theme of every area one after another. Taking one theme at a time for each of the four life periods within a theme treatment the procedure would be as follows:

Reread in Part II the delineation of the area and delineation of the particular theme to be analyzed. This will prepare curriculum planners to maintain proper focus within the theme, and to provide adequate coverage of the theme in the development of correlations for content.

809

Examine the theme treatment for affinities among meanings and experiences—dimension one of the first sections of the treatment (1-a). Describe these affinities.

In light of the defined affinities, examine dimension two of the first section of each theme treatment to see how these 1-a affinities draw to themselves statements on the readiness of the learners for these meanings and experiences. Add the 1-b statement to the 1-a affinities, thus beginning to build the correlation.

🔖 In light of the defined affinities (1-a), together with the statements on the readiness of the learner (1-b), examine the second section of the theme treatment to see how these 1-a affinities draw to themselves statements on modes of communication (2) appropriate to the meanings and experiences. Add the 2 statements to the (1-a + 1-b) partial correlation, yielding (1-a + 1-b + 2). This gives, then, a statement of related meanings and experiences, related to the readiness of the learner facilitated by appropriate modes of communication.

🔖 In light of the defined affinities (1-a), examine the third section of each theme treatment to see how these 1-a affinities draw to themselves statements on the appropriate range of learnings (3). Add the 3 statements to (1-a + 1-b + 2) to complete the correlation (1-a + 1-b +2 + 3). These five steps carried out for every life period of every theme within the five areas yield the curriculum for all the settings of the educational ministry of the church.

Denominational curriculum planners would now have determined the settings of the educational ministry and the curriculum to be offered through the educational ministry in its variety of settings. There remain two major steps to complete the task of the denominational curriculum planners. The first is to particularize for each setting the part of the curriculum which is appropriate to that setting; that is, describe the teaching-learning units in particular which are to be offered through each setting in terms appropriate to the description of that setting. The last remaining step is to organize these described teaching-learning units into an ordered plan for the various settings with adequate concern to provide balance, comprehensiveness, and flexibility.

Particular Teaching-Learning Units for Various Settings

It is at this stage in the derivation of teaching-learning units that the answers to the two foundational questions come into relationship. The settings through which the educational ministry is offered and the content of the curriculum are now considered together in order to take maximum advantage of the distinctive contribution of each setting for communicating the meanings and experiences appropriate to the setting in terms of each of the four life periods.

This confluence may be achieved by combining the ten factors describing the setting with the affinities of meanings and experiences, readiness of the learner, modes of communication and range of appropriate outcomes. In this process of combining, the denominational curriculum planner describes specifically the teaching-learning units for each setting making particular the content, methods, and what the learner may achieve. Further, the implications for the required resources may emerge.

The "since-then" formula (see Weekend Family Retreat example below) illustrates one possible way of approaching this task. Arriving at teaching-learning units for a setting may be facilitated by the use of a series of "since-then" propositions in which the "since" dimension of a proposition reflects the specification of the setting on the ten factors and the "then" dimension reflects the implications of these factors for curriculum in that setting. Notice that the resources of Part IV, Administration, are brought in at the appropriate point as well as the resources of Part III.

SINCE	THEN
We agreed that the distinctive contribution of this setting is in the field of relationships— "fellowship" (designated)	We will focus our attention on the themes and areas dealing primarily with the relational aspects of the gospel.

We agreed that the duration of this setting would be a three-day weekend

We agreed that the frequency was only one meeting

We agreed that the time span was thirty-six hours, in which there would be six particularly planned learning opportunities

We will select the following outcomes to guide us in stating our main purpose.

We will be able to deal with this (designated) amount of content for which (designated) learners are considered to be ready.

812

We agreed the location was to be a camp

We should examine the second section of the selected themes to find suggested modes of communication most appropriate to a camp.

We agreed that the constituency would be families with teen-age children

We agreed that the grouping would be both broadly based and peer grouping at various times

We will particularly examine these (designated) life-period treatments to help narrow our focus on content and on our methods of communication.

We agreed that this was primarily a family-life concern

The sponsoring and guidance of this teaching-learning opportunity should come from the Family Life subcommittee of the Christian Education Committee (or its equivalent) in each congregation[2]

We agreed that this (designated) leadership was good to have

We will need persons with this (designated) training and this (designated) experience, therefore we must provide this (designated) guidance now in order to have such leaders by (designated) time[2]

We agreed that these (designated) types of resources are necessary } We will recommend these (designated) resources, secure and make available these (designated) resources, and produce these (designated) resources[2]

Completing the Organization of Curriculum

The final step in denominational curriculum planning is the ordering of all teaching-learning units for each setting into a plan for that setting. The ordering will be done with a view toward balance within and among the settings, comprehensiveness among the settings, and movement toward fulfillment of the Objective for all persons at the various stages of lifelong engagement in learning.

After this ordering is achieved, the basis is laid for providing resources for the curriculum.

Continuing Curriculum Development

Denominational curriculum planners can continue to use this Curriculum Plan to assess their work and to improve the guidance and resources offered the church for its educational ministry. New insights into God's will and into the demands of the world will continue to call the church to reshape radically its Curriculum Plan. In his call to mission God lays upon the church the necessity to cast its educational ministry in forms relevant to the times, confident that God's Spirit is at work to fulfill his purpose through the church in and among men.

813

----

[2]Not expressly in Part III. Some guidance may be implied by the second section in each theme treatment.

Glossary

This Glossary comprises a list of words each of which is employed with a specialized meaning in Parts I through IV of *The Church's Educational Ministry: A Curriculum Plan*. Every use of each word entered in the Glossary is consistent with its meaning indicated below. Definitions of the words usually are limited to telling what the word means; occasionally a further annotation shows in brief how the word functions as it is used in the book. Words in this book used only in their dictionary sense are not included in the Glossary. An effort has been made in the Plan not to use words of an esoteric, peculiar, or private nature. Referring to the Glossary will answer many questions of the reader, and facilitate his understanding and use of this book.

815

ADMINISTRATION (OF CHRISTIAN EDUCATION)

That service which provides for relating persons and groups to one another and to their available resources in such a way that the church's aim for its educational ministry may be achieved.

ADULT

The life period whose span is from the completion of high school to the time of death, recognizing there are differences within the adult group because of chronological and experiential factors.

CELEBRATION

An act of pure enjoyment and participation enhanced by words, physical attention, courtesy, ceremony, art, and gratuitous care. It is perhaps the purest form of love because it has no utilitarian value.

CHILDREN

The life period from birth through approximately 12 years of age. This life period has been subdivided into early childhood (preschool children—those years from birth to approximately 6 years); elementary years (grades 1 through 6—or approximately 6-12 years of age).

CHRISTIAN EDUCATION

That ministry of the church that provides the educational undergirding for the entire life and work of the church.

COMMUNICATION (IN CHRISTIAN EDUCATION)

That process of personal interaction which is characterized by intelligent and sensitive concern for one another and understanding and acceptance of one's self.

CONTENT

A selected portion of the Scope (meanings and experiences) of the curriculum for Christian education to be included within a particular plan (cf. SCOPE).

CONTEXT (FOR CURRICULUM)

The fellowship of persons who owe allegiance to Jesus Christ; the milieu for learning.

CROSSING POINTS

The dynamic interaction between the gospel (the meanings—

data and experiences inherent in the gospel) and the concerns of the learner in his whole field of relationships.

CURRICULUM

The sum of all learning experiences resulting from the curriculum plan under the guidance of the church and directed toward accomplishing the church's objective (cf. CURRICULUM PLAN).

CURRICULUM AREA

A perspective on the Scope resulting from an analysis of the elements of Scope in light of the Objective.

CURRICULUM PLAN

The formulation and graphic representation of the overall construct for curriculum, distinguishing among component sections and relating these sections to one another in due proportion; particularly the product of the Cooperative Curriculum Project —*The Church's Educational Ministry: A Curriculum Plan,* a kind of high-operational tool to assist in the process of constructing curriculum plans at each level on which provision for learning is made; "Curriculum Plan" is not to be confused with "Curriculum" since a curriculum plan is resident in the resources, while the curriculum happens in the teaching-learning situation.

817

CURRICULUM THEME

A major motif within a curriculum area that has significance throughout the life-span. It describes in greater detail the intersection of the concerns of the Christian faith and basic persistent life issues.

CURRICULUM DESIGN

The basic principles, foundations, and framework which shape the Curriculum Plan, experienced in five interrelated components: Objective, Scope, Context, Learning Tasks, Organizing Principle.

EDUCATIONAL MINISTRY

All educational opportunities which the church provides for the undergirding of the entire life and work of the church.

ELEMENTS

The dimensions of reality in man's field of relationships: the divine experience of man under God, the Christian experience of man's relation to man, the Christian experience of man within the world.

EVALUATION

Assessment of the church's educational ministry on the basis of pertinent information systematically gathered concerning structures, procedures, and outcomes in that ministry.

FIELD OF RELATIONSHIPS

The sphere or arena of association and reciprocity within which a person lives: between a person and God, other persons, the natural world, and the continuum of history.

GOSPEL

God's whole continuous redemptive action toward man, known especially in Jesus Christ.

HOLISTIC

The concept that the determining factors of a reality (being, thing, entity) are of a whole, such as an organism, and not a series of constituent parts. In this Plan "holistic" is a characteristic of the Scope, a view toward the learner and a view toward the gospel.

The perspective for viewing man's whole field of relationships, given by God's self-revelation.

LEADERSHIP

That responsible action and being by which the decisions and actions of persons in groups are influenced, motivated, or changed. Christians are obligated to exhibit such responsible action and being, sometimes as a responsible member of a group, sometimes as the designated head of a group.

LEARNING

Changes in life characteristics that result from experience in the whole field of relationships, whether such changes fulfill or deter the fulfillment of the Objective.

LEARNING TASKS

Phases of the process of human change in which the learner is engaged. In this Curriculum Plan these phases are cast in light of the gospel and are undertaken within the Christian community. This concept underlies the five general learning tasks.

LIFE PERIOD

A segment of human existence defined by specified upper and lower chronological limits and/or educational placement.

LIFE-SPAN

The period of human existence from birth to death; in Part III of the Curriculum Plan the life-span is considered to have four major segments (life periods): early childhood, elementary years, youth, adult.

MEANINGS AND EXPERIENCES

Personal perception of the significance of events on which a range of connotations of reason or mind is brought to bear.

MISSION

A duty or function imposed on or assumed by one or more persons. In this Curriculum Plan—those duties and functions which God calls his people to undertake, individually and collectively.

NEEDS

A person's state or condition of being which serves to influence his behavior directed toward an intrinsic goal basic to personhood such as achievement of competence, release of tension, restoration of psychological and physiological equilibrium.

OBJECTIVE

The ultimate end or purpose which the church strives to fulfill.

ORGANIZING PRINCIPLE

The rationale for relating the components of the Curriculum Design to one another.

SCOPE (OF THE CURRICULUM)

The field over which the church has legitimate purview for its educational ministry, that is, God's redemptive action and its implications for man in the whole field of relationships. The church draws from Scope the content (information and experience) for its curriculum.

SETTING

A particular structure planned and organized to provide teaching-learning opportunities within the total educational ministry. It is a construct, the form of which is determined by such factors as: distinctive contribution, duration, frequency, constituency, administrative connection (cf. Afterword).

A planned and organized event, providing to particular persons in various groupings occasions for engagement in learning in the Christian faith and life. It is a segment of curriculum, one of numerous composite educational events under the church's guidance in a person's lifelong process of becoming. As a segment of curriculum, the teaching-learning unit partakes of the Curriculum Plan; it has focus, content, procedures of communication, form; it is organized according to the principle affirmed by the Design of the Curriculum Plan; and it is actualized within the Christian community.

THEME

See "Curriculum Theme"

THEME TREATMENT

In Part III, the analysis and explication by each life period of the themes within each curriculum area, in terms of: the significance of the theme for the person, the way in which the theme may be communicated, and what learnings within the theme may result from a person's engaging in the learning tasks.

VANTAGE POINT

821

A perspective on the Scope that is embraced by a curriculum area.

YOUTH

The life period which extends from a lower limit of approximately 12 years (beginning the 7th grade of school) to an upper limit of approximately 18 years (completing senior high school).

Appendix

DEVELOPING FUNCTIONS
OF LEADERSHIP
IN THE CHRISTIAN COMMUNITY[1]

The gospel calls all persons to live in meaningful relationship with God and their neighbors. This ministry of reconciliation is the church's mission. All Christians, as members of the body of Christ, are called to assume responsibilities in this ministry of reconciliation in the world and within the Christian community. When the church seeks to move toward its objective, it is confronted with the necessity of aiding each Christian in preparation for volunteer leadership. What is leadership? Who is a leader? What are the church's goals as it prepares persons for leadership?

823

This paper offers foundational concepts and direction concerning leadership needed to undergrid the church's ministries and mission. This will be a resource for denominations singly and together as they develop a plan for the training of persons for leadership, a plan integral to the curriculum and based upon the curriculum design. Such a plan should concern itself with preparing two groups of persons for leadership: a) all Christians called by God to exercise responsible leadership in their group experiences within the world and the church, and b) persons

---

[1]This is a paper developed by the Task Group on Leadership for the Project.

called to places of designated leadership on a volunteer basis within the life and work of the church. These suggestions, their implications, and implementation require further study and development through denominational efforts singly and/or cooperatively.

Leadership and the Leader

824   Providing leadership in the church is seen as both a human and a divine process. The New Testament frequently refers to functions of leadership as gifts to the church, given as the Spirit wills for the common good of the church and for equipping the church to undertake its mission.

Leadership is that quality of action and being by which the decisions and actions of persons in groups are influenced, motivated, or changed. That quality of action and being known as leadership is the result of a constellation of factors such as the person's life experiences, his philosophy of life, his Christian faith and values, his emotional maturity, his capacity for analyzing a situation and making intelligent choices and decisions regarding that which is appropriate for the occasion. Leadership may be provided by any person within the group, irrespective of who has been officially designated as a chairman for the group. When the performance of the group as a whole is influenced, leadership has been exercised.

The response of persons to leadership is influenced both by factors within the person offering leadership and factors inherent within the group and the situation it confronts. When leadership is exercised, there is a response by persons which indicates that they have been influenced, motivated, or changed. This response may take such forms as decisions, actions, changed attitudes, setting of goals, movement toward a goal, unity and cohesiveness among members in a group, improved quality of relationships, or use of resources and guidance which are available.

In this paper, the term *leader* refers to any person who is influencing, guiding, or directing the goals, attitudes, and actions of a group of persons so that they may achieve their objectives. The use of the term *leader* is not equated with a designated chairman. Certain general characteristics tend to make it easier for a person to fulfill the functions of leadership, but do not guarantee that he shall exercise leadership. They tend to distinguish him from others in the group quite apart from the composition of the group and its varying tasks. Personality characteristics, skills, experience, knowledge, and resources are illustrative of those things which enable him to perform functions needed by the group.

The situation (internal and external) and the task being faced by a group significantly affects the choice of any person to whom the group will turn for leadership. The leader at a given moment is the person who is helping the group achieve its task. The nature of the general situation and the specific task cause the one who is providing leadership to restrict his behavior to that which appears to be appropriate for the occasion. More than one person normally serves a group as it moves toward its objective. The situation in which the group finds itself and the task it confronts largely determine who is perceived as a leader and how he is able to function.

825

The composition of the group and the relationships which exist between its members also help determine whose leadership is followed. Some influential factors within the group are the theological and value systems of the members, the psychological climate within the group, the image the members have of a leader and leadership (especially as it relates to a status and authority figure), the performance of the group acting as a whole, changes in the composition of the group, and changes in interpersonal relations within the group. Some of the outside factors in the situation which influence the behavior of the group in its choice of leadership are the nature of the situation faced by the group, the climate within the social milieu, the immediate context of the group, and outside pressures on the group.

A person may be formally designated as chairman or head of the group by virtue of his assignment, appointment, or election as a teacher, officer, executive, or staff member. Such a designated person performs a function in the life of the group which might be described as headship or chairmanship. As head of the group he may or may not be one who provides leadership as defined in this paper. It is the spontaneous recognition by the group members of the head's contribution to group goals that enables him to lead as well as head up a group. An effective head of the group sees it as his function to encourage others in his group to take leadership roles. He moves from headship to leadership as his group members recognize the contribution which he makes to the group's goal and progress, and willingly cooperate with him in its achievement. Headship and leadership are not necessarily the same thing although they are not mutually exclusive.

Faith, experience, and knowledge which grow out of a commitment to God through Jesus Christ, an openness to the work of the Holy Spirit, an understanding of the Bible, an acquaintance with theology and ethics rooted in the faith are viewed by Christians and the church as essential in the persons chosen to take places of designated responsibility in the Christian community and the world. This dimension and way of life result in Christians bringing to their leadership resources beyond those brought by persons not grounded in the Christian faith. This rootage enables them to minister to others and to interpret, conserve, and transmit the heritage of the Christian faith essential to the life and mission of the church.

Within the Christian fellowship are many groups—some organized by design, others the result of informal clustering. Christian commitment and discipleship call for these groups to exercise Christian responsibility and leadership in the life and work of the congregation as a whole as its engages in mission. Just as a single individual has responsibility to the group, so each group has responsibility for the unity and mission of the whole body of Christ. A crisis may arise when a group with designated responsibility fails to provide mature leadership within the life and mission of the total congregation. Other groups, as they become aware of this weakness, should not allow the total congregation to suffer but should take initiative themselves.

Any committee, board, or group within the congregation should, at times, take leadership initiative in the implementation of a concern which has not been assigned to them when other groups in the congregation, whether designated or not, fail to see the need and a way to meet it. Health in the body of Christ cannot be maintained apart from each group's feeling a sense of responsibility for the total mission as well as for its own particular group and its task.

Groups also should take initiative in disbanding when they have fulfilled their purpose so that the energies and time of persons will not be dissipated.

Beyond the organized church Christians cluster informally and formally in the community to help achieve goals which are beneficial to the community and consistent with goals of the church. In this context these groups provide leadership in the community on behalf of important causes, bringing to this leadership all the resources of the Christian faith. These groups of Christians should seek to act responsibly within the community to bring about reconciliation and healing in the world.

827

The Church's Goals
in the Development of Leadership

If congregations are to fulfill their mission in the world, they should seek to achieve the following goals in the development of leadership:

To recognize the gifts of the spirit within the Christian community which enable persons to serve effectively in leadership.

To provide leadership in the community which will minister to the world and bear witness to Christ.

To provide experiences whereby individual Christians may become motivated to assume leadership responsibility for the achievement of the church's mission in the world and to seek out educational experiences which would equip them for this mission.

To help members become aware of their responsibility for ministering to persons in the world.

To provide opportunities for educational experiences which will equip each Christian for assuming leadership within the church and community.

To develop among the congregations a better understanding of the nature of leadership, with an emphasis upon a concerned leadership witnessing and serving in the world in obedience to Christ.

It is recognized that there will always be a need for leadership within the organized church but that an increased emphasis must be placed upon leadership in life situations beyond the organized church. The Christian motivated to give service must be equipped to provide leadership in the achievement of goals consistent with his Christian faith but not necessarily assigned to him formally by the church or some group within the community.

Persons Needed to Implement Goals

Each congregation has primary responsibility for developing a strategy for achieving the goals outlined above for the development of leadership. In the development of leadership locally each congregation should seek the assistance of the following persons from within its fellowship.

Persons capable of diagnosing the contemporary involvement of the congregation in mission in the world, determining the tasks to be done if the congregation is to be seriously involved in mission in the future, clarifying the kind and number of leaders needed during the next decade, determining the problems related to leadership which must be resolved, and planning a strategy of education and training. These persons would have resources available from the denomination to assist in this analysis and planning.

Persons capable of inspiring others in the congregation to commit themselves more fully to Jesus Christ and his will, to live in mission, and to engage in educational experiences within the congregation and community which equip them for providing leadership.

Persons to supervise and counsel those who are engaged in on-the-job training in places of leadership in the congregation and community.

Each denomination has responsibility for undergirding the program of its constituent congregations with adequate study, research, experimentation, counsel, and resources. Some persons helpful to denominations in this service to congregations are:

Capable persons, representing the total life and work of the church as well as specialists in leadership education, who could prepare a design for the development of leadership in congregations. This design, when adapted to the various congregations, could provide the kind of leadership needed for congregations in mission. These persons must be capable of diagnosing leadership in the contemporary situation in which the church finds itself, projecting problems and needs likely to be encountered in the next few decades, and planning a strategy of education and training which is supportive of the efforts of congregations in adapting the design to their own situations.

Persons capable of interpreting the design and strategy for the development of leadership to key persons within each congregation and winning their support and involvement in adapting such a design to their local situation.

Persons informed on the theory and practice of leadership to serve as counselors for curriculum builders and writers who must incorporate insights and values for leadership into the church curriculum.

Persons who can suggest and develop creative experiences for congregational use with those undergoing training in leadership.

Trainers for the supervisors and instructors who are to work in each congregation with persons engaged in on-the-job training in leadership.

Persons to develop instruments and criteria for use by each congregation in the evaluation of the effectiveness of leaders, the selection of leaders, the contribution of groups within the congregation to the mission of the church, and the determination of needs in light of the congregation's desire to provide leadership for fulfilling its mission.

Denominational Tasks
in the Development of Leadership

If the church is to carry out its mission, each denomination must assist the members of its constituency to learn the skills of leadership and to engage in a ministry of reconciliation in the world. In this ministry and the congregation's accompanying program for developing leadership there is a place for all persons with undesignated responsibilities and for a smaller but important number of persons who have designated responsibilities.

The total church curriculum should contribute to the preparation of each member for leadership by strengthening his understanding of the nature of leadership through a body of knowledge and information about leadership and the Christian faith, by providing a climate which supports responsible participation within groups, by clarifying a person's role in the total mission of the church, by encouraging positive attitudes toward leadership and leaders, and by providing some experience in leadership through the ongoing work and life of the church. The curriculum should also provide educational experiences for persons who have or are about to assume designated responsibilities of leadership within the congregation or the community.

Basic Assumptions

As the congregation fosters within each member the potential for leadership, it and the denomination should consciously build upon a few basic assumptions:

> The program for developing leadership should focus upon concerned and trained leaders who are to witness and serve in the world in obedience to Christ. It should not be unduly weighted in the direction of training persons for tasks within the organized life of the church.
>
> The development of skills in leadership is a continuous process over the life span. Maturity in leadership unfolds gradually and its pace cannot be precisely controlled or forced into a limited span of time.
>
> Training should be given to all persons at each age level in the skills and art of leadership, with additional training being provided for those who have been given or are about to assume designated responsibilities for leadership.
>
> In-service experience under the supervision and guidance of a mature leader is essential for those persons in training for special responsibilities. Supervision supports the inexperienced

831

person as he struggles with problems connected with his responsibility in the ongoing life and work of the community and church.

Group support is needed for a person in training. This support may come through either a group of fellow trainees or a group to whom the person is assigned as a leader in training. In either event, support is experienced by unity of mind and purpose of trainee and group, readiness of the group to move with the trainee in a given direction, the quality of relationship between the trainee and members of the group, and commonality of beliefs and mores between trainee and group.

Motivation is a key to growth in leadership. Training programs must be designed so that tasks assigned to a trainee will be of significance to him and tend to draw upon his present interests, abilities, and personality assets.

It is important to recognize that personality change may be necessary in persons before they can make significant gains in developing skills in leadership.

Tasks

Denominations, singly or cooperatively, must undergird the development of leadership by addressing themselves to the following tasks:

Agreement upon hypotheses about leadership which will indicate the stance to be taken as leadership is included in the church's educational curriculum. These hypotheses should be consistent with the gospel, taking into account the results of study, research, and evaluation by denominations and by educational, business, government, and other nonchurch agencies. Provision must be made in the curriculum plan for everyone to have opportunities for education in the skills of leadership. Opportunities also must be provided for training persons for specialized responsibilities. These should be integral to the curriculum plan, comprehensive enough to take place in a variety of settings and to accommodate the needs of persons with responsibilities in various situations in the world and in the church's life and work.

Provision of material and personal resources to undergird the congregations' development of leadership in its constituency. These resources might include: guidance for the congregations in their appraisal of their needs for leadership in light of what they conceive their mission to be; assistance in the development of an indigenous program; proposals for criteria for the selection and evaluation of leaders; and suggestions on how to use resource personnel, materials, and events as sources for guidance and counsel.

Provision for the cooperation of the denomination's congregations with congregations of other traditions, and cooperation with other denominations in carrying out the church's mission in the world.

833

Index

835

836

Evaluation, 591, 633, 797
  in educational program, 799
  of denominational curriculum
    planning, 798
  of learning opportunities, 798
Evangelism, *see* Outreach
Evil, 551, 572
Exhibits, 610
Experience, 45, 602, 648, 671
Experimentation, 471
Exploration, 473, 480, 481, 521, 553

Failure, 346, 647
Fair play, 671
Faith, 23, 78, 117, 143f., 151, 351,
    437, 445, 482, 543, 548,
  Christian, 290, 291, 293, 298, 307,
    318, 323, 328, 332, 333, 347,
    516, 723, 786
  in God, 338, 343
  need for, 733, 737
  spread of, 622
Family, 47, 64, 66f., 77f., 155f.,
    222, 282, 286, 291, 294, 297,
    298, 317, 322, 537, 560, 588,
    681
  devotions, 562
  love of, 278, 288, 289, 319, 323,
    324, 326, 327, 332, 340, 343,
    346, 351, 372, 375, 505, 509,
    513
  rituals, 671
  separation from, 677
Family-life situations, 602
Fears, 382, 516, 572, 576, 582, 603
Fear of the unknown, 341, 343, 516,
    572, 576, 582
Feelings of inadequacy, 781
Fellowship, 11, 131, 214, 217, 289,
    294, 391, 397, 423, 456, 460,
    465, 527, 535, 543, 545, 548,
    556, 557, 565, 611, 654, 668,
    764
  Christian, 281, 293, 351, 398,
    429, 453, 689, 692, 693, 695,
    696, 698, 702, 760, 785; re-
    stored, 727
  groups, 431
  of the church, 292, 344, 349, 352,
    392, 655, 658, 687, 688, 704,
    707, 709, 710

Fellowship, continued
  with God, 101, 137f., 151, 153,
    378, 383, 384, 387f., 390, 395,
    400, 401, 402, 576, 621
  worldwide, 659, 671
Field of relationships, 12ff., 23, 25,
    35, 47f., 54, 59ff., 63f., 261,
    262, 271, 560
Field trips, 329, 381, 413, 471, 475,
    480, 541, 610, 660, 674, 683
Films, 361, 381, 644, 648, 650, 682
Finances, 242f.
Focus, 374
  of curriculum areas, 43, 93, 129,
    162, 205, 259, 483, 586, 685
Folklore, 610
Forgiveness, 46, 47, 135, 153, 260,
    263, 264, 268, 278, 279, 280,
    281, 283, 288, 291, 292, 294,
    298, 348, 353, 381, 391, 404,
    405, 406, 408, 410, 411, 412,
    414, 417, 418, 452, 486, 487,
    489, 490, 491, 492, 493, 496,
    497, 505, 507, 508, 510, 511,
    512, 514, 525, 527, 530, 535,
    539, 547, 589, 600, 603, 611,
    644, 645, 650, 674, 718, 727,
    729, 741, 749, 751
Freedom, 52, 53, 73f., 85, 131, 133,
    138, 149, 153, 172, 179, 277,
    280, 290, 291, 292, 339, 342,
    344, 345, 348, 352, 353, 354,
    430, 514, 528, 530, 533, 535,
    587, 599, 614, 640, 643, 644,
    645, 647, 670
  appreciation of, 604
  Christian, 534
  from guilt, 532
  from prejudice, 605
  moral, 351
  of choice, 350, 396, 400, 407,
    415, 425, 429, 433, 454, 488,
    506, 507, 510, 511, 589, 594,
    600
Friendliness, 451, 610, 711
Friendship, 278, 289, 523, 541, 658,
    687, 691
Frustrations, 366, 369, 516, 735,
    737
Fulfillment, 513
Funerals, 579, 583

839

Futility, 57, 352
Future, 600
  needs, 637

Games, 610, 641
Germination, 467
Geography, 654
Goals, 30, 32f., 192, 528, 533, 535, 539, 543, 563, 568, 667, 673, 676, 677, 683, 692, 694, 733, 768
God, 12, 15f., 25, 31f., 35, 40ff., 49ff., 52, 53, 54, 58, 79, 81, 84, 93, 94-128, 130ff., 147ff., 216ff., 226ff., 232, 260, 262, 264, 268f., 271f., 273, 274f., 275f., 278, 288, 299, 304, 309, 314, 319, 323, 327, 331f., 336, 337, 338, 355, 356, 358f., 363f., 372, 375, 378, 396, 430, 449, 655, 705, 708, 715, 720
  Absolute, the, 352
  Absolute value, 340, 342, 344, 345, 347
  activity of, 461, 470
  authority of, 577, 582
  availability of, 340, 378, 382, 420, 534
  belief in, 426
  children of, 581
  concern of, 453
  creativity of, 368
  creator, 472, 627, 745
  dependability of, 344, 355, 375, 401, 466, 476, 481, 492, 497, 639
  dependence on, 354, 756
  faith in, 745
  gifts of, 548, 631, 672
  goodness of, 469, 472
  grace of, 107, 143, 235, 345, 411, 413, 415, 418, 599, 650
  graciousness of, 407
  greatness of, 425
  guidance of, 752, 756
  handiwork of, 467, 472, 477, 481, 498
  holiness of, 196, 407, 408, 410, 411, 415, 419
  imminence of, 111f.
  in history, 383, 387, 399, 417, 446, 495

God, continued
  judgment of, 387, 453, 457
  laws of, 408, 410
  lordship of, 136, 340, 367, 386, 422
  love, 345, 393, 415, 434, 436, 484-503, 519, 686, 745
  loving Father, 343
  message of, 436, 439, 444, 447
  nature of, 752
  need for, 428, 431
  omnipotence of, 110f.
  power of, 581
  presence of, 396, 421, 422, 425, 427, 428, 432, 450, 707, 749
  purpose of, 335, 344, 350, 354, 382
  Redeemer, 407
  redemptive action, 503-519
  redemptive love, 400, 414, 418
  redemptive mission, 414
  reliability of, 411
  rule of, 672, 675, 670
  Ruler, 338, 577, 582
  sacrificial love of, 496
  seeking love of, 399, 401, 402, 403
  self-disclosure of, 94-128, 210, 374, 445, 461, 464, 465, 803
  son of, 135
  Source of Power, 579, 582, 744
  Sovereign Ruler, 85, 344, 350
  sovereignty of, 429
  Supreme Authority, 340, 342, 352
  Supreme Ruler, 342, 343
  Supreme Sovereign, 348
  Triumphant, 569, 585
  Ultimate Authority, 343
  Ultimate Reality, 344, 347
  Ultimate Value, 345, 348, 349, 350, 352
  vulnerability of, 104f.
  will of, 346, 352, 354, 428, 576
  word of, 34, 440, 750, 755
Good news, 497, 503
Goodwill, 714, 718
Gospel, 84, 94f., 231, 238, 327, 331, 332, 334, 335, 354, 395, 599, 603, 604
Grace, 511
  means of, 646, 651, 750, 755
Gratitude, 468, 477, 482, 609, 743

840

Group activities, 623, 687
  participation, 597, 608, 660, 661,
    664, 709, 747
  projects, 620
  study, 461
Groups, 561, 567, 618
  significant, 566
  youth, 678
Growth, 150-153, 366, 341, 356,
    376, 412, 465, 467, 468, 472,
    476, 479, 512, 519, 520, 530,
    536-552, 553, 622, 625, 640,
    645, 671, 675, 739, 770
  personal, 506, 507
Guidance, 440, 444, 446, 560, 595,
    599, 600, 603, 751, 780
Guilt, 420, 428, 514, 516, 714

Habits, 623
Handicaps, 266, 610
Hardships, 619
Harmony, 733
Headship, 795, 826
Healing, 219, 465, 470, 472, 473,
    474, 476, 478, 481, 735
Health, 629
Helpfulness, 607, 687, 713
Heritage, 51f., 525, 763
  Christian, 495, 500
  of the church, 712
Heroes, 557, 611, 703, 761
Hikes, 541, 748
Historical study, 786
History, 12, 25, 41f., 44, 51, 76,
    79f., 116, 206, 325, 327, 329,
    331, 333, 380, 382, 385, 394,
    426, 429, 500, 573, 577, 578,
    583, 596, 627, 647, 659, 665,
    694, 695, 704, 705, 707, 709,
    776
  Lord of, 102, 383, 387
  of the church, 211ff., 246f., 458,
    462, 463
Hobbies, 627
Holy Spirit, 151, 248, 426, 427, 444,
    445, 525, 544, 547, 548, 578,
    582, 599, 600, 603, 618, 621,
    646, 648, 697, 721, 722, 761,
    767, 769, 784, 785
  awareness of, 773, 778
  guidance of, 777
  presence of, 651

Home, 23, 155, 338, 366, 367, 372,
    550, 559, 563, 565, 568, 572
Hope, 53, 158-161, 350, 414, 446,
    569-585, 684
Hostility, 603, 727
Human need, 733, 768
Human relations, 618, 741, 734
Human rights, 614
Humility, 535, 645
Hurt, 588
Hymnody, 578, 583

Idealism, 561
Identity, 31, 228f., 297, 324, 328,
    379, 380, 489, 512, 516, 524,
    552-571, 612, 616, 623, 652,
    664, 665, 669, 692, 701, 725
Imagination, 88, 356, 359, 360, 364,
    365, 369, 451, 672
Imitation, 280, 553
Impermanence, 82f., 343
Inactivity, 458
Inadequacy, 775
Incarnation, 115, 230, 383, 440,
    492
Inconsistencies, 530
Independence, 32, 411, 512, 694
Indeterminacy, 83
Individuality, 60ff., 270, 273, 276,
    288, 294, 323, 359, 379, 537,
    538, 554, 587
Influence, 462
Initiative, 568
Injustice, 730, 733
Insecurity, 516
  economic, 351
Institutions, 619, 627
Integrity, 602, 636, 681
Intelligence, 309, 314
Intercession, 747
Interdenominations, 565, 779, 787
Interest in learning, 771
  in others, 296, 771
Interpretation, 440, 459
Interrelations, 323
Interviews, 649, 650
Intimacy, 66f.
Invention, 88
Investigation, 682
Isolation, 178, 222, 616

Man, continued
  goodness of, 415
  nature of, 271, 275
  significance of, 400
Management, 88, 222
Manpower, 241f.
Marriage, 275, 349, 397, 516, 595, 597
Materialization, 70ff.
Materials, use of, 623
Maturity, 432, 504, 539, 543, 544, 546, 548, 550, 551, 576, 619
Mechanics, 366, 371
Meditation, 495, 501, 748
Membership, 566, 600, 707
Memorization, 439, 442, 448, 449
Memory, 45
Mental capacities, 264, 268, 272, 273
Message, 115ff., 208f.
Messiah, 578, 582
Method of using Part III, 809ff.
Ministry, 3, 11, 23, 25, 194, 223, 245-250, 454, 461, 463, 558, 583, 635, 650, 722, 724, 759, 770-788
Ministry, educational, 791, 794, 803, 806
  evaluation of, 799
  structure for, 795
Ministry of reconciliation, 823, 830
Minorities, 612
  persecution of, 614
Mission, 206, 208f., 238-244, 563, 659, 675, 704, 714, 715, 731, 758, 770
  of Christian Community, 567, 722
  of God, 433
  world, 614, 622, 705
Mistakes, 412, 594, 644
Money, 632, 635
  handling of, 633
  use of, 627, 631
Moral problems, 397
Moral values, 282, 288, 290
Motivation, 564, 573
Movies, 542, 704, 705
Music, 421, 424, 438, 471, 476, 480, 509, 514, 518, 537, 545, 550, 554, 558, 578, 583, 615, 641, 649, 660, 705, 742, 747, 753
Mutation, 473, 478

Mutuality, 80, 334, 426, 568
Mystery, 126, 314, 315, 318, 376, 478, 746

Natural order, 12, 14f., 25, 44, 50f., 116, 124-128, 302, 303, 304, 305, 306, 309, 310, 311, 312, 313, 314, 315, 316, 318, 349, 354, 357, 420, 465-482
  dependability of, 308, 313
  use of, 304, 306
Natural processes, 301
Natural World, 570, 573, 574, 575, 622, 623, 627, 633, 634, 670, 671, 679, 681, 683, 748
Need, 606
  areas of, 769
  for redemption, 415
  for redemptive power, 416
  for respect, 566
  of others, 658
Needs, material, 614, 616, 681
  of others, 293, 359, 452, 456, 519, 608, 627, 631, 656, 665, 761, 777, 785
  of persons, 780
  of young people, 562
  spiritual, 616
  world, 666
Needy, 622
  sympathy for, 763
Neighbor, 174-180, 343, 519, 544, 548, 551, 604-622
New Testament, 142, 160, 174, 181, 214, 234, 334, 434, 529, 534, 578, 582, 618
New Testament Church, 211, 212, 217, 231

843

Obedience, 152, 189, 196, 217, 324, 334, 410, 457, 461, 491, 492, 495, 501, 504, 505, 508, 510, 516, 523, 643, 644, 645, 649, 650, 654, 659, 755, 781
Objective of Christian Education, 4, 7, 34, 39, 253, 768, 795, 804
  characteristics of, 9
  evaluation of, 601
  functions of, 8f.
  implications of, 10f.
  statement of, 8
  value of, 11

844

Psychology, 77, 734
Pursuit, 103

Quantum theory, 74

Race relations, 650
Rationalization, 296
Reading, 436, 649
  program, 620
Reading, devotional, 495
Reality of God, 426
  of gospel, 617
  of life, 578
Reason, 117, 591
Reassessment, 527, 532
Rebellion, 138, 275, 705
  feelings of, 751
Recognition, 7, 15, 735
Reconciliation, 65f., 72, 226ff.,
  228ff., 446, 465, 489, 493, 621,
  666, 684, 726-740, 750
  ministry of, 823, 830
  need for, 730
Recreation, 615, 639, 654
Redemption, 130-161, 228ff., 388,
  408, 413, 416, 726-740
Reflection, 678, 682, 683
Reformation, 211, 681
Rejection, 598, 609, 727
Relationships, 178, 261, 279, 284,
  285, 286, 295, 377, 379, 381,
  388, 405, 412, 416, 423, 436,
  438, 451, 493, 501, 545, 665,
  671, 718, 723, 725
  broken, 559, 746
  interpersonal, 283, 288, 289, 292,
    554, 555, 561, 562, 566, 568,
    604, 608, 623, 636, 704, 731
  personal, 731, 745
  with God, 340, 345, 563, 568,
    592, 596, 598, 599, 604, 704,
    731, 745
Relativity, 67
Reliance, 721
Religions, other, 442, 529, 533, 542,
  579, 583
Remorse, 746
Renewal, 677
Repentance, 75, 78, 80, 408, 414
Research, 620
Resentment, 609
Reserve, 63, 294

Resources, 540, 619, 638
  material, 242, 621
  natural, 627, 630, 635
  use of, 637
Respect, 621, 623, 687
  for law, 292, 298
Response, 132, 134, 144, 172, 235f.,
  320, 336, 345, 402, 536, 570,
  573, 577, 593, 785
  to God, 351
  lifelong, 531
Responsibility, 265, 267, 270, 272,
  277, 284, 286, 288, 289, 292,
  298, 306, 308, 309, 310, 313,
  317, 318, 323, 326, 335, 340,
  346, 359, 360, 363, 365, 366,
  367, 369, 372, 384, 462, 500
Routines, 771
Restlessness, 582
Results, 572
Resurrection, 572, 574, 575, 576,
  578, 581, 582
Retirement, 354, 654
Revelation, 93-128, 440
  of God, 390
Reverence, 746
Reverie, 90, 365
Ridicule, consequences of, 603
Right and wrong, 343, 348, 375,
  377, 380, 381, 382, 388, 423,
  451, 516, 544
  ability to distinguish between, 405
  discernment between, 414
  knowledge of, 339, 419
  standards of, 341
  understanding, 406
Right choices, 405
Right of possession, 278, 281, 287
Righteousness, 101
  God's, 415
Rights of others, 280, 292, 297, 298,
  330, 542
Rituals, 658
Role, of God, 577
  of pastor, 777
  -playing, 633
Routine, 87f., 355-373

Sacraments, 234f., 452, 463, 501,
  648, 650, 654, 747, 749, 750,
  752, 754, 755, 756
Sacrifice, 228, 552, 613, 618
Salvation, 581

845

847

Values, 83f., 353, 529, 530, 533, 542, 562, 563, 580, 598, 631, 635, 726, 745, 751
  judgments, 583
  of others, 713
  spiritual, 753
Value system, *see* System of Values
Victory, 584
Violation of neighborliness, 615
Visiting, 660
Visitors, 712
Visual materials, 317
Vocation, 80, 349, 354, 397, 577, 663
Volunteers, 724, 774
Vulnerability, 400

Welfare, 658
  agencies, 619
  of others, 600, 643
  of society, 723
Well-being of others, 654, 658, 777
Witness, 3, 81, 193, 210, 329, 372, 399, 403, 432, 447, 486, 490, 509, 517, 533, 534, 551, 556, 616, 621, 622, 631, 635, 639, 646, 649, 653, 654, 663, 677, 699, 710, 719, 720, 724, 738
Word, 12, 33, 94, 114, 140, 159, 234, 241
Work, 83, 88, 267, 280, 623, 625, 629, 631, 632, 635, 639, 655, 658, 673
  appreciation of, 634
  of the church, 562, 728, 739

World community, 219
World, God's, 642
  outreach, 329, 659
  situation, 576, 582, 775
Worship, 3, 90, 153, 232-237, 266, 278, 280, 285, 292, 309, 312, 313, 314, 317, 334, 347, 349, 354, 360, 365, 370, 375, 376, 377, 378, 380, 381, 384, 387, 388, 412, 417, 419, 421, 424, 463, 464, 471, 476, 480, 485, 535, 537, 539, 546, 551, 556, 558, 571, 574, 579, 583, 597, 615, 640, 641, 646, 647, 648, 650, 653, 654, 660, 674, 675, 695, 698, 713, 728, 740-758, 772, 777, 781
  corporate, 233f., 313, 384, 385, 389, 441, 447, 450, 451, 453, 457, 461, 496, 509, 513, 517, 521, 525, 529, 541, 545, 550, 562, 601, 642, 644, 658, 661, 690, 691, 765
  group, 296, 427, 431, 680, 684
  family, 545, 550, 601, 642, 655
  meaning of, 463
  need to, 388
  private, 384, 385, 389, 431, 496, 545, 550, 601, 642, 644
  value of, 770
Worth, 591
Wrongdoing, 263, 264, 407, 410

848